CORPORATE SOCIAL RESPONSIBILITY IN DEVELOPING AND EMERGING MARKETS

Corporate social responsibility (CSR) has emerged as a tool for public and private institutions to promote sustainable development in developing and emerging markets. This work brings together contributors from a variety of fields and international perspectives to assess and improve the effectiveness of CSR by addressing the following questions: What are the linkages between CSR and sustainable development? What does CSR mean for developing or emerging economies and in what ways does this deviate from orthodoxies and universalist approaches? What institutional factors and actors influence the effectiveness of CSR in developing and emerging economies? How can developing and emerging economies promote a flexible, diverse and reconstructed form of CSR that leads to inclusive and sustainable development? This book should be read by anyone interested in understanding what normative factors, theoretical models, policy strategies and corporate practices best facilitate effective CSR and sustainable development.

Onyeka K. Osuji is a Reader in Law at the University of Essex. As a qualified barrister and solicitor in Nigeria and England, he has advised individuals, corporations, and national and international governmental and non-governmental organisations. Dr. Osuji has published extensively in books and reputable international journals addressing issues ranging from corporate social responsibility and governance to globalization and consumer protection. He is also member of the College of Advisors of the ESRC-funded Sustainable Finance, the Law and Stakeholders Network.

Franklin N. Ngwu is Senior Lecturer in Strategy, Finance and Risk Management at Pan-Atlantic University Lagos Business School. He has worked with Barclays Bank, consulted for local and international organisations, and lectured at multiple institutions including Glasgow Caledonian University, University of Salford and University of Manchester. He has multi-disciplinary teaching and research interests and has published books, many book chapters and papers in peer-reviewed journals. Dr. Ngwu's membership of professional bodies includes the Society of Corporate Governance Nigeria, British Academy of Management, Institute of Operational Risk and Expert Network, World Economic Forum.

Dima Jamali is Professor at the Olayan School of Business, American University of Beirut and currently the National Representative for Global Compact Network Lebanon (GCNL), a network of businesses committed to advancing Sustainability and the Sustainable Development Goals (SDGs) in Lebanon. She has a PhD in Social Policy and Administration from the University of Kent in Canterbury, UK. Her research and teaching revolve primarily around Corporate Social Responsibility (CSR) and Social

Entrepreneurship (SE). She is the author and editor of four books: *CSR in the Middle East* (Palgrave, 2012); *Social Entrepreneurship in the Middle East* (Palgrave, 2015); *Development Oriented CSR* (Greenleaf, 2015); and *Comparative Perspectives on Global Corporate Social Responsibility* (IGI, 2016), and over 80 high level international publications, focusing on different aspects of sustainability and sustainable development and CSR in developing countries in general and in the Middle East specifically. She was elected in May 2018 as member of the Lebanese Parliament.

Corporate Social Responsibility in Developing and Emerging Markets

INSTITUTIONS, ACTORS AND SUSTAINABLE DEVELOPMENT

Edited by

ONYEKA K. OSUJI

University of Essex School of Law

FRANKLIN N. NGWU

Lagos Business School, Pan-Atlantic University (Nigeria)

DIMA JAMALI

Olayan School of Business, American University of Beirut

CAMBRIDGE
UNIVERSITY PRESS

CAMBRIDGE
UNIVERSITY PRESS

University Printing House, Cambridge CB2 8BS, United Kingdom

One Liberty Plaza, 20th Floor, New York, NY 10006, USA

477 Williamstown Road, Port Melbourne, VIC 3207, Australia

314-321, 3rd Floor, Plot 3, Splendor Forum, Jasola District Centre, New Delhi - 110025, India

103 Penang Road, #05-06/07, Visioncrest Commercial, Singapore 238467

Cambridge University Press is part of the University of Cambridge.

It furthers the University's mission by disseminating knowledge in the pursuit of education, learning and research at the highest international levels of excellence.

www.cambridge.org
Information on this title: www.cambridge.org/9781108459006
DOI: 10.1017/9781108579360

© Cambridge University Press 2020

First published 2020
First paperback edition 2022

A catalogue record for this publication is available from the British Library

Library of Congress Cataloging in Publication data
NAMES: Osuji, Onyeka, editor. | Ngwu, Franklin N., 1975– editor. | Jamali, Dima, editor.
TITLE: Corporate social responsibility in developing and emerging markets : institutions, actors and sustainable development / edited by Onyeka Osuji, University of Essex Law School, Franklin N. Ngwu, Lagos Business School, Pan-Atlantic University (Nigeria), Dima Jamali, Olayan School of Business, American University of Beirut.
DESCRIPTION: Cambridge, United Kingdom ; New York, NY : Cambridge University Press, 2020. | Includes bibliographical references.
IDENTIFIERS: LCCN 2019029248 | ISBN 9781108472111 (hardback)
SUBJECTS: LCSH: Social responsibility of business – Developing countries. | Sustainable development – Developing countries.
CLASSIFICATION: LCC HD60.5.D44 C674 2020 | DDC 338.9/27091724–dc23
LC record available at https://lccn.loc.gov/2019029248

ISBN 978-1-108-47211-1 Hardback
ISBN 978-1-108-45900-6 Paperback

To the loving memories of my brother, Okechukwu Kenneth Osuji (died 7 February 2017), and sister, Egondu Madonna Ukachukwu (died 4 August 2017), who died when this book was being conceived
– Onyeka K. Osuji

To my dad (Ozor Jacob I. Ngwu), my mum (Lolo Anthonia C. Ngwu), my wife (Chisom Ngwu) and daughter (Chinelo Ngwu)
– Franklin N. Ngwu

With loving memories of my dad (Rashid Jamali) who was the most ardent supporter of my career in academia, and currently my family and two adorable children (Omar and Leya), who are the inspiration for everything good I do in my life.
– Dima Jamali

Contents

Figures

Tables

Notes on Contributors

Dr Paul Abba gained a PhD in Environmental Law and Policy from the University of Exeter, UK. He obtained his first degree in Law with first class honours in 2008 and thereafter obtained a master's degree in Energy and Environmental Law and Policy at the Centre for Energy, Petroleum, Mineral Law and Policy (CEPMLP), University of Dundee, UK with a Distinction in September 2012. Paul is currently a research consultant to the Constitution Review Committee of the Senate of the Federal Republic of Nigeria and consults with various governmental policy bodies in Nigeria. His areas of interest include environmental law and policy, energy law, oil and gas law, practice and labour and industrial relations. He has written several published and unpublished articles on energy law, environmental law, and policy and labour law. He is the author of an award-winning book on labour law relations in Nigeria.

Dr F. Pinar Acar is an associate professor of Organisations and Management at Middle East Technical University, Turkey. She received her PhD from Texas Tech University, USA. Her research aims to investigate the relationship between various dimensions of group diversity and group processes such as intra-group conflict, and the association between individual dissimilarity, salient identities and individual behaviours in diverse team settings Dr Acar's work distinguishes between diversity as an objective construct versus a subjective, perceived construct and identifies potential group-level and organisational phenomena that may alleviate negative effects and facilitate positive effects of diversity. Currently, Dr Acar is examining biases and barriers faced by female leaders. She is interested in understanding the effects of sexist attitudes on glass cliff emergence and differential attributions of transformational leadership and abusive leadership to female leaders versus male leaders. Finally, she is studying abusive leadership and workplace incivility as forms of discrimination towards women.

Dr Nubi Achebo is the Director of Instructional Design and Technology at Lagos Business School, Nigeria, where he also teaches sustainability courses online.

Dr Achebo is passionate about providing learning and development solutions to organisations. He has extensive leadership and management development experience working at Lagos Business School and other organisations worldwide. He is actively involved in the design and delivery of custom Executive Education programmes for Lagos Business School clients. Dr Achebo has over 21 years' technology and management consulting experience working with Andersen Worldwide and Arthur Andersen. He taught as an adjunct professor of Training and Development (MBA programme) for six years at Graham School of Management, Saint Xavier University, Chicago, USA. His areas of teaching and research interests include training and development, learning design, business process analysis, performance management, stakeholder engagement, sustainability conflicts and corporate sustainability. Dr Achebo received his PhD in Instructional Technology from Southern Illinois University, Carbondale, USA. He is an alumnus of the LBS Advanced Management Program (AMP) and has an MBA in Leadership and Sustainability from the University of Cumbria, UK.

Dr Ogechi Adeola is an Associate Professor of Marketing at the Lagos Business School (LBS), Pan-Atlantic University, Nigeria and also the Academic Director, LBS Sales & Marketing Academy. Her research interests include tourism and hospitality marketing, strategic marketing, sustainable entrepreneurship and digital marketing strategies in sub-Saharan Africa. She has published academic papers in top scholarly journals. Her co-authored papers won Best Paper Awards at conferences in 2016, 2017 and 2018. She holds a doctorate in Business Administration (DBA) from Manchester Business School, UK and started her career at Citibank Nigeria, spending approximately 14 years in the financial sector before moving into academia.

Dr Frederick Ahen is a senior research fellow at the University of Turku, Finland. Dr Ahen's research straddles the areas of sustainable global health governance and the role of corporations in changing and being changed by institutions. Other related areas of focus include corporate responsibility, ethics and firm–stakeholder relations. Frederick's research has been published in international peer-reviewed journals such as *critical perspectives on international business; Foresight; Social Responsibility Journal; Technology and Innovation Management Review* and the *Humanistic Management Journal*. In addition to several conference papers, Frederick has had book chapters published by *Springer, Emerald, Palgrave MacMillan, Routledge, Edward Elgar Publishing*, and *Greenleaf Publishing*.

Dr Mohammed Alshaleel is a lecturer at the University of Essex, UK. He was awarded his PhD in International Financial law in 2017. He has an LLM in International Trade law from the University of Essex, and an LLB from the University of Damascus, Syria where he graduated as the Best Student of the

Faculty of Law. Dr Alshaleel has particular interests in international financial law, international trade law and Islamic banking and finance law

Dr Ugochi C. Amajuoyi is a lecturer in the Department of Law at the University of Essex. She gained extensive experience of the consumer financial services sector whilst working at the Financial Ombudsman Service for the past six years. Her research interests include the implications of digital technologies on consumer protection law and regulation, commercial and financial law, general commercial law and development law. Dr Amajuoyi completed her PhD with a thesis entitled, 'Online Peer-to-Peer Lending Regulation: Justification, Classification and Remit in UK Law'. She has written a journal article on the topic in the highly regarded *Journal of Business Law* entitled 'Online Peer-to-Peer Lending: Challenging Consumer Protection Rationales, Orthodoxies and Models?' (2015) 6 *Journal of Business Law*.

Dr Ebes Aziegbe-Esho is a postdoctoral research fellow at the College of Business and Economics, University of Johannesburg, South Africa. She had a stint at Covenant University where she facilitated courses at the undergraduate and post-graduate levels. Ebes has a first degree in Accountancy from University of Nigeria and a PhD, MPhil and an MBA from the Lagos Business School, Pan-Atlantic University, Nigeria. Her areas of research interest broadly include human capital, financing of SMEs, and internationalization of African businesses; with a general focus on Africa and performance of African firms. Prior to entering academia, she worked in treasury operations, domestic operations and internal control unit at Zenith Bank Plc and United Bank for Africa (UBA) for close to a decade. Ebes has consulted widely for firms in Nigeria and on World Bank–assisted projects.

Dr Durand M. Cupido is a lecturer at the University of Essex, where he teaches in the areas of maritime law and international trade law. He previously taught at the Universities of East Anglia and Stellenbosch. He received his PhD from the University of Southampton, UK and holds an LLM (Shipping), from the University of Cape Town, South Africa. Dr Cupido is a qualified attorney of the High Court of South Africa and has practised as an attorney and acted as a consultant in commercial and maritime law.

Dr Luis Alfonso Dau is an associate professor of International Business and Strategy at the D'Amore-McKim School of Business, Northeastern University, USA. His research and teaching interests include global strategy, emerging market firms, institutional changes, pro-market reforms, business groups, family firms, firm per-formance, international corporate social responsibility, sustainability, formal and informal entrepreneurship and the implications of culture on international strategy. He is also a John H. Dunning Visiting Fellow at Henley Business School, University of Reading, UK, as well as a Peter J. Buckley International Visiting Fellow at University of Leeds Business School, UK.

Oserere Eigbe is a management scholar and research assistant at the Lagos Business School, Pan-Atlantic University, Nigeria. She holds a master's degree in Information Science and a bachelor's degree in Economics, both from the University of Ibadan, Nigeria. Her areas of research interest include but are not limited to teaching, technology and innovation.

Dr Yan Feng received her PhD in Applied Economics and Managerial Sciences from University of Pennsylvania, the Wharton School, USA. She is currently an assistant professor of Economics/Management at the HSBC Business School of Peking University, PRC. Her research interest is in the field of applied economics, especially topics in health economics, health policy and management. She is interested in the application of economic understanding in managerial issues related to sustainable strategic development of organisations. She has also been involved in multiple governmental and industrial research projects covering broader strategy and development issues.

Dr Ayse Gozde Gozum completed two master's degrees related to Management after gaining a BSc degree in Business Administration. Following this, she completed her PhD studies during which she specialized in organisational behaviour. She has also one year's UK experience through the Erasmus Exchange Programme which has also contributed to her academic writing skills. As for her academic work experience, she worked as a research assistant in Ufuk University, Turkey for four years. Having produced several publications, which include both qualitative and quantitative data analysis that have been accepted in peer-reviewed journals, she was promoted to an assistant professorship. Currently, she is teaching courses entitled Introduction to Business, Organisational Behaviour, and Management and Organisation at the same university.

Dr Rose Hiquet is a Swiss National Science Foundation (SNF) Postdoctoral Research Fellow at Cambridge Judge Business School, UK. Her research interests include stakeholder relations, corporate social responsibility and sustainable value creation.

Professor Dima Jamali is Professor in the Olayan School of Business, American University of Beirut and currently holding the Kamal Shair Chair in Responsible Leadership and serving as Associate Dean for Research and Faculty Development. She has a PhD in Social Policy and Administration, from the University of Kent in Canterbury, UK. Her research and teaching revolve primarily around corporate social responsibility (CSR) and social entrepreneurship (SE). She is the author/editor of four books: *CSR in the Middle East* (Palgrave, 2012); *Social Entrepreneurship in the Middle East* (Palgrave, 2015); *Development Oriented CSR* (Greenleaf, 2015); and *Comparative Perspectives on Global Corporate Social*

Responsibility (IGI – 2017), and over 65 international publications, focusing on various aspects of CSR in developing countries in general and in the Middle East region specifically. She is the winner of the 2016 National Council for Scientific Research Excellence Award, and the 2015 Aspen Institute Faculty Pioneer Award, dubbed by the *Financial Times* as 'the Oscars of the Business School World' for a pioneering faculty who are at the cutting edge of teaching and scholarship in their field. She is also winner of the Shield of Excellence for the Arab Region and designated as Personality of the Year for CSR by the Arab Organisation for Social Responsibility in 2015. She is also winner of the 2010 Shoman Prize for best young Arab researcher, which recognizes distinctive scientific works that contribute to addressing priority issues at the local, regional and international levels. In 2013, Dr Jamali was selected for the Eisenhower Fellows Program, joining a global network of leading professionals committed to collaborate for a more prosperous, just and peaceful world; she was also selected in 2007 for the British Academy of Management Fellowship for South Asia and the Middle East which identifies and supports scholars with exceptional potential and trajectory from the Middle East. Dr. Jamali is also winner of the AUB Teaching Excellence Award in 2006, which recognizes outstanding educators from across the AUB campus. She worked as an expert consultant for the United Nations on Social Policy and CSR as well as various projects funded by the World Bank, the US Agency for International Development, and major private and public firms in Lebanon and the region.

Kikelomo Kila is a current doctoral researcher at the University of Exeter focusing on Climate Change, Renewable Energy and Corporate Regulation in Developing Countries. She obtained her bachelor's in law degree from the University of Buckingham in 2009 and obtained an LLM in Oil and Gas Law from Robert Gordon University, Aberdeen in 2012. She received full sponsorship from the Petroleum Technology Development Fund to undertake her Doctoral research in Climate Change and Renewable Energy Law at the University of Exeter in 2015. She is a qualified barrister and solicitor of the Supreme Court of Nigeria. She is also a senior research consultant (Policy, Consultation and Legislative Drafting) to the Constitution Review Committee of the Nigerian Senate. Kikelomo currently teaches at the University of Exeter and has presented papers at academic conferences in the United Kingdom and Canada. She is a principal partner of P&K Associates, Legal Consultants and Arbitrators, Nigeria.

Dr Hedda Ofoole Knoll completed her doctoral studies at the University of Hamburg, Germany in September 2018. Hedda has worked as a research assistant at the Eberswalde University for Sustainable Development, mainly on CSR in Global Supply Chains issues. Other areas of research interest include the role of Human Resource Management on Sustainable Global Supply Chains and the impact of political CSR on society – focusing mainly on African countries.

Wenli Liu is currently a project manager at the organisational development department of Tencent, the leading Shenzhen-based hi-tech company. She received her master's degree in Management from Peking University HSBC Business School and a master's degree in Finance from the University of Hong Kong. Before she joined Tencent in 2016, she had served as a human resource management consultant for Aon Hewitt for four years.

Dr Elizabeth M. Moore is a visiting assistant professor in International Business & Strategy at the D'Amore-McKim School of Business, Northeastern University. She recently finished her PhD in Political Science. Her research and teaching interests include formal and informal entrepreneurship, corporate social responsibility, institutional changes, institutional disruptions, transnational institutions, pro-market reforms, firm performance, emerging market firms, and international organisations.

Dr Deborah Motilewa is an innovative business professional with several years' experience as a business lecturer and researcher. At 25, she was the youngest PhD graduate from Covenant University, Nigeria. She currently teaches human resources management, organisational behaviour and change management courses at Bow Valley College, Alberta Canada. Dr Motilewa is particularly interested in human capital development from the developing and developed countries' perspectives. Her current research area is the intersection of Human resources management and corporate social responsibility, specifically, human capital development, sustainable HR, ethical HR and managing diversity in the modern business world. Debbie is passionate about topical issues on nation building, especially leadership and education, and this has influenced her current choice of career. She is the founder and executive director of The VolunteerNG, a non-profit organisation that is bridging the gap in education by connecting children without access to education to volunteers that are able and willing to provide both financial and moral support. As at 2018/2019 session, The VolunteerNG has 26 children on scholarship, and has mentored over 800 young adults. She has also spoken twice on BBC Africa on national issues, and she has lived on three different continents: Europe, Africa and North America.

Omotayo Muritala manages the research department at the Lagos Business School, Pan-Atlantic University, Nigeria. He obtained a master's degree in Economics from the University of Ibadan, Nigeria, with a special interest in Development Economics. Before joining Lagos Business School, he worked as a Deputy Research Executive at ValueFronteira Ltd where he was engaged in consulting studies for USAID, NESG/World Bank and private organisations in Nigeria. In 2014/15 he was a member of the team that produced technical requirements for 'Strengthening Advocacy and Civic Engagement': a nationwide study that examined media strategies for strengthening advocacy programmes and public policy reforms in Nigeria. He is a passionate economist and was a Development Knowledge Facilitator (DKF) for the Millennium Development Goals. He received the Federal Government Scholarship Award in 2010.

Dr Franklin N. Ngwu is a senior lecturer in Strategy, Finance and Risk Management, Lagos Business School, Pan-Atlantic University, Nigeria. He has a PhD in Law and Economics of Banking Regulation, an MSc in Economics and a Postgraduate Diploma in Development Economics from University of Manchester, UK. In addition, he has an MSc in Comparative Political Economy from Cardiff University, UK, and a BSc in Sociology from University of Lagos, Nigeria. He has over 15 years' experience in teaching, business, policy research and consulting both in Nigeria and the UK. He has consulted for both local and international organisations and worked in Barclays Bank, UK for over five years. He has lectured at the Glasgow School of Business and Society, Glasgow Caledonian University; School of Built Environment and Business, University of Salford and the Department of Economics and School of Law, University of Manchester, UK. His teaching and research interests are multidisciplinary in nature. He has presented papers at international/local conferences, contributed many book chapters and published papers in peer-reviewed journals. His latest paper on Securitisation and Financial Crisis was published by the *Research in International Business and Finance* Journal. He is the author/editor of the corporate governance handbook titled *Corporate Governance in Developing and Emerging Markets* (Routledge, 2017). He is working on a second book titled *Enhancing Board Effectiveness-Institutional, Regulatory and Functional Perspectives for Developing and Emerging Markets*. He is a member of several professional bodies including Society of Corporate Governance Nigeria, British Academy of Management and Institute of Operational Risk, UK.

Professor Won-Yong Oh is the Lee Professor of Strategy at the Lee Business School, University of Nevada, Las Vegas in the USA. His research interests include corporate governance, strategic leadership (CEO and top management team), corporate social responsibility (CSR) and international management. He earned his PhD in Management at the University of Kansas.

Dr Adaeze Okoye is a senior lecturer at the University of Brighton. She holds a PhD from the University of Hull and a master's degree in Environmental Law and Policy from the University of Dundee. Dr Okoye is also a barrister and solicitor of the Supreme Court of Nigeria and an academic fellow of the Honourable Society of the Inner Temple. She was a visiting fellow at the Institute of Advanced Legal Studies, University of London in 2015–16. She is a 2010 alumnus of the Institute for Global Law and Policy (IGLP) workshop, Harvard Law School. Her recent book, *Legal approaches and corporate social responsibility* (Routledge Research in Corporate Law, 2016) explores legal approaches to law and the corporate social responsibility relationship. She has also written about law and development, corporate govern-ance, joint development agreements, and environmental management systems in the oil industry.

Dr Onyeka K. Osuji is a reader in Law at University of Essex, UK. He has a PhD in law from the University of Manchester (as a School of Law Scholar); a BCL (Law) from the University of Oxford (as a Shell Centenary/FCO Chevening Scholar) and an LLB from the University of Nigeria. He is a fellow of the Higher Education Academy. He was previously at the University of Exeter and has taught at the University of Manchester and University of Wolverhampton, all in the UK. Dr Osuji previously practised in corporate and commercial law before becoming an academic. He is qualified as a barrister and solicitor of Nigeria and a (non-practising) solicitor of England and Wales and has advised individuals, corporations, and national and international governmental and non-governmental organisations. He has presented papers in several international conferences and has published extensively in books and reputable international journals in the areas of corporate governance, corporate social responsibility, globalization, regulation, consumer protection, social and non-financial reporting, banking and asset management and multinational enterprises. Dr Osuji has taught company law, corporate social responsibility and law, corporate social responsibility, globalization, law and regula-tion, law of contract and commercial law.

Dr Viviana Pilato is a postdoctoral fellow of the Centre for Social and Sustainable Innovation (CSSI) at Peter B. Gustavson School of Business, University of Victoria. She earned her doctorate in 2017 at Università Cattolica del Sacro Cuore, Milan, Italy, and she has also been visiting scholar in 2016 at Cass Business School, UK. Dr Pilato's researches lie at the intersection of two domains – corporate social responsibility (CSR) and international business (IB). Her current research is focused on understanding the headquarter–subsidiary relationship and their CSR. More precisely, her research agenda investigates how MNCs' subsidiaries manage the conflicting demands from their headquarters and local stakeholders in the imple-mentation of CSR practices in developing countries (Africa) and how stakeholder dialogue depends upon the institutional contexts in which the companies operate.

Professor Ting Ren is associate dean and associate professor at Peking University HSBC Business School. He received his PhD in Human Resources and Industrial Relations from the Carlson School of Management, University of Minnesota. Professor Ren's research focuses on industrial organisation, corporate governance, human resources and labour studies. He has published broadly in world-class academic journals. His recent research involves the application of big data and smart robotization in organisation and people studies. He has led numerous con-sulting projects in the Greater Bay Area for policymaking and business practice. He also serves as advisor to both public and private sectors.

Olamide Shittu is a PhD candidate at the Centre for Urban Transitions, Swinburne University of Technology, Australia. He was formerly a management scholar and research assistant at Lagos Business School, Nigeria. He studied Sociology (Bsc) at the University of Ibadan, Nigeria where he graduated with first class honours. He also completed his MSc in Sociology of Development at the same university with distinction. He is a recipient of several awards including the Addax Petroleum National Merit Scholarship Award, the University of Ibadan Postgraduate Scholarship and the Lagos Business School Management Scholar Academy. His research interests include sustainability, development studies and strategy among others. He has previously worked as a teaching assistant at the Department of Sociology, University of Ibadan and has consulted for several organisations including Oxford Policy Management Limited. His works have been published in various peer-reviewed journals including the African Journal for the Psychological Study of Social Issues.

Dr Radek Stech is the founder of the Sustainable Finance, the Law and Stakeholders (SFLS) Network and a lecturer in Law at the University of Exeter. Dr Stech is currently leading on an ESRC-funded global impactful research project on sustainable finance in partnership with the Global Alliance for Banking on Values (GABV) and the World Bank and is an Observer of the Green Bond Principles. Dr Stech has more than a decade of solid research, consultancy and advisory experience in sustainable banking and environmental law in collaboration with such stakeholders as the US Chamber of Commerce Institute for Legal Reform, the Welsh Government, WWF UK, United Kingdom Environmental Law Association and leading international law firms. His PhD project on costs barriers to justice in England and Wales was launched in the House of Lords (2010), published by the UNECE and referred by the Aarhus Convention Compliance Committee. He was a visiting fellow at George Washington University Law School and a researcher at the World Bank (Global Themes). Between 2012 and 2013, he worked as a senior evidence analyst in the Welsh Government, where he was developing, through policy and legal instructions, the Well-being of Future Generations (Wales) Act 2015.

Mallika Tamvada is a doctoral candidate at the Law School, University of Essex. Her research interests are in Corporate Social Responsibility and Business and Human Rights. She has a master's in Law from the University of Houston, USA, and a BA LLB (Hons) from Maharshi Dayanand University, India. Previously, she worked at the Jindal Global Law School, Amity University, Kochhar & Co and practised at the High Court of Delhi and Supreme Court of India.

Dr Uchenna Uzo is a senior lecturer of Marketing Management at Lagos Business School, Nigeria. He received his BSc and MSc in Sociology from the University of Lagos, Nigeria and his Master of Research in Management degree as well as PhD in

Management from the IESE Business School, Barcelona. He is currently the Director of MBA Programmes at Lagos Business School and teaches courses in marketing management, personal selling, sales and channel management. His research and consulting assignments span several industries focusing mainly on retail marketing management, sales and distribution channel management. His academic articles have been published in the *Strategic Entrepreneurship Journal* and the *Journal of Personal Selling and Sales Management*. His cases won the 2013 EFMD Case Writing Competition in the 'African Business Cases' category and the 2016–2017 Emerald/AABS Case Study Competition. He is currently a member of the Management Board of the Lagos Business School.

Dr David T. A. Wesley is a lecturer and research manager in the D'Amore-McKim School of Business at Northeastern University in Boston, where he has managed the business case collection since 1999. His principal fields of academic research focus on cross-cultural adaptation, technology and innovation, and international business and strategy. He has published more than 100 case studies, articles and book chapters, and a leading book on marketing and strategy in the video game industry. His case studies have won numerous awards in Canada, the United States and Europe.

Youzhi Xiao is doctoral student in economics at Peking University HSBC Business School. His research field mainly focuses on international economic management and empirical industrial organisation.

Professor Hongyan Yang is currently an associate professor of strategic management in Lingnan University, Hong Kong. She received her PhD in Strategic Management from Foster Business School, University of Washington at Seattle. Her research interests include corporate strategy, international business, innovation and entrepreneurship. She has published in prestigious journals such as *Academy of Management Journal, Journal of Management, Research Policy, Management and Organisation Review*, among others.

Foreword[1]

It is most important that developing and emerging markets (DEMs) are complemented by corporate social responsibility (CSR). Where there is exposure to environmental degradation and extreme environmental events and conditions; poverty; oppression; and power inequality, then responsible business can be most valued. This is true whether in circumstances where economic growth is flat (some of the developing markets) or where growth is in the double digits (some of the emerging markets). CSR's importance can be seen in the most cursory reference to the roles of responsible business in industrialization of the global North. In circumstances of rapid transformations, uprooting and impoverishment of huge sections of societies, many businesses were set on accumulation at any cost. Robber barons were adept at exploitation of the commons, the people, technology and still-adolescent democratic polities. But equally, responsible businesses (for a variety of reasons) raised standards of social, environmental and political responsibility (Boswell, 1983; Husted, 2015; Moon, Murphy and Gond, 2017), and provided models for governments in the provision of public goods. So the challenge today in developing and emerging markets (DEMs – and elsewhere!) is to 'accentuate the positive and eliminate the negative' (Mercer, 1944).

None of this is to say that any model of CSR alone is a palliative for the challenges that DEMs face. As Collier observed '[t]he state can use narratives, laws, taxes and subsidies to restore the *ethical firm*' (2018: 210 – see Kourula, Moon, Salles-Djelic & Wickert (2019) on the role of government in the governance of business conduct; see Gond, Kang and Moon (2011) for how government roles in regulating CSR may play out comparatively; and Hofman and Moon (2017) on how these roles can bring out different understandings of CSR outside the global North). So, corporations, through CSR, can be part of a propitious governance mix in a variety of circumstances, as well as a cousin in cronyism and misappropriation of public resources.

[1] Thanks to Maha Atal and Lauren McCarthy for feedback on my first draft.

Responsibility lies primarily with those with power – be they governments in DEMs and elsewhere, oligarchs, investors, consumers, religious and other societal leaders and sometimes even social movements.

But the focus of this collection is clearly on business power and responsibility. As Davis's (1960) 'iron law of oligarchy' – that those who have corporate power need to exercise responsibility or else risk losing that power – plays out all too rarely, the challenge for researchers is to 'speak truth to power' (in government and beyond). In this case, the aspiration is to speak the truths about the costs of business irresponsibility as well as about the benefits of CSR. The task here is immense. To understand the imperatives and circumstances for responsible business in DEMs, there are requirements for theorization and conceptualization, description and specification of societies' values, and norms, of business models and opportunities and of governmental regulation and public provision, including the roles of international government organisations – and even of governments in the global North.

But of course whilst in general terms the global North provides indicators that CSR matters, it can hardly be used as a template (not least as the global North's industrialization was partly enabled by exploitation of resources from the global South). Moreover, few DEMs share the *relatively* stable and benign (but also easily exaggerated) blend of regulated capitalism, liberal societies, rule of law and independent judiciary, property rights and democratic politics, all of which can help frame CSR. So CSR analysis has to be well grounded in the societies, politics and economies of today's DEMs. This collection takes us further along the way on several fronts (see also Jamali and Karam, 2018).

There is wide country coverage including focus on the People's Republic of China, India, Nigeria, Republic of South Africa, Turkey and Thailand. There is a good range of issue coverage including human rights, the Sustainable Development Goals, climate change mitigation, environmental protection, human resource management, and community-level grievances and governance. The actor focus is also wide, including corporations (domestic and multinational), micro and informal enterprise, consumers, governments, the judiciary, social movements and business schools. Sectors receiving specific attention include finance, palm oil, fishing and shipping. There is considerable theoretical reach from institutional theory and development theory (various, including 'capabilities') to social performance and green capitalism, as well the normative orientations of Islamic, Hindu, and specifically Gandhian, thought, and utilitarianism.

Let me conclude with a research challenge that is inspired by the collection.

First, the edition as a whole and the contributing chapters are obviously premised on the differences between the global North and the DEMs. These include: that for the last few centuries (analytical lens depending) the global North has dominated the DEMs; that prominent conceptions of CSR have tended to originate there; and that for various reasons some of the most calamitous effects of global sustainability challenges are focused in the DEMs. But apart from not being in the global North, what is it that unites these markets in terms of institutions, actors and sustainable development, and from what perspective (Jardim, 2017)? I would imagine that they collectively have much less in common than do the markets of the global North (Kim and Moon, 2015). I would imagine that even some of the individual DEMs countries have more internal social, economic and environmental heterogeneity than the countries of global North, whose own variation (e.g. in models of corporate ownership and governance) tend to be vastly overestimated.

Whilst it might have been countered that the developing markets have shared, and continue to share, some systemic exploitation from the global North which remains a point of commonality, the rise of the emerging markets has problematized that equation. Now some of the BRICs are able to flex their muscles in the face of admonitions from the global North, and also to militarily and economically exploit societies in the developing markets; and some scholars even argue that developing markets are able to benefit from playing off traditional donors from the global North and the BRICS (e.g. Alden, 2012; Brautigam, 2009; Mohan, 2014; Taylor, 2014). Moreover, so many sustainable development challenges reflect the inter-dependencies of the global North and the DEMs: climate change most obviously, but even such challenges as those entailed in the institution of gender (McCarthy and Moon, 2018) or the deployment of science and technology (Fejerskov, 2017).

Secondly, and relatedly, the question arises as to the implications for CSR in such a heterogeneity as the DEMs, normatively, conceptually, descriptively and strategically? What issues, by what modes and with what rationales does, can or should CSR address, and in which particular DEMs circumstances? And which businesses should engage in these respective CSR policies, and in alignment with which other institutions? Moreover such research needs to be well-attuned to dynamic possibilities for sustainability in very specific circumstances (e.g. see Muthuri, Moon and Chapple, 2008; Valente, 2012).

My first hope is that this sort of research will be important to ameliorating some of the worst problems, and attaining some of the greatest social, environmental and economic developments, to which CSR can reasonably aspire. My second hope is that this could prove critical for business understanding of their roles in bigger questions such as the nature and limits of their responsibilities for capacity-building in DEMs to address climate change and other environmental threats, and for evaluation of the full social and economic impacts of their value chain impacts on host countries.

Jeremy Moon
VELUX Chair of Corporate Sustainability
Copenhagen Business School

REFERENCES

Alden, C. (2012). China and Africa: The Relationship Matures. *Strategic Analysis* 36(5), 701–7.

Boswell, J. (1983). The Informal Social Control of Business in Britain: 1880 – 1939. *The Business History Review* 57(2), 237–57.

Brautigam, D. (2009). *The Dragon's Gift: The Real Story of China in Africa*, Oxford: Oxford University Press.

Collier, P. (2018). *The Future of Capitalism: Facing the New Anxieties*, London: Allen Lane.

Davis, K. (1960). Can Business Afford to Ignore Social Responsibilities? *California Management Review* 2(3), 70–6.

Fejerskov, A. M. (2017). The New Technopolitics of Development and the Global South as a Laboratory of Technological Experimentation. *Science, Technology, & Human Values* 42 (5), 947–68.

Gond, J-P., Kang, N. and Moon, J. (2011). The Government of Self-regulation: On the Comparative Dynamics of Corporate Social Responsibility. *Economy and Society* 40(4), 640–71.

Hofman, P. S., Moon, J. with Wu, B. (2017). Corporate Social Responsibility under Authoritarian Capitalism: Dynamics and Prospects of State-led and Society-driven CSR. *Business and Society* 56(5), 651–71.

Husted, B. W. (2015). Corporate Social Responsibility: Practice from 1800 – 1914. Past Initiatives and Current Debates. *Business Ethics Quarterly* 25(1), 125–41.

Jamali, D. and Karam, C. (2018). Corporate Social Responsibility in Developing Countries as an Emerging Field of Study. *International Journal of Management Reviews* 20(1), 32–61.

Jardim, C. A. (2017). 'The Prerogative to Problematize, Decolonize and Provincialize the Narrative of a Global South' 6° Encontro Nacional da ABRI Perspectivas sobre o poder em um mundo em redefinição Área temática: Teoria das Relações Internacionais. Available at www.encontro2017.abri.org.br/resources/anais/8/1498059597_ARQUIVO_ABRI2017CamilaJardim.pdf accessed 21 July 2019.

Kim, C. H. and Moon, J. (2015). Dynamics of Corporate Social Responsibility in Asia: Knowledge and Norms. *Asian Business & Management* 14(5), 349–82.

Kourula, A., Moon, J., Salles-Djelic, L. and Wickert, C. (2019). New Roles of Governments in the Governance of Business Conduct: Implications for Management and Organizational Research. https://doi.org/10.1177/0170840619852142.

McCarthy, L. and Moon, J. (2018). Disrupting the Gender Institution: Consciousness Raising in the Cocoa Value Chain. *Organization Studies* 39(9), 1153–77.

Mercer, J. (1944). 'Accentuate the Positive' first released with The Pied Pipers and Paul Weston's orchestra, Capitol Records.

Mohan, G. (2014). China in Africa: Impacts and Prospects for Accountable Development. In S. Hickey, K. Sen and B. Bukenya, eds., *The Politics of Inclusive Development: Interrogating the Evidence*, Oxford: Oxford University Press.

Moon, J., Murphy, L. and Gond, J.P. (2017). Historical Perspectives on CSR. In A. M. Rasche, Morsing and J. Moon eds., *Corporate Social Responsibility: Strategy, Communication and Governance*, Cambridge: Cambridge University Press.

Muthuri, J., Moon, J. and Chapple, W. (2008). Implementing 'Community Participation' in Corporate Community Involvement: Lessons from Magadi Soda Company in Kenya. *Journal of Business Ethics* 85 431–44.

Taylor, I. (2014). *Africa Rising? BRICS – Diversifying Dependency*, Oxford: James Currey.

Valente, M. (2012). Theorizing Firm Adoption to Sustaincentrism. *Organization Studies* 33 (4), 563–91.

Endorsement

In looking at how corporate social responsibility and sustainable development configure themselves in developing and emerging markets, the editors and their contributing authors make a significant contribution to a pressing global issue. Indeed, if corporations are key to sustainable development, and if sustainable development is essential for human well-being, then how they play out in developing and emerging markets has to be of crucial importance.

The book seeks to answer four key questions. These focus on why sustainable development and corporate social responsibility are linked, what those linkages mean for developing and emerging economies, the effect of institutional factors on practice, and how different national contexts have to be accommodated for sustainable development to be delivered. The end product is nineteen chapters, spanning theoretical analysis, normative concerns, and cross-county studies. Each chapter provides a valuable contribution to our knowledge and demonstrate, in their different ways, the challenges to be overcome if we are to realize the benefits that corporate social responsibility and sustainable development will provide for developing and emerging markets.

I would strongly recommend this book to policymakers, academics and students, and anyone with an interest in developing and emerging markets. It covers a rarely studied and important area, and it is to be applauded for the contributions it contains.

David Williamson
Emeritus Professor, Staffordshire University
Honorary Senior Research Fellow, University of Manchester

Preface

There are theoretical, policy and practical challenges associated with corporate social responsibility (CSR) that make it an uncertain subject for practitioners, businesspeople, policymakers and scholars. This is notwithstanding that the complex links and interfaces between the proper governance of companies and CSR practices, and how they spill over to affect society and sustainable development, are increasingly being acknowledged globally in a variety of perspectives, particularly in the context of developing and emerging economies. The differences between CSR orientations in more advanced countries and developing and emerging economies can be explained by the institutional model, which recognizes contextual variations in needs, priorities and solutions in terms of how national institutions shape and mould organisational behaviour. The dissection of institutional level factors (macro), organisational level factors (meso) and individual level factors (micro) can enhance understanding of complex multidimensional variables shaping CSR in the developing and emerging economies. The contributions to this book demonstrate the pivotal sustainable development roles CSR can play in the developing and emerging economies.

Although CSR in developing and emerging economies has been considered in scholarship to an extent, the institutional and sustainable development perspectives of CSR have received almost no attention, particularly in relation to developing and emerging economies. It is important to identify theoretical models, corporate strategies and pragmatic solutions for CSR in the developing and emerging economies, and to identify and tackle barriers to the effectiveness and improvement of CSR conception and practice. This book therefore examines the conceptualization, roles and practices of CSR in the developing and emerging markets and articulates solutions for improving its effectiveness and utilization as a wider tool for individual and society development. Its overarching research questions are: (a) What are the linkages between CSR and sustainable development? (b) What does or can CSR mean for the developing or emerging economies and in what ways does this deviate from orthodoxies and universalist approaches? (c) What institutional factors and actors influence or can influence the effectiveness of CSR in the developing and emerging economies? (d) How can developing and emerging economies promote a flexible, diverse and reconstructed CSR that promotes inclusive and sustainable development?

The book's chapters address these questions from a variety of fields and perspectives including, but not limited to, law, business ethics, corporate governance, economics, development studies, regulation, globalization, management, organisational studies, human resources management, political economy, supply chains management and business education. The contributions compare and synthetize diverse normative factors, theoretical models, institutional factors and policy strategies, and corporate and industry practices to illustrate their relevance to the developing and emerging economies. The analyses of concepts, principles and practices, country studies and comparative, historical and contemporary accounts in the chapters enable the cross-exchange of ideas and innovative solutions for CSR and sustainable development, and improving their effectiveness for those economies.

The suggestions and lessons from this book will benefit policymakers, businesses, scholars, companies, corporate boards, practitioners and other stakeholders and aid the design of appropriate conceptual frameworks, policy strategies, stakeholder engagement models and social performance evaluation strategies that are better tailored for CSR and sustainable development in the developing and emerging economies. This book will be of interest to academics, researchers and students of CSR, sustainable development, corporate law, corporate governance, regulation, economics, public administration, political economy, management, organisational studies, marketing and advertising, and development studies.

Table of Cases

Table of Legislation

Introduction to Corporate Social Responsibility in Developing and Emerging Markets: Institutions, Actors and Sustainable Development

Onyeka K. Osuji, Franklin N. Ngwu and Dima Jamali

1.1 CORPORATE SOCIAL RESPONSIBILITY AND SUSTAINABLE DEVELOPMENT: INSTITUTIONS AND PRACTICES

The growing popularity of, and ongoing debates surrounding, the concept of corporate social responsibility (CSR) and the practice of corporate social and environmental reporting have a lot to do with the inter-exchange of ideas and resources due to global interconnections and interdependencies between countries and regions. Globalization has also moved CSR from a simple matter of corporate practice and corporate governance to a topical issue for national and transnational public governance and socioeconomic development. Scholars, policymakers and national and international NGOs, social movements and civil society groups are continually seeking ways to promote 'universal' CSR principles and international best practices and standards in different jurisdictional contexts. This is especially true in relation to multinational enterprises operating through subsidiaries, affiliates and complicated supply chains in developing and emerging countries where regulatory and institutional standards are comparably weaker. Therefore, the complex links and interfaces between the proper governance of companies and CSR practices and how they spill over to affect society and development are increasingly being acknowledged globally, particularly in the context of developing economies (Jamali et al., 2015; Jamali and Karam, 2018; Jamali et al., 2017; Ngwu et al., 2017; Osuji and Obibuaku, 2016).

Nonetheless, there are theoretical, policy and practical challenges associated with CSR that make it an uncertain subject for practitioners, businesspeople, policymakers and scholars (Amaeshi et al., 2008, 2013; Osuji, 2011, 2012). For instance, a common definition of the concept of CSR is still contested, especially in its application to developing and emerging markets, due to variations in institutional and contextual factors that can trigger different individual and society needs, priorities and practices (Jamali and Karam, 2018). This is exemplified by the Sustainable Development Goals (SDGs) agreed upon by the United Nations in 2015 which contain a range of aspirational goals that recognize different needs and priorities for countries at different stages of development. It follows that businesses and society may maintain a relationship of interdependence in the developing and emerging economies different from what may be obtainable in the more advanced economies, thus challenging the founding cornerstone logics of neoliberalism that seem to be the bedrock of the dominant shareholder primacy corporate governance model in the more advanced economies (Jamali et al., 2017).

Similarly, regulatory developments in developing and emerging countries like Indonesia, Mauritius and India challenge the orthodoxy of voluntariness for CSR and corporate self-regulation widely accepted in the more advanced economies. The backdrop is the lack of a binding code of corporate responsibility at the global level that allows national governments to set local priorities and adopt solutions to local needs. Nonetheless, some scholars and policymakers in developing and emerging countries are therefore increasingly regarding CSR as a development tool, with the private sector serving as an important engine or catalyst for national economic development (Jamali et al., 2015; Osuji, 2015; Osuji and Obibuaku, 2016).

The differences between CSR orientations in the more advanced countries and those in developing and emerging economies can be explained by the institutional model, which recognizes contextual variations in needs, priorities and solutions in terms of how national institutions actually shape and mould organisational behaviour (Jamali and Karam, 2018; Osuji, 2015). For example, corporate irresponsibility in developing and emerging countries can be traced to regulatory and institutional factors and institutional gaps and voids in a significant number of cases (Jamali and Karam, 2018; Osuji, 2015).

1.2 DEVELOPING AND EMERGING MARKETS: CONTEXTS AND RECONCEPTUALIZATION OF CSR?

CSR and sustainable development are themes that have infiltrated the global lexicon and have been linked to proper governance of companies and countries in a variety of perspectives. Although CSR in developing and emerging economies has been considered in scholarship to an extent, the institutional and sustainable development perspectives of CSR have received almost no attention, particularly in relation to developing and emerging economies. This is an important void especially in the context of developing and emerging markets that are in the different developmental stages of growing and bolstering their public and private institutions and incentivizing and regulating various aspects of CSR to reap the benefits. Against this backdrop, it is increasingly clear that the peculiar institutional contexts of the developing and emerging markets present both challenges and opportunities for CSR, especially as a mechanism for advancing sustainable development. It is important to identify theoretical models, corporate strategies and pragmatic solutions for CSR in developing and emerging economies. It is also imperative to turn attention to how barriers to effectiveness and improvement of

CSR conception and practice can be identified and tackled and how we need to dissect institutional level factors (macro), organisational-level factors (meso) and individual-level factors (micro) to gain a better understanding of the complex multidimensional variables and influencing factors shaping CSR in developing countries.

This book therefore seeks to examine the conceptualization, roles and practices of CSR in the developing and emerging markets and articulate solutions for improving its effectiveness and utilization and adaptation as a wider tool for individual and society development. It addresses the following central questions:

(1)　What are the linkages between CSR and sustainable development?
(2)　What does or can CSR mean for developing or emerging economies and in what ways does this deviate from orthodoxies and universalist approaches?
(3)　What institutional factors and actors influence or can influence the effectiveness of CSR in developing and emerging economies?
(4)　How can developing and emerging economies promote a flexible, diverse and reconstructed CSR that promotes inclusive and sustainable development?

These questions are tackled by the nineteen substantive chapters from a variety of fields and perspectives; including, but not limited to, law, business ethics, corporate governance, economics, development studies, regulation, globalization, management, organisational studies, human resources management, political economy, supply chains management and business education. The chapter contributions are organised in three parts.

In Part I: 'Institutions, CSR Conceptualizations and Sustainable Development', there are six chapters that investigate the meanings, theorizations and scope of CSR and possible implications for developing and emerging countries. In Chapter 2 'Institutional Theory and Corporate Social Responsibility in Developing Countries: A Comparative Institutional Perspective', Viviana Pilato offers an insightful new conceptual framework that shows how differing expressions of CSR in developing countries are shaped by the institutional dimensions of the developing country's institutional context. The chapter proposes a review of the application of institutional theory for CSR in developing countries and how the different comparative CSR frameworks have been used mostly for developed countries. Rather than using existing comparative institutional models such as Varieties of Capitalism (VOC) or National Business System (NBS), the chapter proposes a new theoretical lens to explore CSR in developing countries. Varieties of Institutional Systems (VIS) aims to expand the conversation on comparative institutional perspectives for CSR in developing countries. The chapter proposes a novel conceptual framework that combines VIS theoretical framework with the heterogeneous expressions of CSR in developing countries. This novel conceptual framework is used to explore which expressions of CSR should be implemented by firms in developing countries, depending on the VIS institutional dimensions. Based on the developing country's institutional context and its institutional dimensions, described by the VIS framework, firms need to adopt a specific expression of CSR in developing countries.

Adaeze Okoye's Chapter 3 entitled 'CSR and a Capabilities Approach to Development: CSR Laws as an Allocative Device?' examines whether the CSR concept and its emerging legal framework can become an allocative device for assigning responsibility for certain aspects of development to business and channelling business conduct on development issues. The chapter proceeds on the basis that CSR is a concept which often captures dimensions of the relationship between business and society in context. On the one hand, it covers aspects which focus on the mitigation of corporate impacts on a range of issues including the environment, health, labour, human rights and corruption. On the other hand, it also covers the ability of corporations to contribute constructively to societal objectives in the above areas and beyond. It is consequently argued that, in a developing country context, CSR could be invariably linked to some development objectives such as optimal health, well-being, education and jobs, because these objectives form the bedrock of capabilities which the individuals in these societies would like to achieve. The chapter references Sen's capabilities conception of development as permitting the consideration of institutions and frameworks, including legal mechanisms geared towards human development objectives which also have a bearing on wider sustainable development goals. The chapter examines examples of emerging legal frameworks to reveal the potential and limitations of this perspective, which indicates how CSR can contribute to development.

Chapter 4 'Domestic Adjudicative Institutions, Developing Countries and Sustainable Development: Linkages and Limitations', by Onyeka K. Osuji and Paul U. Abba, draws insights from the institutional theoretic model, particularly Scott's (2001, 2008) regulatory, normative and cognitive/cultural institutions framework, to investigate the role of courts and other formal adjudicative institutions of developing countries in promoting sustainable development. The tripartite institutions framework emphasizes the knowledge and communicative elements of sustainable development flowing from key social actors such as adjudicative institutions to other segments of society. Using environmental protection as a case study and making references to national laws and judicial decisions, the chapter demonstrates that adjudicative institutions can manifest a commitment to sustainable development, affirm applicable global standards and vertically and horizontally influence other actors in, and segments of, society. It is argued that the regulatory role of adjudicative institutions includes constitutionalization of sustainable development, empowerment of individuals and stakeholder groups and addressing vulnerability of actual and potential victims of unsustainable practices; while the normative role ensures the internalization and transmission of sustainable development values. The cognitive role includes reshaping local practices by promoting effective glocalization and appropriate corporate governance and CSR for sustainable development. The chapter proposes solutions which overcome impediments to the effective involvement of adjudicative institutions in sustainable development. These barriers include lack of explicit provisions, narrowly focusing on compensatory remedies, locus standi, *forum non conveniens* and choice of law. A central message is that adjudicative institutions are a key stakeholder group that champions sustainable development in the public and private spheres.

In Chapter 5 'The Informal Economy: CSR and Sustainable Development', Ogechi Adeola, Oserere Eigbe and Omotayo Muritala investigate how CSR and sustainability practices play a significant role across diverse sectors of an economy. By examining CSR and sustainable development in the informal economy and through a review of the literature, the chapter establishes that unregistered micro, small, and medium enterprises mainly dominate the informal sector particularly in developing and emerging economies. The low degree of formalization and other specific attributes common to small and medium enterprises (SMEs) operating in the informal sector influence their CSR approach and strategies. The chapter discusses the need to build social capital (trust, reputation and legitimacy) and culture as motivating factors that promote SMEs involvement in CSR practices, while legislation and institutional context are major drivers of sustainability practices. The chapter highlights how the informal economy, particularly SMEs, can be positioned to be more socially and environmentally responsible.

In Chapter 6 'Human Resource Management and Political CSR in Global Supply Chains: Causes and Consequences of Host Communities' Enduring Struggles', Hedda Ofoole Knoll and Frederick Ahen argue that little is known about how subsidiaries of multinational corporations (MNCs) implement political CSR across the African continent. The purpose of this chapter is to determine how corporations respond to many 'pressures' to align competing socioeconomic demands through political CSR and how that affects local communities in global supply chains. Based on field work in an emerging economy, the authors focus on a subsidiary of one of the world's largest multinational palm oil producers and its human resources (HR) management. Contrary to what extant literature presents as pressures on MNCs to fulfil demands that are neither related to their raison d'être nor competence, they found that socioeconomic demands in low-income countries are rather the local communities' natural response to shocks emanating from the presence of the subsidiary in their community. The ensuing dramatic changes in the socio-cultural, political and economic institutions underpinning their way of life are articulated as '5Ds': dispossession of land; displacement of people; destruction of the environment; desperation; and de-democratization through disenfranchisement. The chapter's micro-level analysis reveals the dilemma facing HR managers. They are mostly torn between responding to community's grievances and the profit-maximization intents of the firm. They make attempts to liaise and create dialogue but, ultimately, loyalty to the subsidiary is privileged over social demands.

In Chapter 7 'Navigating the CSR Discourse from a Developing Country's Perspective: a Shift to Human Capital Development?' by Deborah B. Motilewa,

Ebes Aziegbe-Esho and Franklin N. Ngwu, it is argued that several sources of today's pressure on managers operating in developing and emerging economies (DEMs) are more associated with social issues than profit-making concerns. Managers are thus faced with the issue of understanding and embedding solutions to societal challenges in their core business strategies in order to be sustainable. Consequently, solutions that go beyond the traditional focus of the CSR discourse on philanthropy in DEMs have become much more imperative as companies strive to use CSR to re-engineer their value chain. As lack of adequate human skills remains a major problem to firms and society, the existing challenges of human capital in many DEMs present businesses (both small and big firms) with the opportunity to use CSR to increase the knowledge, skills and abilities of both their workforce and the society in general. A firm that is able to invest in human capital development across the entire spectrum of its several stakeholders is more likely to achieve a higher competitive advantage and sustainable growth. In this chapter, the authors present case studies of two different approaches to using CSR as a tool for human capital development in Africa and given the success of the companies. It is recommended that firms operating in DEMs should place emphasis on developing and utilizing CSR policies and strategies for human capital development.

Part II 'CSR and Sustainable Development Cross-Country Studies' is composed of six chapters containing country studies of CSR-related practices, experiments and experiences in some developing and emerging economies. The chapters in Part II present comparative, historical and contemporary accounts and highlight developments in those jurisdictions that will enable the cross-exchange of ideas, practices and innovative solutions for CSR and improving its effectiveness for developing and emerging economies.

In Chapter 8 'Firm Ownership and Corporate Social Responsibility in China: from a Multiple Stakeholder Perspective', Ting Ren, Yan Feng, Youzhi Xiao, Hongyan Yang and Wenli Liu adopt multiple stakeholder orientation as a measurement for CSR. Using the data of publicly listed Chinese firms from 2011 to 2016, the authors examine how firms allocate attention to the five key stakeholders' interests under potential resource constraints across different ownership types. Their results suggest that privately owned firms are more likely to prioritize the societal orientation, compared to state-owned and foreign-invested firms; while foreign-invested firms are more likely to attend to investor-orientation, consumer-orientation and environment-orientation, compared to the other two types. Weak difference is detected in employee orientations across the three types of firms, which may be due to a general attention to employee benefits. In the context of potential conflict of interests, the results suggest that different types of ownership lead the firm to make different choices in trading off different stakeholder interests, with foreign-invested firms trading off between internal stakeholder interests and external stakeholder interests, privately-owned firms trading off investor and employee interests for customer interests, and all firms trading off customer interests with environment interests.

Mallika Tamvada in Chapter 9 'The Dynamics of CSR, Mandatory CSR laws, and Corporate Social Performance in India' examines the social and cultural factors influencing CSR in India, the key drivers shaping the legislation mandating CSR in the country, and the impact of this legislation on corporate social performance. The chapter underscores the influence of culture, values, religion, traditions and the role of 'Dharma' for CSR in India. It sheds light on the dynamics of CSR over time by examining how its nature evolved from the Gandhian trusteeship model into a more strategic version of CSR in the face of increasing foreign direct investment (FDI) and growth of MNCs in India. The chapter suggests that such a shift in CSR has impacted the social contributions of firms, necessitating formal legislation covering CSR in India. Furthermore, it highlights that the lack of a binding code at the global level along with the voluntary nature of CSR has compelled the Indian government to reshape CSR to prioritize local needs. It examines the impact of this mandatory CSR legislation on CSR activities along with its limitations. The chapter concludes by discussing the role of legal transplant theory, inventive interventionism and reflexive law for the development of global CSR policy framework.

In Chapter 10 'Nigeria's Informal Economy, Social Responsibility and Sustainable Development', Uchenna Uzo and Olamide Shittu show that the informal economy is the source of livelihood for the teeming population of low-income earners in developing economies. While several studies have been conducted on the impact of the informal economy on Africa's economic development and the neglect of the sector by the government in policy decisions, the authors, however, argue that studies on social responsibility in businesses have largely neglected discourse on socially responsible practices in the informal sector, especially in Nigeria. In this regard, the chapter seeks to contribute to the small extant literature on small business social responsibility in developing economies – specifically Nigeria – and how the exposition of such practices could contribute immensely to the sustainable development of the country. Employing the qualitative research methodology, the study explores how informal businesses conceive of socially responsible practice; what specific social responsibility they adopt; and how these practices could advance the sustainable development of Nigeria. Findings from the study highlight apprenticeship and credit sales as the major practices informal businesses engage in while also noting that such practices are integrated into the day-to-day activities and operations of informal businesses rather than as a separate department. The chapter also establishes some linkages between informal social responsibility and sustainable development while advancing some recommendations on the subject matter.

Durand M. Cupido's Chapter 11 titled 'The Environment in Shipping Incidents: Salvage Contracts and the Public Interest' focuses on South Africa to highlight demands for environmental services in the context of property salvage operations that have seen environmental clauses being added to standard-form salvage contracts. The chapter examines these standard-form salvage contracts against the backdrop of sustainable development and whether they provide an appropriate balance between environmental protection and commercial outcomes in the narrow (the interests of salvors and property owners) and wider sense, i.e. the promotion of shipping and marine commerce in general. Salvors want to get paid for their services while property owners have an interest in their property being saved and the minimization of potential liability. States, representing the public interest and the environment as stakeholders, want their coastlines protected while also having an interest in efficient property salvage operations. As such, modern salvage operations involve at least two of the three recognized interdependent and mutually reinforcing pillars of sustainable development (economic development, social development and environmental protection). The chapter illustrates the challenges faced by salvors in commercial salvage operations as the ones tasked with the furthering of potentially divergent interests (environmental and commercial) and explores the linkages between salvage operations and sustainable development. It examines environmental provisions in the Lloyd's Open Form Salvage Contract (LOF) and Special Compensation Protection and Indemnity Clause (SCOPIC) demonstrating that while these contracts provide a de facto furthering of environmental outcomes, this is incidental to the commercial interests of the contracting parties. The contracts provide no direct basis to promote the environmental protection interests of third-party stakeholders. The chapter argues that the use of the *stipulatio alteri* could provide such a direct legal basis to address external stakeholders' interests in environmental protection, while ensuring an integrated and sustainable balancing with economic endeavour.

In Chapter 12 'Filling Institutional Voids in Thailand: the Case of Nestlé and the Seafood Coalition', David Wesley, Luis Alfonso Dau and Elizabeth M. Moore build on the institutional void's perspective within the institutional theory scholarship by highlighting the role that multinational corporations can play when policy voids are severe, as is the case in many developing countries. The authors utilize an in-depth narrative case study of Nestlé's operations in Thailand to elucidate the institutional and policy voids and then to show how Nestlé worked to fill these voids. Specifically, the chapter documents the history of slavery and child labour in Thailand and how international and domestic policy efforts have failed to address these issues in a political environment that is rife with corruption and abuse. Instead, corporations like Nestlé are filling this policy void with efforts like the Seafood Task Force, which aims to alleviate human rights abuses by eliminating them at the source.

Chapter 13 'Gender Composition of the Upper Echelons and Firm Sustainability Performance: an Examination of Istanbul Stock Exchange Companies' by F. Pinar Acar and A. Gozde Gozum examines the link between the composition of the upper echelons and firm sustainability performance. Gender composition is considered to be the level of women on top management teams (TMTs) and boards. Specifically, the chapter considers whether the presence of three or more women on company boards as well as on TMTs can influence sustainability performance. In undertaking this task, the study incorporates new theoretical developments by conceptualizing gender level using the critical mass concept. The sample consists of the top performing 100 firms in Turkey's Istanbul Stock Exchange (ISE) known as BIST 100. A data set containing information on the BIST 100 companies' TMT members, boards of directors and CEOs as well as firm size, profitability, sustainability performance and industry among others were constructed by using the data provided in the Public Disclosure Platform (PDP). The findings of the study indicate that a critical mass of women on boards of directors is important for sustainability performance. In line with the token theory and critical mass proposition, the chapter's sample shows that having three or more women directors on boards of directors improves the sustainability performance of companies.

The final Part III 'Normative and Utility Perspectives' contains seven chapters that present a picture of CSR and sustainable development from a variety of normative and utility perspectives that can help to improve their conception and practice in the developing and emerging markets. In Chapter 14 'Islamic Finance, Sustainable Development and Developing Countries: Linkages and Potential', Mohammed K. Alshaleel considers the role of Islamic finance in promoting the SDGs in developing countries. Since the SDGs require unprecedented mobilization of funds to support their implementation and given the social and moral ethos and emphasis on prohibition of *riba* (interest) and asset-backed financing, it is argued that Islamic finance offers an effective non-traditional means of financing for sustainable development activities and projects in developing countries. The chapter demonstrates that the ideology of Islamic finance and its attributes, principles, products, instruments and institutions all tend to be well-suited to boosting the SDGs. It shows that Islamic finance has great potential in supporting developing countries efforts to finance the SDGs' agenda. The chapter outlines sustainable development from an Islamic perspective, and the principles of Islamic finance, before assessing the role of Islamic financial institutions, *sukuk* (Islamic bonds), and Islamic social finance (*zakat* and *waqf*) in promoting the SDGs.

Nubi Achebo in Chapter 15 'Developing Countries' Business Schools and Socially Conscious Business Leaders' highlights that organisations and managers are increasingly being held accountable for CSR in their spheres of operation. The author notes that while a few organisations already have structures to deal with competing demands from stakeholders with regard to corporate social responsibilities, some are caught flat-footed. The chapter looks at the theoretical underpinning of CSR and CSR education in the literature. It provides insights into how leaders or managers acquire the sensibilities around CSR in organisations, how managers acquire the necessary knowledge to handle CSR expectations and how MBA institutions are handling the critical task of preparing managers as decisionmakers in charge of CSR for the future. The paper proposes a model that can guide CSR education practitioners.

Chapter 16 'Corporate Participation in Climate Change Mitigation in Developing Countries: "Green Capitalism" as a Tool for Sustainable Development' by Kikelomo Kila shows that tackling the global climate change problem entails navigating complex interwoven links between public and private actors, governments and regulators and, importantly, redirecting corporate and individual behaviours along pathways consistent with environmental sustainability. Corporations are rational calculators and always act in their own business interests while incorporating social and environmental objectives in their business portfolio to improve their 'green credentials'. In developing countries, the weak regulatory systems allow corporations to ignore environmental sustainability in their business activities with little or no repercussions. The author posits that one way of tackling this problem is to make corporate investments in environmental sustainability in developing countries economically attractive to the corporations and in the process enable them to contribute to the achievement of the SDGs in the developing countries while reaping economic rewards for doing so. It is argued that 'green capitalism' as a concept merges economic capitalism with green objectives and, when appropriately utilized, can be an effective tool for achieving the SDGs in developing countries. The chapter analyses the application of green capitalism in developing countries and how it merges the profit-focus of capitalism with environmental sustainability. Utilizing the 'environment contestation approach', it examines how 'green capitalism' reconciles the seemingly antagonistic notions of free-market enterprise on which capitalism is built and the SDGs desired by developing countries. it discusses the regulatory steps needed to prevent potential 'greenwashing' by corporations while incentivising increased investments in SDGs-related projects within these jurisdictions. Using available statistics, the chapter examines the success of 'green bonds' issuance for environmental projects as a reflection of the increasing reliance on green capitalist tools for achieving the SDGs in developing countries.

Rose Hiquet and Won-Yong Oh in Chapter 17 'Ethics Issues in Outsourcing to Emerging Markets: Theoretical Perspectives and Practices' note that offshoring has become a popular practice for MNCs, with the emerging markets being regarded as attractive locations. Although offshore outsourcing has economic benefits, it also involves several ethical issues, such as poor working conditions, child labour and environmental pollution. To identify implications for how to establish ethical practices in MNCs' offshoring operations, the authors discuss theoretical perspectives (i.e. institutional, instrumental and normative) on MNCs' motivations for being socially and environmentally responsible. Based on a review of these perspectives, the chapter provides practical guidelines for both MNCs and policymakers, including (1) redesigning governance, (2) establishing industry-level action and (3) developing institutional capacity. The chapter highlights the importance of developing both public (e.g. government regulation) and private (e.g. corporate code of conduct) governance mechanisms and the need for MNCs to take collective action at the industry level. Lastly, another suggestion is that MNCs should provide resources and capacity to outsourcing companies and local communities to contribute to alleviating ethical concerns in emerging markets.

In Chapter 18 'Promoting Sustainability in Business and Management Education', Ijeoma Nwagwu, Chris Ogbechie and Franklin N. Ngwu acknowledge a broad consensus following the recession of 2008 that ethically challenging practices have permeated the world of today's businesses. They also note that, in many cases, business leaders and entrepreneurs fail to understand their discretionary responsibilities to care for the ecosystem on which lives and businesses depend in enjoying the fruits of the free market and taking advantage of weak governance mechanisms and poor leadership, especially in the developing and emerging economies. The authors argue that the tenets of sustainability, which emphasize the purpose of business as economic advancement coupled with concerns for socio-environmental well-being, offer some direction towards filling the ethical gap in management education to ensure sustainable development in the emerging economies. The chapter therefore examines how sustainability education can be more deliberately advanced in business and management education institutions in the emerging and developing countries.

Chapter 19 'Sustainable Finance, the Law and Stakeholders: Towards Responsible Social Movements' by Radek Stech provides an original and innovative insight into sustainable finance by analysing social movements' interaction with complex finance dynamics (CFDs) through elements of trustworthiness. In doing so, the paper draws on data from an empirical qualitative study that traced the involvement of social movements in shaping three major legal CFDs, namely project finance, bond finance and pension finance on the sustainable finance market between 2015 and 2018. The author argues that social movements, who, by tradition, are in conflict with dominant paradigms, pose a perceptible competitive challenge to major stakeholders who shape the finance dynamics. Whilst the utilization of the trustworthiness analytical framework proves useful in uncovering the conflict, it serves the main purpose of demonstrating the analytic competition between social movements and the major stakeholders. The author also argues that social movements should take a more responsible stance towards sustainable finance and, logically, adopt a form of responsible principles that will govern their relationship with the major stakeholders shaping the CFDs. Further, the author provides draft principles and argues that, if adopted by social movements, these will improve their competitive advantage on the fast-paced sustainable finance market.

Chapter 20 'Sustainable Consumption, Consumer Protection and Sustainable Development: Unbundling Institutional Septet for Developing Economies' by Onyeka K. Osuji and Ugochi C. Amajuoyi draws on the legal, institutional and stakeholder perspectives as well as the SDGs to develop a septet framework for a contextual analysis of the concept of sustainable consumption and production. It uniquely unbundles sustainable consumption and production in a developing country context consisting of six foundational components: (a) sustainable consumption by proximate (existing) consumers for future generations; (b) sustainable production for future generations; (c) sustainable consumption by/for proximate consumers; (d) sustainable production for proximate consumers; (e) participation by proximate consumers; and (f) corporate social responsibility. The septet framework challenges conventional approaches to the concepts of consumer vulnerability, disclosure regulation, contract law, consumer responsibilization, stakeholder, corporate governance, institutional voids and international cooperation. The chapter demonstrates the need for an interventionist 'consumer protection model' for sustainable consumption that includes public interest-oriented disclosure regulation, distributive justice-oriented contract law, resolution of business-to-consumer information asymmetry, credible corporate social reporting and certification standards, distributed/shared consumer responsibilization model, stakeholder enforcement rights, obligations and protection, independent stakeholder determination of standards, resolution of related agency problem through a stakeholder approach to corporate governance and international cooperation in regulatory standards and enforcement. It is also argued that a consumer protection approach to sustainable development can promote stakeholder engagement and meaningful corporate social responsibility. The septet framework therefore provides clarity to the concept of sustainable consumption and production and aligns consumer protection to sustainable development in developing countries by contextualizing the roles of consumers and corporations as institutional actors and consumption as an institution.

The contributions to this book therefore demonstrate the pivotal development roles CSR can play in the developing and emerging economies. The contributions compare and synthetize diverse normative factors, theoretical models, institutional factors and policy strategies, and corporate and industry practices to illustrate their relevance to those economies. Through the three complementary parts combined (I, II and III), and the comprehensive coverage, we shed light on the institutional landscape shaping CSR in the developing world, zooming on specific country experiences (e.g. India, Nigeria, South Africa, Thailand), while also considering normative and utility perspectives that can help in improving both the conception and practice of CSR in the developing and emerging world. The analyses of concepts, principles and practices, country studies and comparative, historical and contemporary accounts in the chapters enable the cross-exchange of ideas and innovative solutions for CSR and sustainable development and improving their effectiveness for developing and emerging economies. The book's multidimensional approach reflects theoretical, socioeconomic, historical, empirical, comparative and interdisciplinary perspectives with some practical suggestions for more effective approaches to CSR and sustainable development in the developing and emerging markets. The suggestions and lessons from this book will benefit policymakers, businesses, scholars, companies, corporate boards, practitioners and other stakeholders and aid the design of appropriate conceptual frameworks, policy strategies, stakeholder engagement models and social performance evaluation strategies that are better tailored for CSR and sustainable development in the developing and emerging economies. This book will be of interest to academics, researchers and students of CSR, sustainable development, corporate law, corporate governance, regulation, economics, public administration, political economy, management, organisational studies, marketing and advertising, and development studies. Through the in-depth and multi]disciplinary account of CSR in the developing world that we offer, we leave the door open for further research and studies that can shed light on the specificities of CSR in the developing world, and hope that this field of research will continue to gain the traction and momentum it deserves to advance and flourish. We need to learn more about CSR in developing and emerging countries, to allow drawing of inferences and substantive contributions over time to the broader business-society field.

REFERENCES

Amaeshi, K., Nnodim, P. and Osuji, O. (2013). *Corporate social responsibility, entrepreneurship, and innovation.* New York: Routledge.

Amaeshi, K., Osuji, O. and Nnodim, P. (2008). Corporate social responsibility in supply chains of global brands: A boundaryless responsibility? Clarifications, exceptions and implications. *Journal of Business Ethics,* 81, 223–4.

Jamali, D. and Karam, C. (2018). Corporate social responsibility in developing countries as an emerging field of study. *International Journal of Management Reviews,* 20(1), 32–61.

Jamali, D., Karam, C. and Blowfield, M. (2015). *Development-oriented CSR.* Sheffield: Greenleaf Publishing.

Jamali, D., Karam, C. M., Soundararajan, V. and Yin, J. (2017). CSR logics in developing countries: Translation, adaptation and stalled development. *Journal of World Business,* 52 (3), 343–59.

Jamali, D. and Neville, B. (2011). Convergence versus divergence of CSR in developing countries: An embedded multi-layered institutional lens. *Journal of Business Ethics,* 102, 599–621.

Ngwu, F., Osuji, O. and Stephen, F., eds., (2017). *Corporate governance in developing and emerging markets.* New York: Routledge.

Osuji, O. (2011). Fluidity of regulation-CSR nexus: The multinational corporate corruption example. *Journal of Business Ethics,* 103, 31–57.

Osuji, O. (2012). Corporate social responsibility: Fairness and promise as the fundaments for juridification of social disclosures. *Contemporary Issues in Law,* 12(1), 46–76.

Osuji, O. (2015). Corporate social responsibility, juridification and globalization: 'Inventive interventionism' for a 'paradox'. *International Journal of Law in Context,* 11, 265–98.

Osuji, O. and Obibuaku, U. (2016). Rights and corporate social responsibility: Competing or complementary approaches to poverty reduction and socioeconomic rights? *Journal of Business Ethics,* 136(2), 329–47.

Osuji, O. and Umahi, O. (2012). Pharmaceutical corporations, developing countries and access to medicine: Social integration and ethical CSR resolution of a global public choice problem. *Journal of Global Ethics,* 8(2–3), 139–67.

Scott, W. (2001). *Institutions and organizations.* Thousand Oaks: Sage Publications, Inc.

Scott, W. (2008). Approaching adulthood: The maturing of institutional theory. *Theory and society,* 37(5), 427–42.

PART I

Institutions, CSR Conceptualizations and Sustainable Development

2

Institutional Theory and Corporate Social Responsibility in Developing Countries: a Comparative Institutional Perspective

Viviana Pilato[1]

2.1 INTRODUCTION

Corporate Social Responsibility (CSR), which refers to 'actions that appear to further some social good, beyond the interests of the firm and that which is required by law' (McWilliams and Siegel, 2001: p. 117), has diffused worldwide. Nevertheless, despite a growing body of literature (Corrigan, 2018; Jamali and Neville, 2011; Osuji and Obibuaku, 2016), it remains challenging to define CSR because it has been studied from different perspectives and therefore defined in disparate ways. Most prior research (Egri and Ralston, 2008) on CSR has mainly focused on developed economies, including Europe and North America. Previous comparative studies showed how CSR differs across different institutional contexts (Jackson and Apostolakou, 2010; Matten and Moon, 2008), explaining how CSR is influenced by national-level institutions (Campbell, 2007; Matten and Moon, 2008). However, this has not been studied in developing countries (Jamali and Karam, 2018; Kolk and Lenfant, 2010).

As compared to developed countries, CSR in developing countries is reported to be 'less embedded in corporate strategies' (Baskin, 2006), 'less formalised' and 'more philanthropic in nature' (Jamali and Neville, 2011; Visser, 2008). Developing economies are also characterised by a range of institutional voids, referring to 'situations where institutional arrangements to support markets are weak or absent' (Khanna and Palepu, 1997, 2010; Mair and Marti 2009: p. 422). As previous studies have shown that CSR is less likely in such circumstances (Amaeshi et al., 2016; Campbell, 2007), comprehending CSR implementation includes also the institutional contexts in which corporations operate (Aguilera et al., 2007), especially in developing countries.

[1] Viviana Pilato conducted this research as a post-doctoral fellow at the Centre for Social and Sustainable Innovation (CSSI) at the Peter B. Gustavson School of Business. CSSI receives funding from Newmont Goldcorp Inc. The author would like to thank Kristin Brandl, Assistant Professor in International Business, Peter B. Gustavson School of Business, University of Victoria, for her support and editorial guidance.

Research on CSR in developing countries remains exiguous (Jamali and Mirshak 2007), and most previous comparative CSR frameworks refer to developed economies (Albareda et al., 2007; Kang and Moon, 2012; Matten and Moon, 2008). For that reason, more research is needed in order to explore how the different institutional dimensions of the institutional context influence the different expressions of CSR implemented in developing countries.

The aim of this chapter is to show how differing expressions of CSR in developing countries are shaped by the institutional dimensions of the developing country's institutional context. Following an overview of how institutional theory has been used to study CSR in developing countries, the chapter describes the use of National Business Systems (NBS) (Whitley, 1999) and Varieties of Capitalism (VOC) (Hall and Soskice, 2001) as comparative CSR frameworks in developed economies. The more detailed Varieties of Institutional Systems (VIS) framework (Fainshmidt et al., 2018) is then introduced, extending the scope of comparative analysis by incorporating Jamali and Karam's (2018) heterogeneous expressions of CSR in developing countries. This novel conceptual framework is used to explore which expression of CSR should be implemented, depending on the VIS institutional dimensions.

The remainder of the chapter, following this introduction, is organised as follows. The next section explores institutional theory and CSR in developing countries. The subsequent section explains the comparative CSR frameworks, mainly applied for developed countries. The following section introduces the VIS framework in developing countries and the different expressions of CSR in developing countries. The subsequent section proposes a novel conceptual framework that combines the VIS framework and the expressions of CSR in developing countries. The conclusion summarises the arguments of the chapter.

2.2 INSTITUTIONAL THEORY AND CSR IN DEVELOPING COUNTRIES

Institutional theory is used to explain 'organisations and management practices as the product of social rather than economic pressures' (Suddaby, 2013: p. 379). This theory is widely used in management studies because it can illustrate 'organisational behaviours that defy economic rationality' (Suddaby, 2013: p. 379). Institutional theory and the new institutionalism foster the belief that organisations must conform to their institutional environment in order to become legitimate (DiMaggio and Powell, 1983; Meyer and Rowan, 1977). In CSR studies, institutional theory has largely been applied to explain how organisations respond to a combination of institutional pressures from different actors within their institutional environment (DiMaggio and Powell, 1983), and to show that CSR differs across institutional contexts (Brammer et al., 2012; Kang and Moon, 2012; Matten and Moon 2008). According to Hall and Taylor (1996), neo-institutionalism is characterised by three approaches: sociological, historical and rational choice institutionalism. Each is based on different premises, and previous studies of CSR in developing countries have relied on different types of institutionalism. As well as depending on institutional theory, referring to the above forms of institutionalism, such studies have been informed by other perspectives within institutional theory, such as institutional logics (Friedland and Alford, 1991; Thornton et al., 2012) and Scandinavian institutionalism (Boxenbaum, 2006; Boxenbaum and Pedersen, 2009). Table 2.1 summarises the three types of institutionalism described by Hall and Taylor (1996), as well as institutional logics (Friedland and Alford, 1991; Thornton et al., 2012) and Scandinavian institutionalism (Boxenbaum and Pedersen, 2009; Czarniawska and Joerges, 1996), including key implications of each theoretical perspective and examples of prior research on CSR in developing and emerging countries.

TABLE 2.1 *Overview of institutional theory as applied to CSR in developing countries*

Institutional theory	Key implications	Studies of CSR in developing countries
Sociological (Hall and Taylor, 1996); DiMaggio and Powell, 1983	• Institutions are viewed more broadly as 'not only formal rules or norms but also a symbol system, cognitive scripts and moral template that provide the frame of meaning to human action'. • Highlights 'how practices are diffused through organisational fields'. • Isomorphism, which indicates similarities across organisations, arises from three types of pressure: coercive, mimetic and normative.	Beddewela and Herzig (2013); Holm et al. (2017); Jamali, Lund-Thomsen and Khara (2017b); Momin and Parker (2013); Park et al. (2014); Yin (2017); Yin and Zhang (2012)
Historical (Hall and Taylor, 1996)	• Differences in practices across institutional contexts; cross-national differences. • Institutions are 'formal or informal procedures, routines, norms and conventions embedded in the organisational structure of the political economy'. • The relationship between institutions and actions can use both calculus and cultural approaches.	Amaeshi and Amao (2009); Jamali and Neville (2011); Muthuri and Gilbert (2011); Preuss et al. (2016)

(continued)

TABLE 2.1 *(continued)*

Institutional theory	Key implications	Studies of CSR in developing countries
Rational choice (Hall and Taylor, 1996)	• Relevant actors 'behave instrumentally to maximise their preferences' following an 'extensive calculation'. • Institutions are perceived as social structures for enforcing mechanisms that reduce uncertainty, by reducing transaction costs.	N/A
Scandinavian (Boxenbaum, 2006; Boxenbaum and Pedersen, 2009; Sahlin and Wedlin, 2008; Czarniawska and Joerges, 1996)	• Focuses on understanding 'how organisations perceive and interpret institutional pressures'. • Centres on the concept of translation, referring to the modification of a practice or idea when implemented in a new organisational context. • Relies on the concept of 'editing to describe and explain how translation proceeds'.	Jamali et al. (2017a)
Institutional logics (Friedland and Alford, 1991; Thornton et al., 2012; Thornton and Ocasio, 1999)	• 'The socially constructed, historical patterns of cultural symbols and material practices, including assumptions, values and beliefs, by which individuals and organisations assign meaning to their daily activities, organise time and space and reproduce their lives and experiences.'	Jamali et al. (2017a); Reddy and Hamann (2018)

2.3 COMPARATIVE INSTITUTIONAL ANALYSIS IN CSR RESEARCH

Within the perspective of historical institutionalism, Comparative Institutional Analysis (Ahmadjian, 2016) distinguishes countries' business systems in terms of National Business System (NBS) (Whitley, 1999) and Varieties of Capitalism (VOC) (Hall and Soskice, 2001). The VOC distinguishes between two main types of advanced economy: liberal market economies (LMEs) and coordinated market economies (CMEs) (Hall and Soskice, 2001). The NBS addresses four sets of institutional players: (1) the 'political system', (2) the 'financial system', (3) the 'education and labour system' and (4) the 'cultural system' (Whitley, 1999).

Based on the above perspectives, Matten and Moon (2008) identified two distinct forms of CSR, the 'explicit' approach of North American LMEs (characterised by voluntary and formalised corporate policies assuming responsibility for societal interests) and the 'implicit' approach of European CMEs (mandatory social obligations for companies, motivated by the societal consensus). This implicit CSR approach has been further investigated by Albareda et al. (2007), who proposed four variants: (1) the 'Partnership model', in which partnership is a key strategy in addressing social challenges; (2) the 'Business in the Community model', characterised by limited intervention policies to 'encourage corporate involvement in governance challenges affecting the community'; (3) the 'Sustainability and Citizenship model', where governments promote CSR by supporting companies; and (4) the 'c model', which proposes the involvement of different stakeholders to reach public consensus on CSR. Figure 2.1 describes the evolution of comparative CSR frameworks in developed economies.

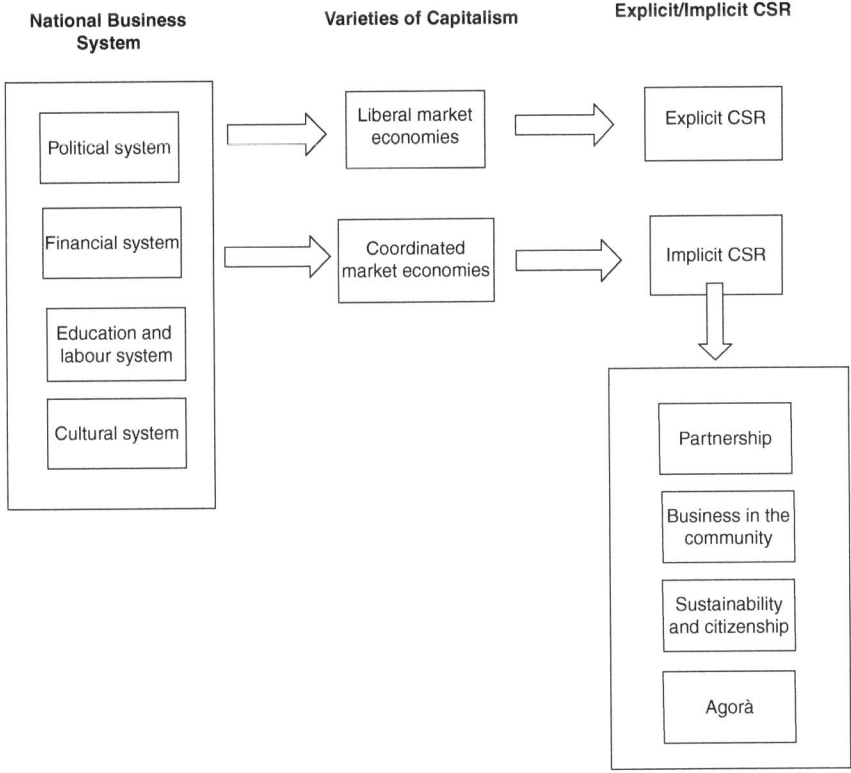

FIGURE 2.1 Comparative CSR frameworks (based on Whitley (1999), Hall and Soskice (2001), Matten and Moon (2008) and Albareda et al. (2007), adapted from initial illustration by Turkina et al. (2017))

The above frameworks have largely been applied to developed countries and fail to capture the distinctiveness and heterogeneity of developing countries.

2.4 COMPARATIVE INSTITUTIONAL ANALYSIS AND CSR IN DEVELOPING COUNTRIES

2.4.1 *Varieties of Institutional Systems in Developing Countries*

Fainshmidt et al.'s (2018) VIS framework represents a first step towards acknowledging the diversity of institutional contexts in developing countries. Integrating VOC and NBS, the VIS framework addresses five institutional dimensions that characterise such institutional contexts: (1) the role of the state, (2) the role of financial markets, (3) the role of human capital, (4) the role of social capital and (5) the role of corporate governance.

According to Fainshmidt et al. (2018), *the role of the state* (i.e. the country's government) can influence a country's economy through direct intervention (Carney and Witt 2014; Whitley, 2003), through majority or minority state-owned enterprises (Zhang and Whitley, 2013) or through indirect intervention (Carney and Witt, 2014; Whitley 2003) in the private sector (e.g. capital provision, favouritism and/or participation in corporate governance) (Boyer, 2005; Kang and Moon, 2012). The four types of states are not considered for the purpose of the analysis.

The role of financial markets, how 'capital is acquired and distributed' (Davis and Marquis, 2005), include 'equity' and 'credit' markets, to acquire financial capitals (Hall and Soskice, 2001; Whitley, 1999), as well as through state-provided capital (Lazzarini et al., 2015) and 'family wealth' (Schneider, 2009; Steier, 2009; Fainshmidt et al., 2018).

The role of human capital refers to the 'organisation of labour markets' and to employees' knowledge (Fainshmidt et al., 2018). Coordination with labour through 'legal arrangements' (Botero et al., 2004) or may be 'more fragmented with high employee turnover and flexibility' (Witt and Redding, 2013). Knowledge capital includes employee skills and competences acquired through education and skill formation systems (Morgan, 2007; Fainshmidt et al., 2018: p. 311).

The role of social capital refers to the 'extent of trust among the members of a society and in society at large' (Inglehart, 1999; Fainshmidt et al., 2018), involving a range of institutional actors that include individuals, organisations, non-government organisations (NGOs) and governments. In developing countries, a lack of trust is explained by 'corruption' and an 'ineffective state' (Fainshmidt et al., 2018).

Finally, *the role of corporate governance* refers to how 'corporations are controlled and managed', including 'ownership concentration', which 'shapes how owners, labour and management interact with each other' (Aguilera and Jackson, 2003), and it involves also 'wealthy family dominance' and 'family intervention in management' (Fainshmidt et al., 2018: p. 313). In this way, institutional actors include owners, individuals, employees and families.

2.4.2 *Expressions of CSR in Developing Countries*

According to Jamali and Karam (2018), CSR in developing countries can be categorised into four expressions: (1) Relational CSR, (2) Developmental CSR, (3) Decoupled CSR or (4) Hybrid CSR.

Relational CSR expression refers to strategies that emphasise the initiation of 'collaborative relationships with others inside and outside the corporation' (Muller and Kolk, 2009). This expression is 'governed by social relations' (Huemer, 2010), with tailored CSR practices to address cultural expectations and local needs (Jamali and Karam, 2018). This expression of CSR emphasises effective 'local engagement, partnering and collaboration' (e.g. Cruz and Boehe, 2010).

Developmental CSR expression is used by corporations to bridge institutional voids and to promote engagement with local stakeholders concerns (Jamali and Karam, 2018; Kolk and Lenfant, 2013). This expression highlights development and sustainability as main priorities (Jamali and Karam, 2018).

Decoupled CSR expression is primarily 'legitimacy-oriented', seeking to maintain legitimacy while engaging in 'business as usual' (Jamali et al., 2017b), such as 'symbolic CSR' (Jamali and Neville, 2011), 'strategic CSR' (Wiig and Kolstad, 2010) or 'greenwash CSR' (Hamann and Kapelus, 2004). This expression promotes the 'logic of efficient systems with profit-oriented business' (Jamali and Karam, 2018).

In conclusion, *hybrid CSR expression* combines elements of both implicit and explicit CSR described above. This expression of CSR reflects the difficulty of a clear distinction between implicit or explicit CSR in developing countries, highlighting the variety of CSR forms in this context (Jamali and Neville, 2011). This expression focuses on CSR forms in developing countries that are not solely explicit or implicit, but combine elements of both, such as international standards of CSR that explicitly specify corporate obligations (more explicit CSR) (Azizul Islam and Deegan, 2008), associated with CSR practices driven by cultural traditions (more implicit CSR) (Balasubramanian et al., 2005).

2.4.3 *Varieties of Institutional Systems and Expressions of CSR in Developing Countries*

The VIS framework by Fainshmidt et al. (2018) and Jamali and Karam's (2018) classification of expressions of CSR can be integrated to provide a novel conceptual framework that explains variations in expressions of CSR in developing countries in terms of specific characteristics of VIS. Figure 2.2 visualises this discussion.

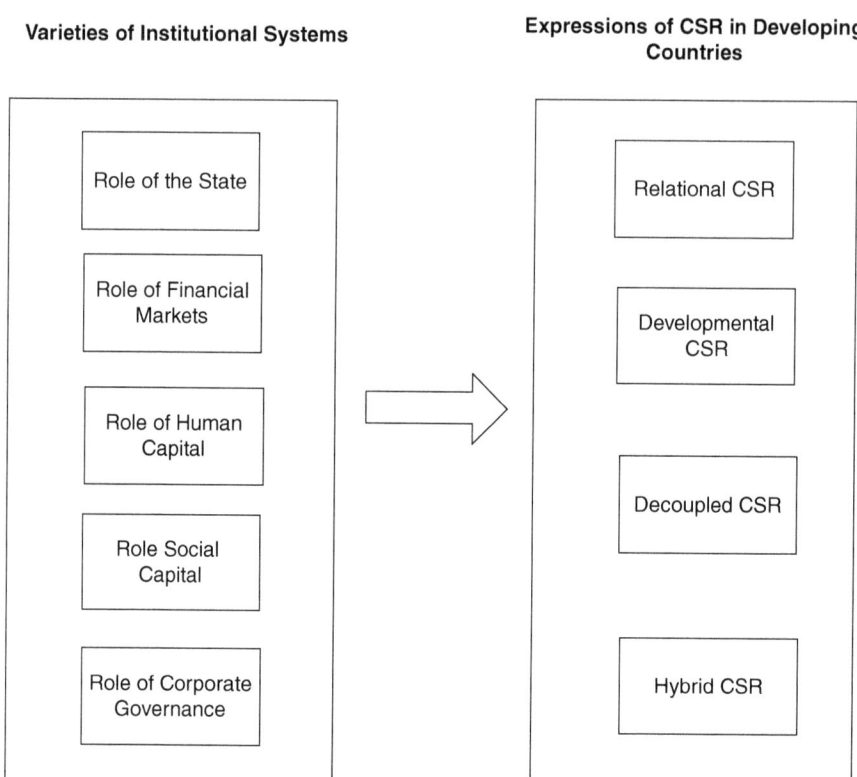

FIGURE 2.2 Varieties of Institutional Systems (Fainshmidt et al., 2018) and CSR expressions in developing countries (Jamali and Karam, 2018)

This section discusses each of the institutional dimensions in the VIS framework to clarify which expression of CSR should be implemented by firms in developing countries. For the purpose of the chapter, the firm considered may be local or international.

State. In developing countries where the state is dominant and plays a direct and active role in the economy, hybrid CSR expressions may be appropriate. In such cases, the government drives the adoption of CSR practices inside the firm through mandatory requirements and policies. This approach reflects implicit CSR. However, notwithstanding the strong requirements from the governments, firms in developing countries might also pursue philanthropic and voluntary CSR practices, that emphasise the explicit side and thus reflecting the combination of both approaches, as hybrid CSR expression. In contrast, if the indirect state intervention is high, favouritism and corruption might indicate a relational CSR expression, because CSR emerges from local relations, emphasising collaborations and engagement to meet local needs. Where direct state dominance and indirect state intervention are either low, a decoupled or even a hybrid CSR expression should be considered. In the absence of regulations, firms may adopt a symbolic CSR or greenwash CSR in the developing country, while continuing their business, only in order to maintain their legitimacy reflecting a decoupled CSR expression. Moreover, in this situation, firms might also respond to stakeholder pressures, developing voluntary CSR practices that respond to the needs of local communities and of the country in question, and thus, a hybrid CSR expression might be most applicable.

Financial Markets. In the case of well-developed financial markets, firms may consider adopting a hybrid CSR expression, combining both implicit and explicit elements. In this situation, strong equity and credit markets, together with state-provided capital, might allow firms to develop voluntary CSR programmes at the firm's discretion or also the state-provided capital might encourage mandatory requirements for firms to address CSR issues. Where financial markets are under-developed and firms tend to rely on internal capital markets based on accumulated family wealth (Steier, 2009), a relational CSR expression may be appropriate, emphasising the importance of collaborative relationships outside the corporation (e.g. with families). Moreover, in this case, also a developmental CSR expression should be considered by firms that might want to fill the institutional void (the lack of well-developed financial markets).

Human Capital. High availability of human capital means strong labour coordination and knowledge capital. In such countries, a relational CSR expression may again be useful. Labour is organised and activities involving this labour force can be coordinated by promoting collaborations within the firm. The engagement fostered by the high collaboration within employees, with strong educational skills, will promote CSR through partnerships rather than impose it, allowing CSR to arise from the local relationship established within employees. On the other hand, if knowledge capital is low and there is poor coordination, the labour force may not engage in collaborations, and a decoupled CSR expression may be more appropriate. In this case, employees who are not properly informed about CSR issues and do not collaborate might just engage in legitimacy-oriented CSR practices, in order to maintain the profit-oriented business.

Social Capital. High levels of social capital indicate a high level of trust among members of society, inviting a relational CSR expression that promotes collaborations and local engagement. The high level of trust motivates the creation of social relations that promote partnerships. In contrast, a lack of trust can lead towards a decoupled CSR expression. Local stakeholders who do not trust each other might encourage firms to consider greenwash or symbolic CSR, in order to maintain the profit priority of the business.

Corporate Governance. Finally, if a country's ownership structure is concentrated and dominated by wealthy families, firms might usefully adopt a relational CSR expression, emphasising the importance of the creation of family social relations within the firm. This expression of CSR emerges from the local relationships developed between family members and informed by sociocultural values and family traditions. In contrast, if ownership is dispersed and there is low family ownership, firms should consider a developmental CSR expression, due to lack of managerial control and overcome institutional voids arising from the lack of concentrated ownership. Moreover, the lack of trust and coordination given by the dispersed and with low family ownership might induce firms to consider a decoupled CSR expression, focused on legitimacy purposes to maintain their business, and developing a strategic CSR.

In conclusion, based on the developing country's institutional context and its institutional dimensions described by the VIS framework, firms need to adopt a specific expression of CSR in developing countries.

2.5 CONCLUSION

The novel conceptual framework proposed here facilitates the exploration of how expressions of CSR in developing countries are influenced by the country's institutional configurations. The VIS framework proposed by Fainshmidt et al. (2018) facilitates an analysis of the role of institutional dimensions to be considered in developing economies, including the role of the state, the role of financial markets, the role of human capital, the role of social capital and the role of corporate governance. This discussion is combined with the work of Jamali and Karam (2018) on expressions of CSR in developing countries, resulting in a novel conceptual framework that further extend comparative CSR literature for developing countries. The chapter illustrates how several institutional dimensions can influence the variations in expression of CSR in developing countries and provides a review of how institutional theory has been used to study CSR in such settings. The evolution of comparative institutional frameworks in CSR-related studies is also described. Future research can usefully apply the developed framework in further empirical studies to classify the expressions of CSR in developing countries according to the country's institutional dimensions.

REFERENCES

Aguilera, R. V. and Jackson, G. (2003). The Cross-National Diversity of Corporate Governance: Dimensions and Determinants. *Academy of Management Review*, 28(3), 447–65. http://doi:10.5465/AMR.2003.10196772.
Aguilera, R. V., Rupp, D. E., Williams, C. A. and Ganapathi, J. (2007). Putting the S Back in Corporate Social Responsibility: A Multilevel Theory of Social Change in Organizations. *The Academy of Management Review*, 32(3), 836–63. http://doi:10.2307/20159338.

Ahmadjian, C. L. (2016). Comparative Institutional Analysis and Institutional Complexity. *Journal of Management Studies*, 53(1), 12–27. http://doi:10.1111/joms.12178.

Albareda, L., Lozano, J. M. and Ysa, T. (2007). Public Policies on Corporate Social Responsibility: The Role of Governments in Europe. *Journal of Business Ethics*, 74(4), 391–407. http://doi:10.1007/s10551-007-9514-1.

Amaeshi, K., Adegbite, E. and Rajwani, T. (2016). Corporate Social Responsibility in Challenging and Non-enabling Institutional Contexts: Do Institutional Voids Matter? *Journal of Business Ethics*, 134(1), 135–53. http://doi:10.1007/s10551-014-2420-4.

Amaeshi, K. and Amao, O. O. (2009). Corporate Social Responsibility in Transnational Spaces: Exploring Influences of Varieties of Capitalism on Expressions of Corporate Codes of Conduct in Nigeria. *Journal of Business Ethics*, 86(2), 225. http://doi:10.1007/s10551-009-0192-z.

Balasubramanian, N. K., Kimber, D. and Siemensma, F. (2005). Emerging Opportunities or Traditions Reinforced? An Analysis of the Attitudes towards CSR, and Trends of Thinking about CSR, in India. *The Journal of Corporate Citizenship*, 17, 79–92.

Baskin, J. (2006). Corporate Responsibility in Emerging Markets. *The Journal of Corporate Citizenship*, 24, 29–47.

Beddewela, E. and Herzig, C. (2013). Corporate Social Reporting by MNCs' Subsidiaries in Sri Lanka. *Accounting Forum*, 37(2), 135–49. http://doi:10.1016/j.accfor.2012.09.001.

Botero, J. C., Djankov, S., Porta, R. L., Lopez-de-Silanes, F. and Shleifer, A. (2004). The Regulation of Labor. *The Quarterly Journal of Economics*, 119(4), 1339–82. http://doi:10.1162/0033553042476215.

Boxenbaum, E. (2006). Lost in Translation: The Making of Danish Diversity Management. *American Behavioral Scientist*, 49(7), 939–48. http://doi:10.1177/0002764205285173.

Boxenbaum, E. and Pedersen, S. S. (2009). Scandinavian Institutionalism – A Case of Institutional Work. In T. B. Lawrence, R. Suddaby and B. Leca, eds., *Institutional Work: Actors and Agency in Institutional Studies of Organizations*. Cambridge: Cambridge University Press, pp. 178–204. http://doi: 10.1017/CBO9780511596605.007.

Boyer, R. (2005). How and Why Capitalisms Differ. *Economy and Society*, 34(4), 509–57. doi:10.1080/03085140500277070.

Brammer, S., Jackson, G. and Matten, D. (2012). Corporate Social Responsibility and Institutional Theory: New Perspectives on Private Governance. *Socio-Economic Review*, 10(1), 3–28. https://doi:10.1093/ser/mwr030.

Campbell, J. L. (2007). Why Would Corporations Behave in Socially Responsible Ways? An Institutional Theory of Corporate Social Responsibility. *The Academy of Management Review*, 32(3), 946–67. http://doi:10.2307/20159343.

Carney, R. W. and Witt, M. A. (2014). The Role of the State in Asian Business Systems. In M. A. Witt and G. Redding, eds., *The Oxford Handbook of Asian Business Systems*. Oxford: Oxford University Press, pp. 538–60.

Corrigan, C. C. (2018). Corporate Social Responsibility and Local Context: The Case of Mining in Southern Africa. *Resources Policy*, 55, 233–43. http://doi:10.1016/j.resourpol.2017.12.007.

Cruz, L. B. and Boehe, D. M. (2010). How Do Leading Retail MNCs Leverage CSR Globally? Insights from Brazil. *Journal of Business Ethics*, 91(2), 243–263. http://doi:10.1007/s10551-010-0617-8

Czarniawska, B. and Joerges, B. (1996). Travels of Ideas. In B. Czarniawska and G. Sevón, eds., *Translating Organizational Change*. Berlin: Walter de Gruyter, pp. 13–47.

Davis, G. F. and Marquis, C. (2005). The Globalization of Stock Markets and Convergence in Corporate Governance. In V. Nee and R. Swedberg, eds., *The Economic Sociology of Capitalism*. Princeton: Princeton University Press, pp. 352–90.

DiMaggio, P. J. and Powell, W. W. (1983). The Iron Cage Revisited: Institutional Isomorphism and Collective Rationality in Organizational Fields. *American Sociological Review*, 48(2), 147–60. http://doi:10.2307/2095101.

Egri, C. P. and Ralston, D. A. (2008). Corporate Responsibility: A Review of International Management Research from 1998 to 2007. *Journal of International Management*, 14(4), 319–39. http://doi:10.1016/j.intman.2007.09.003.

Fainshmidt, S., Judge, W. Q., Aguilera, R. V. and Smith, A. (2018). Varieties of Institutional Systems: A Contextual Taxonomy of Understudied Countries. *Journal of World Business*, 53(3), 307–22. http://doi:10.1016/j.jwb.2016.05.003.

Friedland, R. and Alford, R. (1991). Bringing Society Back. In Symbols, Practices and Institutional Contradictions. In W. Powell and P. DiMaggio, eds., *The New Institutionalism in Organizational Analysis*. Chicago: University of Chicago Press, pp. 232–63.

Hall, P. A. and Soskice, D. W., eds. (2001). *Varieties of Capitalism: The Institutional Foundations of Comparative Advantage*. Oxford: Oxford University Press.

Hall, P. A. and Taylor, R. C. R. (1996). Political Science and the Three New Institutionalisms. *Political Studies*, 44(5), 936–57. http://doi:10.1111/j.1467-9248.1996.tb00343.x.

Hamann, R. and Kapelus, P. (2004). Corporate Social Responsibility in Mining in Southern Africa: Fair accountability or just greenwash? *Development*, 47(3), 85–92. http://doi:10.1057/palgrave.development.1100056.

Holm, A. E., Decreton, B., Nell, P. C. and Klopf, P. (2017). The Dynamic Response Process to Conflicting Institutional Demands in MNC Subsidiaries: An Inductive Study in the Sub-Saharan African E-Commerce Sector. *Global Strategy Journal*, 7(1), 104–24. http://doi:10.1002/gsj.1145.

Huemer, L. (2010). Corporate Social Responsibility and Multinational Corporation Identity: Norwegian Strategies in the Chilean Aquaculture Industry. *Journal of Business Ethics*, 91 (2), 265–77. http://doi:10.1007/s10551-010-0618-7.

Inglehart, R. (1999). Trust, Well-Being and Democracy. In M. E. Warren, ed., *Democracy and Trust*. New York: Cambridge University Press, pp. 88–120. http://doi:10.1017/CBO9780511659959.004

Islam, M.A. and Deegan, C. (2008). Motivations for an Organisation within a Developing Country to Report Social Responsibility Information: Evidence from Bangladesh. *Accounting, Auditing & Accountability Journal*, 21(6), 850–74. http://doi:10.1108/09513570810893272.

Jackson, G. and Apostolakou, A. (2010). Corporate Social Responsibility in Western Europe: An Institutional Mirror or Substitute? *Journal of Business Ethics*, 94(3), 371–94. https://doi.org/10.1007/s10551-009-0269-8.

Jamali, D. and Karam, C. (2018). Corporate Social Responsibility in Developing Countries as an Emerging Field of Study. *International Journal of Management Reviews*, 20(1), 32–61. http://doi:10.1111/ijmr.12112.

Jamali, D., Karam, C., Yin, J. and Soundararajan, V. (2017a). CSR Logics in Developing Countries: Translation, Adaptation and Stalled Development. *Journal of World Business*, 52 (3), 343–59. http://doi:10.1016/j.jwb.2017.02.001.

Jamali, D., Lund-Thomsen, P. and Khara, N. (2017b). CSR Institutionalized Myths in Developing Countries: An Imminent Threat of Selective Decoupling. *Business & Society*, 56(3), 454–86. http://doi:10.1177/0007650315584303.

Jamali, D. and Mirshak, R. (2007). Corporate Social Responsibility (CSR): Theory and Practice in a Developing Country Context. *Journal of Business Ethics*, 72(3), 243–62.

Jamali, D. and Neville, B. (2011). Convergence Versus Divergence of CSR in Developing Countries: An Embedded Multi-Layered Institutional Lens. *Journal of Business Ethics*, 102 (4), 599–621.

Kang, N. and Moon, J. (2012). Institutional Complementarity between Corporate Governance and Corporate Social Responsibility: A Comparative Institutional Analysis of Three Capitalisms. *Socio-Economic Review*, 10(1), 85–108. http://doi:10.1093/ser/mwr025.

Khanna, T. and Palepu, K. (1997). Why Focused Strategies May Be Wrong for Emerging Markets. *Harvard Business Review*, 75(4), 41–51.

Khanna, T. and Palepu, K. G. (2010). *Winning in Emerging Markets: A Road Map for Strategy and Execution*. Boston: Harvard Business Press.

Kolk, A. and Lenfant, F. (2010). MNC Reporting on CSR and Conflict in Central Africa. *Journal of Business Ethics*, 93(2), 241–55. http://doi:10.1007/s10551-009-0271-1.

Kolk, A. and Lenfant, F. (2013). Multinationals, CSR and Partnerships in Central African Conflict Countries. *Corporate Social Responsibility and Environmental Management*, 20 (1), 43–54. http://doi:10.1002/csr.1277.

Lazzarini, S. G., Musacchio, A., Bandeira-de-Mello, R. and Marcon, R. (2015). What Do State-Owned Development Banks Do? Evidence from BNDES, 2002–09. *World Development*, 66, 237–53. http://doi:10.1016/j.worlddev.2014.08.016.

Mair, J. and Marti, I. (2009). Entrepreneurship in and around Institutional Voids: A Case Study from Bangladesh. *Journal of Business Venturing*, 24(5), 419–35. http://doi:10.1016/j.jbusvent.2008.04.006.

Matten, D. and Moon, J. (2008). 'Implicit' and 'Explicit' CSR: A Conceptual Framework for a Comparative Understanding of Corporate Social Responsibility. *Academy of Management Review*, 33(2), 404–24. http://doi:10.5465/AMR.2008.31193458.

McWilliams, A. and Siegel, D. (2001). Corporate Social Responsibility: A Theory of the Firm Perspective. *Academy of Management Review*, 26(1), 117–27. http://doi:10.2307/259398.

Meyer, J. W. and Rowan, B. (1977). Institutionalized Organizations: Formal Structure as Myth and Ceremony. *American Journal of Sociology*, 83(2), 340–63.

Momin, M. A. and Parker, L. D. (2013). Motivations for Corporate Social Responsibility Reporting by MNC Subsidiaries in an Emerging Country: The Case of Bangladesh. *The British Accounting Review*, 45(3), 215–28. http://doi:10.1016/j.bar.2013.06.007.

Morgan, K. (2007). The Learning Region: Institutions, Innovation and Regional Renewal. *Regional Studies*, 31 (5), 491–503. http://doi:10.1080/00343409750132289.

Muller, A. and Kolk, A. (2009). CSR Performance in Emerging Markets Evidence from Mexico. *Journal of Business Ethics*, 85(2), 325–37. http://doi:10.1007/s10551-008-9735-y.

Muthuri, J. N. and Gilbert, V. (2011). An Institutional Analysis of Corporate Social Responsibility in Kenya. *Journal of Business Ethics*, 98(3), 467–83. http://doi:10.1007/s10551-010-0588-9.

Osuji, O. K. and Obibuaku, U. L. (2016). Rights and Corporate Social Responsibility: Competing or Complementary Approaches to Poverty Reduction and Socioeconomic Rights? *Journal of Business Ethics*, 136(2), 329–47. http://doi:10.1007/s10551-014-2523-y.

Park, B. I., Chidlow, A., and Choi, J. (2014). Corporate social responsibility: Stakeholders influence on MNEs' activities. *International Business Review*, 23(5), 966–80. https://doi.org/10.1016/j.ibusrev.2014.02.008.

Preuss, L., Barkemeyer, R. and Glavas, A. (2016). Corporate Social Responsibility in Developing Country Multinationals: Identifying Company and Country-Level Influences. *Business Ethics Quarterly*, 26(3), 347–78. http://doi:10.1017/beq.2016.42.

Reddy, C. D. and Hamann, R. (2018). Distance Makes the (Committed) Heart Grow Colder: MNEs' Responses to the State Logic in African Variants of CSR. *Business & Society*, 57(3), 562–94. http://doi:10.1177/0007650316629127.

Schneider, B. R. (2009). Hierarchical Market Economies and Varieties of Capitalism in Latin America. *Journal of Latin American Studies*, 41(3), 553–75. http://doi:10.1017/S0022216X09990186.

Sahlin, K., and Wedlin, L. (2008). Circulating ideas: Imitation, translation and editing. In R. Greenwood, C. Oliver, R. Suddaby, and K. Sahlin, eds., *The SAGE Handbook of Organizational Institutionalism*. London: Sage Publications, pp. 218–42.

Steier, L. P. (2009). Familial Capitalism in Global Institutional Contexts: Implications for Corporate Governance and Entrepreneurship in East Asia. *Asia Pacific Journal of Management*, 26(3), 513. http://doi:10.1007/s10490-008-9117-0.

Suddaby, R. (2013). Institutional theory. In E. Kessler, ed., *Encyclopedia of Management Theory*. Thousand Oaks: SAGE Publications, Ltd., pp. 380–384. doi:10.4135/9781452276090.n132.

Turkina, N., Neville, B. A., and Bice, S. (2017). Rediscovering divergence in developing countries' CSR. In D. Jamali, C. Karam, and M. Blowfield, eds., *Development-Oriented Corporate Social Responsibility: Volume 2*. Routledge, pp. 13–36.

Thornton, P. H. and Ocasio, W. (1999). Institutional Logics and the Historical Contingency of Power in Organizations: Executive Succession in the Higher Education Publishing Industry, 1958–1990. *American Journal of Sociology*, 105(3), 801–43. http://doi:10.1086/210361.

Thornton, P. H., Ocasio, W. and Lounsbury, M. (2012). *The Institutional Logics Perspective: A New Approach to Culture, Structure and Process*. Oxford: Oxford University Press.

Visser, W. (2008). Corporate Social Responsibility in Developing Countries. In A. Crane, D. Matten, A. McWilliams, J. Moon, and D. S. Siegel, eds., *The Oxford Handbook of Corporate Social Responsibility*. Oxford: Oxford University Press, pp. 473–9.

Whitley, R. (1999). *Divergent Capitalisms: The Social Structuring and Change of Business Systems*. Oxford: Oxford University Press.

Whitley, R. (2003). Competition and Pluralism in the Public Sciences: The Impact of Institutional Frameworks on the Organisation of Academic Science. *Research Policy*, 32 (6), 1015–29. http://doi:10.1016/S0048-7333(02)00112-9.

Wiig, A. and Kolstad, I. (2010). Multinational Corporations and Host Country Institutions: A Case Study of CSR Activities in Angola. *International Business Review*, 19(2), 178–90. http://doi:10.1016/j.ibusrev.2009.11.006.

Witt, M. A. and Redding, G. (2013). Asian Business Systems: Institutional Comparison, Clusters and Implications for Varieties of Capitalism and Business Systems Theory. *Socio-Economic Review*, 11(2), 265–300. http://doi:10.1093/ser/mwt002.

Yin, J. (2017). Institutional Drivers for Corporate Social Responsibility in an Emerging Economy: A Mixed-Method Study of Chinese Business Executives. *Business & Society*, 56(5), 672–704. http://doi:10.1177/0007650315592856.

Yin, J. and Zhang, Y. (2012). Institutional Dynamics and Corporate Social Responsibility (CSR) in an Emerging Country Context: Evidence from China. *Journal of Business Ethics*, 111(2), 301–16. http://doi:10.1007/s10551-012-1243-4.

Zhang, X. and Whitley, R. (2013). Changing Macro-structural Varieties of East Asian Capitalism. *Socio-Economic Review*, 11(2), 301–36. http://doi:10.1093/ser/mws029.

3

CSR and a Capabilities Approach to Development: CSR Laws as an Allocative Device?

Adaeze Okoye

3.1 INTRODUCTION

The challenge of achieving development is the key indicator which forms the dividing line between the developing countries and the developed countries. The United Nations 2030 Agenda for Sustainable Development (Agenda 2030) identifies the global scale of this challenge. It suggests that this requires 'an intensive global engagement . . . bringing together governments, the private sector, civil society, the United Nations system and other actors and mobilizing all available resources' (General Assembly Resolution 2015, para. 39). The means of such engagement for achieving development, amongst the various stakeholders including the private sector, is open to examination. This chapter examines whether CSR through its emerging legal frameworks could become an allocative device which allocates some responsibility for certain aspects of development and thereby channels conduct.

The concept of development is often contested and difficult to measure. Furthermore, there are difficulties in the terminology which may cause problems for its use. For example, the World Bank in its 2016 World Bank Indicators (WDI) report stopped distinguishing between developing and developed countries in the presentation of its data set (World Bank Indicators, 2016) because of the questions raised about criteria.[1] However to achieve 'development' and gain favourable indicators remains the task for a significant number of countries irrespective of exactitude of the measure. Thus development irrespective of definition is important for the benchmarking of states and their peoples. It is linked to their lives, freedoms, incomes, growth, wealth or poverty and identities.

---

[1] 'Therefore, in WDI 2016, there is no longer a distinction between developing countries (defined in previous editions as low-income and middle-income countries) and developed countries (previously high-income countries)' see http://blogs.worldbank.org/opendata/2016-edition-world-development-indicators-out-three-features-you-won-t-want-miss. This was in response to the article by Tariq Khokhar and Umar Serajuddin 'Should we continue to use the term developing world?' http://blogs .worldbank.org/opendata/should-we-continue-use-term-developing-world; see also https://data .worldbank.org/products/wdi accessed 30 October 2018.

Amongst the existing country classifications is the UN classification of least developed countries (UNCTAD, 2017), the IMF classification of advanced economies, emerging market and developing economies (IMF, 2018) and the UNDP human development index which ranges from very high to low human development (HDR, 2016). These measures all hinge on the achievement or non-achievement of development as defined by the parameters of the user of the terminology.

Sen in his key work on development established a radical reconceptualisation of development. His work forms the basis of the human development paradigm. He suggested a rather different focus from the growth of gross national product or of individual income. For him, 'development can be seen . . . as a process of enlarging the real freedoms that people enjoy' (1999: p. 3). This concept of freedoms and capabilities coincides with the focus on the human aspect of development. This reconceptualisation can also be seen in tandem with the changing global space where a state-centric focus to development misses a large part of the picture. The emphasis on enlarging freedoms is also a focus on a capabilities approach that widens the potential scope for actors including key actors such as companies. To reinforce the 'freedom to choose' and enhance functionings (Nussbaum, 2011: p. 25), there is the need for institutional frameworks. The challenge of enhancing educational opportunities, life expectancy, health etc. for large and diverse populations requires institutions and frameworks at different levels including public institutions, non-governmental institutions and private institutions.

Although there is a necessary link between the capabilities approach and the enabling done by public sector institutions and state institutions, it is not the only necessary one. Sen points out that these institutions could include legal mechanisms among others and that such institutions can incorporate private initiatives, public initiatives or mixed ones (1999, p. 53). Nussbaum, whilst recognising the significance of institutions including those of existing nations for the achievement of 'central' capabilities, also acknowledges that 'corporations and non-governmental organisations can play a part in promoting human capabilities in the regions in which they operate' (2011: p. 122).

In spite of earlier debates on whether CSR should or can contribute to development in developing countries (Ite, 2004; Frynas, 2005; Blowfield and Frynas, 2007), it is now acknowledged that most developing states lack the capacity to carry out the actualisation of all development outcomes entirely on their own (World Bank, 1997). This is also why the 2030 Agenda for Sustainable Development recommends that the 17 Sustainable Development Goals be achieved by 'all countries and all stakeholders, acting in collaborative partnership' (General Assembly Resolution, 2015).

This lack of state capacity can stem from the joint realities for many developing countries which involve on the one hand, the inheritance of post-colonial institutions that engenders dichotomised political interests which often results in lack of support for development, for example in African states (Levy, 2004: p. 5) and on the other hand, the questions over the role of the state in a neoliberal globalising world

(World Bank, 1997). While efforts for capacity building of many weak developing countries continues to be encouraged (Acemoglu, Garcia-Jimeno and Robinson, 2015), there is an acceptance of the need for inclusive solutions which includes bringing in the capacities of all institutions: private, non-governmental and public. This is exemplified in the use of the stakeholder approach for planned achievement of Sustainable Development Goals. For example: the Joint Implementation Unit in 2017 reported on The United Nations System – Private Sector Partnerships Arrangement, in the context of the 2030 Agenda for Sustainable Development.[2]

Nevertheless a key question remains: how can CSR contribute to development objectives? Utting (2003) raises two pertinent issues, when he points out that 'if CSR is to make a more significant contribution to development, its proponents face two major challenges: first, there needs to be a better integration between voluntary approaches and law or government regulation ... second the CSR agenda needs to become more "south-centred"'. This means that law has to step into the arena of CSR-development coordination and framing, and that these laws should emerge from a position that takes on objectives that are development focused. Law can also bridge the link between the state as the central and coordinating institution for development and other stakeholders with capacity and interests in achieving development. Law in this space, can use a range of regulatory mechanisms – mandatory or hybrid.

This chapter therefore argues that there are responses to this challenge beginning to emerge from global Southern states.[3] CSR regulation which integrates CSR funds/activities towards development goals often framed in terms of human development goals. The chapter explores this capabilities approach as a conception of development which could permit a larger role for non-state actors through CSR. It examines CSR as an allocative device which could lead to emerging legal frameworks which attempt to harness CSR concept as a vehicle towards development objectives. This potential is examined in this chapter against the emerging CSR legal frameworks of developing countries where these frameworks attempt to co-opt CSR levies and funds towards development objectives.

The first section analyses the capabilities approach to development, the next section then examines CSR and its potential to play this allocative role. The third section tackles the 'how' question, by looking at some emerging ways and tools to actualise this partnership. It examines the existing CSR laws in the first three countries – Indonesia, Mauritius and India – to legislate for CSR. It evaluates what type of goal setting is made in the context of CSR legislation and whether this links to a capabilities view of development. The chapter concludes by highlighting the allocative function that CSR could play within a given developing country context.

---

[2] www.unjiu.org/sites/www.unjiu.org/files/jiu_rep_2017_8_english_1.pdf accessed 30 October 2018.
[3] This refers to global South which is often used as a preferred term to developing countries.

3.2 CAPABILITIES APPROACH TO DEVELOPMENT

In general terms, development can refer to economic development, human development or sustainable development. Economic development is often defined in terms of economic growth. Nafziger points out that 'economic growth refers to increases in a country's production or income per capita . . . production is usually measured by the gross national product (GNP), an economy's total output of goods and services. Economic development refers to economic growth accompanied by changes in output distribution and economic structure' (2012: p. 14).

Nonetheless since the 1990s there has been a marked shift towards human development. The 1990s push for liberalisation and privatisation on a global scale conversely highlighted the gaps in attaining many human objectives in countries across the world. Annan succinctly captured this when he referred to 'a human face to the global market' (1999). He suggested that 'the spread of markets outpaces the ability of societies and their political systems to adjust to them' (1999).

The UNDP had also introduced its human development reports in 1990. The report pointed out that 'while growth in national production (GDP) is absolutely necessary to meet all essential human objectives, what is important is the study of how growth translates – or fails to translate – into human development in various societies' (p. iii). This seminal 1990 UNDP Human Development Report defined human development as 'a process of enlarging people's choices – The most critical of these wide ranging choices are to live a long and healthy life, to be educated and to have access to resources needed for a decent standard of living' (p. 1 and p. 10).[4] This adopts what is also known as Sen's capability approach to development,[5] fully spelt out in his book *Development as Freedom* (1999).

This Human Development Report (HDR) introduced three measurement indicators for the Human Development Index (HDI) which are: life expectancy, education (adult literacy – mean years of schooling and expected years of schooling) and gross national income (GNI) per capita (HDR, 2016: p. 3). They attempt to measure three key aspects of human life: longevity, knowledge and decent living standards (HDR, 1990: p. 12). This approach emphasised the major role which the human aspect of development plays in assessing the impact of development on people's lives and lived experiences.

Sustainable development, on the other hand, attempts to harness the triple aspects of development: economic, human (social) and environmental, taking into account

---

[4] It goes further to point out: 'additional choices include political freedom, guaranteed human rights and personal self-respect' (p. 1).

[5] Sen originally suggested this basic capability framework in his 1979 Tanner Lectures on Human Values (Stanford University) titled 'Equality of What?': 'It is arguable that what is missing in all this framework is some notion of "basic capabilities": a person being able to do certain basic things' p.218, https://tannerlectures.utah.edu/_documents/a-to-z/s/sen80.pdf accessed 17 July 2019.

current and future generations.[6] Sustainable development as a terminology was first used in 1987 in the report of the World Commission on Environment and Development (often referred to as the Brundtland Report). It was then defined by the report as 'development that meets the needs of the present without compromising the ability of future generations to meet their own needs. It contains within it, two key concepts: the concept of "needs", in particular the essential needs of the world's poor, *to which overriding priority should be given*; and the idea of limitations imposed by the state of technology and social organisation on the environment's ability to meet present and future needs' (emphasis added) (1987: p. 41).

The concept of 'needs' as an area of priority coincides with this focus on the human aspect of development. There are linkages between the sustainable developments 'needs' categorisation and the capabilities theory by Sen, but as Lessmann and Raushmayer (2013) indicate there are complexities in a direct substitution of the word 'needs' for 'capabilities' because needs in sustainable development were conceptualised at societal level and with inter-generational aspects, whereas capabilities are more individualised.

Nevertheless, the HDR 2016 recognises this interconnectedness. The report points out that: 'The human development approach also provided the analytical bedrock of the Millennium Declaration and the Millennium Development Goals – the time bound development objectives and targets agreed on in 2000 by 189 heads of states and governments to reduce basic human poverty by 2015. And it informed and influenced the 2030 Agenda and the Sustainable Development Goals' (HDR, 2016: p. 3).

In any case, individuals are the subset of the societal unit and the ultimate recipient of development goals. Sen proposes that their freedoms are essential to process of development for two different reasons: '1. The evaluative reason: assessment of progress has to be done primarily in terms of whether the freedoms that people have are enhanced 2. The effectiveness reason: achievement of development is thoroughly dependent on the free agency of people' (Sen, 1999: p. 4).

Sen suggests freedom as both 'the primary end' and 'the principal means' of development (1999: p. 36) because it has an instrumental role in contributing to the goal of development and also in this sense of 'overall freedom people have to live the way they would like to live' (Sen, 1999: p. 38). He gives examples to include: political freedoms, economic facilities, social opportunities, transparency guarantees and protective security (Sen, 1999: p. 38). There is a correlation between these freedoms which are interconnected and the 'need to develop and support a plurality of institutions, including democratic systems, legal mechanisms, market structures, educational and health provisions, media . . .' (Sen, 1999: p. 53).

---

[6] Following the Brundtland Report definition, https://sustainabledevelopment.un.org/content/docu ments/5987our-common-future.pdf accessed 17 July 2019.

This approach identifies the modern challenge of recognising and developing the functionings of individuals which make up diverse and complex societies within the states that exist today. Therefore these 'institutions can incorporate private initiatives as well as public arrangements and also more mixed structures such as nongovernmental organisations and cooperative entities' (Sen, 1999: p. 53). Nussbaum further clarifies this approach by stressing the role of functionings as the active realisation of capabilities (2011: p. 25). She gives a threshold of ten central capabilities as a requirement for a life worthy of human dignity (2011: p. 32). These include (1) life (lengthy), (2) Bodily health, (3) Bodily integrity, (4) Senses, imagination and thought, (5) Emotions (6) Practical reason, (7) Affiliation, (8) Other species, (9) Play, (10) Control over one's environment – political and material (2011: pp. 33, 34).

She also extends her interpretation to non-humans in view of animal capabilities although this is not the main focus here but it ties in with other ecosystem development approaches (2011: p. 18; 2004). Aspects of the capabilities approach can be traced back to the writings of Aristotle on human flourishing (Nussbaum and Sen, 1993) and Adam Smith on necessities and conditions of living (Sen, 1999: p. 24).

Notwithstanding that this is a radical reconceptualisation of development, the underlying arguments are still essentially liberal. Therefore this may not be satisfactory to critical scholars who critique capitalism's ability to fix its own problems (Dean, 2009). It can also be somewhat difficult to evaluate, as Sen himself admits when discussing lists of capabilities (Sen, 2005) because 'the different functionings have to be assessed and weighted in relation to each other, and the opportunities of having different combinations of functionings also have to be evaluated' (2005: p. 157). Finally, Pogge points to the undercurrent of normative individualism running through the theory, where the criterion for measuring the success of the institutions is the individual and not a communal unit (2002). This may have some import for issues of social justice and persistent under-representation of certain groups such as females or racial groups.

Yet the flexibility that this conception of development gives for collaboration with stakeholders through institutional frameworks is immense, not least because the lists of capabilities are not cemented and can be contextualised. They allow for social realities, prioritisation and dialogue. Sen captures this necessity for fluidity and contextualisation in this succinct statement:

> My scepticism is about fixing a cemented list of capabilities that is seen as being *absolutely complete (nothing could be added to it)* and *totally fixed (it could not respond to public reasoning and to the formation of social values)*. I am a great believer in theory, and certainly accept that a good theory of evaluation and assessment has to bring out the relevance of what we are free to do and free to be (the capabilities in general), as opposed to the material goods we have and the commodities we command. But I must also argue *that pure theory cannot 'freeze' a list of capabilities for all societies for all time to come, irrespective of what the citizens come to understand and value.* That would be not only a denial of the reach

of democracy, but also a misunderstanding of what pure theory can do, *completely divorced from the particular social reality that any particular society faces.* (Sen, 2005, p. 158)

This is therefore an argument for a contextual lists of development priorities for societies. The country or region can prioritise a list of capabilities in response to the social reality that particular society faces. In order to achieve the enhancement of functionings of these capabilities in individuals, the frameworks could co-opt private actors such as companies and this is where CSR could play a role.

3.3 CSR AS A POTENTIAL ALLOCATIVE DEVICE

Corporate social responsibility is a product of the twentieth century (Carroll, 2008). It differed in substance from nineteenth century corporate philanthropy because it was not driven merely by individual religious and ethical charity but by a bigger rationale which can be defined thus: 'a concept of relationship of business to the community in which social responsibility was clearly seen as a charge not merely upon individual conscience and concern but upon corporate resources as well' (Heald, 1970: p. 19).

The emergence of CSR on a global scale is aligned to the weight attached to persuading more states to adopt a neoliberal governance model in the 1990s. These were models 'based on the precepts of macroeconomic stability, liberalization of markets and privatization of economic activity' (UNDP, HDR 2003: p. 16). This resulted in the expansion of markets and the role of the private sector. The effect of the globalisation of such governance regimes transformed public sector and private sector relationships in many developing countries. Cutler observes that these 'forces of globalisation and the privatisation and deregulation of industries, sectors, commodities and services are transforming authority relations locally and globally' (2003: pp. 19–20).

This trend of global integration has been intense, varied, with uneven benefits, significant tensions and contradictions (Santos, 2002). The opening up of markets has been of immense benefit to companies, especially multinationals, which became leading drivers of the integration of the global economy (Jones, 2005). This affected the production of goods, services and financial markets (Santos, 2002: p. 178) thereby projecting multinational companies (MNCs) to the global stage as international actors. This increase in authority and the resulting revenues for the corporate group has led to claims that they possess more economic power than certain states (UNDP, HDR, 1999: pp. 31–2). This has also meant that the private decisions of business regarding questions of investment can affect whole communities as well as states. This 'ability to affect' has resulted in countervailing demands for corporations to take on social responsibility.

The World Business Council for Sustainable Development in 2010 pointed out that 'business has a critical role to play as an engine of economic growth and employment, and a driver of innovation and technology development. Particularly important is the private sector's role as a source of capital for developing countries: globally private sector investments make up over 85% of investment and financial flows' (p. 23).[7] This role can and should be captured by the CSR vehicle. CSR is the outgrowth of the necessity of capitalism to respond to extended societal demands beyond the traditional taxation (Okoye, 2009). It comprises both the voluntary and the mandatory responsibilities which emanate from business's extended role and impacts on various aspects of society. The frameworks used to capture the exact nature of this responsibility to society are contextual and reflective of the expectations of all stakeholders as to which roles business can play in its contribution to society (Okoye, 2012). Therefore in many developing countries, CSR and its mechanisms are geared towards developmental objectives in that context.

CSR may not be amenable to a 'fixed universal definition' because what is socially responsible is driven by contemporary needs and concerns, which cannot be pinned down in precise unchanging terms (Kerr, Janda and Pitts, 2009). This lends credence to contextual definitions of CSR which covers the common reference point of business and society relationships (Okoye, 2012). Therefore CSR in developing countries must be geared towards development objectives and integrated towards development goals. This is shown by the role which the private sector is expected to play in the achievement of the Sustainable Development Goals (General Assembly Resolution, 2015; Joint Implementation Unit, 2017).

Visser also captured this in relation to the previous millennium development goals (MDGs) – (predecessor to the current SDGs). He points out that the challenge of CSR in developing countries was framed by a vision that was distilled in 2000 into the MDGs: 'a world with less poverty, hunger and disease, greater survival prospects for mothers and their infants, better educated children, equal opportunities for women and a healthier environment' (Visser, 2008: p. 473).

Increasingly the past contestations about whether CSR should play a role in development (Ite, 2004; Frynas, 2005; Blowfield and Frynas, 2007) and whether such companies are performing the role of governments (Frynas, 2005) is giving way to more pragmatic questions of how companies can perform these roles. This is because the shift in global role of the state and the focus on markets has moved the questions on to how the private sector can play a role in development.

This interface has already been identified in the potential corporate role in achieving the Sustainable Development Goals (Schönherr, Findler and Martinuzzi, 2017; KPMG, India, 2017). Business was identified as a major actor as early as 1992 in the Earth Summit (United Nations Conference on Environment and Development). The role of business and industry as one of the stakeholders in the SDGs is now centrally acknowledged in Agenda 2030.[8]

---

[7] http://wbcsdservers.org/wbcsdpublications/cd_files/datas/business-solutions/social-impact/pdf/
    BusinessAndDevelopment.pdf accessed 30 October 2018.
[8] https://sustainabledevelopment.un.org/mgos accessed 30 October 2018.

Corporate social responsibility as an allocative device can then play the role of allocating what responsibilities the business enterprise can handle in the task of enlarging human freedoms and promoting sustainable growth. The measure of the companies' social responsibility in a developing context will be framed by how it contributes to enlarging human capabilities. This conception when viewed through Sen's lens will cover processes and opportunities. In more specific terms: 'the processes that allow freedom of action or decisions and the actual opportunities people have, given their personal and social circumstances' (Sen 1999: p. 17). This is because these capabilities depend on 'economic, social and political arrangements' (Sen, 1999: p. 53).

The intrinsic element for CSR is that society and business set objectives through law, partnerships and dialogues of various forms on issues of mutual concern and need (Okoye, 2017). This potential to be an allocative device allows for CSR to serve as a conduit through which set objectives can be achieved and the law can be a tool in creating the facilitative frameworks for such interaction. Teubner suggests the potential of identifying CSR as a decentralised integrative device 'which places restrictions on economic action in the interest of other subsystems – trees and people included' (Teubner, 1984: p. 162).

This is also the sense in which I had previously advocated for a legal perspective of CSR where it is capable of performing 'law-jobs' through the use of legal and quasi-legal frameworks (Okoye, 2017).[9] In this given context, this would be the law-job of channelling conduct on development and allocating responsibility or co-responsibility for development. This law-job of channelling conduct in CSR is not exclusively focused on voluntary codes. It can and has been harnessed by mandatory laws with explicit focus on CSR. There are examples in Indonesia, Mauritius and India of law explicitly focused on CSR. These countries were forerunners in passing CSR-centred legislation. The next section will study these examples briefly.

3.4 CSR LAWS

3.4.1 *Indonesia CSR Laws*

Indonesia was the first country to attempt to use company laws to frame a distinct role for CSR as a commitment to participate in development. This is captured in Article 1(3) of the Indonesian Law No. 40 of 2007 on Limited Liability Companies (Company Law) which specified that: 'Social and Environmental Responsibility means the commitment from company to participate in the sustainable economic development, in order to increase the quality of life and environment, which will be valuable for the Company itself, the local community, and the society in general.'[10]

[9] This adopted Karl Llewellyn's law-jobs approach within CSR (see Okoye, 2017).
[10] A copy of the law can be found on: www.indonesia-investments.com/business/foreign-investment /company-law-indonesia/item8311 accessed 30 October 2018.

More specifically, Article 74 (Chapter V, Social and Economic Responsibility) requires that:

(1) The Company having its business activities in the field of and/or related to natural resources, shall be obliged to perform its Social and Environmental Responsibility. (2) Social and Environmental Responsibility as referred to in paragraph (1) shall constitutes the obligation of the Company which is budgeted and calculated as the cost of the Company, implementation of which shall be performed with due observance to the appropriateness and fairness. (3) The Company which fails to perform its obligation as referred to in paragraph (1) shall be imposed with sanction in accordance with the provision of regulation. (4) Provision regarding Social and Environmental Responsibility shall be further regulated with a Government Regulation.

The implementing regulation is Government Regulation No. 47 of 2012 on Social and Environmental Responsibility for Limited Liability Company (Yunari et al., 2018). The implementing regulation places the burden on the board of directors with a threat of penalty if the company does not fulfil the obligations.[11]

In a wider investment sense, there is further legislation that encourages every investor to implement CSR. Article 15 of Indonesian Law No. 25 of 2007 on Capital Investment[12] specifies that 'every investor shall have obligations: a. to apply the principle of good corporate governance; b. to implement corporate social responsibility; c. to make a report on investment activities and submit it to the Investment Coordinating Board'.[13]

The laws capture a framing of CSR in its infancy. The law identifies that the companies need to contribute to development and then stipulates a financial value of contribution on a sectoral basis but it fails to be specific about what would be an appropriate cost to the company (Chang, 2018).

There is also a dichotomy within Article 74 with the focus on natural resource companies. This was challenged by Indonesian business groups as unconstitutional.[14] The law was however upheld as constitutional in the 2008 decision of the court[15] (Waagstein, 2011). The constitutional court interpreted this as an acknowledgement of

---

[11] 'The board of directors in any company that utilizes or impact natural resources must consider the appropriateness and reasonableness in preparing and setting action plans and budgets. If a company conducting business in the field of or relating to natural resources does not carry out its social and environmental responsibilities, it will be penalized. If it does, it may be given an award by the authority' (Chang, 2018: p. 155).

[12] www.indonesia-investments.com/business/foreign-investment/investment-law-indonesia/item8322 accessed 30 October 2018.

[13] The Elucidation of Article 15 item b: '"Corporate social responsibility" means a responsibility mounted in every investment company to keep creating relationship which is in harmony, in balance and suitable to the local community's neighbourhood, values, norms, and culture.' See Chang, 2018, p. 153.

[14] Chang (2018) points out these the case was instituted by business interests represented by the Indonesian Chamber of Commerce, see p. 154.

[15] Decision No. 53/PUU-VI/2008.

the risks posed by that particular sector (2011, p. 456). The court also recognised that 'mandatory CSR represents the value of social justice' (Lambooy et al., 2013: p. xxvi). Indonesia is a South East Asian nation made up of islands. Its unique geography and vulnerability to environmental harm and harm to indigenous peoples has been cited as a key driving force of the regulations (Chang, 2018: pp. 12, 149).

Recent research on Indonesian companies still seems to indicate a discord between the practices recommended statutorily (norms) and the practice on the ground (implementation) as there is evidence of CSR still running in a somewhat philanthropic form (Chang, 2018: p. 161).

Nevertheless Chang also identifies a range of other sectoral regulations in Indonesia that require CSR activity from business geared towards development. For example: Mining Law No. 4 Year 2009 requires a percentage of profits to be used on CSR and Article 58(1) & (2) of Law No. 39 2014 on Plantations specifies that at least 20 per cent of plantation area is to be used for development of community gardens (Chang, 2018: pp. 156–7).

Chang describes this as 'buck-passing' (2018: p. 157), but it nonetheless represents a systematic approach of apportioning responsibility through legislative frameworks that attempt to use sectoral and financial approaches within law. The argument here is that governments are using these CSR schemes to allocate a share of responsibility for development to business. In Indonesia the sectoral approach recognises that the companies may be best in enhancing sector-specific capacities. The lack of specificity may be either because of a lack of governmental capacity for oversight or a recognition that companies could be best placed to decide within sectoral areas. However if this flexible approach does not yield desired results, it may lead to more specificity in future. This can be seen in the Mauritian example.

3.4.2 *Mauritius CSR Law*

Mauritius has also enacted a CSR legislative framework which appears slightly more developed in its allocative capacity than the previous example because responsibilities and values are assigned and the framework is evaluated, with consequent changes to the framework.

The current law[16] – the Finance (Miscellaneous Provisions) Act 2016 amending the Income Tax Act 50L. CSR Fund requires that:

---

[16] See Ministry of Finance and Economic Development, Mauritius for a copy of the amending legislation: http://mof.govmu.org/English/Legislation/Documents/Finance%20(Miscellaneous%20Provisions)%20Act%202016.pdf, s. 27 from p. 61. See also the extract from the Finance (Miscellaneous Provisions) Act 2016 on the CSR Mauritius website www.csr.mu/download/2016/Extract%20from%20Finance%20Miscellaneous%20Provisions%20Act%202016.pdf accessed 30 October 2018; Ministry of Finance and Economic Development (MOFED), The New CSR Framework Background Document (11 August 2016), http://mof.govmu.org/English/Documents/New%20CSR%20Framework%202016.pdf accessed 30 October 2018.

Every company shall, in every year, set up a CSR Fund equivalent to 2 per cent of its chargeable income of the preceding year. Businesses will be required to contribute, through MRA (Mauritius Revenue Authority), at least 50% of their CSR money to the new National CSR Foundation at the start of their next accounting year, for example, for companies with accounting period ending 31 December 2016, the new CSR framework will be applicable as from 01 January 2017. The rate of contribution will be changed to at least 75% in the following year.

To follow some of the law's past history, it was in 2009 that the Income Tax Act was amended to make CSR mandatory. This is confirmed by the Ministry of Finance and Economic Development, Mauritius CSR Framework Document which states[17]:

> The Corporate Social Responsibility (CSR) system was introduced in the Income Tax Act in 2009, whereby profitable companies were required to devote 2% of their book profits for carrying out CSR activities under approved programmes as per published guidelines. These activities could be carried out either directly by the companies or through the following: i. An approved NGO ii. A Special Purpose Vehicle (SPV) – such as a Foundation iii. A Corporate partner 2. The Programmes approved by the then CSR Committee in 2009 were in the following areas of intervention: i. Socio economic development ii. Health iii. Leisure and sports iv. Environment v. Education & training vi. Natural Catastrophes.

This provision was later amended in 2012 to 'profits chargeable to income tax'.[18] This was in response to the ministerial direction given in a 2010 budget speech which was as follows:

> To focus on most urgent social problems and enhance aim is to focus on the most urgent problems so as to maximise the social benefits and ensure national coverage. We will therefore use 50 percent of the CSR resources to focus on the three National Programmes. Government will add to the CSR resources to implement these three programmes which are: ¬ Social Housing ¬ Welfare of Children from Vulnerable Groups ¬ Eradication of Absolute Poverty.[19]

Yet 2015 saw the removal of all guidelines but following feedback, a new CSR Framework was announced in the Budget 2016/17[20] setting up the National CSR Foundation under the aegis of the Ministry of Social Integration and Economic Empowerment which will handle allocation of CSR among the six priority areas. These six priority areas also indicate areas of shared responsibility. They are:

---

[17] Ministry of Finance and Economic Development (MOFED), The New CSR Framework Background Document (11 August 2016), http://mof.govmu.org/English/Documents/New%20CSR%20Framework%202016.pdf accessed 30 October 2018.
[18] The CSR Framework Document also notes the addition of a further health priority area 'prevention of non-communicable diseases' p. 2.
[19] Budget Speech of November 2010 (para. 333), CSR Framework (n. 17), p. 3.
[20] CSR Framework (n. 17), p. 3.

Poverty Alleviation – targeting families in the Social Register of Mauritius (SRM); Educational Support – targeting families in the SRM; Social Housing – targeting families in the SRM; Supporting persons with severe disabilities; Dealing with health problems resulting from substance abuse and poor sanitation; and Family protection i.e. protection to victims of domestic violence.[21]

Mauritius is an island state in the African continent. It is regarded as an African success story (Bissoon, 2018). There is an explicit connection between CSR and development in this context. Pillay in 2015 pointed out the definition of CSR which had existed under the CSR guidelines: 'the concept whereby companies act to balance their own economic growth with sustainable social and environmental development of the country' (p. 247). She found evidence of a difference made to daily lives but also of a practice that is not yet fully embracing this contextual normative definition of CSR, rather still ameliorative and conservative (2015, p. 245).

Nevertheless the constant evaluation of the CSR framework and the re-definition of priority areas for CSR funding as well as the overall coordination by the foundation indicates that CSR is being effectively used as an allocative device. It evidences a level of evaluation towards areas of priority as defined development objectives and then resulting changes in legal framework in response. Overall it indicates a very obvious desire to continue to channel business conduct towards desired development goals through the CSR legal framework.

3.4.3 India CSR Law

India passed its CSR law in 2013. Section 135 of the Companies Act 2013 (India) specifies:

135. Corporate Social Responsibility[22]
(1) Every company having net worth of rupees five hundred crore or more, or turnover of rupees one thousand crore or more or a net profit of rupees five crore or more during any financial year shall constitute a Corporate Social Responsibility Committee of the Board consisting of three or more directors, out of which at least one director shall be an independent director.

. . .

(5) The Board of every company referred to in sub-section (1), shall ensure that the company spends, in every financial year, at least two per cent. of the average net profits of the company made during the three immediately preceding financial years, in pursuance of its Corporate Social Responsibility Policy: Provided that the company shall give preference to the local area and areas around it where it operates, *for spending the amount earmarked for Corporate Social Responsibility activities*: Provided further that if the company fails to spend such amount, the

---

[21]   CSR Framework (n. 17), p. 4.
[22]   See Ministry of Corporate Affairs Government of India website for a copy of the Act www.mca.gov.in /SearchableActs/Section135.htm accessed 30 October 2018.

Board shall, in its report made under clause (*o*) of sub-section (3) of section 134, specify the reasons for not spending the amount.

[This incorporates a comply-or-explain approach]

The Indian adoption of CSR law was heralded, not because it was the first, but perhaps because of the scale. India is a large South Asian country with a population of over a billion. Therefore the implications of such adoption are significant. Section 135 took effect in 2015 fiscal year [2014–15][23] (Dharmapala and Khanna, 2018). The list of activities that are permissible under Schedule VII of the Companies Act, 2013 to be counted towards CSR spending are decidedly focused on development objectives include:

> Eradicating hunger, poverty and malnutrition; Promoting education; Promoting gender equality; Ensuring environmental sustainability; Protection of national heritage, art and culture; Measures for the benefit of armed forces veterans; Training to promote rural sports; Contribution to the Prime Minister's National Relief Fund; Contributions or funds to technology incubators; and Rural development projects. (Varottil, 2018)

The hybrid pattern (involving comply or explain) was introduced as a compromise for what is a very large coverage of companies (Dharmapala and Khanna, 2018). This compromise may have become necessary in view of the monitoring implications for state institutions tasked with oversight.

Although the Act only took effect in the 2015 fiscal year (2014–15), Varottil in 2018, found some evidence of an increase in CSR spending but also a significant amount of non-compliance (Varottil, 2018). The hybrid regime was criticised as weak for lack of enforcement (Varottil, 2018). Nonetheless the legal framework itself is an attempt to allocate some responsibility and channel some funds specifically towards development related objectives within the scope of CSR. It also represents further evidence of the attempts to channel business conduct towards desired development goals through a CSR legal framework.

3.5 CONCLUSION: THE EMERGENCE OF LEGAL FRAMEWORKS AS AN ALLOCATIVE DEVICE

The World Development Report in 1997 pointed out that the radical shift in thinking over the role of the state in the last 50 years from state-dominated model to minimalist state, and the adoption of market-friendly policies while reducing the scope of state intervention, has resulted in a fundamental crisis of state effectiveness (World Bank 1997: pp. 23–5).

---

[23] Varottil points out more specifically that 'These requirements, enshrined under section 135 of the Companies Act, 2013 and in the Companies (Corporate Social Responsibility Policy Rules), 2014 (the "CSR Rules"), came into effect from April 1, 2014, such that companies (to which these provisions applied) were required to comply with the CSR spending requirement commencing the financial year 2014–15, i.e. ending March 31, 2015' p. 232.

This minimal development state may then be using CSR law in unique ways to coordinate and allocate responsibility for development. The use of such normative legal frameworks is still in its infancy as can be seen from the examples of CSR laws in Indonesia, Mauritius and India. What is emerging is a picture where a percentage of spend or profits is expected to be allocated towards CSR activities channelled towards some development objectives. This seems an open acknowledgement of the need for collaborative partnership for the task ahead. State use of legislation to coordinate such activities has often followed on from what was a voluntary platform for companies to be socially responsible. The legal framework may use mandatory or hybrid mechanisms to achieve such allocation or channelling.

The issues with state capacity may mean that weak government enforcement mechanisms will affect the ability to translate normative ideals in the law into practice. Yet it is clear that an experiment is happening. CSR expectations in those contexts is becoming more concrete and framed in legal terms with identified development objectives.

This allocation acknowledges a capabilities approach on two levels: to enhance capabilities of individuals (as seen by areas often specified by government) but also to allocate responsibility for this objective by examining institutions with the capacities. In this case, private institutions with economic capacities to improve the results in the identified lists of capabilities the governments wish to target. This potential of legal approaches is not only being explored in developing countries but also in developed countries as part of responses to the challenges thrown by the changing landscape of global affairs.

They can be used in positive allocative manner (that is to contribute or to act) or negative manner (to refrain from or to take due care to avoid). The expectation for companies to contribute to society is a key aspect of the global governance framework. The ongoing debate on mandatory human rights due diligence legislation for large corporations following the French Duty of Vigilance law 2017 recognises this challenge of allocating responsibility for contextual challenges to development.[24]

There is a strong link between allocating responsibility and channelling conduct. The evaluation of the success or failure of such legal schemes will come with the passage of time and further evidence in future. However it is important to identify the indications of continued experimentation and the evolution of CSR in this direction.

---

[24] Décision no. 2017–750 DC du 23 Mars 2017 du Conseil Constitutionnel www.conseil-constitutionnel.fr /decision/2017/2017750DC.htm accessed 30 October 2018; see also Developments in the Field https:// corporate-responsibility.org/wp-content/uploads/2017/08/french_law_on_duty_of_care_a_historic_ step_towards_making_globalization_work_for_all.pdf accessed 30 October 2018.

REFERENCES

Acemoglu, D. Garcia-Jimeno, C. and Robinson, J. (2015). State Capacity and Economic Development: A Network Approach. *American Economic Review*, 105(8), 2364–409.

Annan, K. (1999). 'Secretary-General Proposes Global Compact in Human Rights, Environment and Labour in Address to World Economic Forum in Davos' UN Press Release 1 February 1999 SG/SM/6881.

AU/UNECA (2011). 'Minerals and Africa's Development: An Overview of the Report of the International Study Group on Africa's Mineral Regimes', https://au.int/sites/default/files/newsevents/workingdocuments/14499-wd-overview_of_the_isg_report.pdf.

Bissoon, O. (2018). Corporate Social Responsibility in Mauritius: An Analysis of Annual Report of Multinational Hotel Groups. *Asian Journal of Sustainability and Social Reporting*, 3(2). https://doi.org/10.1186/s41180-017-0017-4.

Blowfield, M. and Frynas, J. G. (2005). Setting New Agendas: Critical Perspectives on Corporate Social Responsibility in the Developing World. *International Affairs*, 81(3), 499–513.

Carroll, A. (2008). A history of Corporate Social Responsibility: Concepts and Practices. In A. Crane et al., eds., *The Oxford Handbook of CSR*. New York: Oxford University Press, pp. 19–46.

Crane et al. (2008). *Corporate Social Responsibility: Readings and Cases in Global Context*. Abingdon: Routledge.

Cutler, A. C. (2003). *Private Power and Global Authority: Transnational Merchant Law in the Global Political Economy*. Cambridge: Cambridge University Press.

Dean, H. (2009). Critiquing Capabilities: Distractions of a Beguiling Concept. *Critical Social Policy* 29(2), 261–78.

Dharmapala, D. and Khanna, V. S. (2018). The Impact of Mandated Corporate Social Responsibility: Evidence from India's Companies Act of 2013 (September 8, 2018). U of Chicago, Public Law Working Paper No. 601; University of Chicago Coase-Sandor Institute for Law & Economics Research Paper No. 783; U of Michigan Law & Econ Research Paper No. 16–025; U of Michigan Public Law Research Paper No. 526. Available at SSRN: https://ssrn.com/abstract=2862714 or http://dx.doi.org/10.2139/ssrn.2862714.

European Union (2011). *A Renewed EU Strategy for CSR* (COM/2011/0681 final).

Frynas, J. (2005). The false developmental promise of corporate social responsibility: evidence from multinational oil companies. *International Affairs*, 81(3), 581–98.

GA Resolution (2015). Agenda 2030 Transforming Our World: The 2030 Agenda for Sustainable Development, Resolution adopted by the General Assembly on 25 September 2015, A/RES/70/1.

HDR (1990). *Human Development Report*. New York: UNDP/Oxford University Press.

HDR (2003). *Millennium Development Goals, a Compact to End World Poverty*. New York: UNDP/Oxford University Press.

HDR (2016). *Human Development for Everyone*. New York: UNDP.

Heald M. (1970). The *Social Responsibilities of Business Company and Community*. New Brunswick: Transaction Publishers.

Idemudia, U. (2008). Conceptualizing the CSR and Development Debates. *The Journal of Corporate Citizenship*, 29(1), 91–110.

IMF (2018). *World Economic Outlook*.

Ite, U. E. (2004). Multinationals and Corporate Social Responsibility: A Case Study of Nigeria. *Corporate Social Responsibility and Environmental Management* 11(1), 1–11.

Joint Implementation Unit (2017). JIU/REP/2017/8 The United Nations System – Private Sector Partnerships Arrangements in the Context of the 2030 Agenda for Sustainable Development www.unjiu.org/sites/www.unjiu.org/files/jiu_rep_2017_8_english_1.pdf.

Jones, G. (2005). *Multinationals and Global Capitalism: From the Nineteenth to the Twenty-First Century*. Oxford: Oxford University Press.

KPMG India (2017). Leveraging CSR to Achieve SDGs https://assets.kpmg.com/content/dam/kpmg/in/pdf/2017/12/SDG_New_Final_Web.pdf.

Lambooy, T. et al., eds., (2013). *CSR in Indonesia: Legislative Developments and Case Studies.* Malang. Indonesia: Konstitusi Press/Utrecht University and Brawijaya University.

Lessmann,O. and Rauschmayer, F. (2013). Re-conceptualizing Sustainable Development on the Basis of the Capability Approach: A Model and Its Difficulties. *Journal of Human Development and Capabilities*, 14 (1), 95–114.

Levy, B. (2004). Governance and Economic Development in Africa: Meeting the Challenge of Capacity Building. In B. Levy and S. Kpundeh, eds., *Building State Capacity in Africa New Approaches and Emerging Lessons*. Washington DC: IBRD/World Bank, pp. 1–42.

Nussbaum, M. (2004). Beyond 'Compassion and Humanity': Justice for Non-Human Animals. In M. Nussbaum. and C. Sunstein, eds., *Animal Rights: Current Debates and New Directions*, pp. 299–320.

McBarnet, D. et al., eds., (2007). *The New Corporate Accountability: Corporate Social Responsibility and the Law*. Cambridge: Cambridge University Press.

Nafziger, E. W. (2012). *Economic Development*, 5th ed. New York: Cambridge University Press.

Nussbaum, M. and Sen, A., eds., (1993). *Quality of Life*. New York: Oxford University Press.

Nussbaum, M. C. (2011). *Creating Capabilities: The Human Development Approach.* Harvard: Belknap Press.

Okoye, A. (2012). Exploring the Relationship between Corporate Social Responsibility, Law and Development in an African context: Should Government Be Responsible for Ensuring Corporate Responsibility? *International Journal of Law and Management*,54 (5), 364–78.

Okoye, A. (2017). *Legal Approaches and Corporate Social Responsibility: Towards a Llewellyn's Law-Jobs Approach*. Abingdon: Routledge.

Okoye, A. (2009). Theorising Corporate Social Responsibility as an Essentially Contested Concept: Is a Definition Really Necessary? *Journal of Business Ethics*, 89 (4), 613–27.

Pillay, R. (2015). *The Changing Nature of Corporate Social Responsibility: CSR and Development – The Case of Mauritius*. Abingdon: Routledge.

Pogge, T. W. (2002). Can the Capability Approach Be Justified? *Philosophical topics*, 30 (2), 167–228.

Santos, B. D. (2002). *Towards a New Legal Common Sense*, 2nd ed. Oxford: Butterworths.

Schönherr, N., Findler, F. and Martinuzzi, A. (2017). Exploring the Interface of CSR and the Sustainable Development Goals. *Transnational Corporations*, 24 (3), 33–47.

Sen, A. (2005). Human Rights and Capabilities. *Journal of Human Development*, 6 (2), 151–66.

Sen, A. (1999). *Development as Freedom* Oxford: (Oxford University Press.

Teubner, G. (1984). Corporate Fiduciary Duties and Their Beneficiaries: A Functional Approach to the Legal Institutionalisation of Corporate Responsibility. In K. J. Hopt and G. Teubner, eds., *Corporate Governance and Directors Liabilities: Legal, Economic and Sociological Analyses of Corporate Social Responsibility*. Berlin: De Gruyter, pp. 149–77.

UNCTAD (2017). Least Developed Countries Report.

Utting, P. (2003). 'Promoting Development through Corporate Social Responsibility – Does It Work?' Global Future, Third Quarter.

Varottil, U. (2018). Analysing CSR Spending Requirements under Indian Company Law. In J. J. du Plessis, U. Varottil and J. Veldman, eds., *Globalisation of Corporate Social Responsibility and Its Impact on Corporate Governance*. Switzerland: Springer International Publishing, pp. 231–53.

Villiers, C. (2008). Corporate Law, Corporate Power and Corporate Social Responsibility. In N. Boeger, R. Murray and C. Villiers, eds., *Perspectives on Corporate Social Responsibility*. Cheltenham: Edward Elgar, pp. 85–112.

Waagstein, P. R. (2013). The Mandatory Corporate Social Responsibility in Indonesia: Problems and Implications. *Journal of Business Ethics*, 98 (3), 455–66.

World Bank (1997). *World Development Report: The State in a Changing World*. New York: Oxford University Press.

World Bank (2016). World Bank Development Indicators, Washington DC World Bank Group http://documents.worldbank.org/curated/en/805371467990952829/World-development-indica tors-2016.

World Commission on Environment and Development (1987). Report 'Our Common Future', available at https://sustainabledevelopment.un.org/content/documents/5987our-common-future.pdf accessed 21 July 2019.

Yunari, S. B. et al. (2018). Re-conception of Mandatory Based Corporate Social and Environmental Responsibility, IOP Conference Ser.: Earth Environ. Sci. 106 012098, available at www.researchgate.net/publication/322823490_Reconception_of_mandatory-based_corporate_social_and_environmental_responsibility_in_Indonesia   accessed 21 July 2019.

4

Domestic Adjudicative Institutions, Developing Countries and Sustainable Development: Linkages and Limitations

Onyeka K. Osuji and Paul U. Abba[1]

4.1 INTRODUCTION

This chapter investigates the role of courts and other formal adjudicative institutions of developing countries in promoting sustainable development. A consistent message from several international instruments and forums such as the Sustainable Development Goals (SDGs) 2015 and the 2015 Paris Agreement of the United Nations Framework Convention on Climate Change (UNFCCC) is that sustainable development requires the efforts and contributions of every part of society, including the public and private sectors at the national level. This message is implicit from the meeting of the Intergovernmental Panel on Climate Change (IPCC) held in Incheon, South Korea on 6 October 2018.[2] Under the umbrella of 'strengthening the global response in the context of sustainable development', the IPCC's Special Report on Global Warming of 1.5°C[3] noted the need for 'adaptation options specific to national contexts'. In stressing the need for '[s]trengthening the capacities for climate action of national and sub-national authorities, civil society, the private sector, indigenous peoples and local communities [to] support the implementation of ambitious actions' the IPCC highlighted the importance of participatory public and private institutions in sustainable development. It may be noted that participatory institutions have made a real difference to the effectiveness of public health programmes in regions like Western Europe and Latin America (Falletti and Cunial, 2018). Nonetheless, while the IPCC itself epitomises the interaction of scientific knowledge and policy involving different powerful actors at the global level, there is the question of the attitude, responsibility, influence and

[1] We thank Professor Chris Willett and Dr Durand Cupido of the University of Essex for their comments on previous drafts of this chapter.

[2] The 48th session of the Intergovernmental Panel on Climate Change (IPCC 48) held from 1–5 October 2018 in Incheon, Republic of Korea. http://sdg.iisd.org/events/48th-session-of-the-ipcc/ accessed 7 November 2018.

[3] IPCC's Special Report on Global Warming2018 file:///F:/sr15_headline_statements%20Climate% 20change,%20sustainable%20development,%20consumption,%20CSR%20report%202018.pdf, D3, D7 accessed 28 October 2018.

decisionmaking processes of key formal and informal actors within national jurisdictions where sustainable development policies are practically implemented. Bansal (2002), for example, argued that one of the challenges to effective corporate participation in sustainable development is its institutionalisation in 'the regulations, norms and mindsets'.

At the national level, the courts and other formal adjudicative institutions act in establishing, clarifying and regulating the nature and interaction of different components of society. Different segments of the public and private sectors interact with other persons and organisations within and outside their sectors and sub-sectors and enforce rules and standards with contractual parties. In the context of sustainable development, the adjudicative institutions play a vital role in ensuring the enforcement of standards. As Burger et al. (2017: p. 8) observed, '[l]itigation has arguably never been a more important tool to push policymakers and market participants to develop and implement effective means of climate change mitigation and adaptation'. Stakeholders such as public interest organisations are increasingly resorting to judicial intervention in climate change and other sustainable development matters, especially in the more developed countries (Ghaleigh, 2010: pp. 34–5; Bähr et al., 2018: pp. 194–221). For instance, the US Supreme Court recently dismissed the federal government's attempt to halt a flagship climate change litigation, *Juliana v. United States*,[4] from proceeding to trial at the lower court.[5] *Juliana* alleged that the United States government's affirmative actions caused climate change, violated the younger generation's constitutional rights to life, liberty and property, and failed to protect essential public trust resources.

Nonetheless, when adjudicative institutions are limited by endogenous factors such as incompetence, corruption and detached attitude to the public interest, the result can be detrimental to the global and national sustainable development priorities and to victims of harmful and unsustainable practices. The recent *Agouman v. Leigh Day* case illustrates this.[6] The original cause of action arose from the dumping of harmful waste by a multinational company (Trafigura) in Cote d'Ivoire which caused personal injuries and environmental damage. The dumping was facilitated by the country's inefficient regulatory institutions and occurred after several other countries refused to permit Trafigura to offload the toxic waste within their jurisdictions. Although it claimed that the toxic waste was dumped by an independent contractor it appointed in good faith, Trafigura settled the legal proceedings brought by a group of victims and paid a substantial compensation.[7] However, the victims could not access the compensation fund when it was transferred to public authorities in Cote d'Ivoire by their UK-based legal representatives. The compensation fund was mostly diverted by powerful actors in Cote d'Ivoire in

---

[4] *Juliana* v. *United States* 6:15-cv-1517 -TC US D. Or, (2016).
[5] *United States* v. *Juliana* U.S. District Court for District of Oregon 18–73014 SC (2018).
[6] *Agouman* v. *Leigh Day* [2016] EWHC 1324.
[7] See *Motto* v. *Trafigura Ltd* [2011] EWCA Civ 1150 (on costs).

collusion with the nation's corrupt judiciary. An English High Court held that the legal representatives were in breach of a duty of care to the victims because they ought to have foreseen that Cote d'Ivoire's judicial administration system would abuse the compensation fund. In other words, the legal representatives ought to have considered the prevailing institutional circumstances.

Fijabi v. Nigeria Bottling Company Plc[8] provides a contrasting perspective on the role of adjudicative institutions. In that case, the Nigerian regulatory authorities declined to act despite evidence that the local franchisee of the global multinational, Coca-Cola, was selling beverages containing very high levels of benzoic acid preservative. Notwithstanding that the benzoic content was much higher than the maximum level considered unsafe for consumption by the regulatory authorities of the UK and other European jurisdictions, the company insisted that the beverages were suitable for the Nigerian market. Local regulators acquiesced to the company's position and even refused to demand relevant warning labels on the products. A Nigerian court, however, referenced the available best international standards in its decision to uphold the consumers' right to health in the circumstances. Both the company and the regulators have appealed the judgment.

The cases suggest the existence of adjudicative institutions that are disconnected from the ideals and mechanisms of sustainable development in those developing countries. The consequences can be far-reaching. As the *Johannesburg Principles on the Role of Law and Sustainable Development* adopted the by the Global Judges Symposium (2003) held in August 2002 noted with respect to environmental protection:

> an independent Judiciary and judicial process is vital for the implementation, development and enforcement of environmental law, and that members of the Judiciary, as well as those contributing to the judicial process at the national, regional and global levels, are crucial partners for promoting compliance with, and the implementation and enforcement of, international and national environmental law …

The vital position of adjudicative institutions in sustainable development has been recognised in different jurisdictional contexts. On the one hand, the relatively high standards of environmental protection in EU policy can be attributed to the role of the European Court of Justice (ECJ) in confirming the approach in several cases (Jacobs, 2006). On the other hand, the modest interest in sustainable development in the USA has been traced to the attitude of the country's Supreme Court (May, 2009).

Focusing mainly on environmental protection in Nigeria, this chapter provides a robust account of the linkages between sustainable development and adjudicative institutions and highlights the latter's roles in the interaction of public and private stakeholder groups. It proceeds on the basis that adjudicative institutions are a key

---

[8] Suit No. LD/13/2008 of 15 February 2017.

stakeholder group for sustainable development that can undertake regulatory, normative and cognitive roles as defined in Scott's (2001, 2008) typology of institutions. The close connection between science and policy in environmental governance (Lidskog and Sundqvist, 2015), for example, highlights the imperativeness of effective knowledge-based policy and practice and its communication to formal and informal segments of society. The tripartite institutions model developed here (based on the above discussed regulatory, normative and cognitive elements of institutions) helps in this chapter for identifying appropriate mechanisms for the creation, diffusion and dissemination of sustainable development knowledge across different (public and private) strata of society. Adjudicative institutions that embrace their normative and cognitive institutional roles will see the cases before them as only a template and can, for example, make statements having wider significance than those cases. The statements can reference individual and organisational behaviours and existing legal, cultural and business practices arising within and outside the cases before the adjudicative institutions and compare them to other practices, research findings, scientific debates and even theoretical models of sustainable development. The tripartite framework developed in this chapter shows that existing scholarship reflects a limited application of the institutional model and highlights the need for framing interpretation in its broader institutional contexts. In focusing mainly on explicit constitutional and statutory provisions, existing scholarship arguably signposts the regulatory role of the courts whereas the wider institutional ambit of their roles includes conscious normative and cognitive influences on public and private institutional actors. We argue that the roles of the adjudicative institutions include the constitutionalisation, universalisation, globalisation and enforcement of standards, norm internalisation and transmission, stakeholder empowerment, reshaping of customs and acting as institutional champions for sustainable development. Nonetheless, we identify some obstacles to effective sustainable development roles for adjudicative institutions and propose solutions for tackling them. These barriers include lack of explicit provisions, narrowly focusing on compensatory remedies, locus standi, *forum non conveniens* and choice of law.

While it is generally acknowledged that the law occupies a central role in advancing environmental protection (Gunningham, 2009) and other sustainable development agendas, the role of the courts is subject to an ongoing debate (Pedersen, 2019). One of the earliest contributions to the role of adjudication institutions in environment protection is Joseph Sax's (1971) *Defending the environment*, in which he championed the notion of using private court actions to protect the public trust. Gunningham (2009) argued that the concept of environmental governance has emerged to demonstrate the role of both public and private actors in advancing environmental protection. McAuslan (1991) adopted the institutional approach in examining the role of the courts in environmental matters. Nonetheless, this chapter is unique in applying Scott's (2001, 2008) tripartite classification of institutions to investigate the role of adjudication institutions in sustainable development. The classification facilitates concrete proposals for pro-grammatic participation of public and private institutions in sustainable develop-ment. The chapter therefore provides original contributions to the debate in identifying the formal and informal roles of adjudicative institutions and demon-strating the complementarity of those roles with certain limitations imposed by legal frameworks. The primary reference to developing countries is another distinguish-ing feature from existing studies which mostly focus on environmental matters before the courts of the more advanced countries (e.g. McAuslan, 1991; May, 2009; Pedersen, 2019). Similarly, Jacobs (2006) examined the role of the ECJ in environmental protection. The modest number of works that address the developing country context (e.g. Preston, 2005; Kameri-Mbote and Odote, 2009) are often limited in scope to the formal interpretative functions of the courts as opposed to their wider regulatory, normative and cognitive institutional roles.

The chapter is organised as follows. It, firstly, examines the meaning of institu-tions and locates adjudicative institutions within the framework of institutions for promoting of sustainable development. It demonstrates that adjudicative institutions are a stakeholder group for sustainable development before outlining their roles in a developing country context. The chapter then highlights impediments to the effec-tiveness of adjudicative institutions for sustainable development and offers solutions to conclude that these obstacles are not insurmountable.

4.2 INSTITUTIONS AND ADJUDICATION

A starting point for understanding the role of the courts and formal adjudicative institutions is the institutional theoretic model. As Misangyi et al. (2008) explained, the institutional theory confirms that actions and behaviours are determined or influenced by the institutional environment. Li et al. (2008: p. 328) similarly argued that the theory 'offers a powerful explanation of both individual and organisational actions and processes'. The institutional theory is centred around the concept of 'institutions' which Hoffman (1999) described as 'rules, norms, and beliefs that describe reality for the organisation, explaining what is and is not, what can be acted upon and what cannot' (Hoffman, 1999: p. 351). The institutional theory is, therefore, mostly applied to investigate intra- and inter-organisational behaviour and interaction (Misangyi et al., 2008). However, the theory can have a broader applica-tion to social relationships. In this regard, institutions are explicit and implicit rules and norms (Powell and DiMaggio, 1991) that guide and provide standards of, and impose constraints on, behaviour of actors within society (North, 1990; Scott, 2001).

Although they all potentially influence behaviour, institutions do so in different ways. Consequently, Scott (2001, 2008) has suggested the existence of regulatory, normative and cognitive or cultural institutions as the pillars of the institutional framework. Regulatory institutions are formal laws, rules and regulations and their coercive enforcement. Unlike the informal normative and cognitive institutions, regulatory institutions are explicit and, as a result, potentially more easily amended or adaptable in changing circumstances. While normative institutions refer to consciously shared norms, values, beliefs and expectations for behaviour and social interaction, cognitive/cultural institutions provide implicit, unconscious and symbolic interpretative frames (see also Zucker, 1977; Scott, 2001; Pillay and Kluvers, 2014).

The three categories of institution are not mutually exclusive – regulatory institutions can influence normative and cognitive institutions and equally be influenced by them. Due to the complementary nature of the three categories of institution and their comparable potential to influence behaviour, the desired goal may not be achieved if one category, especially regulatory institutions, is prioritised over and above the others. This is demonstrated by anti-corruption studies (Goddard et al., 2016; Pillay and Kluvers, 2014; Persson et al., 2013; Misangyi et al., 2008; Uberti, 2016), which have linked the apparent ineffectiveness of Nigeria's anti-corruption drive to its focus on regulatory institutions (Ijewereme, 2015). The new institutional economics approach similarly highlights the importance of efficient formal and informal institutions for development, particularly in developing countries (Acemoglu and Robinson, 2008; Rothstein, 2011).

Within the regulatory category are adjudicative institutions that are meant to establish public structures for ensuring the rule of law. For sustainable development, these institutions can be general courts or specialised tribunals such as India's National Green Tribunal and Kenya's Environment and Land Court established in 2010 and 2011 respectively. Ideally, the rule of law refers to an effective legal system which, among other things, protects rights, enforces obligations and ensures prompt, fair, transparent, credible and consistent dispute adjudication. As a governance indicator (Davis and Trebilcock, 2008; Desta and Hirsch, 2012), the rule of law can influence other governance indicators (Kaufmann et al., 2009) such as governmental effectiveness, equality of opportunity and development within countries. Due to its impact on public and private good governance, the rule of law is fundamental to the achievement of sustainable development (Sachs, 2012). As demonstrated by a study on judicial attitude to environmental protection in different jurisdictions (Kotzé, 2009: p. 3), a legal system that provides a framework for the effective application and enforcement of rights and obligations is an essential complement to constitutional and legislative provisions.

In addition to clarifying the structural aspects of institutions, the institutional theory reflects a contextual approach. This is an acknowledgment of diversity of needs between countries and regions (Kang and Moon, 2012) that can affect the identification and prioritisation of sustainable development agendas. For example, sustainable development as defined by the Brundtland Report (United Nations, 1987) is a compromise (Rajamani, 2003) between environment protection and economic growth to reflect sensitivity to local needs, including poverty alleviation in developing countries. Similarly, Principle 7 of the Rio Declaration acknowledged a principle of common but differentiated responsibility which sought to impose greater obligations on developed countries for achieving sustainable development relative to their contributions to global environmental pollution.[9] Furthermore, while paragraph 1 of the 2015 SDGs Declaration suggests a global standardisation objective, paragraph 22 states that '[e]ach country faces specific challenges in its pursuit of sustainable development' and paragraph 56 refers to 'different national realities, capacities and levels of development and respecting national policies and realities'.

The institutional theoretic model, therefore, has a two-fold role in sustainable development. First, it is useful in identifying the types, levels and complementarity of public and private structures for achieving a collective goal such as sustainable development. Second, it highlights the need for local sensitivity in sustainable development. The next part of this chapter considers the roles of formal domestic adjudicative institutions in this regard.

4.3 DOMESTIC ADJUDICATIVE INSTITUTIONS AND SUSTAINABLE DEVELOPMENT

A key role of domestic adjudicative institutions is the interpretation and clarification of laws, regulations and principles and proactively applying them in enforcing or promoting internationally agreed sustainable development principles. However, the role of adjudicative institutions may depend on the content of the national constitution, their interpretation of constitutional provisions and the relationship between international instruments and national law. The third condition largely depends on the extent national law permits direct enforcement of international instruments (Coomans, 2006; Liebenberg, 2007). In Nigeria, for example, the Constitution is the supreme law and prevails over any other laws which are invalid to the extent of their inconsistency with it.[10] The Constitution provides the legal basis for the division of governmental powers and enshrines the principle of separation of powers between the federal, state and local governments.[11] Legislative powers are conferred on the National Assembly and the House of Assembly for the federal and state governments respectively[12] while the President and Governors exercise the respective executive powers.[13]

Nigeria's Constitution confers the judicial powers on federal and state courts, which can review laws, including written and unwritten laws.[14] In this respect, the Constitution specifically empowers the judicial institutions to review laws and

---

[9] See also Arts. 3(1) and 4(1) of the United Nations Framework Convention on Climate Change 1992.
[10] Constitution of the Federal Republic of Nigeria, 1999 (as amended), ss. 1(1) (3).
[11] Ibid., s. 4, Second Sch.
[12] Ibid., s. 4.
[13] Ibid., s. 5.
[14] Ibid., s. 6.

regulations and executive actions and decisions. Section 4(8), for instance, stipulates that 'the exercise of legislative powers by the National Assembly or by a House of Assembly shall be subject to the jurisdiction of courts of law and of judicial tribunals established by law' while section 6(6)(b) extends judicial powers to 'to all matters between persons, or between government or authority and to any persons in Nigeria, and to all actions and proceedings relating thereto, for the determination of any question as to the civil rights and obligations of that person'. These provisions confirm the jurisdiction of adjudicative institutions and the application of constitutional principles in determining rights and obligations in horizontal and vertical disputes. For example, in *Agbai* v. *Okogbue*,[15] the Supreme Court held:

> [A]ny customary law that sanctions the breach of an aspect of the rule of law as contained in the fundamental rights provisions guaranteed to a Nigerian in the Constitution is barbarous and should not be enforced by our courts.

Arguably, sustainable development claims can invoke civil rights in relation to the SDGs and involve legislative and executive actions for the implementation of appropriate strategies. In these circumstances, the Nigerian adjudicative institutions can review the decisions, actions and practices of the legislative and executive arms of government and those of other persons and groups, including in matters of sustainable development. The adjudicative institutions can interpret sustainable development provisions and standards in the wider context of legal, political and constitutional complexities and, in that regard, can undertake regulatory, normative and cognitive institutional roles (see Figure 4.1) as outlined below.

4.4 CONSTITUTIONALISATION OF SUSTAINABLE DEVELOPMENT

Constitutionalisation is the entrenchment of rights or protections in a written constitution because they are deemed to be fundamental in acting as a platform from which the expression and vindication of other rights or other interests can be founded and is a measure of the importance of the rights or interests protected (Hirschl, 2004). There are a few instances of constitutional references to sustainable development, however, in the constitutions of several jurisdictions, sustainable development does not enjoy the same level of significance like 'traditional' human rights. For instance, sustainable development-related matters contained in Chapter II of Nigeria's Constitution are unenforceable and merely aspirational unlike Chapter IV's fundamental rights. Furthermore, only Chapter IV rights are capable of expeditious judicial enforcement through a special fast-track mechanism.[16]

---

[15] [1992] 7 NWLR (Part 204) 391 at 442 *per* Wali JSC.
[16] S. 46 of the Constitution and the Fundamental Rights Enforcement Procedure Rules (FREPR) 2009 made pursuant to s. 46.

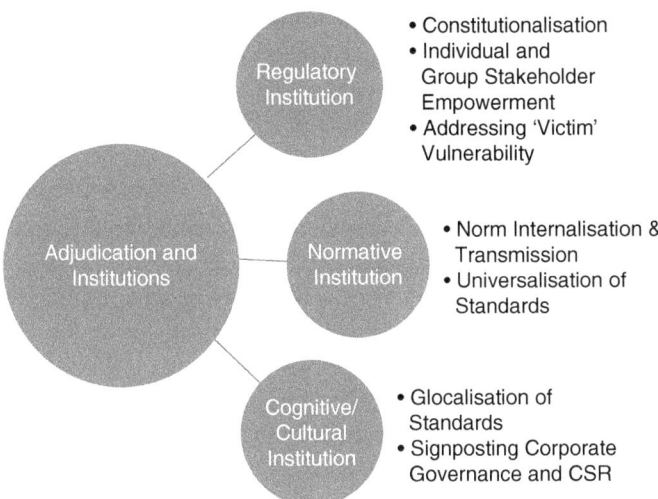

FIGURE 4.1 Adjudicative institutions and sustainable development

Nonetheless, adjudicative institutions can play a regulatory institutional role by facilitating the constitutionalisation of sustainable development despite a lack of explicit constitutional provisions. This is by providing indirect furthering of sustainable development as a constitutional ideal through the fundamental (human) rights provisions. For instance, while the Associated Gas Re-injection Act 1979 permitted gas flaring despite its adverse environmental impact, in *Gbemre v. Shell Petroleum Development Company Nigeria Limited*,[17] a Nigerian court invalidated the statute for violating the right to life guaranteed by section 33 of the Constitution. The court's holding that the right to life includes a right to a safe environment free from noxious pollution by gaseous substances constitutes an indirect promotion of sustainable development as a constitutional right. It confirms Lord Reid's (1972: p. 22) assertion that 'the practical answer is that *the law is what the judge says it is*' (emphasis added).

Another indirect method for constitutionalisation of sustainable development is by using international human rights instruments to interpret constitutional provisions. This anthropocentric approach flows from Principle 1 of the 1972 Stockholm Declaration on the Human Environment (United Nations, 1973) which stated that 'man's environment, the natural and the man-made, are essential to his well-being and to the enjoyment of basic human rights – even the right to life itself'. The 1987 Brundtland Report (United Nations, 1987) similarly confirmed that 'every human being has the right to a clean and safe environment conducive to their health and well-being'. International human rights instruments can, therefore, be a reference source for directly enforceable remedies or act as an interpretative guide to relevant

[17] (2005) AHRLR 151 (NgHC 2005).

national law provisions (Viljoen, 2007). For instance, the Netherlands court partly decided the *Urgenda* case with reference to the European Convention on Human Rights.[18]

Nonetheless, indirect constitutionalisation may depend on how national law treats international treaties. For instance, in a dualistic system like Nigeria, section 12(1) of the Constitution provides that a treaty must be expressly incorporated by domestic legislation to be part of local law. For this reason, the African Charter on Human and Peoples Rights 1981 is part of Nigerian law, having been expressly incorporated by the African Charter on Human and Peoples' Rights (Ratification and Enforcement) Act. Constitutionalisation may be difficult in the absence of a local implementing legislation and, in fact, some may regard it as judicial usurpation of legislative powers. Lawmaking powers are conferred on the legislature which include the enactment of legislation to incorporate supranational rights and obligations into the domestic legal system. Judicial intervention to constitutionalise such rights without explicit legislation may be viewed as an encroachment into the legislative sphere and a violation of the principle of separation of powers between the arms of government.

Furthermore, there are substantive and procedural aspects of constitutionalisation of international instruments. Substantively, adjudicative institutions need to recognise that treaties have moved from their original conception as instruments for regulating only inter-state behaviour to encompassing the rights and obligations of private persons (Yoo, 1999: p. 1968). There is the need to acknowledge that the 'real object' of some treaties is to 'regulate the activities of individuals and private entities' (Chayes and Chayes, 1995: p. 14). This realisation may make it easier for the adjudication of sustainable development matters and resolution of interests therein.

Constitutionalisation can also remove procedural barriers to enforcement and allow rights guaranteed by international instruments to be claimed using a procedure similar to the constitutionally guaranteed rights. For example, while the African Charter confers a direct right of action on aggrieved persons, neither it nor the domestic enabling legislation provides a specific procedure for its enforcement. However, Nigeria's Supreme Court has held that the African Charter can be enforced like a local legislation[19] and claims can be commenced by a writ or other permissible procedure such as the Fundamental Rights (Enforcement Procedure) Rules.[20] While there is no express provision in the Constitution or a statute to justify the decision of Nigeria's Supreme Court, the direct application of the African Charter under the incorporation legislation would have been meaningless in the absence of any enforcement procedure. Order II Rule 1 of the Fundamental Rights (Enforcement Procedure) Rules 2009 implemented this decision by making the

---

[18] *Urgenda Foundation v. The Netherlands (Ministry of Infrastructure and Environment)* [2015] Verdict, The Hague District Court C/09/456689/HA ZA 13–1396 (2015), paras. 4.51–4.53.
[19] *Nemi v. The State* [1994] 1 LRC 376.
[20] *Abacha v. Fawehinmi* [2000] 6 NWLR (Part 660) 228 at 293–4; 348–9.

African Charter rights enforceable through the Rules in the same manner as the fundamental rights in Chapter IV of the Constitution.

4.4.1 *Norm Internalisation and Transmission*

Adjudicative institutions can undertake normative and cognitive institutional roles by championing sustainable development in their interpretative functions. Nonetheless, they will need to internalise appropriate sustainable development norms before transmitting those norms to other social actors. Internalisation refers to the sense of compliance through voluntary acceptance triggered by personal motivations (Viljoen, 2007: p. 23). Motivational postures, which determine whether social actor display commitment, resistance, engagement or game-playing towards a goal, are the

> sets of beliefs and attitudes that sum up how individuals feel about and wish to position themselves in relation to another social entity … Postures are subjective – they bind together the cognitive, emotional and behavioural components of attitude. They provide the narrative within which the authority's message is given meaning. They have coherence for the self and are socially acceptable to significant others. (Braithwaite, 2009: p. 20)

Motivations are necessary for the horizontal and vertical sharing of shared norms, trust, identity and objectives among social actors even in regulatory arenas (Etienne, 2013). It is an implicit reference to the intuitive, emotional and other human aspects of judges (Brennan, 1998: p. 3; Schauer, 2009: p. 114) as the adjudicative institutions, a point acknowledged by some judges. For example, the US judge, Judge Benjamin Cardozo (1921: p. 167), observed that 'deep below consciousness are other forces, the likes and dislikes, the predilections and the prejudices, the complex of instincts and emotions and habits and convictions which make the man, whether he be litigant or judge'. More recently, a UK judge, Sir Terence Etherton (2010: p. 740), highlighted the potential influence of judges' 'personal outlook based on personal experience, and their judicial philosophy' on judicial decisions.

In other words, adjudicative institutions need to demonstrate and apply a belief in the SDGs. This is particularly due to the need to balance sustainable development against competing private and national economic goals. The co-existence of sustainable development and competing economic goals is implicit in the Brundtland Report's definition of sustainable development (United Nations, 1987) as 'development that meets the need of the present without compromising the ability of future generations to meet their own need'. However, the definition does not advocate the pre-eminence of economic priorities. The 2002 Johannesburg World Summit on Sustainable Development's declaration that economic, social and environmental factors are 'interdependent and mutually reinforcing pillars of sustainable development' (United Nations, 2002, Resolution 1, para. 5) reinforces the point that economic factors should not be a sole determinant for decisions.

In relation to environment-polluting gas flaring, for example, the Global Gas Flaring Reduction Partnership suggested that 'in theory, the economics of associated gas dictates that operators will reduce flaring and venting until the marginal costs of gas utilization in a field exceed the marginal benefits' (World Bank, 2004: p. 25). When the cost of facilities and programmes for preventing pollution exceeds the potential liability, in fact, pollution then becomes an economically viable option for oil companies. This may explain the persistence of environmental pollution in oil-producing developing countries like Nigeria (UNEP Report, 2009).[21] In *SERAP*,[22] the Court of Justice of the Economic Community of West African States confirmed that Nigerian authorities often refrain from enforcing environmental regulations against oil companies operating in the Niger Delta region.

Therefore, even when sustainable development goals are constitutionalised or embedded in national law, it still rests on adjudicative institutions to balance the goals against private property rights and national economic considerations (Kysar, 2012). The motivation of adjudicative institutions is central in determining the wider significance of sustainable development in this context. For example, the Costa Rican Supreme Court in *M. M. Levy y Asociacion Ecologista Limonense v. Ministerio del Ambiente y Energia*[23] and the Chilean Supreme Court in *Pablo Orrego Silva v. Empressa Pange SA*[24] demonstrated a pro-sustainable development approach by applying constitutional environmental rights provisions to respectively invalidate major oil and gas and hydroelectric dam projects.

However, adjudicative institutions are constrained in their normative and cognitive institutional roles if they favour economic and other factors over sustainable development. For example, the US federal courts routinely favour constitutional protection of property rights over environmental rights (Wald, 1992; O'Leary, 1989) and the Nigerian judiciary's pro-economic bias relegates environmental considerations to the background (Ebeku, 2007). This attitude has, in turn, brought about the relatively low success rates of environmental litigation in Nigeria and an increasing resort to transnational environmental litigation mainly against major corporate polluters. Several environmental pollution cases have been instituted in jurisdictions like the USA, UK and Netherlands due to a perceived lack of access to justice in Nigeria.[25] In contrast to the largely pro-economic position of Nigerian courts, a

---

[21] See *Gbemre v. Shell Petroleum Development Company Nigeria Limited* (2005) AHRLR 151 (NgHC 2005).
[22] *SERAP v. Federal Republic of Nigeria* ECW/CCJ/JUD/18/12.
[23] Supreme Court of Colombia Decision 2001–13295, Expediente 00–007280-0007-CO, 21/12/2001.
[24] *Pablo Orrego Silva v. Empressa Pange SA* Supreme Court of Chile 5 August 1993.
[25] See *Ken Saro Wiwa et al. v. Royal Dutch Petroleum Co et al* (2008) No. 96 Civ 8386 (KMW); *Kiobel v. Royal Dutch Petroleum Co.*, (2013)133 S.Ct. 1659; *The Bodo Community and others v. Shell Petroleum Development Company of Nigeria Ltd* [2014] EWHC 1973 (TCC; *A.F. Akpan v. Royal Dutch Shell, Plc & SPDC* Court of Appeal of the Hague (December 18, 2015) Arrondisse- mentsrechtbank Den

South African court in *BP Southern Africa (Pty) Ltd v. MEC for Agriculture, Conservation and Land Affairs BP*[26] insisted:

> Pure economic principles will no longer determine, in an unbridled fashion, whether a development is acceptable. Development, which may be regarded as economically and financially sound, will, in future, be balanced by its environmental impact, taking coherent cognisance of the principle of intergenerational equity and sustainable use of resources in order to arrive at an integrated management of the environment, sustainable development and socio-economic concerns.

The pro-sustainable development approaches of the South African, Costa Rican and Chilean courts prove that adjudicative institutions in developing countries can play an important role in curtailing economic development goals in favour of sustainable development, notwithstanding the pressure from the governments at domestic levels to accelerate developmental pursuits regardless of its impact on sustainable development goals.

The question may arise as to the practical consequences of the interpretative role of adjudicative institutions in sustainable development. The attitude of these institutions will determine the rights and obligations of private persons as well as the powers of administrative agencies. Pedersen (2019) found that the UK courts, in balancing competing interests in environmental protection, often adopt the position of administrative agencies being challenged by private claimants. The courts appear to interpret pro-sustainable development provisions strictly especially when the provisions conflict with economic development programmes of public and private persons. This is exemplified by a recent decision of the Court of Appeal regarding the 'presumption in favour of sustainable development' in paragraph 14 of the National Planning Policy Framework (NPPF). The ministerial foreword to the NPPF confirms that '[d]evelopment that is sustainable should go ahead, without delay – a presumption in favour of sustainable development that is the basis for every plan, and every decision … ' The court, however, decided that the NPPF is a policy instrument that does not have statutory force and as such the policy presumption of sustainable development cannot override the statutory 'presumption of development plan' in section 38(6) of the Planning and Compulsory Purchase Act 2004.[27]

Haag [District Court of The Hague], Jan. 30, 2013, Case No. C/09/337050/HA ZA. 09–1580; *Okpabi and Others v. Royal Dutch Shell Plc and Shell Petroleum Development Company of Nigeria (SPDC) Ltd* and *Lucky Alame and Others v. Royal Dutch Shell plc, The Shell Petroleum Development Company of Nigeria Ltd* [2017] EWHC 89 (TCC).

[26] 2004 (5) SA 124 (WLD) www.saflii.org/za/cases/ZACC/2007/25.html accessed 8 April 2015.

[27] *Barwood Strategic Land II LLP v. East Staffordshire Borough Council & Anor* [2017] EWCA Civ 893. See also *City of Edinburgh Council v. Secretary of State for Scotland* [1997] 1 WLR 1447 (p. 1449H, Lord Craig), (p. 145B, Lord Hope); *Secretary of State for Communities and Local Government v. BDW Trading Ltd. (T/A David Wilson Homes (Central, Mercia and West Midlands)* [2016] EWCA Civ 493 para. 21 (Lindblom LJ).

4.4.2 Universalisation of Standards

The adjudicative institutions' normative and cognitive roles include the promotion of universalisation of sustainable development standards by basing their reasoning on applicable international instruments. The backdrop is the requirement by the 1969 Vienna Convention on the Law of Treaties for 'good faith' interpretation of 'the ordinary meaning' of expressions used in treaties and to reflect their 'context' and 'object and purpose'. Universalisation may be possible even when relevant international treaties are not directly enforceable in national law. In *Urgenda*, for instance, the Netherlands court acknowledged the 'reflex effect'[28] of international instruments notwithstanding that the claimant could not directly ask for their enforcement. Another illustration is Nigeria which, although it has not incorporated the Convention on the Elimination of All Forms of Discrimination against Women 1979 (CEDAW), is a signatory state. A court suggested that 'in view of the fact that Nigeria is a party to the convention, courts of law should give or provide teeth to its provisions'.[29] This indicates that CEDAW standards can be applied in determining whether rules and practices are discriminatory. Some African national courts have also referenced international instruments 'seamlessly, without noting or explaining the binding nature or level of persuasive authority' (Adjami, 2002).

Universalisation of standards helps to 'create a template which can be applied only if we infuse them with the factual circumstances of a given society, of its own patterns of disadvantage, the structure of its ruling elites, and its prevailing symbolic meanings of stigma' (Sadurski, 2004: p. 154). It has, for instance, facilitated the recognition of 'the value of human rights vocabulary as a discourse – as an international language of claim against an oppressive state or an oppressive culture' and demonstrated that 'human rights language is today used everywhere around the world to linguistically frame resistance to oppression' (Stacy, 2004: p. 174). While some may object to universalism in areas such as human rights (Mutua, 2004; Osiatynski, 2004) as being mainly Western ideological or cultural imposition, international instruments can help to establish common minimum standards and principles within the global diversity of societies and cultures (Schwartz, 1990). Universalism can, for instance, tackle the existence of 'regulatory arbitrage' (UNEP, 2016) arising from inconsistent standards that corporations and other social actors can exploit.

Therefore, while international instruments can provide a framework for the universalisation of sustainable development standards, the interpretative role of adjudicative institutions is critical, especially when the institutions are confronted by incompatible or challenging national rules and practices. In *SERAP* v. *Federal*

---

[28]   *Urgenda Foundation* v. *The Netherlands (Ministry of Infrastructure and Environment)* [2015] Verdict, The Hague District Court C/09/456689/HA ZA 13-1396 (2015) para. 4.43.
[29]   *Muojekwu* v. *Ejikeme* [2000] NWLR (Part 657) 402 at 436 *per* Tobi JCA.

Republic of Nigeria,[30] the African Commission on Human and Peoples Rights referred to Article 4 of the African Charter in holding that persistent environmental pollution of Nigeria's Niger Delta region through oil extraction constitutes an infringement on the people's right to life. Similarly, Nigerian courts[31] have upheld the superiority of the African Charter over local laws, except the Constitution which is the supreme law. In *Abacha v. Fawehinmi*,[32] the Supreme Court held:

> The African Charter on Human and Peoples' Rights (Ratification and Enforcement) Act … is a statute with international flavour. Being so, therefore, [sic] … if there is a conflict between it and another statute, its provisions will prevail over those of that other statute for the reason that it is presumed that the Legislature does not intend to breach an international obligation … But that is not to say that the Charter is superior to the Constitution …

This decision enables the application of the African Charter rights over inconsistent and conflicting local legislation and creates a platform for the universalisation of sustainable development standards in line with international standards by Nigeria's adjudicative institutions.

4.4.3 Glocalisation of Standards

While universalism may reject the cultural relativist notion that standards are determined by different cultures (Brems, 2004: p. 214), the reality is the existence of diverse cultures globally. This creates a tension between universalism and cultural identity rights in matters such as human rights (Brems, 2004: p. 214; Stacy, 2004: p. 165). Due to different governance indicators (Desta and Hirsch, 2012; Kaufmann and Kraay, 2015), development can be country-specific and reflect culturally adapted practices (Robertson, 2009). In fact, Principle 7 of the Rio Declaration acknowledged disparities in the relative sustainable development obligations and contributions of developed and developing countries.[33] The SDGs also acknowledge that 'different approaches, visions, models and tools available to each country, in accordance with its national circumstances and priorities' (paragraph 59). Paragraph 63 further asserts that 'each country has primary responsibility for its own economic and social development'. These provisions suggest that, despite the overall universalism objective of paragraph 1, the SDGs recognise the need for glocalisation – combined international and local standards – of sustainable development.

This raises the question of whether international sustainable development standards can be combined effectively with local priorities. The attitude of adjudicative

---

[30] *Socio-Economic Rights and Accountability Project (SERAP) v. Federal Republic of Nigeria* Judgment No. ECW/CCJ/Jud/18/12.

[31] For example, *Fawehinmi v. Abacha* [1996] 9 NWLR (Part 475) 710; *Ubani v. Director, S.S.S.* [1999] 11 NWLR (Part 625) 129; *Abacha v. Fawehinmi* [2000] 6 NWLR (Part 660) 228.

[32] [2000] 6 NWLR (Part 660) 228 at 289.

[33] See also Arts. 3(1) and 4(1) of the United Nations Framework Convention on Climate Change, 1992.

institutions is likely to be critical in this regard. If an attitude is 'a relatively enduring organisation of beliefs, feelings, and behavioural tendencies towards socially significant objects, groups, events or symbols' (Hogg and Vaughan, 2005: p. 150), effective glocalisation can be determined, to a large extent, by the adjudicative institutions' pronouncements and actions which can signpost appropriate standards for other social actors. Adjudicative institutions can acknowledge certain minimum standards to which local rules and practices must be subject. For example, while most of the human rights provisions of the African Charter are also contained in Chapter IV of Nigeria's Constitution[34] and can be enforced like national laws,[35] some national and sub-national rules and practices can be contrary to the Charter. In that regard, Nigerian courts have declared the superiority of the Charter in several human rights cases.[36]

Another glocalisation role of adjudicative institutions is to acknowledge, enforce and promote national rules and practices that exceed minimum international sustainable development standards. For example, in *Juliana*, the court insisted that '[t]here is no contradiction between promising other nations the United States will reduce CO_2 emissions and a judicial order directing the United States to go beyond its international commitments to more aggressively reduce CO_2 emissions'.[37]

4.4.4 Stakeholder Empowerment

A consistent sustainable development theme is the necessity of involving all segments of society, including individuals and groups, in promoting sustainable development. On the one hand, individuals are encouraged to adopt more 'sustainable' life choices leading to the growing influence of sustainable consumption messages directed at consumers and other persons. This constitutes 'a simple pathway for engaging and involving the public at large in the development of lifestyle changes that are considered necessary to achieve sustainable development' (Warren, 2003: p. 78). On the other hand, individuals are also being encouraged to take sustainable production into consideration as a sustainable development 'obligation'. In the more advanced economies, business practices seem to equate sustainable development with environmentally friendly products and services (Cho, 2015) while sustainability reporting along the lines of sustainable production and consumption is increasingly popular even beyond the more environment proximate sectors (Higgins et al., 2015; KMPG, 2011).

---

[34] See the observation of Ogundare JSC in *Abacha* v. *Fawehinmi* [2001] 51 WRN 29 at 83.
[35] *Nemi* v. *The State* [1994] 1 LRC 376 (Supreme Court).
[36] For example *Fawehinmi* v. *Abacha* [1996] 9 NWLR (Part 475) 710; *Ubani* v. *Director, S.S.S.* [1999] 11 NWLR (Part 625) 129; *Abacha* v. *Fawehinmi* [2000] 6 NWLR (Part 660) 228.
[37] *Juliana* v. *United States of America*, Opinion and Order [2016] The United States District Court for the District of Oregon 6:15-cv-01517-TC US D. Or, (2016), 15.

In other words, individuals are expected to participate actively in promoting sustainable development. It is increasingly being recognised that participation rights for individuals can be essential for the promotion of sustainable development. For example, Principle 10 of the Rio Declaration[38] confirms that

> Environmental issues are best handled with the participation of all concerned citizens, at the relevant level. At the national level, each individual shall have appropriate access to information concerning the environment that is held by public authorities, including information on hazardous materials and activities in their communities, and the opportunity to participate in decision-making processes.

Participation requires the recognition of 'rights' for individuals and groups as stakeholders. Essentially, individuals and groups are recognised as 'right-holders' for their own benefit, for the benefit of other persons like the future generations, or for the benefit of some things such as the environment. According to Merrills (1996: p. 31), '[r]ights cannot exist as free-floating abstractions, but need rights' holders, for the function of rights ... is to mark out protected areas for the benefit of someone or something, and so the concept of a right without a rights-holder is a contradiction in terms'. Therefore, the individual participation rights can include collective goals such as sustainable development and, in fact, need not reflect anthropocentrism or be constrained to individual benefits or interests. Dworkin (1978: p. 12) similarly noted that '[i]ndividual rights are political trumps held by the individuals. Individuals have rights when, for some reason, a collective goal is not a sufficient justification for denying them what they wish, as individuals, to have or to do, or not a sufficient justification for imposing some loss or injury upon them.' Individual participation rights can be enforced against public and private persons using the instrumentality of adjudicative institutions.

4.4.5 *Addressing Vulnerability of Sustainable Development 'Victims'*

Sustainable development discourse suggests that unsustainable practices are not 'victimless' activities. The future generations[39] are key stakeholders and potential victims, hence the Brundtland Report (United Nations, 1987: p. 43) asked countries to 'ensure that the environment and natural resources are conserved and used for the benefit of present and future generations'. The living are also stakeholders in

---

[38] Report of the United Nations Conference on Environment and Development (Rio De Janeiro, 3-14 June 1992).

[39] See *Urgenda Foundation v. The Netherlands (Ministry of Infrastructure and Environment)* [2015] Verdict, The Hague District Court C/09/456689/HA ZA 13-1396 (2015); *Juliana v. United States of America*, Opinion and Order [2016] The United States District Court for the District of Oregon 6:15-cv-01517-TC US D. Or, (2016); *Greenpeace Nordic Association & others v. Norway Ministry of Petroleum and Energy* [2016] Oslo District Court.

sustainable development.[40] Unsustainable practices can reduce life enjoyment and opportunities for people, increase poverty and lead to adverse physical and mental health. In *Legality of Threat or Use of Nuclear Arms* case,[41] the International Court of Justice pointed out that the environment 'is not an abstraction but represents the living space, the quality of life and the very health of human beings, including generations unborn'. The *Agouman v. Leigh Day* case cited above illustrates the direct impact of unsustainable practices on the health of workers, residents and host communities. Nonetheless, the case also demonstrates the vulnerability of victims to whims and exploitative conduct of powerful social actors like corporations and regulatory authorities. Although provided in relation to fiduciary duties, Justice Wilson's reference to vulnerability in the Canadian case of *Frame v. Smith* (1987) is pertinent here. The judge referred to vulnerability as 'the inability of the bene-ficiary (despite his or her best efforts) to prevent the injurious exercise of the power or discretion combined with the grave inadequacy or absence of other legal or practical remedies to redress the wrongful exercise of the discretion or power'.[42] The contrast-ing libertarian approach ignores vulnerability factors existing between stakeholders who are viewed as having equal power of awareness and enforcement of their rights.

In the context of sustainable development, victim vulnerability includes impedi-ments imposed by national legislation and regulatory authorities. Notwithstanding these obstacles, the adjudicative institutions may be able to refer to international best standards for determining human rights to life, health and safe environment and tortious duty of care which may be closely linked to some aspects of sustainable development. After all, as Lord Bridge stated in *Caparo v. Dickman*, a duty of care incorporates the concepts of proximity and fairness that are 'convenient labels to attach to the features of different specific situations which … the law recognises pragmatically as giving rise to a duty of care of a given scope'.[43] In *Fijabi* cited above, the Nigerian court overcame the position of the local regulatory authorities by referring to an international human right to health.

The awareness of vulnerability factors will enable adjudicative institutions to promote sustainable development related corrective and distributive justice in the substance and procedures of adjudication. Corrective justice (Weinrib, 2002: p. 349) in this regard justifies the provision of remedies for stakeholder victims of wrongful conduct. On the other hand, distributive justice allows reference to sustainable development principles in the allocation of stakeholder rights and obligations. As Frederick Douglass (1955: p. 434) stated, 'where justice is denied, where poverty is enforced, where ignorance prevails, and where any one class is made to feel that

---

[40] See *Greenpeace Nordic Association & others* v. *Norway Ministry of Petroleum and Energy* [2016] Oslo District Court; *KlimaSeniorinnen* case discussed in Bähr et al. (2018).
[41] *Legality of Threat or Use of Nuclear Arms*, ICJ Advisory Opinion of 8 July 2006, para. 28.
[42] *Frame* v. *Smith* (1987) 42 DLR (4th) 81, para. 45 (Wilson J).
[43] *Caparo Industries Plc* v. *Dickman* [1990] 2 AC 605, [14], *per* Lord Bridge.

society is an organised conspiracy to oppress, rob and degrade them, neither persons nor property will be safe'.

4.4.6 *Promoting Appropriate Corporate Governance and Corporate Social Responsibility*

As noted above, sustainable development requires stakeholder involvement. A prominent stakeholder group is that of corporations. While corporations are one of the primary agents for national economic development and can assist in tackling sustainable development issues such as poverty eradication (which is Goal 1 of the SDGs), they can perpetrate unsustainable practices having a huge impact on present and future generations, such as persistent oil pollution by oil companies in Nigeria's Niger Delta region leading to the destruction of entire ecosystems in the region.

Corporate activities can be constrained by regulatory authorities and when these authorities are incapable of imposing, or unwilling to impose, sustainable standards on corporations, it may be left to individuals and groups in a weak regulatory institutional context to approach the adjudicative institutions. The effective awareness of their triple institutional role by adjudicative institutions is critical to ensuring that corporations adopt pro-sustainable development corporate governance models. In this regard, corporate governance can be described as 'the system of checks and balances, both internal and external to companies, which ensures that companies discharge their accountability to all their stakeholders and act in a socially responsible way in all areas of their business activity' (Solomon, 2007: p. 14). In a foreword for *Global Corporate Governance Forum*, Adrian Cadbury similarly suggested that corporate governance 'is concerned with holding the balance between economic and social goals and between individual and communal goals ... The aim is to align as nearly as possible the interests of individuals, corporations and societies' (World Bank, 2003).

The extent to which corporations are willing to demonstrate a wider responsibility for sustainable development may be dependent on the institutional environment. If corporate governance can be regarded as 'the determination of the broad uses to which organisational resources will be deployed and the resolution of conflicts among the myriad participants in organisations' (Daily et al., 2003: p. 371), the determination can be influenced by the existence and effectiveness of formal and informal institutions in what is likely to be a balancing act. As the stakeholder model acknowledges, 'companies have to operate within a complex [structure] of social and economic relationships, and that the most successful companies attempt to get each of these rights in what is often a difficult balancing act' (Waterman Jr, 1994: p. 26). Corporations may be more amenable to adopting appropriate practices if they can predict that the adjudicative institutions will frown upon unsustainable practices and impose sanctions, including compensatory and punitive ones.

However, if sustainable development plays little or no role in the decisions and processes of adjudicative institutions, corporations will feel unfettered and decline a stakeholder approach while allowing 'competitive individualism' to reign, with its lack of attention to the collective interest in sustainable development. In a debate in the UK House of Lords, Lord Avebury even acknowledged that under the shareholder primacy model 'in most cases, the success of the company is dependent on its ability to continue damaging the environment'.[44] As Hamilton and Clarke (1996: p. 39) argued, however, the stakeholder model can be 'the most viable alternative to the competitive individualism which has left many casualties in society, and arguably damaged the quality of life for everyone'. The conflict theory similarly suggests that corporate managers are more likely to be opportunistic and selfish (Gautier and Pache, 2015; Osemeke and Adegbite, 2016) if there are inter-stakeholder struggles for limited resources (Ford and Hess, 2011).

When corporations are confronted by pro-sustainable development adjudicative institutions, they may adopt a corporate social responsibility (CSR) approach that aligns with it. The common pool resources studies (Gabaldon and Gröschl, 2015), suggest that corporate sustainable development obligations and CSR often reference similar moral justifications. CSR of this type will normally reference compliance with both national rules and international best standards to avoid liability under explicit national legislation and judge-made rules such as a tortious duty of care that could easily be stretched to include international best standards. The orthodox view is that CSR 'actions basically are voluntary, that is, they go beyond what is legally required' (Dam and Scholtens, 2012). CSR has been, therefore, been defined as 'a firm's voluntary actions to mitigate and remedy social and environmental consequences of its operation' (Fransen, 2013: p. 213). Nonetheless, CSR is not entirely motivated by altruistic reasons and is often in response to institutional pressures, which could include adjudicative institutions. The European Commission (2011: p. 3) has therefore observed that '[c]ertain regulatory measures create an environment more conducive to enterprises voluntarily meeting their social responsibility'.

4.5 OVERCOMING LIMITATIONS OF ADJUDICATIVE INSTITUTIONS

The preceding discussions have shown that adjudicative institutions are a critical component of sustainable development promotion. Nonetheless, the adjudicative institutions' potential roles can be impeded by a few substantive and procedural factors. While the substance of rules can indicate the standards of behaviour, procedural matters can equally signpost conduct that is acceptable or discouraged. As DiMaggio and Powell (1991: p. 20) noted, institutions also include 'rules of

---

[44] House of Lords debate, 6 February 2006, col.6C266. Available at: https://publications.parliament.uk/pa/ld200506/ldhansrd/vo060206/text/60206-32.htm.

procedures that actors employ flexibly and reflexively to assure themselves and those around them that their behaviour is reasonable'. Procedural rules that prevent the enforcement of substantive standards of behaviour can, in effect, demonstrate a lack of those standards. The substantive and procedural obstacles will now be discussed.

4.5.1 *Explicit Standards*

At the substantive level, explicit provisions are required to promote sustainable development. When express provisions for sustainable development exist in written law, it is easier for adjudicative institutions to declare acts, decisions or practices unenforceable or an infringement of the law.[45] Moreover, legislation can be quicker and more direct than judicial decisions which depend on the claimants' ability and willingness to institute proceedings. Suggesting the merits of legislative intervention in the context of gender discrimination, a Nigerian court stated:

> [T]he abrogation of such obnoxious practice ... rests absolutely with the legislature of the state that still clings to such absurdity ... [and the legislative] authorities that are in a position to do so will hasten the interment of a custom that has outlived its usefulness and has become counter-productive.[46]

Nigeria's Constitution comprises of eight chapters, seven of which provide enforceable provisions on governance, civil and political rights and judicial matters. Chapter II contains some sustainable development-related objectives and policy foundations, including section 20 which refers to a governmental duty to 'protect and improve the environment and safeguard the water, air and land, forest and wildlife of Nigeria'. However, section 6(6)(c) explicitly declares the unenforceability of these aspirational objectives.[47] Placing sustainable development among the enforceable traditional fundamental rights in Chapter IV will, therefore, evince the significance attached to it and render it less susceptible to short-term economic goals of policymakers. This is a realistic prospect due to the attitude of Nigerian courts. Unlike their largely conservative approach to interpreting civil rights, Nigerian courts adopt a more liberal and proactive approach to Chapter IV fundamental rights. In the Chapter IV case of *Nweke* v. *State*, the Supreme Court reiterated that

> it is a formidable prescription that their provisions should not be subjected to 'the austerity of tabulated legalism.' On the contrary, [the provisions] ... call for a generous interpretation ... suitable to give to individuals the full measure of the fundamental rights and freedoms referred to ...[48]

---

[45]　See the observation of Tobi JCA in *Muojekwu* v. *Ejikeme* at 430.
[46]　*Muojekwu* v. *Ejikeme* [2003] 5 NWLR (Part 657) 402 at 438-9 (Olagunju JCA).
[47]　See *NNPC* v. *Fawehinmi* (1998)7 NWLR (Part 559).
[48]　*Nweke* v. *State* (2017) LPELR-42103(SC). See also *Odubu* v. *Stephen* (2012) LPELR-19792.

An explicit incorporation of sustainable development goals, as opposed to indirect promotion, amongst the traditional fundamental rights will, therefore, open these goals to a 'generous interpretation' by adjudicative institutions in a proactive and liberal manner geared towards the fulfilment of the internationally recognised SDGs within the domestic arena.

4.5.2 *Locus Standi*

A major procedural hurdle to the promotion of sustainable development in several countries is the locus standi doctrine (the right or capacity to bring a claim). Usually, claimants are required to demonstrate a direct personal interest in, and personal loss arising from, a cause of action. For example, in *Oronto Douglas* v. *Shell Petroleum Development Company Limited*,[49] the claimant sought to compel the defendant to carry out an environmental impact assessment before oil drilling. The Nigerian court dismissed the claim on the basis that the claimant was not directly affected and thus lacked the locus standi.

While some jurisdictions have watered down locus standi through statutes[50] and judicial decisions,[51] it remains a significant obstacle to environmental protection (Kameri-Mbote, 2009) and other sustainable development claims. Unless it is possibly disguised as a personal injury or human rights claim like some climate change cases (see Ghaleigh, 2010: pp. 34–5; Bähr et al., 2018), sustainable development is usually targeted at protecting the public interest which may disqualify claims by individuals and stakeholder groups who are not public authorities. A jurisdiction desirous of promoting sustainable development therefore needs to relax locus standi rules. For instance, aimed at easing access to the courts,[52] Order XIII of Nigeria's Fundamental Rights Enforcement Procedure Rules 2009 (FREPR) made pursuant to section 46(3) of the Constitution, allows claims by any 'concerned' persons whether they have a personal interest or not. This has opened opportunities for NGOs and advocacy groups to file claims on behalf of individuals and for public interest matters. However, this relaxed approach to locus standi is strictly limited to

---

[49] (1998) LPELR-CA/L/143/97.
[50] See section 32(1)(e) of the National Environmental Management Act 107 of 1998 (NEMA) of South Africa, section 3(4) of the Environmental Management and Coordination Act (EMCA) No. 18 of 1999 of Kenya and the Fundamental Rights Enforcement Procedure Rules (FREPR) 2009 of Nigeria.
[51] See for example the Kenyan case of *Albert Ruturi and Another* v. *Minister for Finance and Others* (*Albert Ruturi*) [2002] 1 KLR 51 at 54, where the court stated that 'as part of the reasonable, fair and just procedure to uphold constitutional guarantees, the right of access to justice entails a liberal approach to the question of locus standi'. In the UK case of *R* v. *Inspectorate of Pollution, ex p Greenpeace (No. 2)* [1994] All ER 329, the Court of Appeal applied a liberal interpretation of the locus standi principle in environmental rights cases, stating that 'a responsible body with a bona fide concern about the subject matter of the proceedings may be regarded as being more than a mere "busy body". This decision was applied in the more recent UK case of *Cherkley Campaign Ltd, Regina (on The Application of)* v. *Longshot Cherkley Court Ltd* [2013] EWHC 2582.
[52] Para. 3 of the Preamble to the Fundamental Rights Enforcement Procedure Rules 2009.

the fundamental rights in Chapter IV of the Constitution and does not to apply to sustainable development claims brought under any other constitutional provisions or in accordance with international instruments. For example, in *The Registered Trustees of the Socio-Economic Rights & Accountability Project* v. *Attorney General of the Federation*[53] the court confirmed that public interest groups could not rely on the FREPR for claims under the African Charter.

A relaxed locus standi rule will also enable the protection of the environment and the interests of future generations and other sustainable development stakeholders that are unable to bring their own claims. For example, in *Urgenda*, a Netherlands court allowed a claim by a group set up 'to stimulate and accelerate the transition processes to a more sustainable society, beginning in the Netherlands'.[54] In *Minors Oposa* v. *Secretary of the Department of the Environment and Natural Resources*,[55] the Philippines' Supreme Court allowed 44 minors to sue for themselves and on behalf of future generations. The court accepted that unsustainable logging could affect the future generations' ability to benefit from the country's natural resources. In granting standing to sue, the court stated: 'We find no difficulty in ruling that they can, for themselves, for others of their generation and for succeeding generations, file a class suit. Their personality to sue on behalf of the succeeding generations can only be based on the concept of intergenerational responsibility in so far as the right to a balanced and healthful ecology is concerned … '[56] In *Juliana*,[57] a US Federal District Court permitted a claim by 21 children on behalf of future generations. The court acknowledged the need for judicial mechanisms to protect the climate change-related environmental interests of future generations.[58] Judge Aiken observed that 'Federal courts too often have been cautious and overly deferential in the arena of environmental law, and the world has suffered for it.' Similar litigations on behalf of future generations have been instituted in some places. For instance, Greenpeace and the Nature and Youth environmental group filed a lawsuit in November 2017 over Norway's failure to abide by its constitutional obligation to safeguard the environment for future generations. The claimants challenged and sought the nullification of ten licences issued by the Norwegian government for exploration in the Barents Sea in order to protect the interests of future generations (Leestma, 2017).

---

53 Suit No. FHC/ABJ/CS/640/2010, Judgment of the Federal High Court, Abuja, delivered on 29 November 2012.
54 *Urgenda Foundation* v. *The Netherlands (Ministry of Infrastructure and Environment)* [2015] Verdict, The Hague District Court C/09/456689/HA ZA 13-1396 (2015) paras. 2.2, 4.10.
55 *Minors Oposa* v. *Secretary of the Department of the Environment and Natural Resources* (S.C., January 1994) (Phil.), 33 ILM 173 (1994).
56 Ibid., 835.
57 United States District Court, D. Oregon, Eugene Division, 217 F.Supp.3d 1224 (D. Or. 2016).
58 *Juliana* v. *United States of America*, Opinion and Order [2016] The United States District Court for the District of Oregon 6:15-cv-01517-TC US D. Or, (2016), 18-28.

4.5.3 *Remedies*

A critical factor for enforcing rules or instituting litigation before the adjudicative institutions is the availability of appropriate remedies for claimants. It has been noted that claimants' recourse to tort law may be due to its compensatory nature (Ward, 2003) while financial outcome is often a key factor for legal representatives (Meeran, 2011). In the case of multinational corporations and other corporate defendants, there may be significant financial rewards for claimants and their representatives even when cases are settled out of court. For example, in respect of environmental pollution and human rights claims for its operations in Nigeria, the Royal Dutch Shell settled the US case of *Ken Saro Wiwa*[59] and the English case of *Bodo Community*[60] after paying significant sums as compensation. In *Ajuwa* v. *Shell Petroleum*,[61] a Nigerian trial court awarded US$1.5 billion as compensation for oil pollution-related personal injuries, destruction of farmlands and contamination of streams. Following the intermediate court's reversal of the decision, a subsequent appeal is pending before Nigeria's Supreme Court.[62]

While a compensatory remedy, especially if coupled with an environment clean-up order, may be regarded by claimants and their legal representatives as a successful outcome of a national or transnational adjudication, its overall suitability for sustainable development is doubtful. Financial awards to private claimants, who are not required to advance sustainable development, can be used for addressing personal socioeconomic concerns. As a reactive remedy, compensation may not provide a comprehensive, sustainable and long-term framework due to its backward-looking nature and narrow scope while harms to the sustainable development cause can be long-lasting and take many years to redress. Moreover, certain classes of claimant, such as NGOs and public interest groups, may be unable to demonstrate sufficient financially ascertainable losses to be compensated. A more holistic and proactive approach is therefore necessary to provide and entrench responsibility and accountability for sustainable development for and across different segments of society. As Lozano et al. (2008, pp. 35–6) observed, 'only if responsibilities are shared in areas of common interest, assuming the active collabora-tion of all social actors, society itself and enterprise, in collaboration with the state, can today's social and environmental challenges be met'.

This may require a range of remedies, including injunctive reliefs, orders for regulatory changes and enforcement. According to the New Zealand court in *Thomson*, it is important that '[r]emedies are fashioned to ensure appropriate action is taken while leaving the policy choices about the content of that action to the appropriate state body'.[63] A good range of remedies can also render 'surrogate

---

[59] *Ken Saro Wiwa et al.* v. *Royal Dutch Petroleum Co et al* (2008) No. 96 Civ 8386.
[60] *The Bodo Community and others* v. *Shell Petroleum Development Company of Nigeria Ltd* [2014] EWHC 1973 (TCC).
[61] *Dr Pere Ajuwa* v. *Shell Petroleum* (2011) 11 SC 207.
[62] See also *Shell Petroleum Development Company (Nigeria) Ltd* v. *Abel Isaiah* (2001) 5SC (Pt. 11) 1.
[63] *Thomson* v. *Minister for Climate Change Issues* (2017) NZHC 733, 133.

protection' of sustainable development unnecessary by providing direct protection routes. 'Surrogate protection' (Taylor, 1998) applies, for instance, when a right to a clean environment is not claimed and the environment, which is not being protected per se, is sought to be protected by establishing claims to property or other environmental goods that entitles one to a peaceful enjoyment of such property and the environment it is attached to. A more direct route through remedies will enable the needs of future generations to be protected in line with the Brundtland Report's definition of sustainable development (United Nations, 1987). This is also reinforced by the Rio Declaration which states that '[t]he right to development must be fulfilled so as to equitably meet developmental and environmental needs of present and future generations' (United Nations, 1992). Furthermore, the Philippines' case of *Juan Antonio Oposa v. Fulgencio S. Factoran Jr*,[64] demonstrates that private claimants can seek to restrict environmentally harmful activities for future generations.

4.5.4 Forum Non Conveniens

Another procedural barrier is the *forum non conveniens* doctrine which, like its application in transnational human rights and tort litigation (Baldwin, 2007; Meeran, 2011; Aristova, 2018), can ultimately affect the substance and results of sustainable development claims arising in developing countries. As formulated by the House of Lords in *Spiliada Maritime Corp v. Cansulex*,[65] foreign courts can decline jurisdiction over a claim when a court in another jurisdiction is clearly a more suitable forum, due to the parties' interests and the interest of justice. Nigerian claimants have been frustrated by *forum non conveniens* after approaching foreign jurisdictions to prosecute environmental pollution claims, often against Nigerian companies and their foreign parent companies. Lack of access to justice is one of the reasons claimants adduce for seeking remedies in the courts of the more advanced countries where a defendant corporation's corporate base or parent company is located. An example is *Bodo Community*[66] which the parties settled out of court.

Although *Lungowe v. Vedanta Resources Plc*,[67] the cause of action which arose in Zambia, suggested that the English jurisdiction was possible for environmental pollution occurring in a developing country, the more recent case of *Okpabi v. Royal Dutch Shell Plc*[68] demonstrates a firm stand by the English courts against such transnational litigations. In that case, the English court declined jurisdiction because of *forum non conveniens* over claims against a UK-based parent company

---

[64] *Juan Antonio Oposa v. Fulgencio S. Factoran, Jr* G.R. No. 101083 (Supreme Court of the Philippines 9 Aug. 1993).

[65] [1987] AC 460.

[66] *The Bodo Community and others v. Shell Petroleum Development Company of Nigeria Ltd* [2014] EWHC 1973 (TCC).

[67] *Lungowe & others v. Vedanta Resources PLC and Konkola Copper Mines PLC* [2016] EWHC 975.

[68] The case was jointly filed with *Lucky Alame and Others v. Royal Dutch Shell plc, The Shell Petroleum Development Company of Nigeria Ltd* [2017] EWHC 89 (TCC).

(Royal Dutch Shell) for environmental pollution allegedly committed by its Nigerian subsidiary (Shell Petroleum Development Corporation (SPDC)). The court reasoned that a foreign court should be circumspect in passing qualitative judgments on other sovereign nations' legal systems and insisted that 'claims by Nigerians against a Nigerian company about events in Nigeria, governed by Nigerian law, should be heard in a Nigerian court'. Justice Fraser stressed:

> There is simply no connection whatsoever between this jurisdiction and the claims brought by the claimants, who are Nigerian citizens, for breaches of statutory duty and/or in common law for acts and omissions in Nigeria, by a Nigerian company.[69]

In the USA, claimants once relied on the Alien Torts Act in relation to environmental pollution and personal injury cases occurring in Nigeria. An example was *Ken Saro Wiwa v. Royal Dutch Petroleum Co*[70] which the parties settled out of court. However, the Supreme Court later decided in *Kiobel v. Royal Dutch Petroleum Co.*[71] to decline US jurisdiction on *forum non conveniens* grounds. In *Kiobel*, Chief Justice Roberts explained that the *forum non conveniens* doctrine is to prevent judicial interference in foreign policy.

To overcome the obstacles posed by *forum non conveniens*, legislators and courts of the more advanced countries need to recognise the global imperative of sustainable development. This includes the acknowledgement that certain claims of environmental pollution, personal injury or human rights are practically for the advancement of global sustainable development. This can be achieved by regional or multilateral treaties. For instance, the Brussels Convention,[72] the Brussels Regulations[73] and the Lugano Convention[74] on jurisdiction in civil and commercial matters prevent the application of *forum non conveniens* in matters affecting signatory EU and European Free Trade Association members. However, the intention to exclude the doctrine from sustainable development claims needs to be explicit. For instance, the application of the Brussels Regulation to the Environmental Liability Directive[75] based claims by public authorities is contentious due to the lack of explicit provisions (Bogdan, 2009; Collins and Harris, 2012; Dickinson, 2008).

---

[69] Ibid., 123.

[70] *Ken Saro Wiwa et al v. Royal Dutch Petroleum Co et al* (2008) No. 96 Civ 8386.

[71] *Kiobel v. Royal Dutch Petroleum Co* (2013)133 S.Ct. 1659.

[72] Art. 5(3)(5) and Art. 6(1) of the 1968 Brussels Convention on jurisdiction and the enforcement of judgments in civil and commercial matters. Consolidated version CF OJ 1972 No. L299, 31 December 1972, pp. 32–42.

[73] Art. 7(2)(5) of the Brussels Regulation No. 1215/2012 of the European Parliament and of the Council of 12 December 2012 on jurisdiction and the recognition and enforcement of judgments in civil and commercial matters.

[74] Convention on jurisdiction and the recognition and enforcement of judgments in civil and commercial matters OJ 2007 No. L339, 21 December 2007, pp. 3–41 (Lugano Convention).

[75] Directive 2004/35/EC of the European Parliament and the Council of 21 April 2004 on environmental liability with regard to the prevention and remedying of environmental damage OJ 2004 No. L143, p. 56.

Even among developing countries, it may be useful to establish regional or multilateral treaties to ensure a wider jurisdictional scope for sustainable development. Treaties of this kind will disallow courts from declining jurisdiction if sustainable development is explicitly stated as a non-excludable matter. In *Owusu v. Jackson*,[76] for example, the ECJ held that *forum non conveniens* is incompatible with article 4 of the Brussels Regulation, a position two later decisions reiterated.[77] A *forum non conveniens* limiting treaty exemplifies the need for international cooperation for sustainable development as acknowledged in several forums. The recent meeting of the IPCC stressed the importance of international cooperation in creating a global 'enabling environment' for sustainable development and as a 'critical enabler for developing countries and vulnerable region'.[78]

Forum non conveniens can also be overcome by unilateral or multilateral provisions ascribing sustainable development responsibility to certain classes of social actors. In the Netherlands (Ryngaert, 2013), for example, the courts exercise jurisdiction based on attribution of responsibility to parent companies for their subsidiaries' acts and omissions. This has been applied to environmental pollution cases from Nigeria.[79] Consequently, the Netherlands has become attractive to transnational environmental claims against multinational corporations, particularly from oil-producing developing countries such as Nigeria (Enneking, 2012, 2014; Ryngaert, 2013).

4.5.5 *Choice of Law*

Under international law, jurisdiction is almost entirely territorial and exercised by domestic regulatory institutions, which creates possible disparities in laws. International law (De Jonge, 2011; Omoteso and Yusuf, 2017) does not really intervene even when there are lax regulatory standards arising from governance failures, especially in developing countries. For instance, it was reported in 2016 that some Swiss companies profited from 'regulatory arbitrage' between the European regulations and lax standards of African countries (UNEP, 2016). The companies sold 'Africa-standard' fuels that greatly exceeded the sulphur levels permitted by Switzerland and other European countries (Guéniat et al., 2016). *Agouman v. Leigh Day*[80] and the Rana Plaza building collapse in Bangladesh (Taplin, 2014)

---

[76] *Owusu v. Jackson* C-281/02 Judgment of the Court (Grand Chamber) 1 March 2005 ECLI:EU: C:2005:120.

[77] *Turner v. Grovit* Case C-159/02 and *Gasser v. Misak* Case C-116/02.

[78] IPCC's Special Report on Global Warming 2018 file:///F:/sr15_headline_statements%20Climate% 20change,%20sustainable%20development,%20consumption,%20CSR%20report%202018.pdf, D7.

[79] See *Milieudefensie v. Royal Dutch Shell PLC and Shell Petroleum Development Company of Nigeria Ltd*, District Court of The Hague [2013] ECLI.NL.RBDHA.BY9854; *A.F. Akpan v. Royal Dutch Shell, Plc & SPDC* Court of Appeal of the Hague (18 December 2015) Arrondissementsrechtbank Den Haag [District Court of The Hague], 30 January 2013, Case No. C/09/337050/HA ZA. 09-1580.

[80] *Agouman v. Leigh Day* [2016] EWHC 1324.

also highlight the respective lax standards of Cote d'Ivoire and Bangladesh in environmental and personal injury matters.

In adjudication, 'choice of law' rules determine the applicable substantive law when the elements or effects of a cause of action concern two or more territorial jurisdictions such as cases involving multinational companies. In EU Member States, the law of the place of the cause of action is normally the applicable law.[81] Nonetheless, insistence on the place of the cause of action can encourage 'double standards' (Meeran, 2011: p. 14) when the standards are clearly lax or lacking. This can also be problematic when the law of the place contains access to justice obstacles such as short limitation periods, statutory prohibition of claims and restriction and assessment of remedies (Meeran, 2011: pp. 16–17).

As suggested above with regard to *forum non conveniens*, there can be a two-fold solution to the choice of law difficulties in sustainable development claims. First, provisions in national law can trigger the application of best international standards when a choice of law situation arises. In *Fijabi*,[82] a Nigerian court considered the UK beverages content rules and implicitly referenced international best standards in determining the scope of a tortious duty of care. The second solution is for a multilateral treaty that explicitly permits reference to international best standards.

4.6 CONCLUSION

Sustainable development is a long-term collective action issue. Just like anti-corruption, the need for a 'role model' (Persson et al., 2013: p. 465) is imperative across different strata of society in developing countries. This chapter, therefore, draws insights from the institutional theoretic model, particularly Scott's (2001, 2008) regulatory, normative and cognitive/cultural institutions framework, to investigate the roles of adjudicative institutions in promoting sustainable development in developing countries. The tripartite institutions framework makes a significant contribution in emphasising the knowledge and communicative elements of sustainable development flowing from key social actors such as adjudicative institutions to other segments of society. This may not be possible if, as in scholarly and policy discussions, the role of adjudicative institutions is regarded as regulatory only and is concentrated on explicit constitutional and statutory provisions. The tripartite framework demonstrates the broader institutional contexts of adjudication with practical consequences for the sustainable development agenda. If, in addition to their regulatory function, adjudicative institutions accept their normative and cognitive institutional roles they can, for example, consciously provide interpretative frames with wider significance than the cases before them. When adjudicative institutions make references to theoretical models, scientific evidence, scholarly debates and

---

[81]   Arts. 4 and 7 of the Rome II Regulation on the Law Applicable to Non-contractual Obligations, No. 864/2007.

[82]   Suit No. LD/13/2008 of 15 February 2017.

practices from other jurisdictions and sectors, it can signpost appropriate individual and organisational behaviours and direct public and private actors on whether changes need to be made to advance sustainable development. The nature of the relationship between scientific knowledge and policy at the global level is in fact debated in environmental governance studies (Lidskog and Sundqvist, 2015). In any event, it is critical that sustainable development knowledge is shared by key public and private social actors such adjudicative institutions and corporations.

Using environmental protection as a case study and making references to national laws and court decisions, the chapter provides original arguments that contribute significantly to the advancement of sustainable development. It demonstrates that adjudicative institutions have core roles in manifesting a commitment to sustainable development, affirmation of applicable global standards and vertically and horizontally influencing other social actors and segments of society. The regulatory role of adjudicative institutions includes constitutionalisation of sustainable development, empowerment of individuals and stakeholder groups and addressing vulnerability of actual and potential victims of unsustainable practices. In their normative role, adjudicative institutions can ensure the internalisation and transmission of sustainable development values. Their cognitive role includes reshaping local practices by promoting effective glocalisation and appropriate corporate governance and social responsibility for sustainable development.

Nonetheless, there are impediments to the effectiveness of adjudicative institutions as this chapter singularly demonstrates. First, adjudicative institutions are better equipped with explicit sustainable development provisions in national law. The technical hurdle of locus standi needs to be relaxed to allow individuals[83] and public interest groups[84] to bring claims to protect the environment, future generations and other stakeholders who may not be able to protect themselves. In addition to compensation, the range of remedies can be broadened to include remedies other than financial compensation that can directly promote sustainable development goals. A relaxed approach can tackle obstacles posed by *forum non conveniens* and choice of law doctrines to sustainable development. Moreover, the support of other regulatory institutions is essential to the effectiveness of adjudicative institutions. It does not augur well for sustainable development if, for example, governments routinely ignore decisions and pronouncements of adjudicative institutions.

What is not in doubt is the fact that adjudicative institutions can be institutional champions for sustainable development in developing countries. The adjudicative institutions can frame sustainable development standards and national priorities by reference to scientific evidence and best international and local standards. They can influence other regulatory institutions and social actors by recognising their

---

[83] See *Asghar Leghari* v. *Republic of Pakistan* [2015] WP No 25501 Lahore High Court Green Bench [2015] Orders of 4 September 2015 and 14 September 2015.

[84] See *Greenpeace Nordic Association & others* v. *Norway Ministry of Petroleum and Energy* [2016] Oslo District Court.

symbolic position and using it to proactively advance sustainable development. The role of adjudicative institutions is, therefore, not simply the enforcement of standards but extends to scrutinising, reviewing and directing appropriate actions, including preventive measures. Adjudicative institutions need to assume responsibility for sustainable development and demand accountability from other public and private institutions and social actors.

The role of the courts in the developing country context has received modest attention in the mass of studies on environmental protection and sustainable development. This chapter is unique in applying the institutional approach to identify adjudicative institutions within both formal and informal structures and processes for promoting sustainable development in the developing country context. The institutional theoretic model has also enabled the advancement of arguments that cut across the public-private law divide and demonstrate that the formal and informal roles of the adjudicative institutions are complemented by the substantive and procedural legal impediments that are not insurmountable.

Although this chapter is primarily focused on adjudicative institutions, it aims to make a contribution of much broader significance in terms of scholarship and practical effects. It provides a framework grounded on regulatory, normative and cognitive classification for understanding and advancing sustainable development by public and private actors beyond those undertaking adjudicative functions. For example, government agencies, industry associations and non-governmental organisations addressing poverty reduction, labour standards, renewable energy and other aspects of sustainable development may be more effective if they comprehend the broader significance of their roles transcending expressions of regulatory standards. The framework reflects the wider formal and informal institutional context of sustainable development and does not focus exclusively on explicit constitutional and statutory roles of formal institutions. In discussing the role of an administrative agency, for instance, the framework will help to demonstrate the agency's normative and cognitive institutional roles in addition to highlighting its formal regulatory functions in other areas of sustainable development and not just the protection of the environment. Similarly, for private actors like corporations with the capacity to research, create, track, apply and disseminate knowledge and use it to address social challenges, the regulatory, normative and cognitive framework developed here can assist in the design and implementation of sustainable development-themed CSR programmes to operate within and outside the organisation, for example, within the supply and purchasing chains. It can help corporations and policymakers to ensure that CSR programmes have a meaningful impact on the attitudes, decisions and behaviours of corporate insiders like employees and managers as well as the supply and purchasing chains and other external persons.

REFERENCES

Acemoglu, R. and Robinson, J. (2008). *The Role of Institutions in Growth and Development*. Washington DC: World Bank.

Adjami, M. (2002). African courts, international law, and comparative case law: Chimera or emerging human rights jurisprudence? *Michigan Journal of International Law*, 24(1), 103–68.

Aristova, E. (2018). Tort litigation against transnational corporations in the English courts: The challenge of jurisdiction. *Utrecht Law Review*, 14(2), 6–21.

Bähr, C. Brunner, U. and Casper, K. (2018). KlimaSeniorinnen: Lessons from the Swiss senior women's case for future climate litigation. *Journal of Human Rights and the Environment*, 9 (2), 194–221.

Baldwin, J. (2007). International human rights plaintiffs and the doctrine of forum non conveniens. *Cornell International Law Journal*, 40(3), 749–80.

Bansal, P. (2002). The corporate challenges of sustainable development. *Academy of Management Perspectives*, 16(2),122–31.

Bogdan, M. (2009). The treatment of environmental damage in Regulation Rome II. In J. Ahern, and W. Binchy, eds., *The Rome II Regulation on the Law Applicable to Non-Contractual Obligations: A New International Litigation Regime*. Leiden: Martinus Nijhoff, pp. 224–5.

Braithwaite, V. (2009). *Defiance in Taxation and Governance: Resisting and Dismissing Authority in a Democracy*. Cheltenham: Edward Elgar.

Brems, E. (2004). Reconciling universality and diversity in international human rights law. In A. Sajó, ed., *Human Rights with Modesty: The Problem of Universalism*. Leiden: Martinus Nijhoff, pp. 213–30.

Brennan Jr, William, J. (1988). Reason, passion, and the progress of the Law. *Cardozo Law Review*, 10, 3–23.

Burger, M. Gundlach, J. Kreilhuber, A. Ognibene, L. Kariukia, A. and Gachie, A. (2017). *The Status of Climate Change Litigation: A Global Review*. UNEP/Sabin Centre for Climate Change Law: Columbia University.

Cardozo, B. (1921). *The Nature of the Judicial Process*. Connecticut: Yale University Press.

Chayes, A. and Chayes, A. (1995). *The New Sovereignty: Compliance with International Regulatory Agreements*. Cambridge: Harvard University Press.

Cho, Y. (2015). Different shades of green consciousness: The interplay of sustainability labelling and environmental impact on product evaluations. *Journal of Business Ethics*, 128, 73–82.

Collins, Lord and Harris, J., eds., (2012). *Dicey, Morris & Collins on the Conflict of Laws*. 15th ed. London: Sweet & Maxwell.

Commission of the European Communities (CEC). (2011). *A Renewed EU Strategy for Corporate Social Responsibility*. EU Doc. COM (2011) 681 final, 3.

Coomans, F., ed., (2006). *Justiciability of Socio-Economic Rights: Experiences from Domestic Systems*. Antwerp: Intersentia.

Daily, C. Dalton, D. and Cannella Jr, A. (2003). Corporate governance: Decades of dialogue and data. *Academy of Management Review*, 28(3), 371–82.

Dam, L. and Scholtens, B. (2012). Does ownership type matter for corporate social responsibility? Corporate governance. *An International Review*, 20(3), 233–51.

Davis, K. and Trebilcock, M. (2008). The relationship between law and development: Optimists versus sceptics. *American Journal of Comparative Law*, 56(4), 895–946.

De Jonge, A. (2011). Transnational corporations and international law: Bringing TNCs out of the accountability vacuum. *Critical Perspectives on International Business*, 7(1), 66–89.

Desta, M. and Hirsch, M. (2012). African countries in the world trade system: International trade, domestic institutions and the role of international law. *International and Comparative Law Quarterly*, 61(1), 127–70.

Dickinson, A. (2008). *The Rome II Regulation: The Law Applicable to Non-contractual Regulations*. Oxford: Oxford University Press.

Douglass, F. (1955). 'Southern barbarism' 24th anniversary of emancipation. In P. Foner, ed., *The Life and Writings of Frederick Douglass*. New York: International Publishers.

Dworkin, R. (1978). *Taking Rights Seriously*. Cambridge: Harvard University Press.

Ebeku, K. (2007). Constitutional right to a healthy environment and human rights approaches to environmental protection in Nigeria: Gbemre v. Shell revisited. *Review of European, Comparative & International Environmental Law*, 16(3), 312–20.

Enneking, L. (2012). *Foreign Direct Liability and Beyond – Exploring the Role of Tort Law in Promoting International Corporate Social Responsibility and Accountability*. The Hague: Eleven International Publishing.

Enneking, L. (2014). The future of foreign direct liability? Exploring the international relevance of the Dutch Shell Nigeria case. *Utrecht Law Review*, 10, 44–54.

Etherton, T. (2010). Liberty, the archetype and diversity: A philosophy of judging. *Public Law*, October, 727–46.

Etienne, J. (2013). Ambiguity in relational signals in regulator-regulatee relationships. *Regulation & Governance*, 7(1),30–47.

Falletti, T. G. and Cunial, S. L. (2018). *Participation in Social Policy: Public Health in Comparative Perspective*. New York: Cambridge University Press.

Ford, C. and Hess, D. (2011). Corporate monitorship and governance regulation. In theory, in practice, and in context. *Law and Policy*, 33(4), 509–41.

Fransen, L. (2013). The embeddedness of responsible business practice: Exploring the interaction between national-institutional environments and corporate social responsibility. *Journal of Business Ethics*, 115, 213–27.

Gabaldon, P. and Gröschl, S. (2015). A few good companies: Rethinking firms' responsibilities toward common pool resources. *Journal of Business Ethics*, 132, 579–88.

Gautier, A. and Pache, A. (2015). Research on corporate philanthropy: A review and assessment. *Journal of Business Ethics*,126, 343–69.

Ghaleigh, N. (2010). 'Six honest serving men': Climate change litigation as legal mobilisation and the utility of typologies. *Climate Law* 31, 34–5.

Global Judges Symposium (2003). Johannesburg principles on the role of law and sustainable development. *Journal of Environmental Law*, 15(1), 107–10.

Goddard, A., Assad, M., Issa, S., Malagila, J. and Mkasiwa, T. (2016). The two publics and institutional theory: A study of public sector accounting in Tanzania. *Critical Perspectives on Accounting*, 40, 8–25.

Grušić, U. (2016). International environmental litigation in EU courts: A regulatory perspective. *Yearbook of European Law*, 35(1), 180–228.

Guéniat, M., Harjono, M., Missbach, A. and Viredaz, G. (2016). *Dirty Diesel. How Swiss Traders Flood Africa with Toxic Fuels. A Public Eye Investigation*. Lausanne: Public Eye.

Gunningham, N. (2009). Environment law, regulation and governance: Shifting architectures. *Journal of Environmental Law*, 21(2), 179–212.

Hamilton, L. and Clarke, T. (1996). The stakeholder approach to the firm: A practical way forward or a rhetorical flourish? *Career Development International*, 1(2), 39–41.

Higgins, C., Milne, M. and van Gramberg, B. (2015). The uptake of sustainability reporting in Australia. *Journal of Business Ethics*, 129, 445–68.

Hirschl, R. (2004). The political origins of the new constitutionalism. *Indiana Journal of Global Legal Studies*, 11(1), 71–108.

Hoffman, A. (1999). Institutional evolution and change: Environmentalism and the U.S. chemical industry. *The Academy of Management Journal*, 42(4), 351–71.

Hogg, M. and Vaughan, G. (2005). *Social Psychology*. 4th ed. Prentice-Hall.

Ijewereme, O. (2015). Anatomy of corruption in the Nigerian public sector: Theoretical perspectives and some empirical explanations. *Sage Open*, 5(2), 1–16.

Jacobs, F. (2006). The role of the European Court of Justice in the protection of the environment. *Journal of Environmental Law*, 18(2), 185–205.

Kameri-Mbote, P. (2009). Kenya. In L. Kotzé and A. Paterson, eds., *The Role of the Judiciary in Environmental Governance: Comparative Perspectives*. London: Kluwer, pp. 451–67.

Kameri-Mbote, P. and Odote, C. (2009). Courts as champions of sustainable development: Lessons from East Africa. *Sustainable Development Law and Policy*, 10, 31–8, 83–4.

Kang, N. and Moon, J. (2012). Institutional complementarity between corporate governance and corporate social responsibility: A comparative institutional analysis of three capitalisms. *Socio-economic Review*, 10(1), 85–108.

Kaufmann, D. and Kraay, A. (2015). Worldwide governance indicators. Available at http://info.worldbank.org/governance/wgi/index.aspx#home accessed 11 July 2018.

Kaufmann, D., Kraay, A. and Mastruzzi, M. (2009). Governance matters VIII: Aggregate and individual governance indicators 1996–2008. Policy Research Working Paper 4978, Washington DC: World Bank.

KMPG (2011). *The KMPG Survey of Corporate Social Responsibility Reporting*. London: KPMG.

Kotzé, L. and Paterson, A., eds., (2009). *The Role of the Judiciary in Environmental Governance: Comparative Perspectives*. London: Kluwer Law International.

Kysar, D. (2012). Global environmental constitutionalism: Getting there from here. *Transnational Environmental Law*, 1(1), 83–94.

Leestma, D. (2017). Groups sue Norway over failure to protect environment for future generations. Available at www.ecowatch.com/norway-climate-lawsuit-2510288916.html accessed 10 July 2018.

Leventhal, H. (1974). Environmental decision-making and the role of the courts. *University of Pennsylvania Law Review*, 122,509–55.

Li, J., Moy, J. Lam, K. and Chu, W. (2008). Institutional pillars and corruption at the societal level. *Journal of Business Ethics*, 83(2), 327–39.

Lidskog, R. and Sundqvist, G. (2015). When does science matter? International relations meets science and technology studies. *Global Environmental Politics*, 15(1), 1–20.

Liebenberg, S. (2001). The protection of economic social and cultural rights in domestic legal systems. In A. Eide, C. Krause and A. Rosas, eds., *Economic Social and Cultural Rights*. 2nd ed. London: Kluwer, pp. 55–84.

Lozano, J., Albareda, L. and Ysa, T. (2008). *Governments and Corporate Social Responsibility: Public Policies Beyond Regulation and Voluntary Compliance*. London: Palgrave Macmillan.

May, J. R. (2009). Not at all: Environmental sustainability in the Supreme Court. *Sustainable Development Law and Policy*, 10, 20–29, 81–2.

McAuslan, P. (1991). The role of courts and other judicial type bodies in environmental management. *Journal of Environmental Law*, 3(2), 195–208.

Meeran, R. (2011). Tort litigation against multinational corporation for violation of human rights: An overview of the position outside the United States. *City University of Hong Kong Law Review*, 3(1) 1–41.

Merrills, J. (1996). Environmental protection and human rights: Conceptual aspects. In A. Boyle and M. Anderson, eds., *Human rights approaches to environmental protection*. Oxford: Oxford University Press, pp. 25–42.

Misangyi, V., Weaver, G. and Elms, H. (2008). Ending corruption: The interplay among institutional logics, resources, and institutional entrepreneurs. *Academy of Management Review*, 33(3), 750–70.

Mutua, M. (2004). The complexity of universalism in human rights. In A. Sajó, ed., *Human Rights with Modesty: The Problem of Universalism*. Leiden: Martinus Njihoff. 51–64.

North, D. (1990). *Institutions, Institutional Change, and Economic Performance*. New York: Cambridge University Press.

O'Leary, R. (1989). The Impact of Federal Court Decisions on the Policies and Administration of the U.S. Environmental Protection Agency. *Administrative Law Review*, 41(4), 549–74.

Omoteso, K. and Yusuf, H. (2017). Accountability of transnational corporations in the developing world: The case for an enforceable international mechanism. *Critical Perspectives on International Business*, 13(1), 54–71.

Osemeke, L. and Adegbite, E. (2016). Regulatory multiplicity and conflict: Towards a combined code on corporate governance in Nigeria. *Journal of Business Ethics*, 133, 431–51.

Osiatynski, W. (2004). On the universality of the universal declaration of human rights. In A. Sajó, ed., *Human Rights with Modesty: The Problem of Universalism*. Leiden: Martinus Njihoff. pp. 33–50.

Palmer, E. (2007). *Judicial Review, Socio-Economic Rights and the Human Rights Act*. Oxford: Hart Publishing.

Pedersen, O. W. (2019). A study of administrative environmental decision-making before the courts. *Journal of Environmental Law*, 23 January 2019. https://doi.org/10.1093/jel/eqy026.

Persson, A., Rothstein, B., and Teorell, J. (2013). Why anticorruption reforms fail: Systemic corruption as a collective action problem. *Governance*, 26(3), 449–71.

Pillay, S. and Kluvers, R. (2014). An institutional theory perspective on corruption: The case of a developing democracy. *Financial Accountability & Management*, 30(1), 95–119.

Powell, W. and DiMaggio, P. (1991). *The New Institutionalism in Organizational Analysis*. Chicago: University of Chicago Press.

Preston, B. J. (2005). The role of the judiciary in promoting sustainable development: The experience of Asia and the Pacific. *Asia Pacific Journal of Environmental Law*, 9(2/3), 109–211.

Rajamani, L. (2003). From Stockholm to Johannesburg: The anatomy of dissonance in the international environmental dialogue. *Review of European Community and International Environmental Law*, 12(1),23–32.

Reid, Lord. (1972). The Judge as lawmaker. *The Journal of the Society of Public Teachers of Law*, 12(1), 22–9.

Robertson, D. (2009). Corporate social responsibility and different stages of economic development: Singapore, Turkey, and Ethiopia. *Journal of Business Ethics*, 88(4), 617–33.

Rothstein, B. (2011), Can markets be expected to prevent themselves from self-destruction? *Regulation and Governance*, 5, 387–404.

Ryngaert, C. (2013). Tort litigation in respect of overseas violations of environmental law committed by corporations: Lessons from the Akpan v Shell litigation in the Netherlands. *McGill International Journal of Sustainable Development Law and Policy*, 8(2), 245–60.

Sachs, J. (2012). From millennium development goals to sustainable development goals. *Lancet*, 379, 2206–11.

Sadurski, W. (2004). Universalism, localism and paternalism in human rights discourse. In A. Sajó, ed., *Human Rights with Modesty: The Problem of Universalism*. Leiden: Martinus Njihoff. pp.141–60.

Sax, J. (1971). *Defending the environment: A strategy for citizen action*. New York: Knopft.

Schauer, F. (2009). *Thinking Like a Lawyer: A New Introduction to Legal Reasoning*. Cambridge: Harvard University Press.

Schwartz, R. (1990). Human rights in an evolving culture. In A. An-Na'im, and F. Deng, eds., *Human Rights in Africa: Cross-Cultural Perspectives*. Washington, DC: Brookings Institution, pp. 368–82.

Scott, W. (2001). *Institutions and Organizations*. Thousand Oaks: Sage Publications, Inc.

Scott, W. (2008). Approaching adulthood: The maturing of institutional theory. *Theory and Society*, 37(5), 427–42.

Solomon, J. (2007). *Corporate Governance and Accountability*. Hoboken: John Wiley & Sons.

Stacy, H. International Human Rights in a Fragmenting World. In A. Sajó, ed., (2004). *Human Rights with Modesty: The Problem of Universalism*. Leiden: Martinus Njihoff.

Taplin, I. (2014). Who is to blame? A re-examination of fast fashion after the 2013 factory disaster in Bangladesh. *Critical Perspectives on International Business*, 10(1/2), 72–83.

Taylor, P. (1998). From environmental to ecological human right: A new dynamic in international law? *Georgetown Environmental Law Review*, 10, 309–11.

Uberti, L. (2016). Can institutional reforms reduce corruption? Economic theory and patron–client politics in developing countries. *Development and Change*, 47(2), 317–45.

United Nations (1973). UN Conference on the Human Environment, Stockholm, Sweden, 5–16 June 1972, Report of the UN Conference on the Human Environment, 2–7, UN Doc. A/Conf.48/14/Rev.1.

United Nations (1987). Report of World Commission on Environment and Development: Our common future (Brundtland Report). Available at www.un-documents.net/our-com mon-future.pdf (accessed 10 July 2018).

United Nations (1992). Report of the United Nations Conference on Environment and Development (Rio De Janeiro, 3–14 June 1992). A/CONF.151/26.

United Nations (2002). Report of the World Summit on Sustainable Development. UN Doc A/Conf 199/20.

United Nations Environment Programme (UNEP). (2016). Diesel fuel sulphur levels: Global status June 2016. Available at www.unep.org/Transport/New/PCFV/pdf/Maps_Matrices/world/sulphur/MapWorldSulphur_June2016.pdf accessed 1 July 2018.

Viljoen, F. (2007). *International Human Rights Law in Africa*. Oxford: Oxford University Press, 33, pp. 540–42.

Wald, P. (1992). The role of the judiciary in environmental protection. *Boston College Environmental Affairs Law Review*, 19(3), 519–46.

Ward, H. (2003). Towards a new convention on corporate accountability? Some lessons from the Thor Chemicals and Cape PLC Cases. *Yearbook of International Environmental Law*, 12, 136–47.

Warren, L. (2003). Sustainable development and governance. *Environmental Law Review*, 5 (2), 77–85.

Waterman Jr, R. (1994). *The Frontiers of Excellence: Learning from Companies that Put People First.* London, Brealey.

Weinrib, E. (2002). Corrective justice in a Nutshell. *The University of Toronto Law Journal*, 52 (4), 349–56.

World Bank (2003). *Global Corporate Governance Forum.* Washington, DC: World Bank.

World Bank (2004). 'Regulation of associated gas flaring and venting: A global overview and lessons from international experience'. Report number 3. Washington, DC: World Bank.

Yoo, J. (1999). Globalism and the constitution: Treaties, non-self-execution, and the original understanding. *Columbia Law Review*, 1955–2090.

Zucker, L. (1977). The role of institutionalization in cultural persistence. *American Journal of Sociology*, 42, 726–43.

5

The Informal Economy: CSR and Sustainable Development

Ogechi Adeola, Oserere Eigbe and Omotayo Muritala

5.1 INTRODUCTION

The relevance of corporate social responsibility (CSR) to the attainment of sustainability in the different sectors of an economy cannot be underestimated (Behringer and Szegedi, 2016). The concepts of CSR and sustainable development have been enshrined in the corporate practice of many organisations in emerging and developed countries. As there are variations in CSR practice between developed countries and emerging economies (Muller and Kolk, 2009), similarly there are distinctions in the CSR practices of the informal and formal sectors within emerging economies. The informal economy which relates to economic activities that are not based on government regulation or under government taxation has become a major employer of labour in the world (Hudson et al., 2012). The informal economy comprises small and medium enterprises (SMEs) that account for 90 per cent of all the enterprises and at least 50 per cent of employment (Fjose et al., 2010). Several millions of people work and trade in the informal sector, with activities in emerging economies significantly bigger than the formal sector in terms of employment and output.

There are several perspectives on the informal economy: one school of thought associates it with low income, unfair competition, low productivity, human rights abuses and environmental degradation (Wilson, 2011). Another school of thought gives it a positive connotation, linking it with entrepreneurship, innovation, creativity and resilience. There is now increasing awareness that the informal economy can be better positioned to be more innovative and productive than the formal economy.

In this twenty-first century where every country needs to achieve the United Nations' Sustainable Development Goals (SDGs), sustainable development must be rooted in a sound understanding of the informal economy, especially if actions taken in the direction of the SDGs are to be inclusive and beneficial to the poor. It is in this context that this chapter examines corporate social responsibility and sustainable development in the informal economy with a focus on emerging economies. It attempts to understand CSR in the context of small and medium enterprises (SMEs).

The chapter is organised as follows: the next section provides a background on CSR and sustainable development. In the third section, the informal economy is examined, while the fourth section provides some insights into the engagement of informal businesses in CSR and sustainable development. The motivations for small and medium businesses' involvement in CSR and sustainable development are discussed in the fifth section. The sixth section concludes the chapter.

5.2 CSR AND SUSTAINABLE DEVELOPMENT

There have been several definitions of CSR by different scholars, which vary in content, context, process and value (Inyang, 2013); and as described by Industry Canada (2009), it is an evolving concept that to date does not have a generally accepted definition. Likewise, Meehan, Meehan and Richards (2006) affirmed that defining CSR has been debatable since its inception. Carroll (1979) defined CSR as encompassing the economic, legal, ethical and discretionary expectations the society has of organisations at a certain period. The World Business Council for Sustainable Development (WBCSD) (2009) defined CSR as 'the commitment of business to contribute to sustainable economic development, working with employees, their families, the local community and society at large to improve their quality of life'.

CSR, according to the European Union Commission (2011), implies the duty of firms to take responsibility for their impacts on the society; this involves certain activities by firms beyond their legitimate obligations towards the society and environment in which they operate. Furthermore, Liu and Fong (2010) asserted that CSR entails diverse voluntary initiatives, apart from legal and contractual requirements, which employees, their families and local communities would benefit from if effectively embarked on, thereby improving the overall welfare of the community, and contributing to economic development. Likewise, according to Inyang, Awa and Enuoh (2011), CSR is defined as an obligation of business managers/owners to pursue desirable policies that would add value to the society where the business is located. CSR can, therefore, be best understood from the perspective of the changing relationship between businesses and the society; hence, while companies aim at making a profit, they must also take cognisance of how their actions can affect their communities and the world at large.

The triple bottom line propounded by Elkington (1997) is a concept that can be used to describe and explain sustainability (Coşkun Arslan and Kisacik, 2017). The triple bottom line consists of three main dimensions of sustainability which are closely linked – the economic, environmental and societal dimensions. According to Iyigun (2015), economic sustainability refers to how a firm is able to manage its capital, stock and funds; environmental sustainability describes how firms are to operate without causing harm within the ecosystem; while societal sustainability emphasises that firms manage their business operations to meet the needs of stakeholders, which should also be in line with the firm's value system. Stakeholders refer to those who are affiliated with the firm, who benefit or suffer damage from the firm, and whose rights are either considered or ignored (Coşkun Arslan and Kisacik, 2017).

Primarily, the triple bottom line focuses on 3Ps, which are People (societal sustainability), Planet (environmental sustainability) and Profit (economic sustainability) as depicted in the figure below. Coşkun Arslan and Kisacik (2017) concluded in their study that adoption of the triple bottom line approach by firms will not only manage the economic, environmental and social impacts of their activities but will also provide an avenue to disseminate the outcomes of these impacts with the stakeholders to maintain corporate sustainability performance.

Sustainability has thus become a major focus of many CSR practices (Bhagwat, 2011). The United Nations Brundtland Commission in 1987 defined sustainability as the 'development that meets the needs of the present without compromising the ability of future generations to meet their own needs' (World Commission, 1987: p. 44). Bhagwat (2011) defined sustainability as a voluntary organisation's activities that include social and environmental concerns in business operations and interactions with stakeholders. Corporate sustainability enhances the relationship between the

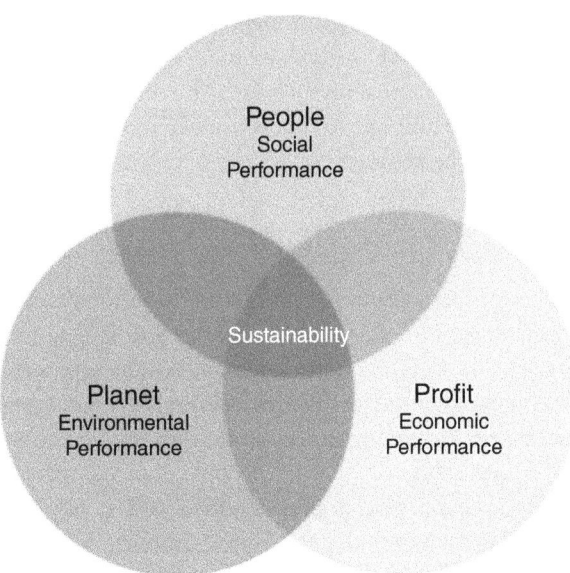

FIGURE 5.1 The triple bottom line formulation of sustainability (Coşkun Arslan and Kisacik, 2017)

strategies of firms and their stakeholders and also minimises risky behaviours (Altınay, 2016).

Increasingly, it appears pressure is being mounted on businesses to pay attention to societal issues (Johnson and Greening, 1999; Aguilera, Rupp, Williams and Ganapathi, 2007); and as a result, the businesses are faced with rising expectations from various stakeholders (Arvidsson, 2010; Basu and Palazzo, 2008). In essence, they are being persuaded to take into cognisance their impact on society more than ever before (Lee, 2011). In contrast, a study carried out on CSR among Latin American SMEs found that pressure from stakeholders such as the civil society and public sector incentives did not seem to motivate CSR practices (Vives, 2006).

Although the two concepts, corporate social responsibility and sustainable development, have been used interchangeably, some scholars consider them as two distinct concepts (Strand, Freeman and Hockerts, 2015) due to the fact that the term 'sustainable development' has many different interpretations (Bhagwat, 2011). Sustainable development can be regarded as corporate sustainability at the corporate level, which is based on three pillars (economic, ecological and social) wherein the social dimension is called corporate social responsibility (Bhagwat, 2011). Accordingly, CSR can be viewed as an organisation's contribution to sustainable development (Bansal, 2005).

Das and Rangarajan (2017) in their review of literature, ascertained that the three terms – corporate citizenship, CSR and corporate sustainability – denote the same meaning and are being used interchangeably in the literature. Das and Rangarajan (2017) further conceptualised corporate sustainability as a term that describes the need for organisations to get involved in and focus on social and environmental development in order to improve the sustainability of their business operations in the long run. By implication, organisations are to be socially and environmentally responsible, and should not only focus on how to make profits since CSR is germane to the very sustenance of the business.

5.3 THE INFORMAL ECONOMY

The informal economy emanates from the informal sector that comprises of activities that are unprotected, unregulated, unrecorded and largely unrecognised by public authorities. The informal economy is a broadly used term that covers various sectors. According to Becker 2004: p. 8, 'The informal sector is increasingly being referred to as the informal economy to get away from the idea that informality is confined to a specific sector of economic activity but rather cuts across many sectors.' The informal economy hence refers to all economic activities carried out by workers and economic units that are not under any formal arrangements either in law or in practice. It is often referred to as the shadow economy and is characterised by the small scale of operations; labour-intensive methods of production and adapted technology; low entry requirements; and skill acquisition through informal education (International Labour Organisation (ILO), 1972). Hence, informal economic activities have been defined as legally unregulated processes of generating income, predominantly carried out in very small enterprises (Cheng and Gereffi, 1994).

Generally, informal enterprises or businesses are referred to as informal because they are often unregistered, they do not pay tax, there are generally no regulations guiding their employment conditions, and they also do not comply with regulations regarding their licence of operations. In a similar vein, Garcia-Bolivar (2006) defined informal businesses as being characterised by little differentiation of ownership of means of production, low level of technology, very little capital base, as well as the simple division of labour. Additionally, informal businesses do not only comprise businesses that hire labour but also include individuals who work as self-employed (Becker, 2004). Examples of these self-employed individuals include taxi drivers, street vendors, hair stylists, shoe cobblers, amongst others. They hardly engage in transactions, sign contracts or incur liabilities since they have insufficient capital resources (Becker, 2004).

Across developing and emerging economies, the informal sector is expanding (Hudson, Williams, Orviska and Nadin, 2012). This can be attributed to the fact that when formal enterprises are shut down or downsized, the laid-off workers often end up in the informal economy (Chen, 2012). Since informal businesses are not registered, determining their size and contribution to the economy might be complicated. However, it has over time been established in literature, and statistical reports that small businesses make a huge contribution to economic development in both developed and developing or emerging economies. This contribution is visible in terms of job creation as well as development impacts such as poverty alleviation, particularly in developing countries (Inyang, 2013; Deijl, de Kok and Essen, 2013). In developing and emerging economies, SMEs account for 90 per cent of enterprises and at least 50 per cent of employment (Luetkenhorst, 2003; Fjose, Grünfeld and Green, 2010). According to a 2017 report on the SME sector in India, SMEs account for about 95 per cent of total industry units in the country and also employ 40 per cent of India's workforce (Dolly, 2017). Also, small businesses provide employment for 80 per cent of the urban population in China as well as contribute 60 per cent to the country's GDP (Sham and Pang, 2014). In sub-Saharan Africa, SMEs account for over 95 per cent of all businesses (Fjose, Grünfeld and Green, 2010).

Studies have revealed that SMEs drive economic growth, promote private sector development, provide the platform for equitable income distribution and create employment opportunities (Jamali, Lund-Thomsen and Jeppesen, 2017). More so, some studies carried out in Africa provided claims for the contribution of SMEs to economic development through their social responsibility activities (Dzansi, 2011; Oguntade and Mafimisebi, 2011; Viviers and Venter, 2007). In the year 2000, it was reported that the informal sector accounted for 20–50 per cent of the non-agricultural GDP in sub-Saharan Africa, excluding South Africa. In developing countries, informal businesses accounted for 41 per cent of gross national income (GNI) (Garcia-Bolivar, 2006). In Nigeria, it accounted for 76 per cent of GDP from 1989 to 1990 (Johnson, Kaufmann, Shleifer, Goldman and Weitzman, 1997).

In Nigeria, the National Bureau of Statistics (NBS) reports that small businesses account for 97 per cent of all businesses and employ 50 per cent of the total labour force (Nwankwo, Ewuim and Asoya, 2012). Furthermore, Kongolo (2010) reported that small businesses account for about 91 per cent of business entities and provide about 60 per cent of employment in South Africa. The activities and prevalence of small businesses in developing economies can appear similar to what exists in the developed world. As of 2016, small businesses accounted for more than 99 per cent of all businesses in the United States and employed 48 per cent of US employees (US Small Business Administration Office of Advocacy, 2016). Globally, SMEs represent about 90 per cent of businesses, 50–60 per cent of global employment and more than half of gross domestic product (Luetkenhorst, 2004; Inyang, 2013).

In this chapter, we categorised small and medium-sized enterprises (SMEs) under informal economy since SMEs cover series of enterprises including established traditional family business and survivalist self-employed people probably lacking a formalised administrative structure (Inyang, 2013). Although SMEs are mainly focused on meeting daily needs; to a great extent, they cultivate close relationships with communities where they operate (Spence and Lozano, 2000; Enderle, 2004). Lepoutre and Heene (2006) further characterised SMEs in terms of the responsibilities of a small business, which include: treating customers, business partners and competitors with fairness and honesty; caring about the general well-being of employees and customers; motivating its employees via training and development opportunities; regarding natural resources and the environment; and demonstrating patriotism in the local community. It is against this backdrop that the next section examines the engagement of informal businesses in the context of small and medium business in CSR and sustainable development.

5.4 ENGAGEMENT OF INFORMAL BUSINESSES IN CSR AND SUSTAINABLE DEVELOPMENT

Many previous studies on CSR practices have focused on large firms, thereby underestimating CSR engagement of small firms (Turyakira, 2017). Morsing and Perrini (2009) highlighted the need to understand the engagement of SMEs in CSR and how they differ from large firms. It is important to understand CSR in the context of small and medium businesses since their attributes, particularly those described earlier, have clearly set them apart from large businesses. It is typical to find micro businesses, in respective economic locations, developed and non-developed, with a low degree or non-existence of formalisation, whose CSR strategy never evolves into a specific management approach (Russo and Tencati, 2009). Interestingly, the term CSR is rarely used by SMEs even though their activities suggest the practice, albeit in an informal way (Russo and Tencati, 2009).

The institutional context of SMEs' CSR operation can be influenced by compulsion, norms and values within the environment, which approach is categorised as implicit, as against voluntary disposition to social responsibility (Matten and Moon, 2008). In general, there is little regulatory oversight for compliance with CSR among SMEs in developing countries (Tewari and Pillai, 2005), and they are equally difficult to regulate (Blackman, 2006). Formal laws, regulations and enforcement agencies do not really exercise control over SME-CSR engagement in developing countries (Jamali et al., 2017). Formalising CSR practice in SMEs would be limiting the CSR operation in that sector for failure in developing countries where, in most cases, micro business owners are out of reach of information and knowledge required to accomplish particular areas of CSR practice (Allet, 2017).

Sustainability practices among SMEs in developing societies, particularly in terms of environmental practices are often being neglected (Hoogendoorn, Guerra and van der Zwan, 2014). Environmental practices, according to Uhlaner, Berent-Braun, Jeurissen and de Wit (2012), refer to all efforts or actions taken by firms in order to minimise the impact of their activities on the environment. Such actions could include waste reduction, recycling, saving on resources and developing organically produced products (Hoogendoorn et al., 2014). Most SMEs are reluctant to implement environmentally friendly practices (Johnson, 2015), and their activities contribute significantly to global pollution (Hillary, 2000; Revell, Stokes and Chen, 2010)

5.5 MOTIVATIONS FOR SMALL AND MEDIUM BUSINESSES' INVOLVEMENT IN CSR AND SUSTAINABLE DEVELOPMENT

There are many motivating factors for small and medium businesses and their owner-managers to act responsibly within the community they operate. The need to grow and expand the business operation by building trust, reputation and legitimacy, i.e. social capital, makes it beneficial for small businesses to engage in CSR (Jamali et al., 2017; 2011; Russo and Tencati, 2009). SMEs can enter new markets and introduce innovative services and products and be open to new business opportunities in the wake of CSR demands (Morsing and Perrini, 2009). An earlier study by Hockerts, Morsing, Eder-Hansen, Krull, Midttun, Halme, Sweet, Davidsson and Nurmi (2008), examined how Nordic SMEs created innovations related to their CSR engagement. The study revealed that the SMEs understudied regarded CSR as a business opportunity to set a new stage for competitiveness. Worthington, Ram and Jones (2006) explored CSR in the UK Asian small business community, using the social capital theory. Their findings revealed that these small businesses possess a high level of CSR engagement, thereby indicating that social responsibility is seen as an important business concern, which in turn creates value for the organisation.

The interpersonal relationship that exists between SME owners and employees, the business partners and the local community clearly reveals that they possess a naturally responsible approach to business thereby making them no less responsible than large firms in CSR practices (Inyang, 2013). Also, the fact that micro companies maintain close contact, have extensive knowledge of customers' needs and can respond with great flexibility give them the opportunity to influence CSR practice (Sanchez and Benito-Hernandez, 2015). For big businesses, the media has been a major influencer for CSR practice – the need to project the organisation's brand. Small businesses operating in local communities, on the other hand, are less visible and more likely to be driven by the needs in the communities that they maintain social ties and business relationship with (Besser, 2012). In a study on micro firms and their CSR operations in the Italian economy by Russo and Tencati (2009), virtues and moral ethics on the part of sole owners were found to have influenced CSR operations of micro firms. The owners considered the need to act responsibly on the basis of moral ethics in matters relating to social service.

In addition, Pastrana and Sriramesh (2014) sought to understand the perceptions and practices of CSR among SMEs in Colombia, a developing economy. Findings from the study revealed that the SMEs' CSR practices were influenced by cultural and contextual aspects of the society. According to Worthington et al. (2006) and Jamali, Zanhour and Keshishian (2009), CSR of SMEs in developing economies is characterised by personal and religious motivations, which reflects in a natural philanthropic CSR orientation.

The interesting findings by Vives (2005) summarise the motivations for CSR practice among SMEs. The study found CSR practices among the Latin American SMEs, in most cases, are limited to factors such as ethical and religious beliefs, concern for employees, the need to maximise profits and the desire to possess inter-personal relations with customers, business partners and the community at large.

Legislations and institutional context have been the sole drivers for small and medium businesses that engage in environmental practices. The study by Hoogendoorn et al. (2014) finds strict environmental legislation as a driver for SMEs to be environmentally responsible both in production (greening) processes, and service offerings. In addition, the size of a firm also contributes to and deter-mines the likelihood of the firm to engage in greening processes. Furthermore, AboelImaged (2018) establishes that institutional context influences the disposition of firms to environmental issues.

5.6 CONCLUSION

This chapter examined corporate social responsibility and sustainable development in the informal economy. The review of previous studies laid a foundation for the classification of informal businesses to consist of micro, small and medium-sized enterprises that operate outside formal or regulatory structure and are dominant mostly in developing economies. However, while the informal sector is dominated by micro, small and medium-sized enterprises, it is acknowledged that not all SMEs are covered in the informal sector. Notably, a majority of successful SMEs operate within the formal sector.

The contribution of SMEs to economic productivity and employment is enormous and cannot be underestimated. Small businesses are particularly focused on meeting the needs of local communities, and have other responsibilities, and maintain relationships with the local people. The formation and characterisation of small business in developing countries show that there is little or no formalised structure that governs their operations. The chapter identified motivating factors that promote SMEs' CSR. Businesses respond to communities' needs in order to build social capital – trust, reputation and legitimacy, and promote their businesses for economic returns. By building social relationships with the community, a small business can establish and expand market operation via other activities including innovation, finding new opportunities and setting the stage to compete effectively. Some entrepreneurs view this as the duty of firms to give back and assist communities to meet some social and environmental needs, which is based on personal virtues and moral ethics. Culture also plays a role as it influences the natural philanthropic disposition of firms. It is the expectation in some societies, particularly Africa, that indigenous organisations should have a positive influence on their communities. However, small and medium businesses do not show concerns for environmental issues in general except where the practice is mandated through legislation.

With adequate information and motivation, micro, small and medium-sized enterprises can be properly positioned to become committed to the economic and social needs as well as environmental protection of their communities. According to Inyang (2013), the efforts to properly position SMEs should include the provision of adequate resources to ensure the availability comprehensive information about CSR, including other CSR practices not common with SMEs; provision of training programmes to educate on CSR themes such as business ethics, citizenship and responsible practices; and government providing a level playing field through suitable legal framework and incentives. Such efforts should also incorporate sustainability practices for small and medium firms.

With the above efforts in place, SMEs will be encouraged and motivated to place social responsibility and sustainable development at the core of daily business decisions. Engagement in CSR and sustainable development by SMEs will, therefore, become more of 'just the way we do things' and less of 'an add-on', as professed by Jenkins (2009).

REFERENCES

Aboelmaged, M. (2018). The drivers of sustainable manufacturing practices in Egyptian SMEs and their impact on competitive capabilities: A PLS-SEM model. *Journal of Cleaner Production*, 175, 207–21.

Aguilera, R. V., Rupp, D. E., Williams, C. A. and Ganapathi, J. (2007). Putting the S back in corporate social responsibility: A multilevel theory of social change in organizations. *Academy of Management Review*, 32(3), 836-63.

Ali, W., Frynas, J. G. and Mahmood, Z. (2017). Determinants of corporate social responsibility (CSR) disclosure in developed and developing countries: A literature review. *Corporate Social Responsibility and Environmental Management*, 24(4), 273–94.

Altınay, T. A. (2016). Integrated sustainability reporting and accounting. *Süleyman Demirel University Institute of Social Sciences Journal*, 25,47–64.

Arvidsson, S. (2010). Communication of corporate social responsibility: A study of the views of management teams in large companies. *Journal of Business Ethics*, 96(3), 339–54.

Bansal, P. (2005). Evolving sustainably: A longitudinal study of corporate sustainable development. *Strategic Management Journal*, 26(3), 197–218.

Basu, K. and Palazzo, G. (2008). Corporate social responsibility: A process model of sensemaking. *Academy of Management Review*, 33(1), 122–36.

Becker, K. F. (2004). The informal economy in developing countries: a fact finding study. Available at www.rrojasdatabank.info/sida.pdf accessed 21 July 2019.

Behringer, K. and Szegedi, K. (2016). The role of CSR in achieving sustainable development: Theoretical approach, *European Scientific Journal*, 12(2), 10–25.

Besser, T. L. (2012). The consequences of social responsibility for small owners in small towns. *Business Ethics: A European Review*,21(2).

Bhagwat, P. (2011, March). Corporate social responsibility and sustainable development. In *Proceedings of the Articles and Case Studies: Inclusive & Sustainable Growth Conference* 1(1).

Carroll, A. B. (1979). A three dimensional concept model of corporate social performance. *Academy of Management Review*, 4, 487–505.

Castka, P., Balzarova, M. A., Bamber, C. J. and Sharp, J. M. (2004). How can SMEs effectively implement the CSR agenda? A UK case study perspective. *Corporate Social Responsibility and Environmental Management*, 11(3), 140–9.

Chen, M. A. (2012). The informal economy: Definitions, theories and policies. WIEGO Working Paper. (Vol. 1, No. 26, 90141–4).

Cheng, L. L. and Gereffi, G. (1994). The informal economy in East Asian development. *International Journal of Urban and Regional Research*, 18(2), 194–219.

Clemens, B. (2006). Economic incentives and small firms: Does it pay to be green? *Journal of Business Research*, 59(4), 492–500.

Coşkun Arslan, M. and Kisacik, H. (2017). The Corporate Sustainability Solution: Triple Bottom Line. *Journal of Accounting & Finance*. July special issue, 18–34.

Das, M. and Rangarajan, K. (2017). Corporate Sustainability as a Business Strategy in SMEs - A Literature Review in the Emerging Market Context. Proceedings of International Conference on Strategies in Volatile and Uncertain Environment for Emerging Markets 14–15 July, 2017, Indian Institute of Technology Delhi, New Delhi,505–11.

Deijl, C., de Kok, J. and Essen, V. V. (2013). Is small still beautiful? Literature review of recent empirical evidence on the contribution of SMEs to employment creation. Deutsche Gesellschaft für Internationale Zusammenarbeit (GIZ) GmbH.

Dolly (2017). SME sector in India – Statistics, Trends, Reports, 28 September 2017, available at https://evoma.com/business-centre/sme-sector-in-india-statistics-trends-reports/ accessed 21 July 2019.

Dzansi, D. Y. (2011). Social responsibility of small businesses in a typical rural African setting: Some insights from a South African study. *African Journal of Business Management*, 5(14), 5710.

El Baz, J., Laguir, I., Marais, M. and Stagliò, R. (2014). Influence of national institutions on the corporate social responsibility practices of small- and medium-sized enterprises in the food-processing industry: Differences between France and Morocco. *Journal of Business Ethics*, 134(1), 117–33.

Elkington, J. (1997), *Cannibals with Forks: The Triple Bottom Line of 21th Century Business*. Oxford: Capstone Publishing.

Enderle, G. (2004). Global competition and corporate responsibilities of small and medium-sized enterprises. *Business Ethics: A European Review*, 13(1), 50–63.

European Commission (2011). *Communication from the Commission to the European Parliament, the Council, the European Economic and Social Committee and the Committee of the Regions: A renewed EU strategy 2011–14 for Corporate Social Responsibility*. Available at www.europarl.europa.eu/meetdocs/2009_2014/documents/com/com_com(2011)0681_/com_com(2011)0681_en.pdf accessed 21 July 2019.

Fjose, S., Grunfeld, L. A. and Green, C. (2010). SMEs and growth in Sub-Sahara Africa: Identifying SME role and obstacles to SME growth. MENON-Publication, 14, 1–28 available at www.norfund.no/getfile.php/133983–1484571386/Bilder/Publications/SME%20and%20growth%20MENON%20.pdf accessed 16 July 2017.

Frynas, J. G. (2005). The false developmental promise of corporate social responsibility: Evidence from multinational oil companies. *International Affairs*, 81(3), 581–98.

Garcia-Bolivar, O. E. (2006). Informal economy: Is it a problem, a solution or both? The perspective of the informal business. *bepress Legal Series*, 1065.

Gelbmann, U. (2010). Establishing strategic CSR in SMEs: An Austrian CSR quality seal to substantiate the strategic CSR performance. *Sustainable Development*, 18(2), 90–8.

Grayson, D. and Hodges, A. (2004). *Corporate Social Opportunity! Seven Steps to Make CSR Work for Your Business*. Sheffield: Greenleaf.

Hillary R. 2000. *Small and Medium-Sized Enterprises and the Environment*. Sheffield: Greenleaf Publishing.

Hockerts, K., Morsing, M., Eder-Hansen, J., Krull, P., Midttun, A., Halme, M. ... and Nurmi, P. (2008). *CSR-Driven Innovation: Towards the Social Purpose Business*. Frederiksberg: Center for Corporate Social Responsibility, CBS.

Hoogendoorn, B., Guerra, D. and van der Zwan, P. (2015). What drives environmental practices of SMEs? *Small Business Economics*, 44(4), 759–81.

Hudson, J., Williams, C., Orviska, M. and Nadin, S. (2012). Evaluating the impact of the informal economy on businesses in South East Europe: Some lessons from the 2009 World Bank Enterprise Survey. *South East European Journal of Economics and Business*, 7(1), 99–110.

ILO (1972). Employment, income and equality: A strategy for increasing productivity in Kenya. Geneva: International Labour Organization.

Industry Canaa. (2009). Corporate social responsibility guide project leader. Available at www.ioc.gc.ca/eic/site/csr-rse.ns/eng/rs00128.html accessed 22 July 2019.

Inyang, B. J. (2013). Defining the role engagement of small and medium-sized enterprises (SMEs) in corporate social responsibility (CSR). *International Business Research*, 6(5).

Inyang, B. J., Awa, H. O. and Enuoh, R. O. (2011). CSR-HRM nexus: Defining the role engagement of the human resources professionals. *International Journal of Business and Social Science*, 2(5), 118–26.

İyigün, N. Ö. (2015). What could entrepreneurship do for sustainable development? A corporate social responsibility-based approach. *Procedia-Social and Behavioural Sciences*, 195, 1226–31.

Jamali, D., Lund-Thomsen, P. and Jeppesen, S. (2017). SMEs and CSR in developing countries. *Business & Society*, 56(1), 11–22.

Jamali, D. and Neville, B. (2011). Convergence versus divergence of CSR in developing countries: An embedded multi-layered institutional lens. *Journal of Business Ethics*, 102(4), 599–621.

Jamali, D., Zanhour, M. and Keshishian, T. (2009). Peculiar strengths and relational attributes of SMEs in the context of CSR. *Journal of Business Ethics*, 87(3), 355–77.

Jenkins, H. (2009). A 'business opportunity' model of corporate social responsibility for small- and medium-sized enterprises. *Business Ethics: A European Review*, 18(1), 21–36.

Johnson, R. A. and Greening, D. W. (1999). The effects of corporate governance and institutional ownership types on corporate social performance. *Academy of Management Journal*, 42(5), 564–76.

Johnson, M. P. (2015). Sustainability management and small and medium-sized enterprises: Managers' awareness and implementation of innovative tools. *Corporate Social Responsibility and Environmental Management*, 22(5), 271–85.

Johnson, S., Kaufmann, D., Shleifer, A., Goldman, M. I. and Weitzman, M. L. (1997). The unofficial economy in transition. *Brookings Papers on Economic Activity*, 1997(2), 159–239.

Kongolo, M. (2010). Job creation versus job shedding and the role of SMEs in economic development. *African Journal of Business Management*, 4(11), 2288–95.

Lee, M. D. P. (2011). Configuration of external influences: The combined effects of institutions and stakeholders on corporate social responsibility strategies. *Journal of Business Ethics*, 102(2), 281–98.

Lepoutre, J. and Heene, A. (2006). Investigating the impact of firm size on small business social responsibility: A critical review. *Journal of Business Ethics*, 67(3), 257–73.

Liu, H. and Fong, M. (2010). The corporate social responsibility orientation of Chinese small and medium enterprises. *Journal of Business Systems, Governance & Ethics*, 5(3).

Luetkenhort, W. (2003). Corporate social responsibility and the development agenda: Should SMEs care? Working Paper, No. 13. Vienna: United Nations Industrial Development Organization.

Luetkenhorst, W. (2004). Economic development, the role of SMEs and the rationale for donor support: Some reflections on recent trends and best practices. Keynote Presentation to UNIDO at the SME Partnership Group Meeting, Hanoi, 19 November.

Meehan, J., Meehan, K. and Richards, A. (2006). Corporate social responsibility: The 3C-SR model. *International Journal of Social Economics*, 33(5/6), 386–98.

Morsing, M. and Perrini, F. (2009). CSR in SMEs: Do SMEs matter for the CSR agenda? *Business Ethics: A European Review*, 18(1), 1–6.

Muller, A. and Kolk, A. (2009). CSR Performance in Emerging Markets: Evidence from Mexico. *Journal of Business Ethics*, 85, 325–37.

Nwankwo, F., Ewuim, N. and Asoya, N. P. (2012). Role of cooperatives in small and medium scale enterprises (SMEs) development in Nigeria: Challenges and the way forward. *African Research Review*, 6(4), 140–56.

Oguntade, A. and Mafimisebi, T. (2011). Contributions of corporate social responsibility to agriculture and rural development in Nigeria. *Journal of sustainable Development in Africa*, 13(4), 110–28.

Pastrana, N. A. and Sriramesh, K. (2014). Corporate social responsibility: Perceptions and practices among SMEs in Colombia. *Public Relations Review*, 40(1), 14–24.

Renaud, D., Bouché, P., Gartiser, N., Zanni-Merk, C. and Michaud, H. P. (2010). Knowledge transfer for supporting the organizational evolution of SMES: A case study. In R. J. Howlett, ed., *Innovation through Knowledge Transfer* Berlin, Heidelberg: Springer, pp. 293–302.

Revell, A., Stokes, D. and Chen, H. (2010). Small businesses and the environment: Turning over a New Leaf? *Business Strategy and the Environment*, 19(5), 273–88.

Russo A. and Tencati A. (2009). Formal vs. informal CSR strategies: Evidence from Italian micro, small, medium-sized, and large firms. *Journal of Business Ethics*, 85, 339–53.

Sanchez P. E and Benito-Hernandez S. (2015). CSR policies: Effects on labour productivity in Spanish micro and small manufacturing companies. *Journal of Business Ethics*, 128, 705–24. http://doi: 10.1007/s10551-013-1982-x.

Sham, T. and Pang, I. (2014). China's SMEs development. OCBC Wing Hang Monthly Newsletter, September, 1–4, available at www.ocbcwhhk.com/webpages_cms/files/Investment%20Newsletter/English/Investment%20Newsletter_Sep_e(1).pdf accessed 21 July 2019.

SME sector in India – statistics, trends, reports (2017). Available at https://evoma.com/business-centre/sme-sector-in-india-statistics-trends-reports/ accessed 16 July 2018.

Spence, L. J. (1999). Does size matter? The state of the art in small business ethics. *Business Ethics: A European Review*, 8(3), 163–74.

Spence, L. J. (2007). CSR and small business in a European policy context: The five C's of CSR and small business research agenda 2007. *Business and Society Review*, 112(4), 533–52.

Spence, L. J. and Lozano, J. F. (2000). Communicating about ethics with small firms: Experiences from the UK and Spain. *Journal of Business Ethics*, 27(1–2), 43–53.

Spence, L. J. and Rutherfoord, R. (2003). Small business and empirical perspectives in business ethics: Editorial. *Journal of Business Ethics*, 47(1), 1–5.

Strand, R., Freeman, R. E. and Hockerts, K. (2015). Corporate social responsibility and sustainability in Scandinavia: An overview. *Journal of Business Ethics*, 127(1), 1–15.

Turyakira, P. K. (2017). Small and medium-sized enterprises (SMEs) engagement in corporate social responsibility (CSR) in developing countries: Literature review. *African Journal of Business Management*, 11(18), 464–9.

Uhlaner, L. M., Berent-Braun, M. M., Jeurissen, R. J. and de Wit, G. (2012). Beyond size: Predicting engagement in environmental management practices of Dutch SMEs. *Journal of Business Ethics*, 109(4), 411–29.

United States Small Business Administration Office of Advocacy (2016). Small Business Profile. Available at www.sba.gov/sites/default/files/advocacy/United_States.pdf accessed 30 July 2018.

Vives, A. (2006). Social and environmental responsibility in small and medium enterprises in Latin America. *The Journal of Corporate Citizenship*, 21, 39–50.

Viviers, S. and Venter, D. J. L. (2007). Corporate social responsibility: A SMME perspective. *African Journal of Business Ethics*, 2(1), 20–7.

Wilson, T. D. (2011). Introduction: Approaches to informal economy. *Urban Anthropology and Studies of Cultural Systems and World Economic Development*, 40 (3), 205–21.

World Business Council for Sustainable Development, WBCSD. (2009). Business role: Corporate social responsibility (CSR). Available at www.wbcsd.org/templates/TemplateWBCSD5/layout.asp?type=Menuld-E00 accessed 21 July 2019.

World Commission on Environment and Development (1987).*Our Common Future*. Oxford: Oxford University Press.

Worthington, I., Ram, M. and Jones, T. (2006). Exploring corporate social responsibility in the UK Asian small business community. *Journal of Business Ethics*, 67(2), 201–17.

6

Human Resource Management and Political CSR in Global Supply Chains: Causes and Consequences of Host Communities' Enduring Struggles

Hedda Ofoole Knoll and Frederick Ahen

6.1 INTRODUCTION

Understanding the implementation and governance of CSR practices in global supply chains in middle and low-income countries is becoming an increasingly important area of research (Soundararajan and Brown, 2014). McWilliams and Siegel (2001: p. 117) define CSR as 'actions that appear to further some social good, beyond the interest of the firm [and by extension all organisations] and that which is required by law'. The global and highly complex supply chains of multinational corporations (MNCs) present many challenges in identifying and managing CSR at different phases of the supply chain. This is especially true in middle and low-income countries where governance is not always stable, and labour laws lack strong enforcement mechanisms due to the weak state capacity. These issues prompt key questions about the intensification of the globalization of CSR agenda (Rotter et al., 2014). The attribution of responsibilities to corporations and their managers in the changing geopolitical context is coupled with the absence of enforceable global governance regimes in many countries (e.g. enforcing human rights and providing public goods and services). This raises the question of the legitimization of political influence for businesses in their global supply chains as discussed by Scherer and Palazzo (2011) and Scherer et al. (2014). Scherer and Palazzo (2011) for example, argue that CSR has not sufficiently integrated the aspects of private businesses which have become politically important in global society (Scherer, 2006). '[…] political CSR suggests an extended model of governance with business firms contributing to global regulation and providing public goods' (Scherer and Palazzo, 2011: p. 901). The purpose of the chapter is to determine how corporations respond to the many 'pressures' to align socioeconomic practices with the prevailing form of globalization through political CSR and how that affects local communities in global supply chains. Consequently, we investigate the micro-level use of political CSR governance mechanisms of global supply chains [for the purposes of this chapter, CSR governance mechanisms in global supply chains are defined as voluntary multi-stakeholder cooperation with a set of contracts,

guidelines, norms and institutions used to govern and shape corporate responsibilities when addressing societal or ecological activities and issues within global supply
chains (Jastram and Prescher, 2014, Soundararajan and Brown, 2014, Knoll and
Jastram, 2018). We achieve this aim by addressing the noted gaps in the literature
about CSR identified above. In so doing, we present a case study examining the
potential contribution of human resource (HR) managers in the process of implementing political CSR in a subsidiary of an MNC in a lower middle-income
country, Ghana. This study answers the question:

> *How does the implementation of political CSR by HR managers of MNC subsidiaries
> affect the host communities in Ghana?*

In spite of the study's context-specific data (from Ghana), this chapter focuses
broadly on West, East, Central and Southern Africa (WECS Africa, henceforth)
and emergent Africa more widely. This is because given the dispersion of international production, MNCs mostly negotiate their legal, socioeconomic demands
across vast geographical spaces.

In this chapter, we posit that many advocates of political CSR in MNCs are
universalizing assumptions about a set of conditions that do not exist or are irrelevant
in countries where the implications of a complex history of social, political, and
economic imperialist exploitations still reverberate. Ignoring these issues diverts
attention away from addressing the real political and socioeconomic problems
that workers face in regions such as WECS Africa (Frynas, 2005; Knoll and
Jastram, 2018). Orock (2013) concludes that there has not been a sufficient response
from MNCs with respect to social needs and labour conditions in WECS Africa.
MNCs in WECS Africa still negotiate issues concerning land purchase with their
immediate and vulnerable stakeholders. This has led to displacement and socioeconomic issues in rural areas, as the following case study will elaborate. This, in
turn, has led to socioeconomic and political CSR activities by MNCs. These
emergent questions include the demand for the provision of education, housing
and healthcare from MNCs in WECS Africa. The result is the risk of MNCs being
overburdened with demands unrelated to their economic purpose. The question
that arises is, how did they find themselves in this quagmire in the first place?
Moreover, the legitimacy of managerial authority towards social governance
mechanisms, and the marginalization of democratic political processes raise new
questions. Thus, the self-regulation of MNCs on issues of social welfare, without a
wider democratic participation, needs further critical examination (Smith, 2013;
Nèron, 2013; Kourula and Delalieux, 2014; Mäkinen and Kasanen, 2016).

The remainder of the chapter is structured as follows: First, we examine how the
concepts of CSR in global supply chains are addressed with regard to the interdependence between CSR, HRM and stakeholder involvement. Subsequently, we
explain the method of our enquiry into the outcomes created by political CSR in a
palm oil supply chain through a synthesis of the analysed data from the field studies.

For the purpose of brevity, we present only the synthesis as a case study. Finally, the chapter concludes with a discussion about the observations and data analysis from the field, the contribution and managerial implications, the limitations of this chapter, and potential future research directions.

6.2 LITERATURE: CONCEPTUALIZING CSR IN GLOBAL SUPPLY CHAINS

The conceptualization of political CSR beyond immediate shareholder interests in profit maximization and mere legal compliance generates a number of ethical challenges. These include the articulation and endorsement of acceptable working conditions for employees along the entire supply chain. Working conditions are often handled across diverse jurisdictions with inconsistent regulations and strategies for control. These challenges could involve the actions of HR managers as socially connected actors who are engaged in practices that impact communities (Driscoll and Hofman, 1998; Fuentes-Garcia et al., 2007; Young, 2011). This is especially important in terms of impact and possible ethical violations (Wiley, 2000; Fuente-Garcia et al., 2007; Garavan and McGuire, 2010). In an ideal situation, HR managers can be seen as 'enablers' and 'stewards' of the CSR policies of their organisations and promoters of appropriate behaviour as required of corporate citizens (Voegtlin and Scherer, 2014: p. 4, Jamali et al., 2015). Scherer (2017) points out that the implications of the emerging political responsibility of HR managers need to be explored further. This exploration must include aspects of 'the influence of HR management and HR functions (selection, development, assessment and compensation) on individuals, groups and leaders and their response to changing or growing corporate responsibilities' (Scherer 2017: p. 6; see also Greenwood, 2002 and Voegtlin and Scherer, 2014). Direct and indirect discussion of CSR in the literature includes (i) the application of CSR to human resource management (HRM) (Francis and Keegan, 2006; Cohen, 2010; Morgeson et al., 2013; Jamali et al., 2015; Fuentes-Garcia et al., 2010); (ii) the role of HR development in embedding CSR and ethics in organisations (Garavan and McGuire, 2010); (iii) stakeholder perspective on HRM (Ferrary, 2009); (iv) the impact of socially responsible HRM on employees' organisational citizenship behaviour (Newman et al., 2016); and (v) political CSR as well as the challenges and implications for HRM (Voegtlin and Scherer, 2014). Maak et al. (2016) and Scherer (2017) report a dearth of empirical explanations of 'how' and 'why' corporations engage in political CSR in countries that they (as many others) uncritically refer to as 'less developed', and that there is still a lack of data from inside corporations and about the micro-level foundations of political CSR (Campbell and Slack, 2008; Kourula and Delalieux, 2014; Scherer et al., 2017). More prominently, what has been left out from the discourse is the role of HR managers in implementing political CSR in the subsidiaries of MNCs in low-income countries (Wiley, 2000; Voegtlin and Scherer, 2014; Jamali et al., 2015).

Carter and Easton (2011) imply that over the past two decades, the conceptualization and management of sustainable international supply chains through CSR governance mechanisms has undergone immense changes. Expectations about sustainable supply chains transformed from defensive philanthropy concepts towards an affirmative 'corporate social integration' approach within supply chains (Porter and Kramer, 2006). Research on supply chain governance has demonstrated that voluntary CSR governance mechanisms – in particular instruments such as codes, guidelines, reporting certifications or audits – still fail, in practice. This is especially true of attempts to improve working conditions throughout international supply chains, particularly in low-income countries (Amazeen, 2011; Lund-Thomsen and Lindgreen, 2014). Controversial scandals within supply chains, documentations of poor CSR practices, and companies connecting CSR to public relations (PR) and marketing departments have led stakeholders to accuse corporations of using CSR as window dressing (Ellerup Nielsen and Thomsen, 2009). In this regard, we underline issues concerning weak institutional environments, vulnerable stakeholders within supply chains and instruments that may be unable to adequately capture the issues surrounding beneficiaries of ethical trade in global supply chains (Blowfield, 2004; Locke et al., 2013). There is also a lack of empirical research concerning the right tools and processes for managing social issues along supply chains. Additionally, there is a lack of deeper analysis of CSR governance and implementation mechanisms (Scherer and Palazzo, 2011). More recently, researchers have broadened the debate on CSR towards a version of political CSR in global supply chains (Scherer and Palazzo, 2011). Greenwood and De Cieri (2007) and later Scherer (2017) postulate that the link between political CSR and HRM deserves special attention. They propose that a stronger connection can expand the debate on political CSR. HR managers who appear to be sandwiched between the corporation's profit mandate and the aspirations of its internal and external stakeholders could make an important contribution to solving CSR issues in global supply chains. However, literature on CSR has a strong focus on employment relationships but not particularly on HRM (Greenwood and De Cieri, 2007).

HRM, with its focus on executing organisational strategies, provides a managerial framework in implementing CSR strategies into practical actions and outcomes successfully (Jamali et al., 2015). Thus, Jamali et al. (2015) as well as Voegtlin and Scherer (2014) propose more systematic links between CSR and HRM theories and suggest research bridging the two strands of literature. The question regarding the identification of stakeholders, how to tend to stakeholder groups as well as what consequences these actions could have in terms of the interdependence between political CSR and HRM is of much greater importance than it appears. Soundararajan and Brown (2014) argue that successful implementation of CSR governance mechanisms in global supply chains is dependent on effective stakeholder management. Furthermore, research attention has moved towards the issue of stakeholder dialogue and collaboration throughout a supply chain. Following the concept of stronger cooperation and collaboration (Drake and Schlachter, 2008) with stakeholders throughout the supply chain, the present study takes inspiration from Soundararajan and Brown's (2014) perspective of moving HRM towards an inter-organisational HRM in global value chains (Helfen, 2014), in the quest to determine whether or not this occurs in our particular case study.

6.3 METHODOLOGY: A NESTED SINGLE CASE STUDY DESIGN

The qualitative research from which our discussion is generated is based on a nested single case study design. The empirical component entails a primary exploratory research using triangulation of data from observations, document analysis and interviews regarding political CSR and HRM within supply chains in Ghana. We adopted a purposive sampling methodology, with an emphasis on a well-known subsidiary. This is because the chosen corporation interacts internationally within its supply chains, and is therefore particularly useful/suitable as a source of data on CSR issues in low-income countries (O'Higgens, 2003).

The Benso Oil Palm Plantation is a subsidiary of one of the biggest multinational corporations in palm oil production, Wilmar International. After intensive desk research and literature review, a research protocol was designed. Subsequently, data collection took place from July to September 2014 in Ghana and from October to December 2014 in Germany with phone calls. These included 47 semi-structured interviews with palm oil farmers, palm oil production workers and managers from the multinational palm oil producer in Ghana and a small- and medium-sized fair-trade and organic palm oil producer. This was accompanied by observations at their palm oil fields and palm oil production sites along with in-depth interviews with experts in Ghana. The information gathered was documented in audio and written forms in field diaries. The interviews were complemented with a review of secondary sources including relevant corporate documents, and reports including the Roundtable on Sustainable Palm Oil's (RSPO) Social Impact Assessment (SIA) report, websites, literature reviews and other documents published by the corporations about CSR. The reports proved especially important because they gave an in-depth understanding of relevant issues that would not have come up during the interviews. At the end of the first round of research, emerging issues were highlighted and the focus of the next interviews was to refine these issues in greater depth. The content analysis was undertaken with inspiration from the phases developed by Mayring (2000). Thus, the findings were clustered into three key issues concerning HR and supply chain management in host communities: (i) political CSR governance; (ii) socioeconomic CSR activities; and (iii) the impact of the above on internal and external stakeholders.

6.4 FINDINGS

6.4.1 *Political CSR Governance in Supply Chains*

In what follows, we supply a synthesis of the analysis of CSR governance mechanisms of the MNC and its subsidiary in Ghana in a narrative that explains the current state of affairs. Benso Oil Palm Plantation (BOPP) was founded in 1976 as a joint venture between the Government of Ghana and Unilever. In 2004, the Government of Ghana sold its 40 per cent stake at the Ghana Stock Exchange. Wilmar Africa Ltd acquired the majority stake after acquiring Unilever's share of BOPP in 2011 and took over management control of BOPP (TÜV Rheinland, 2014; SIA, 2014; Wilmar, 2016a). Wilmar Africa is a wholly owned subsidiary of Wilmar International (Wilmar), based in Singapore. Wilmar is one of the leading global producers, processors and merchandisers of palm oil and lauric oils worldwide. BOPP is divided into two divisions forming the nucleus plantation producing fresh palm fruits: the smallholder scheme and independent palm fruit producers, and the palm oil mill engaged in the production of crude palm oil (SIA, 2014). The BOPP concession hosts the nucleus estate and smallholder scheme. It is comprised of 6,799 hectares of contiguous land of the western region of Ghana including a 1,650-hectare smallholder project with 438 farmers producing around 17,000 metric tons of crude oil in 2014 (SIA, 2014; BOPP Presentation, 2014; Interview 23, Estate Manager). In total 1,373 employees work for BOPP of which 72 are management and senior staff, 488 are unionized workers and 798 are third-party contract workers who work for sub-contractors (BOPP Presentation, 2016).

Wilmar's sustainability approach is directed by being part of the RSPO since 2005, the United Nations Global Compact (UNGC), and it also has the International Sustainability and Carbon Certification (Wilmar, 2016b). BOPP was awarded its RSPO certification in 2014 and the HR department played a key role in the progress towards it. The RSPO is a global multi-stakeholder sustainability initiative, which promotes and guides sustainable palm oil production. It offers a certification system (Wilmar, 2016c) with standards, associated principles and criteria to guide corporations for a sustainable palm oil production. Moreover, it guides companies to ensure that they improve socioeconomic conditions of the communities within the operational areas and of the workers (SIA, 2014). In addition to the global CSR governance mechanisms BOPP is also guided by internal CSR governance policies. It is their HR manager and general management of BOPP who established it in order to remain sustainable in their daily work. The major policy areas include: CSR, child labour, compensation procedure, education and scholarship, housing, occupational health & safety and road maintenance. The committees are responsible for advancing sustainability programmes, developing policies and acting as gatekeepers of policies. Any information regarding CSR activities and issues is documented by the head of the committees and finalized in a report by the management who finally submits it to the most senior management of Wilmar. The firm is not monitored in any stringent way since the government is uninvolved. The above good intentions then look more like the programme of a municipal assembly than that of a subsidiary. How this works in practice is analysed below.

6.4.2 Socioeconomic Activities of HR Department

BOPP's HR department plays a key role in implementing CSR governance mechanisms through a multi-stakeholder approach. The HR managers of the subsidiary are involved in, or looking forward to, hard governance reporting initiatives designed by the Ghanaian government to implement precise CSR reporting regulations. The new prominent political role of MNCs in low-income countries also carries inherent dangers that are described in more detail below. However, before that the following paragraphs will outline how the HR department deals with socioeconomic activities together with internal and external stakeholders.

BOPP's HR department runs all the CSR activities and community issues with the support of other heads of departments and functional managers depending on the activity or issue. The CSR approach follows a specific procedure: the activities are initially negotiated directly with the community leaders who can express their wishes. Subsequently, the HR manager studies the financial budget of the year and decides together with the other managers what can be prioritized and what needs to be rescheduled. This part can be safely interpreted as a form of convenience CSR and subversion of the people's will. This is because community demands for CSR actions are jettisoned due to the arbitrary decisions of managers using financial constraints or budget allocations as the main justification, although the firm consistently reports profits.

With reference to the internal CSR activities to date, BOPP provides employees and their family members with free accommodation, drinking water, subsidized electric power (90 per cent subsidized), a clinic on the estate and free bus services to and from markets and churches for employees and dependents. They have a preschool for the workers' children and they offer scholarship schemes and other professional training facilities to employees and dependents. These measures represent mere philanthropic gestures compared to the value captured in acquiring thousands of hectares of land with timber, bodies of water and flora and fauna; as well as the loss of culture, history and a sense of community whose traditional structures are now lost for good. In the present case, the subsidiary is seen as an integral part of the community. A key part of this is the duty to give back to society due to its privileged financial position and the need to maintain 'harmony' between the company and its community (Young, 2011). This integrative orientation influences decisionmaking but does not mean that the HR manager will disregard economic performance. As strategic HR practices have an impact on business results

(Ulrich, 1997), the subsidiary's decisionmaking process naturally relies on instrumental strategies using cost-benefit analysis.

In theory, the HR manager enables social innovation in the search for solutions to societal problems. The objective is to improve the socioeconomic conditions in areas such as education, health and poverty reduction. In political CSR studies, such a role is discussed as 'private actors placed in a prominent political role' (Scherer and Palazzo, 2007; 2011). Managers in such political CSR-oriented corporations fill the void left by weak governments in areas such as health, education and social security. They practise self-regulation procedures especially with regard to difficult political CSR issues that require immediate attention and need to be solved competently to ensure organisational legitimacy (Matten and Crane, 2005; Gilbert et al., 2011; Rasche et al., 2013; Maak et al., 2016). However, Ghana, our research context, is not a failed state and neither is the community a refugee camp lacking any social order and institutional structures. This means that some of these social problems did not exist previously but are the results of displacement and dispossession of land.

6.4.3 Corporate Town or Total Institutional Control

The work environment is an extended version of corporate citizenship towards a so-called 'company town' formed around BOPP's operational milieu, with managers and staff who are responsible for the entire lives of the employees and family members. This can be seen as 'socially benign', but also as a 'total institution' (Gofman, 1961) of dissolved spheres between private life and work (Mäkinen and Kourula, 2014). The workers can be left quite vulnerable, having no boundaries between their work and private lives. This leads to a situation whereby the subsidiary's control over human resources extends beyond the work environment. There is a danger of being drawn towards domination of the company in all central aspects of the workers' lives. For example, if one is fired by the subsidiary, this could also mean that one loses his/her direct social environment and essentially becomes homeless or internally displaced person (Mäkinen and Kasanen, 2016). The challenge seems not to be if the company engages in CSR with genuine interest, but rather if their CSR activities solve issues they have either created or are indirectly involved in creating.

6.4.4 Impact Analysis of Political CSR

The harmony that the firm seeks to create is not to solve an existing conflict but the one created by the firm's very presence in the community, which locals consider an unjust appropriation of resources. Here, we provide empirical examples of how the subsidiary attempts to solve self-generated problems.

Building a community centre. For more than 15 years, a nearby community had tried to build a community centre. They were unable to complete the centre and asked BOPP for support to complete the project. The amount of investment was calculated to be around 230,000 GHC, representing a lot of money for BOPP to complete the project in one year. However, BOPP stated that they would be able to achieve it in two to three years. But in-depth analysis only raises questions. Is building a community center a fair demand on the firm in term of priorities and are there more pressing needs?

Housing and accommodation issues. The SIA Report of the RSPO revealed that in 2013, the company provided 150 fewer houses than needed for their employees, contract workers and their family members, comprising around 3,479 people in total in the three BOPP villages. The result was overcrowding: around ten people were living in houses built for four. This was a major issue for the workers in addition to the poor housing conditions, both of which can have an impact on the community's health (SIA, 2014).

Recreational facilities. In addition to such social welfare activities, BOPP has diverse recreational facilities such as a swimming pool, tennis courts, a golf course, recreational centres, clubhouses, estate shops, soccer fields and volleyball pitches (SIA, 2014). With regard to health and safety activities, BOPP has a weekly meeting called 'safety talk'. Here the divisions discuss health and safety topics such as fire safety, road safety, childcare or illnesses such as Ebola, to create awareness. This seems to wrongly suggest that there is neither a government in Ghana nor any municipal governance system, apart from the informal governance structures made up of chiefs. Therefore the firm must take over these roles; although the reality however is slightly different.

Community development. The external CSR activities include initiatives that help to improve infrastructure, reduce poverty and develop the community. A special focus lies in the provision of education and healthcare. Notable among the CSR activities for external stakeholders is financial assistance to communities for the provision of social activities. This includes royal funerals and festivals, and social amenities such as electricity infrastructure, road maintenance and renovation of rundown schools, scholarships for brilliant but financially less well-off children, and access to BOPP's clinic. However, this is clearly more complicated, as seen in the following examples:

- Health issues: Farm labourers who are only manual workers on the farm are not provided for by BOPP. Their health insurance for example, is their own responsibility and not deemed a concern of BOPP, one farmer explains.
- Destroyed social fabric and issues of child safety: Many nearby rural communities lack higher educational facilities. The consequences are that their children have to travel long distances to school. Moreover, low quality

transportation facilities and poor roads led parents to decide to rent rooms near the school. The consequence was that these children are living alone without any parental or adult supervision. The effect was that many school-aged girls were getting pregnant and many school-aged boys were getting into illegal independent mining businesses and encountering social problems (SIA, 2014).

Compensation for displacement. After the BOPP estate was established, villages in this area were divided or relocated, with the result that quite a number of households and farms were physically displaced (Interview 26–29, BABSA: smallholder association; SIA, 2014). These displacements came with compensation in some cases without consultation with the affected individuals. Moreover, only displaced households were paid compensation but not those who lost their farms. Others were not paid anything at all. In general, compensation was paid almost 28 years after the land was acquired, without interest (Interview 26–29, BABSA: smallholder association; SIA, 2014). In a country where life expectancy now stands at 62 years, it means most older people never lived to see their compensation.

In 1995, a smallholder initiative was started in collaboration with governmental and financial institutions. It was planned for a 25-year period on land that was within the BOPP estate for farmers who had to be displaced from their farms when BOPP was established. The objective was to set up sustained income and means of livelihood, to reduce poverty and to be a channel for transfer of technology and skills in oil palm cultivation (Interview 26–29, BABSA; SIA, 2014, BOPP Presentation, 2014). In addition to a four-hectare land parcel, and oil palm seedlings for each farmer, technical support was provided by BOPP. This was part of their CSR towards the community. In this case, however, the farmers are required to sell their palm fruit bunches to BOPP. A relevant question is: to what extent does a four-hectare palm oil farm on land now owned by someone else improve the livelihood of families compared to having one's own land that provides a decent livelihood, a sense of worth and dignity when one goes to work, a source of nutraceuticals and game, herbal medicines and the maintenance of traditions and culture?

Employment issues. With regard to socioeconomic improvements in the nearby area over the years, BOPP achieved employment of over 3,500 people in the plantation and the surrounding area, which contributed to an increase in the demand for goods and services. Although job opportunities have been created through BOPP, the proportion of local workforce at BOPP is about 11 per cent, due to the number of unskilled workers in this area (SIA, 2014). Dissatisfaction of the community and its leaders with the situation led to several complaints. They argued that the community is not informed whenever job vacancies are available and that formal structures of communication with the company with regard to job opportunities are lacking (SIA, 2014). Does the firm need workers? Who is helping whom? CSR is framed as a means of elevating living conditions. How does a plantation job compare to the independence of land ownership and production of food crops? Under normal circumstances, life in the local communities meant a sense of belonging to families and tribes, traditions and cultural practices, now separated by evictions.

The current situation means that there is a net loss for the community and a net gain for the subsidiary (see the synthesis in Table 6.1). This is exemplified by the fact that 43 years (since the establishment of the subsidiary in 1976) is too long a period for a community to still wallow in poverty despite being endowed with resources. There are reasons for this. All the value-adding processes are conducted outside the community because there is still no factory for diversification into manufacturing. The underdevelopment is therefore expected because the initial endowment (the land) was stripped away. By implication, the firm offers constant first aid to a problem that requires a surgical operation. More prominently, the social problems were created by the presence of the subsidiary because most of them did not exist prior to their arrival. Compounding this is the complicity of the government. The idea that the firm provides jobs does not tally with the empirical observation because prior to the arrival of BOPP there were farming communities with land ownership and that guaranteed a decent livelihood.

TABLE 6.1 *Critical incidents in the supply chain and political CSR, impact on firms and local community*

Supply chain phase	Subsidiary	Community	Synthesis of impact
Land acquisition	Firm gains territory for control and cash crop farming	Dispossession of land, loss of the sources of nutraceuticals and water, wildlife, flora and fauna, herbal medicine, etc.	Negative impact on biodiversity, environmental degradation contributing to climate change
Geographical change and ownership	Guaranteed possession of land for future production of palm fruit	Displacement: loss of livelihood, community, history, institutions and future well-being	A starting point of local population being rendered powerless
Change in the nature of labour	Cheap source of labour for basic farm work	Employment gains minimal compared to the freedom to till one's own land and independence; no high level or influential position	Delayed compensation and alternative sources of livelihood for a long period strips locals of human rights

TABLE 6.1 *(continued)*

Supply chain phase	Subsidiary	Community	Synthesis of impact
Political CSR practices using PR and legitimating tactics	Based on cost-benefit analysis and budget provision solely decided by HR managers	A new situation is created reinforcing the helplessness and dependency on HR manager and corporate fiat	Dependency responded to with boutique projects and diversionary corporate practices
Solidification of political CSR	Easy control of farm workers allowing exertion of political and economic power over the community	Total institution that now dissolves both the working and social life of workers, e.g. company town	A totally weakened working population ensures the lack of alternatives and hence the guarantee of cheap labour for the subsidiary under the same unfavourable conditions
The firm as a de facto political institution (without mandate or election)	Gradual takeover of governance and decisionmaking on welfare and public utility issues	Subversion of local authority, under-mining democracy via subtle means of negotiations in which subsidiary has lopsided power	HR boss as a de facto governor representing the corporation – due to the absence of government control
Farm and community as simple supply chain input	Harvest and export, no value-added activity	No opportunity for political, civil or economic independence – net exporters of raw materials	The loss of land and independence translates into a modern-day plantation

Below in Figure 6.1 is the livelihood analysis of the structure of accumulation inherent in dispossession in global supply chains and its consequences on communities. For example, building a community centre, a swimming pool, a golf course, or repairing roads that are mainly heavily trafficked by the heavy-duty trucks of the firm appear to be more diversionary than sustainable acts. None truly answers the root question and structural problem of poverty alleviation. Consider this statement that encapsulates the tragedy of the affected community and punches massive holes into claims of CSR practices: 'The displacement came with indirect impact to the villagers; it affected their daily diets and income. It affected livelihoods, traditional household structures, artisanal independent gold mining opportunities and natural

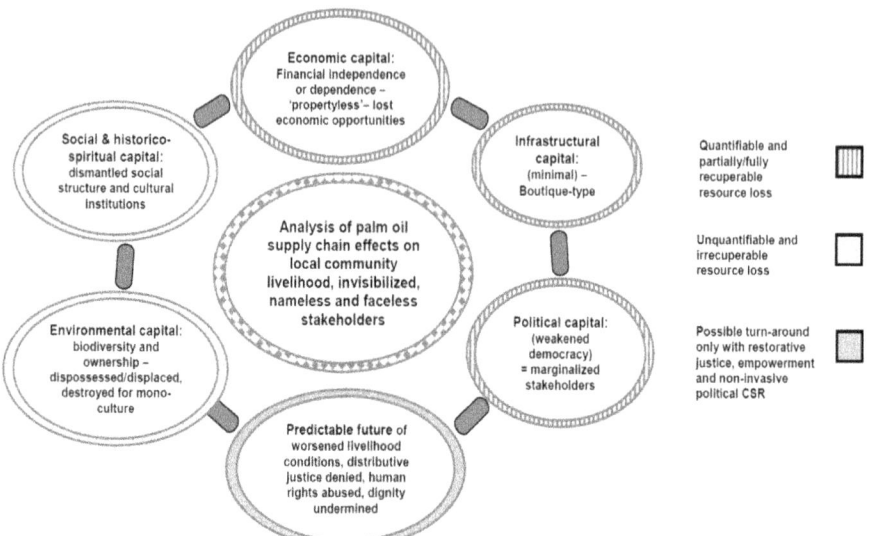

FIGURE 6.1 The effects of subsidiary's accumulation by dispossession on host community's capitals

resources such as food crops, natural water sources, fishing and hunting' (Interview 26–29, BABSA: smallholder association, SIA, 2014). Furthermore, many managers think that an improvement in CSR can evolve if reporting is not only internal or to a global multi-stakeholder initiative such as the RSPO, but also obligatory in a transparent and regulated manner to the government and the people. This means the whole political CSR process misses the point of serving its immediate constituents.

6.5 DISCUSSIONS

6.5.1 *Political CSR and Neocolonialism in WECS Africa*

This study fills an important gap in literature focusing on MNC–stakeholder relationship in WECS Africa. It provides new insights into how behavioural processes influence political CSR (Scherer, 2017) through a micro-level analysis of HR managers. In general, CSR debates have been mostly driven by stakeholders and MNCs from Western countries with fewer representations from low-income countries (Knoll and Jastram, 2018). It appears that the subsidiary of Wilmar, BOPP, is an active partner in political CSR. This kind of practice is what Lock and Seele (2017) refer to as politicized CSR or Scherer and Palazzo (2011) as 'the new political role of the corporation' in weaker institutions. The subsidiary works on initiatives towards poverty reduction in their direct environment through increased employment among others. However, this can be immediately interpreted as a non-market strategy to gain legitimacy and not necessarily an attempt to solve a social problem even if it was created by the firm and the government. Furthermore, what also needs to be considered in political CSR in low-income countries across Africa is the risk of moving towards neocolonial constructions (Vertigans, 2011; Ehrnström-Fuentes, 2016). As the first president of Ghana, Dr Kwame Nkrumah, states in his books (1965, 1973), there lies a danger of governments precipitating towards the grip of outsiders. This can result in economic dependency and powerless governments having less control over the destinies of their own countries across Africa (Nkrumah, 1965). Therefore, we need further investigations into political CSR activities of MNCs with their subsidiaries in the former colonies. Thus, MNCs can be partners for economic growth but cannot be depended on for economic development. There is also the need to consider concerns regarding the corporate political power that is now rivalling the state and the lack of accountability even in cases of clear abuses (Kapferer, 2004; Young, 2008; Orock, 2013). The major risk in political CSR is that the firm is gradually replacing the state.

6.5.2 HRM and Political CSR: Towards an HRM-Model of Shared Responsibility

This paper expands research on HRM in political CSR. Looking at HRM from an inter-organisational perspective (Helfen, 2014) the results showed the lack of social impact of the company regarding their workers and the local community that could have led to shared responsibility strategies of alternative livelihoods, skills development and diverse mitigation measures. The use of a multi-stakeholder approach and control mechanisms can be seen as a foundation for deriving moral legitimacy from the internal and external stakeholders towards an environment of shared responsibility, as presented in the proposed model below (Figure 6.2).

The model is derived from the analysis of the data from the field work. It depicts the ideal situation of political CSR in which inputs come from competing interest groups in order to produce the optimal outcome. The current situation however deviates substantially from the above representation. Nonetheless, this model could serve as the appropriate guide-post for firm–stakeholder relations in global supply chains where political CSR plays a major role. Thus, we propose that responsible HR managers should take the role as inter-organisational enablers in embedding a political CSR approach into the organisation. This would significantly impinge on the successful operationalization and governance of political CSR. Preuss et al. (2009) postulate that such a complex and interactive link of HRM and CSR through different constellations of various stakeholders in shaping governance mechanisms plays a pivotal role in enabling a mutual overlap between the concept of political CSR and HRM (Voegtlin and Greenwood, 2016).

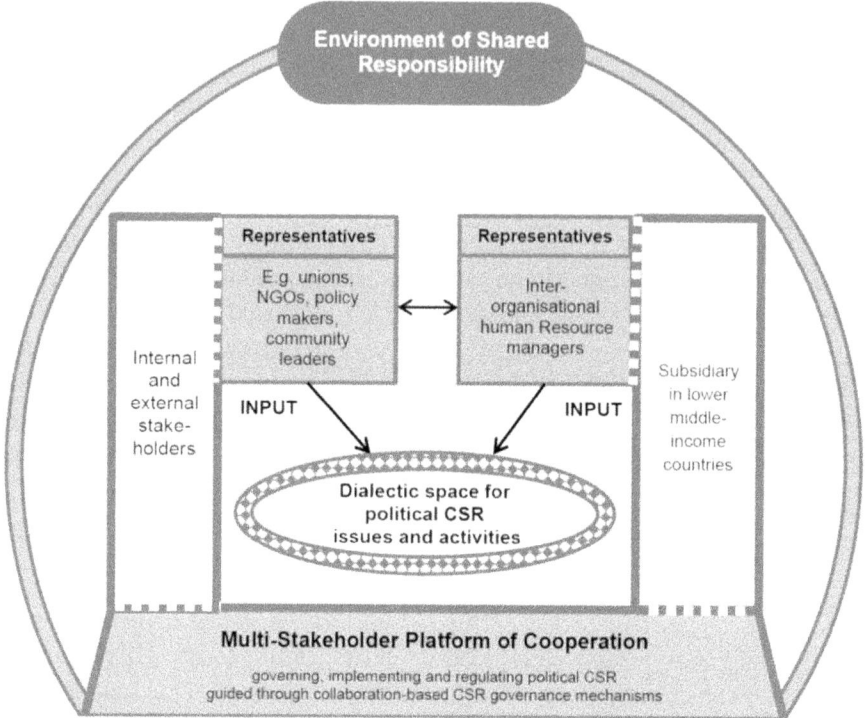

FIGURE 6.2 An ideal inter-organisational HRM model of shared responsibility in low-income countries

Put together, we argue that the interdependence of CSR, multi-stakeholder involvement and HR must start internally with the duty of care of employee governance, thus generating the necessary room for social innovation. Our model explains the possible interdependence between the firm and its HR manager on one hand, and the community and the national and local government on the other. HR managers are seen as intermediaries between the firm and its diverse stakeholder groups on political CSR issues. This makes them responsible for governing, implementing and regulating diverse political CSR issues and activities. Here, they work with representatives of internal and external stakeholders such as unions, non-governmental organisations or governments. This concept is grounded in an inter-organisational perspective of HRM, moving the responsibility of HRM beyond the corporation. It is centred on a cooperative multi-stakeholder platform and collaboration-based CSR governance mechanisms such as the RSPO.

However, the above model is a hopeful ideal. This is because until the community becomes a corporative member with shared gains from the firm's operations, there cannot be a shared responsibility because there is no shared decision-making power. Thus, the final decision on budget allocation, timing, planning, quality and quantity of projects depends on the HR manager and the subsidiary.

6.6 CONCLUSIONS

This study addressed the question: *How does the implementation of political CSR by HR managers of MNC subsidiaries affect the host communities?* The chapter offers three contributions for research and practice: First, the observations point to the importance of socioeconomic CSR issues and activities in low-income countries. Second, the study proposes a refined interpretation of the quality of the interdependencies between political CSR and the potential contribution of HR managers, and third, it illuminates the potential and the risks of political CSR in an under-explored research area in an under-studied geographical setting.

Contrary to what extant literature presents as the pressures on MNCs to fulfil demands that are neither related to their raison d'être or competence, we found that socioeconomic demands in low-income countries are rather the local communities' natural response to shocks emanating from the presence of the subsidiary in their community. The ensuing dramatic changes in the socio-cultural, political and economic institutions underpinning their way of life can be articulated as '5Ds': (i) *dispossession* of land without immediate provision for replacement; (ii) *displacement* of people and the cutting of their connection with their only known ancestral home; (iii) *destruction* of the environment as a result of mono-culture, resulting in climate change that affects biodiversity. This then leads to (iv) *desperation* that only forces the local population to succumb to a superficial and inadequate alternative solution labelled as political CSR. The hierarchy of projects that count towards social change and development indicate that most of what is labelled CSR is essentially boutique projects and diversionary attempts that do not produce structural changes. The enduring power asymmetry between the subsidiary and the local community means that decisionmaking about resource control and distribution lies 'lop-sidedly' with the subsidiary and its HR manager in the presence of other weak stakeholders and mostly ineffective capacity in enforcing regulations. This disenfranchisement results in the (v) *de-democratization* of the local governance and the social system. Thus, corporate self-regulation *sans* democratic participation and monitoring systems by the government leads firms to pursue self-interest as the most optimal trade-off while warding off public outrage with diversionary CSR tactics. This discovery completely changes the direction and meaning of the discourse of political CSR, from firms pursuing CSR to mostly damage control practices using non-market strategies. Affected areas of global palm oil supply chains that are not accounted for include the lack of protection for virgin forests, wildlife and bodies of water.

The '5Ds' as a conceptual framework crystalizes our understanding of the artificially engineered socioeconomic conditions of local communities. This refers to a situation whereby the communities are no longer in control of the natural resources that used to sustain them. Here, they are denied the fundamental human rights, given the extent to which national institutional structures and MNCs in cohorts operate to maximize their bottom line while treating the people as simple means of production bereft of humanity (Ahen and Amankwah-Amoah, 2018).

Micro-level analysis reveals that HR managers are mostly torn between responding to community's grievances and the profit-maximization intents of the firm they represent. They make attempts to liaise and create dialogue but ultimately loyalty to the subsidiary comes first. This conflict of interest is not unexpected for most economic agents (Ahen, 2014, 2018). We have no data on an HR manager who sacrificed his job or antagonized the subsidiary on behalf of the local community. Rather, there are records of perpetual community–firm conflicts where there is always one winner – the subsidiary.

The main problem with political CSR is the absence of checks and balances to ensure any form of accountability by those who have voluntarily obligated themselves to provide welfare goods and services to the host community (Ahen, 2018; Ahen and Amankwah Amoah, 2018). MNCs and HR departments mostly make the rules and decide about conformity to same. HR representatives act as de facto governors and the corporation as a state. This is what the CIA predicted that by 2015, most corporations will have more say in governance than states themselves (Carlson, 2015). Shared responsibility requires shared power in decisionmaking. However, the power asymmetry is very evident in this particular case. Political CSR as a prescribed governance system as in extant literature for neglected communities in low-income countries has two main features: (i) corporate political power with greater bargaining power and (ii) governments' neglect of local peoples adversely affected by weak institutions.

6.6.1 Managerial Implications

The managerial implications centre on the broader issues of distributive justice, HR manager selection and the overall governance of CSR that must be geared towards a more humanistic approach to produce optimal outcomes. Our findings indicate that an HR manager is seen as an enabler with moral duties to bring about improvements in the social performance of the organisation. The proposed HRM model of shared responsibility would ideally enable an inter-organisational HRM system that not only creates wealth for the corporation but also for the society in its operational milieu while keeping harmony between its internal and external stakeholders. Consequently, it would support changing the balance of power between 'strong' MNCs and 'weak' vulnerable stakeholders. In that context, HR managers, seen as positive role models for employees could encourage, educate and provide opportunities for social innovations. However, this is partly wishful thinking as the HR manager is constrained by the profit-maximization intents of the firm and not the 'higher calling' with a moral duty for social advancement. This means the onus lies with the host country of any subsidiary to fully fulfil its role of regulating firms and providing public goods through public-private partnerships, when necessary.

6.6.2 *Limitations and Directions for Future Research*

The local conditions, time and resource constraints limited a comprehensive engagement with all stakeholders affected directly or indirectly by the company. In addition, we do not have information about pension plans for farmers. In spite of all that, our analytical approach reveals how MNCs' subsidiaries deal with political CSR issues and activities in particular in a lower middle-income country in WECS Africa. This provides a useful lens especially for researchers, managers, union leaders, NGOs and other stakeholders studying political CSR.

Given the growing importance of political CSR within supply chains, the role of employee governance and vulnerable stakeholders in low-income countries, it is surprising how little is known about CSR governance mechanisms and political CSR of subsidiaries of MNCs in low-income countries in WECS Africa. This chapter contributes to filling this gap. Nevertheless, further research on the relevance of implementing political CSR and handling CSR issues in Africa is needed. Finally, there is still an open debate about whether corporations are the best actors to protect and implement social welfare through political CSR in a collectively beneficial way (Smith, 2013; Mäkinen and Kasanen, 2016). What impact will this new powerful and prominent political role of MNCs have on labour rights, human rights and social welfare in low-income countries? In this context, HRM and political CSR research has not yet provided sufficient answers. Critical analysis of the complex effects of political CSR of MNCs is needed. We also need more long-term research on the legitimacy of managerial authority of HR managers as inter-organisational enablers on political CSR in low-income countries.

REFERENCES

Ahen, F. (2014). Ethically constrained optimization of dynamic capabilities: Towards sustainable global health. *Social Responsibility Journal*, 10(3), 436–54.

Ahen, F. (2018). Dystopic prospects of global health and ecological governance: Whither the eco-centric-humanistic CSR of firms? *Humanistic Management Journal*. https://doi.org/10.1007/s41463-018-0034-1

Ahen, F. and Amankwah-Amoah, J. (2018) Institutional voids and the philanthropization of CSR practices: Insights from developing economies. *Sustainability*, 10, 2400.

Amazeen, M. (2011). Gap (RED): Social responsibility campaign or window dressing? *Journal of Business Ethics*, 99, 167–82.

Blowfield, M. (2004). Implementation deficits of ethical trade systems. *Journal of Corporate Citizenship*, 13, 77–90.

BOPP Presentation (2014). Company Overview of BOPP. 4th August 2014.

BOPP Presentation (2016). Company Overview of BOPP.

Campbell, D. and Slack, R. (2008). Corporate 'philanthropy strategy' and 'strategic philanthropy': Some insights from voluntary disclosures in annual reports. *Business & Society*, 47 (2), 187–212.

Carlson, N. (2015) Back in 2000, the CIA made these predictions for 2015. *Business Insider Singapore*. Available at www.businessinsider.sg/cia-predictions-for-2015-from-2000–2015-1/#.Vcup4flN2z6 accessed 29 June, 2018.

Carter, C. R. and Easton, P. L. (2011). Sustainable supply chain management: Evolution and future directions. *International Journal of Physical Distribution & Logistics Management*, 41, 46–62.

Cohen, E. (2010). *CSR for HR. A Necessary Partnership for Advancing Responsible Business Practices*. London: Greenleaf Publishing Limited.

Drake, M. J. and Schlachter, J. T. (2008). A virtue-ethics analysis of supply chain collaboration. *Journal of Business Ethics*, 82(4), 851–64.

Driscoll, D.M. and Hofman, W. M. (1998). HR Plays a Central Role in Ethics Programs. *Workforce*, 77 (4), 121–23.

Ehrnström-Fuentes, M. (2016). Delinking Legitimacies: A pluriversal perspective on political CSR. *Journal of Management Studies*, 53(3), 433–62.

Ellerup Nielsen, A. and Thomsen, C. (2009). CSR communication in small and medium-sized enterprises: A study of the attitudes and beliefs of middle managers. *Corporate Communications: An international Journal*, 14(2), 176–89.

Ferrary, M. (2009). A stakeholder's perspective on human resource management. *Journal of Business Ethics*, 87,31–43.

Francis, H. and Keegan, A. (2006). The changing face of HRM: In search of balance. *Human Resource Management Journal*, 16(3), 231–49.

Frynas, J. G. (2005). The false development promise of corporate social responsibility: Evidence from multinational oil companies. *International Affairs* 81, 581–98.

Fuentes-Garcia, F. J., Nunez-Tabales, J. M. and Veroz-Herradon, R. (2008). Applicability of corporate social responsibility to human resources management: Perspective from Spain. *Journal of Business Ethics*, 82(1), 27–44.

Garavan, T. N. and McGuire, D. (2010). Human resource development and society: Human resource development's role in embedding corporate social responsibility, sustainability, and ethics in organizations. *Sage*, 12(5), 487–507.

Gilbert, D. U., Rasche, A. and Waddock, S. (2011). Accountability in a global economy: The emergence of international accountability standards. *Business Ethics Quarterly*, 21(1), 23–44.

Greenwood, M. R. (2002). Ethics and HRM: A review and conceptual analysis. *Journal of Business Ethics*, 36, 261–78.

Greenwood, M.R. and De Cieri, H. (2007). Stakeholder theory and the ethics of HRM. In A. Pinnington, R. Macklin and T. Campbell, eds., *Human Resource Management. Ethics and Employment*. Oxford: Oxford University Press, pp. 119–136.

Helfen, M. (2014). Netzwerkförmige Tertialisierung und triangularisierte Beschäftigung: Braucht es eine interorganisationale Personalpolitik? In J. Sydow, D. Sadowski, P. Conrad, eds., *Managementforschung*. Wiesbaden: Springer Fachmedien 24, pp. 171–206.

Jamali, D. R., El Dirani, A. M. and Harwood, I. A. (2015). Exploring human resource management roles in corporate social responsibility: The CSR-HRM co-creation model. *Business Ethics: A European Review*, 24, 125–43.

Jastram, S. and Prescher, J. (2014). Legitimizing corporate social responsibility governance. In S. O. Idowu, C. S. Frederiksen, A. Y. Mermod and M. E. J. Nielsen, eds., *Corporate Social Responsibility and Governance Theory and Practice*. Heidelberg, New York, Dordrecht, London: Springer, pp. 39–62.

Knoll, H. O. and Jastram, S. M. (2018). A pragmatist perspective on sustainable global supply chain governance – The case of Dr. Bronner's. *Society and Business Review*, https://doi.org/10.1108/SBR-12-2017-0122.

Kourula, A. and Delalieux, G. (2014). The micro-level foundations and dynamics of political corporate social responsibility: Hegemony and passive revolution through civil society. *Journal of Business Ethics*, 135, 769.

Lock, I. and Seele, P. (2017) Politicized CSR: How corporate political activity (mis-)uses political CSR. *Journal of Public Affairs*, e1667. https://doi.org/10.1002/pa.1667.

Locke, R. M., Rissing, B. A. and Pal, T. (2013). Complements or substitutes? Private codes, state regulation and the improvement of labour standards in global supply chains. *British Journal of Industrial Relations*, 51, 519–52.

Lund-Thomsen, P. and Lindgreen, A. (2014). Corporate social responsibility in global value chains: Where are we now and where are we going? *Journal of Business Ethics*, 123, 11–22.

Maak, T., Pless, N. M. and Voegtlin, C. (2016). Business statesman or shareholder advocate? CEO responsible leadership styles and the micro-foundation of political CSR. *Journal of Management Studies*, 53, 463–93.

Mäkinen, J and Kasanen, E (2016). Boundaries between business and politics: A study on the division of moral labor. *Journal of Business Ethics*, 134 (1), 103–16.

Mäkinen, J. and Kourula, A. (2014). Globalization, national politics and corporate social responsibility. In R. Tainio, S. Meriläinen, J. Mäkinen and M. Laihonen eds., *Limits to Globalization: National Borders Still Matter*. Copenhagen: Copenhagen Business School Press, pp. 219–35.

Matten, D. and Crane, A. (2005). Corporate citizenship: Toward an extended theoretical conceptualization. *Academy of Management review*, 30(1), 166–79.

Mayring, P. (2000). *Qualitative Inhaltsanalyse. Grundlagen und Techniken* (7th ed., first ed. 1983). Weinheim: Deutscher Studien Verlag.

Morgeson, F. P., Aguinis, H., Waldman, D. A. and Siegel, D. A. (2013). Extending corporate social responsibility research to the human resource management and organizational behavior domains: A look to the future. *Personnel Psychology*, 66, 805–24.

Nèron, P. Y. (2013). Toward a political theory of the business firm? A comment on 'Political CSR'. *Business Ethics Journal Review*, 1(3), 14–21.

Newman, A., Miao, Q., Hofman, P. S. and Zhu, C. J. (2016). The impact of socially responsible human resource management on employee's organizational citizenship behaviour: The mediation role of organizational identification. *International Journal of Human Resource Management*, 27, 440–55.

Nkrumah, K. (1973). *Revolutionary Path*. London: Panaf.

Nkrumah, K. (1965). *Neo-Colonialism: The Last Stage of Imperialism*. London: Thomas Nelson and Sons.

Orock, R. T. E. (2013). Less-told stories about corporate globalization: Transnational corporations and CSR as the politics of (ir)responsibility in Africa. *Dialect Anthropol*. 37, 27–50.

Porter, M. E. and Kramer, M. C. (2006). Strategy and society: The link between competitive advantage and corporate social responsibility. *Harvard Business Review*, 84, 78–92.

Rasche, A., Waddock, S. and Mcintosh, M. (2013). The United Nations Global Compact: Retrospect and prospect. *Business & Society*, 52, 6–30.

Rotter, J. P., Airike P.-E. and Mark-Herbert C. (2014). Exploring political corporate social responsibility in global supply chains. *Journal of Business Ethics*, 124, 581–99.

Scherer, A. G. (2018). Theory assessment and agenda setting in political CSR: A critical theory perspective. *International Journal of Management Reviews*, Vol. 2018, 1–24.

Scherer, A. G. and Palazzo, G. (2007). Toward a political conception of corporate responsibility: Business and society seen from a Habermasian perspective. *Academy of management review*, 32(4), 1096–120.

Scherer, A. G. and Palazzo, G. (2011). The new political role of business in a globalized world: A review of a new perspective on CSR and its implications for the firm, governance, and democracy. *Journal of Management Studies*, 48, 899–931.

Scherer, A. G., Palazzo, G. and Matten, D. (2014). The business firm as a political actor: A new theory of the firm for a globalized world. *Business & Society*, 53, 143–56.

SIA (Social Impact Assessment) (2014). *Social Impact Assessment of Benso Oil Palm Plantation Adum Banso Estate*. Accra: FISAMO Development Associates.

Smith, J. (2013). Corporate human rights obligation: Moral or political? *Business Ethics Journal Review*, 1 (2), 7–13.

Soundararajan and Brown (2014). Voluntary governance mechanisms in global supply chains: Beyond CSR to a stakeholder utility perspective. *Journal of Business Ethics*, 1–20.

TÜV Rheinland (2014). *RSPO Certification Assessment Report: Benso Oil Palm Plantation Limited (BOPP) Palm Oil Mill – Takoradi, Republic of Ghana, West Africa*. Indonesia: PT TUV Rheinland Indonesia.

Vertigans, S. (2011). CSR as corporate social responsibility or colonial structures return? A Nigerian case study. *International Journal of Sociology and Anthropology*, 3(6), 159–63.

Voegtlin, C. and Greenwood, M. (2016). Corporate social responsibility and human resource management: A systematic review and conceptual analysis. *Human Resource Management Review*, 26(3), 181–97.

Voegtlin, C. and Scherer, A. G. (2014). MNCs as political actors in a post-national world: challenges and implications for human resource management (January 2014). University of Zurich Chair of Foundations of Business Administration and Theories of the Firm, Working Paper No. 205. Available at http://ssrn.com/abstract=1972339 or http://dx.doi.org/ 10.2139/ssrn.1972339 accessed 19 March 2017.

Wiley, C. (2000). Ethical standards for human resource management professionals: A comparative analysis of five major codes. *Journal of Business Ethics*, 25, 93–114.

Wilmar (2016a). Consumer products available at www.wilmar-international.com/our-busi ness/og/consumer-products/countries/ghana/ accessed 5 May 2016.

Wilmar (2016b). Sustainability Available at www.wilmar-international.com/sustainability/ accessed 5 May 2016.

Wilmar (2016c) Certifications. Round Table on Sustainable Palm Oil available at www .wilmar-international.com/sustainability/progress/certifications/roundtable-on-sustainable-palm-oil/ accessed 5 May 2016.

Young, I. M. (2008). Responsibility and global justice: A social connection model. In Scherer, A. G. and Palazzo, G. eds., *Handbook of Research on Global Corporate Citizenship*. Cheltenham: Edward Elgar, pp. 137–65.

Young, I. M. (2011). *Responsible for Justice*. Oxford: Oxford University Press.

7

Navigating the CSR Discourse from a Developing Country's Perspective: a Shift to Human Capital Development?

Deborah B. Motilewa, Ebes Aziegbe-Esho and Franklin N. Ngwu

7.1 INTRODUCTION

Economic growth and productivity depend on people (Schultz, 1961). Consequently, adequate investment in human capital, notably in healthcare and education, are important and helpful in addressing the development problems of developing and emerging economies (DEE). The different theories of human capital have established positive correlation between human capital and economic growth (Ritter, 2016; Barney, 1991), entrepreneurial performance and competitive advantage (Wu, 2013) and lifetime income and poverty reduction (Anyanwu and Erhijakpor, 2009). Although various strategies of human capital investment have proven more effective than others (Ritter, 2016), the underlying suggestions all point to the efficacy of education and skill development at its core.

Given the positive impact that human capital improvements can make on the development challenges of developing and emerging economies, the question then is how these impacts can be effectively made through both public and private sectors interventions. Focusing on the private sector, these interventions are mainly done under the banner of corporate social responsibility (CSR) of firms. While CSR practices in DEE emanated from firms' responses to 'institutional void' – the lack or underdevelopment of key institutions – triggered by public governance failures, an emerging line of argument is that firms' CSR should be evocative (reflective) through building of human capital (skills) rather than a mere philanthropic gesture to assuage the society's demand.

In their early forms, CSR interventions were developed on the *'family virtue model'* characterized mainly by philanthropic actions relying on the managers' goodwill and ethical considerations (Lompo and Trani, 2013). Studies have shown that the outcome of CSR initiatives geared towards the provision of basic infrastructural amenities have been of limited benefit in terms of human development and capabilities (Lompo and Trani, 2013). This is because CSR has been widely adopted by major multinational corporations (MNCs) in response to the vitriolic accusations by civil society organisations from mainly developed economies regarding the environmental impact of their activities and poor treatment of the labour force in DEE (Jenkins, 2005). Consequently, these companies are increasingly being encouraged by United Nations agencies, international NGOs and other developing partners to participate in development initiatives of their host nations (Lompo and Trani, 2013; Idemudia, 2010).

The appealing aspect of the evocative demand on firms to be more impactful through their CSR activities is that the problems emanating from the institutional voids of developing and emerging markets are not selective in their impacts. The problems affect both the communities and the firms and as human capital development is a core necessity of firms, it is therefore also in their interest to develop the human capital potential of their host and wider communities. The aim of this chapter therefore is to examine and show that CSR interventions of firms through human capital development is not only appropriate but a necessity for both firms and society due to the wide derivable benefits. Using two cases – General Electric (GE) and Private Sector Alliance of Nigeria (PHN), the immense benefits of CSR intervention through human capital and how these benefits are felt across other sectors through their interconnectedness with human capital are properly demonstrated. The remaining sections of the chapter is structured as follows: while section two examines the human capital issues and challenges in developing and emerging economies, section three analyses the role of corporation as institutional actors. Using GE and PHN as case studies, section four provides detailed examples of how CSR interventions in human capital development leads to wide and interconnected benefits to both the firms and the society. Section five provides further discussion and conclusion.

7.2 HUMAN CAPITAL ISSUES AND CHALLENGES IN DEVELOPING AND EMERGING CONTEXTS

The human capital endowment of any nation is, no doubt, an important determinant of long-term economic growth and prosperity. This is even more so for DEE as human capital has both been theorized (e.g. Asefa and Huang, 1994; Danquah and Quattara, 2014; Mincer, 1984) and empirically shown (e.g. Jones 1996; Barro, 1991, 2001) to aid economic development. Human capital development is thus very germane to the development of any nation. It is no surprise that UNDP's Human Development Index (HDI) shifts attention to people, and inherently peoples' human capital, in recognition of the importance of people and their human capital. However, DEE are faced with numerous human capital issues and challenges, some of which are so enormous that substantial progress is almost impossible without complementary efforts of both the government and the private sector.

Consequently, and indeed unsurprisingly DEE, such as those in Africa, consistently rank lower than their developed counterparts on the World Economic Forum (WEF)'s Human Capital Index (HCI). For example, seventeen of the bottom twenty countries on the recent WEF HCI are African countries (HCI, 2017), a pattern that has been rather consistent in all previous annual reports of the Index. In the midst of the numerous human capital issues facing emerging countries, we identify four major ones that are of considerate importance because of their potential to directly affect peoples' level of knowledge and skills, and general application of their human capital. Moreover, many other human capital challenges in DEE contexts can almost successfully be subsumed under these four main issues.

First is the low enrolment rates in school generally, and specifically in science, technology, engineering and mathematics (STEM) subjects. Even more disheartening is the completion rate of those that somehow manage to get enrolled into primary, secondary and tertiary schools. In Africa, for example, more than 35 per cent of children have no access to secondary school education and about 30 million children do not attend school (ADB, 2018). According to the World Bank, enrolment rates into universities is a mere 7 per cent compared to a global average of 29 per cent. Indeed, extant research has also reported that Africa has the lowest enrolment rates in the world (Shuaibu and Oladayo, 2016). These low enrolment rates are even far worse for STEM subjects where only 30 per cent of students in tertiary education graduate in STEM courses (Annunziata and Kramer, 2015). Low enrolment rates is not a challenge faced by only developing economies of Africa. Emerging economies such as India also have low enrolment rates that have considerably hindered human capital levels (Rastogi and Gaikwad, 2017). Given that formal education is the primary measure of human capital, low enrolment rates invariably connotes low levels of human capital.

A second human capital issue in DEE contexts is poor healthcare and the resultant high correlation of low life expectancy rates at birth. A core component of human capital that is sometimes largely overlooked in the discourse on human capital is health. Becker (1993, 2002) identifies health as a primary measure of human capital. Good healthcare is fundamental to human capital development (Oster et al., 2013). At the very basic level, individuals cannot put their knowledge and skills to any use without having good health. Unfortunately, many DEEs still grapple with basic health challenges that have been largely overcome in the developed economies. Diseases such as malaria, HIV/AIDS and different sporadic viral outbreaks, are still common – affecting the potential workforce in these contexts. Relatedly, average life expectancy is lowest in developing and emerging contexts. The average life expectancy in Africa is only 60 years, compared to 71.4 years, the world average life expectancy (WHO, 2017). In addition, lack of health workers, due partly to brain drain, and general poor health infrastructure, all contribute to poor healthcare in developing and emerging economies.

Indeed it is difficult to talk about the challenges of emerging economies without a mention of poor infrastructure. Almost all facets of life and economy are beset with poor physical and organisational facilities, where available. Buildings, books and other education materials are almost non-existent in many developing economies.

Indeed, many schools have no physical or virtual libraries. In addition, curriculum for all three levels of education are rarely updated to meet international standards and national needs. Clearly, education infrastructure requires more funding. Paradoxically, available data reveals that while the world average for government expenditure on education as a percentage of total government expenditure is 14 per cent; that for sub-Saharan Africa, for example, is a little higher at 16 per cent (World Bank, 2018). Perhaps, emerging economies need to investigate specific areas of education expenditure to better improve education infrastructure.

Finally, enabling institutions that enhance human capital development are also lacking in developing and emerging contexts, a situation regarded as institutional voids (Khanna and Palepu, 1997; Mair and Marti, 2009). The formal rules of engagement that facilitate education and related activities aimed at building human capital are sometimes non-existent. Sometimes if they do exist, they are neither respected nor made to function as they should. Adequate formal and legal frameworks are missing. Consequently, large informal sectors emerge even within the education sector. Thus, lack of enabling institutions has a great effect on the quality, rather than the quantity of human capital.

Summarily, human capital challenges in emerging contexts are intricately complex as the many issues are interconnected. Consequently, on a cursory consideration, these challenges may appear enormous. However, the solutions also lie in the intricacy of the challenges as solving one challenge inadvertently leads to partly solving another. Thus this presents a clear opportunity to CSR professionals to contribute to the development of human capital using bold and clear CSR strategies.

7.3 THE ROLE OF CORPORATIONS AS INSTITUTIONAL ACTORS

Developing and emerging economies are usually characterized by formal institutional deficiencies where the regulatory, economic, social and political institutions of the society are unfavourable to business organisations and citizens generally. The business environment in Nigeria, for instance, although the largest economy in Africa is depicted by intensified insecurity, economic degradation, political risk and poverty, weak infrastructural facilities, poor governance, feeble public sector, incompetent private property protection, corruption, weak enforcement of agreements and high cost of doing business (Amaeshi, Adegbite, Ogbechi, Idemudia, Seny Kan, Issa and Anakwue, 2015).

Resulting from these ill-formed formal institutions, corporations operating in DEEs with little or no infrastructure available to effectively run their businesses are playing the role of informal institutional actors by performing CSR activities such as building roads and providing healthcare facilities for their staff, amongst other activities which ordinarily should be provided by the government. Within this framework, the definition of CSR becomes the continuing commitment by business to behave ethically and contribute to economic development while improving the quality of life of the workforce and their families as well as of the local community and society at large (World Business Council for Sustainable Development, 1999). In a study of corporate social responsibility across the globe, Idowu and Leal-Filho (2009) revealed that corporate entities in Africa mostly engage in CSR activities in areas such as healthcare, manpower development and capacity building, youth development schemes, staff welfare, provision of basic infrastructure, microcredit, business development and economic empowerment. Likewise, Eranda and Abeysekera (2011) showed that the CSR philosophy of most companies in Nigeria for example encompasses activities that consider social issues generally. This is generally due to the present state of decadence in several sectors of the Nigerian economy: the terrible road and rail system, the outdated state of the country's secondary and tertiary public institutions, the security situation in the country, especially around the North and the oil producing states, which constitute a global concern that appears to defy all solutions.

Similarly, De Oliveira (2006), Newell and Muro (2006) and Vivarta and Canela (2006) ascribe CSR in DEEs such as Mexico, Brazil and Argentina to be heavily shaped by socioeconomic and political conditions, such that environmental and social problems like deforestation, unemployment, inequality and crime are largely addressed by CSR practices, thereby creating a hope for positive change in the face of persistent poverty, environmental degradation, corruption and stagnation. Consequently, CSR in Africa, and other developing economies are inherent appearance of institutional works guided by a socio-cultural ethic. Thus, this aids the new concept of CSR in the DEEs contexts, as it enhances development and fills institutional gaps (Motilewa, Worlu, Agboola and Olokundun, 2016).

7.4 CASE STUDIES[1]

In this section, we present case studies of two different approaches to using CSR as a tool for human capital development. The first is General Electric (GE)'s strategic focus to improve the knowledge and skills of potential future workforce by investing in STEM education in Africa. The second case study is on Private Sector Health Alliance of Nigeria (PHN), an embodiment of how creative partnerships can be formed across firms in the corporate world and across governments in proffering solutions to human capital challenges.

7.4.1 *Developing Workforce through Investment in STEM Education: the Case of General Electric (GE)*

GE's focus on STEM education rests on a three-pronged strategy to strengthen Africa's education system, increase localization of talent, and build a pipeline of

[1] Materials for the case studies have been sourced from available public sources.

technological skills for the future. In a bid to improve STEM education in Africa, the company has chosen to make substantial investments in education in three African countries: Nigeria, Mozambique and South Africa.

In Nigeria, GE's investment in STEM education involves upgrading some facilities in technical colleges by providing mechanical and electrical engineering workshops so that students are able to practise theoretical knowledge gained in the classroom. Students are thus able to acquire hands-on technical skills. The engineering workshops are equipped with ultra-modern equipment. Lecturers in these technical colleges are also being trained on how to adequately deliver up-to-date knowledge to students. Similarly, in Mozambique, GE is collaborating with two universities to provide scholarships. Oil and gas equipment are also being supplied to the universities to enhance hands-on learning of STEM subjects. The curriculum of STEM courses is also being upgraded in these universities to meet international standards. As a commitment to the quality of these strategic human capital CSR initiatives in Mozambique, GE engages these universities to train its employees.

In 2009, GE formed a joint venture called GE South Africa Technologies (GESAT) with South Africa's Mineworkers Investment Company (MIC), a company that is 100 per cent owned by black South Africans. In a continental first, GESAT produces locomotives and has a 30 per cent local content input from South Africa. GESAT has successfully produced locomotives for South Africa's state-owned rail company, Transnet. Local content is provided by black-owned small and medium scale Enterprises (SMEs) that are continuously trained on innovation, technology, project management, general support skills and how to improve operational efficiency. In addition to creating over 5,000 jobs, GE's initiative in South Africa is helping to transfer knowledge and technology to locals, thus building capabilities and aiding in quality human capital development.

7.4.2 *Creative Partnerships: Private Sector Health Alliance of Nigeria (PHN)*

In a first of its kind, private sector health alliance of Nigeria (PHN) is a private-sector led coalition that seeks to advance health care in Nigeria. Unlike other CSR initiatives that are usually spearheaded by a single company, PHN is a multi-stakeholder platform put together by top corporate leaders in Nigeria. The stakeholders include founder and chairperson of the Dangote Group, Aliko Dangote; chairperson and founder of Zenith Bank Plc, Jim Ovia; and the former managing director of Access Bank Plc, Aigboje Aig-Imoukhuede. Others include a former minister of Health in Nigeria, Mohammed Ali Pate, and a former CEO at Stanbic IBTC Holdings, Sola David-Borha. PHN is also strongly supported by billionaire Bill Gates, and his wife, Melinda Gates, founders of The Bill and Melinda Gates Foundation. The goal of PHN is to help attain all health-related millennium development goals in Nigeria. Consequently, the three areas of focus are child mortality, maternal health, and HIV/AIDS and malaria.

PHN also operates via partnerships with education and health institutions. It currently has five such partnerships, which include Nigeria Healthcare Quality Initiative; the Healthcare Leadership Academy; Maternal, Neonatal and Child health; Africa Resource Centre for Supply Chain; and the Private Providers Network. These platforms serve as vehicles for various health programmes. For example, through the Healthcare Leadership Academy, PHN has partnered with top schools and universities such as Cambridge University, Duke University, the Lagos Business School and the Institute for Health Improvement Boston (IHI) to provide training to healthcare personnel. Senior executives and leaders in public health sector are offered fellowships in partner schools and universities to enable them build capabilities.

PHN strives to use technological innovation to solve healthcare challenges in its three main areas of focus – child mortality, maternal health, and HIV/AIDS and malaria. However, rather than using a strict CSR and philanthropic approach, it uses a business approach. PHN makes impact investments in healthcare innovations that have been successfully incubated in the Nigeria Health Innovation Marketplace (NHIM). An important aspect of NHIM is the hack-a-thons that seeks to find and fund innovative solutions to healthcare challenges in Nigeria and beyond. Successful products from the marketplace include Fyodor urine malaria test, a device that can detect malaria parasites in urine, and 'omomi', an application that helps expectant mothers to monitor their health and access healthcare personnel when needed.

The two case studies presented above may appear different. However, there is a common thread between the two. Both have involved developing human capital through creative partnerships. However, while GE has focused its partnerships directly along its supply value chain such as employees, potential employees and other equipment suppliers, PHN has created partnerships with other firms and institutions in different sectors. Thus, despite having no business, and consequently no value chain, PHN has been able to forge partnerships in its bid to develop healthcare and human capital.

7.5 DISCUSSION AND CONCLUSION

Some literature on CSR in DEEs focused on the investigation and analysis of 'what MNCs and other firms do' (Yin and Jamali, 2016) and 'why firms act' (Husted et al., 2016). With respect to the first question, proceeding from the failure of the government in developing economies to provide what is regarded as the core public goods, the MNCs started to assume enlarged responsibilities such as provision of education, public health, social security and ancillary issues in their globally expanded business environment. As apparent in many developing economies lacking government functions, these firms perform public governance functions both within and outside their communities of operation (Doh et al., 2015; Husted, 2015).

For the second part, there are managerial and institutional perspectives to CSR motivation (Jain et al., 2017 p. 702). While the firms' CSR practices can be influenced by the managerial perception of stakeholder responsibilities which may emanate from the climate and culture of the organisation, there are institutional pressures from communities, private sector and governmental bodies. Drawing from the two perspective, Jain (2017) reframed the Aupperle's (1984) Corporate Social Orientation (CSO) as a legitimacy-signalling posture where the CSO is determined from the managerial perception in the face of institutional pressures of coercion or mimetic nature. Fear of bad reputation forced many MNCs to adopt good human development practices. In the face of multiple internal and external stakeholder pressures, firms are more likely to respond to institutional factors that are strongly linked to their social legitimacy.

Despite the global appeal and theorizations of CSR, references to institutional necessities and local priorities are indicative of the need to contextualize or operationalize CSR discourse. The institutional logic links CSR operationalization to sustainable and socioeconomic development of developing economies (Jamali et al., 2017). This approach advocates for a distinction between CSR as a management tool and CSR as a development approach (Newel and Frynas, 2007).

Hence, CSR practices must be promoted in accordance with human development principles. The emergence of CSR as a human capital-centric agenda resulted from the increased globalization drive and the intensification of MNC's roles in the process. The renewed focus is a product of the shift in attention of development agencies such as the UN and World Bank from promoting economic growth to placing emphasis on structural issues such as poverty eradication, promoting access to essential services, enhancing equality of opportunities, social justice and empowering the most vulnerable in line with the SDG.

To date, the overall impact of development projects implemented by MNCs' through CSR initiatives on human development of local population remains limited (Lompo and Trani, 2013; Idemudia, 2010). These companies are not genuinely motivated to promote human development concerns but rather the pursuit of their capitalistic goals. Rather, only a more effective action, with sufficient financial resources, that is based on authentic participation and genuine involvement of the communities geared towards development of a complete person through education, and skill development, might change the current trend where the most vulnerable are not even reached by the 'development' interventions. This will ensure a win-win situation for all parties concerned as demonstrated by the two cases – GE and PHN.

Through the interventions and collaborations pursued by GE across three African countries – Mozambique, Nigeria and South Africa, one of the major problems (human capital deficit) of GE and the three economies, is being addressed. Interestingly, the impact does not stop with improved human capital for both GE and the economies, there are other wider socioeconomic benefits.

Not only will unemployment reduce, social inclusiveness will increase with reduced inequality. Expectedly with the improved skills of the beneficiaries some of which will work with GE and some outside GE, the general productivity of GE and other firms that will recruit the beneficiaries and the economies will improve. As GE is mainly focused in the provision of infrastructure which is at the core of DEEs' development challenge, the improved productivity of GE will expectedly lead to higher infrastructural provision across these economies. Moreover, as infrastructure can be argued to be a kind of fulcrum for the rapid socioeconomic development of economies, the provision of higher infrastructure by GE will ultimately result into wider and sustainable development of the intervened economies. The interesting aspect of these multi-faceted benefits is that all the positive outcomes can be traced to GE's intervention in one societal problem – human capital deficit.

The wide benefits derivable from GE's intervention is also applicable in PHN involvement in the health sector. As the productivity of every economy is highly related to the state of the health sector, the impacts of PHN's health sector intervention cannot be overemphasized. Even though the focus is on four key areas – child mortality, maternal health, and HIV/AIDS and malaria, the positive impacts can be described as holistic as they go beyond the health sector affecting almost every sector of the economy. Moreover, focusing on four core areas which Nigeria cannot be said to have done or doing well, the intervention goes to the core of the health and wider socioeconomic challenges of Nigeria. Expectedly, effective training and upskilling of health professionals in Nigeria will ultimately lead to better, wider and cheaper service delivery especially reduction in child mortality, improved maternal health and early detection and cure of prevalent diseases such as HIV/AIDS and malaria. With the interconnectedness of the health sector and other sectors of the economy, it means that this singular intervention principally in the human capital of the health sector will lead to improved socioeconomic development of Nigeria and other DEEs that experience such human capital interventions as done by both PHN and GE.

REFERENCES

African Development Bank [ADB] (2018). Human Development, Report by Africa Development Bank. Available at www.afdb.org/en/documents/document/tracking-africas-progress-in-figures-47710 accessed 23 July 2019.

Amaeshi, K., Adegbite, E. and Rajwani, T. (2014). Corporate social responsibility in challenging and non-enabling institutional contexts: Do institutional voids matter? *Journal of Business Ethics*. http://doi:10.1007/s10551-014-2420-4.

Amaeshi, K., Adegbite, E., Ogbechie, C., Idemudia, U., Seny Kan, K. A., Issa, M. and Anakwue, O. (2015). Corporate social responsibility in SMEs: A shift from philanthropy to institutional works? *Journal of Business Ethics*. doi:10.1007/s10551-015-2633-1.

Amaeshi, K., Osuji, O. and Nnodim, P. (2008). Corporate social responsibility in supply chains of global brands: A boundary less responsibility? Clarifications, exceptions and implications. *Journal of business Ethics*, 81(1), 223–4.

Annunziata, M. and Kramer, S. (2015). Building strong workforces to power Africa's growth: The future of work in Africa. Available at http://files.publicaffairs.geblogs.com/ideas-lab/files/pdfs/building-strong-workforces-to-power-africas-growth.pdf accessed 21 July 2019.

Asefa, S. and Hunag, W. (1994). Introduction. In S. Asefa and W.-C. Huang, eds., *Human Capital and Economic Development*. Kalamazoo, MI: UpJohn Institute for Employment Research, pp. 1–10. http://doi:10.17848/9780880995689.ch1.

Anyanwu, J. C. and Erhijakpor, A. E. O. (2009). Health expenditures and health outcomes in Africa. *African Development Review*, 21(2), 400–433.

Barney, J. B. (1991). Firm resources and sustained competitive advantage. *Journal of Management*, 17(1), 99–129.

Barro, R. J. (1991). Economic growth in a cross-section of countries. *Quarterly Journal of Economics*, 106(2), 407–43.

Barro, R. J. (2001). Human capital and growth. *American Economic Review*, 91(2), 12–17.

Becker, G. S. (1993). Nobel Lecture: The economic way of looking at behavior. *Journal of Political Economy*, 101(3), 385–409.

Becker, G. S. (2002). The age of human capital. In E. P. Lazear, ed., *Education in the Twenty-First Century*. Palo Alto, California: Hoover Institution Press, pp. 3–8.

Danquah, M. and Quattara, B. (2014). Productivity growth, human capital and distance frontier in Sub-Saharan Africa. *Journal of Economic Development*, 39(4), 27–48.

De Oliveira, J. A. P. (2006). Corporate citizenship in Latin America: New challenges to business. *Journal of corporate citizenship*, 21(Spring), 17–20.

Doh, J. P., Littell, B. and Quigley, N. (2015). CSR and sustainability in emerging markets: Societal, institutional, and organizational influences. *Organizational Dynamics*, 44(2). Doi:10.1016/j.orgdyn.2015.02.005.

Eranda, N. B. A. and Abeysekera, N. (2015). Strategic corporate social responsibility through redefining the firm's value chain. *International Journal of Business and Social Research*, 5 (6), 23–32.

HCI. (2017). The global human capital report. *World Economic Forum*.

Husted, B. W. (2015). Corporate Social Responsibility practice from 1800 - 1914: Past initiatives and current debates. *Business Ethics Quarterly*, 25(1), 1–17.

Husted, B. W., Montiel, I. and Christmann, P. (2016). Effects of local legitimacy on certification decisions to global and national CSR standards by multinational subsidiaries and domestic firms. *Journal of International Business Studies*, 47(3), 382–397.

Idemudia, U. (2010). Rethinking the role of corporate social responsibility in the Nigerian oil conflict: The limits of CSR. *International Development*, 22(7), 833–845.

Idowu, S. O. and Leal Filho, W. (2009). *Global Practices of Corporate Social Responsibility*. Berlin Heidelberg: Springer-Verlag.

Jenkins, R. (2005). Globalization, corporate social responsibility and poverty. *International Affairs*, 81(3), 525–540.

Jones, C. I. (1996). *Human Capital, Ideas, and Economic Growth*. California: Stanford University.

Khanna, T. and Palepu, K. G. (1997). Why focused strategies may be wrong for emerging markets. *Harvard Business Review*, 75, 41–51.

Lompo, K. M. and Trani, J. (2013). Does corporate social responsibility contribute to human development in developing countries? Evidence from Nigeria. *Journal of Human Development and Capabilities*, 14(2), 241–265.

Mincer, J. (1984). Human capital and economic growth. *Economics of Education Review*, 3(3), 195–205.

Motilewa, B. D., Rowland, E. K., Agboola, G. M. and Olokundun, A. M. (2016). An Analysis of Institutional Environments on Corporate Social Responsibility Practices in Nigerian Renewable Energy Firms. World Academy of Science, Engineering and Technology. *International Journal of Social, Behavioral, Educational, Economic, Business and Industrial Engineering*, 10(8), 2410–16.

Newell, P. and Muro A. (2006). Corporate social and environmental responsibility in Argentina. *Journal of Corporate Citizenship* 2006(24), 49–68.

Oster, E., Shoulson, I. and Dorsey, E. R. (2013). Limited life expectancy, human capital and health investments. *American Economic Review*, 103(5). http://doi: 10.1257/aer.103.5.1977

Rastogi, C. and Gaikwad, S. M. (2017). A study on determinants of human capital development in BRICS Nations. *FIIB Business Review*, 6(3), 38–50.

Ritter, B. (2016). Human Capital Development in Developing Countries, International Centre for Global Leadership, available at www.icglconferences.com/articles/human-capital-development-in-developing-countries/ accessed 23 July 2019.

Schultz, T. W. (1961). Investment in human capital. *The American Economic Review*, 51(1), 1–17.

Shuaibu, M. and Oladayo, P. T. (2016). Determinants of human capital development in Africa: A panel data analysis. *Oeconomia Copernicana*, 7(4), 523–49. http://doi:10.12775/OeC.2016.030.

Vivarta, V. and Canela, G. (2006). Corporate social responsibility in Brazil: The role of the press as watchdog. *Journal of Corporate Citizenship*, 21(Spring), 39–50.

WHO (2017). World Health Statistics: Monitoring Health for the SDGs. Available at http://apps.who.int/iris/bitstream/10665/255336/1/9789241565486-eng.pdf?ua=1 accessed 21 July 2019.

World Bank. (2018). School Enrollment Data. https://data.worldbank.org/indicator/SE.PRM.ENRR

World Business Council for Sustainable Development (2002). The Business Case for Sustainable Development: Making a Difference Towards the Johannesburg Summit 2002 and Beyond.

Wu, J. (2013). The antecedents of corporate social and environmental irresponsibility. *Corporate Social Responsibility and Environmental Management*, 21(5), 286–300.

Yin, J. and Jamali, D. (2016). Strategic corporate social responsibility of Multinational companies subsidiaries in emerging markets: Evidence from China. *Long Range Planning*, 49(5), 541–558.

PART II

CSR and Sustainable Development Cross-Country Studies

8

Firm Ownership and Corporate Social Responsibility in China: from a Multiple Stakeholder Perspective

Ting Ren, Yan Feng, Youzhi Xiao, Hongyan Yang and Wenli Liu

8.1 INTRODUCTION

The initial serious consideration of CSR arises with the concern around quality issues of food, manufacturing products and of environmental problems in general. How firms maintain their relationship with the customers and local communities becomes not just an image management issue, but rather the strategic choices related to CSR have extended value that determine a business organisation's long-term survival and development.

As was reported in the 2013 *Bluebook on Corporate Social Responsibility of Chinese Firms*, published annually by Chinese Academy of Social Sciences with a focus on the highest performing firms since 2009, Chinese firms are still in quite an early stage of incorporating CSR as an operational target and creating CSR value in the real sense. Among the investigated state-owned, privately owned and foreign-invested firms, state-owned enterprises (SOEs) have the highest CSR scores, especially, central government–affiliated firms, followed by foreign-invested firms (FOEs). Privately owned firms (POEs) seem to care the least for CSR. From the analysis of the six-year trend, for all three types of firms, they are paying more and more attention to their societal stakeholders. In this study, we investigate the influence of the company's ownership on its attainment and practices of CSR. In a broad CSR definition context, our rationale is that different stakeholders may pursue their own interests depending on the different ownership type of a company, which leads to different firm choices and performance.

Scholars have studied CSR from the perspective of stakeholders because of a basic consensus: enterprises bear certain responsibilities and obligations to stakeholders who are essential for the survival and development of the firm (Freeman, 1984; Clarkson, 1995). By establishing a trust relationship with its stakeholders, a firm will greatly reduce the operational costs and improve its performance (Barney and Hansen, 1994; Hill, 1995; Jones, 1995; Wicks, Berman and Jones, 1999). On the other hand, the interests of the corporate stakeholders are broad and diverse, and failure to resolve this divergence may endanger the sustainability of a firm (Freeman,

1984; Harrison and St John, 1994; Clarkson, 1995). Due to the scarcity of resources, it is impossible to meet the desire of all stakeholders; hence, a balance between different stakeholders' interests is called for (Barney, 1991; Mahoney and Pandian, 1992; Amit and Schoemaker, 1993). Companies with different ownership structures are subject to different internal and external conditions, which may lead to different bias towards different stakeholders (Anderson, 1982; Webster, 1993).

More recently, the impact of the ownership structure on CSR has started to draw scholarly attention (Donaldson and Preston, 1995; Thompson and Driver, 2002; Aguilera and Jackson, 2003; Aguilera and Cuervo-Cazurra, 2004; Grandori, 2004). Several previous studies attempted to investigate CSR within Chinese firms in the context of the substantiality of CSR reporting and CSR initiatives (Lin, 2010; Marquis and Qian, 2014). Given the distinct complexity of institutional structure of China and the large number of state-owned firms, this research questioned whether Chinese firms just symbolically use CSR as window dressing or the firms are genuinely interested in their societal stakeholders' benefits. In this chapter, we take the perspective of multiple stakeholder orientation and attempt to identify evidence of different level of attention a firm pays to CSR that varies with the ownership structure of the firms. Indirectly our results also serve as evidence of firms' practice of incorporating CSR into their corporate governance.

This chapter provides a distinct look at a firm's decision related to its prioritization of different stakeholder orientation and associated interests based on different ownership types. For the firm of different ownerships that we investigate, namely, SOEs, POEs and FOEs, we identify five key stakeholders and evaluate the stakeholder orientation with financial and operational indicators. We then use a hierarchical regression model to analyse 1,580 listed firms on the Chinese market and discuss the impact of ownership on the five stakeholder orientations. We further correlate firms' decisions regarding stakeholder interests to the context of a possible trade-off scenario and obtain confirmatory results that firms do choose differently between two potentially conflicting interests, implied by different stakeholder orientations. Our findings suggest that, among the three types of firms, POEs are more likely to attend to societal orientation, FOEs are more likely to attend to investor orientation, consumer orientation and environmental orientation. A weak difference is detected in employee orientations across different types of firms. In a context of potential conflicting interest, our results suggest that different types of ownership leads to different choices in trading off different stakeholder interests, with FOEs trading off between employee and social interests, SOEs trading off customer interests with social interests, and all firms trading off customer interests with environment interests.

In what follows we will discuss some basic theory on CSR and stakeholders and provide previous literatures that relate stakeholder interests to CSR, upon which we establish our hypotheses. Empirical model analysis and results are presented following the theoretical discussions. Then we discuss the findings and conclude.

8.2 THEORETICAL FRAMEWORK AND LITERATURE BACKGROUND

8.2.1 *CSR in Context*

The general concept of CSR incorporates the idea that firms take action according to society goals and values; or, in other words, firms should bear more responsibilities beyond economic and legal obligations (Bowen, 1953; McGuire, 1963; Davis and Blomstrom, 1975).

As the theory about corporations and stakeholders develops with the dramatic change of macro environment in which the firms operate, the CSR concept is more involving, covering multiple angles of corporate responsibilities. For example, Epstein (1987) argued that CSR is about having a positive impact on all stakeholders of a firm, reflecting the 'citizenship' of firms, and as a citizen of a society, the core standard of good corporate citizenship is the involvement in the community (Epstein, 1989). In his 'corporate performance three-dimension conceptual model', Carroll (1998) divided CSR into four aspects: economic responsibility, legal responsibility, ethnic responsibility and charitable responsibility. Beyond the relations between corporations and employees or communities, Carroll (1998) pointed out that the corporate citizenship was also the corporate responsiveness to all key stakeholders.

8.2.2 *Key Stakeholder Identification*

As was first defined by the Stanford Research Institute in 1963, stakeholders are any groups that include multiple internal and external parties upon which the success of an organisation depends (Freeman and Reed, 1983). The definition of key stakeholders varies and is generally defined by their relationship with the firms (Freeman, 1984; Cornell and Shapiro, 1987; Alkhafaji, 1989; Thompson et al., 1991; Carroll, 1993; Starik, 1994; Donaldson and Preston, 1995). According to Freeman (1984), Clarkson (1995), and Donaldson and Preston (1995), stakeholders are any groups or anyone who can affect the organisation or are affected by the organisation. In a broad stakeholder map described by Freeman (1984), key stakeholders include at least shareholders, employees, customers, competitors, unions and suppliers. Likewise, Greenley and Foxall (1997) argued that key stakeholders should include customers, competitors, employee relations, unions and shareholders.

Thompson, Wartick and Smith (1991) argued that stakeholders are the people or groups who have relations with firms. Alkhafaji (1989) believed that stakeholders are the groups for whom firms should be responsible. Berman et al. (1999) suggested that there are five stakeholder areas: employees, the natural environment, the diversity of a work place, customers, product safety and community relations. Agle, Mitchell and Sonnenfeld (1999) proposed that key stakeholders should include shareholders, employees, customers, the government and communities. The broadly used Kinder,

Lydenberg and Domini (KLD) Social Rating Database evaluates CSR from nine dimensions, in which there are five dimensions used by scholars: communities, women and minorities, employee relations, the natural environment, and the quality of product and service (Graves and Waddock, 1994; Turban and Greening, 1997).

In order to clarify the scope of the stakeholder concept, scholars have provided various classifications (Turker, 2008; Charkham, 1995; Wheeler and Sillanpaa, 1997; Wherther and Chandler, 2005; Jensen and Meckling, 1976). There are several useful classifications such as primary and secondary stakeholders (Freeman, 1984; Clarkson, 1995), contracting and public stakeholders (Charkham, 1995), and internal, external and societal stakeholders (Wherther and Chandler, 2005). Wheeler and Sillanpaa (1997) suggested four dimensions in CSR including primary social, secondary social, primary non-social and secondary non-social stakeholders. The primary social stakeholders are the parties influenced directly by the firm strategic choices and the secondary social stakeholders are the ones influenced less directly including civil society, business at large and various interest groups. The primary non-social and secondary non-social stakeholders are also classified by direct and indirect influence including the natural environment, non-human species, future generations and their defenders in pressure groups. This classification of CSR broadens the understanding of the concept of CSR by considering the non-social stakeholders, and increases the recognition of these stakeholders in the business community (Turker, 2008). Another more direct CSR classification is proposed by Carroll (1991), classifying CSR by different stakeholders including owners (investors), customers, employees, community, competitors, suppliers, social activist groups, public at large and others. This classification provides a more direct method to identify the CSR.

In general, broader stakeholders are more difficult to define and quantify; therefore, some scholars have proposed a narrower spectrum of stakeholders. Cornell and Shapiro (1987) defined the key stakeholders all potential claimants for firms (investors and non-investors). Carroll (1993) argued that key stakeholders are the groups or people who interact with firms and enjoy the right or the interest in the firms. The narrow stakeholder concept in general highlights the economic interests of stakeholders.

As Clarkson et al. (1994) pointed out, the narrower concept only includes the stakeholders directly involved with company business outcomes, but the broader concept also covers potential stakeholders, making it possible for firms to balance their relations with key stakeholders. Since firms have an interrelated connection with various parties from the consumers to the suppliers to the overall society, key stakeholders beyond investors play an important role in linking the corporate strategy to the corporate financial performance (Williamson, 1975; Jensen and Meckling, 1976; Cornell and Shapiro, 1987). Given the literature and our intended measurement for CSR realization, we adopt a broad definition of CSR and identify five key stakeholders: investors, employees, customers and the society and environment. For each stakeholder we proxy-measured the relevant activities of CSR.

After defining the stakeholders, in order to study the CSR it is necessary to measure CSR for different stakeholders. Therefore, how to measure CSR for different stakeholders is a topic of growing academic and management interest (Maon et al., 2010). Carroll (2000) argued that it is important to measure the CSR and the real matter is to develop valid and reliable measures. Recently, some attempts have been made to measure CSR both in academic and business communities including reputation indices or databases, forced-choice survey instruments, single-issue and multiple-issue indicators, content analysis of corporate publications, scales measuring CSR at the individual level, and scales measuring CSR at the organisational level. However some experts (Waddock and Graves, 1997) pointed out that finding a proper way to do so is a task of great difficulty. Across the research, reputation indices and databases are widely used methods. The Kinder, Lydenberg, and Domini (KLD) Database, the Fortune Index and the Canadian Social Investment Database (CSID) are most widely used to measure the CSR. These kinds of database provide an index which can evaluate the CSR in different dimensions such as community, diversity, employee relations, environment, international operations, product and business practices, and corporate governance (Mahoney and Thorne, 2005). But it is a pity that there is no data relating to Chinese companies in the database available.

Using single-issue and multiple-issue indicators is also a popular method. The commonly used indicators include the pollution control performance (e.g., Bragdon and Marlin, 1972; Chen and Metcalf, 1984; Freedman and Jaggi, 1982) and corporate crime (Baucus and Baucus, 1997; Davidson and Worrell, 1990) and so on. This method has a significant limitation in that the indicators are always uni-dimensional (Maignan and Ferrell, 2000) and are always reported by countries and regions; when there is no information reported for firms, the research cannot study the differences between companies. In recent years, content analysis is increasingly being used and a growing body of literature uses this method to measure the CSR. Content analysis is based on corporate social reporting and the information about CSR becomes more and more accessible. The method has an 'objective rating of companies since once the social attributes are selected, the process of rating is standardized' (Ruf, Mende-Christie and Brown, 2004). However the companies may prefer to provide some more favourable images to mislead the readers and different countries may have different disclosing standards, hence the corporate social reporting may not be an accurate resource, for example poor performers provided longer environmental disclosures (Ingram and Frazier, 1980).

In conclusion, in the context of our research we adopt a broader and more combined perspective of CSR, in the sense that we regard firms' activities in the context of economic contributions and internal and external communities all as relevant representations of the realization of firm CSR, including investors, employees, customers, the society and the environment. After choosing the dimensions, it is necessary to select the proper methods to measure the CSR in every dimension. In this chapter, based on the concept of CSR towards different stake-holders, we choose different financial indices from the firm's financial statement, which is readily available, to measure the CSR.

8.2.3 Multiple Stakeholder Orientation

The interests of different stakeholders vary widely. With limited resources, firms are unlikely to be able to address and satisfy all the stakeholders. The attempt to perfectly balance the interests for all can negatively impact a firm's overall performance (Barney, 1991; Mahoney and Pandian, 1992; Amit and Schoemaker, 1993; Greenley and Foxall, 1997). In this light, a firm will always place more weight and attention on certain stakeholder groups. The findings about firms' orders of priority vary across different literatures. Anderson (1982) and Webster (1992) considered consumers the most important stakeholders. Posner and Schmidt (1984) proposed that employees and consumers be considered the most important group. The relative attention that firms pay to their stakeholders can be defined as firms' orientation to each stakeholder (Greenley and Foxall, 1997). To identify a firm's prioritized orientation and use this priority indicator to argue for our measurement of firms' CSR-related aspects, we rely on the literatures dealing with stakeholder orientation and firm performance.

It was concluded in a significant amount of research that firm performance is associated with the firm's orientation to multiple stakeholders, in the sense that higher performance may be strongly associated with firms' ability to focus on certain orientations (McGuire, Sundgren and Schneeweis, 1988; Webster, 1993; Clarkson, 1995; Donaldson and Preston, 1995; Greenley and Foxall, 1997). Previous studies identified two different types of CSR activities, i.e., institutional CSR and technical CSR, and argued that different CSR activities essentially were targeted at different stakeholders, which may contribute differently to the outcomes of firm operations in terms of firm financial performance and firm risk (e.g., Brammer and Millington, 2008; Godfrey, Merrill and Hansen, 2009; Chang, Kim and Li, 2014).

Following this line of reasoning, it is reasonable for our study to conceptualize the different orientations with different focus activities that target different stakeholders that we identified. Given the proposed association between CSR activities, orientations and targeted stakeholders, the measurement of different activities that are highly associated with certain stakeholder groups may serve as indicators of the underlining orientation priority preferences.

8.2.4 Institutional Theory and CSR

Institutional theory indicates that the firm's behaviour is governed by its institutional environment, including the organisation's social context, the scope of activities and the network of social relationships (Doshi and Khokle, 2012). For example, peer pressure may force the firms to comply with the social norms and behave according to other firms' practices; the broader a firm's activities extend, the more intricate connections it will face and this potentially changes the parameters of decisionmaking. CSR is also found to be institutionally contingent and the forms and standards adopted are different across institutional contexts (Habisch et al, 2005; Aguilera et al, 2007; Kostova, Roth and Dacin, 2008). For example, MNCs may apply different strategies in their home country and the host country. The business norms across different institutional settings can vary and influence the choices of CSR.

In the extant literature, scholars tend to be more concerned about the relationship between institutional environment and business practices. There are three major forces through which institutional factors bring conformity in business practices: the coercive force (e.g. local government or the industrial association requirements), the mimetic force (e.g. competitors' adoption of certain standards or strategies) and the normative force (e.g. the suppliers/customers' adoption of certain standards or government promotion of certain standards) (DiMaggio and Powell, 2000). The coercive force brings business practices in line with societal expectations. The mimetic force drives firms to take certain actions under peer pressure. The normative force drives firms to take certain actions according to common beliefs. In other words, institutional forces will influence the agents' behaviour by aligning their beliefs with societal norms, internal norms and external norms. Besides that, more and more literature begins to analyse the heterogeneity and practice variation occurring in a pluralistic institutional environment (Kraatz et al., 2008). CSR is a kind of business practice which will be affected by different institutional environments.

Three major institutional models further elaborate the aforementioned forces, including the institutional entrepreneurship model (DiMaggio, 1988; Maguire, Hardy and Lawrence, 2004), the institutional work model (Clegg et al., 2006), and the institutional logic model (Friedland and Alford, 1991). The institutional entrepreneurship model emphasizes the change and the mobilization of institutions. In this model, the administrator of an institution is of great importance. Therefore, this model mainly focuses on how administrators strategize, mobilize and coordinate tangible and intangible resources for institutional change (Meek, Pacheco and York, 2010). The institutional work model indicates a broad category of actions aiming to create, maintain or disrupt institutions (Clegg et al., 2006). This model explains how individuals' activities affect institutions (Lawrence, Suddaby and Leca, 2009), such as employees, investors and more. The institutional logic model is always used to explain how society-level factors influence the individual preferences and organisational interests; such societal level factors include capitalism, the bureaucratic state, democracy and nuclear family (Friedland and Alford, 1991). Formally speaking, the institutional logic model is defined as socially constructed factors including historical patterns of material practices, assumptions, values and beliefs (Thornton and Ocasio, 1999). There are two important conclusions in this model: (1) society as an inter-institutional and multilevel institutional system and (2) interests, assumptions and practices as embedded within prevailing institutional logics (Thornton and Ocasio, 2008).

To further apply all these theories and models to firm-level CSR phenomena, two main models of CSR can be deduced: the explicit versus implicit model, and the liberal market versus coordinated market model. The explicit versus implicit model focuses on performing CSR in the context of social issues or corporate issues. The liberal market model emphasizes social issues related to the moral and physical characteristics of the communities, while the coordinated market model emphasizes a relatively narrow range of social issues such as health and safety at the workplace.

In the multiple stakeholder perspective, the explicit versus implicit model or the liberal market versus coordinated market model will divide stakeholders into two contexts: the social context and the organisational context. The social context includes the environment, charity and consumers, while the organisational context includes employees and investors. Multiple stakeholder theory indicates that different stakeholders can exert different influences on CSR orientation in two ways: withholding strategy and usage strategy (Freeman, 1999). Specifically, the stakeholders can affect the flow of the particular resources to the firms and can affect the way the firms use the resources.

Hence, integrating institutional theories and models with multiple-stakeholder orientated CSR models, the institutional environment and the structure of the stakeholders are diversified across institutions, which will make institutions render different incentives to implement CSR orientation for different stakeholders. Therefore, there are institutional rationales to study CSR from firm ownership and multiple-stakeholder perspective.

8.2.5 Firm Ownership and CSR

Ownership plays an important role in corporate governance, since ownership determines the control rights and influences the financial performance and the realization of shareholders' goals (Yan and Gray, 1994). At the same time, ownership also determines the principal-agent relationship between owners and managers and affects the effectiveness and efficiency of the corporate governance, which may or may not impact the operating performance. Firms with different ownership types have different goals. Ownership types determine the practices of firm operation, and dominant shareholders tend to steer the operation to benefit themselves (Jensen and Meckling, 1976; Claessens et al., 2002). Since CSR activities are associated with stakeholder targeting for a firm, it will reasonably be (significantly) influenced by the ownership of a firm. There are so far limited literatures talking about the impact of ownership types on a firm's CSR activities. One reason is because in most of the international markets, ownership type tends to be relatively homogeneous, therefore many studies focus on the ownership concentration. For example, Lopez-Iturriaga and Lopez-de-Foronda (2009) argued that the largest shareholding ratio will affect the firm's performance in terms of CSR activities and CSR funds will decrease with the increase in the proportion of the largest dominant shareholder. Thus, in order to protect the interests of other stakeholders, many firms will fragment their ownership.

Chinese firms' ownership types can be broadly distinguished as state-owned or non-state-owned, with the second type divided into foreign invested and privately-owned firms (Deng and Dart, 1999; Peng and Luo, 2000; Tang and Tang, 2003; Tse et al., 2003). Given the diversity of ownership type, the impact of firm types is more interesting and worth exploring in the Chinese context. There are a few studies on the relationship between ownership and CSR activities for Chinese firms. For example, Deng and Dart (1999) found that the priority on market orientation of state-owned firms is lower than that of privately owned firms, which may be because state-owned firms have a governmental affiliation, so they have both economic goals and distinct political goals. Apparently, the three different types of firms attend to different stakeholder orientation with different priority preferences.

The reasons why different types of Chinese firms behave differently regarding stakeholder orientation may be due to their different characteristics. State-owned firms may have economic goals and political goals, and the managers in the state-owned are appointed by the government, so they do not have incentives to pursue better performance, whereas foreign-invested firms have more advanced governance structure and care about the financial performance and customer relations (Peng and Luo, 2000; Li and Zhang, 2007; Marquis and Qian, 2014). Privately owned firms face a competitive market with less and possibly more restricted access to capital resources and they are also more likely to have less advanced governance structure than foreign investor-owned firm, which lead them to focus intensively on customers and competitors (Peng and Luo, 2000; Li and Zhang, 2007).

8.3 HYPOTHESES DEVELOPMENT

8.3.1 *Impact of Ownership Type on Stakeholder Orientations*

As was discussed previously, firms have many internal and external stakeholders, such as the investors, employees, customers, suppliers and more. Dealing with the relations with various stakeholders is critical. Firms should ideally implement CSR activities and coordinate the relations between various stakeholders. However, due to the scarcity of resources, firms cannot meet all the requirements from stakeholders. Donaldson and Preston (1995) argued that not all the requirements of stakeholders are rational; firms have to balance the interest between stakeholders. For the listed firms, different ownership structure determines the influence and the bargaining power of shareholders, and then affects the operation performance and the realization of shareholders' goals. The largest shareholders can use their power to influence the firm operation and pursue their interests, and maybe at the expense of other stakeholders. Similarly, firms with different owner-ship types are driven by different internal and external conditions such as the tax benefit packages, responsibilities towards the investors, the potential financing constraints etc., so they will have different actions and a different stakeholder orientation priority. Specifically, firms with different ownership types are usually more closely monitored by different stakeholders, for example, state-owned firms report to the government and are expected to benefit the broader society, and other types of firms establish their legitimacy and pursue values through taking care of internal stakeholders such as shareholders and employees (Hong, 2004; Ma and Parish, 2006).

The weight that each firm puts on different stakeholders varies, and the specific importance of and orientation to stakeholders rely on stakeholders' power, legiti-macy and urgency (Donaldson and Preston, 1995; Mitchell, Agle and Wood, 1997; Peng and Luo, 2000; Harvey and Schaefer, 2001). Given the varieties and the distinct features of Chinese firms closely associated with the firm type, we expect the orientation to multiple stakeholders to vary according to their ownership type, which will be reflected through different CSR activities priority. Overall a large part of Chinese economy is under state control, the institutional environment impacts firms in different ways. Management structures and paradigms may vary across firms; social harmony is emphasized for firm practices regardless of the firm type. Based on the broader definition of stakeholders, we identify five key stake-holders for Chinese firms: investors, employees, customers, the society and the environment, which essentially correspond to the previously identified fields of firm CSR aspects (Epstein, 1989; Carroll, 1998).

In China, SOEs are controlled by the government, which naturally leads to their focus on economic goals and political goals. The governmental affiliation serves as a double-edged sword. On the one hand, because of the abundant and easy access to capital sources and the state-owned status, these firms are believed to enjoy more policy benefits and privileges, which may come from the industrial monopoly status, credit concessions, supplies of key resources, state purchasing orders and more (Luo and Tan, 1998; Peng and Luo, 2000; Faccio, Masulis and McConnell, 2006; Buckley et al., 2007; Li and Zhang, 2007; Nguyen, Le and Bryant, 2013). On the other hand, SOEs' business practices are also limited by some elements of state policy because of their state affiliation. Additionally, the managers of SOEs are usually appointed by the government whose evaluation is not entirely based on the business performance, so they have relatively fewer incentives to pursue profits (Deng and Dart, 1999; Peng and Luo, 2000).

FOEs are set up according to the Chinese laws and are invested by Chinese investors and foreigners (joint ventures), or solely by foreigners. In order to attract foreign investors, the government will generally provide tax incentives. Additionally, most of the FOEs (especially MNCs) are believed to have better governance structures and governance quality (Estrin and Perotin, 1991; Wang and Coffey, 1992; Coffey and Wang, 1998).

POEs play an increasingly important role in the development of the Chinese economy. They in general do not have tax incentives (except for rare cases of a particular product or industry) and the governance structure is believed to be less advanced than FOEs. POEs also are believed to be relatively more influenced by general government policies. Research has found that POEs exchange societal CSR (e. g. donations) for better political connections and are also benefiting more (in terms of market performance) from their CSR activities (Hong, 2004; Ma and Parish, 2006; Wang and Qian, 2011, Marquis and Qian, 2014). From these discussions, we may deduce that the main characteristics of POEs are customer oriented and profit oriented.

Based on the characteristics of the different type of firms, we therefore submit our first main hypothesis about the impact of ownership type on the stakeholder orientation:

Hypothesis 1 (H1): Different ownership types have different impact on stakeholder orientations.

On the basis of the above argument, we further elaborate the potential difference in CSR orientation across ownership types as follows:

For investor orientation, state-owned firms can use their ownership to pursue political goals which may harm their investors (Shleifer and Vishny, 1994; Frye and Shleifer, 1997). Consequently, the higher the proportion of state-owned capital, the more negative the impact on investor orientation will be, whereas the higher the proportion of foreign investor-owned capital, the more positive the impact on investor orientation will be. For POEs, they face a competitive market with less capital and less competitive corporate governance, their profitability does not lead to bigger margin for their investors, relatively speaking, and they are also constrained with having to attend to customers for profit (Deng and Dart, 1999). In this sense, they will have to give the investor relatively prioritized consideration with a certain level of concern for customers, and we predict that they follow FOEs in terms of investor CSR orientation. For employee orientation, scholars have found that the higher the level of state-owned capital, the more negative the impact on employee orientation; the higher the level of foreign investor-owned capital, the more positive the impact on employees. Hence FOEs placed more priority on employee interests than SOEs (Yan and Gray, 1994). POEs face a competitive market; they may try to reduce labour costs to survive. It is commonly known that SOEs have better benefits for their employees than POEs in China (except for perhaps a very small number of private giants), so for the employee orientation, SOEs out-run POEs.

Some researchers have proposed that customers are the most important stakeholder group (Posner and Schmidt, 1984). We expected that ownership type will influence the firm customer orientation. Specifically, for POEs, they are often small in size and have to try their best to satisfy customers to maintain their market share.

For SOEs, profit is not necessarily the ultimate goal; they can utilize their ownership to pursue political goals (Shleifer and Vishny, 1994; Frye and Shleifer, 1997). Customers are also not their top priority. It is expected that the attention to the customer orientation for POEs is stronger than SOEs (Deng and Dart, 1999).

In respect of the society orientation, all the firms know that a contribution to society can help build their brand and win trust. SOEs can use their ownership to pursue political goals, and contribution to society is considered one of the political goals, therefore we expect SOEs to emphasize societal interests more than the other two types (Tan, 2002). There is traditionally an emotional link between POEs and the Chinese society, and the private owners of the firms consider the legitimacy of their businesses based on the ideology of kinship, which points to inherent social responsibility from their private businesses, so the owners of POEs are willing to contribute to society (Lin, 2010). We predict that POEs put considerable priority on society orientation, although maybe less so compared to SOEs that bear the pre-determined social responsibility due to their nature.

For the environment orientation, the government makes sustainable development part of the national strategy, and so as an agent for the government participating in business, SOEs are expected to fully conform to the standards set by the government. And if the companies cause pollution, they will face a degree of punishment by the authorities. In recent years, a lot of issues related to pollution have arisen in China, which have posed an adverse influence on people's health. Therefore, a growing number of people have started to pay more attention to the environment. Some researchers have proven that being environmentally friendly may help companies build a good reputation and win trust from the public (Kolk, 2016). Therefore more and more companies pay more attention to the environment. SOEs are controlled by governments and they are always supervised by governments; hence, they have to conform to the regulation of the law of environment, and especially some SOEs that tend to incur pollution are supervised closely and urged to pay extensive attention to their potential pollution problems. Besides that, FOEs, since most of them are big companies investing in China, tend to adopt more up-to-date technologies and represent more advanced production and management skills (the initial purpose of welcoming foreign investors is exactly due to these comparative advantages). They also tend to follow their home country's protocol of environmental regulations, and all of these reasons make them in general more environmentally friendly.

To summarize, in a relative context, we expect that SOEs should care the most about how they perform for social targets, but the least about what benefits their direct customers and business investors, whereas FOEs care the most about their internal stakeholders (employees and investor) and environment, and the least about the external overall environment (society). POEs are expected to care the most about their customers which are the lifeline of the firms, and the least about their employees. We list the expected results in Table 8.1:

TABLE 8.1 *Summary for hypothesis 1*

Stakeholder Orientation	Hypothesis
CSRI	FOE > POE > SOE
CSRE	FOE > SOE > POE
CSRC	POE > FOE > SOE
CSRS	SOE > POE > FOE
CSREN	FOE > SOE > POE

8.3.2 *Stakeholder Orientation Priority: Trade-Off Selection*

Hypothesis 1 interrogates firms' priority in relation to the five key stakeholder groups' interests. In order to verify the existence of different weightings put on different stakeholder interests for different ownership types, we wish to prove that the priority sequences do indeed exist, using firm choice preference in the situation where the firms have to trade-off between different stakeholders' interests.

We separate our overall samples into three sub-samples by ownership type for this test: POEs, FOEs and SOEs. We test for firm choices of stakeholder orientation priority in the context of potential conflicting interest; that is, we check the result of firm choices between managing, for example, outputs for the environment and outputs for customers, or between any other pair of (potentially conflicting) stakeholder interests. Presumably, a negative correlation between stakeholder interests indicates a trade-off since it indicates that when firms prioritize the interest of one stakeholder they may have to sacrifice the interest of another stakeholder, whereas a positive correlation indicates no conflicting priority order. Most importantly, we compare the results among the three different types of firms in terms of their choices regarding CSR versus other stakeholder interests.

In general, if we assume that the outputs a firm contributes towards the environment orientation will also benefit the society as a whole because of the environment's inherent social responsibility (Tan, 2002; Lin, 2010), it is then reasonable to expect that environment and the social orientation will not be considered a pair of trade-off relationships for any type of firm. This expectation is also indicated by the consistent priority sequence that every type of firms attribute to the social orientation and environment orientation. For the trade-off relationship between the environment and social orientations, we propose that:

Hypothesis 2 (H2): Regardless of ownership type, a firm treats environment orientation and the societal orientation as a consistent pair of interests.

However, among other stakeholder interests, there might still exist trade-off relationships. As was discussed in the previous section, POEs face severe competition and are expected to pay special attention to profits and customer relations (Deng and Dart, 1999). Therefore, when facing possible trade-off choices between these stakeholder interests, a POE will be likely to choose customer interests over other stakeholder orientations. However, a POE may also consider contributing to the society (especially in the form of donations) a gesture of goodwill that will promote the reputation of the firm among the customers, which, in return, benefits their expected profitability (Hong, 2004; Brammer Millington and Pavelin, 2006; Campbell and Slack, 2006; Ma and Parish, 2006; Lin, 2010; Wang and Qian, 2011; Marquis and Qian, 2014). Consequently, even though a privately owned firm may treat customer orientation as its top priority, when it comes to consider customer orientation and social orientation, the trade-off conflict is not necessarily significant, therefore we hypothesize:

Hypothesis 3 (H3): POEs will trade off the environment orientation, the investor orientation and the employee orientation for the customer orientation.

Hypothesis 4 (H4): For POEs, the customer orientation and the societal orientation are not always a conflicting choice.

For SOEs, we expect them to specifically prioritize government and social orientations over other interests. We know that environmental protection is written into many government regulations and environmental protection is also set by government objectives. Therefore, it is reasonable to treat environmental orientation as consistent with the government orientations. And it is reasonable to assume that they may choose to trade off other stakeholder orientations for their environmental orientation and social orientations when facing potential conflict (Shleifer and Vishny, 1994; Tan, 2002; Lin, 2010). Therefore, we posit that:

Hypothesis 5 (H5): SOEs will trade off the customer orientation, the investor orientation and the employee orientation for environment and societal orientations.

As for FOEs, we expect them to care the most about their internal stakeholders and the least about the regulatory body and the external overall environment (Yan and Gray, 1994). We propose that:

Hypothesis 6 (H6): FOEs will trade off the customer, the societal and the environment orientations for either the investor orientation or the employee orientation.

8.4 SAMPLE, VARIABLES AND DESCRIPTIVE STATISTICS

8.4.1 Sample

Samples are from CSMAR and the Genius Finance Database and all firms are listed in the Shanghai and Shenzhen stock market from 2011 to 2016. We exclude firms with abnormal financial performance in consecutive years. In order to get an accurate estimation, we winsorize the extreme values by the highest 5 per cent and

TABLE 8.2 *Sample industry distribution*

Industry	Samples	Rate (per cent)
Agriculture, forestry, livestock production and fishing	25	1.58
Extraction	47	2.97
Manufacturing	907	57.41
Electricity, heat, gas and water production and supply	72	4.56
Constructing	46	2.91
Wholesale and retail trade	113	7.15
Transportation, warehousing and logistics	54	3.42
Accommodation and catering industry	10	0.63
IT	74	4.68
Finance	45	2.85
Real estate	101	6.39
Renting	20	1.27
Scientific research and technical service	4	0.25
Management of water conservation, environment and public facilities	16	1.01
Education	4	0.25
Health and social work	5	0.32
Culture, sports and entertainment	17	1.08
Miscellaneous	20	1.27
Total	1580	

Note: Samples are from CSMAR and the Genius Finance Database

the lowest 5 per cent. The final sample includes 9,353 observations representing 1,580 firms. Theses samples are distributed in 13 industries based on the SFC industry classification.[1] Table 8.2 shows the industry distribution; manufacturing firms accounts for a large proportion of our sample firms.

8.4.2 *Variables*

8.4.2.1 Dependent Variables: the Responsibility of Firms to Key Stakeholders and Financial Indicators

Normally, a firm's CSR activity/performance is measured using indicators issued by official organisations or an index composed by the researcher. However, as pointed out by Carroll (1998) and Brammer, Jackson and Matten (2012), CSR should be considered in a broader field of economic governance, since the social responsibility of a firm is closely related to the institutional framework of the business and therefore is embedded in a broader field of institutions. In the sense that firm orientation to different stakeholders is reflected through and associated with the firms' performance, CSR activities may be grossly captured by economic activities relevant to different stakeholders (McGuire, Sundgren and Schneeweis, 1988; Anderson, 1982; Webster, 1992; Webster, 1993; Clarkson, 1995; Donaldson and Preston, 1995; Greenley and Foxall, 1997). For example, institutional CSR activities targeting secondary stakeholders (such as activities related to community involvement, environmental consideration and more) may bring a benefit and act as a cushion to protect firms whereas the technical CSR activities targeting the primary stakeholders (such as activities related to corporate governance, employee relationships, etc.) do not necessarily render such benefit. A knowing firm may intentionally cater the CSR practices towards certain stakeholders and thus the economic activities relevant to different stakeholders may serve as the indication of corresponding CSR activities (for instance, increasing philanthropic donations, paying out greater dividends and more). Also based on the grounds of quantifiability and data availability, we adopt accounting indicators to proxy the 'CSR activities' and use the 'CSR activities to operating income ratio' to measure the five key stakeholder orientations. Recent literature has suggested that accounting information reflects diverse stakeholder interests, although the information is subject to proper interpretation (Andon, Baxter and Chua, 2015). An approach comparable to the present study has also been used to measure the stakeholder orientation of social enterprises and non-profit organisations by adopting the Social Return on Investment indicator (Hall, Millo and Barman, 2015).

Investor Orientation (CSRI). 'Investors' generally refers to the natural or legal persons who invest in firms and expect gains for the investment, they are mainly shareholders and creditors. The broader spectrum of investors includes shareholders, creditors and stakeholders; and the narrow concept for investors refers only to shareholders. In this chapter, we have considered shareholders and creditors as investors. Investors care the most about the gains and profits, therefore the CSR expenses (financial resources that are allocated towards CSR purposes regarding investor stakeholders) for the investor orientation include profits or gains, such as dividends, interests etc. Our proxy CSR activities for the investor orientation are the dividend, the profit distribution and the interest paid to investors.

$$\text{Investor orientation} = \frac{\text{Dividend, profit distribution and interests}}{\text{Operating income}}$$

Employee Orientation (CSRE). Employees are the major foundation of a firm's operation. As firms enjoy the labour and contribution of their employees, in return they should be responsible for their employees. The main responsibility towards employees is to provide a solid career platform and development opportunities, occupational safety, competitive wages and good benefits, among other things. CSR activities for employees thus could include: wages, fringe benefits, and other costs of manpower, materials and financial resources for staff development, such as investment in training. Our proxy CSR activities for the employee orientation are mainly the wages paid to and fringe benefits paid for employees, as they are more consistent across firms and are better explicitly disclosed, and they represent the major part of benefits from their employment, therefore:

$$\text{Employee orientation} = \frac{\text{Benefits paid for employee}}{\text{Operating income}}$$

Customer Orientation (CSRC). Customers are the basic driver for the firms to achieve their strategic objectives. In order to get recognition from customers, firms should safeguard the interests of customers, and from time to time they may want to provide products and services that are beyond customer expectations. The CSR activities for customers are broadly speaking as follows: R&D costs, costs for direct services and costs for after-sales services. Our proxy CSR activities for the customer orientation are mainly the expense that firms pay for R&D, productions and services. Together, these expenses are the operating costs, therefore the indicator for customer orientation is business cost ratio.

$$\text{Business cost ratio} = \frac{\text{Operating cost}}{\text{Operating income}}$$

Additionally, since the higher the sales growth rate is, the more stable the customer relationship is, we also use the sales growth rate in the past three years to evaluate the firm's customer orientation:

$$\text{Sales growth in past 3 years} = \sqrt[3]{\frac{\text{Operating income this year}}{\text{Operating income in 3 years ago}}} - 1$$

To simplify the analysis, we calculate the customer orientation using an equal-weighted combined indicator with these two ratios; therefore:

$$\text{Customer orientation} = 1/2 \text{ business cost ratio} + 1/2 \text{ Sales growth in past 3 years}$$

Society Orientation (CSRS). Firms set up their business on the foundation of the infrastructure, market security and good social order, all of which are provided to the firms as the external environment. But firms also contribute back to the society, which is considered the basic responsibility of firms. The main ways that firms can contribute to society are through the following channels: providing more job opportunities, reducing the harm to the environment, and rationally using resources. Another direct way that firm contributes to the society is through donations (Zhang, Rezaee and Zhu, 2009). The society orientation essentially measures whether and how much firms are willing to contribute to the society. We define the society orientation as the ratio of the donations in the current operating year to the operating income. A higher ratio indicates a higher priority in society orientation.

$$\text{Society orientation} = \frac{\text{Donations this year}}{\text{Operating income}}$$

Environment Orientation (CRSEN). In the financial statement of companies, some companies disclose the operating fee paid for the environmental protection and the pollutant drainage fee. Some research has treated this information as the measure for CSR directed towards the environment (Schaltegger, 2002). The pollutant drainage fee, used to eliminate the influence of the environment, is a penalty for the companies who cause the environmental pollution. The fee will be used for environmental protection or pollution control projects. The purpose of collecting this fee is to encourage polluters to raise their resource management efficiency, prevention and control of pollution and improve the environment. Therefore, research has used this variable to identify the environmental-protecting efficiency of companies (Stanwick and Stanwick, 1998; Konar, 2001; Zhang, 2010). The payment of the environmental protection and pollutant drainage fee also represents the amount of the pollution emission. The higher fee means that the companies cause more pollution. Conversely, the lower ratio of environmental protection and pollutant drainage fee means a higher priority in environment orientation.

$$\text{Environment orientation} = \frac{\text{Environmental protecting fee or pollutant drainage fee}}{\text{Operating income}}$$

All orientation indicators have a positive relationship with orientation priority, which suggests that the higher the ratio, the higher priority a firm puts on a certain orientation. For the environment orientation, it is negatively correlated with the CSR for environment.

8.4.2.2 Independent Variables

The independent variables for our research are the ownership type (represented by the type of the largest dominant shareholder): state-owned firms (SOE), foreign-invested firms (FOE) and privately owned firms (POE).

8.4.2.3 Control Variables

Based on the previous literature, we control for a series of factors that may influence the firm choice of CSR activities. Firm size matters in terms of prioritizing performance indices: small or mid-size firms need to respond to customers more effectively, to pay more attention to shareholders, to keep good relations with employees and suppliers, and to respond to competitors more quickly, so that the stakeholder orientation for small or mid-size firms will be higher than large firms (Deng and Dart, 1999). In different periods of a firm's lifecycle, firms will focus on different aspects of development/strategy; for example, the firms in a period of growth will pay more attention to profit to survive in the market, therefore, firm age is an important factor (Peng and Luo, 2000). Industry category will also affect the stakeholder orientation, for example the stakeholder orientation in manufacturing industry is higher than that in the service industry (Kaynak and Kara, 2004). In China, there are many cities with different economic development levels and business cultures, it is thus reasonable to assume that the firms in different regions may pay attention to different stakeholder orientation and to different extents. Therefore, in our model we include five control variables: firm size (SIZE), in the logarithm form of the value of assets; firm age (AGE); industries (IND), a set of dichotomous variables denoting 13 industries; regions (REGION), a set of dichotomous variables; and a set of dichotomous variables of years (YR).

8.4.2.4 Descriptive Statistics

Table 8.3 is a description of our sample. Overall, the data indicates a relatively large difference between different orientations.

The descriptive statistics in Table 8.4 show a rough picture of the stakeholder orientations for different ownership types. Indeed, we can identify that there are apparent differences between different ownership types.

8.4.3 *Pearson Correlation and Analysis of Variance*

Table 8.5 shows the result of Pearson correlation analysis using the Sidak test to adjust for the significance. The result shows that the correlations of state-owned firms and privately owned firms is relatively large; that is because SOE, POE and FOE are exclusive dummy variables, in order to avoid multi-collinearity, SOE is then used as the baseline variable. Table 8.6 shows the result of analysis of variance and the Scheffe test, which indicate that most of the mean comparison is significant. The results are partially inconsistent with our expectations based on hypotheses; however, major results are all consistent. Given that this test is preliminary and

TABLE 8.3 *Descriptive statistics for stakeholder orientation and firm size*

Variables	Mean	S. D.	Min	Max
CSRI	0.054	0.070	0.000	1.406
CSRE	0.093	0.066	0.002	0.724
CSRC	0.534	0.202	-0.145	3.956
CSRS	0.001	0.001	0.000	0.033
CSREN	0.066	0.061	-0.130	0.583
SIZE	3.577	1.242	0.531	9.838

TABLE 8.4 *The measurement of stakeholder orientation for different ownership types*

Ownership	Item	CSRI	CSRE	CSRC	CSRS	CSREN
SOE	Mean	0.0409	0.269	0.0332	3.83E-08	0.00504
	S.D.	0.114	0.92	0.043	1.34E-07	0.0112
	Min	0.000	0.000394	0.000	0.000	5.29E-05
	Max	0.483	4.229	0.227	6.95E-07	0.0472
POE	Mean	0.0412	0.319	0.0515	7.43E-08	0.00663
	S.D.	0.116	0.991	0.0621	1.81E-07	0.0117
	Min	0.000	0.000394	0.000	0.000	5.29E-05
	Max	0.483	4.229	0.227	6.95E-07	0.0472
FOE	Mean	0.0522	0.11	0.0603	4.42E-08	0.00395
	S.D.	0.125	0.51	0.0649	1.28E-07	0.00348
	Min	0.000	0.000394	0.000	0.000	7.06E-05
	Max	0.483	4.01	0.227	6.95E-07	0.012
Total	Mean	0.0414	0.306	0.0484	6.37E-08	0.00625
	S.D.	0.116	0.97	0.0596	1.69E-07	0.0116
	Min	0.000	0.000394	0.000	0.000	5.29E-05
	Max	0.483	4.229	0.227	6.95E-07	0.0472

important factors such as the firm size and the industry category are not considered, we will further explore more statistically accurate results in the following section.

8.5 MODELS AND REGRESSION RESULTS

8.5.1 Impact of Ownership Type

We use the OLS model and revise the heteroskedasticity with the method of White (1980) to test the impact of ownership types on stakeholder orientations. Multi-collinearity and model bias have been tested and ruled out. Table 8.7 summarizes the regression results for all the firms.

From the table, we find that the ownership impacts the CSR. The results show that the majority of our hypotheses for firms of different types of ownership are supported by the empirical results. Compared with the SOE companies, the POE companies and the FOE companies have shown preferred priority to internal investors, society and their consumers. As for the employees and environment, compared with the SOE companies, the FOE companies show preferred priority to the employees and environment, while the POE companies show lower priorities.

TABLE 8.5 *Pearson correlations*

	CSRI	CSRE	CSRC	CSRS	CSREN	SIZE	AGE	SOE	POE	FOE
CSRI	1									
CSRE	0.147***	1								
CSRC	−0.004***	0.006	1							
CSRS	0.929***	−0.004	−0.001	1						
CSREN	0.997***	0.953***	−0.001	0.002***	1					
SIZE	0.01	0.006	0.009	0.001	−0.021	1				
AGE	0.021**	0.046**	−0.001	0.028	−0.02	0.31***	1			
SOE	0.003	−0.004	−0.011	−0.018	−0.12	0.201***	0.056***	1		
POE	0.005	0.001	−0.012	0.019	0.013	−0.16***	−0.041***	−0.918***	1	
FOE	−0.004	−0.009	−0.004	−0.004	−0.003	−0.078***	−0.30***	−0.078***	−0.323***	1

Note: N = 9353; p < 0.1, ** p < 0.05, *** p < 0.01, two-tailed tests.

TABLE 8.6 *One factor analysis of variance and Scheffe test*[1]

Stakeholder orientation	Mean				Scheffe test[1] (p value)			Sequential comparison
	Total	SOE	FOE	POE	FOE vs. SOE	POE vs. SOE	POE vs. FOE	
CSRI	0.0414	0.0409	0.0522	0.0412	0.024	0	0	FOE > POE > SOE
CSRE	0.306	0.269	0.11	0.319	0.012	0.009	0	POE > SOE > FOE
CSRC	0.0484	0.0332	0.0603	0.0515	0.8	0	0.014	FOE > POE > SOE
CSRS	6.37E-08	3.83E-08	4.42E-08	7.43E-08	0.334	0.011	0.97	POE > FOE > SOE
CSREN	0.00625	0.00504	0.00395	0.00663	0.008	0.024	0	POE > SOE > FOE

Note: 1. Scheffe multiple comparison test: compare the mean of variables, two-tailed tests. 2. '>' Indicates that the mean is larger.

TABLE 8.7 *Impact of ownership type on stakeholder orientations*

	(1) CSRI	(2) CSRE	(3) CSRC	(4) CSRS	(5) CSREN
POE	0.00790**	0.0697	0.0116***	4.03e-08***	0.00156*
	(0.00296)	(0.0591)	(0.00128)	(6.08E-09)	(0.000719)
FOE	0.0148*	−0.122	0.0191***	2.40e-08	−0.00456*
	(0.00775)	(0.0931)	(0.00407)	(−2.14E-08)	(0.00233)
SIZE	0.00553***	−0.0574***	−0.00323***	7.75e-09***	−0.00135***
	(0.00122)	(0.0166)	(0.000454)	(2.177E-09)	(0.000285)
AGE	0.0430***	0.439***	−0.0162***	−2.10e-08*	0.00601***
	(0.00296)	(0.0584)	(0.00164)	(9.42E-09)	(0.000936)
INDUSTRY	CONTROL	CONTROL	CONTROL	CONTROL	CONTROL
YEAR	CONTROL	CONTROL	CONTROL	CONTROL	CONTROL
REGION	CONTROL	CONTROL	CONTROL	CONTROL	CONTROL
F-test	112.33	187.21	118.73	162.24	153.32
N	8795	1996	8795	2851	1394

Note: $^*p < 0.1$, $^{**}p < 0.05$, $^{***}p < 0.01$, two-tailed tests; robust standard error; robust standard errors are in the parentheses.

What is more, compared with the POE companies, the FOE companies have shown to attach lower priorities towards societal interests, however, the FOE companies have paid more attention to their consumers and environment. We also use the hypothesis test to determine whether the coefficients of the FOE and POE are significantly different and the results are shown in the table. According to the results, we can know the coefficients before the POE and FOE are significantly different except for the CSR for employee (CSRE).

Tables 8.8 and 8.9 more clearly represent our results. In terms of investor interests measured by the dividend and interests to their operating income, FOEs take first place, which is consistent with our hypothesis. The results also reflect that the FOEs have a more mature dividend policy and pay more attention to their investors. Also for consumers' interests measured by the sales expense to their operating income, FOEs take first place again and the POEs take second place, which is partially consistent with our hypothesis. Also, firm size and firm age both have a negative influence on the CSRC, which means the smaller and younger companies may favour their consumers.

For employee orientation, the result is not significant for FOEs and POEs. We use benefit for employees over operating income as the measure of employee orientation, and the results are not significant. But when we use the wage over operating

TABLE 8.8 *Sequence of stakeholder orientation for different ownership types*

Ownership	CSRI	CSRE	CSRC	CSRS	CSREN
SOE	3	2	3	3	2
FOE	1	3	1	2	1
POE	2	1	2	1	3

Note: Figures indicate the sequence of priority.

TABLE 8.9 *Summary results for hypothesis 1*

H1	Stakeholder orientation	Hypothesis	Regression result	Hypothesis supported?
1a	CSRI	FOE > POE > SOE	FOE > POE > SOE	Yes
1b	CSRE	FOE > SOE > POE	FOE > SOE > POE	Yes
1c	CSRC	POE > FOE > SOE	FOE > POE > SOE	Partially
1d	CSRS	SOE > POE > FOE	POE > FOE > SOE	Partially
1e	CSREN	FOE > SOE > POE	FOE > SOE > POE	Yes

Note: '>' indicates that the stakeholder orientation is larger than that behind, two-tailed tests.

income, we find that FOEs are placed highest and POEs lowest, which is consistent with our hypothesis. When we calculate the average of the benefit to the firms, we find that the difference among the SOEs, FOEs and POEs is not significant. Only a small portion of firms announce benefit expenses in the financial statement. The majority of companies put wage and benefits together. We calculated the correlation between wage and benefits and found a significantly positive correlation. Therefore, we suggest using cash paid to employees as a proper proxy to measure the employee orientation.

In terms of societal interests measured by the firm donation proportion to their operating income, privately owned firms surprisingly take first place again, and again inconsistent with our hypothesis. To find a possible explanation, we calculated the sample average donations for different ownership types and the results show that the mean annual donation per SOEs of our research period is 1,712,773 RMB, higher than POEs' 992,020 RMB and FOEs' 787,444 RMB.

As is indicated by the average donation magnitude, even among firms with different ownership types, the donations vary to a large extent, and we actually find the expected sequence of our hypothesis. Combining this set of numbers with our regression results which control for the firm size and other firm characteristics, we can conclude that state-owned firms are indeed major social donators in terms of the absolute magnitude of donations.

However, when taking into account the 'capability' factors such as the firm size, the firm age and so on, POEs seem to have done a better job in contributing towards the societal interests, compared to the other two types of firms. For example, the adjusted 'willingness' of donating seems to put POEs in the spotlight. Zhang, Rezaee and Zhu (2009) identified quite similar patterns for state-owned and privately owned firms. In their study of firm response to the Sichuan earthquake, the finding was that SOEs are less likely to respond to natural disasters compared with POEs, everything else being equal.

As for the environment orientation measured by environment-protecting expenses in relation to income, POEs take last place and the FOEs take first place which is consistent with our hypothesis. Besides that, firm size has a negative impact on CSREN and firm age has a positive impact on CSREN, which means the smaller firms and older firms will cause more pollution. We can know from this result that bigger firms have scaling economy which means they can utilize their resources much more efficiently. Also the younger companies will likely use more advanced technology which is more environmentally friendly. Some papers have shown that the size and pollution have a negative relation in the United States and our paper also reaches the same conclusion (Grant, Bergesen and Jones, 2002).

8.5.2 Trade-Off Test

Next we moved to test the trade-off effects. Table 8.10 summarizes the results for our test on possible trade-off relationships between different stakeholder orientations. A negative sign is an indication of potential trade-off relationship, and we find all our hypotheses supported by the results, with the exception of the result for H2: the sign is correct but is of no statistical significance.

As we can see from Table 8.10, the societal orientation and environment orientation are two consistent interests for all type of firms. This is evidenced by the significantly positive coefficient of the CSREN/CSRS pair.

The POEs give customer interests the highest priority among all tested stakeholder interests and would be willing to trade off other stakeholder interests to achieve better results in terms of customer orientation. The negative sign of the coefficients for the relevant pairs of stakeholder orientations indicate the trading-off pattern, and for CSRC/CSRI, CSRC/CSRE and CSREN/CSRC, the test is significant.

SOEs exhibit priority towards environment interests, the significant negative coefficients are the indication of the preferred choice of them facing potential conflicts of interest. As for societal orientation, the results do not show the conflicting interest between societal interests and other interests, rather the results show the consistency between societal interests and other interests. The reason may be that

TABLE 8.10 *Results for trade-off test*

	CSREN	CSREN	CSREN	CSREN	CSRI	CSRI	CSRI	CSRE	CSRE	CSRC
SIZE	−0.0006* (0.00034)	−0.00005 (0.00038)	−0.00096** (0.000417)	−0.0011*** (0.000441)	0.0089*** (0.00158)	0.0168*** (0.0022)	0.0884*** (0.0255)	0.0019 (0.00179)	−0.00091 (0.00184)	−0.0054*** (0.000969)
AGE	0.0057*** (0.0015)	0.005545*** (0.00163)	0.00648*** (0.00182)	0.00231* (0.012)	0.0039 (0.00696)	0.0227** (0.0085)	0.017 (0.0129)	0.027*** (0.00631)	0.0305*** (0.0084)	−0.011** (0.00368)
SOE CSRI	0.816*** (0.0076)									
CSRE		0.117*** (0.0124)			0.904*** (0.0579)					
CSRC			−0.0779*** (0.0181)			−0.063* (0.0364)		0.017 (0.071)		
CSRS				0.654 (0.104)			3.936*** (0.539)		2.91*** (0.393)	2.35* (1.367)
N	311	311	311	139	1567	1666	1567	1568	742	742
	CSREN	CSREN	CSREN	CSREN	CSRI	CSRI	CSRI	CSRE	CSRE	CSRC
SIZE	0.002** (0.00078)	0.0017** (0.00069)	0.00221** (0.00095)	−0.0036 (0.0102)	0.0187* (0.00974)	0.018* (0.0099)	−0.0203 (0.0257)	−0.0002 (0.005)	0.0143 (0.0196)	0.0105*** (0.00031)
AGE	−0.0013 (0.00036)	−0.0007 (0.003)	−0.00059 (0.00421)	0.021 (0.0382)	0.834*** (0.0162)	0.097*** (0.0196)	0.146** (0.056)	0.0606*** (0.0147)	0.869** (0.0343)	−0.039*** (0.0094)
FOE CSRI	0.0373** (0.01759)									

	CSREN	CSREN	CSREN	CSREN	CSRI	CSRI	CSRI	CSRE	CSRE	CSRC
CSRE		0.0186** (0.0834)			0.531*** (0.1463)					
CSRC			−0.0182* (0.00929)			−0.194 (0.124)		0.179 (0.111)		
CSRS				0.217 (0.3145)			−1.28* (0.757)		−1.64* (0.845)	5.703 (2.11)
N	14	231	231	47	231	231	47	231	47	47
SIZE	−0.0012*** (0.00028)	−0.00011 (0.00031)	−0.00104*** (0.00034)	−0.0017 (0.00065)	0.0063*** (0.00123)	0.0052*** (0.00148)	0.0056* (0.00248)	−0.00498*** (0.00101)	−0.0026 (0.00182)	−0.00934 (0.00117)
AGE	0.00335*** (0.00079)	0.00216** (0.00085)	0.0059*** (0.001)	0.004 (0.0022)	0.285*** (0.00258)	0.061*** (0.00323)	0.0627*** (0.00793)	0.489*** (0.0026)	0.526*** (0.00569)	−0.016*** (0.0037)
POE										
CSRI	0.742*** (0.0048)									
CSRE		0.848*** (0.00663)			0.7431*** (0.027)					
CSRC			−0.00246* (0.00124)			−0.15*** (0.024)		−0.059*** (0.0191)		
CSRS				0.221*** (0.526)			1.77*** (0.2258)		15.71*** (1.84)	−7.353 (7.003)
N	1069	1069	1069	334	6938	6938	1944	6876	1,944	1944

Note: * p < 0.1, ** p < 0.05, *** p < 0.01, two-tailed tests; we also controlled for IND, REGION and YR in all the regressions; robust standard errors are in the parentheses.

the SOEs undertake a great deal of responsibilities including for society, investors (the government) and for consumers, therefore these interests show consistency. This might also be an indication of the broader consideration of 'customers' due to the firms' state affiliation. For the environment state-owned firms have to conform to the regulations and laws and they have a responsibility to reduce pollution, therefore they have to trade off other interests for environmental orientation, and the negative sign before the CSREN and CSRC shows the trade-off between the environment and consumers.

The results for FOEs are consistent with our hypotheses also. We can draw conclusions according to the sign before the CSRI/CSRE, CSRI/CSRC, CSRI/CSRS, CSRE/CSRS and CSRE/CSRC. However, due to the relative smaller sample size, the results serve as a reference and should be interpreted and generalized with caution.

8.6 DISCUSSIONS AND CONCLUSION

We study the ownership impact on stakeholder orientations and verify the existence of trade-off among multiple stakeholder interests. Our findings provide evidence that ownership type will influence firms' priority setting on stakeholder orientations, reflected by both the performance result and choice preferences. Testing the stakeholder orientations in a trade-off context, we also find evidence supporting our hypotheses about different priority setting based on the type of ownership, these trade-off choices are consistent with our expectation of firm indicators that are related to different stakeholder orientations. All of our results confirm that firms do not try to balance all stakeholder interests but attach different levels of importance to different stakeholders. The findings are consistent with the majority of the previous literatures (McGuire, Sundgren and Schneeweis, 1988; Webster, 1993; Clarkson, 1995; Donaldson and Preston, 1995; Greenley and Foxall 1997). With the consideration of firm ownership, the observed CSR activities (measured by different attributes of financial activities and performance) are significantly associated with firm features denoted by their ownership types.

In terms of the investor orientation, the first priority choice sequence is FOEs, POEs and SOEs. These results are quite relevant to the governance structure of different type of firms (Deng and Dart, 1999; Peng and Luo, 2000; Tang and Tang, 2003). Investors intend to pursue profits. The governance structure for FOEs and POEs are better aligned with such pursuit. For SOEs, due to the multi-dimensional nature of organisational goals, and the most senior managers being appointed by the government may not have all the incentives linked with business performance, so the investor orientation is not always the firm's top priority.

Our results suggest that among the three types of firms, FOEs care the most for the employee orientation, followed by SOEs and then POEs, which indicates that FOEs probably pay more attention to and actively invest more in their employees. POEs seem to be 'less proactive' in offering employees' benefits due to their size, resource constraints and competitive disadvantages. SOEs are in between the other two types. Since the employee orientation is represented by the ratio of cash paid to or for employees with regard to the operating income, which considers wages and fringe benefits, our empirical results indicate that employee benefits of SOEs is better than POEs.

The fact that we do not find a significant difference among the three types of ownership on the customer orientation indicates a general emphasis on customer relations for all types of firms. However, when facing potential conflicts firms of different ownership types still choose differently in terms of the customer orientation, sometimes over other stakeholder interests. Our trade-off test indicates that POEs will choose customer interest over other orientations.

We find that POEs prioritize their attention to the society orientation, which is inconsistent with our common belief that SOEs in general treat society orientation as their first priority. It is apparent from our results that POEs and SOEs both care about the benefit of society, this result is also consistent with the CSR Bluebook reports. FOEs rank last whether in terms of rough average or firm characteristics adjusted absolute magnitude. This is not surprising since it is reasonable to expect firms with domestic origins to have a higher level of attachment to the Chinese society as a whole, whereas firms with foreign roots are relatively less connected both culturally and in a more general sense. However, FOEs have become more involved with the Chinese communities. As was noted in 'China Business Report of 2018' (publicized by the American Chamber of Commerce in Shanghai), 61.6 per cent of surveyed firms intend to increase the magnitude of investment in China, and at least in Shanghai, one quarter of the GDP and one third of the tax revenues were contributed by FOEs. FOEs also brought new technologies and R&D facilities into China and cultivated a group of local talent. In terms of CSR specifically, FOEs have contributed to the improvement of sense of corporate citizenship, introduced into China a high level of environmental protection protocols, and actively participated in philanthropic activities. Similarly, in the report of 'Top 500 in CSR in China 2017' (publicized by China Enterprises Evaluation Association, an organisation established by Development Research Center of the State Council), 22 per cent of the firms are FOEs, indicating the positive role of FOEs on Chinese market. Among all the firms, SOEs tend to choose societal interest consistent with the customer benefits. This is due to the society being treated as an even broader group of 'customers', so their benefits are consistent with the limited group of customers served directly by the firms.

As for the environment orientation, we find that the FOEs care more about the environment, while POEs care less about the environment and SOEs feature in the middle. Because of the limitation of capital and technology, in order to get more profit, POEs tend to opt for less advanced technologies and are more likely to be less capital intensive in production, which may cause much more pollution. For SOEs, they can always get subsidies or tax preferences from the government to renew their equipment and technology because that constitutes environmentally friendly practice. Hence, they tend to cause less pollution. For FOEs, they always have the latest technology and enough capital; hence, they tend to be more environmentally friendly.

From the trade-off test, we can know the different types of ownership lead firms to make different choices in trading-off different stakeholder interests. SOEs prioritize societal interests and environmental interests, and POEs place the highest priority on customer interests and would like to trade off other interests for customer. FOEs prefer the internal to external interests, and trade off external interests for the internal interests such as those of employees and investors.

Despite the interesting findings, there are several aspects of our study that can be improved in further exploration of the topic. The first limitation of the study is perhaps the measurement for the CSR orientation, since there is no consensus on measurement in the CSR orientation. The index we used is selected by the definition of the CSR for different orientation. A more precise measurement that can represent initiatives is desirable.

Using operating costs/operating income as the customer orientation is also a rough proxy for the real measurement of how dedicated a firm is towards customer interests, given that the operating costs are broad categories of expenses including costs relating to customer services and customer relation maintenance. Heterogeneity of the structure of operating costs could exists across firms of different ownership types, which further affects the preciseness of this measurement.

Since CSR is important both from a theoretical and practical perspective, especially from the perspectives of stakeholder orientations, more accurately quantifiable indicators of CSR activities which relate to multiple stakeholder orientations are desirable for future research.

REFERENCES

Agle, B. R., Mitchell, R. K. and Sonnenfeld, J. A. (1999). Who matters to CEOs? An investigation of stakeholder attributes and salience, corporate performance, and CEO values. *Academy of Management Journal*, 42 (5), 507–25.

Aguilera, R. V. and Cuervo-Cazurra, A. (2004). Codes of good governance worldwide: What is the trigger? *Organization Studies*, 25, 417–46.

Aguilera, R. V. and Jackson, G. (2003). The cross-national diversity of corporate governance: Dimensions and determinants. *Academy of Management Review*, 28, 447–65.

Aguilera, R. V., Rupp, D. E., Williams, C. A. and Ganapathi, J. (2007). Putting the s back in corporate social responsibility: a multilevel theory of social change in organizations. *Academy of Management Review*, 32(3), 836–63.

Alkhafaji, A. F. (1989). *A stakeholder approach to corporate governance: Managing a dynamic environment*, New York: Quorum Books.

Amit, R. and Schoemaker, P. (1993). Strategic Assets and Organizational Rent. *Strategic Management Journal*, 14, 33–46.

Anderson, P. E. (1982). Marketing strategic planning and the theory of the firm. *Journal of Marketing*, 46, 15–26.

Andon, P., Baxter, J. and Chua, W. F. (2015). Accounting for stakeholders and making accounting useful. *Journal of Management Studies*, 52 (7), 986–1002.

Barney, J. B. (1991). Firm resources and sustained competitive advantage. *Journal of Management*, 17, 99–120.

Barney, J. B. and Hansen, M. H. (1994). Trustworthiness as a source of competitive advantage. *Strategic Management Journal*, 15, 175–90.

Berman, S. L., Wicks, A. C., Koth, S. and Jones, T. M. (1999). Does takeholder orientation matter? The relationship between stakeholder management models and firm financial performance. *Academy of Management Journal*, 42, 488–506.

Bowen, H. R. (1953). *Social Responsibility of the Businessman*, New York: Harper & Row.

Bragdon, J. H. and Marlin, J. (1972). Is pollution profitable. *Risk Management*, 19(4), 9–18.

Brammer, S., Jackson, G. and Matten, D. (2012). Corporate social responsibility and institutional theory: new perspectives on private governance. *Socio-Economic Review*, 10(1), 3–28.

Brammer, S. and Millington, A. (2008). Does it pay to be different? An analysis of the relationship between corporate social and financial performance. *Strategic Management Journal*, 29(12), 1325–43.

Brammer, S., Millington, A. and Pavelin, S. (2006). Is philanthropy strategic? An analysis of the management of charitable giving in large UK companies. *Business Ethics: European Review (Chichester England)*, 15(3), 234–45.

Buckley, P. J., Clegg, L. J., Cross, A. R., Liu, X., Voss, H. and Zheng, P. (2007). The determinants of Chinese outward foreign direct investment. *Journal of International Business Studies*, 38(4), 499–518.

Campbell, D. and Slack, R. (2006). Public visibility as a determinant of the rate of corporate charitable donations. *Business Ethics: European Review (Chichester England)*, 15(1), 19–28.

Carroll, A. B. (1993). *Business and society: ethics and stakeholder management*, Cincinnati: South-Western.

Carroll, A. B. (1998). The four faces of corporate citizenship. *Business and Society Review*, 100/101, 1–7.

Chang, K., Kim, I. and Li, Y. (2014). The heterogeneous impact of corporate social responsibility activities that target different stakeholders. *Journal of Business Ethics*. 125(2), 211–34.

Charkham, J. (1995). Keeping good company: a study of corporate governance in five countries. Oxford University Press.

Chen, K. H. and Metcalf, R. W. (1980). The relationship between pollution control record and financial indicators revisited. *The Accounting Review*, 55(1), 168–77.

Claessens S., Djankov S, Fan, J. P. H. and Lang, L. (2002). Disentangling the incentive and entrenchment effects of large shareholdings. *Journal of Finance*, 57(6),2741–71.

Clarkson, M. (1995). A stakeholder framework for analyzing and evaluating corporate social performance. *Academy of Management Review*, 20(1), 92–117.

Clarkson, M., Starik, M., Cochran, P. and Jones, T. M. (1994). The Toronto conference: reflections on stakeholder theory. *Business and Society*, 33(1), 82.

Clegg, S. R., Hardy, C., Lawrence, T. B. and Nord, W. R. (2006). *The Sage Handbook of Organization Studies*, 2nd ed., London: SAGE Publications Ltd.

Coffey, B. S. and Wang, J. (1998). Board diversity and managerial control as predictors of corporate social performance. *Journal of Business Ethics*, 17(14), 1595–603.

Cornell, B. and Shapiro, A. C. (1987). Corporate stakeholders and corporate finance. *Financial Management*, 16(1), 5–14.

Davis, K. and Blomstrom, R. L. (1975). *Business and society: environment and responsibility*, 3rd ed. New York: McGraw-Hill.

Deng, S. and Dart, J. (1999). The market orientation of Chinese enterprises during a time of transition. *European Journal of Marketing*, 33(5/6), 631–54.

DiMaggio, P. (1988). Interest and agency in institutional theory. *Institutional Patterns and Organizations: Culture and Environment*, 3–21.

DiMaggio, P. J. and Powell, W. W. (2000). The iron cage revisited: isomorphism in organizational fields. *Advances in Strategic Management*, 48(2), 147–60.

Donaldson, T. and Preston, L. E. (1995). The stakeholder theory of the corporation: concepts, evidence, and implications. *Academy of Management Review*, 20(1), 65–91.

Doshi, V. and Khokle, P. (2012). An institutional perspective on corporate social responsibility. *Vikalpa: The Journal for Decision Makers*, 37(2), 98–102.

Epstein, E. M. (1987). The corporate social policy process: beyond business ethics, corporate social responsibility and corporate social responsiveness. *California Management Review*, 29(3), 99–114.

Epstein, E. M. (1989). Business ethics, corporate good citizenship, and the corporate social policy process: a view from the United States. *Journal of Business Ethics*. 8(8), 583–95.

Estrin, S. and Perotin, V. (1991). Does ownership always matter? *International Journal of Industrial Organization*, 9(1), 55–72.

Faccio, M., Masulis, R. W. and McConnell, J. J. (2006). Political connections and corporate bailouts. *Journal of Finance*, 61(6), 2597–635.

Freeman, R. E. (1984). *Strategic management: A stakeholder approach*, Boston: Pitman.

Freeman, R. E. (1999). Divergent stakeholder theory. *Academy of Management Review*, 24(2), 233–6.

Freeman, R. E. and Reed, D. L. (1983). Stockholders and stakeholders: a new perspective on corporate governance. *California Management Review*, 25(3), 88–106.

Freedman, M. and Jaggi, B. (1982). Pollution disclosures, pollution performance and economic performance. *Omega*, 10(2), 167–76.

Friedland, R. and Alford, R. R. (1991). *Bringing society back in: symbols, practices, and institutional contradictions*, Chicago: University of Chicago.

Frye, T. and Shleifer, A. (1997). The invisible hand and the grabbing hand. *American Economic Review*, 87(2), 354–8.

Godfrey, P. C., Merrill, C. B. and Hansen, J. M. (2009). The relationship between corporate social responsibility and shareholder value: an empirical test of the risk management hypothesis. *Strategic Management Journal*, 30, 425–45.

Grandori, A. (2004). *Corporate governance and firm organization*. New York: Oxford University Press.

Grant, D. S., Bergesen, A. J. and Jones, A. W. (2002). Organizational size and pollution: the case of the US chemical industry. *American Sociological Review*, 67(3), 389–407.

Graves, S. B. and Waddock, S. A. (1994). Institutional owners and corporate social performance. *Academy of Management Journal*, 37(4), 1034–46.

Greenley, G. E. and Foxall, G. R. (1997). Multiple stakeholder orientation in UK companies and the implications for company performance. *Journal of Management Studies*, 34(2), 259–84.

Habisch, A., Jonker, J., Wegner, M. and Schmidpeter, R. (2005). *Corporate Social Responsibility Across Europe*. Berlin Heidelberg: Springer.

Hall, M., Millo, Y. and Barman, E. (2015). Who and what really counts? Stakeholder prioritization and accounting for social value. *Journal of Management Studies*, 52 (7), 907–34.

Harrison, J. S. and St John, G. H. (1994). *Strategic management of organizations and stakeholders*. St Paul: West.

Harvey, B. and Schaefer, A. (2001). Managing relationships with environmental stakeholders: a study of UK water and electricity utilities. *Journal of Business Ethics*, 30(3), 243–60.

Hill, C. W. L. (1995). National institutional structures, transaction cost economizing and competitive advantage: the case of Japan. *Organization Science*, 6(1), 119–31.

Hong, Z. (2004). Mapping the evolution and transformation of the new private enterprises in China. *Journal of Chinese Political Science*. 9(1):23–42.

Ingram, R. W. and Frazier, K. B. (1980). Environmental performance and corporate disclosure. *Journal of Accounting Research*, 18(2), 614–22.

Jesen, M. and Meckling, W. (1976). The theory of the firm: managerial behavior, agency cost and ownership structure. *Journal of Financial Economics*, 3(4), 305–60.

Jones, T. M. (1995). Instrumental stakeholder theory: a synthesis of ethics and economics. *Academy of Management Review*, 20(2), 404–37.

Kaynak, E. and Kara, A. (2004). Market orientation and organizational performance: a comparison of industrial versus consumer companies in mainland China using market orientation scale (markor). *Industrial Marketing Management*, 33(8), 743–53.

Kolk, A. (2016). The social responsibility of international business: from ethics and the environment to CSR and sustainable development. *Journal of World Business*, 51(1), 23–34.

Konar, S. and Cohen, M. A. (2001). Does the market value environmental performance? *Review of Economics and Statistics*, 83(2), 281–89.

Kostova, T., Roth, K. and Dacin, M. T. (2008). Institutional theory in the study of multi-national corporations: a critique and new directions. *Academy of Management Review*, 33 (4), 994–1006.

Kraatz, M. S., Block, E. S., Davis, J., Glynn, M. A., Hoffman, A. and Jones, C., et al. (2008). Organizational implications of institutional pluralism. *Journal of Pharmacy & Nutrition Sciences*, 5(1), 5–13.

Lawrence, T. B., Suddaby, R. and Leca, B. (2009). *Institutional work: actors and agency in institutional studies of organizations*. AMDISA Secretariat.

Li, H. and Zhang, Y. (2007). The role of managers' political networking and functional experience in new venture performance: evidence from China's transition economy. *Strategic Management Journal*, 28(8),791–804.

Lin, L. (2010). Corporate social responsibility in China: window dressing or structural change? *Berkeley Journal of International Law*, 28(1), 64–100.

López-Iturriaga, F. J. and López-de-Foronda, Ó. (2009). Corporate social responsibility and large shareholders: an analysis of European firms. *Transnational Corporations Review*, 3(3), 17–33.

Luo, Y. and Tan, J. J. (1998). A comparison of multinational and domestic firms in an emerging market: a strategic choice perspective. *Journal of International Management*, 4 (1), 21–40.

Ma, D. and Parish, W. L. (2006). Tocquevillian moments: charitable contributions by Chinese private entrepreneurs. *Social Forces*. 85(2), 943–64.

Maguire, S., Hardy, C. and Lawrence, T. B. (2004). Institutional entrepreneurship in emer-ging fields: HIV/AIDS treatment advocacy in Canada. *Academy of Management Journal*, 47 (5), 657–79.

Mahoney, J. T. and Pandian, J. R. (1992). The resource-based view within the conversation of strategic management. *Strategic Management Journal*, 13(5), 363–80.

Mahoney, L. S. and Thorne, L. (2005). Corporate social responsibility and long-term com-pensation: evidence from Canada. *Journal of Business Ethics*, 57(3), 241–53.

Maignan, I. and Ferrell, O. C. (2000). Measuring corporate citizenship in two countries: the case of the United States and France. *Journal of Business Ethics*, 23(3), 283–97.

Maon, F., Lindgreen, A. and Swaen, V. (2010). Organizational stages and cultural phases: a critical review and a consolidative model of corporate social responsibility development. *International Journal of Management Reviews*, 12(1), 20–38.

Marquis, C. and Qian, C. (2014). Corporate social responsibility reporting in China: symbol or substance? *Organization Science*, 25(1), 127–48.

McGuire, J. W. (1963). *Business and Society*. New York: McGraw-Hill.

McGuire, J. B., Sundgren, A. and Schneeweis, T. (1988). Corporate social responsibility and firm financial performance. *Academy of Management Journal*. 31(4), 854–72.

Meek, W. R., Pacheco, D. F. and York, J. G. (2010). The impact of social norms on entrepreneurial action: evidence from the environmental entrepreneurship context. *Journal of Business Venturing*, 25(5), 493–509.

Mitchell, R. K., Agle, B. R. and Wood, D. J. (1997). Toward a theory of stakeholder identification and salience: defining the principle of who and what really counts. *Academy of Management Journal*, 22(4), 853–86.

Nguyen, T. V., Le, N. T. B. and Bryant, S. E. (2013). Sub-national institutions, firm strategies, and firm performance: a multilevel study of private manufacturing firms in Vietnam. *Journal of World Business*, 48(1), 68–76.

Peng, M. W. and Luo, Y. (2000). Managerial ties and firm performance in a transition economy: the nature of a micro-macro link. *Academy of Management Journal*, 43(3), 486–501.

Posner, B. C. and Schmidt, W. H. (1984). Values and the American manager: an update. *California Management Review*, 26(3), 202–16.

Ruf, B. M., Meade-Christie, N. L. and Brown, R. M. (2004). The relationship between the existence of antitakeover devices and corporate social performance. *Academy of Accounting & Financial Studies Journal*, 8(9), 2898–902.

Schaltegger, S. (2002). A framework for ecopreneurship: leading bioneers and environmental managers to ecopreneurship. *Greener Management International*, 38, 45–58.

Shleifer, A. and Vishny, R. W. (1994). Politicians and firms. *Quarterly Journal of Economics*, 109(4), 995–1025.

Stanwick, P. A. and Stanwick, S. D. (1998). The relationship between corporate social performance, and organizational size, financial performance, and environmental perfor-mance: an empirical examination. *Journal of Business Ethics*, 17(2), 195–204.

Tan, J. (2002), Impact of ownership type on environment-strategy linkage and performance: evidence from a transitional economy. *Journal of Management Studies*, 39(3), 333–54.

Tang, Y. and Tang, Y. (2003). An exploratory study of market orientation in China. *Asian Business & Management*, 2(1), 91–110.

Thompson, G. and Driver, C. (2002). Corporate governance and democracy: the stakeholder debate revisited. *Journal of Management and Governance*, 6(2), 111–30.

Thompson, J. K., Wartick, S. L. and Smith, H. L. (1991). Integrating corporate social performance and stakeholder management: implications for a research agenda in small business. In J. E. Post ed., *Research in corporate social performance and policy*, 12(2), 207–30. Greenwich: JAI Press.

Thornton, P. H. and Ocasio, W. (1999). Institutional logics and the historical contingency of power in organizations: executive succession in the higher education publishing industry, 1958– 1990. *American Journal of Sociology*, 105(3), 801–43.

Thornton, P. H. and Ocasio, W. (2008). Institutional Logics. In R. Greenwood, C. Oliver, R. Suddaby, K. Sahlin, eds.,*The SAGE Handbook of Organizational Institutionalism*, pp. 99–128. London: SAGE Publications Ltd.

Tse, A. C. B., Sin, L. Y. M., Yau, O. H. M., Lee, J. S. Y. and Chow, R. (2003). Market orientation and business performance in a Chinese business environment. *Journal of Business Research*, 56(3), 227–39.

Turban, D. B. and Greening, D. W. (1997). Corporate social performance and organizational attractiveness to prospective employees. *Academy of Management Journal*, 40(3), 658–72.

Wang, J. and Coffey, B. S. (1992). Board composition and corporate philanthropy. *Journal of Business Ethics*, 11(10), 771–8.

Wang, H. and Qian, C. (2011). Corporate philanthropy and corporate financial performance: the roles of stakeholder response and political access. *Academy of Management Journal*, 54 (6), 1159–81.

Webster, F. E. (1992). The changing role of marketing in the corporation. *Journal of Marketing*, 56(4), 1–17.

Webster, C. (1993). Refinement of the marketing culture scale and the relationship between marketing culture and profitability of a service firm. *Journal of Business Research*, 26(2), 111–31.

Wherther, W. B. and Chandler, D. (2005). *Strategic corporate social responsibility*. Sage Publications.

White, H. (1980). A heteroskedasticity-consistent covariance matrix estimator and a direct test for heteroskedasticity. *Econometrica*, 48(4), 817–38.

Wicks, A. C., Berman S. L. and Jones, T. M. (1999). The structure of optimal trust: moral and strategic implication. *Academy of Management Review*, 24(1), 99–116.

Williamson, O. E. (1975). *Markets and hierarchies*. New York: The Free Press.

Yan, A. and Gray, B. (1994). Bargaining power, management control, and performance in United States-China joint ventures: a comparative case study. *Academy of Management Journal*, 37(6), 1478–517.

Zhang, R., Rezaee, Z. and Zhu, J. (2010). Corporate philanthropic disaster response and ownership type: evidence from Chinese firms' response to the Sichuan earthquake. *Journal of Business Ethics*, 91(1), 51.

9

The Dynamics of CSR, Mandatory CSR Laws, and Corporate Social Performance in India

Mallika Tamvada

9.1 INTRODUCTION

The responsibility towards the society is an integral part of the socio-cultural fabric of Indian way of living (Dhanesh, 2015). The fundamental basis for such responsibility is 'Dharma' – a concept that explains the duty to do good karma or righteous action (Dhanesh, 2015). Good karmas include charities and philanthropic contributions. As this sense of duty is ingrained in the Indian culture and way of life, it is also embedded into corporate routines and businesses. Thus, by spending their profits on social goals, Indian corporations often took responsibility for community development by supporting charities for the poor and underprivileged, constructing schools, developing roads, amongst other things. These contributions can be linked to the religious, cultural and social beliefs of the country. However, the economic liberalisation in the 1990s that resulted in an economic boom has shifted the corporates' focus on responsibility from societal benefit to strategic models of CSR. The longstanding debates on CSR have drifted from the traditional social contract of philanthropic engagement. Such a shift in CSR has had significant implications on the social responsibility, necessitating formal legislation around CSR in India.

India legislated on CSR by mandating CSR spending along with CSR disclosures.[1] The Act and the rules provide for the manner in which CSR activities shall be formulated, undertaken, reported and monitored. It is estimated that 5,097 companies in India spent INR 9,822 crores, approximately equal to US$1.5 billion, towards CSR activities in the fiscal year 2015–16 under the new CSR regime.[2] The overall spending on CSR by 500 listed companies in the financial year 2017–18 is estimated to be INR 11,000 crores.[3] Thus, the mandatory CSR legislation may have contributed positively to 'corporate social performance' in India (Boodoo, 2016) while meeting the goal of CSR activities leading to community goodwill, creating

[1] S. 135, The Company Act, 2013; Sch. VII, The Company Act, 2013; Companies (CSR Policy) Rules, 2014.
[2] https://csrbox.org/India_CSR_news_Estimated-Prescribed-CSR-IN-FY-2018–in-Large-500-Listed-Companiesin-India-_63 accessed 29 June 2018.
[3] Ibid.

social impact and visibility (Sharma, 2013) in the face of greater transparency. However, several concerns were raised about how regulations 'risk tick box behaviour, tokenism, or corruption while masking the data and the real engagement of corporates in delivering their social duties'.[4] The aim of this chapter is to examine the social and cultural factors influencing CSR in India, the key drivers shaping the mandatory legislation, the impact of this legislation on corporate social performance, and the need of legal transplants for strengthening CSR.

The remaining chapter is structured as follows. Section 2 presents the Indian concept of CSR and how it was part of the socioeconomic fabric of the country for several centuries. This section discusses CSR in India, how it was operationalised, and the impact of economic liberalisation on its nature. Section 3 presents the key factors that influenced the mandating of CSR in India and discusses the main provisions of CSR to highlight the main aspects of the mandatory legislation. Section 4 critically evaluates CSR practices following the mandatory CSR legislation while discussing the impact of the legislation on corporates' social performance. Section 5 discusses the theory of legal transplant, its importance and necessity while suggesting a mechanism for legal transplant to create a universally applicable CSR law. Section 6 summarises the discussion on Indian CSR and concludes the chapter.

9.2 NATURE OF CSR IN INDIA AND THE TRANSITION

CSR is not a new concept in India. In India, the idea of the role of business for society is imbued with culture, values, religion and traditions of the country. Many well-known business entities or business families like Tata, Birla, Godrej and others have made significant contributions to the society, consistent with the long tradition of working for social welfare. In the following discussion, the conceptual roots of the socio-culturally driven social responsibility of businesses in India and the nature of such responsibility are provided. More specifically, the discussion demonstrates the transition of a culturally ingrained concept of CSR to a more Western-influenced CSR in due course of time.

9.2.1 Indian Culture Vedic Times and CSR

9.2.1.1 Dharma

Dharma – 'righteous duty' is a core part of the Indian culture and can be found in the ancient Vedic literature of India. 'The objectives of dharma are to lead society to material progress, cultural development and general welfare of its diverse population' (Deep, 2017). According to the Vedic texts, Dharma includes charitable

---

[4] nonprofitquarterly.org/2017/02/17/mandatory-corporate-social-responsibility-india-working/ accessed 29 June 2018.

activities and philanthropic contributions. They result in good karma. In addition to this, Dharma can be found in the Vedic debt theory which 'inspires to give back to society as a part of one's duty' (Deep, 2017). Thus, 'Indian society has had an ethos of giving, instilled through cultural, religious traditions and practices', and this is 'ingrained in the collective psyche of the Indian commercial communities' (Dhanesh, 2015). Wealthy merchants contributed from their wealth towards wider society through various activities like 'by way of setting up temples for a religious cause',[5] or by 'helping society in getting over phases of famine and epidemics by providing food from their godowns and money thereby securing an integral part in the society'[6] and this was known as merchant charity (Sundar, 2013). It can, therefore, be asserted that the commercial history in India can be traced since Vedic times (1500-600 BCE) (Sundar, 2000; Dhanesh, 2015) with deep traditions of social responsibility, and Dharma has been instrumental in shaping such social engagement of business. For these reasons, social responsibility was a Dharma that businesses need to follow in India, and CSR was its manifestation (Deep, 2017).

The great Indian philosopher Kautilya (in the fourth century BC) in his book *Arthashastra* – manuals of statecraft and economic management for kings (Trauntmann, 1979)[7] has described in detail the norms, ethics and fundamentals of business in various sectors during the time of Mauryan empire in 322-187 BC. This ancient text has greatly influenced governance in India. Here, Kautilya emphasised the ethical practices and contributions to society while conducting business.[8]

9.2.1.2 Guilds

The social contributions and developmental initiatives by business entities found in the early Vedic and later Vedic periods were made by individuals as well as through 'merchant guilds'.[9] The social contributions of the guilds were related to 'the rich tradition and ethos of giving'.[10] They worked 'collaboratively with the state within the broader values framework of *Artha*'.[11] These merchant guilds enabled the rulers

---

5   D. Vajpeyi and R. S. Rai, 'Corporate social responsibility in India: Implications of governmental Intervention through the new Companies Bill of India'. Available at: paperroom.ipsa.org/papers/ paper_33361.pdf accessed on 29 June 2018.
6   Ibid.
7   T. R. Trauntmann (1979). Traditions of statecraft in ancient India. In R. J. Moore ed., *Tradition and politics in South Asia*, New Delhi, Vikas Publishing House; B. Jane (2016). Guilds and governance in ancient India: historical practices of corporate social responsibility. In B. Jane and V. Nilakant, eds., *Managing responsibly: alternative approaches to corporate management and governance*, Routledge.
8   B. Jane (2016). Guilds and governance in ancient India: historical practices of corporate social responsibility. In B. Jane and V. Nilakant, eds., *Managing responsibly: alternative approaches to corporate management and governance*, Routledge.
9   The association of corporations of traders, manufacturers and other economic participants.
10 M. Mitra (2007). *It's only business!: India's corporate social responsiveness in a globalized world*, Oxford: Oxford University Press.
11 *Artha* is the part related to earnings in the Dharma Sutras, a Vedic text enumerating the principles of Dharma.

to design 'mechanisms for wealth creation and labour regulation' that were consistent with 'the specific ethics' of individuals' socioeconomic class.[12] The core objective of these was the well-being of all people as everyone was expected to care the poor and other needy communities (Dhanesh, 2015). The guilds and local communities maintained a close link and reflected each other's values. 'CSR was not separated from the ordinary activity of guilds because guild activities were embedded in the well-being of the local community of which they were a part'.[13] Thus, the guilds were intertwined with community, and furthered the 'traditions of gift giving, particularly to institutions which provided ritual, educational and charitable services to the community'.[14] Similar engagement of business in social development through guilds is seen in the Gandhian trusteeship model.

9.2.1.3 Trusteeship: Gandhian Philosophy

The end of the nineteenth century paved the way for Gandhi's trusteeship model. The businesses social engagement now included 'broader humanitarian needs like poverty alleviation efforts, disaster relief, reforestation, and building of schools and temples' (Mohan, 2001; Husted, 2015). Furthermore, business entities started using their financial, managerial and human resources for their direct involvement in community welfare and development rather than donating (Gautam, 2010). By the early twentieth century (Chahoud et al., 2007; Husted, 2015), the Gandhian trusteeship model gained prominence and offered a remarkable shift in CSR during the colonial era in a country that was socially vulnerable. The Gandhian model was instrumental in the 'consolidation and amplification of social development' (Singh and Verma, 2014). It emphasised the relationship between business and wealth as a form of trusteeship where businesses were treated as trustees of wealth on behalf of society having a duty to use wealth for the benefit of the public good (Husted, 2015). Gandhi's influence led to the active involvement of several industrialists in nation-building. Under his influence, leading business houses such as Tata, Bajaj and Birla proactively contributed to the socioeconomic development of India. They established foundations to support institutions such as educational, health etc. (Gautam, 2010; Husted, 2015; Pillay, 2017) and facilitated the setting up of training and scientific institutions. These foundations took part in a wide range of social activities like hospital building, providing disaster aid and so on.[15] Their actions demonstrated a shift from merchant charity rooted in religious commitments to philanthropy to an active involvement of business in social development (Husted, 2015). It is believed

---

[12]   See above (n. 8).
[13]   Ibid.
[14]   Ibid.
[15]   D. Vajpeyi and R. S. Rai, 'Corporate social responsibility in India: Implications of governmental Intervention through the new Companies Bill of India'. Also available at: paperroom.ipsa.org/papers/paper_33361.pdf accessed 20 June 2018.

that Gandhi's trusteeship concept drew inspiration from the Vedic texts (Husted, 2015).

Colonial rule did have an impact on the way the businesses contributed to the social goals. During this period, 'business philanthropy was characterised by a sense of enlightened self-interest' where participation in the freedom struggle along with social upliftment initiatives were the core social goals of Indian businesses (Dhanesh, 2015). Although this business engagement was not based on a sustainable model (Chapparia and Jha, 2017), the approach towards CSR changed during this period. Thus, culture, social values and colonialism had a substantial effect on the nature of CSR. While charity and philanthropic contributions remained primary drivers of CSR, the focus shifted away from religious sentiments to social development goals and nation-building ideals.

9.2.2 *Global Market, Economic Liberalisation and CSR*

The Indian CSR model gradually changed from a philanthropic to a multi-stakeholder concept following India's independence in 1947 from colonial rule and subsequent industrialisation (Chapparia and Jha, 2017). In the period between 1950 until economic liberalisation in the 1990s, much was 'characterised by cen-tralisation, competition to survive in private sector and corrupt practices' (Chapparia and Jha, 2017). During this period, 'legal rules and regulations on industrial licen-sing, high taxes and restrictions on the private sector' and the emergence of Public Sector Undertakings (PSUs) led to several corporate malpractices.[16] This led to the enactment of formal legislations on corporate governance, labour and environmen-tal issues (Chahoud et al., 2017). Although a large public sector emerged during this period, it initially played a limited role, and the involvement of private sector in the socioeconomic development of the country continued to be a compelling necessity (Rishi and Moghe, 2013).[17]

In the 1990s, the Indian government initiated reforms to liberalise and deregulate the Indian economy to address the glitches arising from post-independence policies of industrial licensing, high taxes and restricting the private sector. This paved the way for integrating the Indian economy into the global market. Consequently, 'controls and license systems were partly abolished, and the Indian economy experi-enced a pronounced boom' (Gouda et al., 2017). The economic boom and increased share in the global market led to the change of attitude of businesses towards their social responsibility. Indian companies started moving from their traditional philan-thropic engagement following their global influence (Pillai, 2017). Furthermore, to maintain competitiveness, it became imperative on them to follow international standards regarding labour, environment and other social issues, and the CSR

---

[16]   Ibid.
[17]   Ibid.; P. Rishi, S. Moghe, Integrating corporate social responsibility and culture as a strategy for holistic corporate success in India. *The Journal of Corporate Citizenship*, 2013(51), 17.

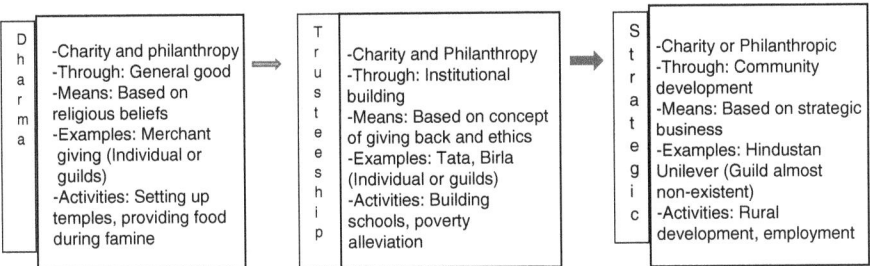

FIGURE 9.1 The transitory nature of CSR in India

evolved from a philanthropic to a multi-stakeholder concept (Chapparia and Jha, 2018). Parallel to this, a growing number of corporations in India started treating CSR as a strategy for 'protecting the goodwill and reputation', 'defending attacks' and a 'branding and promotional tool'.[18] Thus, corporates began using CSR for strategic reasons like in the West and started reporting their CSR activities on their official websites, annual reports and so on.[19]

Although the philanthropic roots of CSR started to dry up, 'a combination of extreme social need, limited public finance, improved returns to Industry, a pro-business environment, and the emergence of a strong civil society' (Dhanesh, 2015) necessitated participation of business entities. Businesses believed it was imperative for them to contribute to society for their own business good. Thus, they were engaged in social welfare programmes and schemes; however, in the absence of a global law on CSR engagement and voluntarism, Indian CSR began to take the shape of strategic and pro-business CSR models like in Western countries. While working through guilds was relegated to a back seat, business started using social responsibility as a strategic tool to meet competitiveness in the global era of business. However, post-liberalisation, businesses were expected to adopt the triple bottom line approach,[20] as an inseparable part of their strategy to attain both shareholder and social value (Galliara, 2011).

---

[18] Vajpeyi and Rai, Corporate social responsibility in India: Implications of governmental intervention through the new Companies Bill of India; for example 'Project Shakti' undertaken by Hindustan Unilever Limited (HUL) to penetrate and tap rural markets in India is a classic example of innovative business strategy with societal concerns. The project works on the model of appointing underprivileged rural women from self-help groups as selling agents of the FMCG giant's products in their villages. While Project Shakti resulted in the empowerment of these women and helped to position HUL as a socially responsible organisation, it also gave the company much broader and deeper penetration in the rural markets for sales.

[19] Vajpeyi and Rai, Corporate social responsibility in India: Implications of governmental Intervention through the new Companies Bill of India.

[20] Triple bottom line (TBL) is a tool to measure corporate performance along the interrelated dimensions of profits, people and the planet. It 'captures the essence of sustainability by measuring the impact of an organisation's activities on the world ... including both its profitability and shareholder values and its social, human and environmental capital', A. Savitz (2013). *The triple bottom line: how today's best-run companies are achieving economic, social and environmental success-and how you can too,* John Wiley & Sons.

9.3 TOWARDS MANDATORY CSR

9.3.1 *Key Factors Necessitating Legislation*

Globalisation has had a significant impact on the traditional notion of CSR in India. Under its influence, the pressure exerted by the international business code of conduct along with the voluntary nature of CSR has drifted philanthropic CSR into strategic CSR. Consequently, business attitudes towards CSR has turned away from community needs to reputational returns. The Indian government took initiatives like by providing CSR voluntary guidelines (2009), national voluntary guidelines on social, environmental and economic responsibilities of business (2011), DEP guidelines, and so on. However, the lack of adequate monitoring and implementation mechanisms has further complicated the delivery of CSR in India. As noted by Zile in 2012, around 80 per cent of the private internationals and 50 per cent of the private national companies in India claim to have a CSR policy in place (Mukherjee, 2013). However, a study by Karmayog[21] in 2008 suggested that 49 per cent of 1,000 companies studied across 35 per cent of sectors have not undertaken any CSR activity.[22] Here, lack of transparency and corporate scams are hampering the real contribution of companies towards CSR while the companies are not willing to be transparent on the volume of their expenses on CSR. Thus, the absence of regulation and the voluntarist nature of CSR undermined the real spirit of CSR in India like in other parts of the world.

India has struggled with problems related to poverty, unemployment, illiteracy and malnutrition. Large inequities between the haves and have-nots persist in the country. Corporates have the know-how, strategic thinking, workforce and financial strength to enable a widespread social transformation (Singh and Verma, 2014) that can reduce such inequities. As proactive corporate engagement alongside public developmental initiatives can fast-track socioeconomic transformation, the Indian government made CSR mandatory by introducing CSR provision in the Company Law Act, 2013. Thus, the Act sets out provisions for proactive business engagement, greater transparency with regard to companies' CSR contributions, and to reinstate the traditional approach of CSR rooted in the duty to give back for a more holistic contribution by corporates to society.

9.3.2 *The Mandatory CSR Legislation of India*

On 1 April 2014, the provisions relating to mandatory CSR came into effect. Section 135 of India's Companies Act 2013, mandates CSR spending followed by

---

[21] It is a platform for the Indian non-profit sector providing research on CSR activities of Indian Companies. www.karmayog.org/csr/.

[22] www.karmayog.org/csr/ accessed on 29 June 2018; G. Meena (2010). Corporate Social Responsibility in India. In G. Williams, ed., (2010). *Responsible management in Asia: perspectives on CSR*, Springer, p. 33; R. Gautam and A. Singh (2010). Corporate social responsibility practices in India: A study of top 500 companies. *Global Business and Management Research: An International Journal*, 2(1), 41-56.

accountability provisions. The Companies (Corporate Social Responsibility Policy) Rules, 2014 (the (CSR Policy) Rules) provide the manner in which companies can undertake their CSR activities and Schedule VII of the Act enumerates the activities that can be undertaken under the remit of CSR. Thus, India became the first country to mandate CSR spending in the world.

9.3.2.1 Applicability

Every company having a net worth of INR 500 crores or more, or turnover of INR 1000 crores or more, or a net profit of INR 5 crores or more during any financial year is mandated to spend on CSR.[23] Such companies must spend at least 2 per cent of the average net profits of the company made during the three immediately preceding financial years in pursuance of its CSR policy[24] unless it shows a compelling reason for not being able to comply.[25]

9.3.2.2 Strategising CSR/Planning and Implementing CSR

BOARD AND COMMITTEE. Section 135 of the Companies Act, 2013 provides the first step towards formalising CSR projects in a corporate structure. According to the provision, the board of directors of a qualifying company shall constitute a CSR Committee of the board consisting of three or more directors, of which at least one director is required to be an independent director.[26] The Committee so constituted has to formulate and recommend to the board a CSR policy which sets out the activities and the amount of expenditure to be incurred on those CSR activities.[27] The CSR activities formulated by the Committee must be within the ambit of activities listed under the Schedule VII of the Act.[28]

The board has to take into account the recommendations made by the CSR Committee and approve the CSR policy of the company. Such policy must be part of the board's CSR report and must be placed on company's website.[29] The board of directors must ensure that the company undertakes those CSR activities with the minimum required spending towards the CSR policy.[30] Furthermore, the board of directors must ensure that activities under the CSR policy are within the ambit of activities listed under Schedule VII of the Act. If the company fails to spend the

[23]　S. 135(1) of the Companies Act, 2013.
[24]　S. 135(5) of the Companies Act, 2013.
[25]　Second proviso to s. 135(5) of the Companies Act, 2013.
[26]　S. 135(1) of the Companies Act, 2013.
[27]　S. 135(3) of the Companies Act, 2013.
[28]　Sch. VII of the Act/ s. 135(3)(a) of the Companies Act, 2013.
[29]　S. 135(4) of the Companies Act, 2013.
[30]　S. 135(5); Second proviso to s. 135(5) of the Companies Act, 2013.

minimum required amount, the board must specify the reasons for not spending the amount in its report.[31]

For effective implementation following approval of the CSR policy by the board, the committee must monitor the company's CSR policy from time to time. Thus, it must oversee the application of CSR policy by conducting an impact assessment or due diligence, monitoring project development and so on.[32]

REPORTING CSR. The board must include the CSR report in its annual report.[33] The CSR Rules provide a format for the board to annually report on CSR. In this report, the board must provide details of the activities undertaken along with complete specifications of the expenditure on such activities. This is required, in particular, to the spends within 2 per cent of the average net profits of the previous three years. The board is also required to ensure a responsibility statement that shows compliance of CSR objectives by the company in letter as well as spirit. This has to be signed by an authorised individual of the company.

9.3.2.3 CSR Activities

Schedule VII of the Companies Act, 2013 provides the activities that qualify as CSR activities. They include undertakings related to environment sustainability, empowering women and promoting gender equality, education, poverty reduction and eradicating hunger, social business projects, reducing child mortality and improving maternal health, improvement of health, imparting of vocational skills, contribution towards central and state government funds for socioeconomic development and relief, and so on.

The law does not prevent a company from initiating a CSR activity beyond the activities prescribed under Schedule VII of the Act nor does it stop a company from pursuing CSR activities outside India. However, the amount spent on activities as specified under Schedule VII in Indian Territory alone is construed as CSR for meeting the regulatory requirement of spending 2 per cent of average net profit on CSR.[34]

9.3.2.4 Mode of Operation

SOCIETY/TRUST/SECTION 8 COMPANY. The Act provides three forms of charitable entities namely, a Society, Trust and Company with charitable objects through which companies can discharge their CSR obligations. These entities can be registered under the Societies Registration Act, 1860, Indian Trusts Act, 1882 and

---

[31] Second proviso to s. 135(5) of the Companies Act, 2013.
[32] S. 135(3) of the Companies Act, 2013.
[33] Rule 8(1) of the Companies (CSR Policy) Rules, 2014.
[34] Rule 3(1) of the Companies (CSR Policy) Rules, 2014.

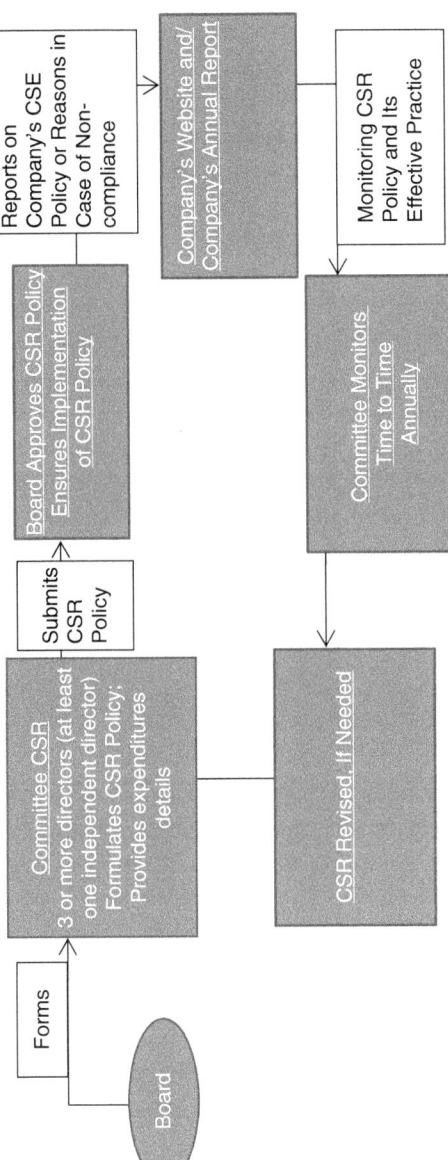

FIGURE 9.2 The pictorial depiction of the process of developing and implementing CSR in India

section 8 of the Companies Act, 2013 respectively. According to Rule (2) of the Companies (CSR Policy) Rules, 2014, a profit-making organisation can undertake CSR initiatives either through a registered trust or through a registered society or through forming a company under section 8 (Companies with Charitable Objects) depending on the purpose and mandate of the organisation either established by the company, singly or along with any other company,[35] or institution established by the central government or state government or any entity established under an Act of Parliament or a State legislature.[36] If such a company or trust or society is established by a company then such a company must have an established track record of three years in undertaking similar programmes or projects and the company must specify the projects or programmes to be undertaken, the modalities of utilisation of funds of such projects, and the monitoring and reporting mechanisms.[37]

DIRECTLY ON ITS OWN. Companies in India engage themselves in CSR through active participation on their own or through their CSR department or by setting up their own NGOs and pooling money for CSR activities.

THROUGH NGOS. Companies can channel their resources through independently registered non-governmental organisations (NGOs) that have a record of at least three years in similar related activities. 'There are numerous NGOs which are working in various sectors like women empowerment, literacy, eradication of poverty, sanitation, skills development, etc.' (Sinha, 2017). The companies, based on their CSR policy, can select an appropriate implementing partner who can initiate CSR activity on behalf of the company (Sinha, 2017). This facilitates companies without expertise or knowledge being able to undertake CSR activities through these NGOs.

Furthermore, many companies in India are located mostly in cities and more developed towns. For these companies, reaching out to remote areas is not always practical. However, they can contribute towards CSR through these NGOs which work in remote areas of the country. The expenditure of such company must be according to the company's CSR policy. 'The spending companies are required to monitor the progress of the CSR initiative, utilization of funds and receive periodical report' (Sinha, 2017).

COLLABORATING WITH OTHER COMPANIES. 'A company may also collaborate with other companies for undertaking projects or programs or CSR activities in such a manner that the CSR committees of respective companies are in a position to report separately on such projects or programs.'[38] Companies can undertake CSR

---

[35] Rule 4(2) of the Companies (CSR Policy) Rules, 2014.
[36] Rule 4(2) of the Companies (CSR Policy) Rules, 2014.
[37] Proviso to Rule 4(2) of the Companies (CSR Policy) Rules, 2014.
[38] Rule 4(3) of the Companies (CSR Policy) Rules, 2014.

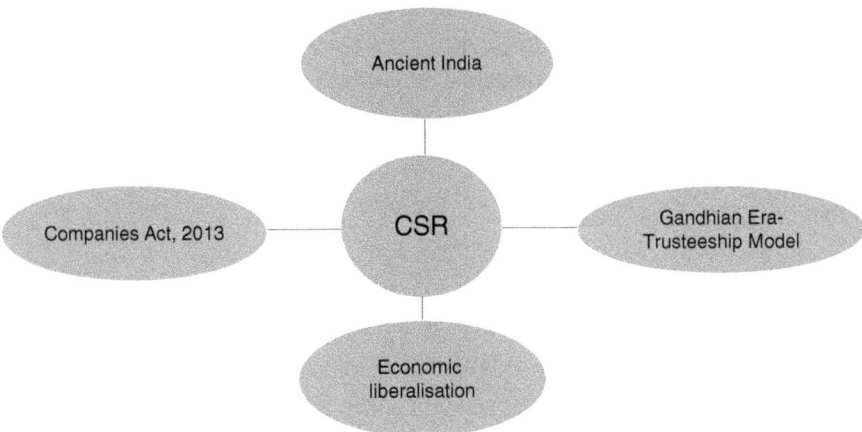

FIGURE 9.3 Traditional link of CSR in India

activities together with other entities through a separate legal entity by incorporating a trust, society or another third company for CSR activities.

As observed by Sinha (2017), the collaborative CSR efforts between unrelated corporate entities can enhance the scale of CSR projects that are undertaken by corporates. It can enable companies to raise more funds for carrying out specific projects without budgetary constraints. Furthermore, companies with the same vision can collaborate among themselves to create a greater impact if the resources of individual companies are not sufficient to accomplish their CSR vision (Sinha, 2017).

Although CSR has taken various dimensions in the Indian context, Figure 9.3 depicts that it has maintained a close link with the Indian traditions that emerged from the concept of 'Dharma' that encompasses charity or philanthropy as a righteous duty for both individuals as well as businesses. As mentioned before, merchant charity was prevalent in India since Vedic times. This form of social contribution by businesses was based on religious grounds rooted in Dharma. The Gandhi's trusteeship model was also influenced by Vedic texts, and Gandhi's concept of giving back to society was through charity and philanthropic contributions of businesses for nation-building and social development. After economic liberalisation, social contributions by corporates had some form of philanthropy and charity for community development; however, the main focus of CSR shifted to realising strategic gains.

Global developments and initiatives, like global compact, Global Reporting Initiatives, voluntary codes and so on, started having influence on CSR policies in India. Companies stated getting more conscious about their business reputation and social role. However, CSR remained voluntary and restricted to social disclosures. Hence, companies began to formulate CSR policies strategically or through random pick and choose mechanisms than through a systematic approach recognising the core concept of CSR and its relation to law. This has prompted the Indian government to adopt the CSR law by resorting to institutional factors than dealing with varying, unclear, ambiguous, non-mandatory forms of CSR. Thus, the mandatory CSR provision under the Companies Act, 2013, has attempted to bring back the traditional motives by enlisting CSR activities for philanthropic and social causes rather than for strategic reasons.

9.4 IMPACT OF CSR LEGISLATION AND CORPORATE SOCIAL PERFORMANCE IN INDIA

9.4.1 *Impact and Corporate Social Performance (CSP)*

Following the enactment of the mandatory CSR provision, the Indian Institute of Corporate Affairs has estimated that at least 6,000 Indian companies have to undertake CSR projects[39] under the Companies Act, 2013 leading to a CSR spending of INR 140 billion in 2014–15 (Mukherjee et al., 2016). This has fundamentally altered the landscape of CSR contributions in India. Several companies that were not previously pursuing CSR started to undertake CSR initiatives. Companies that never reported or spent on CSR started reporting CSR activities due to regulatory reasons. It is estimated that 5,097 companies in India spent INR 9822 crores, approximately equal to US$1.5 billion, towards CSR activities in the fiscal year 2015–16 under the new CSR regime.[40] The overall spending on CSR by 500 listed companies in the financial year 2017–18 is estimated to be INR 11,000 crores.[41] Furthermore, analysing the CSR performance of 3,973 companies over financial years 2015, 2016, 2017, the annual report of the Confederation of Indian Industries (CII) 2017, suggests a significant increase in CSR activities in the areas of environment, gender equality, national heritage and sports development.[42] A report by the CRISIL Foundation (30 January 2017) suggests that the total spending by India Inc. on CSR has risen by 22 per cent in the fiscal year 2016 from its previous year (Allirajani, 2017; Chhaparia and Jha, 2018). This increase in CSR spending is confirmed by analysing the CSR reporting on websites and annual reports of the companies listed in the BSEIT sector index (Bird et al., 2017) and a report from a study of the paper industry (Pandey and Rishi, 2016). Thus, the reports suggest that

---

[39] www.cii.in/ accessed on 29 June 2018; P. Ashok, (2014) 'Business and the sustainability development goals'. Available at: www.theguardian.com/sustainable-business/india-csr-law-debate-business-ngo accessed 26 June 2018.

[40] csrbox.org/India_CSR_news_Estimated-Prescribed-CSR-IN-FY-2018–in-Large-500-Listed-Companiesin-India-_63 accessed 29 June 2018.

[41] Ibid.

[42] See Annual CSR Tracker 2017: From Commitment to Impact, April 2009, 2018, Confederation of Indian Industry https://cii.in/PublicationDetail.aspx?enc=hC7wCLSqd8ajyMN6o3vEsDoGI5hWg8gh8WsFs ZaqxLY accessed 26 June 2018; www.cii.in accessed 29 June 2018.

mandatory CSR in India has made a significant positive impact on business engagements in discharging their social obligations.

However, the Act has tilted the balance of social engagement of business towards specific CSR activities. Several companies have chosen the easiest and most readily available options for their CSR activities. The reports suggest that corporate CSR is concentrated in a handful of areas like education, sanitation, sports, gender equality, among others, while other major areas are ignored or severely underfunded. For example, 90 per cent of all the companies in the top 100 based on their CSR spending that are listed on India's BSE 500 Stock Exchange, have a CSR programme focused on education, sanitation or skills and livelihoods.[43]

Furthermore, the Act provides that companies must engage in CSR giving preference to the local areas where they operate. However, 'the investments are often in regions close to corporate headquarters, which frequently doesn't match where financial support is most needed'[44] leading to 'a further divide between those states which do not have industries or have very few industries and the states which have most of the industries located in their geographical area' (Gautam and Singh, 2010). For example, areas such as Bihar are in need of intervention; however, they have inadequate CSR participation (Gautam and Singh, 2010). Although the states of Karnataka and Maharashtra are energy-sufficient, they have a large number of energy access programmes in corporates' CSR in these regions.[45] A KPMG report points out that the CSR projects are increasingly being implemented in and around industrialised areas, which ignores the needy and poor regions (Richa and Gautam, 2010).

Thus, the social engagement of business remained mostly voluntary, and businesses often have a choice in designing their CSR activities, paving the way to choose convenient activities and meeting regulatory requirements rather than community needs. Such actions indicate, 'firstly, that companies are more inclined to formally meet the regulatory requirements than social needs; secondly, the regulation has the gap that facilitates corporates to opt any of their options than the potential need, the corporates are concerned with their corporate image than being philanthropic'.[46]

43 www.ey.com/Publication/vwLUAssets/EY-Government-and-Public-Sector-Corporate-Social-Responsibility-in-India/%24File/EY-Corporate-Social-Responsibility-in-India.pdf accessed 29 June 2018.
44 N. Priyanka (2018). Corporate Social Responsibility in India A meaningful Organisational initiative for Sustained Business Presence and Growth, also available at: www.shrm.org/shrm-india/pages/corporate-social-responsibility-in-india-a-meaningful-organisational-initiative-for-sustained-business-presence-and-growth.aspx accessed 29 June 2018.
45 Ibid.
46 N. Priyanka (2018). Corporate Social Responsibility in India A meaningful Organisational initiative for Sustained Business Presence and Growth, also available at: www.shrm.org/shrm-india/pages/corporate-social-responsibility-in-india-a-meaningful-organisational-initiative-for-sustained-business-presence-and-growth.aspx accessed 29 June 2018.

9.4.2 Challenges Ahead

It is believed that Indian CSR has moved from a philanthropic form of business donations and contributions to a more structured practice addressing the urgent developmental challenges of the country (Gatti et al., 2018). Indeed, the new legislation has given a direction to the practice of CSR in India that was previously ridden with complexity and ambiguity with regard to its scope and contribution. However, the practice of CSR is restored to its traditional roots, as India has now brought back its age-old theory with a more modern outlook by attempting to provide clear ambit and scope of social responsibilities that the corporates are obligated and mandated to perform. However, this bold attempt towards the active involvement of companies alongside the government faces several challenges that need to be addressed going forward.

One such challenge relates to non-compliance. The CSR provision under the Companies Act has relaxed the terms of CSR spending by making it 'comply-or-explain' (Dharampala and Khanna, 2018; Gatti et al., 2018). According to it, the board is required to give reasons in its report if a company fails to spend the required minimum amount. Thus, it has diluted the much-intended mandatory form of CSR. Furthermore, the Act does not provide effective accountability for non-compliance with CSR duties. Under the CSR provision, failure on the part of the board to report on CSR activities make the company liable to a penalty in the form of a fine ranging from fifty thousand rupees but which may extend to 25 lakh rupees. Furthermore, every officer in default would be punishable with imprisonment up to three years and/or a fine (Gopalan and Kamalnath, 2015). However, with 'comply or explain' status, the company can always find its way out. Thus, the absence of adequate accountability mechanisms coupled with the 'comply-or-explain' provision make CSR mostly discretionary even in the face of these new regulations and increase the probability of reducing it to the status of 'tick the box' paperwork.

Furthermore, the mandatory CSR provision allows companies to pursue CSR activities in association with NGOs. Such association with registered NGOs can be enriching as investments are based on need assessments of the local community by these NGOs to implement CSR activities. Also, if different companies are investing in an NGO for CSR activities, each partner adds value to the entire process and learns from each other. However, there is a dearth of efficient and trained organisations that can contribute to the development of society by giving a helping hand in the CSR activities. The lack of proper training personnel serves as a hindrance to the CSR activities embraced by the company. For these reasons, there is a compelling need for building the local capacity of the non-governmental organisations to complement the CSR activities of corporates (Parvin, 2018).

Finally, the Schedule VII list of CSR activities, when interpreted liberally, has a wide scope and includes almost everything in its ambit. There are no clear-cut guidelines and directions to lead the CSR initiatives of the companies. This is a considerable challenge for the companies' CSR decisionmaking (Gopalan and Kamalnath, 2015). Thus, the intended mandatory CSR echoes back to the era of voluntary CSR practices (Gopalan and Kamalnath, 2015). Thus, a systematic and rigorous needs assessment and proper design of intervention strategy are missing. Furthermore, while the activities listed are in alignment with the government's welfare services, several areas such as human rights and corporate accountability are not in the list.

9.5 CSR, LAW AND LEGAL TRANSPLANTS

The relationship between CSR and law has been in discussion for several decades with an aim to have a universal framework on CSR to regulate the activities of firms towards their social obligations. However, institutional differences and voluntarism crept into the CSR models leading to confused notions of CSR that do not provide a concrete framework to deliberate business obligations towards society meaningfully. This has exacerbated the differences in CSR orientations in more advanced countries and the rest of the world. When countries begin adopting CSR to their contextual needs, they place priorities on shaping organisational behaviour, and add more complexities to CSR. The legal transplant theory, as propounded by Watson (1978), offers a powerful approach for developing dynamic elements in CSR while bringing uniformity in its application. According to Watson (1978), legal transplant is 'the transfer of legal rule and institutions from one legal system to another'. It propagates that most changes in a legal system happen through the borrowing of legal systems from other systems. Legal transplant has been a useful tool in developing legal systems in the past, as in the case of property laws, contract law (Kahu, 2015; Ogus and Garoupa, 2006) or other internationally available legal instruments in global interactions. Thus, it is a useful source of legal development (Watson, 1974).

However, studies on possible legal transplants for harmonising and unification of CSR laws across jurisdictions have been relatively rare and less explored. Furthermore, the extent studies have overlooked the dynamic socio-legal-economic capacities of developing countries. This has resulted in transplanting laws from developed countries to developing countries while ignoring global developments and the legal-economic potentials of developing countries in a multicultural world. Garoupa and Ogus (2006) have pointed out that the cross-interaction and interchange is needed for better legal transplants. By putting the notion of transplant as uni-directional from developed countries to developing ones, the idea of legal transplants can overlook the dynamic capacity of developing countries. For example, Indian CSR supports the views of Amartya Sen that there is a 'need to balance the traditional human rights thinking by giving a more prominent place to matters relating to development' in the human rights agenda (Karhu, 2015). It contains several elements responding to the needs of development unlike the Western models that concentrate more on individual rights and environ-mental protection. Thus, developed countries can imbibe worthy elements of legal-institutional aspects of CSR from the developing countries into their domestic laws. On the other hand, Indian policymakers ignored fundamental aspects related to individual rights that are directly affected by business operations in their scope of CSR policy. For example, businesses in India have had several cases of causing negative impact through pollution and other devastations caused by the ancillary activities associated with industries such as mining, chemicals, oil, tobacco, bev-erages and cement. By prioritising the needs of development and GDP growth over human rights, policymakers cannot ignore these negative consequences of develop-ment. The gravity of these impacts that involve blatant violation of individual rights needs to draw immediate attention. The United States and the European Union have developed a stronger CSR policy framework to ensure that business activities do not adversely impact individual rights. Thus, India can learn and transplant such dynamic elements of western CSR policies to protect and promote individual rights from the impacts of business activities. In this process of exchange and transplant, countries are likely to find better mechanisms for implementing CSR policies along with a decent degree of harmonisation in the application of CSR to promote uniformity in CSR.

In doing so, as Mousourakis (2013) suggests, 'relativity must be considered when the comparative law is used in the search for similarities between different legal systems' or 'is employed in the process of harmonising law'. Furthermore, 'the relativity is imposed by the special relationship of the law to its cultural, political and socio-economic environment and its effect on the meaning and function of legal rules, institutions and principles must be addressed' (Mousourakis, 2013). This provides a model of interaction between jurisdictions based on the balance between the distinctions of their laws on the one hand, and the pressure for convergence generated by transboundary trade of goods and services on the other hand if there is transboundary interaction between different sets of legal rules and practices. However, studies on the likelihood of convergence in the sense of adoption of, or adjustment to, norms from other sets of legal rules and practices of legal rules through relativity are limited.

In addition to this, the nature of relationship of CSR to law is not clear and this has raised difficulties in regulating CSR. Over time, several legal theories linking CSR to law were sought for regulating CSR. Prominent among them are reflexive law, responsive regulation, inclusive regulation and prescriptive laws. However, these theories have limitations and are unlikely to provide a concrete proposition for a universally applicable regulation on CSR. To bridge this gap, Osuji (2015) sug-gested *inventive interventionism* (II) as a regulatory approach with new conceptual and functional ways to effectively regulate CSR. For this purpose, he examined and evaluated reflexive and responsive regulation, prescriptive law, voluntary self-regulation, and developed the conceptual and functional roots while building on legal transplant theories. Importantly, Osuji (2015) suggests a new functional approach that requires 'appropriate institutional support for regulatory CSR, recognising the distinctive features and goals of CSR and social disclosure and separating them in regulatory design, and linking performance and disclosure particularly through stakeholder empowerment'. For example, this can include 'recognition of self-regulatory bodies, endorsement of guidelines issued by independent, public or private bodies, establishment of CSR-specific regulatory, administrative and independent bodies' to set standards (Osuji, 2015). Through this process, inventive interventionism takes a particular care in importing jurisdiction's non-governmental actors such as individuals, corporations and other organisations and its conditions and environment.

Thus, 'inventive interventionism places regulatory CSR in an institutional framework that provides for CSR-related legal powers for public and independent agencies and rights for stakeholders, while enabling effective exercise of such powers and rights' (Osuji, 2015). This can be a powerful tool for achieving uniform law in CSR; however, inventive interventionism incorrectly assumes institutional support even in the absence of any incentives to gain support from the institutions in cases of complex and conflicting institutional differences. Furthermore, it does not consider the tricky zones of institutions with weak governance who do not have equal say, particularly when power is imbalanced. This can be addressed by considering reflexive law alongside the inventive interventionism. 'Reflexive law offers a theoretical framework for understanding public–private regulation on CSR' (Buhmann, 2010). It 'refers to learning and exchanging of demands, expectations and best practices between social systems' (Buhmann, 2010). This can complement the dynamic approach of inventive interventionism for realising a mechanism that can facilitate the development of substantive law on CSR in transboundary operations while ensuring some flexibility to avoid pitfalls of strict or prescriptive regulations. It can bridge the gaps of both the theories to provide a mechanism for a collective interplay and more efficient legal transplants that can gradually lead to juridification of CSR. However, there are some pitfalls when reflexive law alone is applied as it weakens the sanctions and monitoring mechanisms. Hence, a combination of inventive interventionism and reflexive law can offer a solution here.

Reflexive law assumes that 'institutional procedure mechanisms should be designed to neutralize power disparities in order to limit abuse of power by stronger participants in the process' (Tubner, 1986; Buhmann, 2010). Thus, social actors have an opportunity to learn and 'reflect on the consequences of their actions in relation to the community and to integrate societal needs and demands through self-regulation' (Buhmann, 2010). Reflexive law, therefore, achieves 'substantive results through co- and self-regulation by societal actors' (Buhmann, 2010). Through this approach, a law that can facilitate ways of working with the subsystems, for example, by seeking 'the alignment of regulatory norms set by legislators, legal norms generated as a response by the legal subsystem, and activities over which control is sought' (Amao, 2007). It avoids direct regulation while shaping the processes of self-regulation resulting in the 'benefits of better adaptation to conditions of uncertainty and those requiring compromise' (Amao, 2007). Thus, adding this legal approach to inventive interventionism adds substantive elements that are built through the process of engagement and support from institutional stakeholders. Furthermore, this approach harmonises the advantages of laws and self-regulation in order to minimise the disadvantages of both approaches.

As Buhmann (2010) observed, reflexive law theory 'does not claim that substantive, top-down regulation should be abandoned, but supplements statutory law as a regulatory strategy by offering an alternative'. Here, authorities can continue to exercise control by 'establishing procedures that guide self-reflection but leave organisations, such as companies, the freedom and choice to determine their own norms of conduct discursively' (Buhmann, 2010). With inventive interventionism, this autonomy defines the scope within which the freedom to self-regulate is exercised. Achieving substantive results through reflexive regulatory process and inventive interventionism, CSR contributions are best realised in cooperation with stakeholders through a degree of business self-regulation. The analysis indicates a gradual juridification of CSR and provides novel perspective to the common ideals that bind CSR and law.

This gives incentives to the countries to gradually provide their support for regulating CSR, leading to a stronger legal approach that results in a more effective universal legal mechanism of CSR that can motivate countries, including developing ones, to adapt it to their institutional set-up; while keeping the universal frame and ambit in view but refraining from opting to their own institutional schemes. In order to transform CSR from its current state rooted in institutional differences and voluntarism, it is a necessity to give institutions a chance to understand CSR, its importance, flexibility and its applications with more flexibility and acceptability while understanding their normative values and realising the legal values attached to it.

Some scholars, however, argue that legal transplants, in general, do not devise the socio-cultural position of the society that they transplant to. According to them, by the time transplant occurs, it loses its significance as the original rule undergoes change during its adoption (Legrand, 1997; Berkowitz et al., 2003). This assumption cannot be completely validated. Mousourakis (2013) argues that 'there is a degree of uniformity with respect to the emergence of certain needs as societies progress through similar stages of development and a natural tendency exists towards imitation, which may be precipitated by a desire to accelerate progress or pursue common political and socio-economic objectives'. As pointed out by Garoupa and Ogus (2006) legal transplant for CSR aims to realise a centrally recognised legal culture by harmonising legal rules. They observed that it has the potential to provide a uniform system that is globally applicable if the rules, regulations and norms existing across different institutions are integrated thus recognising legal culture by harmonising legal rules (Garoupa and Ogus, 2006; Osuji, 2015). As Osuji (2015) suggests, supporting 'legal and institutional infrastructure, including adequate enforcement and verification mechanisms, are required to ensure that responsibility is accompanied by ability and willingness to abide by the rules'. This can be done effectively, if the transplants are done in line with inventive interventionism while bringing reflexive laws dimensions into the discussion. 'Legal transplants have enabled various systems of law and legal orders to benefit from the legal innovations made elsewhere' Osuji, 2015). Thus, legal transplants with an inventive interventionism regulatory approach along with reflexive law can facilitate the desired outcomes. What is important is to reach a common underpinning of CSR understanding and its relation to law. The dynamic mutual absorptions of distinct law and CSR elements can ultimately lead to a universal framework gradually over time and thus prevent countries from shielding under their own institutional set-ups. Thus, transplanting CSR from each other and adapting it to their geographical contexts can provide a stronger and balanced approach to CSR and this could promote a centrally recognised legal culture on CSR.

In summary, CSR in India can benefit from this approach by tackling its various institutional flaws using the lens of the global context and thus become part of global CSR.

9.6 CONCLUSION

Corporate social responsibility was weaved into the socioeconomic fabric of India several centuries ago. It existed in the form of charity or philanthropy for cultural as well as religious reasons. In the course of time, its nature evolved into different models like the Gandhian trusteeship model. It retained a close nexus with the Indian culture of 'giving' until market liberalisation in the 1990s when CSR in India went through a transition to shape into strategic CSR. In this context, corporations in India started treating CSR as another tool for profit maximisation. As CSR is not regulated in most jurisdictions, it exists in different forms and lacks a mechanism for its effective implementation. Furthermore, the institutional differences across different nations had a huge impact on CSR in a newly liberalised economy of India that was attracting foreign firms. Weak monitoring and implementing mechanisms along with the absence of accountability led to corporate irresponsibility in many cases. The ethos of giving now shifted to strategic investments for companies as they linked CSR to their financial performance. Along with this, the growing gap between the haves and have-nots necessitated a change and a more systematic form of CSR in India.

Following these developments, the government of India recognised giving back to the society as one of the core responsibilities of businesses. As corporates have the know-how, strategic thinking, workforce and financial strength to enable widespread social transformation, they can be instrumental in achieving sustainable developmental goals. The constitution of India has enshrined the duty to take welfare measures for the social and economic development of the country as one of the state's core duties.[47] The Indian government, in the exercise of its power under the constitution, enacted the law on the social responsibility of corporates under the company law to restore the culturally driven social responsibility of business in the Indian context. The provision makes CSR mandatory and provides a mechanism to formulate, implement and monitor CSR practices for its effective discharge of duties.

The enactment has made India the first country to regulate and mandate CSR spending. This has provided a systematic approach towards corporate's duty towards society while retaining its traditional roots. Mandatory CSR spending does have a positive and statistically significant impact on firm value,[48] and companies in India now increasingly undertake CSR activities that are resulting in positive impact on society. While corporate social commitments have improved when compared to their CSR performance before the enactment, some concerns related to the risk of tick boxing, the provision to comply or explain, and effective accountability mechanisms are growing concerns that need to be addressed going forward.

It is well known from the past that companies make huge impact on society and the environment. India has not given required importance to the adverse impact that companies have on society. It emphasised community development while ignoring the protection and promotion of individual rights or human rights. This may result in situations where companies engage in community development as part of their mandatory CSR requirements while blatantly violating human rights. Here legal transplant theory along with inventive interventionism and reflexive law can enable a superior regulatory framework wherein the Indian legal system transplants the strengths of Western laws on business human rights while Western legal systems learn from the experience of India about regulating CSR. This can lead to positive socioeconomic outcomes by viewing firms, as part of society, having a duty towards its advancement. In the process of harmonising law and CSR through legal transplants, this chapter provides a conceptual analysis by bringing reflective theory into the inventive interventionism to provide a fundamental basis for transplant mechanism.

---

[47] www.mea.gov.in/Images/pdf1/Part4.pdf accessed 29 June 2018.
[48] P. Bhagawan and J. Mukhopadhya (2018). Does mandatory CSR expenditure affect firm value? Evidence from Indian firms, *Ideas for India*, 4 January 2018, available at www.ideasforindia.in /topics/macroeconomics/does-mandatory-csr-expenditure-affect-firm-value-evidence-from-indian-firms.html accessed 29 June 2018.

REFERENCES

Amao, O. O. (2007). Reflexive law: Does it have any relevance to the corporate social responsibility (CSR) debate? *Cork Online Law Review*, 6, 55–64.

Allirajani, M. (2017). 'India Inc's CSR spending rises 22% in FY16', *Times of India*, 30 January 2017, available at http://timesofindia.indiatimes.com/business/India-business /India-incs-csr-spending-rises-22-in-fy 16/aticleshow/56869682.cms accessed on 29 June 2018

Berkowitz, D., Pistor, K. and Richard, J. F. (2003). Economic development, legality, and the transplant effect. *European Economic Review*, 47(1), 165–95.

Bird, R. G., Mukherjee, A. and Duppati, G. (2017). Mandatory corporate social responsibility: The India experience. 8th Conference on Financial Markets and Corporate Governance (FMCG) 2017.

Boodoo, M. U. (2016). Does mandatory CSR reporting regulation lead to improved corporate social performance? *Evidence from India.*

Buhmann, K. (2010). Reflexive regulation of CSR to promote sustainability: Understanding EU public-private regulation on CSR through the case of human rights. University of Oslo Faculty of Law Research Paper No. 2010-07. Available at SSRN: https://ssrn.com /abstract=1712801.

Chahoud, T., Emmerling, J., Kolb, D., Kubina, I., Repinski, G. and Schläger, C. (2007). *Corporate social and environmental responsibility in India-assessing the UN global compact's role* Vol. 26 Bonn: Deutsches Institut für Entwicklungspolitik GmbH, p. 127.

Chhaparia, P. and Jha, M. (2018). Corporate social responsibility in India: The legal evolution of CSR policy. *Amity Global Business Review*, 13(1).

Deep, A. (2017). Vedic theory of debts and CSR, legal regulations and CSR initiative by Maharatna Company – Gail (India) Ltd. *International Journal of Current Research*, 9(07), 54263–24268.

Dhanesh, G. S. (2015). Why corporate social responsibility? An analysis of drivers of CSR in India. *Management Communication Quarterly*, 29(1), 114–29.

Dharmapala, D. and Khanna, V. (2018). The impact of mandated corporate social responsibility: Evidence from India's Companies Act of 2013. *International Review of law and Economics*, 56, 92–104.

Galliara M. (2011). Corporate social responsibility in India. In G. Williams, ed., *Responsible management in Asia: Perspectives on CSR*. London: Palgrave Macmillan, pp. 27–43.

Garoupa, N. and Ogus, A. (2006). A strategic interpretation of legal transplants. *The Journal of Legal Studies*, 35(2), 339–63.

Gatti, L., Vishwanath, B., Seele, P. and Cottier, B. (2018). Are we moving beyond voluntary CSR? Exploring theoretical and managerial implications of mandatory CSR resulting from the New Indian Companies Act. *Journal of Business Ethics*, 1–12.

Gautam, R. and Singh, A. (2010). Corporate social responsibility practices in India: A study of top 500 companies. *Global Business and Management Research: An International Journal*, 2 (1), 41–56.

Gopalan, S. and Kamalnath, A. (2015). Mandatory corporate social responsibility as a vehicle for reducing inequality: An Indian solution for Piketty and the millennials. *Northwestern Journal of Law & Social Policy*, 10, 34.

Gouda, S., Khan, A. G. and Hiremath, S. L. (2017). *Corporate social responsibility in India. Trends, issues and strategies*. Hamburg: Anchor Academic Publishing.

Husted, B. W. (2015). Corporate social responsibility practice from 1800–1914: Past initiatives and current debates. *Business Ethics Quarterly*, 25(1), 125–41.

Karhu, J. (2015). Corporate social responsibility and the law: Ideas for developing dynamic elements in mandatory CSR. *Review of Market Integration*, 7(1), 62–74.

Legrand, P. (1997). The impossibility of 'legal transplants'. *Maastricht Journal of European and Comparative law*, 4(2), 111–24.

Mohan A. (2001). Corporate citizenship: Perspectives from India. *Journal of Corporate Citizenship*, 1 Jun(2), 107–17.

Mousourakis, G. (2013). Legal transplants and legal development: A jurisprudential and comparative law approach. *Acta Juridica Hungarica*, 54(3), 219–36.

Mukherjee, A. and Bird, R. (2016). Analysis of mandatory CSR expenditure in India: a survey. *International Journal of Corporate Governance*, 7(1), 32–59.

Mukherjee, A. and Chaturvedi, R. (2013). From CSR to MCSR: The journey towards mandatory corporate social responsibility in India. *Golden Research Thoughts* 3(2), 2231-5063.

Osuji, O. K. (2015). Corporate social responsibility, juridification and globalisation: 'Inventive interventionism' for a 'paradox'. *International Journal of Law in Context*, 11(3), 265–98.

Parvin, K. K. (2018). Corporate social responsibility: Dimensions and challenges in selected software companies in India. *International Journal of Research in Commerce & Management*, 9(2).

Pillai, K. R. (2017). Corporate social responsibility in India: A journey from corporate philanthropy to governance mandate. *Indian Journal of Corporate Governance*, 10 (2),176–84.

Pandey, S. and Rishi, P. (2016). Logical framework analysis of corporate social responsibility initiatives of Indian paper industry. *Journal of Organisation & Human Behaviour*, 5(4).

Rishi, P. and Moghe, S. (2013). Integrating corporate social responsibility and culture as a strategy for holistic corporate success in India. *The Journal of Corporate Citizenship*, (51), 17.

Sharma, S. (2013). Corporate social responsibility in India: The emerging discourse & concerns. *Indian Journal of Industrial Relations*,582–96.

Singh, A. and Verma, P. (2014). From philanthropy to mandatory CSR: A journey towards mandatory corporate social responsibility in India. *International Journal of Business and Management Invention* 3(8).

Sinha, S. N. (2017). A critical analysis of the provisions of corporate social responsibility. *IUP Journal of Corporate Governance*, 16(3).

Singh, A. and Verma, P. (2014). CSR@ 2%: A new model of corporate social responsibility in India. *International Journal of Academic Research in Business and Social Sciences* 4(10).

Sundar, P. (2000). *Beyond business: From merchant charity to corporate citizenship: Indian business philanthropy through the ages.* Indian Centre for Philanthropy: Tata McGraw Hill Publishing Company.

Sundar, P. (2013). *Business and community: The story of corporate social responsibility in India.* New Delhi: Sage Publications.

Teubner, G. (1983). Substantive and Reflexive Elements in Modern Law. *Law and Society Review* 17(2), 239–85.

Trautmann, T. R. (1979). Traditions of statecraft in ancient India. In R. J. Moore ed., *Tradition and politics in South Asia.* New Delhi: Vikas Publishing House, pp. 86–102.

Watson, A. (1978). Comparative law and legal change. *The Cambridge Law Journal*, 37(2), 313–36.

Nigeria's Informal Economy, Social Responsibility and Sustainable Development

Uchenna Uzo and Olamide Shittu

10.1 INTRODUCTION

The informal economy is an integral part of every developing country. According to Mbaye (2014: p. 3), the informal economy contributes to 'about half of the national output, more than 8 per cent of total employment and 90 per cent of new jobs in African low-income countries'. The important role the informal economy plays in developing countries makes academics, practitioners and policymakers view it as a driver of sustainable development in developing economies, especially in Africa (Onwe, 2013). In a continent with the majority of the people surviving at a low standard of living (Ibrahim and Wertheimer, 2018), the informal economy continues to serve as a means of last resort to the masses (Truong, 2018). Beyond its provision of a source of livelihood, the informal economy serves as a platform where economic activities interact with community practices (Gibson, Hill and Law, 2018). As a result of this, the informal economy gives its actors a sense of belonging, community participation, and moral norms and values. The actors view themselves as important members of the community and they contribute to its development through their various socioeconomic activities (Gibson, Hill and Law, 2018).

Unlike the formal sector, this array of activities in the informal economy are largely unregulated by formal and legal institutions, thus mostly outside the government's control (Bromley and Wilson, 2017). This neglect perhaps also is reflected in the non-involvement of informal sector actors in matters of world sustainability (Organisation for Economic Co-operation and Development [OECD], 2017). At best, informal sector workers are viewed by policymakers as needing intervention and thus, government programmes are mostly designed to disrupt their economic activities in urban centres. However, the few studies on the informal economy have shown that they are very organised and interwoven into the fabrics of community norms and values (Bromley and Wilson, 2017; Gibson, Hill and Law, 2018; Uzo and Adigwe, 2016). Embedded in their economic operations, therefore, are various activities that could be considered as promoting social development through familial, community, ethnic, associational and religious configurations (Bromley and Wilson, 2017; Gibson, Hill and Law, 2018).

Given the dearth of literature on social responsibility activities in the informal sector in developing economies, this chapter documents the unique ways informal businesses practise social responsibility and how such activities could be the key to uncovering new strategies for achieving sustainable development. Thus, this study focuses on unpacking the nature of social responsibility activities in firms within the informal economy and its viability for sustainable development in Nigeria – a typical developing economy. The qualitative method of data collection was adopted for the study (Mason, 2010). This was important in order to explore the in-depth understanding of socially responsible practices in the informal economy context. Qualitative data was gathered from informal businesses in the retail and movie (Nollywood) industries in Nigeria through interviews and observations. An extensive exploration of existing literature on informal businesses, CSR and sustainable development was also conducted in order to situate the study in the current research endeavour. The hermeneutic analysis was used to analyse primary and secondary data. The questions this chapter attempts to answer include how informal businesses understand corporate social responsibility and why; what specific social responsibility activities informal businesses engage in; and, in what ways these activities address the Sustainable Development Goals.

10.2 EXPLORING THE INFORMAL ECONOMY

For decades, the informal economy has been an enduring aspect of almost all economies – more enduring and significant in developing countries than developed economies. Cheru (2002: pp. 48–9) defined the informal economy as a 'dynamic and enduring force' that represents 'an alternative society, with parallel social and religious institutions alongside the official ones'. A significant feature of the informal economy agreed by scholars in literature is its lack of recognition from governments (Gërxhani, 2004), with Cheru (2002: p. 49) describing it as 'a node of resistance and defiance against state domination'. However, literature is quick to separate the discussion of informal economy's activities outside government's control from illegal business activities (International Institute for Environment and Development [IIED], 2016; Larson, 2002; Busso, Fazio and Levy, 2012). For instance, Mbaye (2014) suggested that the operation of the informal sector outside the scope of the official legal and fiscal systems is as a result of the absence of valid statistics on its activities.

Even with this, the differentiation of informal and formal sectors in an economy should be considered as more of a range than a distinction (Mbaye, 2014; Steel and Snodgrass, 2008). This is because several studies have shown that many informal enterprises pay informal taxes, form pressure groups and sustain contractual relationships with corporate firms (Auriol and Warlters, 2005; Gordon, 2009; Mbaye, 2014).

However, the informal sector has been said to characterize those enterprises that are not formally registered, small in size and constitute of jobs that serve as sources of living for those who are less privileged, especially in developing economies (International Conference of Labour Statisticians [ICLS], 2003). This makes the informal economy very diverse and these small enterprises can be found in various sectors including farming, trade, crafts, production, mining, construction and services among others (IIED, 2016).

The diversity of the informal economy makes it worth trillions of dollars worldwide which accounts for about 13 per cent of world GDP. In several developing countries including Nigeria, Benin, Burkina Faso, India, Colombia and Togo, the total value-added created by the informal economy form about one-third of the gross value added (GVA) of these countries (International Labour Organisation [ILO], 2013; IIED, 2016). Informal employment has been found to be more than 50 per cent of non-agricultural employment in Asia, Africa and Latin America (ILO, 2013; IIED, 2016) thus representing more than half of the workforce in developing economies (Vanek, Chen, Carré, Heintz and Hussmanns, 2014; IIED, 2016). This means that about 80 per cent of households in cities in developing countries rely on informal employment such as home-based work, street vending and waste picking as their primary source of income (Inclusive Cities and WIEGO, 2012).

Thus, due to the huge importance of the informal economy in developing countries, a discussion of sustainable development and CSR in these countries cannot overlook the informal sector's contribution. However, with so many studies of CSR focused on formal organisations, the questions this chapter hopes to answer include: Do enterprises in the informal sector engage in social responsibility? Are there ways informal enterprises view social responsibility that are different from formal organisations? What are the socially responsible practices that informal enterprises engage in? How can their socially responsible practices, if any, promote the efforts of developing countries towards sustainable development?

10.3 INFORMAL ECONOMY AND BUSINESS SOCIAL RESPONSIBILITY

Although the concept of corporate social responsibility (CSR) started in the 1930s, scholars are yet to find an acceptable definition for it (Castka, Bamber, Bamber and Sharp, 2004; Obalola, 2010; Rahman, 2011; Sweeney, 2007). However, current literature has agreed that CSR should be an organisation's contribution to the socioeconomic development of society. According to Efiong, Usang, Inyang and Effiong (2013), CSR:

> Is the promise by business organisations to behave in a way that is ethically acceptable and at the same time contributing to the economic development and improvement of the living conditions of the employees, the catchment community and the larger society. (p. 119)

The CSR is important because it represents the avenues through which an organisation projects its impact on society. Made more prominent with the recent global discussion on driving sustainable development through stakeholders' participation in developing economies, CSR is a tool adopted by organisations to facilitate sustainable development and contribute to the political, economic, educational and health advancement of such of their host community or country (Efiong et al., 2013; Ismail, 2009; Moon, 2007). Early discussions on the role of CSR in an organisation led to the emergence of two schools of thought – the 'classical view' which sees CSR only as activities that should be embedded in the company's primary economic activities and the 'stakeholder view' which believes CSR activities should be beyond economic considerations to include socially responsible activities (Branco and Rodriques, 2007; Crowther, 2004).

In other words, classical theorists advocate that corporate organisations should always consider the profitability of their CSR activities which means whatever socially responsible practice an organisation engages in should be ultimately to recoup profits for the organisation (Coelho, McClure and Spry, 2003; Hailong, 2010; Jamali and Mirshak, 2007; Mang'unyi and Chege, 2014; Quazi and O'Brien, 2000). On the other hand, the proponents of the stakeholder perspective argue that corporate entities should look beyond making profits to include philanthropic activities that have positive impacts on communities. In this sense, CSR activities should be beyond only protecting the interests of shareholders to include stakeholders which may be environmental groups, communities outside local operations, customers, government agencies and so on (Coelho, 2003; Hailong, 2010; Jamali and Mirshak, 2007; Mang'unyi and Chege, 2014; Pirsch, Gupta and Landreth, 2007). However, a strategic school of thought emerged after these previous two in a bid to synthesize their viewpoints by arguing that CSR should be practised strategically in order to boost the overall competitive advantage of the organisation (Hailong, 2010; Jamali and Mirshak, 2007).

Studies have also shown that organisations benefit from CSR (Baena, 2018; Barrett, 1998; Fan, Haq, Moeriera and Virk, 2018; Harrison and Freeman, 1999). CSR activities, carried out effectively, help to create a strong corporate brand recognition and increased reputation for the company, brand loyalty and government and community support (Baena, 2018). In this regard, several types of research have been conducted across the world on CSR, mostly focusing on corporate organisations and multinational companies whilst research on small and medium enterprises (SMEs) is very scarce (Cantele and Zardini, 2018; Russo and Tencati, 2008; Spence and Rutherfoord, 2003). Thus, the arguments that have shaped CSR discourse over the years and the attendant policies have only been from and consequently focus on formal organisations.

The neglect of SMEs in mainstream CSR literature has manifested in several ways. First, the 'corporate' in the term CSR has ensured its limitation to formal organisations without regard for SMEs that cannot take on the 'corporate' label. This means that CSR discussion may seem irrelevant to SMEs who hardly have the financial and operational capacity to delineate a CSR department. Also, because of scholastic and political emphasis on CSR reporting, SMEs may have difficulties in producing reports on financial and socially beneficial activities (Visser, 2012). Therefore, 'socially responsible enterprises' is a better term for SMEs as it captures the essence of their activities without placing stringent ethical considerations on them as compared to formal organisations (Visser, 2012). To reflect this reality, Visser (2012) adopted the IDEARSE Centre's definition of CSR which is:

> A permanent and continuous commitment, voluntarily adopted by the business, to respond to the economic, social and environmental impacts of its activities, and to guarantee the sustainable and human development to all its stakeholders.

The above definition encapsulates the purpose of a socially responsible business – whether a corporate organisation or a small enterprise – which is to give back some goodwill to its stakeholders who ensure its survival. However, due to the narrowness of the definitions of CSR and its inability to adequately capture informal enterprises' activities, scholars have found it helpful to distinguish between the CSR carried out by large organisations and the social responsibility of SMEs (Russo and Tencati, 2008; Visser, 2012). Therefore, the literature on CSR has conceptualized corporate organisations' CSR as formal or explicit while that of SMEs are referred to as informal or implicit social responsibility (Russo and Tencati, 2008; Visser, 2012).

The major differences between these two forms of social responsibility are the level of formality and resources dedicated to social responsibility activities. SMEs are more likely to engage in socially responsible practices that are embedded in their daily routine activities, unlike large organisations that usually create a separate department for CSR activities. Also, SMEs tend to be more integrated into local communities than large organisations. SMEs usually have a local level of operations and most times controlled by their owners and depend on personal sources of income (Russo and Tencati, 2008). This means they are more likely to feel the need to act in a socially responsible way as a part of the community than corporate organisations. For the latter, issues of CSR are more complex and such decisions are influenced by consideration for the industry, resource availability, corporate ethical values, product nature and organisational commitment among others (Fortis, Maon, Frooman and Reiner, 2018; Obalola, 2007).

SMEs are not compelled to have all these structures in place and mostly emphasize being connected with the cultural practices of their local communities and focus on traditional values such as good employee relations, communal sharing and consensus (Miranda and Miranda, 2018; Helg, 2007). This is not to say that corporate organisations do not have informal CSR in their internal operations, however, the level is more intensified in SMEs than the former (Russo and Tencati, 2008). According to Russo and Tencati (2008), SMEs hardly label their activities as informal social responsibility although it forms a significant part of their operations.

The authors further found out that SMEs informal social responsibility activities are part of their attempts to gain recognition and acceptance at the community level for their activities (Russo and Tencati, 2008). Therefore, although SMEs may not have comprehensive plans and strategies, they also have commitments towards environmental protection, eco-efficiency, and employees and stakeholder engagement (Russo and Tencati, 2008).

Another way SMEs galvanize actions on social responsibility is through the formation of associations and indigenous organisations (Visser, 2012). These organisations give SMEs a platform to form collective efforts at creating exchanges that promote social and cultural benefits instead of personal profits consideration (Jackson, 2016; Peredo and McLean, 2010). According to Berkes and Adhikari (2006):

> The individual profit motive no doubt exists but it seems to be subordinate to meeting community needs and objectives. The social role of many of these enterprises are [sic] apparent in terms of providing local employment, making use of talents and resources locally available, and sharing profits among community members. (p. 11)

Peredo and McLean (2010) noted that most SMEs in developing economies conduct ethnic-based social responsibility activities. That is, their informal socially responsible practices are targeted at providing social benefits to members of their ethnic groups (Peredo and McLean, 2010). In terms of employment, SMEs employ traditional apprenticeships and community-based entrepreneurship to mentor younger ones in their communities in their line of business (Jackson, 2016). The apprenticeship system is one in which owners of informal businesses take children of community members under them in order to mentor and teach them their trade. The young apprentice receives this training in exchange for his/her loyalty, voluntary service and dedication. After the apprentice service, which can span a number of years, the business owner then sets the young apprentice up for his/her own business or sometimes opens up a new branch of the business with the apprentice as a manager. This strategy not only helps to provide SMEs with an adequate human resource for smooth operations of their businesses but also promotes community or ethnic values by empowering and mentoring youths in entrepreneurship, thus increasing people's standard of living.

10.4 AN EXPOSITION OF THE INFORMAL ECONOMY'S SOCIAL RESPONSIBILITY ACTIVITIES IN NIGERIA

As with other SMEs as discussed above, socially responsible activities among informal businesses in Nigeria are ingrained in their day-to-day activities. As a result of this, and stemming from their relative size to corporate organisations, informal businesses do not have separate organisational departments that oversee socially responsible activities in neighbouring communities. Sometimes, informal business owners make attempts to recognize the socially responsible activities they engage in and therefore bring up innovative business strategies that have an impact on the sustainable development of their immediate communities. Studies have shown that informal economic activities such as tailoring, shoe cobblers, retailing, carpentry and vehicle repair among others are avenues through which they earn a living, train their young ones and improve society (Onokala and Banwo, 2015; Onwe, 2013). However, for this research, we focused on informal businesses in the Nollywood movie industry and retail sector in Nigeria. Therefore, with the data conducted through in-depth interviews and observations, the researchers were able to identify apprenticeship and credit sales services that are part of informal business operations which could also count as being equivalent to a CSR. These are discussed below.

10.5 APPRENTICESHIP AS INFORMAL BUSINESS SOCIAL RESPONSIBILITY

Findings from observations and interviews of Nollywood business owners reveal that a socially responsible practice that informal business owners in Nigeria engage in is apprenticeship. In this regard, informal business owners would take greenhorns under their tutelage and teach them the profession in exchange for their unpaid service. This arrangement usually occurs in businesses that require special skills and training. In most of the cases, the apprentice is usually from the same social group with the business owner such as ethnic, religious and neighbourhood affiliations. In some instances, the apprentices are young people whose parents could perhaps not send them to schools. On other occasions, the parents pay the business owners some advance payments for registration. Data from Nollywood show that after graduation, the apprentice becomes part of the network of the master and although the former is paid for his/her services, such payment is heavily discounted due to the established relationship between both parties.

In the same vein, findings from street sellers in Lagos identify family, friendship and ethnic associations as important factors that influence their entrance into the business. This phenomenon was observed in 11 instances among the respondents. Also, the majority of the respondents acknowledged that the difficult economic situation in Nigeria made them get into the business after seeking recommendations from friends and/or relatives. A respondent explained his situation as follows:

> Previously, I worked in tower aluminium company and I discovered that the payment structure couldn't help me cater for my family and also pay some bills, so I decided to quit the job. Later, I met a friend of mine who introduced me to this business and asked me to try for some weeks in which I obeyed and since then I have been in the business. (IDI/Male/Street Seller/Sausage Roll/Lagos)

Data from interviews show that some of the respondents migrated from other parts of Nigeria due to the unavailability of job opportunities and in search of greener pastures in Lagos. However, their inability to also find paid employment in Lagos led them to approach retailers who then introduced them into the business. A street seller explained his situation thus:

> When I came into Lagos state, I searched around for a job but could not find a job and I also searched for business but could not find a good one, so I started this sunglass business with little money. This business was introduced to me by my elder brother and I checked and noticed it was profitable. (IDI/Male/Street Seller/ Apparels/Lagos)

As in Nollywood, street sellers also work for some retailers or wholesalers for some years before branching out to be independent. Like in the movie industry, business owners in the study location charge little or nothing when accepting apprentices that will work for them in exchange for mentorship. A respondent described his story thus:

> Actually, I learned the trade from my master and after I got my freedom, I started selling on my own. (IDI/Male/Street Seller/Fashion and Accessories/Lagos)

Aside from selling the goods for their mentors, the street sellers are able to make some profits off the wares they parade for their bosses. When asked how street sellers make money from working for retailers, a respondent explained thus:

> The hawkers earn their profit from sales. Whatever they carry, it is left for them to know how much to sell. But they must return my own money. The more you sell, the more you make money. Averagely, most of them earn or make 2,000 Naira daily. A serious hawker can make 2,000 Naira per day. (IDI/Male/Retailer/Magazines/ Lagos)

Another respondent who also served as an apprentice for some years and hawked his wares on the street after a while reflected on his journey thus:

> I paid someone to learn this business. After learning I sold for a while, that is, I also hawked on the streets then I got a shop of my own when KAI (Kick Against Indiscipline) officials started disturbing. (IDI/Male/Retailer/Electric Shavers/Lagos)

After such an apprenticeship period, the business owners would set up the graduating apprentice with his/her own independent business or as an extension of the master's business. The new business owner then carries on the tradition of recruiting new street sellers as apprentices. Asked how he got into the business, a respondent replied as follows:

> After being an apprentice with one of my bosses, I left there and I was able to raise little money to buy an umbrella and phone. That was how I started the phone call business. And gradually I moved into a shop and became a retailer of recharge cards. (IDI/Male/Retailer/Recharge Cards/Lagos)

Although it could be said that retailers employ the street sellers in order to promote the sales of their goods, findings from the study revealed that a large part of such endeavours by retailers is their consideration for the plights of the young ones especially given the backdrop of the economic difficulties faced by the country. A respondent expressed his thoughts thus:

> most people that finished their secondary school, maybe they don't have someone to send them to a higher institution, may decide to start hawking or some who are waiting for their result could do the same thing. At the times when there are no jobs, one has to create a job for himself. Some of these boys are part-time students or people who don't have anything doing, taking it as a fulltime job. (IDI/Male/Retailer/Books/Lagos)

10.6 CREDIT SALES AS INFORMAL BUSINESS SOCIAL RESPONSIBILITY

Another socially responsible practice observed in the study area is the selling of goods to street sellers on credit. Findings show that even though this practice is a strategy by informal business owners to get more share of the market by recruiting street sellers, they also engage in credit sales to hawkers due to the latter's lack of access to adequate business capital. These store owners permit the street sellers to sell their wares in the city and pay back after completing sales. In this regard, some store owners who sell yoghurts, popcorns and the like also provide the hawkers with bicycles or wheelbarrows with which they convey their goods. A respondent reflected on this:

> Firstly I would want to say that the hawkers we are referring to do not have large funds to establish big, so they decide to start with the little funds or money they have in order to grow. They cannot afford money for a shop and that is why you see them hawking the product. We know that presently, the economic situation is not encouraging and that is why they hawk. There are no jobs for graduates and some of them go out to hawk. (IDI/Male/Retailer/Recharge Cards/Lagos)

After the day sales, the street sellers return to pay up the retailers for the purchase of the goods while keeping the profits for themselves. Credit sales social responsibility was reported in 14 cases among the respondents. In this case, long working relationships, goodwill and trust play important roles in determining the number of credit sales and duration of debt settlement. However, some of the street sellers do not reciprocate the retailers' trust, as explained by a respondent below:

> Some of them do take the products given to them and run away. There is one of the hawkers that owes me and I saw him on a bus then I came down to make sure he sees me. He did not even return the amount sold. There was another case whereby someone cheated me and made away with the cash and magazine. Unfortunately for him, I caught him one day and he started pleading so late, I had to leave him. (IDI/Male/Retailer/Journals/Lagos)

Unfavourable situations like the one described above had made some retailers create a different type of systems around credit sales and repayment. For instance, findings show that some retailers in the study area make street sellers pay for their initial purchase but permit the latter to return some of the purchased goods that they cannot sell in exchange for cash after the day provided the goods are still in good condition. As such, both the retailer and street seller are able to recoup their cost without breaching any repayment agreement. Also, although not as common as the other processes, another method adopted by retailers identified in the study area is outlined by a respondent as follows:

> It is a risky business, but whoever wants to join me must bring a guarantor to sign on behalf of that person in case of any eventuality. So you are to come with a guarantor from where you live. Although if anything negative happened, you may not hold the guarantor responsible because he might not be the one that instigated that person to defraud the business. Also, any bad person is a bad person even if the guarantor is good. Most of them sign some documents which include passports, name, address, phone number and the guarantors' name/addresses. (IDI/Male/Retailer/Magazines/Lagos)

The respondent's explanation above shows that retailers in the study area have tried to bring in legal procedures into their credit sales social responsibility in order to make it formal and reduce risk possibilities. Although respondents noted that they may not take any legal action in the case of a breach of contract, they nonetheless believed that such documentation usually works because street sellers are afraid of being prosecuted if they do not honour the agreements.

10.7 DISCUSSION OF FINDINGS AND RECOMMENDATIONS

From the findings presented above, the study has shown that socially responsible practices are integral to the functioning of informal businesses in the study area. This, therefore, has implication for the discourse and implementation of sustainable development in developing economies. For instance, the socially responsible practices informal businesses engage in ensure that developing economies are able to find alternatives to the scarcity of white-collar and government jobs for the teeming unemployed young populations. Efforts towards ensuring sustainable development in developing countries and across the world cannot continue to ignore informal economy's contribution to the business social responsibility dialogue not just because of its size but also considering its impact on employment, productivity and economic growth (Mbaye, 2014).

The chapter has as its theoretical underpinning the belief that informal businesses in developing countries are vital to the achievement of sustainable development through their socially responsible practices. Adopting the stakeholder perspective, the authors agree with Mang'unyi and Chege (2014) and Hailong (2010) that social responsibilities in organisations, whether corporate or informal, should be beyond the pure consideration of profits to include and reflect the socioeconomic realities of the community or society they operate in. As a result, the chapter explored the idiosyncrasies in the way informal businesses practice social responsibility in Lagos Megacity thus extending the growing interests and studies in developing countries' informal economies (Uzo and Adigwe, 2016; Uzo and Mair, 2014).

It should be noted that although this chapter is about the exposition of the otherwise inconspicuous elements of the sector that could represent socially responsible practices, there have been several studies that are critical of the informal economy and street selling. For instance, Adedeji, Fadamiro and Adeoye (2014) explored the consequences of street trading on special arrangements in a city and they highlighted space inaccessibility, traffic congestion, illegal structures, unmanageable waste generation and defacement of urban spaces as some of the features of public space misuse in developing economies. Others have suggested that street selling is the resultant consequence the flooding of the market with middlemen to the advantage of large retailers and petty capitalists that benefit from the effects of rural-urban migration and resource-strain in urban centres (Bromley, 2000).

However, the findings presented in this chapter are important as a means of expanding the scope of social responsibility beyond corporate organisations. Thus, this study will ensure that the contributions of grassroots to sustainable development through their social practices in SMEs are recognized and acknowledged in academic and policy discourse. Furthermore, the findings in this chapter show that socially responsible practices could be incorporated into the activities and strategy of the organisation instead of as a separate department as most corporate organisations have (Gazzola, 2014; Guadamillas-Gómez, Donate-Manzanares and Škerlavaj, 2010). Therefore, governments across all levels need to create a platform that will encourage and incentivize SMEs to put more efforts and dedicate more resources into socially responsible practices that promote galvanizing local resources for economic growth and sustainable development.

Also, corporate organisations, especially those in the fast-moving consumer goods industry, could formally recognize the social responsibility practices of informal businesses and thereby provide concessions to retailers that engage in these social responsibility practices on the purchase of goods in order to ease the burden of capital loss on the latter. The authors would also like to suggest that informal business owners adopt a more formal means of social responsibility practices as observed among a few of the retailers in the study area, as this would reduce the likelihood of a breach of agreements among the apprentices or street sellers. For instance, as adopted by some of the retailers, the provision of guarantors by street sellers and filling out of some legal documents would to a large extent prevent the thoughts of betrayal of trust and loyalty among the hawkers.

Lastly, the authors would propose that further studies be conducted on other social responsibility practices among informal businesses in emerging economies or as a comparative analysis between developing and developed economies in order to better situate the phenomenon in academic discourse. Also, these types of research would provide more empirical evidence for a robust theoretical analysis while also enshrining policy implications of the practices in grounded research. The authors believe there should be conscious attempts among scholars, especially in the field of sustainability, to theorize about concepts that are reflective and representative of the nature of social responsibility practices in the informal sector. This would reduce the level of confusion in the academic literature on the difference, in substance and practice, between corporate social responsibility and small businesses social responsibility.

10.8 CONCLUSION

The objectives of this chapter were to examine the nature of social responsibility in the informal economy; types of socially responsible practices that informal businesses in Nigeria engage in; and how such practices could promote sustainable development in developing economies. The study was conducted among informal businesses in the Nollywood industry and retail sector in Nigeria. The chapter sheds some light on the nature of social responsibility in informal businesses while also contributing to the debate on the conceptualization of social responsibility in the informal economy. In particular, the authors argue that the concept of corporate social responsibility does not apply to informal businesses because of their relatively small size and the nature of their operations. Informal businesses mostly do not have separate units in charge of social responsibility and such practices are integrated into their business model.

Stemming from the above and as examples of socially responsible practices in the informal sector, findings from the study showed that informal businesses in Nigeria in the main provide credit sales to their employees and street sellers, and also take on apprentices who they mentor in the art of business in exchange for their workmanship. The study also reveals that some informal business owners provide start-up funds to graduating apprentices and long-time employees that wish to start their own businesses while some other informal business owners give graduating apprentices stake in the business sometimes by opening a new branch office for them.

Finally, in light of the discussions in the chapter, the authors argue that the inclusion of informal businesses into the social responsibility discourse is important for the attainment of sustainable development in Nigeria. As such, the authors advise policymakers to provide incentives to informal businesses in order for them to consciously engage in practices that advance sustainable development in the country.

REFERENCES

Adedeji, J. A., Fadamiro, J. A. and Adeoye, A. O. (2014). Spatial implications of street trading in Osogbo traditional city centre, Nigeria. *Architecture Research*, 4(1A), 34–44. https://doi:10
.5923/s.arch.201401.05.

Auriol, E. and Warlters, M. (2005). Taxation base in developing countries. *Journal of Public Economics*, 89(4), 625–46.

Baena, V. (2018). The importance of CSR practices carried out by sport teams and its influence on brand love: The Real Madrid Foundation. *Social Responsibility Journal*, 14 (1), 61–79. https://doi.org/10.1108/SRJ-11-2016-0205.

Barrett, R. (1998). *Liberating the Corporate Soul: Building a Visionary Organization*, Oxford: Butterworth Heinemann.

Berkes, F. and Adhikari, T. (2006). Development and conservation: Indigenous business and the UNDP Equator Initiative. *International Journal of Entrepreneurship and Small Business*, 3, 671–90.

Branco, M. C. and Rodriques, L. L. (2007). Positioning stakeholder theory within the debate of corporate social responsibility. *Electronic Journal of Business Ethics and Organization Studies*, 12(1).

Bromley, R. (2000). Street vending and public policy: A global review. *International Journal of Sociology and Social Policy*, 20(1/2), 1–28. https://doi.org/10.1108 /01443330010789052.

Bromley, R. and Wilson, T. D. (2017). Introduction: The urban informal economy revisited. *Latin American Perspectives*, 45(1), 4–23. https://doi.org/10.1177/0094582X17736043.

Busso, M., Fazio, M. and Levy, S. (2012). (In)formal and (un)productive: The productivity costs of excessive informality in Mexico. IDB Working Paper Series 1DB-WP-341.

Cantele, S. and Zardini, A. (2018). Is sustainability a competitive advantage for small businesses? An empirical analysis of possible mediators in the sustainability-financing performance relationship. *Journal of Cleaner Production*, 182, 166–76.

Castka, P., Bamber, C. J., Bamber, D. J. and Sharp, J. M. (2004). Integrating corporate social responsibility (CSR) into ISO management systems: In search of a feasible CSR management system framework. *The TQM Magazine*, 16(3), 216–24.

Cheru, F. (2002). *African Renaissance: Roadmaps to the Challenge of Globalization*, London: Zed Books.

Coelho, P. R., McClure, J. E. and Spry, J. A. (2003). The social responsibility of corporate management: A classical critique. *American Journal of Business*, 18(1), 15–24.

Crowther, D. (2004). Corporate social reporting: Genuine action or window dressing? In D. Crowther and L. Rayman-Bacchus, eds., *Perspectives on Corporate Social Responsibility*. Aldershot: Ashgate.

Efiong, J. E., Usang, O. U., Inyang, I. O. and Effiong, C. (2013). Corporate social responsibility in small and medium scale enterprises in Nigeria: An example from the hotel industry. *International Journal of Business and Management*, 8(14), 119–26.

Fan, J., Haq, S. H. I. U., Moeriera, A. G. and Virk, M. M. (2018). Impact of CSR dimensions on consumer satisfaction and brand loyalty in the formation of purchase intentions: Study from Pakistan livestock industry. *Management*, 8(2), 54–63.

Fortis, Z., Maon, F., Frooman, J. and Reiner, G. (2018). Unknown knowns and known unknowns: Framing the role of organizational learning in corporate social responsibility development. *International Journal of Management Reviews*, 20(2), 277–300.

Gazzola, P. (2014). CSR integration into the corporate strategy. *Cross-Cultural Management Journal*, XVI (2[6]), 331–8.

Gërxhani, K. (2004). The informal sector in developed and less developed countries: A literature survey. *Public Choice*, 120(3/4), 267–300. https://doi:196.13.242.252.

Gibson, K., Hill, A. and Law, L. (2018). Community economies in Southeast Asia: A hidden economic geography. *Routledge Handbook of Southeast Asian Development*, 131–41.

Gordon, R. and Li, W. (2009). Tax structures in developing countries: Many puzzles and a possible explanation. *Journal of Public Economics*, 93(7–8), 855–66.

Guadamillas-Gómez, F., Donate-Manzanares, M. J. and Škerlavaj, M. (2010). The integration of corporate social responsibility into the strategy of technology-intensive firms: A case study. *Zbornik radova Ekonomskog fakulteta u Rijeci*, 28(1), 9–34.

Hailong, L. (2010). The schools of thought about corporate social responsibility [J]. *China Nonprofit Review*, 2, 007.

Harrison, J. G. and Freeman, R. E. (1999). Stakeholders, social responsibility, and performance: Empirical evidence and theoretical perspectives. *Academy of Management Journal*, 42(5), 479–85. http://dx.doi.org/10.2307/256971.

Helg, A. (2007). 'Corporate social responsibility from a Nigerian perspective'. Master's thesis, Management and Organisation, Handelshogskolan, 2007.

Ibrahim, M. I. M. and Wertheimer, A. I. (2018). Introduction: Discovering issues and challenges in low- and- middle-income countries. In M. I. M. Ibrahim, A. I. Wertheimer, Z.-U.-D. Babar, eds., *Social and Administrative Aspects of Pharmacy in Low- and Middle-Income Countries: Present Challenges and Future Solutions*, pp. 1–11. London, San Diego, Cambridge and Oxford: Academic Press, Elsevier.

Inclusive Cities and WIEGO (2010). The informal economy monitoring study. www .wiego.org/wiego/informal-economy-monitoring-study-iems-publications

International Conference of Labour Statisticians [ICLS] (2003). Guidelines concerning a statistical definition of informal employment. 17th ICLS. Available at www.ilo.org /wcmsp5/groups/public/–dgreports/–stat/documents/normativeinstrument/wcms_087622 .pdf accessed 28 March 2018.

International Institute for Environment and Development [IIED] (2016). *Informality and inclusive green growth: Evidence from 'The biggest private sector' event*. London: IIED.

International Labour Organization [ILO] (2013). *Women and men in the informal economy: A statistical picture*. Geneva: ILO.

Ismail, M. (2009). Corporate social responsibility and its role in community development: An international perspective. *Journal of International Social Research*, 2(9).

Jackson, T. (2016). Indigenous practices in the informal economy and sustainability in Africa: Cultural Heritage as a Generator of Sustainable Development, in The role of Entrepreneurship: Challenges and Opportunities – Workshop, 2 November 2016, Middlesex University.

Larson, J. E. (2002). Informality, illegality, and inequality. *Yale Law & Policy Review*, 20(1), 137–82.

Mang'unyi, M. S. and Chege, K. (2014). Challenges facing the implementation of corporate social responsibility programs in education sector: A survey of private primary schools in Busia County, Kenya. *International Journal of Innovative Research and Development*, 3(4), 410–25.

Mason, M. (2010). Sample size and saturation in PhD studies using qualitative interviews (63 paragraphs). *Forum: Qualitative Social Research*, 11(3), Art. 8, http://nbn-resolving.de/urn: nbn:de:0114-fqs100387 accessed 28 September 2016.

Mbaye, M. A. (2014). The informal sector, employment, and structural transformation: Some operational recommendations for a productive policy, The Informal Sector, Growth, Employment, and Sustainable Development: Discussion Note, pp. 1–7. International Organization of La Francophonie.

Miranda, A. T. and Miranda, J. L. F. (2018). Status and conditions of small-and medium-sized enterprises as predictors in empowering rural communities in Samar Island, Philippines. *Asia Pacific Journal of Innovation and Entrepreneurship*, 12(1), 105–19.

Moon, J. (2007). The contribution of corporate social responsibility to sustainable development. *Sustainable Development*, 15(5), 296–306.

Obalola, M. A. (2010). 'Ethics and social responsibility in the Nigerian insurance industry: A multi-methods approach'. Doctoral degree thesis, De Montfort University, 2010.

Onokala, U. and Banwo, A. (2015). Informal sector in Nigeria through the lens of apprenticeship, education and unemployment. *American Advanced Research in Management*, 1(1), 13–22.

Onwe, O. J. (2013). Role of the informal sector in development of the Nigerian economy: Output and employment approach. *Journal of Economics and Development Studies*, 1(1), 60–74.

Organisation for Economic Co-operation and Development [OECD] (2017). Enhancing the contributions of SMEs in a global and digitalised economy. *Meeting of the OECD Council at Ministerial Level Paris, 7–8 June 2017*. Available at www.oecd.org/mcm/documents/C-MIN-2017–8-EN.pdf accessed 7 June 2018.

Peredo, A. M. and McLean, M. (2010). Indigenous development and the cultural captivity of entrepreneurship. *Business & Society*, 52(4), 592–620.

Pirsch, J., Gupta, S. and Landreth, G. (2007) A framework for understanding Corporate Social Responsibility programs as a continuum: An explanatory study. *Journal of Business Ethics*, 70, 125–40.

Quazi, A. and O'Brien, D. (2000). An empirical test of a cross-national model of corporate social responsibility. *Journal of Business Ethics*, 25, 33–51.

Rahman, S. (2011). Evaluation of definitions: Ten dimensions of corporate social responsibility. *World Review of Business Research*, 1(1), 166–76.

Russo, A. and Tencati, A. (2008). Formal vs. informal CSR strategies: Evidence from Italian micro, small, medium-sized, and large firms. *Journal of Business Ethics*, 85, 339–53. https//doi:10.1007/s10551-008-9736-x.

Spence, L. J. and Rutherfoord, R. (2003). Small business and empirical perspectives in business ethics: Editorial. *Journal of Business Ethics*, 47(1), 1–5.

Steel, W. F. and Snodgrass, D. (2008). Raising productivity and reducing risks of household enterprises: Diagnostic methodology framework. *World Bank Africa Region Analysis on the Informal Economy*. Washington, DC: World Bank.

Sweeney, L. (2007). Corporate social responsibility in Ireland: Barriers and opportunities experienced by SMEs when undertaking CSR. *Corporate Governance: The International Journal of Business in Society*, 7(4), 516–23.

Truong, V. D. (2018). Tourism, poverty alleviation, and the informal economy: The street vendors of Hanoi, Vietnam. *Tourism Recreation Research*, 43(1), 52–67.

Uzo, U. and Adigwe, J. O. (2016). Cultural norms and cultural agents in buyer-seller negotiation processes and outcomes. *Journal of Personal Selling & Sales Management*, 36(2), 126–43. http://dx.doi.org/10.1080/08853134.2016.1188707.

Uzo, U. and Mair, J. (2014). Source and patterns of organizational defiance of formal institutions: Insights from Nollywood, the Nigerian movie industry. *Strategic Entrepreneurship Journal*, 8, 56–74. http://doi:10.1002/sej.1171.

Vanek, J., Chen, M. A., Carré, F., Heintz, J. and Hussmanns, R. (2014). Statistics on the informal economy: Definitions, regional estimates and challenges. WIEGO Working Paper (Statistics) 2, available at www.wiego.org/sites/default/files/publications/files/Vanek-Statistics-WIEGO-WP2.pdf accessed 28 March 2018.

Visser, W. (2012). Practising social responsibility without the CSR label. *The Guardian*. www.theguardian.com/sustainable-business/blog/smes-social-responsibility-without-csr-label accessed 7 June 2018.

The Environment in Shipping Incidents: Salvage Contracts and the Public Interest

Durand M. Cupido

11. 1 INTRODUCTION

The ideals of sustainable development can conflict with the private goals of private actors in what are traditionally private arenas governed by private property and private contracting rules. A maritime salvage operation, defined as 'any act or activity undertaken to assist a vessel or any other property in danger in navigable waters or in any other waters whatsoever'[1] is one such arena. The key actors in salvage operations, traditionally, have been the owners of maritime property (ship-owners and cargo-owners) and salvors that perform salvage operations for a reward (Rose, 2010). However, environmental protection concerns in the context of salvage operations have led to the involvement of additional actors in that salvors increasingly had to contend with public scrutiny and coastal state intervention in operations threatening pollution (De la Rue and Anderson, 2012).

The 1979 collision between the *Atlantic Empress* and *Aegean Captain*, approximately twenty miles northeast of the island of Tobago in the Caribbean Sea, illustrated how coastal state intervention can frustrate salvors' efforts to obtain a salvage award. In this incident, the *Aegean Captain* was towed to safety by salvors but the *Atlantic Empress*, loaded with 470,000 tons of crude oil, was leaking oil and on fire. There was a point where the oil escaping from the vessel 'was as little as 10 miles from the north coast of Tobago',[2] and 'none of the neighbouring Caribbean States would allow the stricken vessel into their territorial waters' (Gold, 1989). There was the real danger of pollution to the tourist beaches and coral reefs of Tobago and the prevention of pollution was an understandable primary concern.[3] The salvors, following instructions, towed the vessel 300 miles out to sea where it eventually sank (Gold, 1989). While the salvors conferred real benefits by preventing pollution and liability on the part of ship owners and their pollution underwriters, they received no reward because they saved no property. Moreover, their service was

---

[1] The International Convention on Salvage 1989, Art. 1(a).
[2] https://shipwrecklog.com/log/wp-content/uploads/2014/10/mobil-atlanticempress.pdf accessed 19 July 2019.
[3] Ibid.

not assistance to a vessel or other property in navigable water and, therefore, not a salvage operation. More recent examples such as the *Rena K* also show how governments have become more involved and how marine environmental protection has become a primary concern in salvage operations.[4]

Increased public demand for environmental protection outcomes in salvage operations has led to changes to the law regulating salvage operations, such as the entering into force of the International Convention on Salvage of 1989 (the Convention) and amendments to standard salvage contracts devised by the salvage industry. The latter include the industry standard Lloyd's Open Form Salvage Contract (hereinafter referred to as LOF), the most widely used standard contract in maritime salvage, and the Special Compensation Protection and Indemnity Clause (SCOPIC) that was designed to be used in conjunction with LOF.[5] Notwithstanding these legal developments, there is a lack of literature providing analyses of the private law of salvage, or aspects thereof, with reference to the ideals of sustainable development or the Sustainable Development Goals (SDGs) 2015. While discussions of the broader area of environmental law and its connection with other distinct areas of law do exist, the only attempt in relation to salvage law is that of De La Rue and Anderson in their work on 'Shipping and the Environment' (2012). However, while the authors acknowledge the importance of salvage 'as the first line of defence in protecting the environment' they do not explore the possible linkages, practical or academic, between environmental concerns, salvage operations and the ideals of sustainable development. As such, this chapter represents the first attempt to analyse salvage operations against the backdrop of sustainable development and the achievement of the SDGs 2015.

While the Convention and its link with sustainable development certainly merits discussion in its own right, this chapter will focus on the industry devised contractual mechanisms and most recent iterations of the LOF (2011) and SCOPIC (2014). This focus is for two reasons. First, while the right to a salvage award is not based on contract,[6] the bulk of salvage services (including those with an environmental

---

[4] Reports on the grounding of the *Rena K* off the coast of New Zealand provided some insight into approaches and priorities following marine disasters. In this regard, it has been reported that, the Tauranga Mayor Stuart Crosby, following the conviction of the Captain and Navigation officer of the *Rena K*, remarked that '[t]he real concern has always been the damage to the environment and the damage to [Tauranga's] reputation as a tourist destination'. The same report also alludes to the central role of salvors in quoting the employer (Daina Shipping Co.), of the Captain and navigation officer: 'The Rena owners and our insurers continue to be closely involved in managing the response to the grounding, especially through the activities of our salvage and recovery teams – Svitzer & Smit and Braemar Howells.' The employer further noted: 'There are many complex legal, environmental and community issues still to be resolved from the grounding and we are committed to working with all affected parties to achieve a satisfactory conclusion.' www.stuff.co.nz/national/crime/6984980/Rena-captain-and-officer-sent-to-jail accessed 19 July 2018.

[5] See below 13–14.

[6] See discussion below 6–7.

protection dimension) are rendered pursuant to standard form contracts. Secondly, these contracts represent significant private industry effort in the pursuit of sustainable development, which suggests a self-imposed and well-developed sense of social accountability on the part of the industry in relation to public environmental concerns. As such, salvage contracts provide the ideal context for an examination of the viability of private contracting as a means to promote the interests of all stakeholders in salvage operations with an environmental protection dimension. This latter issue can be broken down into two further issues; whether private contracting rules can be used effectively to pursue sustainable development goals and how the public interest, represented by the state, can be integrated effectively into salvage operations via private contracting.

The examination of the LOF and SCOPIC is undertaken against the backdrop of the law of South Africa, an emerging economy with a relatively well-developed system of salvage law. South Africa is among several coastal developing and emerging countries that are confronted with marine environmental pollution and other sustainable development issues. South Africa also pioneered the use of standby Emergency Towing Vessels (ETVs) contracted by the government (Department of Transport), which is now used by many countries.[7] The major providers of marine salvage services in Southern Africa typically operate from South African bases,[8] while South African contract law provides a tried and trusted mechanism for the recognition of third-party interests in private contracts in the form of the *stipulatio alteri*.[9] While, the private industry has taken steps, ostensibly, to promote environmental interests in private salvage contracts, the efficacy of their efforts against the backdrop of sustainable development has not been subjected to academic scrutiny. Consequently, this chapter provides the first attempt to analyse private contracting in salvage operations as a means to integrate the public interest in the environment and to recommend the use of provisions for the benefit of third parties by the industry. Here, the appropriate legislative means or, should we seek international regulation, the appropriate international convention could potentially be used to create the mechanism for the use of private contracting parties, should the industry's efforts fall short of expectations.

The chapter is organised as follows. It commences with an illustration of the challenges faced by salvors in commercial salvage operations where there is also a threat of pollution and the linkages between commercial salvage operations and sustainable development. The chapter then provides a theoretical analysis of the legal nature of salvage and legal developments in response to environmental protection demands. This is done for the sake of completeness and to set the stage for an examination of the LOF and SCOPIC. Particular attention will be paid to environmental provisions in the LOF and SCOPIC in order to highlight their limitations in

---

[7]   https://maritimesa.org/grade-11/2016/09/12/south-african-salvage-operations/ accessed 19 July 2019.
[8]   www.smit.com/#view/map accessed 19 July 2019.
[9]   See discussion below, at Section 11.7.

accounting for the public interest in salvage operations. The chapter then considers the extent to which the *stipulatio alteri* (provision for the benefit of third parties), could be used as a direct means to incorporate the public interest in private salvage contracts, which is an analysis that has not been undertaken in relation to salvage contracts.

11.2 SALVAGE OPERATIONS, ROLE-PLAYERS AND SUSTAINABLE DEVELOPMENT

As mentioned, the 1979 collision between the *Atlantic Empress* and *Aegean Captain*, approximately twenty miles northeast of the island of Tobago in the Caribbean Sea, illustrated the involvement of coastal states in salvage operations and the extent to which divergent interests are potentially at play.[10]

Salvage operations, of course, are economic activities in that professional salvors want to get paid for the services they provide while property owners have a commercial interest in their property being saved and the minimisation of potential liability. States, representing the public interest and the environment as stakeholders, want their coastlines protected while also having an interest in efficient property salvage operations. The latter interest is predicated upon the idea that property salvage operations promote marine commerce in general.[11] For these reasons, modern salvage operations have become a careful balancing exercise between environmental protection concerns and the traditional commercial outcomes of salvage operations. Therefore, modern salvage operations involve at least two of the three recognised interdependent and mutually reinforcing pillars of sustainable development (economic development, social development and environmental protection).[12]

This balancing exercise becomes clearer when one considers the extent to which salvage operations and capacity are recognised as an integral component of a multi-faceted approach to pollution emanating from ships. Following the running aground of the *Sea Empress* just outside the entrance to Milford Haven (southwest coast of Wales) in 1999, with 131,000 tonnes of North Sea crude oil aboard,[13] Lord Donaldson of Tymington[14] reviewed the preparedness of the United Kingdom to deal with oil pollution incidents. He identified salvage as one of 'four main tasks that may be associated with marine pollution incidents'.[15] Aspects of Lord Donaldson's recommendations, including the importance of salvage capacity as a preventive

[10] See discussion above 1.
[11] See below 6.
[12] *Johannesburg Declaration on Sustainable Development* UN Doc. A/CONF.199/20 (2002): para. 5.
[13] www.glaucus.org.uk/News.htm accessed 19 July 2019.
[14] Command and Control: Report of Lord Donaldson's Review of Salvage and Intervention and Their Command and Control, available at https://core.ac.uk/display/40332397?recSetID=accessed 19 July 2019.
[15] Ibid., 45.

measure, were implemented in the United Kingdom's National Contingency Plan for Pollution from Shipping and Offshore installations (NPC) in the year 2000.[16] This take on the importance of salvage operations in the context of marine pollution response plans is also to be observed in other jurisdictions. An example is the National Marine Pollution Contingency Plans of Namibia, which expressly include private salvage providers in the pollution response matrix, recognising that 'operational management of a maritime casualty rests with the commercial sector, i.e. towage and salvage contractors'.[17]

An appreciation of the economic (the immediate commercial interests of salvors and owners, and the promotion of marine commerce in general) and environmental protection aspects of salvage operations allows one to draw definite links between salvage and the 2015 SDGs. The recognition of salvage as an integral component of national marine pollution prevention measures, suggests a definite link between salvage and SDG 14 to the extent that SDG 14 includes the prevention of marine pollution.[18] In relation to the economic dimension of salvage operations, the United Nations International Maritime Organisation (IMO) has acknowledged that the 2030 Agenda for Sustainable Development and the associated SDGs can only be 'realized with a sustainable transport sector supporting world trade and facilitating global economy' [sic]. Therefore, logically, salvage operations can be linked to the relevant 2015 SDGs to the extent that they promote maritime commerce and a sustainable transport sector. This will also become clearer in the discussion of the legal foundations of salvage in the discussion to follow.

11.3 THE LAW OF SALVAGE, ENVIRONMENTAL PROTECTION DEMANDS AND CONSEQUENTIAL DEVELOPMENTS

Salvage has been described as 'a service which confers a benefit by saving or helping to save a recognised subject of salvage when in danger from which it cannot be extricated unaided, if and so far as the rendering of such service is voluntary in the

---

[16] In this regard, in a response to a question directed at the Secretary of State for Transport on 20 January 2003 about the last review of the United Kingdom's coastal waters counter pollution practices, it was noted that the 'National Contingency Plan for Marine Pollution from Shipping and Offshore Installations' was published in January 2000 by the Maritime and Coastguard Agency (MCA), 'following the experiences gained during [the] SEA EMPRESS incident and from the recommendations in Lord Donaldson's review of salvage and intervention and their command and control'. See publications and records of the UK Parliament at https://publications.parliament.uk/pa/cm200203/cmhansrd/vo030120/text/30120w10.htm accessed 19 July 2019. The 2000 NCP was an update of earlier NCPs, the first of which was published in 1968 in response to the Torrey Canyon disaster. The first solely electronic version of the NCP was published in 2014 and last updated on 17 August 2017. This latest version can be accessed at www.gov.uk/government/publications/national-contingency-plancp accessed 19 July 2019.

[17] National Marine Pollution Contingency Plan – Republic of Namibia. www.mwt.gov.na/documents/98944/100185/NMPCP/a77e4969-8f7c-4661-b4ea-ddc39ed56694 accessed 19 July 2019.

[18] See www.globalgoals.org/14-life-below-water accessed 19 July 2019.

sense of being attributable neither to a pre-existing obligation, nor solely for the interests of the salvor' (Rose, 2010: p. 8). This description identifies three basic requirements for a salvor to claim a salvage reward:

(a) danger to the vessel and her cargo;
(b) voluntariness of services; and
(c) success in salvaging at least some property.

The last requirement conveys the idea that a benefit must be conferred and forms the basis of the 'no cure, no pay' principle (NCNP). A salvage award is made from a fund constituted by the value of the salved property and if nothing is saved there will be no fund and, therefore, no award can be paid out.

The right to a salvage award is premised upon two bases. The first is the notion of rewarding salvors for the benefits they confer (Rose, 2010; Rose, 1989: p. 183). These benefits inform the liability of their recipient to pay or contribute to the salvage award. In this regard, 'each and every interest which has received a benefit from the salvage service provided must contribute' (Rose, 2010: p. 15). Rose (2010: p. 207) has suggested that these benefits may be dealt with as a manifestation of the principle of unjust enrichment, also pointing out that salvage has, to an increasing extent, come to be included within the modern law of restitution for unjust enrichment.[19] However, this categorisation of salvage is not uniformly observed (see Wright, 1939; Birks, 1985; Virgo, 1999; Burrows, 2011), because restitution does not explain the reward element of a salvage award that may be inflated for policy considerations (Rose, 2010: p. 21).

The second base of salvage awards, which explains the reward element and distinguishes salvage from unjustified enrichment, is the public policy of encouragement (Rose, 2010: p. 14). In this regard, Lushington in *The Fusilier*[20] remarked that

> [d]irect benefit is not the sole principle upon which salvage reward is required to be paid. I am of the opinion that the payment of salvage depends upon more general principles; and in saying this, I think I am supported both by Lord Stowel and Story J. Salvage is not governed by the ordinary rules which prevail in mercantile transactions on shore. Salvage is governed by a due regard to benefit received, combined with a just regard for the general interests of ships and marine commerce. All owners of ships and cargoes and all underwriters are interested in the great principle of adequate remuneration being paid for salvage services; and none are more interested than the underwriters of the cargo.

The encouragement aspect of salvage and the notion that salvage 'is [partly] governed by . . . a just regard for the general interests of ships and marine commerce',

---

[19] Rose (2010) correctly cites Goff and Jones (1966) and Klippert (1983) as examples of authors that include salvage within the modern law of restitution for unjust enrichment.
[20] (1865) Br. Of Lush. 341, 347.

provides legal reinforcement of the earlier drawn linkages between salvage operations as economic activities and the 2015 SDGs. It also reinforces the notion of
salvage operations as economic activities in a narrow and broader sense; salvors
provide a service to the owners of maritime property for which they get paid and,
besides these immediate commercial interests of salvors and owners of maritime
property, also serve the public interest in the promotion of shipping and broader
marine commerce. It is, of course, these aspects of salvage that may conflict with and
that have to be balanced against the environmental protection aspects of shipping
disasters. It is also this balancing of interests that places salvage within the influence
sphere of sustainable development concerns and the 2015 SDGs.

As mentioned, the bulk of modern salvage operations are performed in terms of
contract. As such, the question of a contractual basis for the right to salvage has also
received academic attention (Stoljar, 1964). Suffice to say that while suggestions
have been made that modern salvage services are contracts implied in fact (Stoljar,
1964: pp. 171–6), the idea of a contractual basis for the right to claim salvage has not
found general support in academic writing (see Gaskell, 1986; Reeder, 2003:
p. 39).[21]

English courts have also dismissed the idea of a contractual basis for the right to
claim salvage. In *The Cargo Ex Port Victor*,[22] the court expressly rejected any attempt
to deal with the right of salvage as arising from an implied request from an owner of
property in danger to salvors or an implied contract. Sir Francis Jeune, in dismissing
the notion of an implied request for help and an implied contract, held:

> [t]he true view is, I think, that the law of Admiralty imposes on the owner of property
> saved an obligation to pay the person who saves it simply because in the view of that
> system of law it is just he should.[23]

11.4 PROPERTY VERSUS ENVIRONMENT: BALANCING NEW
THREATS AND OLD LAW

Although salvage operations are essentially services to property, shipping incidents
such as *The Atlantic Empress*[24] illustrated the tensions between the traditional
commercial property interests in salvage and the more recent and growing public
interest in the protection of the marine environment. However, while salvage
operations had the potential to be a first line of defence in preventing environmental

---

[21]   In particular, note the authorities Gaskell cites in nn. 1–2.
[22]   [1901] P. 243 (confirmed on appeal).
[23]   Ibid., 249. In *The Meandros* [1925] P. 61, the court similarly referred to the legal liability created by
       salvage as arising from the saving of property, where the owner who has had the benefit of such
       a service has to remunerate those who have conferred the service, at 68. See further, *The Toju Maru*
       [1972] A.C 242, 292.
[24]   See above 1.

disasters, salvors had no real incentive to protect the environment, especially where there was no prospect of saving the ship or her cargo (Kerr, 1990: p. 532).[25]

Besides inadequate financial incentives, salvors could expose themselves to possible liability claims if they did not avert or minimise pollution damage (Redgwell, 1990: p. 145; Binney, 1990: p. 643). Thus salvors faced increased risks, while at the same time there was no incentive for them to become involved in environmental protection during salvage operations.[26] Coastal states' intervention in salvage operations also had the potential to complicate salvage operations (Binney, 1990: p. 644), while, as noted in the case of the *Atlantic Empress*, they could also exclude ships in distress from their coastal waters. There was, therefore, a very real possibility that salvors could withhold their expertise as a first line of defence in pollution prevention because of states' potential frustration of salvage operations. This was not ideal as salvors, aside from the general interests of maritime commerce, had a valuable practical role to play in the prevention of pollution. Essentially, the immediate commercial interests of salvors were in conflict with state interests in environmental protection.

The industry responded to the above problem with an amendment to the LOF in 1980. This represented the first practical step towards a revision of salvage law principles in line with environmental protection concerns. The amendment was informed by the perceived need to create adequate incentives for salvors to become involved in rescue operations that could prevent pollution and where there was a real risk that no, or very little, property would be saved (Aberdein, 1994: p. 47). However, while this industry initiative was commendable, it had one key weakness in the form of its limited scope of application (Coulthard, 1983). It applied only to oil and imposed a duty on salvors to 'prevent the escape of oil from the vessel' (Coulthard, 1983: p. 55, citing clause 1(a) of LOF 1980), saying nothing about oil that has already escaped or other polluting substances.

This contractual response was followed by the Salvage Convention, which adopted the 'safety net' approach of the LOF 1980 (Kerr, 1990: p. 538). The Convention, which entered into force on 15 July 1996, was predicated upon an increased concern with environmental protection, expressly '[noting] that substantial developments, in particular the increased concern for the protection of the environment, have demonstrated the need to review the international rules'.[27] The Convention acknowledges the value of 'efficient . . . salvage operations' not only in

---

[25] Here, the law of unjustified enrichment (restitution) would not be of assistance to the salvor because the property owner would not be enriched. Also, while the law of restitution may potentially offer possibilities against the state, it would not provide better financial results to salvors than the maritime law of salvage because of the lack of a reward element.

[26] The salvor may be liable in damages for negligence in carrying out the salvage operations. The House of Lords confirmed the possibility of such a claim in *The Toju Maru* (see above n. 14). Where a vessel threatens to pollute the possible damages that could result are substantially more than in traditional salvage operations, thus greatly increasing the salvor's risks.

[27] Preamble to the Convention.

the traditional property salvage sense, but also for the 'protection of the environment'.[28] Moreover, it acknowledges the 'need to ensure that adequate incentives are available to persons who undertake salvage operations in respect of vessels and other property in danger'.[29] Besides the clear expression of an environmental protection purpose in its Preamble, the Convention also contains a number of environmentally relevant provisions that aim to encourage salvors to act in the interest of the environment (see Binney, 1990: p. 648).

It imposes a duty on the salvor to 'exercise due care to prevent or minimize damage to the environment'[30] and provides for a possible enhanced salvage award based on the 'skill and effort of the salvors in preventing or minimizing damage to the environment'.[31] Article 14 of the Convention also created a mechanism for special compensation of salvors engaging in salvage operations in respect of ships and their cargo that pose an environmental threat. Special compensation functions as a safety net in that salvors are guaranteed a recovery of their expenses in cases where the 'vessel by itself or its cargo threatened damage to the environment' and the salvors failed to earn a traditional salvage award.

Furthermore, salvors who are successful in their efforts to prevent or minimise damage to the environment can earn a bonus up to a maximum of 30 per cent of their expenses. This bonus can be increased to 100 per cent if the tribunal deems it fair and just to do so.[32] Salvors are thus encouraged to perform salvage operations knowing that even if their efforts in protecting the environment fail, they can at the very least recover their expenses (Kerr, 1989: p. 515). As such, Article 14 represented a significant change to the traditional no cure, no pay principle of property salvage operations. In its interpretation of expenses that could be recovered under Article 14, the House of Lords in *The Nagasaki Spirit*,[33] held that the ordinary meaning of 'rate', which would include an element of profit, was not applicable under the Convention. Instead, based on the references to expenses in Article 14 and on the *travaux preparatoires*[34] of the Convention, the term only referred to an amount for personnel and equipment which covered indirect and overhead costs but no profits (See also De La Rue and Anderson, 1989: p. 594). Lord Mustill made short shrift of salvors' argument for the inclusion of a profit element, stating:

> In the first place I do not accept that salvors need a profit element as a further incentive. Under the former regime the undertaking of a salvage service was a stark gamble. No cure-no pay. This is no longer so, even if traditional salvage yields little

---

[28] Ibid.

[29] Ibid.

[30] Art. 8.

[31] Art. 13(1)(b).

[32] Art. 14(2).

[33] *Semco Salvage & Marine Pte Ltd* v. *Lancer Navigation* (The Nagasaki Spirit) [1997] 1 Lloyd's Rep. 323 [HL].

[34] The preparatory documents or documentary evidence of the negotiations, discussions and drafting of the final text of the Convention.

or nothing under article 13 the salvor will, in the event of success in protecting the environment be awarded a multiple not only of his direct costs but also the indirect stand-by costs, yielding a profit. Moreover, even if there is no environmental benefit he is assured of an indemnity against his outlays and receives at least some contribution to his standing costs. Lack of success no longer means 'no pay', and the provisions of this safety net suffice, to fulfill the purposes of the new scheme.[35]

Salvors were understandably unhappy, and the industry's response was again in the form of contract. In addition to the standard LOF, industry devised the SCOPIC clause for use in conjunction with LOF by means of the former's incorporation into the latter. The direct purpose of SCOPIC, of course, was to address the perceived shortcomings of Article 14 of the Salvage Convention.[36] These contractual mechanisms are discussed in the ensuing sections of the chapter.

11.5 SALVAGE CONTRACTS (LOF), SCOPIC AND ENVIRONMENTAL PROTECTION

While standard form of salvage agreements have been promulgated over the years, 'providing for quantification of the salvors' reward by arbitration if it cannot be agreed between the parties' (Miller, 1981: pp. 243–4), the LOF is the most well-known and frequently used (Miller, 1981: p. 243). These contracts have provided the industry with a flexible means to respond to environmental protection demands. While the LOF has been revised over the years,[37] the first environmental provisions only appeared in the 1980 iteration thereof. This chapter, however, focusses on the LOF 2011 and the most recent 2014 iteration of SCOPIC, to determine if their environmental provisions promote all stakeholder interests in salvage operations. Essentially, we assess whether these contracts effectively balance commercial interests and environmental sustainability in salvage operations and if a contract between salvors and salved property can further the public interest in environmental protection.

11.5.1 LOF

The LOF 2011 is a relatively short document when compared with commercial contracts in general. It retains the traditional 'no cure, no pay' principle of salvage in respect of salvage operations,[38] although salvors appear to be of the opinion that the LOF 2011 gives 'priority . . . to the protection of the marine environment'.[39] However,

35   *Semco Salvage & Marine Pte Ltd v. Lancer Navigation* (1997) 1 Lloyd's Rep. 323 [HL].
36   See discussion below, Section 11.5.2.
37   1908, 1924, 1926, 1950, 1953, 1967, 1972, 1980, 1990, 1995, 2000.
38   www.marine-salvage.com/documents/LOF%202011.pdf accessed 19 July 2019.
39   ISU webpage: www.marine-salvage.com/overview/no-cure-no-pay/ accessed 19 July 2019.

while this might be a laudable sentiment, the ensuing discussion will show that this is not necessarily an accurate claim on the part of salvors.

11.5.1.1 Parties to the LOF 2011

The LOF does not refer to salvors and describes those performing the salvage services as the 'salvage contractors' in box number 1. Nevertheless, for this chapter, the term salvor shall be used instead of contractor. Box 2 provides for the property to be salved while box 9 provides for the captain (of the ship) or other person signing for and on behalf of the property. This makes sense if one considers that salvage contracts are typically signed at sea, with property owners (cargo and ship) represented by the captain.

11.5.1.2 Environmental Clauses in LOF 2011

Clause B of LOF 2011 expressly addresses the issue of environmental protection in the context of salvage operations. It provides that 'while performing salvage services, the [salvors] shall also use their best endeavours to prevent or minimise damage to the environment'. This phrasing positions environmental protection as an addition to what is regarded as the salvor's basic obligation under Clause A:

> Contractors' basic obligation: The Contractors identified in Box 1 hereby agree to use their best endeavours to salve the property . . . and to take the property to the place . . . or to such other place as may hereafter be agreed. If no place is inserted . . . and in the absence of any subsequent agreement as to the place where the property is to be taken the Contractors shall take the property to a place of safety.

The Clause B duty only arises in the performance of the traditional salvage operation (the basic obligation of the salvor). Therefore, in the absence of a traditional property salvage scenario, there would be no free-standing duty on a salvor to perform environmental services. The link between Clauses A and B is that once a salvage operation commences, there will be the further obligation to minimise or prevent environmental damage. This reinforces the idea of salvage operations as a service to property.

The need for Clause B might be explained by the fact that salvage operations by their nature represent a threat to the marine environment. It is common knowledge that salvors sometimes release potentially polluting substances into the sea in order to successfully keep vessels afloat. In this context, Clause B could potentially be regarded as an instruction to salvors not to imperil the environment through their decisions on property salvage. The clause can, therefore, be viewed as an instruction to salvors to carefully balance their operational decisions against potential environmental damage. This reading suggests that the protection of the marine environment is not truly prioritised relative to property salvage as suggested by salvors (the

ISU).[40] Instead it functions more as a cautionary backdrop to salvage operations that might otherwise be performed without due concern for the environment.

Clause B, of course, is a contractual promise to the owner of property salved and not to any extraneous parties. As such, any positives for the environment or other third parties are incidental to contractual terms primarily devised for the benefit of salvors and salved property owners. The owner of salved property would certainly have an interest in salvors taking the necessary care during environmentally threatening salvage operations because a failure to do so might result in liability for the owner. Therefore, the duty on the salvor to minimise or prevent environmental damage is predicated upon the commercial interests of the parties to the contract.

However, while a commercial reason for Clause B is apparent, the potential liability of the owner of salved property is not expressed as the contractual quid pro quo for the salvor's award. Of course, there would be no impediment to the contract providing for the prevention of liability as the quid pro quo for the remuneration of the salvor. The contract could even provide for the amount of the remuneration or a formula for remuneration in addition to standard property salvage. Nonetheless, even if the contract was to provide for limitation of liability as a factor in the determination of the award this would not account for the benefit conferred on third party stakeholders that fall outside of the contractual duty owed to property owners.

In this regard, Reeder (2011, p. 326) has correctly suggested that 'principles relating to privity of contract apply to salvage agreements as they do to other contracts' (Reeder, 2010: p. 326). As such, the contractual duty owed to the owner of salved property does not provide a legal basis for the benefits bestowed upon third party stakeholders. A possible exception to this would be if the agreement between the salvor and the recipients of salvage services was intended to confer a benefit on parties outside of the contract (Merkin, 2000). However, as to this possibility, Rose (2010: p. 515) has noted that potential third party beneficiaries of the salvor's Lloyd's Form duty will not acquire rights by virtue of the English Contracts (Rights of Third Parties) Act 1999.

Rose provided no explanation for this view but it is correct because the Act provides that the beneficiary 'may [only] enforce a term of the contract if the contract expressly provides that he may, or ... [a] term [of the contract] ... purports to confer a benefit on him'.[41] However, while, the LOF duty to prevent or minimise damage to the environment confers a de facto benefit outside of the contractual relationship, it does not confer any rights on third parties to enforce the duty. So, while the LOF has certainly introduced de facto environmental protection outcomes into property salvage operations, it does not provide a legal basis for

---

[40]   Ibid.
[41]   Contracts (Rights of Third Parties) Act 1999, s. 1(1)(a) and (b).

the effective integration of third-party stakeholders' interests into salvage operations.

11.5.2 SCOPIC

While environmental concerns in general have led to amendments to the LOF, the immediate commercial and financial interests of salvors and unhappiness with the decision of the House of Lords in *The Nagasaki Spirit*,[42] led to the development of SCOPIC. In this regard Rose (2010: p. 209) mentions salvors' concerns regarding 'the calculation of remuneration for salvage and environmental services and the promptness with which payments were made' (Rose, 2010: p. 209). Additionally, Reeder (2011: p. 613) has suggested that the 'uncertainties surrounding the assessment of Article 14 claims and the necessity to prove a threat of environmental damage or that damage to the environment was averted (to earn an increment on the expenditure) caused salvors to have an interest in the devising of some alternative'.

11.5.2.1 SCOPIC and LOF

SCOPIC 2014 is more a scheme than an actual clause given that it is detailed and made up of 16 so-called sub-clauses. SCOPIC is a voluntary addition to the LOF in that parties have the option to incorporate SCOPIC into their LOF salvage agreement (Bishop, 2012). As such, there is no automatic application of SCOPIC in the absence of its express incorporation into the LOF contract.[43] When parties incorporate SCOPIC, they essentially replace the special compensation regime under Article 14 of the Convention with the remuneration method provided for under SCOPIC. In this regard sub-clause 1 of SCOPIC provides; '[i]f this SCOPIC clause has been incorporated into the Main Agreement the Contractor may make no claim pursuant to Article 14'.

Sub-clause 2 provides that the assessment of SCOPIC remuneration shall commence from the time the written notice is given to the owners of the vessel and services rendered before the notice shall not be remunerated under the clause at all but in accordance with Convention Article 13 as incorporated into the Main Agreement ('Article 13'). Article 13, of course, regulates the calculation of the standard salvage award. Sub-clause 6 also provides that salvage services under the main agreement shall continue to be assessed in accordance with Article 13 of the Convention, even where SCOPIC had been invoked by a salvor. Like Article 14 special compensation, SCOPIC remuneration is payable by 'the owners of the vessel', which is to be expected because it is an agreement between salvors and the owners of salved property. A SCOPIC award is payable to the extent that it exceeds the total Article 13 award.[44]

---

[42]   See discussion above (n. 36) and text thereto.
[43]   Box 7 of the LOF 2011 asks the following: 'Is the Scopic Clause incorporated into this agreement? State alternative: Yes/No'.
[44]   SCOPIC sub-clause 6.

Therefore, SCOPIC distinguishes between salvage operations proper and environmental services rendered in the context of such services. This might indicate a degree of reluctance to erode the traditional understanding of salvage operations. Of course, nothing prevents the contracting parties from departing from basic definitions employed in the law of salvage or in the Convention except that they are not permitted to derogate from any 'duties to prevent or minimize damage to the environment'.[45] Parties could potentially define salvage services to include environmental services for the benefit of the property interests.

SCOPIC's incorporation into the LOF is not the only requirement for it to become operative between the contracting parties. Sub-clause 2 requires that the contractor must invoke 'by written notice to the owners of the vessel the SCOPIC clause ... at any time of his choosing regardless of the circumstances and, in particular, regardless of whether or not there is a "threat of damage to the environment"'. A failure to invoke SCOPIC will, of course, preclude a salvor from using the SCOPIC method of remuneration.

A notable difference between the SCOPIC scheme and the special compensation regime under the Convention is that there is no requirement for a threat to the environment as under the Convention. While one might think that salvors would simply always invoke SCOPIC, this is not the case. SCOPIC contains what might be regarded as a penalty should a salvor unnecessarily invoke the scheme (see also Reeder, 2011: p. 622). Sub-clause 7 provides as follows:

> If the SCOPIC clause is invoked under sub-clause 2 hereof and the Article 13 Award or settlement (before currency adjustment and before interest and costs) under the Main Agreement is greater than the assessed SCOPIC remuneration then ... the said Article 13 Award or settlement shall be discounted by 25% of the difference between the said Article 13 Award or settlement and the amount of SCOPIC remuneration.

The above provision would presumably discourage salvors from unnecessarily invoking the SCOPIC clause. Without this clause, salvors would naturally 'have nothing to lose from invoking the SCOPIC Clause on day one of salvage in every case' (Bishop, 2012: p. 83). However, unnecessarily invoking SCOPIC would result in the discounting of any Article 13 award by 25 per cent of the difference between it and the SCOPIC assessment.[46] In this manner, salvors have to make an honest assessment of the existence or not of an environmental threat.

Sub-clause 9 similarly provides a counter to salvors unnecessarily invoking SCOPIC in that it gives the shipowner the right to withdraw from SCOPIC with five days' notice to the salvors.[47] As such, shipowners are not entirely at the mercy of

---

[45] Art. 6(3) of the Convention.
[46] SCOPIC clause 7.
[47] SCOPIC clause 9(ii).

salvors unnecessarily invoking SCOPIC. However, a shipowner can only withdraw where shore authorities permit them to do so. The contractual balancing of the parties' interests is, therefore, subject to the powers of 'Government, Local or Port Authorities or any other officially recognised body having jurisdiction over the area where the services are being rendered'.[48] Presumably, such powers will be exercised with reference to environmental protection needs as assessed by these authorities.

Sub-clause 9(i), which affords salvors the right to terminate their services under SCOPIC, provides that

> The Contractor shall be entitled to terminate the services under the SCOPIC clause and the Main Agreement by written notice to owners of the vessel . . . if the total cost of his services to date and the services that will be needed to fulfil his obligations hereunder to the property . . . will exceed the sum of:
>
> (a) The value of the property capable of being salved; and
> (b) All sums to which he will be entitled as SCOPIC remuneration.

Therefore, a salvor who runs the risk of operating at a loss can terminate services under the main agreement and SCOPIC. However, this right to terminate is also subject to the powers of governments, local authorities and other officially recognised bodies with jurisdiction over the area where services are rendered.[49] As such, the contract pre-empts possible interference by public authorities in the contractual rights of salvors and shipowners. While this might suggest that the environment is prioritised over the contractual rights of the parties, it amounts to no more than a confirmation of powers that coastal states have to direct salvors anyway.[50] As such, the maximising of profits for salvors remains a primary concern, which is also borne out by the way that SCOPIC remuneration works.

11.5.2.2 SCOPIC Remuneration

SCOPIC introduced a tariff rate (sub-clause 5), which replaced the 'fair rate' as provided for under the Convention. The total SCOPIC remuneration in terms of sub-clause 5(i) includes, 'the total of the tariff rates of personnel, tugs and other craft, portable salvage equipment, out of pocket expenses and bonus due'. The tariffs are set out in Appendix 'A' and the tariff rates used are 'those in force at the time the salvage services take place'.[51] The bonus referred to in sub-clause 5(i) is provided in sub-clause 5(iv):

---

[48] SCOPIC clause 9(iii).
[49] Ibid.
[50] Art. 1 of The International Convention Relating to the Intervention on the High Seas in Cases of Oil Pollution Casualties, 1969, grant coastal states the right to 'take measures on the high seas as may be necessary to prevent, mitigate or eliminate grave and imminent danger to their coastline or related interests from pollution of the sea by oil'.
[51] Sub-clause 5(ii).

In addition to the rates ... and any out of pocket expenses, the contractor shall be entitled to a standard bonus of 25% of those rates and out of pocket expenses.

This addition of a bonus addresses salvors' unhappiness with the decision in *The Nagasaki Spirit* in that salvors can make a profit. This, of course, is in line with an understanding of salvage operations as an economic activity. From the property owner's perspective, this understanding is furthered by sub-clause 12 of SCOPIC, which gives the owners of the vessel the option to appoint a Special Casualty Representative. It appears to be directed at enabling ship-owners and their P&I Club to keep a 'close watch on the salvage operation and the practical fulfilment by the contractor of his SCOPIC duties' (Reeder, 2011: p. 628). This reiterates the idea that SCOPIC is predicated upon the narrow interests of the contractual parties. Nevertheless, given that SCOPIC improves the financial situation of salvors, environmental protection is arguably furthered as a consequence of salvors having better incentives to engage in operations where property present an environmental threat.

11.6 PROVISIONS DIRECTLY ADDRESSING ENVIRONMENTAL PROTECTION

The discussion of SCOPIC thus far suggests that environmental benefits beyond the potential liability of ship-owners are indirect and a consequence of better financial incentives and public oversight mechanisms. The latter, of course, is not because of the agreement and at best a contractual endorsement of already existing public powers. However, there are clauses that appear to be of more direct relevance to environmental protection through the imposition of duties on the contracting parties.

11.6.1 *Sub-clause 10*

The clause reiterates the link between SCOPIC and the LOF by setting out the main duties of the salvor with reference to the LOF obligations:

The duties and liabilities of the Contractor shall remain the same as under the Main Agreement, namely to use his best endeavours to salve the vessel and property thereon and in so doing to prevent or minimise damage to the environment.

This confirms the earlier assertion that environmental protection is an add-on to property salvage services. There is also nothing to suggest that SCOPIC moves beyond the earlier interpretation of the LOF provision. Without traditional property salvage services, there would be no independent duty on a salvor to provide environmental services. This much is clear from the phrase 'and in so doing', which refers to the salvor using best endeavours to salve property, linking the further duty to prevent or minimise damage to the environment with a commenced property salvage operation.

Again, it is difficult to see how this could refer to anything more than a salvor having to exercise the necessary care in the performance of its salvage services. Moreover, given that this deals with a contractual undertaking by a salvor to salve property interests, one is, again, faced with the question of the nature of these interests. As mentioned, the owner of property could only have one real commercial interest in this undertaking from a salvor namely, its potential liability for pollution damage. As such, the provision amounts to an undertaking by a salvor to perform the salvage operation with due regard for the potential liability of the ship-owner. Again, the contractual undertaking is based on the interests of the contractual parties and, quite obviously, the ship-owner who is liable for the payment of SCOPIC remuneration.

It is not clear what the penalty for a breach of this obligation might be. Also unclear is how the term, to prevent or minimise damage to the environment, should be classified. From the ship-owner's perspective, given its interests in the avoidance of potential liability, such a clause would undoubtedly be very important. As such, one may argue that a ship-owner could legitimately withdraw from the contractual arrangement with the salvor. However, unlike contracts in general, there is the substantial public law oversight in salvage operations, which is also acknowledged in SCOPIC. While the shipowner can withdraw from SCOPIC,[52] this would be subject to the approval of the relevant authorities.[53]

Of course, one may argue that this oversight measure only applies in relation to a withdrawal under sub-clause 9(ii) and therefore, that a classification of such a breach as a condition, would afford a shipowner the right to cancel. However, such an approach would run contrary to the public interest in salvage operations. So, there is a tension here between a contracting party's potential rights and the public interest in environmental protection, given that an exercise of the former may impede the pursuit of the latter. Therefore, despite the importance of the term, it is not ideal to regard the right as a condition unless the right to terminate is subjected to the powers of coastal authorities in a manner similar to withdrawals under sub-clause 9. As such, one would, again, have the imposition of outside interests and powers on a private contractual relationship. Given the important public interest dimension, a better approach might be, as Rose (2010: p. 512) suggested, for a breach to impact upon the salvage award. Rose (2010: p. 515) does not consider the potential classification of the term (sub-clause 10) but notes that

> in a situation where the salvee shipowner is subject to liability for causing environmental damage, a salvor who fails to carry out his environmental duties may become liable to indemnify the shipowner for the liability which he (the salvor) has failed to avert.

He notes further that in most cases 'the significance of imposing environmental duties on a salvor will be to affect the payment(s) which may be made to him [the

---

[52] SCOPIC sub-clause 9(ii).
[53] SCOPIC sub-clause 9(iii).

salvor]' (2010: p. 515). This construction, of course, would imply that we are not dealing with a condition of the contract. This consequence to a breach of the duty will also ensure a de facto furthering of third-party stakeholders' interests, albeit incidental to salvors discharging their contractual duties to shipowners.

Again, the operation of sub-clause 10, with the environmental duty owed to salved property interests, reduces the promotion of the public interest to an incident of the private contractual relationship. Those that want the environment and its protection to be more of a priority relative to private property interests may feel that sub-clause 10, as it stands, does not go far enough to prioritise environmental protection relative to private commercial salvor and salved property interests.

11.6.2 *Sub-clause 14*

Sub-clause 14 of SCOPIC is another clause ostensibly directed at pollution prevention and it provides as follows:

> The assessment of SCOPIC remuneration shall include the prevention of pollution as well as the removal of pollution in the immediate vicinity of the vessel insofar as this is necessary for the proper execution of the salvage but not otherwise.

This clause also reinforces the idea that environmental duties are secondary to property salvage as, again, we have a clause, supposedly with an environmental aim, being based upon the narrow commercial property interests of the salvor and salved property interests. Regarding 'removal of pollution', this shall only be taken into account in the assessment of SCOPIC remuneration where the activity takes place in the immediate vicinity of the vessel and 'insofar as this is necessary for the proper execution of the salvage but not otherwise'. Therefore, polluting substances beyond the immediate vicinity of the vessel will not be considered. Cleaning-up services are also only relevant to the extent that they are necessary for the proper execution of the salvage. The wording of the provision suggests that a contractor shall be rewarded for environmental services to the extent that these are undertaken in furtherance of property salvage efforts. Therefore, any efforts beyond this shall effectively not be relevant for the purpose of assessing remuneration. From a purely commercial perspective one may argue that a contractor could validly decide not to provide environmental services, even where pollution emanates from the vessel, once pollution has moved beyond the immediate vicinity of the vessel and is not necessary for the proper execution of the salvage. If the salvor's remuneration is seen as the primary means to encourage salvors to perform environmental services and SCOPIC is truly intended to promote the public interest, as claimed by salvors,[54] then sub-clause 14 appears unduly limited and not geared towards encouragement or the prioritising of the environment.

---

[54] See above (n. 42).

However, one might explain this clause by reading it together with the duty imposed by sub-clause 10. Essentially, should a salvor ignore pollution beyond the immediate vicinity of the vessel, or where not necessary for the proper execution of salvage, it might be guilty of a breach of Clause 10. This is because the shipowner could be exposed to liability in direct contravention of Clause 10. Therefore, the apparent disregard for pollution beyond the immediate vicinity of the vessel or where the removal of pollution is not necessary for the proper execution of salvage is probably not a problem when read together with Clause 10.

Nevertheless, SCOPIC and LOF, at best, only provide for the incidental furthering of the public interest. The benefits conferred on the environment are a de facto consequence of provisions predicated upon the narrow commercial interests of the contracting parties. Should we truly seek the proper balancing and integration of the divergent interests in property salvage operations, a clearer legal basis would go some way to provide a more sustainable foundation for development in that regard. As things stand, the SCOPIC and LOF do not provide such a basis. It is here that the *stipulatio alteri* mechanism may provide a solution.

11.7 STIPULATIO ALTERI (CONTRACT IN FAVOUR OF A THIRD PARTY) AND THE PUBLIC INTEREST IN ENVIRONMENTAL PROTECTION

In the South African context, the contract in favour of third parties (*stipulatio alteri*) is well established and it has been used in numerous contexts (Van Rensburg et al., 2014: para. 350). The device may even be used in favour of a person, not yet in existence and has found good use in the context of companies still to be registered and specifically to secure contracts for such companies to be incorporated (Van Rensburg et al., 2014: para. 350).[55] Pushing the envelope, one might observe some linkages between the device's utility and questions of sustainable development, especially when viewed against the popular definition of sustainable development given by the 1987 Brundtland Report: 'development that meets the needs of the present without compromising the ability of future generations to meet their own needs'.[56] One could possibly substitute the notion of 'a person not yet in existence' as used in relation to the *stipulatio alteri*, for 'future generations', the beneficiaries or otherwise of actions taken today, and imagine the development of the use of the *stipulatio alteri* to secure the interests of future generations (read person not yet in existence) in contracts concluded today.

In South African law, a *stipulatio alteri* exists where A (the stipulans) and B (the promisor) enter into a contract, each in their own names, with the intention of

---

[55] See also *McCullogh* v. *Fernwood Estate Ltd* 1920 AD 204.
[56] World Commission on Environment and Development report 'Our Common Future' (1987) 43, www.un-documents.net/our-common-future.pdf accessed 19 July 2019.

creating an opportunity for C (a third party) to acquire rights and duties, should he (C) so wish, as against B. One may argue that the *stipulatio alteri* operates as an exception to the rule that only the parties to a contract can enforce the contract and be subject to obligations under it.[57] On the other hand, it may simply be regarded as a logical expression of freedom of contract (Sutherland, 2006: pp. 204–7). Applied in the context of SCOPIC, the recipients of salvage services would be the stipulans, the salvor would be the promissor, and the coastal state representing the public interest would be the third party. However, to determine the utility of the *stipulatio alteri* as a means to integrate the public interest into salvage contracts, one must consider its central features and requirements.

11.7.1 *Central Features and Requirements for the* Stipulatio Alteri

A feature of the *stipulatio alteri* in South African law is that the benefit conferred on a third party can have corresponding duties for such a third party attached to it. In *McCullogh* v. *Fernwood Estate*,[58] Chief Justice Innes held:

> It may happen that the benefit carries with it a corresponding obligation. And in such a case it follows that the two would go together. The third person could not take advantage of one term of the contract and reject the other.

In the case of SCOPIC, there is nothing to suggest that any potential rights that might be conferred carry with them any accompanying duties. However, this is one instance where a third party might be required to provide 'consideration' for the benefit conferred. Essentially, it would be possible for any rights acquired by a third party under the salvage contract and SCOPIC to be subject to a corresponding duty to reward the salvor. In *Malelane Suikerkorporasie (Edms) Bpk* v. *Streak*,[59] Marais J found that the above quotation was not consistent with an understanding that the third party will necessarily be better off in a material fashion.[60] Instead, the true benefit obtained by such a third party would be the right to create a contractual link with either or both of the original contractors.[61]

From the aforesaid, the intention of the stipulans and promissor in concluding the contract must involve more than a simple conferring of benefits on a third party.[62] Essentially, the third party must be given an opportunity to become a party to a contract with the promissor (also see Van Rensburg et al., 2014). This was also emphasised by Schreiner JA in *Crookes* v. *Watson*:

---

[57] In England and Wales, the Contracts (Rights of Third Parties) Act 1999, similarly provides for a statutory based exception to the strict application of the rules pertaining to privity of contract.
[58] *McCullogh* v. *Fernwood Estate Ltd* 1920 AD 204.
[59] *Malelane Suikerkorporasie (Edms) Bpk* v. *Streak* [1970] 1 All SA 41 (T).
[60] Ibid., 45.
[61] Ibid.
[62] See *Mpakathi* v. *Kghotso Development CC* 1993 (3) SA 429 (W).

What is not very appropriately styled a contract for the benefit of a third person is not simply a contract designed to benefit a third person; it is a contract between two persons that is designed to enable a third person to come in as a party to a contract with one of the other two.[63]

Another key feature is that the agreement between stipulans and promisors does not by itself vest any rights or impose any duties on a third party.[64] Acceptance of the benefit conferred is required in order for a third party to demand performance of a stipulation in its favour, failing which, there would be no *vinculum iuris* [legal bond] between such a third party and the promisor.[65] Thus, it is generally accepted in South Africa that a 'third party will only acquire rights in terms of a *stipulatio alteri* by acceptance' (Sutherland and Cupido, 2004: p. 558).[66] In *Goldfoot* v. *Meyerson*,[67] Greenberg J stated, 'when it is said that a contract made for the benefit of a third party may be adopted by him what is meant is that the third party, by notice of adoption to the promisor, can create a *vinculum juris* between himself and the latter'.[68] As such, any benefits conferred upon a third party need to be accepted, essentially meaning that the *stipulatio alteri* is structured as an offer that might be accepted or rejected. In this regard, the third party must provide a 'notice of adoption to the promisor',[69] thereby becoming a party to the original contract. Innes CJ, in *Hyams* v. *Wolf & Simpson*,[70] took this idea further, stating that

> The contract must be made, if not in the name of C, then with a view to his benefit, and for that benefit entirely; and C must ratify and accept the contract while it is still open to him to do so. Those are essential conditions of C's right to recover.

Essentially, the 'benefit' which the third person obtains from the contract, is the right to conclude a contract with the promisor if he so wishes.[71] The analysis provided by Marais J, in *Malelane Suikerkorporasie (Edms) Bpk* v. *Streak*,[72] mentioned earlier, also included a comment on the meaning of the phrase 'for that benefit entirely' used in *Hyams* v. *Wolf & Simpson*. Marais J interpreted the phrases 'with a view to his benefit' and 'for that benefit entirely', as placing the emphasis on 'with a view' which functions to distinguish between a contract with a benefit conferred accidentally on the third party as opposed to a contract where the contractual undertaking in favour of the third party is exclusively for its benefit.[73] Marais J concluded that the

---

[63] 1956 (1) SA 277 (AD).

[64] Ibid.

[65] Ibid.

[66] Also see *Mpakathi* v. *Kghotso Development CC*, paras. 15–16.

[67] 1926 T.P.D. 242.

[68] Ibid., 247 quoting with approval from *Mutual Insurance Co.* v. *Hotz*, 1911 A.D. 556 at p. 567.

[69] See above (n. 52).

[70] 1908 T.S. 78.

[71] *Malelane Suikerkorporasie (Edms) Bpk* v. *Streak* [1970] 1 All SA 41 (T).

[72] Ibid.

[73] *Malelane Suikerkorporasie (Edms) Bpk* v. *Streak* 45.

undertaking will only be a stipulation for the benefit of a third party if the main intention or purpose of the undertaking is to confer a benefit on the third party.[74] The right of the third party to elect to accept or reject this undertaking would be the actual benefit conferred not the potentially beneficial consequence flowing from such an acceptance.[75]

Applying the *stipulatio alteri* to SCOPIC, one would have to show that the contracting parties had the intention to confer on the third party the right to elect to become a party to the contract. However, as noted earlier, nothing in the wording of the relevant clauses 10 and 14 suggest the intention to confer benefits on parties outside of the immediate contractual relationship. All extra-contractual benefits are incidental to duties owed as between the primary contracting parties. This is precisely the type of situation which Schreiner J distinguished from a true *stipulatio alteri*.[76] So, '[t]he mere fact that a third party may stand to derive some material advantage from a contract does not necessarily mean that the contract is a stipulation in favour of a third party. It qualifies as such only if the parties intended the person benefited to have the right to become a party to a contract with one of them' (Van Rensburt et al., 2014).

As mentioned, sub-clause 14 of SCOPIC revolves around the performance of traditional property salvage operations. Any attempt to confer benefits on outside parties, logically, would have taken into account pollution outside of the immediate vicinity of operations. Moreover, the concern with cleaning up pollution would not have been subjected to the proviso that it must be necessary for the property salvage operation. sub-clause 10 simply reiterates the position under the main agreement (LOF) with no possibility in its current guise for a potential contractual conferring of benefits on extra-contractual interests.

11.7.2 Stipulatio Alteri *and SCOPIC*

Although SCOPIC involves no *stipulatio alteri*, the latter's use could provide a sound legal basis for the integration of the public interest in a salvage contract. This will be via the agency of the state as trustee for the public interest (Van der Linde, 2010),[77] which would also open further avenues for the remuneration of salvors. Essentially, acceptance by the state could be accompanied by a corresponding duty to remunerate salvors for environmental services in the context of salvage operations. While the legal theoretical basis of such remuneration might not necessarily be within the four corners of traditional salvage law, it will be in line with the understanding that the beneficiary must pay for the benefits received. Of

---

[74] Ibid., 46.
[75] Ibid., referring with approval to *Crookes v. Watson*, above (n. 63).
[76] See above (n. 63) and text thereto.
[77] In the South African context, also see The National Environmental Management Act, Ch. 1, s. 2(1)(o), which expressly provides that '[t]he environment is held in public trust for the people, ... [and] must be protected as the people's common heritage'.

course, there would be a need to amend the SCOPIC clauses to express the intention that the salvor's duty is one in favour of the public interest via the agency of the coastal state. Moreover, the coastal state will have to accept both the contractually conferred benefit and the corresponding duty to pay, to become a party to the contract as trustee for the public interest. In this way, the contract would provide a direct legal basis for the effective integration of the public interest in environmental protection. While a detailed discussion of the ways in which acceptance may take place is beyond the scope of this discussion, this could be addressed via appropriate legislative measures detailing the possible bases for acceptance by the state. Of course, one may also consider an international convention is regulation at international level is sought.

A key problem, should the duties under SCOPIC be amended to allow for the interests of third parties, is that coastal states are, typically, empowered under international law to take measures to prevent pollution.[78] Of course, as the bearers of rights under international law, states may also be obliged under international law to take measures in the prevention of pollution.[79] Given these rights of the state to intervene, a right typically exercised in situations where salvage operations may present a threat to the environment, there would appear to be no incentive to accept benefits conferred under SCOPIC especially where there is a corresponding duty to pay.

However, coastal states would be well advised to keep in mind the essential practical role played by salvors in averting or minimising pollution in shipping incidents.[80] The exercise of power without regard for the narrow and broader commercial and economic realities of salvage operations could frustrate the very reason for the exercise of such power. Intervention may serve as a disincentive to commercial salvors and, although aimed at environmental protection, may impact negatively on broader maritime commerce, world trade and, ultimately, the achievement of the 2015 SDGs. The proper balancing of economic endeavour (in the broad and narrow sense) and environmental protection in salvage operations is a key aspect

---

[78] See for example the International Convention Relating to Intervention on the High Seas in Cases of Oil Pollution Casualties, 1969, which in its preamble 'affirms the right of a coastal State to take such measures on the high seas as may be necessary to prevent, mitigate or eliminate danger to its coastline or related interests from pollution by oil or the threat thereof, following upon a maritime casualty'. See also Art. 221 of the United Nations Convention on the Law of the Sea, which empowers States, 'pursuant to international law, both customary and conventional, to take and enforce measures beyond the territorial sea proportionate to the actual or threatened damage to protect their coastline or related interests, including fishing, from pollution or threat of pollution following upon a maritime casualty or acts relating to such a casualty [this would probably include salvage operations], which may reasonably be expected to result in major harmful consequences'. In this regard, the reference to customary international law would mean that even non-party states would be empowered in the manner provided by the Article.

[79] See the United Nations Convention on the Law of the Sea (UNCLOS), Part XII, Art. 192, which specifically obliges states to 'preserve and protect the marine environment'.

[80] See above pp. 4–5.

of sustainable development. Therefore, it should be approached in a way that incorporates due respect for the dual role of salvors in both the furthering of marine commerce and protection of the environment. We need the technical skills of commercial salvors and they should be encouraged to make their skills available. An approach based on the aforesaid realities, will ensure effective and sustainable public-private cooperation in the balancing of the economic and environmental dimensions of shipping incidents. Moreover, the *stipulatio alteri*, as part of such an approach, will provide a sound legal basis for the effective and sustainable balancing and integration of diverse interests in salvage operations. While we have seen significant steps taken by the private industry in the development of contracts that provide indirect furthering of the public interest, the use of the *stipulatio alteri* might need more proactive legislative intervention, be it at domestic level or at supranational level through an appropriate international convention.

11.8 CONCLUSIONS

While salvors believe that the LOF and SCOPIC prioritise environmental protection this is not borne out by provisions ostensibly aimed at environmental outcomes. Both the LOF and SCOPIC, where incorporated, treat the environmental responsibilities of the salvor as secondary to traditional property salvage operations. While they provide a de facto furthering of third-party interests in the environment, they are still agreements between salvors and the owners of salved property. Environmental protection is predicated upon ship-owner liability with no direct legal technical basis provided for potential third-party interests. As they are, LOF and SCOPIC do not effectively promote the public interest in environmental protection.

However, this is not necessarily due to the inherent unsuitability of private contracting but rather the result of the environment's position as an outside third-party stakeholder in private contracts between salvors and property owners. Nevertheless, as demonstrated, the *stipulatio alteri* could provide a direct legal basis upon which external stakeholder interests can be addressed. However, a coastal state will have to accept the *stipulatio alteri* and any possible duty to remunerate the salvors, in order to become a party to the contract. Of course, as mentioned, the coastal state might not see enough of an incentive to accept the *stipulatio alteri* as it could simply exercise powers of intervention under public international law. However, developing and emerging states may not necessarily be in a position to effectively exercise these powers, while the exercise of such powers may also be a disincentive to salvors, which could impact negatively on the achievement of the 2015 SDGs.

Private contracting and the *stipulatio alteri* can provide a viable direct legal basis to promote the public interest in environmental protection while also providing the necessary financial incentives to professional salvors. Moreover, the contractual benefits (becoming a party to the contract between the salvor and property owners) conferred upon the state as representative of the public interest will ensure an integrated and sustainable balancing of economic endeavour and environmental protection as well as an equitable spreading of the costs in salvage operations. Salvors will also be able effectively to discharge their dual roles namely, the rescue of property at sea in service of general maritime commerce and the protection of the environment.

REFERENCES

Aberdein, D. (1994). Marine Salvage and the Environment: New Zealand and the 1989 Salvage Convention, *Australian and New Zealand Maritime Law Journal*, 10(1), 35–74.

Binney, B. (1990). Protecting the Environment with Salvage Laws: Risks, Rewards, and the 1989 Salvage Convention, *Washington Law Review*, 639–56.

Birks, P. (1985). *Introduction to the Law of Restitution*, Oxford: Oxford University Press.

Bishop, A. (2012). The Development of Environmental Salvage and Review of the London Salvage Convention. *Tulane Maritime Law Journal*, 37, 65–106.

Burrows, A. (2011). *The Law of Restitution*, 3rd ed. Oxford: Oxford University Press.

Chen, L. (2001). Recent Developments in the Law of Salvage of the Marine Environment, *International Journal of Marine and Coastal Law*, 16(4), 686–98.

Coulthard, P. (1983). A New Cure for Salvors? A Comparative Analysis of the LOF 1980 and the C.M.I Draft Salvage Convention, *Journal of Maritime Law and Commerce* 14(1), 45–67.

De La Rue, C. and Anderson, C. (1998). *Shipping and the Environment*, London: Informa.

De La Rue, C. and Anderson, C. (2009). *Shipping and the Environment*, 2nd ed. London: Informa.

De La Rue, C. and Anderson, C. (2012). Environmental Salvage – Plus ça change …? *The Journal of International Maritime Law*, 18,279–92.

Gaskell, N. (1986) The Lloyd's Open Form and Contractual Remedies *Lloyd's Maritime and Commercial Law Quarterly*, 306–49.

Goff, R. and Jones, G. (1966). *The Law of Restitution*, London: Sweet & Maxwell.

Gold, E. (1989). Marine Salvage: Towards a new regime, *Journal of Maritime Law and Commerce*, 20,487–503.

Kerr, D. (1989). The 1989 Salvage Convention: Expediency or Equity, *Journal of Maritime Law and Commerce*, 20(4), 505–20.

Kerr, M. (1990). The International Convention on Salvage 1989 – How It Came to Be, *International and Comparative Law Quarterly*, 39, 530–56.

Klippert, G. (1983). *Unjust Enrichment*, Toronto: Butterworth.

Merkin, R. (2000). *Privity of Contract: The Impact of the Contracts (Rights of Third Parties) Act 1999*, London: Routledge.

Miller, A. (1981). Lloyd's Standard Form of Salvage Agreement – LOF 80: A Commentary *Journal of Maritime Law and Commerce*, 12(2), 243–61.

Redgwell, C. (1990). The Greening of Salvage Law, *Marine Policy*, 142–50.

Reeder, J. (2003). *Brice on Maritime Salvage*, 4th ed. London: Sweet & Maxwell.

Reeder, J. (2011). *Brice on Maritime Law of Salvage*, 5th ed. London: Sweet and Maxwell.

Rose, FD. (1989). Restitution for the Rescuer *Oxford Journal of Legal Studies*. 9, 167–204.

Rose, F. D. (2010). *Kennedy & Rose Law of Salvage*, 7th ed. London: Thomson Reuters.

Stoljar, S. (1964). *The Law of Quasi-Contract*, Law Book Company for New South Wales Bar Association.

Sutherland, P. (2006). Third-Party Contracts. In H. Macqueen and R. D. Zimmermann, eds., *European Contract law – Scots and South African Perspectives*', Edinburgh: Edinburgh University Press, pp. 203–29.

Sutherland, P. and Cupido, D. M. (2004). Insurance Law. *Annual Survey of South African Law*, 540–65.

Van der Linde, M., ed., (2010). *Compendium of South African Environmental Legislation* 2nd ed. Pretoria: Pretoria University Law Press.

Van Rensburg A, Lotz J. G. and Van Rhijn T. A. R. (2014) Contract. In D. Joubert, ed., *The Law of South Africa* 3rd ed. Vol 9.

Virgo, G. (1999). *Principles of the Law of Restitution*, Oxford: Oxford University Press.

Filling Institutional Voids in Thailand: the Case of Nestlé and the Seafood Coalition

David Wesley, Luis Alfonso Dau and Elizabeth M. Moore

12.1 INTRODUCTION

Globalization has reduced the economic and political distances between countries (Mahtaney, 2013). Along with increased cross-border transactions, however, has come increased global problems that pose serious threats to state sovereignty and capacity (Singh, 2012). Additionally, the current era has faced relentless global problems, both man-made and natural. They include, but are not limited to, economic collapse, health crises, such as Ebola and Zika, terrorism, and intense hurricanes and earthquakes (Abrahms, 2008; Baden et al., 2014; Kennedy and Nisbett, 2015). The accumulation of problems exceeds the ability of any single government (Millar, Choi and Chen, 2004; Nayyar, 2011). Therefore, scholars and practitioners have been looking to alternate actors (e.g. non-governmental organisations (NGOs), individuals and, increasingly, firms) as engines of change (Dau et al., 2017; Savitz, 2013). Thus, it is critical that we understand the role that firms play in promoting sustainable development goals through responsible strategic choices.

How can firms set a standard of social responsibility? This research centers on the intersection of firm CSR and sustainable development through strategic choices in developing countries (Amaeshi Adegbite and Raiwani, 2016; Hacking and Guthrie, 2008). Are there certain institutional environments that encourage firms to act responsibly as norm setters? How can academics and practitioners identify the different ways that firms respond to social responsibility standards? What strategies can firms employ to have a more active role in promoting global social responsibility throughout the supply chain, particularly within developing country contexts? Can firms fill policy voids when governments fail to establish norms of social responsibility and sustainable development?

This chapter will contribute to both the literature on CSR and sustainable development (Churie, Sjostedt and Corell, 2005; Elkington, 1998; 2013) and the literature on institutional voids (Doh, et al., 2017; Khanna and Palepu, 2010; Mair,

Marti and Ventresca, 2012). Specifically, we examine Nestlé as a model for labour and human rights in developing countries. Through this case study, we offer prescriptions for both firms and policymakers. Firms can benefit from this study by gaining an understanding of the role that enterprises play in setting norms and global responsibility standards (Lawrence and Beamish, 2012; Osland, 2013), as worldwide problems converge. Policymakers can utilize this research program to understand not only institutional voids around socially responsible behavior (Dau, Moore and Soto, 2016b; Khanna and Palepu, 2005), but also to understand how governments can cooperate with firms (Boddewyn and Doh, 2011) on sustainable development programs.

12.2 GLOBAL SOCIAL RESPONSIBILITY AND INSTITUTIONAL VOIDS

12.2.1 *CSR*

National and sub-national level actors face increased pressure from global actors and organisations to improve social responsibility programs (Churie et al., 2005; Dau et al., 2016b). This pressure structure is outlined in the "triple bottom line" (Elkington, 1998, 2013), a concept that means putting forward a better global effort at balancing three pillars of sustainability: (1) people; (2) planet; and (3) profit (Hacking and Guthrie, 2008; Savitz, 2013). As opposed to classic economic thinking that suggests that the firm's only obligation is to its shareholders, the triple bottom line and the increased global pressure structures imply that firms must be accountable and conscientious of all shareholders and stakeholders (Elkington, 1998, 2013; Amaeshi et al., 2016).

Within this framework, if each pillar is upheld, global sustainability would be possible. People refers to the protection of labour and human rights (Elkington, 1998, 2013). Planet refers to the protection of the environment (Elkington, 1998, 2013). Profit refers to the economic value created by a company for stakeholders, such as employees, shareholders and the public (Elkington, 1998, 2013). Although the current global climate has increased pressure on firms and other actors to engage in socially responsible behavior, CSR is still primarily self-regulated (Dau, Moore Soto, 2016a; Millar et al., 2004; Puffer and McCarthy, 2008). Thus, firms must monitor and promote their own compliance with ethical and environmental standards and regulations in countries where there is a lack of CSR regulation.

12.2.2 *Institutional Voids*

As North's famous articulation reminds us, formal institutions provide guidelines for firm behavior and they influence markets (North, 1990). By setting formal rules and regulations of competition, cooperation and coordination, firms become more efficient at conducting legitimate business practices (Dau, 2011, 2012, 2013, 2016, 2018). As such, formal institutions facilitate opportunities for firms, by clearly defining the costs and risks associated in pursuing one strategy over another. In other words, when rules are clear and transparent, firms have an advantage (Dau, Moore and Bradley, 2019). Colloquially put, playing by the rules is easier when you know them upfront.

Consequentially, when the rules are absent, there are increased risks and costs that firms must consider (Amaeshi et al., 2016; Doh, et al., 2017). The absence of formal rules, of formal institutional voids, creates conditions of uncertainty (Khanna and Palepu, 2010; Puffer and McCarthy, 2008). Where formal institutional voids exist, social needs are unmet by government regulation (Khanna and Palepu, 2005; Mair and Marti, 2009). As such, necessary critical functions and mechanisms to support firm behavior and strategy are lacking (Mair et al., 2012; Stephan Uhlaner and Stride, 2015). Institutional voids can range from lack of infrastructural regulation, corruption and policies to mitigate it, inefficient capital markets, and ill-defined educational systems (Doh, et al., 2017; Khanna and Palepu, 2005, 2010).

The degree to which institutional voids exists depends on the country context (Mair and Marti, 2009; Puffer and McCarthy, 2008). Developing countries are often categorized by an increased propensity to experience formal institutional voids (Dau et al., 2016b; Nayyar, 2011). Developing countries that lack capacity and proper enforcement mechanisms face the most severe institutional voids (Cynamon Fazzari and Setterfield, 2013; IMF, 2010; Leipziger and Canuto, 2012). In these countries, scholars and practitioners must identify actors to fill institutional voids and mitigate market inefficiencies and development challenges.

12.3 THEORETICAL JUSTIFICATION OF THE INTERSECTION OF CSR, INSTITUTIONAL VOIDS AND NORM-SETTING

We assert that amidst institutional voids, multinational corporations (MNCs) can promote CSR and sustainable development (Dau et al., 2016b; Millar et al., 2004; Park, 2005). Specifically, we focus on the role that MNCs can play in promoting positive human and labour rights. Human and labour rights as defined by the United Nation's Global Compact Initiative as two of the primary principles of sustainable development are critical aspects of social responsibility (UNCOP, 2016). In this framework, firms need to support and uphold internationally mandated human rights and pre-determined freedoms surrounding collective bargaining and association (Lawrence and Beamish, 2012). In many developing countries, however, rights are not upheld because governments do not have regulatory mechanisms to ensure that firms promote sustainable development (IMF, 2010; Nayyar, 2011). Thus, institutional voids exist. Illustrating and understanding the pathways and actions that firms can take in developing countries are imperative.

12.4 CONFRONTING SLAVERY AND CHILD LABOUR IN THAILAND: THE NESTLÉ CASE

Having the right policies, procedures and management systems is good and necessary, but it is not enough. It is the implementation, how you behave on the ground and the relationships you establish with different stakeholders, which create the trust necessary to be successful over time, as a company and as a society.

Paul Bulcke, Chairman of Nestlé S.A.

Nestlé Thailand was one of Nestlé's fastest growing subsidiaries with a growth rate of 10 percent annually and exports to 44 countries. It purchased coffee directly from more than 12,000 farmers, contributing significantly to the local economy. And it provided financial assistance, training and other support to help farmers increase productivity and promote economic development. On a trip to Thailand, Nestlé chairman Paul Bulcke reaffirmed his commitment to the country. "Thailand has a very important role to play in Nestlé's Asian and Global strategy," he said. He further asserted that Nestlé operated at the "highest global standards" in Thailand (Nestlé, 2011).

At the same time, Nestlé was under pressure on multiple fronts. In addition to consumer boycotts, it faced lawsuits in US courts over supply chain practices, which critics claimed relied heavily on slavery and child labour, particularly in Thailand (Smith, 2015).

Although most firms claimed to be unaware of forced labour in their supply chains, Nestlé argued that ignorance was not defensible. In 2012, the company commissioned a study to examine its supply chain in Thailand and Malaysia, countries that the US State Department considered among the worst for slavery.

The findings of its supply chain audit, which it published in 2015, confirmed the existence of slavery and child labour and provided examples of the abuses suffered by forced labour victims. Even Nestlé's loudest critics lauded the company's uncommon transparency. More importantly, Nestlé responded with a 10-point plan to eliminate forced and child labour from its seafood supply chain (see Table 12.1). "Nestlé is committed to eliminating forced labour in our seafood supply chain in Thailand, working alongside other stakeholders to tackle this serious and complex issue," the company announced in a press release.

> We believe that our Action Plan will help improve the lives of those affected by unacceptable practices. This will be neither a quick nor an easy endeavour, but we look forward to making significant progress in the months ahead. (Nestlé, 2015)

TABLE 12.1 *Nestlé 10-point plan (abridged)*

1. Based on the current signature of the Nestlé Supplier Code, incorporate new business requirements into commercial relationship.	Work closely with suppliers to ensure development and implementation of capacity building programs and business requirements that address human rights and labour standards and demonstrate compliance on an ongoing basis.
2. Enforce traceable supply chains identifying all potential sources of origins as part of a comprehensive supply chain risk assessment.	Ensure a verifiable supply chain traceability system as part of a comprehensive supply chain risk assessment that is aligned with industry partners and stakeholders within the Thailand Seafood Industry enabling traceability of seafood ingredients from fishing vessels through the complete supply chain to the receiving manufacturing sites and finished products.
3. Define and communicate requirements to boat owners and/or captains, including recruitment practices and living/working conditions for boat workers.	Building on the Marine Catch Purchasing Document, or any other industry recognized best practice; create a set of requirements for boat owners and captains.
4. Implement a training program for boat owners and/or captains.	Based on requirements set [3], and together with industry partners and stakeholders within the Thailand Seafood Industry, create a training hub to generate awareness and provide education to ensure effective worker protections in priority areas as determined by Verité. This training hub may take the form of a "demonstration boat" or "university" where a training program will be given to electable boat owners/captains.
5. Implement an awareness raising campaign on human rights and labour conditions, targeting primarily boat workers.	In cooperation with local authority and industry partners and stakeholders in the Thailand Seafood Industry, create an awareness raising campaign, addressing at 1st the topics of labour standards and health and safety at the workplace.
6. Enable the work of a Migrant Workforce Emergency Response team.	Identify a 3rd party partner [e.g. MWRN, LPN, Project Issara, *to be considered*] experienced in protecting individuals from the worst form of labour conditions. Deploy and empower this partner organisation as the Migrant Workforce Emergency Response Team: Team will be in charge to deploy the necessary assessments (based on [5] and

TABLE 12.1 *(continued)*

	[7]) to identify individuals in need of immediate assistance.
7. Create and implement a fishing vessels verification program.	By leveraging opportunities to collaborate with industry partners and stakeholders in the Thailand Seafood Industry, implement, at first, an internal audit program verifying working (labour and health and safety at workplace) conditions in fishing vessels for 100% of the fleet used.
	Secondly, alongside with monitoring of compliance through Key Performance Indicators, randomly select boats on a monthly basis to undergo a 3rd party verification audit by an independent organisation, executed every quarter. 3rd party verification audit should include interview of boat workers and establish history of their working career in the region and country.
8. Dedicate resources.	Mandate a Nestlé leader to the implementation of the action plan: Part Time or Full Time Job [To be confirmed] profile will include coordination with relevant parties, management of implementation activities, establishment of KPIs and dashboard, effective use of internal and financial resources dedicated, representation to relevant industry parties and stakeholders.
9. Collaborate and scale up.	Leverage opportunities for collaboration with industry partners and stakeholders within the Thailand Seafood Industry and seek to become a member of the Shrimp Sustainable Supply Chain Taskforce, share progresses on implementation of action plan and learning, contribute to testing of innovative solutions and continuously seek to enlarge implementation to other supply schemes and locations in South East Asia.
	Achieve similar aims as part of the Good Labour Practices Working Group, convened by Government of Thailand and supported by the International Labour Organisation.

(continued)

TABLE 12.1 *(continued)*

10. Publicly Report.	Report publicly on progresses, including challenges and failures identified with how to best resolve and solutions to address. This should include ongoing monitoring of business partners' supply chain management systems by independent third-party assessments and identification of risks and issues to be addressed.

Source: Nestlé[1]

12.4.1 Nestlé S.A.[2]

Nestlé was founded in 1867 in Vevey, Switzerland, by German chemist Henri Nestlé. His simple but effective breakthrough, an infant milk formula made from cow's milk, sugar and flour, reduced infant mortality rates among children who could not be breastfed. Shortly afterward, the company expanded into infant cereals and condensed milk products. By the end of the nineteenth century, Nestlé added milk chocolate, a product that would define Nestlé in the twentieth century.

After World War II, Nestlé's growth accelerated as the company's product portfolio encompassed an ever-wider variety of foods and cooking products. Diversification became a cornerstone of expansion efforts. By the end of the century, Nestlé was a leading producer of pharmaceuticals, cosmetics, bottled water and pet food. The company employed 335,000 people in 189 countries.

In recent years, Nestlé came under pressure from human rights organisations for its supply chain practices, which sourced raw materials from companies known to employ child and forced labour. In 2005, a group of child labour victims from Mali sued Nestlé in a US federal court, arguing that the company was aware that its cocoa suppliers in the Ivory Coast were using child slaves. After a series of jurisdictional appeals, the US Supreme Court ruled in 2016 that Nestlé could be tried for human rights abuses in its supply chain (McCarthy, 2016).

In 2016, Nestlé missed its projected growth targets, resulting in the company's lowest growth in two decades (see Tables 12.2–12.4 for financial data). Changing tastes contributed to the decline, as consumers clamored for more healthy offerings and reduced their intake of sugary beverages, chocolate and candy.[3] Although, Nestlé outperformed other consumer product giants, including Unilever, Procter & Gamble and Kraft Heinz, the company promised to address "some of these very

---

[1] www.Nestlé.com/asset-library/documents/library/documents/corporate_social_responsibility/Nestlé-seafood-action-plan-thailand-2015–2016.pdf accessed February 7, 2017.

[2] Nestlé, 2018. All of the factual and historical information in this section comes from the "About Us, Detailed History" section of Nestlé's webpage.

[3] Other factors included low inflation rates, and exchange rate volatility.

TABLE 12.2 *Key financial data*[4]

Results	2015	2014
Sales	88,785	91,612
Trading operating profit	13,382	14,019
as % of sales	15.1%	15.3%
Profit for the year attributable to shareholders of the parent (Net profit)	9,066	14,456
as % of sales	10.2%	15.8%
Balance sheet and Cash flow statement		
Equity attributable to shareholders of the parent	62,338	70,130
Net financial debt	15,425	12,325
Ratio of net financial debt to equity (gearing)	24.7%	17.6%
Operating cash flow	14,302	14,700
as % of net financial debt	92.7%	119.3%
Free cash flow [(a)]	9,945	14,137
Capital expenditure	3,872	3,914
as % of sales	4.4%	4.3%
Data per share		
Weighted average number of shares outstanding (in millions of units)	3,129	3,188
Basic earnings per share	2.90	4.54
Underlying earnings per share	3.31	3.44
Dividend as proposed by the Board of Directors of Nestlé S.A.	2.25	2.20
Market capitalization, end December	229,947	231,136
Number of employees (in thousands)	335	339

TABLE 12.3 *Sales by geographic area (2015, in CHF millions)*[5]

United States	25,293
Greater China Region	7,060
France	4,848
Brazil	3,925
United Kingdom	3,006
Germany	2,929
Mexico	2,749
Philippines	2,645
Italy	1,867
Canada	1,847
Spain	1,668
Switzerland	1,549
Australia	1,498
Japan	1,440
Russia	1,330
Rest of the world	25,131
Total	**88,785**

[4] Source: www.Nestlé.com/asset-library/documents/library/documents/annual_reports/2015-annual-review-en.pdf accessed February 17, 2017.
[5] Source: www.Nestlé.com/asset-library/documents/library/documents/annual_reports/2015-annual-review-en.pdf, accessed February 17, 2017.

TABLE 12.4 *Sales by product category (2015, in CHF millions)*

Powdered and Liquid Beverages	
Total sales	19,245
Trading operating profit	4,100
Water	
Total sales	7,112
Trading operating profit	796
Milk Products and Ice Cream	
Total sales	14,637
Trading operating profit	2,471
Nutrition and Health Science	
Total sales	14,854
Trading operating profit	2,909
Prepared Dishes and Cooking Aids	
Total sales	12,579
Trading operating profit	1,724
Confectionery	
Chocolate	6,365
Sugar confectionery	1,130
Biscuits	1,375
Total sales	8,870
Trading operating profit	1,246
Pet Care	
Total sales	11,488
Trading operating profit	2,386

fundamental changes that we've witnessed in the consumer-goods industry" by focusing on restructuring and cost reduction (Blackstone, 2017).

12.4.2 *Thailand*

Centrally located between the South China Sea to the east and the Bay of Bengal to the west, Thailand was one of the more diverse nations in South East Asia. It shared land borders with Myanmar (also known as Burma), Cambodia, Malaysia and Laos and was less than 200 nautical miles from China, Indonesia and Vietnam. Ethnic Thais, descendants of the Siamese people who immigrated to the peninsula nearly one thousand years ago, had a distinct language and culture (Wyatt, 2003). Of the country's 67 million inhabitants, Thais comprised approximately two-thirds of the population. Among the numerous minorities in Thailand, the largest were Chinese, Malay, Vietnamese, Khmer, Tibetan and Polynesian (see Figure 12.1).

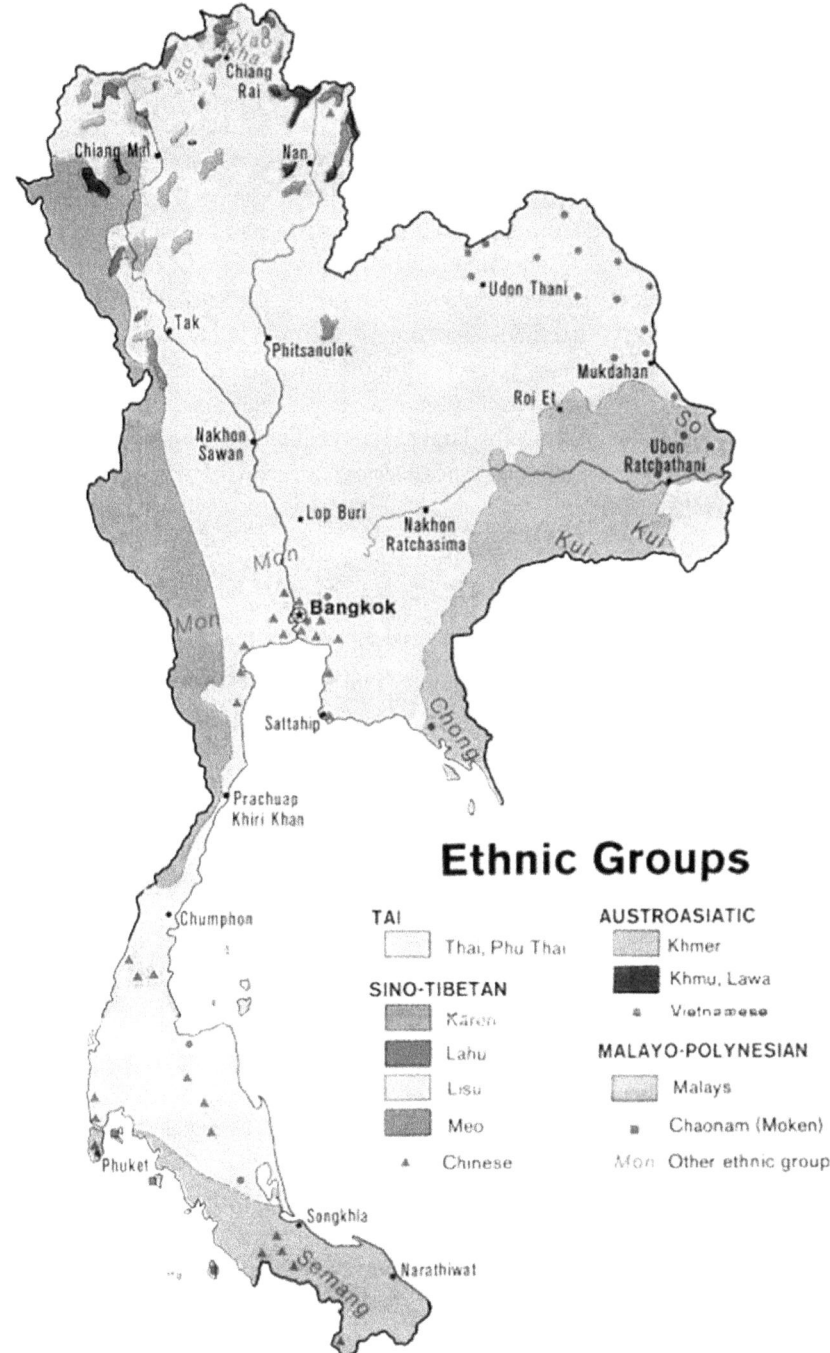

FIGURE 12.1 Map of ethnolinguistic groups of Thailand
Source: US Central Intelligence Agency[6]

6   Public domain map https://commons.wikimedia.org/wiki/File:Ethnolinguistic_map_of_Thailand_1974 .jpg accessed January 25, 2017.

Thailand's modern history began in the late eighteenth century when King Rama the First established Bangkok as the capital of the Kingdom of Siam. In the 1930s, the monarchy was overthrown and the country was renamed Thailand, translated as "Land of the Free" (BBC, 2016). The country was plagued with coups d'état throughout the twentieth century. The latest coup occurred in 2014 when General Prayuth Chan-Ocha seized control and declared himself prime minister.

Despite its political instability, Thailand maintained a favorable investment policy that allowed its economy to grow more quickly than most of its neighbors. The country was a major exporter of automotive parts, electronics and agriculture. Because of its economic growth, Thailand experienced severe labour shortages that were filled by as many as 4 million migrant workers, primarily from neighboring countries (US CIA, 2017).

12.4.3 *The Slave Trade*

Although slavery and child labour were illegal, Thailand was one of the worst offenders of human trafficking, ranking 20th in the world in forced labour prevalence. Among the estimated 45 million slaves worldwide, Thailand was believed to have nearly half a million (Global Slavery Index, 2016). Although actual numbers were difficult to ascertain because slavery was largely hidden, even modest estimates placed Thailand high on the list of offending countries (Kessler, 2015).

Thailand's human trafficking problem was in part due to institutional voids and in part due to geography. Forced labour was prohibited under the country's constitution and Thailand passed a number of laws ostensibly aimed at protecting women and children from exploitation (Datla, 2013). Yet, corruption remained a major barrier to enforcement as human traffickers bribed police and military officers to not enforce anti-slavery laws or, in many cases, to participate in human trafficking. Lawyers who have attempted to help victims have been threatened by the military (Lucas, 2017).

The region's geography, with 5,462 kilometers of mostly undefended borders, made it easier to exploit immigrants. Most victims came from poor neighboring countries, particularly Burma and Cambodia, where economic conditions favored migration to Thailand and Malaysia. Many were promised paid positions by slave traffickers posing as people smugglers or boyfriends. Once in Thailand, they were sold to slave camps, to slave trading ships that operated offshore in international waters and to fishing boats. Those who escaped were often recaptured by police officers and resold to other slave traders and owners. Younger children were used in agriculture, including shrimp processing, or were sold to pedophile sex rings (US Department of Labour, 2015).

12.4.4 *Slavery in the Supply Chain*

Although Nestlé had long been accused of profiting from slave labour in its cocoa supply chain in Africa, the company had recently come under scrutiny for forced and child labour in its seafood supply chain in South East Asia, particularly Thailand (The Environmental Justice Foundation, 2015). Nestlé's primary supplier for shrimp and seafood for its pet products was Thai Union Frozen Products. As one of the largest suppliers of seafood in Thailand, Thai Union exported 28 million pounds of seafood to the United States alone.

Monitoring illegal fishing and slave labour was increasingly difficult as ships operated further away from shore. This was largely driven by unsustainable environmental practices that had decimated coastal fish stocks. Between 1960 and 1980, Thailand's fisheries increased their catch from 64,000 tons to 2 million tons, while over the same period the catch per unit of effort decreased by 84 percent.[7] By 2012, the annual catch per unit of effort was estimated to have declined by another 50 percent. To compensate for declining fish stocks, vessels ventured into international waters, where they competed for limited resources with vessels from other nations. In some cases, this resulted in violent confrontations between fishing vessels and seizures by foreign naval and coast guard vessels (The Environmental Justice Foundation, 2015).

Thai Union operated large motherships in the deep ocean. It also processed, packed and exported seafood. Smaller independently owned fishing vessels met up with the mother ships to offload their catch. Once loaded, fish was mixed in holding containers, thereby making it impossible to trace the source. A single mothership could contain fish from legitimate vessels and slave ships. The motherships then transported fish to shore for sorting and packing (The Environmental Justice Foundation, 2015).

Trash fish (mixed species caught by dredging the ocean floor) were crushed and made into fish meal to fertilize crops and supply shrimp farms. At least three tons of trash fish was required to produce one ton of shrimp. Adult shrimp were then transported to sheds where they were peeled and processed for export. Cases of child and forced labour were documented at each of the points in the supply chain, from fishers who were forced to work at sea for years at a time, to children who spent 16 hours a day in dark sheds peeling raw shrimp (The Environmental Justice Foundation, 2015).

12.4.5 *Forced Labour in the Fishing Industry*

The Environmental Justice Foundation found numerous examples of "horrific abuses" and slavery. Fishers worked an average of 18.8 hours per day, seven days a

---

[7] A "unit of effort" was a measure of time, labour and energy expenditure. For instance, if it takes two similar sized fishing vessels to produce the same catch as one vessel in previous years, the catch remains the same, but the catch per unit of effort is half.

week (Zimmerman et al., 2014). The men and boys were told they would have to work on the fishing boats to pay off their debts to people smugglers. However, once at sea, they were charged fees for food and board that consumed their pay. To prevent escape, fishing boats operated far from shore, often for years at a time. Fishing vessels were resupplied by large refrigeration ships owned by the Thai Union and other companies that sold seafood to major suppliers. This method of resupply allowed fishing boats to operate out of reach of authorities.

Occasionally, slaves escaped or were rescued by foreign NGOs. Escaped slaves told tales of torture and gruesome executions of disobedient workers. Many had never been to sea before. Some could not even swim. Yet, they were expected to learn to manage the nets immediately. If they made mistakes, they were beaten. If they got sick, they were thrown overboard. If they disobeyed the captain, they were tortured or murdered in front of the other fishers to instill fear in the crew and prevent mutinies.

Myint Naing was one of 300 Burmese slaves held in a remote Indonesian island that was secretly being used as a base for Thai fishing vessels.

Naing left home in 1993 searching for a better life in Thailand. His story followed the usual pattern of being offered a position for a fee that would be paid off once he found work in Thailand. Instead, he was sent to a slave camp where he starved for a month. After being sold to a fishing boat, he spent years at sea in cramped conditions with nothing to eat but garbage fish and boiled ocean water. Fishers who did not perform as expected were whipped with poisonous stingray tails. Those who died were thrown overboard or stored in the freezer with the fish. Between expeditions, slaves were kept on an Indonesian island without communication and no means to escape. In 2015, Associated Press journalists uncovered the island where Naing and others were being held and after alerting the Indonesia authorities, the slaves were returned to their home countries (Mason, 2015).

For freed slaves like Naing, escaping captivity was not the end of the ordeal. Slaves suffered from post-traumatic stress disorder (PTSD), as well as numerous health problems. Some had lost fingers and limbs in fishing nets. Others had no employability skills. Neither the Thai government, nor their home governments offered much assistance, leaving survivors dependent on their families and tribes. When Naing returned to Burma after 22 years in captivity, he had forgotten his customs and had difficulty speaking his native tongue. He was nearly penniless and "struggled to convert 15,000 Indonesian rupiahs into about 1,000 Myanmar kyats, both roughly $1" (Mason, 2015).

12.4.6 Shrimp Processing Warehouses

Fishing boats were manned by men, but women and children were also victimized by human traffickers. The "pretty" ones were raped and sent to brothels, while those deemed less attractive were sent to shrimp processing plants, where they pealed and packaged shrimp for 16 or more hours per day. Survivors described life in a shrimp plant.

> Every morning at 2 a.m., they heard a kick on the door and a threat: Get up or get beaten. For the next 16 hours, No. 31 and his wife stood in the factory that owned them with their aching hands in ice water …
>
> They were at the mercy of their Thai bosses, trapped with nearly 100 other Burmese migrants. Children worked alongside them, including a girl so tiny she had to stand on a stool to reach the peeling table. Some had been there for months, even years, getting little or no pay …
>
> Inside the large warehouse, toilets overflowed with faeces, and the putrid smell of raw sewage wafted from an open gutter just outside the work area. Young children ran barefoot through suffocating dorm rooms. Entire families laboured side-by-side at rows of stainless steel counters piled high with tubs of shrimp. (Mason et al., 2015)

When the Associated Press discovered one such slave shed and reported it to Thai authorities, the slaves were treated like criminals.

> No one at the Gig shed was arrested for human trafficking, a law that's seldom enforced. Instead, migrants with papers, including seven children, were sent back there to work. Another 10 undocumented children were taken from their parents and put into a shelter, forced to choose between staying there for years or being deported back to Myanmar alone. Nineteen other illegal workers were detained. (Mason et al., 2015)
>
> Two escaped slaves who confided in the reporters were arrested. Just four days after being reunited, the couple was fingerprinted and locked inside a Thai jail cell without even a mattress. They were held on nearly $4,000 bail and charged with entering the country illegally and working without permits. (Mason et al., 2015)

Although the Thai government claimed to be doing everything in its power to combat slavery, corruption was rampant and officials from local police to high ranking military officers were involved in the slave trade. Some protected slave traders, while others sold escaped slaves. Slave compounds were sometimes ringed with soldiers or police officers who kept slaves from escaping under the guise of providing security. A Harvard University study observed that "local police in the cities treat migrant workers like walking ATMs. The police catch migrants and even if the migrants have official documents as proof that they are in the country legally, they will request a bribe" (Datla, 2013).

12.4.7 Government Policies on Slavery

Under US law, the importation of goods made by slave labour was illegal. Ambassadors were responsible for submitting a Trafficking in Persons (TIP) report each year. Countries with the lowest ranking, those "whose governments do not fully comply with the minimum standards and are not making significant efforts to do so," were classified as Tier 3 nations. Thailand was among 23 nations in the Tier 3 classification. Others included Syria, North Korea and Saudi Arabia (US State Department, 2012).

The US State Department declared that Thailand was making little effort to combat slavery and human trafficking. In 2011, the Thai government "reported that 392 foreign victims were classified as trafficking victims in Thailand," yet Thailand's fishing fleet alone accounted for an estimated 200,000 foreign workers, most of whom worked under forced labour conditions (Mason, 2014).

Although Thailand was on the US State Department's watch list, the country was repeatedly exempted due to its strategic importance and assistance in providing intelligence for the "war on terror" (Mazzella, 2017). In 2002, it also became the CIA's first "black site" for terrorist interrogations (Council of Europe, 2008). Thailand also avoided the US Tariff Act of 1930 due to a loophole that allowed "products that came from forced labour [to] be imported if consumers had a 'consumptive demand' for the product" (Mazzella, 2017).

In 2016, President Obama shocked human rights activists, as well as many congressional Democrats and Republicans, by upgrading Thailand to Tier 2 to pave way for the Trans-Pacific Partnership, a proposed trade deal between the United States and 11 other Pacific nations (Carter, 2015). Because of the upgrade, the Thai government faced less pressure to combat slavery. Nevertheless, the United States was the only foreign country that provided significant police assistance to Thailand, with agents from "the FBI, the Department of Homeland Security, and other U.S. law enforcement" coordinating investigations with the Royal Thai Police (US FBI, 2016).

12.4.8 Nestlé's Supplier Code of Conduct

Nestlé was a member of the UN Global Compact, which outlined ten principles of conduct, including prohibiting the use of forced labour (see Table 12.1). It also required suppliers to adhere to these principles and submit to inspections (see Table 12.1). Specifically, it prohibited suppliers from engaging in "any form of indentured servitude, such as the use of physical punishment, confinement, threats of violence as a method of discipline or control such as retaining employees' identification, passports, work permits or deposits as a condition of employment."

Human Rights

Principle 1: Businesses should support and respect the protection of internationally proclaimed human rights; and

Principle 2: make sure that they are not complicit in human rights abuses.

Labour

Principle 3: Businesses should uphold the freedom of association and the effective recognition of the right to collective bargaining;

Principle 4: the elimination of all forms of forced and compulsory labour;

Principle 5: the effective abolition of child labour; and

Principle 6: the elimination of discrimination in respect of employment and occupation.

Environment

Principle 7: Businesses should support a precautionary approach to environmental challenges;

Principle 8: undertake initiatives to promote greater environmental responsibility; and

Principle 9: encourage the development and diffusion of environmentally friendly technologies.

Anti-Corruption

Principle 10: Businesses should work against corruption in all its forms, including extortion and bribery.

Figure 12.2 Ten principles of the UN Global Compact[8]

The supplier shall only employ workers who are legally authorized to work in their facilities and are responsible for validating employees' eligibility to work through appropriate documentation. All work shall be voluntary, and workers shall be free to leave work or terminate their employment upon reasonable notice. (Nestlé, 2013)

The code also banned the use of child labour and provided clear guidelines on employment hours and conditions. Nestlé's responsible sourcing guidelines further demanded that suppliers ensure

a There is no known sourcing from Illegal, Unreported and Unregulated (IUU) fisheries and vessels.

b There is no known sourcing from aquaculture operations which are not legally licensed for production and sales (Nestlé, 2013).

---

[8] www.unglobalcompact.org/what-is-gc/mission/principles accessed February 21, 2017.

II. Supplier's Acknowledgement (If required by the Nestlé Purchasing Organisation) We, the undersigned hereby confirm that:

• We have received and taken due note of the contents of the Nestlé Supplier Code of 2013, published by Nestlé S.A,
• We are aware of all relevant laws and regulations of the countries in which our company operates,
• We will report to Nestlé S.A any case of violations of the Code.
• We will comply with the Nestlé Supplier Code requirements based on a development oriented approach and without amendment or abrogation.
• We will inform all of our employees/subcontractors of the content of the Nestlé Supplier Code, and that we will ensure that they also comply with the provisions incorporated therein.

We hereby authorized Nestlé S. A or any organisations acting on behalf of the Nestlé S. A to carry out audits with or without notice at our premises and the business premises of our subcontractors at any time to verify compliance with the Nestlé Supplier Code content.

Name of Company

_____

Name of Title

_____

Signature   Company Stamp/Seal

_____

Company's Business Registration/Statutory ID/Code/Number

_____

Date & Place

_____

This document must be signed by an authorized representative of the supplier & returned to the requesting Nestlé Purchasing Organisation

Figure 12.3 Supplier agreement form[9]

However, the company's critics asserted that the "numerous corporate statements intended to show that Nestlé does not tolerate the use of forced labour by its suppliers" were "unlawful, unfair, and/or deceptive" given the "superior

9   www.Nestlé.com/asset-library/documents/library/documents/suppliers/supplier-code-english.pdf accessed February 21, 2017.

As the basis for this approach, we recommend Nestlé develop an integrated anti-trafficking and forced labour strategy with clear measurable objectives (SMART goals). The strategy should:

1. Prioritize the following Key Result Areas (KRAs):
   i. vulnerability of sea-based workers (vessel employment and working conditions);
   ii. migrant legal status in receiving country;
   iii. recruitment-related fees and exploitation by recruiters; and
   iv. worker access to effective grievance channels.
2. Leverage opportunities for collaborative multi-stakeholder action that can drive change from the government and inter-governmental levels (e.g., adoption of ILO Recommendation 203-2014: Recommendation on supplementary measures for the effective suppression of forced labour) to producer levels (e.g., fair, safe and legal employment practices).
3. Ensure verifiable supply chain traceability as the first step in a comprehensive supply chain risk assessment.
4. Ensure that that suppliers can deliver effective worker protections in the following priority areas by strengthening supplier screening, onboarding, and performance management:
   i. Mitigation of debt risk by adoption and implementation of a 'No fees' policy for job seekers;
   ii. Performance management of labour providers (including incentivizing ethical practices and penalizing unethical ones);
   iii. Legalization of employee immigration status without financial burden;
   iv. Unrestricted access of workers to their personal documents including passports;
   v. Transparent, accurate and understandable terms of employment including written contracts;
   vi. Freedom of movement/freedom to quit without penalty;
   vii. Prevention of child labour and hazardous juvenile labour;
   viii. Unfettered and timely access to grievance systems;
   ix. Fair wages and work hours;
   x. Protection from harm, prioritizing vessel-based workers; and
   xi. Humane treatment.
5. Provide sufficient resources for both internal and supplier communication and capacity building programs, to ensure that the trafficking policy is fully understood and that suppliers, including labour providers, are incentivized or supported through external training to develop internal

(cont.)

competencies and business processes for continuously strengthening risk controls and remedies for vulnerable workers.

6. Provide robust, independent risk-based performance monitoring of supplier management of critical forced labour and human rights abuses. The approach should identify and track forced labour risks (proactively), issues (requiring immediate action), and KPIs of business partners' supply chain risk management systems (resulting in continual improvement).

Figure 12.4 Verité's recommended action plan[10]

knowledge of Nestlé's supply chain and the practices of its supplier" (District Court California, 2015).

12.4.9 *Auditing the Supply Chain*

Following a series of news reports on forced labour, in 2012, Nestlé contacted Verité to audit its supply chain in Thailand. Verité was an "independent, non-profit organisation that conducts research, advocacy, consulting, trainings, and assessments with a vision that people worldwide work under safe, fair, and legal conditions" (Verité, 2017). When Verité completed its report in 2015, its findings were "largely consistent with … other assessment work in the Thai seafood sector, as well as with reporting done by media and other organisations" (Verité, 2015).

"These findings of severe labour and human rights abuses present an urgent challenge to any company sourcing seafood," the report noted, namely because "tracing product to its original origins and holding all suppliers accountable to social and environmental sustainability standards [was] challenging" (Verité, 2015). Nevertheless, Verité made a number of recommendations that focused on a combination of traceability, education and monitoring (see Table 12.4).

Many human rights organisations praised Nestlé's transparency. Steve Trent, director of the Environmental Justice Foundation, lauded Nestlé for "own[ing] up to the abuses." "Businesses today have the ability to build the kind of transparency needed to effectively combat these human rights abuses and illegal fishing," he added (Nguyen, 2015).

Nevertheless, not everyone was convinced that the company's intentions were honorable. "It's easy to own up to something that has already been uncovered," exclaimed Andrew Wallis, CEO of labour rights NGO Unseen UK.

---

[10] Verité Assessment of Recruitment Practices and Migrant Labour Conditions in Nestlé's Thai Shrimp Supply Chain, 2015, www.verite.org/wp-content/uploads/2016/11/NestléReport-ThaiShrimp_prepared-by-Verite.pdf accessed February 21, 2017.

By the time Nestlé owned up to slavery in the Thai seafood industry, it was accepted knowledge. It'll be a brave new world when companies are actually doing the real investigation to probe into part of their supply chains that have remained outside the public domain. We need to move into a space where we say, "We're all guilty; let's get past that to a place where we can properly address the problem" – and I don't think we're there yet. (Kelly, 2016)

Nestlé's admission also did not dissuade a class action suit against the company in US federal court. "America's largest and most profitable food conglomerates should not tolerate slave labour anywhere in their supply chains," began the complaint.

These companies should not turn a blind eye to known human rights abuses or shirk from investigating potential human rights abuses by their suppliers, especially when the companies consistently and affirmatively represent that they act in a socially and ethically responsible manner. When these food conglomerates fail to uphold their responsibility for ensuring the absence of slave labour in their supply chains, their misconduct has the profound con-sequence of supporting and encouraging slave labour … Such food conglom-erates should be required to make restitution to the consumers they have deceived and to ensure the absence of slave labour in their supply chains going forward. (District Court California, 2015)

Lead counsel Steve Berman recognized that although Nestlé's report was "a step in the right direction, it does not change the fact that the company has failed to disclose the use of forced labour in its seafood supply chains to consumers. Hagens Berman's litigation stemming from these grave human rights violations will continue, as we believe consumers have the right to know about Nestlé's use of slave labour at the point of sale."

Notwithstanding the enormity of tackling a problem as entrenched as forced labour, Verité was optimistic about Nestlé's ability to bring about meaningful change, despite Nestlé's lack of direct ownership of much of the supply chain.

Nestlé is the biggest food company in the world, it is seen as a leader in the industry, and could have a positive impact on the whole industry by raising the bar on labour protection. (Verité, 2015)

Following the Verité audit, Bulke warned that without government and industry efforts, the ability of Nestlé to combat labour abuses would be limited. "A company, even a sizeable one like Nestlé, cannot resolve alone some of the systemic human rights issues that the world faces: challenges such as child labour in agriculture, food security, access to water and sanitation and – of course – the broadening of the business and human rights agenda to other and more companies, all need the involvement of many other actors" (Bulke, 2014). The question was how much influence Nestlé could exert on suppliers, and how much responsibility should it accept for abuses that occur outside of its direct control.

12.4.10 *Nestlé and the Seafood Task Force*

Following an investigative report published by *The Guardian* in June of 2014 that highlighted the use of forced labour in Thailand in the supply chains of shrimp production for the US and the UK, several corporations implicated in the report, including Nestlé, Charoen Pokphand Foods and Costco, established the Shrimp Sustainable Supply Chain Task Force, which was renamed the Seafood Task Force in 2016 (Seafood Task Force, 2016). Since its inception, the Seafood Task Force has grown to include major US and EU food retailers, Thai production manufacturers, local and international NGOs, and government agencies.

The central objective of the Task Force, which has 53 members, is to oversee and supervise the entire seafood production industry to ensure traceability, international regulation compliance, accountability for abuse, scalability and sustainability (Seafood Task Force, 2016). An independent report by the NGOs the Freedom Fund and Humanity United called the Seafood Coalition, "the most influential and diverse coalition of stakeholders operating in Thailand on this issue" (Stride, 2016).

Nestlé spearheaded the Seafood Task Force in 2015 as part of the corporation's action plan. Nestlé's vision was to "be an industry leader in determining where the seafood is coming from & demand it is sourced responsibly" (Nestlé, 2015). The objectives were to activate management systems to transparently map upstream supply chains and monitor and remediate practices per good labour standards. These objectives were achieved through incorporating business requirements of traceability into relationships with suppliers, conducting a supply chain risk assessment, communicating good business standards to all members of supply chain, implementing training programs for all members of supply chain including boat owners and captains, creating an awareness campaign around human rights and human rights abuses, establishing an emergency respond team for migrant workers, implementing a verification process for fishing boats, assigning resources to developing processes, collaborating with other corporations through membership in the Seafood Task Force and publicly reporting data and progress on objectives (Nestlé, 2015).

Due to its leading role, Nestlé faced external and internal pressure to evaluate and reform its supply chain as well as encourage its competitors and suppliers to do the same. Every year since the development of the action plan, Nestlé has released progress reports detailing the achievements made and objectives maintained. The most recent self-reported data from Nestlé in 2017 claims the following: 99 percent of the tuna and shrimp supply chains have been mapped for traceability; 100 percent of suppliers and suppliers' suppliers have signed Nestlé's Supplier Code; over 10 percent of vessels have been audited to Seafood Task Force standards; and transhipment, a key risk factor for forced labour, has been banned (Bethell, Nestlé, 2017). Additionally, Nestlé has partnered with other NGOs to implement inclusive labour monitoring, create systems of verifiable worker feedback to strengthen supplier relations and reduce labour risks, and initiate worker training programs. Lastly, Nestlé works to align stakeholders to the Code of Conduct, develop fisheries improvement initiatives and create responsible recruitment systems for migrant workers entering the industry (Bethell, Nestlé, 2017).

12.5 CONCLUSION

The purpose of this chapter is to document Thailand's history of slavery and child labour through the lens of the corporate social responsibility framework. Only by documenting the human rights abuses present in Thailand, can scholars and practitioners understand the severe institutional voids that exist in the country. While domestic policy efforts and agendas have failed to correct these human rights abuses, we elucidate the role that corporations, like Nestlé, have in filling this policy void. Using Nestlé's creation and active membership in the Seafood Task Force, we argue that multinational companies can serve not only as policy proxies when institutional voids are present, but also as engines of normative social change. As companies continue to emphasize the triple bottom line of people, planet and profit, their roles as policy advocates becomes increasingly important.

Despite the importance of this chapter, there are several limitations and opportunities for future scholarship that merit attention. First, although this chapter outlines a detailed narrative example of the role that an MNC can have in filling institutional voids, the chapter focuses on primarily one example, Nestlé. Thus, future scholarship can expand upon this research program by examining additional MNCs to understand if others are actively participating in policy shaping. Second, this research program was intentionally designed to examine only Thailand. By focusing on one country, we were able to effectively study the impact that Nestlé had on filling policy voids. Future research can build upon this research by studying additional countries, both developed and developing. By looking at institutional voids in other developing countries, scholars can add to the breadth of the arguments put forth in this chapter.

This chapter contributes to the literature on CSR and sustainable development (Elkington, 1998; 2013) and the literature on institutional voids (Doh et al., 2017). Extant scholarship has looked at the different pressure systems that firms experience as it relates to CSR (Churie et al, 2005; Dau et al., 2016b). These scholars have argued that when firms experience pressure from national governments and consumers, they are more likely to engage in socially responsible behavior. Additionally, the literature on institutional voids posits that when institutional voids exists, firms must figure out how to navigate these voids and act strategically (Khanna and Palepu, 2005; 2010). We build on this literature by suggesting that in developing countries, where institutional voids are often more exaggerated and visible, MNCs can do more than navigate around the voids, but rather they can serve to fill those voids and positively impact policy around CSR through responsible strategic choices. This is critical for policymakers in developing country contexts and for managers. From a policymaking perspective it is imperative that governments understand all the different actors that can shape policy. This research suggests that governments and policymakers in developing countries would benefit from a more horizontal, and less hierarchical, relationship with MNCs. From a managerial perspective, this research indicates that when firms operate in developing countries they have the opportunity not only to maximize profit for their shareholders, but to positively impact all their stakeholders through responsible strategic choices and filling existing institutional voids.

REFERENCES

Abrahms, M. (2008). What terrorists really want: Terrorist motives and counterterrorism strategy. *International Security*, 32(4), 78–105.
Amaeshi, K., Adegbite, E. and Rajwani, T. (2016).Corporate social responsibility in challenging and non-enabling institutional contexts: Do institutional voids matter? *Journal of Business Ethics*, 134(1), 135–153.
Baden, L., Kanapathipillia, R., Campion, E. W., Morrisey, S., Rubin, E. J. and Drazen, J. M. (2014). Ebola – an ongoing crisis. *New England Journal of Medicine*, 371(15), 1458–1469.
BBC (2016). Thailand profile – timeline. *BBC News*.
Bethell, O. (2017) Responsible Sourcing of Seafood at Nestlé – Thailand Action Plan Update. *Nestrade LTD*, 1–2.
Blackstone, B. (2017). Nestlé Drops Targets as Consumer Giants Struggle. *The Wall Street Journal*.
Boddewyn, J. and Doh, J. (2011). Global strategy and the collaboration of MNEs, NGOs, and governments for the provisioning of collective goods in emerging markets. *Global Strategy Journal*, 1(3-4), 345–361.
Bulke, P. (2014). Keynote Statement, United Nations Annual Forum on Business and Human Rights. Nestlé.
Carter, Z. (2015). Obama Shrugs Off Global Slavery to Protect Trade Deal. *The Huffington Post*.
Churie, A., Sjostedt, G. and Corell, E. (2005). *Global Challenges: Furthering the Multilateral Process for Sustainable Development*. Sheffield: Greenleaf Publishing.
CIA (2017). Thailand, The World Fact Book. US Central Intelligence Agency.
Council of Europe (2008). CIA Above the Law? Secret Detentions and Unlawful Inter-state Transfers of Detainees in Europe. Strasbourg, France, p. 152.
Cynamon, B. Z., Fazzari, S. M. and Setterfield, M. (2013). *After the Great Recession: The Struggle for Economic Recovery and Growth*. Cambridge: Cambridge University Press.
Dau L. A. (2011). Reforms, multinationalization, and profitability. In L. Toombs, ed., *Academy of Management Best Paper Proceedings*. Briarcliff Manor: Academy of Management.
Dau L. A. (2012). Pro-market reforms and developing country multinational corporations. *Global Strategy Journal*, 2(3), 262–276.
Dau L. A. (2013). Learning across geographic space: Pro-market reforms, multinationalization strategy, and profitability. *Journal of International Business Studies*, 44(3), 235–262.

Dau L. A. (2016). Knowledge will set you free: Enhancing the firm's responsiveness to institutional change. *International Journal of Emerging Markets*, 11(2), 121–147.

Dau L. A. (2018). Contextualizing international learning: The moderating effects of mode of entry and subsidiary networks on the relationship between reforms and profitability. *Journal of World Business*, 53(1), 403–414.

Dau, L. A., Moore, E. M. and Abrahms, M. (2018). Female Entrepreneurship and International Organizations. In Apostolopoulos et al., eds., *Entrepreneurship and the Sustainable Development Goals*. Bradford: Emerald Publishing Group.

Dau, L. A., Moore, E. M. and Bradley, C. (2019). Regime Structure, Institutional Stability and Pro-Market Reforms: Deepening the Inter-disciplinary Connection. In W. Newburry, ed., *Family and Entrepreneurial Multinational Companies in Latin America: Contexts, Challenges and Perspectives*. London: Palgrave Publishing Company.

Dau, L. A., Moore, E. M. and Soto, M. (2016a). Informal Transnational Political Actors and Emerging Markets: Understanding Entrepreneurship in a Changing Normative Atmosphere. In A. Walsh, ed., *Entrepreneurship and Firm Performance*, pp. 19–41. NOVA Science Publishers.

Dau, L. A., Moore, E. M. and Soto, M. (2016b). The Great Recession and Emerging Market Firms: Unpacking the Divide Between Global and National Level Sustainability Expectations. In *Lessons from the Great Recession: At the Crossroads of Sustainability and Recovery*, pp. 165–187. Bradford: Emerald Group Publishing Limited.

Dau, L. A., Moore, E. M., Figgins, J. and Ault, J. (2017). Firms as Policy Advocates and Institutional Framers: Understanding the Impact of Ethnic and Political Stratification on BRICS MNEs. In W. D. Nelson, ed., *Advances in Business and Management*. New York: NOVA Science Publishers.

Datla, A. (2013). United States and Thailand: Diplomatic Wrangles in the War on Human Trafficking, Case Number 1991.0, John F. Kennedy School of Government, Harvard University, p. 9.

District Court California. (2015). *Barber v. Nestlé USA Inc.* December 9.

Doh, J., Rodrigues, S., Saka-Helmhout, A. and Makhija, M. (2017). International business responses to institutional voids. *Journal of International Business Studies*, 48(3), 293–307.

Elkington, J. (1998). Partnerships from Cannibals with Forks: The Triple Bottom Line of 21st-Century Business. *Environmental Quality Management*, 8(1), 37–51.

Elkington, J. (2013). Enter the Triple Bottom Line. In *The Triple Bottom Line*. New York: Routledge, pp. 23–38.

Environmental Justice Foundation (2015). "Pirates and Slaves: How Overfishing in Thailand Fuels Human Trafficking and the Plundering of Our Oceans". The Environmental Justice Foundation, London, pp. 8–11.

Global Slavery Index (2016). Thailand Country Report.

Hacking, T. and Guthrie, P. (2008). A framework for clarifying the meaning of triple bottom-line, integrated, and sustainability assessment. *Environmental Impact Assessment Review*, 28 (2–3), 73–89.

IMF. (2010). "Mexico Recovering, but Crisis Spotlights Challenges, says IMF". IMF Survey Magazine: In the News, March, pp. 12–38.

Kelly, A. (2016). Nestlé admits slavery in Thailand while fighting child labour lawsuit in Ivory Coast, *The Guardian*.

Kennedy, S. and Nisbett, R. (2015). The Ebola epidemic: a transformative moment for global health. *Bulletin of the World Health*, 93(1), 2–12.

Kessler, G. (2015). Why you should be wary of statistics on "modern slavery" and "trafficking". *The Washington Post*.

Khanna, T. and Palepu, K. G. (2005). *Spotting Institutional Voids in Emerging Markets.* Cambridge: Harvard Business Press.

Khanna, T. and Palepu, K. G. (2010). *Winning in Emerging Markets: A Road Map for Strategy and Execution.* Cambridge: Harvard Business Press.

Lawrence, J. T. and Beamish, P. W., eds. (2012). *Globally responsible leadership: Managing according to the UN global compact.* Thousand Oaks, California: Sage.

Leipziger, D. and Canuto, O. (2012). "Ascent after Decline: Regrowing Global Economies after the Great Recession". *International Bank for Reconstruction and Development,* p. 322.

Lucas, S. (2017). *One Country at a Time: International Human Rights Reform in Asia.* Liberty Law, p. 27.

Mahtaney, P. (2013). *Globalization and Sustainable Economic Development: Issues, Insights, and Inference.* New York: Palgrave Macmillan.

Mair, J. and Marti, I. (2009). Entrepreneurship in and around institutional voids: A case study from Bangladesh. *Journal of Business Venturing,* 24(5), 419–435.

Mair, J., Martí, I. and Ventresca, M. J. (2012). Building inclusive markets in rural Bangladesh: How intermediaries work institutional voids. *Academy of Management Journal,* 55(4), 819–850.

Mason, M. (2014). Thailand's rampant trafficking may carry price, *The Associated Press.*

Mason, M. (2015). Myanmar fisherman goes home after 22 years as a slave. *The Associated Press.*

Mason, M. McDowell, R. Mendoza, M. and Htusan E. (2015). Global supermarkets selling shrimp peeled by slaves. *The Associated Press.*

Mazzella, D. (2017). Slaves No More, *West Virginia University Magazine.*

McCarthy, J. (2016). The child labour lawsuit against Nestlé: what you need to know, *Global Citizen.*

Millar, C. C., Choi, C. J. and Chen, S. (2004). Global strategic partnerships between MNEs and NGOs: Drivers of change and ethical issues. *Business and Society Review,* 109(4), 395–414.

Nayyar, D. (2011). The financial crisis, the great recession and the developing world. *Global Policy,* 2(1), 20–32.

Nestlé. (2011). Nestlé worldwide CEO visits Thailand. Nestlé Press Release.

Nestlé. (2013). The Nestlé Supplier Code.

Nestlé. (2013). Nestlé Responsible Sourcing Guideline.

Nestlé. (2015). Nestlé takes action to tackle seafood supply chain abuses. Nestlé.

Nestlé. (2015) Responsible Sourcing of Seafood – Thailand Action plan 2015–2016. *Nestec S. A.,* 1–6.

Nestlé. (2018). About Us, Detailed History.

Nguyen, K. (2015). Nestlé Admits to Slave Labour, May Prompt Other Companies to Come Clean, *The Huffington Post.*

North, D. C. (1990). *Institutions, Institutional Change and Economic Performance.* Cambridge: Cambridge University Press.

Osland, J. S. (2013). An overview of the global leadership literature. In *Global leadership,* New York: Routledge, pp. 48–77.

Park, S. (2005). Norm diffusion with international organizations: A case study of the World Bank. *Journal of International Relations and Development,* 8(2), 111–141.

Puffer, S. M. and McCarthy, D. J. (2008). Ethical turnarounds and transformational leadership: A global imperative for corporate social responsibility. *Thunderbird International Business Review,* 50(5), 303–314.

Puffer, S. M., McCarthy, D. J. and Boisot, M. (2010). Entrepreneurship in Russia and China: The impact of formal institutional voids. *Entrepreneurship Theory and Practice*, 34(3), 441–467.

Savitz, A. (2013). *The Triple Bottom Line: How Today's Best-Run Companies Are Achieving Economic, Social and Environmental Success – and How You Can too*. New Jersey: John Wiley & Sons.

Seafood Task Force. (2016) Story so far. Seafood Task Force.

Singh, K. (2012). "Does globalization spell the end of the nation-state?" In *Introduction to Global Politics: A Reader*, pp. 327–333.

Smith, S. E. (2015). 5 shocking scandals that prove it's time to boycott Nestlé, *The Daily Dot*.

Stephan, U., Uhlaner, L. M. and Stride, C. (2015). Institutions and social entrepreneurship: The role of institutional voids, institutional support, and institutional configurations. *Journal of International Business Studies*, 46(3), 308–331.

Stride, J. (2016) Assessing government and business responses to the Thai seafood crisis. *The Freedom Fund & Humanity United*, 1–44.

Syrmopoulos, J. (2016). Nestlé Just Admitted to Using Slaves – Here's a List of Their Brands to Stop Buying Right Now. The Free Thought Project.

Verité. (2015). Verité Assessment of Recruitment Practices and Migrant Labour Conditions in Nestlé's Thai Shrimp Supply Chain. *Verité*.

Verité. (2015). About Verité.

US Department of Labour. (2015). Thailand Country Report.

US Federal Bureau of Investigations. (2016). Report from Thailand.

US State Department. (2012). Trafficking in Persons Report.

Wyatt, D. K. (2003). *Thailand: A Short History*. New Haven: Yale University Press, p. 2.

Zimmerman, C., et al. (2014). Health and human trafficking in the Greater Mekong Subregion. Findings from a survey of men women and children in Cambodia, Thailand and Viet Nam. *International Organization for Migration and the London School of Hygiene and Tropical Medicine*. p. 4.

13

Gender Composition of the Upper Echelons and Firm Sustainability Performance: an Examination of Istanbul Stock Exchange Companies

F. Pinar Acar and A. Gozde Gozum

13.1 INTRODUCTION

Responsiveness to environmental and social issues, along with economic performance, have become important components of firms' value (Barton, 2011; Fombrun, 2006; Mun and Jung, 2018). One way organisations attempt to respond to environmental and social issues is through their sustainability efforts (Crane and Matten, 2007; De Bakker, Groenewegen and DenHond, 2005; Gamerschlag, Möller and Verbeeten, 2011). Sustainability refers to "meeting the needs of the present without compromising the ability of future generations to meet their needs" (World Commission on Economic Development, 1987: p. 43). Thus, sustainability means maximizing firm value while ensuring social and environmental quality (Bowen, 1953; Drucker, 1984; Holme and Watts, 2000; McWilliams and Siegel, 2001).

There is an increasing awareness concerning sustainability around the world (Bear, Rahman and Post, 2010; Gamerschlag et al., 2011; Lindgreen et al., 2012; Mun and Jung, 2018). Shareholders, consumers and other stakeholders demand more CSR information from corporations (Mun and Jung, 2018). This is reflected in the increasing number of sustainability reports, as well as the emergence of institutions that provide third-party ratings to global investors on the sustainability performance of firms (Gray et al., 2001; Kolk, 2005; Mun and Jung, 2018). Although sustainability has been receiving quite a lot of scholarly and practitioner attention (Kirsch, 2018; Mun and Jung, 2018), firm-level determinants of sustainability efforts is still an under-researched area (Bansal, 2005; Boulouta, 2013; Campbell, 2007; Galbreath, 2011; Sharma and Henriques, 2005), especially in the context of developing economies (Khan, Lew and Park, 2015).

One firm-level determinant of sustainability performance pertains to the composition of its upper echelons (Glass et al., 2016). Specifically, the board of directors and the top management team (TMT) of an organisation are its ultimate decision-making entities (Finkelstein, Hambrick and Cannella 2009). Enacting a corporate culture and formulating strategies that integrate environmental and social issues fall in the realm of these teams (Finkelstein et al., 2009; Finkelstein and Hambrick,

1996; Hambrick, 2007). Although members of the board and the TMT may bring a variety of different attributes that may bear upon firm decisions and performance, the current research focuses on the influence of gender composition on firm sustainability performance. Thus, the present chapter attempts to contribute to the research on sustainability by investigating gender composition of board of directors and TMTs on firm sustainability performance in an emerging country context, namely Turkey. To this end, this chapter will draw upon the important research streams of upper echelons perspective, token theory and the notion of critical mass, and the group effectiveness literature.

The present study aims to extend the extant research on sustainability performance and upper echelons perspective in several ways. First, although the central role upper echelons play in shaping the economic performance of organisations has been demonstrated (Barsade et al., 2000; Campbell and Minguez-Vera, 2010; Carpenter, 2002; Nguyen and Faff, 2012), their role regarding sustainability performance is scarcely investigated (Cook et al., 2016; Post, Rahman and McQuillen, 2015). This is surprising given the fact that sustainability decisions involve high uncertainty, complexity and information overload, and such decisions are especially prone to the influence of executive characteristics (Carpenter and Fredrickson, 2001; Hambrick, 2007; Hambrick and Mason, 1984). According to the upper echelons perspective, the more uncertain the decisionmaking situation, the stronger is the connection between executive characteristics and firm outcomes (Hambrick, 2007). Decisions regarding sustainability involve high uncertainty making the composition of upper echelons particularly relevant. This chapter attempts to fill this gap by examining the effects of upper echelon characteristics on firm sustainability performance.

Second, studies that examine the effects of elite decisionmaking bodies in organisational settings concentrate either on boards of directors or TMTs (Finkelstein et al., 2009; Nielsen, 2010). This study takes into account both teams. In contemporary organisations, boards are actively involved in setting the strategic direction of the firm together with TMTs (Forbes and Milliken, 1999; Rindova, 1999; Westphal, 1999). Finkelstein and Hambrick (1996: p. 277) state that boards can be seen as "supra management teams" who take an active role in molding the strategic direction of their organisations. Boards share common interest with top managers and support them in value creation (Golden and Zajac, 2001). Thus, TMT shapes the direction of an organisation together with the board.

Nielsen (2010) indicates that research on board effects and TMT effects developed independently, uninformed of each other. One area where the unconnected development of research on TMT and board effects is especially problematic is concerned with gender composition. Gender composition of board of directors attracted quite a lot of attention (Kirsch, 2018), whereas there is very few research on gender composition of TMTs (Nielsen, 2010). Although gender is a highly visible demographic category, it is one of the least frequently examined TMT attributes as part of the upper echelons perspective. By examining TMT gender composition together with the board gender composition, the present study attempts to integrate these two independent research streams.

Third, the present study aims to contribute to the upper echelons literature by incorporating recent developments from research on gender diversity, token theory and representation of women on boards, which are commonly neglected by the upper echelons perspective. This is in line with Hambrick and Mason's (1984) call for incorporating theories from relevant fields into upper echelons research (Nielsen, 2010). For instance, recent diversity research indicates that diversity can take on different meanings with respect to attributes in question (Bell, 2007). However, upper echelons research generally treats diversity as a "general construct" (Nielsen, 2010: p. 307). This study takes into account new developments such as differences in conceptualizations and operationalizations of diversity. Extant research on board gender composition mostly focuses on the proportion of female directors. However, more recent research based on tokenism theory (Kanter, 1977) suggests that attaining a critical mass of female directors may be more relevant, hence this study takes into account this notion of critical mass (Konrad et al., 2008).

Finally, the vast majority of studies on sustainability as well as upper echelons perspective examines firms from developed countries and especially the USA. Thus, existing knowledge on the effects of TMT characteristics on sustainability performance is predominantly based upon findings from developed countries in the West. An important question left unanswered by the extant research is whether the findings generalize to firms and their upper echelons from emerging markets with different cultural settings (Carpenter and Fredrickson, 2001; Hambrick, 2007). Emerging markets may present a context which significantly differs from the context of developed countries (Hoskisson et al., 2000; Khanna et al., 2005; Wright et al., 2005). Thus, the present study puts to test propositions that were built in developed Western country settings in a different economic and cultural context.

In sum, the primary objective of the present study is to investigate whether TMT and board gender composition may distinguish firms with high sustainability performance from those with lower performance. Specifically, this chapter aims to identify whether upper echelons' composition with respect to gender account for differences in sustainability performance.

13.2 TURKISH CONTEXT

The context of the present study is Turkey. Governmental process of CSR in Turkey goes back to the 1950s in parallel with CSR research in the West and following Bowen's (1953: p. 6) proposition that "businesses have the obligation to pursue those [CSR] policies, to make those decisions, or to follow those lines of action which are desirable in terms of the objectives and values of the society." The milestone documents that Turkey signed about CSR include the Universal

Declaration of Human Rights, Convention on the Rights of the Child, OECD Guidelines for multinational enterprises and of International Labour Organisation conventions such as the Equal Remuneration Convention (1951), Discrimination (Employment and Occupation) Convention (1958), Worst Forms of Child Labour Convention (1999), and right to the Organise and Collective Bargaining Convention (1949).

Since 1991, the Ministry of Labour and Social Security of the Turkish Republic has been implementing various projects to decrease the level of child employment in Turkey under the guidance of and cooperation with ILO/IPEC, and within the framework of "Assistance to Enhance the Status of Women Workers and Combat Child Labour Project" (UNDP, Turkey CSR Baseline Report, 2008). Turkey was one of the first countries to sign the United Nations Convention on Biological Diversity (UNCBD) at the Rio Summit in 1992. Turkey, also, signed the Agenda 21 United Nations Convention to Combat Desertification (UNCCD), which was opened for signature in 1994. In 2005, the National Action Plan was published in the Official Gazette (Corporate Social Responsibility for All Project TURKEY Sustainability Reporting National Review Report, EU, 2016).

However, the private sector side of CSR is relatively new in Turkey. Today, more companies operating in Turkey are interested in CSR and they are investing in CSR for medium- and long-term success. The CSR sector is growing with every passing day. The number of stakeholders who are interested in CSR in Turkey has been rapidly increasing in recent years (Corporate Social Responsibility for All Project TURKEY Sustainability Reporting National Review Report, EU, 2016). There is a growing incentive for CSR in Turkey such as sponsorship activities as well as social projects organised with nongovernmental organisations (NGOs), multinational companies (MNCs) and international organisations (UNDP, Turkey CSR Baseline Report, 2008).

Another trend that has attracted scholarly as well as public attention is the presence of women in elite leadership positions, such as boards of directors or TMTs of organisations (Kirsch, 2018). Governments around the world develop laws and guidelines to increase women representation not only in the workforce but also in leadership positions. The primary instrument for improving gender diversity in corporate boards of Turkey is the Capital Markets Board's (CMBT) Corporate Governance Guidelines, which recommend that the companies set a target percentage of women on boards of no less than 25 percent. The communiqué (Series IV, No: 57) regarding women on boards in Turkey, "Communiqué on the Amendment of the Communiqué Pertaining to the setting out and application of the corporate governance principles" (Series IV, No: 56) was published in the Official Gazette numbered 28201, and entered into force by being published on 11 February 2012. According to this communiqué, although mandatory application is not required, "there is at least one-woman member on board" policy adopted. The above-mentioned policy has the characteristics of an advisory policy with an "apply or explain if you cannot apply" principle. The Communiqué on Corporate Governance issued by CMBT on 3 January 2014 advised that a "Corporation shall determine a target rate provided that it is not less than 25% and a target time for membership of women in the board of directors and form a policy for this target, and the board of directors shall annually evaluate the progress in respect to achieving this target." In 2011, CMBT advised that there should be at least one woman member on boards of directors as part of corporate governance principles and started a voluntary application. In 2014, this advice was changed to a minimum of 25 per-cent of the board. According to this principle, although there is no obligation, the reason should be explained to CMBT if there is no women member on the board of a company.

Turkey is 131st among 144 countries in the global gender gap index (World Economic Forum, Global Gender Gap Index, 2017). Although the population gender ratio (female/male) is 1.03 in Turkey, gender ratio for the labour force participation is 0.43 and the ratio among those with advanced degrees is 0.83 (World Economic Forum Report, 2016). According to International Finance Corporation[1] (IFC), while the Eastern Europe average is 18.7 percent and the developed world average is 17.3 percent, Turkey has 11.7 percent representation of women on boards, which means less than one of every eight firms has at least one woman on its board. When looking at family-owned companies, only 22.2 percent of board members are women members of the owning families in Turkey (UNDP & European Union Commission, 2008). According to research conducted in 2014 by Credit Suisse Research Institute, the percentage of women on boards in Turkey shows a decreasing rate: 9.2 percent in 2011, 8.5 percent in 2012, 6.6 percent in 2013, 5.9 percent in 2014 and 8.6 percent in 2015. According to the same research, the gender diversity at management level in Turkey is also decreasing with 7.7 percent in 2014 and 5.4 percent in 2016, compared to the global average of 13.9 percent in 2014 and 13.8 percent in 2016. According to a research conducted by Sabanci University (2017), Istanbul Stock Exchange, Borsa Istanbul (BIST), companies which have only male board members make up 41 percent of the total in 2016, and women held 13.9 percent of all board seats in 2016. Besides, according to the same research, it was found that the smaller Turkish companies have a higher percentage of women on their boards with 14.3 percent compared to BIST Stars Market companies which have only 12.5 percent women. Thus, Turkish women are severely under-represented in leadership positions.

In terms of the cultural context, Turkey is high in conservatism (Arat, 2010; Karakitapoğlu-Aygün and İmamoğlu, 2002; Özdemir, 2016; Schwartz, 1994) and is below the world average in gender egalitarianism (House et al., 2004). Turkish culture is characterized by high levels of patriarchy (Aycan et al., 2000; Aycan, 2004; Öngen, 2007; Sümer, 2006), which puts an emphasis on the care giving and nurturing roles of women (Glick et al., 2016; Öngen, 2007; Sakalli, 2001). Patriarchy

---

[1] IFC is a sister organisation of the World Bank and member of the World Bank Group.

encourages sexist attitudes (Sakalli-Uğurlu and Beydoğan, 2002) and, compared to Western nations, Turkey is relatively high in sexism (Glick et al., 2000; Glick et al., 2016).

Traditional gender roles prevail in Turkish society (Aycan, 2004; Öngen, 2007; Sümer, 2006). Men are depicted as dominant, independent, competitive and capable of leadership whereas women are seen as submissive, dependent, caring, and good at domestic tasks and child rearing (Özkan and Lajunen, 2005; Sakalli-Uğurlu and Beydoğan, 2002). Leadership is construed to be masculine and men are considered the "first choice" for managerial positions (Sakalli-Uğurlu and Beydoğan, 2002: p. 649). Sex segregation continues and is reflected in the division of labour between the sexes (Özkan and Lajunen, 2005), such that Turkish women predominantly occupy jobs that fit the feminine stereotype such as nurses, secretaries and teachers (TurkStat, 2017).

13.3 THEORETICAL FRAMEWORK

13.3.1 *Upper Echelons and Firm Outcomes*

This study draws upon the upper echelons perspective (Finkelstein et al., 2009; Hambrick, 2007; Hambrick and Mason, 1984). The central idea underlying this perspective is that powerful actors such as top executives of an organisation choose firm strategies and through the strategies they influence firm outcomes. Therefore, to understand what happens to a firm, one should examine the characteristics of its top executives (Carpenter, Geletkanycz and Sanders, 2004; Finkelstein and Hambrick 1996; Hambrick, 1989; Hambrick, 2007; Hambrick and Mason, 1984). Most studies that use upper echelons perspective focus on TMTs as powerful actors. Finkelstein and Hambrick (1996: p. 8) define TMTs as "the relatively small group of most influential executives at the apex of an organisation."

Research based on the upper echelons perspective traditionally disregarded the effects of other actors such as boards of directors. However, the actions and decisions of the TMT are also influenced by characteristics of the directors on the board. Both the TMT and the board of directors are at the apex of the firm and they share the same objective of value creation (Finkelstein and Hambrick, 1996; Forbes and Milliken, 1999; Nielsen, 2010; Rindova, 1999; Westphal, 1999). Both teams jointly influence the organisation's strategic decisions and shape its future direction (Carpenter et al., 2004; Finkelstein and Hambrick, 1996; Hambrick, 2007). Thus, an examination of the factors that influence strategic outcomes such as firm sustainability performance should include both TMT effects and board effects (Finkelstein et al., 2009).

To assess upper echelons impact on firm strategies and outcomes, the upper echelons perspective advocates the use of demographic variables as proxies for psychological constructs, such as cognitions, perceptions and values (Hambrick and Mason, 1984). Demographic attributes are easy to measure and highly reliable, whereas psychological constructs are not subject to direct measurement and are difficult to discern (Carpenter, 2002; Hambrick and Mason, 1984; Pitcher and Smith, 2001; Sambharya, 1996; Wiersema and Bantel, 1992). Hambrick and Mason (1984) accept that demographic variables are noisy indicators of the underlying psychological constructs but argue that if they still produce significant results, then it means the propositions of upper echelons perspective have passed more stringent tests.

Upper echelons perspective literature has demonstrated that TMT composition with respect to a variety of characteristics such as age (e.g. Escriba-Esteve et al., 2009), functional background (e.g. Simons, Pelled and Smith, 1999) and education level (e.g. Hermann and Datta, 2005) impact firm strategy (e.g. Michel and Hambrick, 1992) and outcomes such as international expansion (e.g. Carpenter et al., 2004), innovation (e.g. Bantel and Jackson, 1989) and economic performance (e.g. Murray, 1989). In parallel to the TMT research, the research on boards of directors also showed that board composition with respect to characteristics such as gender (e.g. Cook and Glass, 2017), industry experience (e.g. Golden and Zajac, 2001) and functional background (e.g. Eisenhardt, Kahwajy and Bourgeois, 1997) impact firm outcomes such as corporate social responsibility (e.g. Cook et al., 2016), innovation (e.g. Chen, 2014) and strategic change (e.g. Haynes and Hillman, 2010). In sum, composition of both the TMT and the board of directors are expected to influence firm outcomes such as its sustainability performance.

13.3.2 *Composition of Upper Echelons: Level and Diversity*

Group effectiveness research defines team composition as the configuration of member attributes on a team (Levine and Moreland, 1990). One type of configuration refers to the level of demographic traits on a team. Composition configured as levels of demographic characteristics refers to the extent to which certain characteristics are present on a team. The level of a given demographic attribute represents the upper echelons' overall condition regarding the attribute (Bell et al., 2011). Composition as level can be operationalized as mean or proportion depending on the demographic attribute in question. The level of demographic attribute present on the team is assumed to be associated with level of predisposition and psychological tendencies of team members, such as their risk orientation, being receptive to changes and being responsive to stakeholder needs (Bell, 2007; Chuang Nakatani and Zhou, 2009; Michel and Hambrick, 1992). Thus, high team levels of demographic characteristics are proposed to be associated with certain strategies and outcomes (Bell, 2007; Bell et al., 2011; Wiersema and Bantel, 1992).

Team composition can be examined along a variety of demographic characteristics, such as gender. Gender is a highly visible demographic category which can be an important source of differences in traits, values, perspectives, expertise and skills among executives. Long-term association of women with domestic roles and men with provider roles led to the development of gender roles ascribing different traits to men and women (Eagly, 1987). Specifically, women are socialized to display traits such as empathy, altruism, kindness, affection, interpersonal sensitivity and gentleness; whereas men are socialized to display traits such as aggressiveness, ambitiousness, dominance, independence and self-confidence (Eagly and Karau, 2002; Heilman, 2001). Individuals internalize traits and values associated with their gender roles (Eagly and Carli, 2003). In turn, these values and traits spill over to the organisational setting (Glick and Fiske, 2007). In support of the gender role spillover argument, several studies show that women differ from men with respect to traits and values such as competitiveness, risk-taking, moral reasoning and stakeholder orientation (Kidder and Parks, 2001; Lin, 2008; Sexton and Bowman-Upton, 1990; Ward and King, 2018).

In addition to bringing distinct feminine values and traits as a result of internalized gender roles, women executives and board members may emphasize higher stakeholder orientation and CSR activities compared to male members of the upper echelons in order to avoid "backlash" as a result of incongruence between their job roles and gender roles (Rudman and Phelan, 2008: p. 64). Leadership roles such as board membership and executive positions are perceived to be masculine (Eagly and Karau, 2002; Heilman, 2001). Women occupying such incongruent roles may be perceived as not conforming to their gender roles (Rudman et al., 2012). They may be perceived to display counter-stereotypical masculine behavior (Rudman and Phelan, 2008) and lack female-stereotypical attributes (Heilman and Okimoto, 2007; Rudman, 1998). Such women elicit disapproval and hostile reactions (Rudman and Fairchild, 2004). Thus, women leaders may adopt more socially responsive behaviors to avoid being penalized for not being feminine enough (Rudman and Fairchild, 2004; Rudman and Kilianski, 2000; Rudman et al., 2012).

Occupations and industries are gendered in nature and viewed as more appropriate for men or women (Garcia-Retamero and López-Zafra, 2006; Glick, Wilk and Perreault, 1995; Heilman, 1997; Stulmacher and Poitras, 2010). Women executives are likely to follow a different career trajectory than their male counterparts (Kumra and Vinnicombe, 2008) and therefore develop different expertise and skills as well as network ties. In sum, women executives and directors bring different values, personality traits, skills and experiences than men. The variety of experiences, information bases, and internal and external network ties enable the boards and TMTs to engage in more thorough discussions and debates; integrate and synthesize diverse expertise and knowledge; and consider a broader range of alternatives (Ancona and Caldwell, 1992; Bell et al., 2011; Cannella, Park and Lee, 2008, Horwitz and Horwitz, 2007; Jackson et al., 2003; Jehn, Northcraft and Neale, 1999; Pelled, Eisenhardt and Xin, 1999), as a result, leading to better sustainability performance.

For the level of these feminine characteristics to be reflected on the board and TMT decisions, however, the number of women should be above a critical mass (Konrad et al., 2008). Tokenism theory (Kanter, 1977) suggests that if the number of women on a board is very small, problems of tokenism such as hypervisibility, stereotyping and exclusion may arise, limiting the effects of feminine traits on decisions (Glass et al., 2016; Post et al., 2015). Konrad and colleagues suggest that women should make up a critical mass of three, so that they no longer suffer from tokenism and they can have impact on board processes, organisational outcomes and sustainability performances (Erkut, Kramer and Konrad, 2008; Konrad et al., 2008).

Gender composition in terms of proportion of female directors on boards of directors has received quite a lot of attention (Kirsch, 2018), whereas presence of women on TMTs did not receive much attention (Nielsen, 2010). The research on women on boards identified an association between proportion of female directors and firm's financial performance (e.g. García-Meca, García-Sánchez and Martínez-Ferrero, 2015), environmental practices (e.g. Glass et al., 2016) and ethical behavior (e.g. Richardson, Taylor and Lanis, 2016), among other outcomes. Building upon the above discussion, the following hypotheses are proposed:

Hypothesis 1: There is a positive relationship between the critical mass of women executives (at least three women) on the TMT and firm sustainability performance.

Hypothesis 2: There is a positive relationship between the critical mass of women directors (at least three women) on the board of directors and firm sustainability performance.

13.4 METHOD

13.4.1 Sample

The sample of this chapter consists of top-performing 100 firms on the Istanbul Stock Exchange (ISE) known as BIST 100. BIST 100 companies are the largest and most liquid companies listed on the ISE and they account for a significant portion of Turkish economy (TCMA, 2014). The BIST National-100 index is a capitalization-weighted index and the main indicator of the Turkish stock market. BIST stock indices are created to measure the joint performance of group of equities traded on ISE. Information regarding BIST 100 companies are publicly disclosed in an electronic system called the Public Disclosure Platform (PDP). The members of firms' TMT and boards of directors were identified for this chapter based on the data provided in PDP. For the purposes of the current chapter, a firm's TMT is defined as the top executives who have a vice president or higher title. Using the data provided in PDP, the authors constructed a data set containing information on TMT members, boards of directors, CEOs, as well as firm size, profitability, sustainability performance and industry, among others.

13.4.2 Measures

13.4.2.1 Dependent Variable

Firm Sustainability Performance. The dependent variable of the study, sustainability performance, was measured by using the BIST Sustainability Index. The BIST Sustainability Index is a platform for institutional investors to identify companies that are responsive to environmental, social and governance issues. The rating used in the present chapter covers the time duration of November 2016 to October 2017. Firm sustainability performance is coded as 1 when a company is listed in this index and 0 when a company is not listed.

13.4.2.2 Independent Variables

The independent variables include the critical mass of women on boards of directors and TMTs and gender diversity of TMTs and boards of directors.

Board Critical Mass. This variable is coded 1 for companies with three or more women directors on their boards and 0 if otherwise.

TMT Critical Mass. This variable is coded 1 for companies with three or more women executives on their TMTs and 0 if otherwise.

13.4.2.3 Control Variables

A review of research on firms' CSR and sustainability performance revealed a variety of factors that are commonly controlled for, such as firm size, board and TMT size, profitability, industry type, CEO duality, and the proportion of independent board members. To choose among these potential control variables, their correlations with the dependent variable were analyzed. Firm size has significant correlation with firm sustainability performance and therefore is included in further analyses as a control variable. Firm size is operationalized as total number of employees.

13.5 RESULTS

The present chapter aimed to understand the effects of gender composition of upper echelons on the sustainability performance of organisations. Upper echelons of an organisation include both its TMT and board of directors. Gender composition refers to the level of women on the TMT and the board. The level of women executives on the TMT and the board is conceptualized as whether their number reaches or goes above the critical mass of three women.

The sample firms have a mean board size of 8.3400 (SD = 2.62167) and a mean TMT size of 6.8300 (SD = 4.04034). 13 percent of the sample firms had three or more women directors on their boards, whereas 37 percent had no women directors on

TABLE 13.1 *Descriptive statistics and nonparametric correlations* (N = 100)

Variable	Mean	SD	1	2	3
1. Sustainability performance			–		
2. Board critical mass			0.201*	–	
3. TMT critical mass			0.033	0.149	–
6.Firm size	8516.1	22991.9	0.269**	−0.010	−0.189

Note: SD = standard deviation
*p < 0.05; **p < 0.01.

TABLE 13.2 *Regressing firm sustainability performance on size, TMT and board composition* (N = 100)

	β	SE	p	OR
Control variables				
Firm size	0.818**	0.292	0.005	2.266
Independent variables				
Board critical mass	1.631*	0.858	0.057	5.111
TMT critical mass	0.266	0.711	0.708	1.305

Note: OR = Odds ratio
*p < 0.1, ** p < 0.05

their boards. 11 percent of the sample firms had three or more women on their TMTs, whereas 47 percent had no women executives on their TMTs. The mean number of women directors on boards is 1.15 (SD = 1.21); and the mean number of women executives on the TMTs is 0.98 (SD = 1.21). 59 percent of the firms in the sample met the requirements of the sustainability index and qualify to be included in the BIST Sustainability Index List of Constituent Companies.

Table 13.1 shows descriptive statistics and intercorrelations of the study variables. As can be seen in Table 13.1, there seems to be a strong positive association between sustainability performance and firm size and presence of three or more women directors on boards of directors.

The hypotheses of the study were tested using binomial logistic regression, which is appropriate when the dependent variable is dichotomous. The results of the regression analysis can be seen in Table 13.2.

Hypothesis 1 proposed that there would be a positive relationship between the critical mass of women executives (at least three women) on the TMT and firm sustainability performance; and Hypothesis 2 proposed that there would be a positive relationship between the critical mass of women directors (at least three women) on the board and firm sustainability performance. As shown in Table 13.2, the estimated coefficient for TMT critical mass is not significant. Thus, Hypothesis 1 is not supported. The estimated coefficient for board critical mass is marginally significant (B = 1.631 p = .057). Thus, when organisations have three or more women directors on their boards, they seem to have better sustainability performance. Hypothesis 2 is marginally supported. Finally, the results in Table 13.2 shows that firm size is strongly associated with firm sustainability performance indicating that larger firms have better sustainability performance.

13.6 DISCUSSION AND CONCLUSION

The present chapter aimed to investigate how the human side of corporate governance influenced sustainability performance of organisations in an emerging economy context, namely Turkey. The theoretical framework utilized was upper echelons perspective (Hambrick and Mason, 1984). The current chapter examined the link between upper echelons' gender composition and firm sustainability performance. Upper echelons of an organisation consist of its TMT and board of directors. This chapter considered gender composition as the level of women on TMTs and boards. Specifically, it considered whether presence of three or more women on company boards as well as within TMTs influenced sustainability performance. Thereby, the study incorporated new theoretical developments by conceptualizing gender level using critical mass concept (Erkut et al., 2008; Konrad et al., 2008). The findings of the present study indicate that a critical mass of women on board of directors is important for sustainability performance. In line with token theory (Kanter, 1977) and critical mass proposition (Erkut et al., 2008; Konrad et al., 2008), in the present sample, having three or more women directors on boards of directors improves sustainability performance of companies. However, this influence is only marginally significant. One reason for this might be the small sample size. Among the variables considered in the current model, size is another variable that is found to influence sustainability performance. Larger organisations with more resources are expected to have higher sustainability performance, probably because they also have access to greater resources. The present chapter also indicates that critical mass of women on TMTs did not influence sustainability performance.

In conclusion, women bring different traits, values and skills to boards of directors. Women may be particularly sensitive to and may exercise more influence on decisions regarding CSR and sustainability. Thus, women's presence on boards may lead to improved board effectiveness in terms of CSR practices, ethical decisionmaking and sustainability. However, the present study demonstrates that women representation on boards of directors needs to reach a critical mass level, so that feminine traits, values and skills are reflected on the boards' decisionmaking processes and firms' sustainability performance. When this critical threshold is not reached, the board of directors is likely to disregard the different abilities and skills that women bring into the group. Female representation on boards may lead to improvement in ethical decisionmaking, responsiveness to stakeholder demands and CSR practices of firms. Their exclusion from elite leadership positions such as directorships on boards, may result in sub-optimal decisionmaking on CSR and sustainability issues. Finally, promoting female board participation through mandatory quotas for female representation such as those implemented in France, Italy, Norway and Spain may contribute to improvement of sustainability performance.

The present chapter has several strengths. Traditionally, the upper echelons studies focused only on the TMTs and disregarded the effects of other powerful actors such as board of directors. This study focused jointly on boards of directors and TMTs as the ultimate decisionmaking units responsible for meeting the needs of stakeholders. This chapter differed from previous studies by incorporating critical mass concept and consistently conceptualizing and operationalizing gender composition. Finally, research on sustainability is largely conducted in developed countries. This study was conducted in Turkey and thus attempts to expand the modest research on determinants of sustainability in emerging economies.

The current study also has some limitations. First, this study concentrated on a demographic attribute: gender. Thereby, it does not measure team processes. Some may argue that this approach creates a "black box" (Lawrence, 1997: p. 19). Second, although the upper echelons research showed that the executive team has stronger influence on firm outcomes than the CEO (Finkelstein and Hambrick, 1996), the characteristics of the CEO, the most important individual actor who shapes the organisation's direction, should also be taken into account. Members of the upper echelons were determined using public documents. However, other actors may also be involved in sustainability and CSR decisions. Roberto (2003) argues that TMTs are composed of a stable core and dynamic periphery that changes with the decisionmaking situation. Thus, a more thorough method of identifying the upper echelons members might be interviews with insiders rather than using publicly disclosed documents.

REFERENCES

Ancona, D. G., Caldwell, D. F. (1992). Demography and design: Predictors of new product team performance. *Organization Science*, 3, 321–341.
Arat, Y. (2010). Religion, politics and gender equality in Turkey: Implications of a democratic paradox *Third World Quarterly*, 31, 869–884.
Aycan, Z. (2004). Key success factors for women in management in Turkey. *Applied Psychology: An International Review*, 53, 453–477.
Aycan, Z., Kanungo, R. N., Mendonca, M., Yu, K., Deller, J., Stahl, G. and Kurshid, A. (2000). Impact of culture on human resource management practices: A 10-country comparison. *Applied Psychology: An International Review*, 49, 192–221.

Bansal, P. (2005). Evolving sustainably: A longitudinal study of corporate sustainable development. *Strategic Management Journal*, 26(3), 197–218.

Bantel, K. A., Jackson, S. E. (1989). Top management and innovations in banking: Does the composition of the top team make a difference? *Strategic Management Journal*, 10, 107–12.

Barsade, S. G., Ward, A. J., Turner, J. D. F. and Sonnenfeld, J. A. (2000). To your heart's content: a model of affective diversity in top management teams. *Administrative Science Quarterly*, 45, 802–836.

Barton D. (2011). Capitalism for the long term. *Harvard Business Review* 89, 84–91.

Bear, S., Rahman, N., and Post, C. (2010). The impact of board diversity and gender composition on corporate social responsibility and firm reputation, *Journal of Business Ethics*, 97, 207–221.

Bell, S. T. (2007). Deep-level composition variables as predictors of team performance: A meta-analysis. *Journal of Applied Psychology*, 92, 595–615.

Bell, S. T., Villado, A. J., Lukasik, M. A., Belau, L. and Briggs, A. L. (2011). Getting specific about demographic diversity variable and team performance relationships: A meta-analysis. *Journal of Management*, 37, 709–743.

Borsa Istanbul (2018). BIST Sustainability Index. available at www.borsaistanbul.com/en/ indices/bist-stock-indices/bist-sustainability-index, accessed April 18, 2018.

Boulouta, I. (2013). Hidden connections: The link between board gender diversity and corporate social performance. *Journal of Business Ethics*, 113(2), 185–97.

Bowen, H. R. (1953). *Social Responsibilities of the Businessman*. New York: Harper & Row.

Campbell, J. L. (2007). Why would corporations behave in socially responsible ways? An institutional theory of corporate social responsibility. *Academy of Management Review*, 32 (2), 946–967.

Campbell, K. and Minguez-Vera, A. (2010). Female board appointments and firm valuation: Short and long-term effects. *Journal of Management & Governance*, 14, 37–59.

Cannella, A. A., Park, J. and Lee, H. (2008). Top management team functional background diversity and firm performance: Examining the roles of team member co-location and environmental uncertainty. *Academy of Management Journal*, 51(4), 197–237.

Capital Market Boards of Turkey (Sermaye Piyasası Kurulu) (2011). Kurumsal yönetim ilkelerinin belirlenmesine ve uygulanmasına ilişkin tebliğ.

Carpenter, M. A. (2002). The implications of strategy and social context for the relationship between top management team heterogeneity and firm performance. *Strategic Management Journal*, 23, 275–284.

Carpenter, M. A. and Fredrickson, J. W. (2001). Top management teams, global strategic posture, and the moderating role of uncertainty. *Academy of Management Journal*, 44, 533–545.

Carpenter, M. A., Geletkanycz, M. A. and Sanders, W. G. (2004). Upper echelons research revisited: Antecedents, elements, and consequences of top management team composition. *Journal of Management*, 30, 749–778.

Chen, H. (2014). Board capital, CEO power and R&D investment in electronics firms. *Corporate Governance: An International Review*, 22(5), 422–436.

Chuang T., Nakatani K. and Zhou, D. (2009) An exploratory study of the extent of information technology adoption in SMEs: An application of upper echelon theory. *Journal of Enterprise Information Management*, 22, 183–196.

Cook, A. and Glass, C. (2017). Women on corporate boards: Do they advance corporate social responsibility? *Human Relations*, 71(7), 897–924.

Crane, A. and Matten, D. (2007). *Business ethics. Managing corporate citizenship and sustainability in the age of globalization*, 2nd ed. Oxford: Oxford University Press.

Datta, D. K., Gutherie, J. P. and Wright, P. M. (2005). Human resource management and labor productivity: Does industry matter? *Academy of Management Journal*, 48(1), 135-145.

DeBakker F., Groenewegen P. and DenHond F. (2005). A bibliometric analysis of 30 years of research and theory on corporate social responsibility and corporate social performance. *Business and Society*, 44(3), 283–317.

Drucker, P. F. (1984). The new meaning of corporate social responsibility. *California Management Review*, 26(2), 53–63.

Eagly, A. H. (1987). *Gender differences in social behavior: A social-role interpretation.* Hillsdale: Erlbaum.

Eagly, A. H. and Carli, L. (2003). The female leadership advantage: An evaluation of the evidence. *The Leadership Quarterly*, 14, 807–834.

Eagly, A. H. and Karau, S. J. (2002). Role congruity theory of prejudice toward female leaders. *Psychological Review*, 109, 573–598.

Eisenhardt, K. M., Kahwajy, J. L. and Bourgeois, L. J. (1997). Conflict and strategic choice: How top management teams disagree. *California Management Review*, 39(2), 42–62.

Erkut, S., Kramer, V. W. and Konrad, A. M. (2008). Critical mass: Does the number of women on a corporate board make a difference? In S. Vinnicombe, V. Singh, R. Burke, D. Bilimoria and M. Huse, eds., *Women on Corporate Boards of Directors: International Research and Practice*, London: Edward Elgar.

Escriba-Esteve, A., Sanchez-Peinado, L. and Sanchez-Peinado, E. (2009). The influence of top management teams in the strategic orientation and performance of small and medium-sized enterprises. *British Journal of Management*, 20, 581–97.

European Professional Women's Network (2008). 3rd European PWN Board Women Monitor.

European Union [EU] (2016). Corporate social responsibility for All Project Turkey, Sustainability Reporting National Review Report.

Finkelstein, S. and Hambrick, D. C. (1996). *Strategic leadership: Top executives and their effects on organizations.* Minneapolis/St. Paul: West.

Finkelstein, S., Hambrick, D. C. and Cannella, A. A. (2009). *Strategic leadership: Theory and research on executives, top management teams and boards.* New York: Oxford University Press.

Finkelstein, S., Whitehead, J. and Campbell, A. (2009). What drives leaders to make bad decisions? *Leader to leader*, 53, 52–58.

Fombrun, C. J. (2006). Corporate governance. *Corporate Reputation Review*, 8, 267–271.

Forbes, D. and Milliken, F. (1999). Cognition and corporate governance: Understanding boards of directors as strategic decision-making groups. *Academy of Management Review*, 24(3), 489–505.

Galbreath, J. (2011). Are there gender-related influences on corporate sustainability? A study of women on boards of directors. *Journal of Management and Organization*, 17(1), 17–38.

Gamerschlag, R., Moller, K. and Verbeeten, F. (2011). Determinants of voluntary CSR disclosure: Empirical evidence from Germany. *Review of Managerial Science*, 5(2–3), 233–262.

García-Meca, E., García-Sánchez, I. M. and Martínez-Ferrero, J. (2015). Board diversity and its effects on bank performance: An international analysis. *Journal of Banking and Finance*, 53, 202–214.

García-Retamero, R. and López-Zafra, E. (2006). Prejudice against women in male-congenial environments: Perceptions of gender role congruity in leadership. *Sex Roles*, 55 (1–2), 51–61.

Glass, C., Cook, A. and Ingersoll, A. R. (2016). Do women leaders promote sustainability? Analyzing the effect of corporate governance composition on environmental performance. *Business Strategy and the Environment*, 25, 495–511.

Glick, P. and Fiske, S. T. (2007). Sex discrimination: The psychological approach. In F. J. Crosby, M. S. Stockdale and S. A. Ropp, eds., *Sex discrimination in the workplace.* Malden: Blackwell 155–187.

Glick, P., Fiske, S. T. et al., (2000). Beyond prejudice as simple antipathy: Hostile and Benevolent sexism across cultures. *Journal of Personality and Social Psychology*, 79, 763–775.

Glick, P., Sakalli-Uğurlu, N., Akbas, G., Orta, I.M. and Ceylan, S. (2016). Why do women endorse honor beliefs? Ambivalent sexism and religiosity as predictors. *Sex Roles*, 75, 543–554.

Glick, P., Wilk, K. and Perreault, M. (1995). Images of occupations: Components of gender and status in occupational stereotypes. *Sex Roles*, 32, 565–582.

Golden, B. R. and Zajac, E. J. (2001). When will boards influence strategy? Inclination power strategic change. *Strategic Management Journal*, 22, 1087–1111.

Gray R., Javad M., Power D. M. and Sinclair, C. D. (2001). Social and environmental disclosure and corporate characteristics: A research note and extension. *Journal of Business Finance & Account*, 28(3–4), 327–356.

Hambrick, D. (1989). Guest editor's introduction: Putting top managers back in the strategy picture. *Strategic Management Review*, 10, 5–15.

Hambrick, D. C. (2007). Upper echelons theory: An update. *Academy of Management Review*, 32, 334–343.

Hambrick, D. and Mason, P. (1984). Upper echelons: the organization as a reflection of its top managers. *Academy of Management Review*, 9(2), 193–206.

Haynes, K. and Hillman, A. (2010). The effect of board capital and CEO power on strategic change. *Strategic Management Journal*, 31(11), 1145–1163.

Heilman, M. E. (1997). Gender discrimination and the affirmative action remedy: The role of gender stereotypes. *Journal of Business Ethics*, 16, 877–889.

Heilman, M. E. (2001). Description and prescription: How gender stereotypes prevent women's ascent up the organizational ladder. *Journal of Social Issues*, 57, 657–674.

Heilman, M. E. and Okimoto, T. G. (2007). Why are women penalized for success at male tasks? The implied communality deficit. *Journal of Applied Psychology*, 92, 81–92.

Hermann, P. and Datta, D. K. (2005). Relationships between top management team Characteristics and international diversification: An empirical investigation. *British Journal of Management*, 16(1), 69–78.

Holme, R. and Watts P. (2000). *Corporate social responsibility: Making good business sense.* Geneva: The World Business Council for Sustainable Development.

Horwitz, S. K. and Horwitz, I. B. (2007). The effects of team diversity on team outcomes: a meta-analytic review of team demography. *Journal of Management*, 33, 987–1015.

Hoskisson, R. E., Eden, L., Lau, C. M. and Wright, M. (2000). Strategy in emerging economies. *Academy of Management Journal*, 43, 249–267.

House, R. J., Hanges, P. J., Javidan, M., Dorfman, P. W. and Gupta, V. eds., (2004). *Culture, leadership, and organizations: The globe study of 62 societies.* California: Sage Publications, Inc.

International Finance Corporation (2011). *Focus: Women on Boards; A Conversation with Male Directors.* A Global Corporate Governance Forum Publication.

International Labor Office [ILO] (1999). Worst Forms of Child Labor Convention. No. 182.

International Labor Office (1958). Discrimination (Employment and Occupation) Convention. No. 111.

International Labor Office (1951). Equal Remuneration Convention. No. 100.

International Labor Office (1949). Right to Organise and Collective Bargaining Convention. No. 98.

Jackson, S. E., Joshi A. and Erhardt, N. L. (2003). Recent research on group and organizational diversity: SWOT analysis and implications. *Journal of Management*, 29, 801–830.

Jehn, K. A., Northcraft, G. B. and Neale, M. A. (1999). Why differences make a difference:
A field study of diversity, conflict and performance in workgroups. *Administrative Science
Quarterly* 44(4), 741–763.

Kanter, R. M. (1977). Some effects of proportions on group life. *American Journal of Sociology*,
82(5), 965–990.

Karakitapoğlu-Aygün, Z. and İmamoğlu, E. O. (2002). Value domains of Turkish adults and
university students. *The Journal of Social Psychology*, 142, 333–351.

Khan, Z., Lew, Y. K. and Park, B. (2015). Institutional legitimacy and norms-based CSR
marketing practices: Insights from MNCs operating in a developing economy.
International Marketing Review, 32(5), 463–491.

Khanna, T., Palepu, K. G. and Sinha, J. (2005). Strategies that fit emerging markets. *Harvard
Business Review*, 83(6), 63–74.

Kidder, D. L. and Parks McLean, J. (2001). The good soldier: Who is she? *Journal of
Organizational Behavior*, 228, 939–959.

Kirsch, A. (2018). The gender composition of corporate boards: A review and research agenda.
The Leadership Quarterly, 29, 346–364.

Kochan, T., Bezrukova, K., Ely, R., Jackson, S., Joshi, A., Jehn, K. and Thomas, D. (2003). The
effects of diversity on business performance: Report of the diversity research network.
Human Resource Management, 42, 3–21.

Konrad, A. M., Kramer, V. and Erkut, S. (2008). Critical mass: The impact of three or more
women on corporate boards. *Organizational Dynamics*, 37(2), 145–164.

Kolk, A. (2005). Environmental reporting by multinationals from the Triad: Convergence or
divergence. *Management International Review*, 45(1), 145–167.

Kumra, S. and Vinnicombe, S. (2008). A study of the promotion to partner process in
a professional services firm: How women are disadvantaged. *British Journal of
Management*, 19, S65–S74.

Lawrence, B. S. (1997). The black box of organizational demography. *Organization Science*,
8, 1–22.

Levine, J. M. and Moreland, R. L. (1990). Progress in small group research. *Annual Review of
Psychology*, 41, 585–634.

Lin, C. (2008). Clarifying the relationship between organizational citizenship behaviors,
gender, and knowledge sharing in workplace organizations in Taiwan. *Journal of
Business and Psychology*, 22, 241–250.

Lindgreen, A., Maon, F., Reast, J. and Yani-De-Soriano, M. (2012). Guest editorial: Corporate
social responsibility in controversial industry sectors. *Journal of Business Ethics*, 110(4),
393–395.

McWilliams, A. and Siegel, D. (2001). Corporate social responsibility: A theory of the firm
perspective. *Academy of Management Review*, 26(1), 117–127.

Michel, J. G. and Hambrick, D. C. (1992). Diversification posture and top management team
characteristics. *Academy of Management Journal*, 35, 9–37.

Milliken, F. J. and Martins, L. L. (1996). Searching for common threads: Understanding the
multiple effects of diversity in organizational groups. *Academy of Management Journal*, 21,
402–433.

Mun, E. and Jung, J. (2018). Change above the glass ceiling: Corporate social responsibility
and gender diversity in Japanese firms. *Administrative Science Quarterly*, 63(2), 409–440.

Murray, A. I. (1989). Top management group heterogeneity and firm performance. *Strategic
Leaders and Leadership*, 10(1), 125–141.

Nguyen, H. and Faff, R. (2012). Impact of board size and board diversity on firm value: Australian evidence. *Corporate Ownership and Control*, 4, 24–32.

Nielsen, S. (2010). Top management team diversity: A review of theories and methodologies, *International Journal of Management Reviews*, 12(3), 301–316.

Official Gazette (T.C. Resmi Gazete), 11/02/2011, No:28201.

Official Gazette (T.C. Resmi Gazete), 30/12/2011, No:28158.

Öngen, D. E. (2007). The relationships between sensation seeking and gender role orientations among Turkish university students. *Sex Roles*, 57, 111–118.

Özdemir, F. (2016). Çelişik duygulu cinsiyetçilik üzerinde dini yönelim tiplerinin yordayici gücü (The predictive power of religious orientation type on ambivalent sexism), *Nesne*, 4, 89–107.

Özkan, T. and Lajunen, T. (2005). Masculinity, femininity, and the Bem sex role inventory in Turkey. *Sex Roles*, 52, 103–110. PDP (2018). Public Disclosure Platform. Available at www .kap.org.tr/en/, accessed April 11, 2018,

Pelled, L. H. (1996). Demographic diversity, conflict, and work group outcomes: an intervening process theory. *Organizational Science*, 7, 615–631.

Pelled, L., Eisenhardt, K. and Xin, K. (1999). Exploring the black box: An analysis of work group diversity, conflict, and performance. *Administrative Science Quarterly*, 44, 1–28.

Pitcher, P. and Smith, A. D. (2001). Top management team heterogeneity: Personality, power, and proxies. *Organization Science*, 12, 1–18.

Post, C., Rahman, N. and McQuillen, C. (2015). From board composition to corporate environmental performance through sustainability-themed alliances. *Journal of Business Ethics*, 130, 423–435.

Richardson, G., Taylor, G. G. and Lanis, R. (2016). Women on the board of directors and corporate tax aggressiveness in Australia: An empirical analysis. *Accounting Research Journal*, 29(3), 313–331.

Rindova, V. (1999). What corporate boards have to do with strategy: A cognitive perspective. *Journal of Management Studies*, 36, 953–75.

Roberto, M. A. (2003). The stable core and dynamic periphery in top management teams. *Management Decision*, 41, 120–131.

Rudman, L. A. (1998). Self-promotion as a risk factor for women: The costs and benefits of counterstereotypical impression management. *Journal of Personality and Social Psychology*, 74, 629–645.

Rudman, L. A. and Fairchild, K. (2004). Reactions to counterstereotypic behavior: The role of backlash in cultural stereotype maintenance. *Journal of Personality and Social Psychology*, 87, 157–176.

Rudman, L. A. and Kilianski, S. E. (2000), Implicit and explicit attitudes toward female authority. *Personality and Social Psychology Bulletin*, 26, 1315–1328.

Rudman, L. A., Moss-Racusin, C. A., Phelan, J. E. and Nauts, S. (2012). Status incongruity and backlash effects: Defending the gender hierarchy motivates prejudice against female leaders, *Journal of Experimental Social Psychology*, 48, 165–179.

Rudman A. and Phelan, J. E. (2008). Backlash effects for disconfirming gender stereotypes in organizations, *Research in Organizational Behavior*, 28, 61–79.

Sabanci University. (2017). *Women on Board Turkey*, 5th Annual Report, Corporate Governance Forum of Turkey.

Sakalli, N. (2001). Beliefs about wife beating among Turkish college students: The effects of patriarchy, sexism, and sex differences. *Sex Roles*, 44, 599–610.

Sakalli-Uğurlu, N. (2002), Çelişik duygulu cinsiyetçilik ölçeği: geçerlik ve güvenirlik çalışması (Ambivalent sexism inventory: a study of reliability and validity). *Türk Psikoloji Dergisi* (Turkish Journal of Psychology), 17, 47–58.

Sakalli-Uğurlu, N. and Beydoğan, B. (2002). Turkish college students' attitudes toward women managers: The effects of patriarchy, sexism, and gender differences. *Journal of Psychology*, 136(6), 647–656.

Sambharya, R. B. (1996). Foreign experience of top management teams and international diversification strategies of U.S. multinational corporations. *Strategic Management Journal*, 17, 739–46.

Schwartz, S. H. (1994). Beyond individualism-collectivism: New cultural dimensions of values. In U. Kim, H. C. Triandis, C. Kagitcibasi, S.-C., Choi and G. Yoon, eds., *Individualism and collectivism: Theory, method and applications*, pp. 85–119. London: Sage.

Sexton, D. L. and Bowman-Upton, N. (1990). Female and male entrepreneurs: Psychological characteristics and their role in gender related discrimination. *Journal of Business Venturing*, 5, 29–36.

Sharma, S. and Henriques, I. (2005). Stakeholder influences on sustainability practices in the Canadian forest products industry. *Strategic Management Journal*, 26(2), 159–180.

Simons, T., Pelled, L. and Smith, K. (1999). Making use of difference: Diversity, debate, and decision comprehensiveness in top management teams. *Academy of Management Journal*, 42, 662–673.

Sümer, H. C. (2006). Women in management: Still waiting to be full members of the club. *Sex Roles*, 55, 63–72.

Stulmacher, A. F. and Poitras, J. (2010), Gender and job role congruence: A field study of trust in labor mediators. *Sex Roles*, 63, 489–499.

TCMA [Turkish Capital Markets Association] (2014). *The handbook of the Turkish Capital Markets*. Istanbul: TCMA Publication.

TISK (2016). Corporate social responsibility for All Project Turkey, sustainability reporting, National Review Report. available at http://tisk.org.tr/en/wp-content/uploads/192016/04/CSR.pdf accessed February 25, 2018.

TurkStat (2017). Laborforce statistics. Available from www.tuik.gov.tr/PreHaberBultenleri.do?id=24630 accessed August 25, 2017.

UNDP/EU Commission (2008). Turkey Corporate Social Responsibility Baseline Report. available from http://kssd.org/site/dl/uploads/CSR_Report_en.pdf accessed April 28, 2018.

Ward, S. J. and King, L. A. (2018). Gender differences in emotion explain women's lower immoral intentions and harsher moral condemnation. *Personality and Social Psychology Bulletin*, 44, 653–669.

Welbourne, T. M., Cycyota, C. S. and Ferrante, C. J. (2007). Wall street reaction to women IPOs: An examination of gender diversity in top management teams. *Group & Organization Management*, 32, 524–547.

Westphal, J. D. (1999). Collaboration in the boardroom: Behavioral and performance consequences of CEO-board social ties. *Academy of Management Journal*, 42, 7–24.

Wiersema, M. F. and Bantel, K. A. (1992). Top management team demography and corporate strategic change. *Academy of Management Journal*, 35(1), 91–121.

Williams, K. Y. and O'Reilly, C. A. (1998). Demography and diversity in organizations: a review of 40 years of research. *Research in Organizational Behavior*, 20, 77–140.

Wright, M., Filatotchev, I., Hoskisson, R. E. and Peng, M. W. (2005). Strategy research in emerging economies: Challenging the conventional wisdom. *Journal of Management Studies*, 42, 1–33.

World Commission on Economic Development [WCED] (1987). *Our common future*. Oxford: Oxford University Press.

World Economic Forum (2016). The global gender gap report. Available at http://reports.weforum.org/global-gender-gap-report- 192016/ accessed April 25, 2018.

World Economic Forum (2016). Gender parity and human capital. Global gender gap Report. Available from http://reports.weforum.org/global-gender-gap-report- 192016/rankings/ accessed April 25, 2018.

Yang, Q., Xue, Y. and Yurtoglu, B. B. (2007). Does the Strategic Role and the Control Role of the Board of Directors Exist in Chinese Listed Companies? (Project No. 07JC630057) and (Project No. 2008BJB018), Shanghai, China: Social Science of Educational Minister project and Shanghai Social Science.

PART III

Normative and Utility Perspectives

14

Islamic Finance, Sustainable Development and Developing Countries: Linkages and Potential

Mohammed K. Alshaleel

14.1 INTRODUCTION

This chapter aims at investigating the potential role of Islamic finance in fostering and achieving Sustainable Development Goals (SDGs), with particular focus on developing countries. Specifically, it focuses on examining some fundamental tools of Islamic finance, namely Islamic banking, *sukuk* (Islamic bonds), *zakat* and *waqf*, and their potential. Given the ambitious and comprehensive nature of the 2030 plan for the SDGs, this chapter argues that Islamic finance – as an innovative avenue and a nontraditional source of financing – can play a significant role in helping developing countries to achieve the SDGs, by filling potential finance gaps. Sustainable development is a global concept that includes meeting, "the needs of the present without compromising the ability of future generations to meet their own needs" (United Nations, 1987). The foundation of achieving this vision lies in three fundamental pillars: economic growth, environmental protection and social inclusion (United Nations, 2015). SDGs are a collection of 17 global goals set by the United Nations in 2015. Financing needs for achieving SDGs remain significant (United Nations, 2014a). They include eradicating poverty and hunger (the first and second Goals of the SDGs), improving health and education (the third and fourth Goals of the SDGs), providing access to affordable energy (the seventh Goal of the SDGs), promoting gender equality (the fifth Goal of the SDGs), infrastructure and rural development (the ninth and eleventh Goals of the SDGs), and climate resilient development (the thirteenth Goal of the SDGs) (United Nations, 2014a).[1] Importantly, the financing needs differ across countries and regions. In developing countries, for example, financing needs are excessively large relative to the size of their economies. The UN World Investment Report of 2014 calculated that developing countries' financial needs for achieving SDGs would range from US\$3.3 trillion to US\$4.5 trillion per year, giving a total requirement of roughly US\$37.5 trillion, between 2014 and 2030 (United Nations, 2014b).

---

[1] For further information about SDGs, see Chapter 5 of this Volume, 'The Informal Economy: CSR and Sustainable Development'.

Furthermore, sustainable development is multidimensional and results from human actions carried out by institutions, groups or individuals. To succeed, sustainable development requires these institutions, groups and individuals to act in a certain way or direction. Islam, as an institution, is a major cultural, social, political and economic factor in Muslim-majority countries. Islam teaches Muslims the religious and political conception (Dusuki and Abdullah, 2006). While the former includes regulating the relationship between Muslims and God, the latter regulates the relationship among human beings, including, for example, social and economic systems. Islamic teachings potentially support sustainable development, because they facilitate the transformation of cultural believes and attitudes through institutional reform and individual development. The *Qur'an*, for example, in verses 6:141, 28:77 and 7:31, affirms the principles of Islam that direct human beings on the management of natural resources, to ensure the earth is secured for both present and future generations.[2] As a result, the comprehensive teachings of Islam have sufficient scope to influence Islamic financial institutions, and indeed individuals, in a way that promote SDGs.

Islamic finance, with assets expected to exceed US$3.2 trillion by 2020, can play a significant role in helping to fill the SDGs financing gap in developing countries (Gatti, 2018: p. 321). Emerging in the early 1970s, the Islamic financial industry has recorded remarkable growth, exceeding 15 percent per annum (Hassan and Mollah, 2018: p. 27) and is spread across more than 70 countries (Rahman and Sulfia, 2015: p. 116). The industry's assets reached US$2 trillion by the end of 2015 (Hassan and Mollah, 2018: p. 116). These figures demonstrate the potential of Islamic finance as a significant part of international finance. Islamic finance is concentrated geographically in Asia and the Middle East and is present in more than 21 African countries (The Economist Intelligence Unit, 2015). In Africa, there are more than 50 Islamic finance institutions, and several African countries, such as Kenya, Morocco, Niger, Nigeria, Senegal, South Africa, Sudan and Uganda, have recently established legal frameworks for Islamic finance (The Economist Intelligence Unit, 2015). Most Muslim-majority countries are generally income-poor.[3] In fact, most world poverty resides in Asia and Africa, where the Muslim-majority countries are located. There are around 650 million Muslims living on less than US$2 a day and having no access to formal finance (World Bank, 2014).

---

[2] *Qur'an* (6:141, 28:77 and 7:31). Verse 6:141 says "It is He who produces gardens, both cultivated and wild, and date-palms, and crops of diverse tastes, and olives and pomegranates, similar and dissimilar. Eat of its fruit when it yields, and give its due on the day of its harvest, and do not waste. He does not love the wasteful."

[3] There is no international consensus on guidelines for measuring poverty. According to the United Nations Educational, Scientific and Cultural Organisation "In pure economic terms, income poverty is when a family's income fails to meet a federally established threshold that differs across countries. Typically, it is measured with respect to families and not the individual … Similarly, the international standard of extreme poverty is set to the possession of less than 1$ a day." Available at www.unesco.org/new/en/social-and-human-sciences/themes/international-migration/glossary/poverty/ accessed February 9, 2019.

In addition, Muslim wealth accounts for US$11.5 trillion, of which US$9.5 trillion is not currently invested in sharia (Islamic law) compliant investments (Alam et al., 2017: p. 457). Research shows that approximately 72 percent of the Muslim population does not use any formal financial services, and between 20 and 40 percent of Muslims avoid using financial services altogether because of the interest prohibition in Islam (Sadiq and Mushtaq, 2015). Guided by principles and values of sharia, Islamic finance has generated various mechanisms that can support sustainable development financing in developing countries.

The remainder of this chapter is divided into six sections. Section 14.2 explains sustainable development from an Islamic perspective, highlighting that the Islamic law model, based on *maqasid al-sharia* (objectives of Islamic law), represents an effective response to the SDGs. Section 14.3 examines principles of Islamic finance, with a focus on three main principles: prohibition of *riba* (interest), prohibition of *ghara* (uncertainty) and *maysir* (gambling), and asset-backed financing. Section 14.4 analyzes the role of Islamic financial institutions in promoting sustainable development, focusing on the banking industry. Section 14.5 explores the role of *sukuk* (Islamic bonds) in Islamic finance, emphasizing that *sukuk* can be used to mobilize funds from capital market-based sources, to finance sustainable development projects in developing countries. Section 14.6 examines Islamic social finance institutions (*zakat* and *waqf*) and suggests improvements in their role in promoting the SDGs. Section 14.7 concludes with some practical recommendations to maximize the role of Islamic finance, in supporting the SDGs, in developing countries.

14.2 SUSTAINABLE DEVELOPMENT FROM AN ISLAMIC PERSPECTIVE: MAQASID AL-SHARIA

Sustainable development and the proper allocation of finance are fundamental for the Muslim world because, as mentioned above, Muslim-majority countries are poor nations.[4] While the SDGs do not explicitly target financial inclusion, greater access to financial services is a key component of sustainable development. Financial inclusion means that formal financial services, such as bank accounts, loans, payment services and insurance, are available to all people to meet their specific needs (Bhowmik and Saha, 2013: p. 3). A large portion of the poor population does not use formal financial services, either because of religious considerations, or due to economic or social reasons (Mohieldin et al., 2012: p. 58). The prohibition of *riba* in Islam is an important barrier to the poor making use of formal financial services.[5] Therefore, increasing access to financial services in Muslim-majority countries would require sharia-compliant financing. In this regard, Islamic

[4] See Section 1.
[5] As mentioned in the Introduction to this chapter around 72 percent of the Muslim population does not use any formal financial services, and between 20 and 40 percent of Muslims avoid using financial services due to the interest prohibition in Islam.

microfinance institutions can be key in increasing access to financial services and creating sustainable avenues for inclusive finance. In fact, microfinance is more prevalent in Islamic financial institutions than their conventional counterparts and this can be attributed to existing networks of bank branches, which facilitates access to larger number of clients (Sadiq and Mushtaq, 2015: p. 50).

However, any potential role for Islamic finance institutions in achieving SDGs is predicated on finding support for sustainable development in Islam itself. To Muslims, Islam is a complete and integrated code of life comprising all aspects of life. While its fundamentals, including worship and creed, are immutable, Islam's secondary manifestations, including questions of economic, social and business practices, are flexible and develop to meet contemporary needs (Dusuki and Abdullah, 2006: p. 30). The primary sources of sharia (Islamic law) are the *Qur'an* and the *Sunnah*. The process for deriving law from the *Qur'an* and the *Sunnah* is called *ijtihad*. While *ijtihad* plays an important role in resolving contemporary issues (Hallaq, 2009: p. 27), it must comply with the objectives of sharia (*maqasid al-sharia*). Further, Islamic jurists have identified different objectives of sharia, however, the majority recognize social welfare (*maslahah*) as the key objective (Hallaq, 2009: p. 179). This implies that when Muslim scholars interpret the *Qur'an* and the *Sunnah*, they must interpret them in a way that is consistent with broader social welfare, and the best interests of society. According to Imam al-Ghazali, "The very objective of the Sharī'ah is to promote the well-being of the people, which lies in safeguarding their faith, their self, their intellect, their posterity, and their wealth. Whatever ensures the safeguard of these five serves public interest and is desirable, and whatever hurts them is against public interest and its removal is desirable" (Chapra, 2000: p. 118).

In addition, the concept of *maslahah* is divided into three categories: necessities, needs and luxuries (Auda, 2008: p. 4). The necessities category is also divided into sub-categories: preservation of life, faith, intellect, wealth and posterity (Auda, 2008: p. 4). The three categories have evolved over time in response to changing circumstances and global challenges. Yusuf al-Qaradawi, for example, included the concept of human dignity as one of the main objectives of sharia (Auda, 2008: p. 8). Ibn Ashur, a renowned Islamic scholar, also introduced a new understanding of *maqasid al-sharia*, by reconceptualizing each category in modern terminology. For instance, preservation of posterity has evolved into the preservation of family (2006: p. 122). He also introduced the concepts of "orderliness," "natural disposition," "freedom," "rights," "civility" and "equality" as *maqasid* in their own right (Ashur, 2006: pp. 34 and 83). The Islamic scholars' attempts to expand and develop *maqasid al-sharia*, demonstrate that Islamic law is potentially able to respond to contemporary global issues, such as climate change, energy needs, environmental degradation and other sustainable development challenges. In other words, an Islamic law model, based on *maqasid al-sharia*, can respond to the SDGs.

14.3 PRINCIPLES OF ISLAMIC FINANCE

The Islamic finance model has its foundation in the *Qur'an* and *Sunnah*, and it is, therefore, sharia-compliant. It emphasizes equality, as well as aiming to achieve both social justice and economic prosperity, for the whole community. While Islam encourages the right of individuals to trade and pursue financial activities, it strongly emphasizes that they must adhere to strict principles. The fundamental principles are: the prohibition of *riba* (interest), prohibition of *ghara* (uncertainty), prohibition of *maysir* (gambling) and the asset-backed financing principle.

14.3.1 Prohibition of Riba (Interest)

Islamic finance derives its strength fundamentally from the ban on *riba* imposed by the *Qur'an* and the *Sunnah*. *Riba* is an Arabic word that means increment or increase (Hassan and Lewis, 2014: p. 132). Definition of *riba* has been a focus of dispute among Islamic scholars. They disagree over whether it prohibits all forms of interest, therefore representing an absolute prohibition of usury, or just excessive gains associated with high levels of interest (Eisenberg and Nethercott, 2012: p. 41). Nonetheless, there is a consensus among scholars today that *riba* includes, among other things, interest.

In addition, two types of *riba* were formally identified by jurists: *riba al-nasiyah* (interest on delayed payment) and *riba al-fadl* (interest on counter-value in trade) (Karim, 2010: p. 19). The term *nasiyah* comes from the root *nasa'a* which means to postpone or defer (Hassan and Lewis, 2014: p. 113). It refers to a predetermined amount in excess of capital, paid to the lender, in return for lending money. Since this type of *riba* is prohibited by the *Qur'an*, it is also called *riba al Qur'an* (Eisenberg and Nethercott, 2012: p. 41). *Riba al-fadl* refers to the increase which is taken in exchange for specific homogeneous commodities. It includes an exchange of unequal amount of the same commodity simultaneously. It is also called *riba al Sunnah*, because its prohibition was established by *Sunnah* (Eisenberg and Nethercott, 2012: p. 41). The Prophet (*pbuh*) said, "Gold for gold, silver for silver, wheat for wheat, barley for barley, dates for dates and salt for salt-like for like, equal for equal, and hand-to-hand; if the commodities differ, then you may sell as you wish, provided that the exchange is hand-to-hand" (Ullah and Al-Karaghouli, 2017: p. 7).

The precise reason for the *riba* prohibition is unclear. However, scholars agree that one of the prevailing justifications for the prohibition is the prevention of exploitation and injustice (Hasan, 2014: p. 17). The prohibition aims at preventing exploitative practices that interest-charging institutions could deploy against economically vulnerable individuals and to promote justice and equality amongst members of society.

14.3.2 *Prohibition of* Ghara *(Uncertainty) and* Maysir *(Gambling)*

Ghara and *maysir* are terms for expressing the interrelated notions of uncertainty and chance. *Ghara* literally means uncertainty, deception or ambiguity (Eisenberg and Nethercott, 2012: p. 31). *Gharar* may arise in a contract, for example in relation to issues such as uncertainty in value, quality, quantity or existence of the subject matter, uncertainty in the due dates for payments, or uncertainty in the price (Eisenberg and Nethercott, 2012: p. 47). The Prophet *(pbuh)*, for example, has forbidden the purchase of the unborn animal in the mother's womb (Black et al., 2013: p. 178). The rationale of prohibition of *gharar* is the existence of ambiguity in rights and liabilities that might be exploited to delude people in making their decisions. This implies that the prohibition aims at avoiding fraud, and protecting the right of contracting parties, which minimizes disputes.

Maysir literally means gambling (Eisenberg and Nethercott, 2012: p. 31). It refers to the easy acquisition of something by chance without any effort. Gambling also involves lotteries and betting on any game (Housby, 2011: p. 14). In gambling, the winner will take the losers' money, and the losers lose their money without a fair compensation. Clearly, *maysir* is regarded as a source of injustice, since the winner can only win if the other side loses, and this can trigger hatred between the winner and the loser.

14.3.3 *Asset-Backed Financing*

One of the distinctive features of Islamic financial system is that it is based-upon asset-backed financing. Unlike the conventional financial system, where financial institutions deal with money and monetary papers only, Islamic financing recognizes money as a medium of exchange only, without any intrinsic utility in itself (Hasan, 2014: p. 17). Any transaction occurring in the financial market must have a counter-transaction in the real asset market. The emphasis on this linkage is based on the prohibition of *riba*, and encourages Islamic people to generate profit from productive commercial activities. In the conventional financial system, the separation between risk and the underlying assets might cause the risk management and wealth creation to move in different directions (Bellalah and Masood, 2013: p. 13). This can result in greater systemic risk and inequitable concentration of wealth.

14.4 ROLE OF ISLAMIC FINANCIAL INSTITUTIONS IN PROMOTING SUSTAINABLE DEVELOPMENT

Achieving sustainable development requires substantial investment in various essential areas, including renewable energy, infrastructure, environmental technology, education and the healthcare sector. It is increasingly accepted that the ability of the public sector to provide resources to these necessary investments is limited.[6] Therefore, Islamic financial institutions can play a fundamental role in contributing to the achievement of the SDGs. The Islamic financial sector may be divided into Islamic banks, Islamic asset management companies, Islamic bonds (*sukuk*) and Islamic insurance companies (*takaful*) (World Bank, 2017). Islamic banks dominate the Islamic financial industry, amounting to 79 percent of total assets (World Bank, 2017). Unlike its conventional counterparts, the non-bank financial institutions sector is very small. Nonetheless, the non-banking sector contains the largest number of Islamic financial institutions (Islamic Corporation for the Development and Thomson Reuters, 2016). The existence of Islamic banks in the Islamic financial system raises an important question about the role of Islamic banks in financing sustainable development. Significantly, the Islamic banking industry has spread throughout the world, not only in Muslim countries, but also in non-Muslim countries such as the UK (Aldohni, 2012: p. 8). In its activities, Islamic banking is expected to adhere to sharia and apply its principles, unlike conventional banking (Ginena and Hamid, 2015: p. 335). To illustrate, Islamic banks' involvement in banking activities and services is based on the profit and loss sharing (PLS) principle, rather than the interest-based system (Khan and Porzio, 2010: p. 91). Banks do not lend money and receive a predetermined sum on a fixed future date. Rather, they are responsible for ensuring the money is invested in productive projects, with trustworthy borrowers, because if the project is successful the bank shares in the profit, and if it fails the bank suffers losses. Since the profit of the Islamic banks is directly related to the real rate of return, they have real interest in the profitability of the undertaken investment. As discussed previously, the main objective of sharia is to promote public interest and society welfare. Since sharia is the foundation and source of the Islamic banking industry, the implementation of a public interest through the three dimensions of SDGs, economic, environmental and social, should be obligatory for Islamic banks (United Nations, 2014a).

In addition, Islamic banks' social engagement can be demonstrated by two important tools: *zakat* and *al-qard al-hasan* (benevolent loan). *Zakat* is an obligatory social welfare tax on surplus income and wealth of Muslims, which Islamic banks, financial institutions and individuals, who act in a financial capacity, are obliged to give for the benefit of society in order to purify their wealth (*zakat* will be discussed later) (Kettell, 2011: p. 82). *Al-qard al-hasan* is an interest-free loan given for either welfare purposes or for meeting short-term funding requirements (Bovens et al., 2002: p. 59). The borrower is only under an obligation to repay back the principal amount of the loan without paying any interest. Since Islamic banks do not receive any benefit in return, *al-qard al-hasan* can be seen as an important instrument for redistributing wealth in society and promoting poverty

---

[6]   See Section 1.

alleviation, which is the first SDG. Islamic banks also grant *al-qard al-hasan* to individuals to help them meet their social needs such as education, medical treatment and marriage, and this responds to the third SDG (good health and well-being) (United Nations, 2015) and also the fourth (quality education) (United Nations, 2015 and Visser, 2009: p. 62). However, it is significant to emphasize that Islamic banks are not charitable institutions and, like their conventional counterparts, seek profit to survive and continue in business. Therefore, a careful balance needs to be struck between profit maximization and the involvement of Islamic banks in societal economic and social activities.

Furthermore, another potential contribution of Islamic banks to SDGs is sustainable infrastructure development, with resilient infrastructure being the ninth SDG (United Nations, 2015). There is a widespread recognition that high-quality infrastructure plays a fundamental role in promoting economic growth, reducing poverty and improving living standards (Weber et al., 2016: p. 62). In developing countries, poor infrastructure is a major obstacle to development, limiting the economic development and growth of these countries. The direct reason for the investment shortfall in the infrastructure in these countries is lack of funding. While traditionally governments have been responsible for improving infrastructure facilities, in most developing countries they suffer debts, deficits and face difficulty in generating assets. The lack of adequate government resources necessitates the creation of partnerships between the public and private sectors (World Bank, 2017).

Clearly, Islamic banks have the potential to provide financing for the improvement of infrastructure-related sectors in developing countries, but such provision is not straightforward. Islamic banks are relatively small in size, which may be problematic given the large amounts of funding required by infrastructure financing. This raises an important question about the effective method that Islamic banks can employ to finance infrastructure development. Syndicated financing might be the best mechanism that Islamic banks can adopt to finance infrastructure projects in developing countries. In the conventional syndicated loan, a group of banks simultaneously, but severally, provide a loan to a borrower on the basis of one lending document, usually called a loan or facility agreement (Mugasha, 2007: pp. 5–12). Islamic syndicated financing would have similar procedures and arrangements, but with different financing contracts that comply with Islamic finance principles. In the conventional syndicated loan, the relationship between the banks and the other party takes the lenders-borrower format. In the Islamic syndicated loan, the relationship between the parties can take either the PLS form, which includes the *musharakah* (joint venture) and the *mudarabah* (partnership), or, alternatively, the relationship may take the *ijarah* (leasing) form.

This view can be supported by a number of case studies from different developing countries. In Djibouti, for example, the Doraleh Container Terminal project was financed by Islamic syndication.[7] The terminal was developed under a 30-year concession agreement. DP World of the United Arab Emirates provided US$5 million in equity, and US$422 million was raised through Islamic syndication by several banks, including West LB AG, Standard Chartered Bank and Dubai Islamic Bank. The syndicated financing was mainly based on *musharakah* and *ijarah* contracts.

Another successful case of Islamic syndication was the Master Wind Energy Limited project in Pakistan, which financed 33 wind turbines for electricity generation (World Bank, 2017). The project aimed to implement the Government of Pakistan's plan to increase the use of renewables. The total cost of the project was US$132 million, US$100 million of which was financed by external sources. This was divided equally between the US-based Overseas Private Investment Corporation and Islamic syndication. This syndication was also based on *musharakah* and *ijarah* contracts. This case demonstrates that Islamic banks can provide finance to sustainable development projects in partnership with conventional financing. It should be noted that affordable and clean energy is the seventh SDG (United Nations, 2015).

14.4.1 *Islamic Development Bank (IDB)*

International development cooperation is a significant element of achieving the SDGs. In this regard, multilateral financial institutions (MFIs) such as the World Bank, the International Fund for Agricultural Development (IFAD), the African Development Bank (AfDB), the European Investment Bank (EIB), the Inter-American Development Bank (IADB) and the Asian Development Bank (ADB), can serve as effective institutional mechanisms to address the financial needs of SDGs. Their clear mandate to boost development-oriented programs supports their critical role in helping to finance SDGs. When talking about the role of Islamic financial institutions in promoting SDGs, it is significant to talk about the leading role of IBD in fostering sustainable development in developing countries. IDB is a multilateral financial development institution based in Jeddah, Saudi Arabia. The IDB is composed of 57 member countries, located across Asia, Africa, Europe and Latin America.[8] The bank officially started its operations in 1975. IDB was established with the purpose of alleviating poverty and fostering economic development and social progress, which are the main focus of the SDGs, through financing productive projects and programs in both public and private sectors in its member countries. It finances these projects through a number of sharia-compatible modes such as *Ijarah* and *musharakah*. IDB initiated numerous development initiatives

---

[7] For further information about the project see, World Bank, 'MIGA and Islamic finance: Doraleh Container Terminal Project, Djibouti (English)' (2008) available at http://documents.worldbank.org /curated/en/869821468026341157/MIGA-and-Islamic-finance-Doraleh-Container-Terminal-Project-Djibouti accessed August 18, 2018.

[8] See, Islamic Development Bank, About IsDB, available at www.isdb.org/who-we-are/about accessed August 18, 2018.

and programs in member countries. In Africa, for example, IDB launched Special Programme for the Development of Africa (SPDA) in 2008.[9] The IDB allocated US$4 billion over a five-year period, with an additional US$8 billion to be leveraged from other development partners. In its operations, SPDA focused on five key sectors: agriculture to achieve food security; improving health, especially fighting against communicable diseases; water and sanitation to improve life standards; energy and transport infrastructure; the education system to integrate youth in the world of work (the emphasis on these sectors corresponds to the second, third, sixth, eighth, seventh, ninth and fourth SDG) (United Nations, 2015).[10]

Another important initiative financed by IDB is the Lives and Livelihoods Fund (LLF) in 2016 (Islamic Development Bank, 2016). This project, with US$2.5 billion of funding, is considered the largest development program in the Middle East. In a period extending from its launch to 2021, LLF primarily aims to promote health, agriculture and rural infrastructure sectors (the third and ninth Goals of the SDGs) (United Nations, 2015). Importantly, In May 2016, the IDB signed a memorandum of understanding with the United Nations Development Programme (UNDP) to strengthen their partnership, with the purpose of bolstering the effective implementation of the SDGs.[11] Therefore, in its 10-Year Strategy, the IDB aligned its strategic objectives with the SDGs. The majority of the SDGs, namely the first, seventh, eighth, ninth, tenth and eleventh, are reflected directly in the plan, and only three Goals, the second, sixth and sixteenth, are reflected thematically and indirectly (Islamic Development Bank, 2017). In February 2018, the IDB launched Engage, a new digital platform to promote technological and scientific solutions, which will support the acceleration of progress toward the SDG, through connecting the latest scientific and technological innovations, with market opportunities and funding (Islamic Development Bank, 2018). Particularly, the platform focuses on achieving six SDGs: inclusive and equitable education, food security, sustainable management of water, healthier lives, sustainable industrialization, and access to affordable and clean energy.

The discussion above illustrates the pivotal role of IDB in achieving the SDGs. The IDB has recognized that it alone cannot address the whole development needs of its member countries, and therefore it worked on strengthening partnerships with international and regional development partners. The IDB effort reflects the Addis Ababa Action Agenda, which aims at producing an enhanced global partnership that

---

[9]   See The Standing Committee for Economic and Commercial Cooperation of the Organisation of the Islamic Cooperation (COMCEC), 'Report on the Special Program for the Development of Africa (SPDA)' (2017) available at www.comcec.org/en/wp-content/uploads/2017/04/33-FC-IDB-SPDA.pdf accessed August 18, 2018.

[10] See The Standing Committee for Economic and Commercial Cooperation of the Organisation of the Islamic Cooperation (COMCEC), above (n. 9).

[11] The memorandum is available at www.undp.org/content/dam/undp/library/corporate/Partnerships/ UNDP-Islamic%20Development%20Bank%20(IsDB)%20MoU%20and%20Action%20Plan%20 (2016).pdf accessed August 18, 2018.

aims to foster universal, inclusive economic prosperity and promote people's well-being while protecting the environment.[12] The pioneering role of the IDB in financing development programs and projects, through sharia-compliant modes, can be a template for Islamic banks, and other Islamic financial institutions, when looking to finance sustainable development programs. This could happen by seeking advice and technical assistance from the IDB.

14.4.2 Sukuk (*Islamic Bonds*)

Sukuk form another significant pillar of Islamic finance.[13] The Accounting and Auditing Organisation for Islamic Financial Institutions (AAOIFI) defines sukuk as, "certificates of equal value representing, after closing subscription, receipt of the values of certificates and putting it to use as planned, common title to shares and rights in tangible assets, usufructs and services, or equity of a given project or equity of a special investment activity" (Accounting and Auditing Organisation for Islamic Financial Institutions, 2003: p. 298).[14] It is significant to emphasize that *sukuk* must adhere to sharia principles and rules, including structuring, trading, underlying assets for the issuance of *sukuk* and investment of proceeds (Safari et al., 2014: p. 28). In practice, different sharia-compliant contracts are used to govern the relationship between the *sukuk* issuers and *sukuk*-holders, including *ijarah, murabahah, mudarabah, wakalah* (agency) and musharakah. The different types of contracts are created to cater to the investors' needs and that would encourage them to buy *sukuk*. AAOIFI recognizes various types of *sukuk* such as asset-based *sukuk*, debt-based *sukuk* and equity-based *sukuk* (Visser, 2013: pp. 79–88). Asset-based *sukuk* are issued against an existing tangible asset, usufruct, leased asset and/or promise of leasing an asset in the future Visser, 2013: p. 81). This type includes *ijarah sukuk* and *manfah* (usufructs) *sukuk*. Debt-based *sukuk* are certificates arising from transactions that create debt, such as *murabahah sukuk* and *istisna sukuk* (Visser, 2013: p. 83). In equity-based *sukuk*, returns are determined on profit and loss sharing, in the underlying investment. This form of *sukuk* includes *mudarabah sukuk* and *musharakah sukuk*.

In addition, *sukuk* have increasingly played a significant role in Islamic capital markets by bringing Islamic finance closer to modern conventional financial practices, as well as accelerating the growth of Islamic financial industry in terms of its size, and the types and number of investors. *Sukuk* represent the second largest segment of Islamic finance. According to the International Islamic Financial

---

[12]   The Addis Ababa Action Agenda is available at https://sustainabledevelopment.un.org/content/docu ments/2051AAAA_Outcome.pdf accessed August 18, 2018.

[13]   *Sukuk*, plural of Arabic word *sakk*, which means certificate.

[14]   Accounting and Auditing Organisation for Islamic Financial Institutions is an Islamic international autonomous not-for-profit organisation that prepares accounting, auditing, governance and sharia standards for Islamic financial institutions and the industry.

Market (IIFM) report (2018), the total global *sukuk* issuances during the period 2001–17 reached US$979,209 million (International Islamic Financial Market, 2018). The bulk of the *sukuk* (77.6 percent) issued during the period were domestic and more than a fifth was international (International Islamic Financial Market, 2018). The bulk of issuances in 2017 were by sovereign and quasi-sovereign entities (International Islamic Financial Market, 2018).

Furthermore, *sukuk* can be used to mobilize funds, from different capital market sources, to finance sustainable development projects in developing countries. As previously discussed, due to the prohibition of *riba* in Islam, the majority of the Muslim population do not have access to bank accounts or use financial services. *Sukuk*, as a sharia-compliant instrument, can be a viable tool for Islamic financial inclusion, because *sukuk* encourage Muslims to invest their money and be participants in the financial system.[15] This can be demonstrated by the following case. The government of Indonesia issued retail *sukuk* in 2014 to raise US$1.7 billion, to finance building roads, ports and other development projects (World Bank Group, 2015). The *sukuk* were oversubscribed and bought by a variety of investors, including, for example, the self-employed, housewives and private sector employees. Another important example was the US$500 million *sukuk* issued in a non-Muslim country, South Africa in 2011 (The Economist Intelligence Unit, 2015). In this case, the *sukuk* were four times oversubscribed and investors from the Gulf Corporation Council (GCC) bought one-half of the issue. This case shows that *sukuk* are an important tool for raising finance for achieving SDGs not only in Muslim countries, but also in non-Muslim countries. Importantly, *sukuk* are a preferred instrument of investment for institutional investors, due to their tradability, in the sense that *sukuk* certificates can be bought or sold easily.

For governments of developing countries, *sukuk* represent a significant tool for the financing of infrastructure, and other development projects. They can also use *sukuk* to fund budget deficits. In Malaysia, the Ministry of Finance established DanaInfra Nasional Berhad Company to finance infrastructure projects assigned by the government.[16] In its first infrastructure project, DanaInfra raised a total of US$789.14 million by selling different tranches of *sukuk*, including retail *sukuk* to fund Mass Rapid Transit project (rail-based public transport) in Klang Valley. Another important example in Malaysia is the Khazanah sustainable and responsible investment *sukuk* established in 2015.[17] Khazanah issued around US$24 million

---

[15] For further information about Islamic financial inclusion see Section 2.

[16] For further information, see World Bank and Securities Commission Malaysia, 'Report on Islamic Finance and Public-Private Partnership for Infrastructure Development' (2017) available at http://documents.worldbank.org/curated/en/792701518619005045/pdf/123425-WP-P157703-PUBLIC.pdf accessed August 24, 2018. See also, DanaInfra Nasional Berhad (DINB), 'Retail sukuk: exchange traded sukuk investment for everyone' (2014) available at www.danainfra.com.my/images/stories/retailsukuk/ENG_brochure.pdf accessed August 24, 2018.

[17] For further information, see Khazanah Nasional Berhad, 'Khazanah to Issue Second Tranche of Sustainable and Responsible Investment (Sri) Sukuk' Press Release (2017) available at www.khazanah.com.my/Media-Downloads/News-Press-Releases/2017/Khazanah-to-issue-second-tranche-of-Sustainable-an accessed August 24, 2018.

sukuk, to improve the quality of education in Malaysian government schools, through a public-private partnership arrangement between the Ministry of Education and a non-profit foundation, Yayasan AMIR (YA) Trust School Programme. *Sukuk* were fully subscribed by various investors, including management companies, corporations, foundations, banks and pension funds. Further, *sukuk*-holders were given an option to convert their *sukuk* into a donation at any point. Successfully, by the end of 2016, the Trust Schools Programme was implemented at 83 schools in 10 Malaysian states, providing education for over 65,000 students (quality education is the fourth Goal of SDGs) (United Nations, 2015).

In Pakistan, the Water and Power Development Authority (WAPDA) established the Neelum Jhelum Hydropower Company (Private) Limited (NJHPC) to finance construction of the 969 megawatt Neelum Jhelum Hydropower dam (International Islamic Financial Market, 2017). NJHPC issued *sukuk* worth PKR 100 billion to finance the project. The sukuk had a maturity of eight years with a two-year grace period (affordable energy is the seventh Goal of SDGs) (United Nations, 2015).

Moreover, given its leading role in developing Islamic finance through introducing innovative sharia-compliant products, in 2017, Malaysia witnessed the issuance of the world's first green sustainable and responsible investment (SRI) *sukuk* by Tadau Energy Sdn Bhd (Malaysia World's Islamic Finance Marketplace, 2017). Tadau Energy Sdn Bhd is a renewable energy and sustainable technology investment firm that aims to promote and accelerate the development of renewable energy technologies. The green SRI *sukuk* issuance aimed at achieving the company's long-term vision of a low carbon and climate resilient future (affordable, reliable, sustainable and clean energy is the seventh Goal of the SDGs) (United Nations, 2015).

The success of the above cases should motivate the governments of developing countries to develop *sukuk* market in order to promote the implementation of SDGs. This would primarily include creation of an appropriate legal and regulatory framework, to ensure compliance of *sukuk* issuers with sharia principles, which in turn would strengthen the confidence of investors in sharia-compliant products. The legal framework will also regulate the contractual relationships among the parties involved in the process of issuing *sukuk*. Along with Islamic syndicated financing, *sukuk* can play an effective role in partially financing large sustainable development projects in developing countries, where governments find difficulties in allocating sufficient resources.

14.5 ISLAMIC SOCIAL FINANCE: THE POTENTIAL ROLE OF *ZAKAT* AND *WAQF* INSTITUTIONS

Eradicating poverty in all its forms is one of the greatest challenges facing the world, given that one in five people in developing countries live on less than US$1.25 a day (Seear and Ezezika, 2017: p. 64). Therefore, the elimination of poverty is the first

Goal of the SDGs (United Nations, 2015). It is significant to emphasize that poverty should not only be understood as a lack of income or resources, because it has various manifestations, including hunger, limited access to education and other basic needs, and social discrimination, and that should influence the way policies and intervention addressing poverty are designed. In this respect, Islam has introduced social finance institutions – *zakat* and *waqf* – for poverty alleviation and strengthening social welfare. While *zakat* is obligatory for all Muslims, *waqf* is a voluntary charitable act. These Islamic social finance institutions were effective tools in solving the problems of poverty, and the provision social services to the poor, in the past in Muslim countries (Ahmed, 2004: p. 30). The following discussion investigates these institutions and their potential role in advancing SDGs, especially the first, no poverty, goal.

14.5.1 *The Institution of Zakat*

Zakat, which means purity, growth and increase in Arabic, is one of the five fundamental pillars of Islam.[18] It is a mandatory form of alms for all Muslims whose wealth falls above a certain threshold (*nisab*) (Abdulai and Shamshiry, 2014: p. 52). Most of the items that are subject to *zakat* are listed in the *Qur'an* and *Sunnah*, including gold and silver (money), goods for trade, agricultural products, and herds of camels, sheep and cows. The rate of *zakat* depends on the type of assets. The rate of *zakat* on cash, silver, gold, debts and goods for trade is 2.5 percent (Abdulai and Shamshiry, 2014: p. 53). While the basic rate of *zakat* is 5 percent on agricultural products if crops are irrigated, this rises to 10 percent on agricultural products if farmers use water from natural sources such as springs, rain or rivers (Abdulai and Shamshiry, 2014). Furthermore, the *Qur'an* classifies eight categories of beneficiaries to whom *zakat* can be paid (*Qur'an*, 9:60): (1) the poor (*Fuqara*); (2) the needy (*Miskeen*); (3) administrators of *zakat* (*Amil*); (4) sympathizers, those whose hearts are inclined toward or have accepted Islam; (*Muallaf-at-Quloobuhum*); (5) to free slaves or captives (*Riqab*); (6) those who are in debt (*Gharimin*); (7) for the cause of God (*Fisabillillah*); and (8) the wayfarer (*Ibnus Sabil*) (Abdulai and Shamshiry, 2014: p. 52).

In addition, because paying *zakat* is compulsory, the institution of *zakat* is considered as one of the most significant sources of funds available within the Islamic financial system. It has great potential to mobilize additional untapped resources for advancing the SDGs, by addressing the higher poverty and hunger levels in large Muslim-majority countries. Because *zakat* is paid to specific categories, it can also play a key role in redistributing income in favor of the poorest and most vulnerable within a community, as well as fighting diseases and promoting

---

[18] The other pillars are testimony of faith (*shahada*), prayer (*salah*), fasting (*saum*) and pilgrimage (*haj*). See Visser, 2013: p. 31.

health (Ruttan, 2003: p. 223). This demonstrates that the main objective of *zakat*, poverty reduction, is substantially aligned with the SDGs' no poverty goal (United Nations, 2015). Further, in the institution of *zakat*, the payer of *zakat*, and the receiver of *zakat*, are from different classes. *Zakat* payers are deemed to be rich because they possess wealth above a certain threshold, while the receivers of *zakat* are usually poor people.[19] Thus, the distinction between the two classes is based on reaching the *nisab* (the wealth threshold). Since this distinction is based on wealth rather than income, it ensures that the redistribution of wealth reaches the right people, who are usually the poor. Nonetheless, *zakat* should be viewed as a positive measure that aims at preventing poverty, rather than a corrective poverty-reduction tool.

While *zakat* has the potential of advancing the SDGs in the developing countries, especially on poverty eradication, its impact is dependent on the size of *zakat* collections. This raises a significant question about how *zakat* is collected. In the early history of Islam, *zakat* was collected and distributed by the government of the Prophet (*pbuh*). He appointed designated personnel to collect and distribute *zakat* (Ahmed, 2004: p. 30). After the Prophet's death, the first Muslim *caliph*, Abu Bakr, continued using the same system devised by the Prophet (*pbuh*). The most fundamental change to the system of *zakat* management occurred during the time of the second caliph, Umar bin al Khattab, who established the institution of *Bait ul Mal* (State Treasury) for the management of *zakat* funds (Ahmed, 2004: p. 31). At the present time, Muslim countries have different approaches to state involvement in *zakat* collection and disbursement. Only six Muslim countries: Libya, Malaysia, Pakistan, Saudi Arabia, Sudan and Yemen, have a compulsory *zakat* system for citizens (Hasan, 2015: p. 130). In some countries, *zakat* contribution through official organisations is voluntary (Hasan, 2015: p. 129). Many Muslim-majority countries have no *zakat* government system in place, so instead *zakat* is given individually and directly from person to person, because individuals may not be confident that delivering *zakat* through a third party will reach those in need. The non-involvement of state in *zakat* collection and disbursement, is the main obstacle to utilizing *zakat* as a significant source of funding for promoting the SDGs. In order to illustrate the potential of *zakat* in advancing SDGs in Muslim-majority countries, or non-Muslim countries that do not have mandatory system or governmental organisations involved in collecting *zakat*, it is necessary to highlight some case studies from countries that have obligatory and formal systems of collecting and distributing *zakat*.

In Sudan, Diwan al Zakat is responsible for collecting and disbursement of *zakat*. To help the poor in the community, it used *zakat* funds to provide finance to farmers to purchase essential inputs provided the funds are reimbursed after the harvest

---

[19]   The Hanafi jurists, for example, defined the poor as those who have money lesser than the amount on which *zakat* is payable.

(Sadiq and Mushtaq, 2015: p. 52). Consequently, the use of *zakat* funds has increased the profitability of farming for farmers, as well as expanding *zakat* accumulation from agriculture. Increased profitability helps farmers to improve their life conditions, and therefore reduce poverty.

In Indonesia, while *zakat* can be collected by private institutions, a new law in 2011 appointed the National Board of Zakat (BAZNAS) as the national agency for collecting, distributing and coordinating the management of *zakat* through the BAZNAS offices, as well as through private *zakat* institutions. According to BAZNAS, the volume of *zakat* collected annually amounts to approximately US$270 million and, around 6.8 million poor people, 22.6 percent of the poor population in Indonesia, have benefited from *zakat* (Noor and Pickup, 2017). BAZNAS disbursed *zakat* in five major sectors: humanitarian support, education, economy, proselytizing and health. For example, BAZNAS used *zakat* to buy boats and canoes for fisher folk to improve their lives, in terms of their health, income and education. BAZNAS also agreed with the UNDP to support the expansion of electricity access to the poor in Jambi province, by disbursing US$350,000 for renewable energy in rural communities with high poverty levels (Pickup, 2017). This includes developing two micro hydro power plants. The project was the first official disbursement of the *zakat* fund to promote the SDGs. Significantly, around 30 million Indonesians do not have access to electricity, which, of course, is significantly detrimental to their standard of living (Pickup, 2017).

In Kuwait, the International Sharia Board of Zakat of the Zakat House of Kuwait issued a fatwa (ruling) that allowed the House of Zakat to use *zakat* proceeds to construct and operate hospitals, orphanages and clinics to provide health services to poor people (good health and well-being is the third of the SDGs) (Ahmed, 2004: pp. 37–8). Interestingly, the Fatwa Committee in Kuwait also issued a fatwa which considered full-time students, at any level, to be part of the poor and needy people category, so *zakat* funds can be used to finance their living and study needs during their period of education (Ahmed, 2004: p. 37). This fatwa will help poor people to access quality education, which is the fourth SDG (United Nations, 2015).

14.5.2 Challenges and Opportunities

Despite *zakat*'s great potential, many challenges that limit its efficacy remain. In order to improve efficiency and effectiveness in the performance of the *zakat* institution, the collection and disbursement of *zakat* should be through formal institutions. As mentioned above, some Muslims are cautious about paying *zakat* through third parties, so they must be convinced that paying *zakat* through a formal organisation, rather than informal networks, is more efficient, in terms of poverty alleviation and improving living standards. Muslim scholars and Islamic institutions can play a key role in this regard. They can help in clarifying that Islam does not prevent paying *zakat* through formal organisations, and that in the early days of

Islam, the state was responsible for collecting and disbursement of *zakat*. Another significant way to improve *zakat* revenues, and therefore make the desired impact, is through enacting laws that allow formal governmental institutions to collect *zakat* from both individuals and financial/economic entities. However, the management of these institutions should be subject to strict transparency requirements, to avoid misappropriation and abuse of *zakat* funds. This would bolster *zakat* payers' confidence in the institutions. Further, to facilitate the operations of *zakat* institutions, an extensive national database of both target groups and actual beneficiaries, should be established and governed by appropriate laws.

In addition, another possible way to maximize the use of *zakat* funds in promoting SDGs is the establishment of dedicated international or regional *zakat* funds, to channel *zakat* from rich countries, such the Gulf states, to poor countries. The international *zakat* fund could be an illustration of the importance of international cooperation in achieving SDGs. The fund would be responsible for the collection and distribution of *zakat* for sustainable development purposes. This raises a question about the management of the fund. The management of the fund should be entrusted to a reputable entity such as the IDB, or any politically independent entity. This institution should also be subject to independent supervisory committee or board that oversees the management's decisions regarding the disbursement of *zakat* funds.

14.5.3 *The Institution of* Waqf

Waqf is another important institution in Islamic social finance, and clearly has the potential to foster SDGs. *Waqf*, plural *awqaf*, is a voluntary and irrevocable dedication of a movable, or immovable, asset for perpetual social benefit. Once a *waqf* is created, it can never be sold, and exists in perpetuity (Ahmad, 2015: p. 118). Although the institution of *waqf* seems similar to the trust instrument found in common law legal systems, there are differences between them in terms of perpetuity and ownership. While the Islamic law mandates perpetuity for *awqaf*, the English law contains a rule against perpetuity (Moffat et al., 2005: p. 305). Also, while Islamic jurists deem *waqf* to be owned by God, the trustee, conventionally, is seen as the owner of the trust's property (Ahmed, 2004: p. 33). Compared to *zakat*, one of the significant characteristics of *waqf* is that it provides flexibility in fund utilization. As discussed above, in the institution of *zakat*, funds must be utilized for specific groups of recipients. While in *waqf*, the assets can be used to provide a wide spectrum of welfare services to Muslims and non-Muslims such as education, healthcare institutions, environmental preservation programs, infrastructure and other social purposes.

Historically, the *waqf* has been used extensively by Muslim countries to promote public objectives, such as better healthcare, education, roads, clean water and the relief of poverty (Ahmed, 2004: p. 29). The information and data available on the size

of *waqf* institutions, demonstrates the significance of this Islamic financial institution, in serving the poor and enhancing societal welfare. Despite its declined usage
in modern times, the *waqf*'s historical role suggests strongly that this social
institution can again be an effective instrument for the organisation and allocation
of funds to promote the SDGs (Khan and Jareen, 2015: p. 201). This decline in usage
can be variously attributed to misappropriation of *awqaf* properties, changes in
economic and social structures, and the general mismanagement of *awqaf* (Khan
and Jareen, 2015).

Prophet Muhammad (*pbuh*) and his companions established various types of
awqaf. The first *waqf* in the Islamic history was created by the Prophet (*pbuh*), when
he purchased land and constructed a mosque in Madinah, known today as the
Prophet's mosque (Ahmed, 2004: p. 32). Another early example of *waqf* is the
endowment of the Ruma Well as a public utility. When Prophet Muhammad
(*pbuh*) arrived in Madina, he realized that the Ruma Well was one of the few
sources of drinkable water for the city (Abdelhady, 2013: p. 33). The price of water
was high, so he asked his companions to purchase the Well and render it free for
everyone. One of his companions, Uthman, bought the Well and made it free for
everyone. Umar, the second caliph, established a *waqf* on a land, Khaybar, upon the
recommendation of the Prophet (*pbuh*), directed the fruits of the land to be
distributed to the poor guests and wayfarers (McChesney, 2014: p. 7). The Ruma
Well *waqf*, and the land of Khaybar *waqf*, encouraged other companions to establish
various types of *waqf*.

Later, with the spread of Islam, the institution of *waqf* expanded in size, impact and
scope. In the education sector, the leading centers of Islamic learning, such as Al-
Azhar University in Egypt, Al-Qarawiyyin in Morocco and Al-Zaytuna in Tunisia were
established as *awqaf* (Ahmad, 2004: p. 119). These mosques offered, in addition to
religious instruction, education in mathematics and the physical sciences. *Waqf* was
also used to support scientific research in religious and non-religious areas, such as
pharmacology, astronomy and physiology. In the healthcare sector, Al Noori Hospital
in Damascus was established in AD 1145 as a *waqf* and later became a medical school,
where many notable physicians were trained. The list of graduates notably includes
Ibn Nafis, a scholar who made several important contributions to the early knowledge
of pulmonary circulation and discovered the theory of the respiratory system in the
human lung (Leeuwen, 1999: p. 186). The hospital was also the first hospital to adopt
medical records (Ahmad, 2004: p. 120). Another important health *waqf* was the
establishment of Shishli Children Hospital in Istanbul in 1898 (Hasan, 2015: p. 186).
The hospital provided health services and medicines to patients, especially the poor.
Furthermore, in the nineteenth century, around three quarters of the arable land of
the Ottoman empire was *awqaf*, including half of the size of the land in Algeria' and
one third in Tunisia (Ahmad, 2004: p. 119).

The discussion above demonstrates that *waqf* has a history of success in a number
of different circumstances, including essential sectors such as healthcare and

education. The institution of *waqf* was able to serve the poor and the needy without differentiating between Muslims and non-Muslims. This raises a significant question about the current role of this institution in promoting sustainable development objectives. In order to answer this question, it is necessary to investigate the types of *waqf* institution because some types might have bigger roles to play in advancing the SDGs in developing countries.

Awqaf can be categorized, according to their objectives, as public (philanthropic) *waqf*, private (family) *waqf*, or combined/mixed *waqf* (*mushtarak*) (Kahf, 2013: p. 213). Public *waqf* is established for the benefit of society at large. It aims at supporting the poor in a society, including providing educational, environmental and other social services (Ahmad, 2004: p. 39). The private *waqf* is established for the benefit of the founder's family, so that they can enjoy the usufruct of the *waqf*, and the revenues generated from the *waqf* are distributed among the family members and their successors (Ahmad, 2004: p. 123). In mixed *waqf*, both the founder's family and the public benefit from the *waqf* according to its deed. Significantly, the objectives for which the assets of the *waqf* can used, and the way its revenues can be distributed, are determined by the waqf founder. The founder also sets out how the *waqf* is to be managed, and indeed who is responsible for carrying out the management function. In the *waqf* deed, the founder can impose any kinds of restrictions that he/she wants. This shows the flexibility in the *waqf* structure. The philanthropic *awqaf* has the potential to contribute to sustainable development efforts in developing countries, because these *awqaf* are established for the benefit of the community at large. In addition, while most of *waqf* created consist of real estate, the cash *waqf* is also common in Muslim communities. The cash *waqf* is considered as an effective tool for making investments in different agricultural, educational and social services. The cash *waqf* can also be used for free lending to the relevant beneficiaries, or it might be invested, and its net revenue distributed to the beneficiaries (Brown, 2013: pp. 31–3). Since the creation of the real estate *waqf* has become so expensive, and only very rich people can establish it, the cash investment *waqf* can be an effective alternative to revitalize the *waqf* institution in Muslim developing countries. This is because it enables individual people in society to contribute to the creation of *waqf*, and the revenues of these *awqaf* can be used to promote sustainable development objectives.

Revitalizing the role of the institution of *waqf* in supporting sustainable development objectives in developing countries necessitates addressing some existing challenges. Most of the existing *awqaf* objectives, for instance, might not match the SDGs. Therefore, it is necessary to identify which *awqaf* objectives can support or boost the SDGs. People also need to be made aware of the importance of the SDGs in advancing life standards in society and consider that when establishing new *awqaf*. Importantly, many *awqaf* were established centuries ago and their original deeds have become lost for various reasons (Miura, 2015: p. 187). This implies that their objectives are not known. Since SDGs aim at supporting the poor, these *awqaf* can be used to advance the SDGs efforts in developing countries.

Further, another important challenge is management, administration and governance of *awqaf*. Governments in some Muslim countries have attempted to take over the *awqaf* management, exploiting the loss of *awqaf* deeds or records. When governments have taken over the management of *awqaf*, they usually try to establish agencies to manage *awqaf*, making *awqaf* become part of the public sector (Ahmed, 2004: p. 43). It is well-recognized that the public sector in developing countries may suffer from bureaucracy, and lack proper human resources and flexibility, in terms of making urgent decisions. This minimizes the potential role of the *waqf* institution in sustainable development. Therefore, in order to revive the role of *awqaf* in sustainable development, they should be managed by independent professional management institutions. However, *awqaf* can still be subject to external supervision by governments. *Awqaf*, for example, can be supervised by ministry of awqaf, and the *awqaf* mangers should periodically report to the ministry of *awqaf*. In fact, professional management has developed advanced skills through specialized education, experience and professional designations that will improve *awqaf* quality generally, as well as service delivery, which in turn can increase *awqaf* profitability. Nonetheless, professional management should be overseen by independent internal supervisory bodies, to ensure the effectiveness of the operation of *waqf* and compliance of the management with the *waqf* objective. The activities and decisions of the management can, for example, be supervised by a board of trustees or independent directors, and the internal supervisory body can report to external state oversight structures (the government body). It is necessary to emphasize the importance of having laws and regulations that regulate the work of *awqaf* management, to ensure the transparency of *waqf* operation, and management accountability. The appropriate laws and regulations are also essential to facilitate the creation of new types of *awqaf* beyond those traditionally used. For example, *awqaf* could be established through the issuing of special types of *sukuk*, which are available for individuals to purchase. The revenues from these *awqaf* could then be used to finance infrastructure, education, health and poverty alleviation. If the law provides a good framework to the operation of these innovative types, then people will be encouraged to contribute to developing the *waqf* institution.

In this regard, the IDB has taken an important initiative in emphasizing the potential role of the institution of *awqaf* in achieving the sustainable development objectives, in developing countries. Under the IDB guidance, Awqaf Properties Investment Fund (APIF) was established in 2001 (Islamic Development Bank, 2014). The APIF aims to mobilize funds to promote and develop *awqaf* properties worldwide, to support IDB goals of sustainable development in both its member countries and outside. APIF is financed by *awqaf* institutions, ministries, the IDB and Islamic financial institutions. IDB manages the APIF. The APIF has financed many real estate projects including commercial, special purpose buildings and residential projects, in several developing countries.

14.6 CONCLUSION

This chapter has considered how Islamic finance can contribute to the promotion and achievement of the SDGs in developing countries. Given the ambitious and comprehensive nature of the 2030 plan for the SDGs, the mechanisms of Islamic finance can substantially support sustainable development financing. This chapter has demonstrated a harmonious relationship between the SDGs, which revolves around social and human well-being, as well as the Islamic ethos and objectives, which emphasize ethics, justice and equity. The investment products and tools of Islamic finance provide viable alternative sources of financing for fostering the economic, social and environmental dimensions of sustainable development. This chapter has also demonstrated that Islamic social finance institutions like *zakat* and *waqf,* can play important roles in providing additional finance sources for developing countries. Therefore, both institutions should be integrated in the overall development strategy of Muslim developing countries. Islamic finance instruments and products should also be considered by non-Muslim developing countries, due to their innovative ways in which they promote sustainable development. *Sukuk,* for example, could generate extra funding to advance sustainable infrastructure development projects.

Despite the remarkable growth in Islamic finance and its role in promoting the SDGs, further steps should be taken to maximize its potential. Islamic finance should promote innovative products that encourage people to use Islamic financial services, without needing to mimic conventional instruments and products, given that mimicry can cause public concern about sharia compliance. The success of *sukuk* is a demonstration of the importance of creating more Islamic products. Furthermore, one of the main challenges to Islamic finance solutions, is variations in the legal frameworks of countries, such as the variation in collection and distribution of *zakat,* in which it could be deployed. This means that more work is required on the standardization of legal frameworks and guidelines, to aid the structuring of Islamic financial products and institutions. The role of the Accounting and Auditing Organisation for Islamic Financial Institutions, in developing and issuing standards for the global Islamic finance industry, is very significant in this regard.

In addition, it is important to raise awareness about Islamic finance products and institutions. People should be convinced that Islamic products are sharia-compliant, and that their money will be invested according to sharia principles. This would support the growth of Islamic finance, which in turn will increase its contribution to the SDGs.

REFERENCES

Abdelhady, H. (2013). Islamic Finance as a Mechanism for Bolstering Food Security in the Middle East: Food Security Waqf. *Sustainable Development Law & Policy*, 13, 29–35.

Abdulai, A. and Shamshiry, E. (2014). *Linking Sustainable Livelihoods to Natural Resources and Governance: The Scale of Poverty in the Muslim World*. Singapore: Springer.

Accounting and Auditing Organization for Islamic Financial Institutions [AAOIFI] (2003). Shari'a Standards 1424-5H/2003–4.

Ahmad, M. (2015). Role of Waqf in Sustainable Economic Development and Poverty Alleviation: Bangladesh Perspective. *Journal of Law, Policy and Globalization*, 42, 118–130.

Ahmed, H. (2004). Role of Zakah and Awqaf in Poverty Alleviation, Issue 8 of Occasional paper. Jeddah: Islamic Development Bank, Islamic Research and Training Institute.

Alam, N., Gupta L. and Bala S. (2017). *Islamic Finance: A Practical Perspective*. London: Palgrave Macmillan.

Aldohni, A. (2012). *The Legal and Regulatory Aspects of Islamic Banking: A Comparative Look at the United Kingdom and Malaysia*. New York: Routledge.

Auda, J. (2008). *Maqasid Al-Shariah: A Beginner's Guide*, 14 vols. London: International Institute of Islamic Thought.

Bellalah, M. and Masood, O., eds., (2013). *Islamic Banking and Finance*. Newcastle upon Tyne: Cambridge Scholars Publishing.

Bhowmik, S. and Saha, D. (2013). *Financial Inclusion of the Marginalised: Street Vendors in the Urban Economy*. New Delhi: Springer Science & Business Media.

Black, E., Esmaeili, H. and Hosen, N. (2013). *Modern Perspectives on Islamic Law* Cheltenham: Edward Elgar Publishing.

Bovens, M., T'Hart, P. and Peters, B., eds., (2002). *Success and Failure in Public Governance: A Comparative Analysis*, New Horizons in Public Policy Series Cheltenham: Edward Elgar Publishing.

Brown, R. (2013). *Islam in Modern Thailand: Faith, Philanthropy and Politics*, Routledge Contemporary Southeast Asia Series. New York: Routledge.

Chapra, M. (2000). *The Future of Economics: An Islamic Perspective*, 21 vols. Leicester: The Islamic Foundation.

DanaInfra Nasional Berhad (DINB) (2014). 'Retail sukuk: exchange traded sukuk investment for everyone' available at www.danainfra.com.my/images/stories/retailsukuk/ENG_brochure .pdf accessed August 24, 2018.

Dusuki, A. and Abdullah, N. (2006). Maqasid al-Shari'ah, Maslahah, and Corporate Social Responsibility. *The American Journal of Islamic Social Sciences* 24, 25–45.

Eisenberg, D. and Nethercott, C., eds., (2012). *Islamic Finance: Law and Practice*. Oxford: Oxford University Press.

Pickup F. (2017). (UNDP Indonesia Deputy Country Director), 'Islamic finance offers enormous opportunity to support SDGs and address inequality' available at www.id.undp.org /content/indonesia/en/home/presscenter/articles/2017/08/23/islamic-finance-offers-enormous -opportunity-to-support-sdgs-and-address-inequality.html accessed August 31, 2018.

Gatti, S. (2018). *Project Finance in Theory and Practice: Designing, Structuring, and Financing Private and Public Projects*. 3rd ed. Cambridge: Academic Press.

Ginena, K. and Hamid, A. (2015). *Foundations of Shariah Governance of Islamic Banks*, The Wiley Finance Series. Chichester: John Wiley & Sons.

Hallaq, W. (2009). *An Introduction to Islamic Law*. Cambridge: Cambridge University Press.

Hasan, S., ed., (2015). *Human Security and Philanthropy: Islamic Perspectives and Muslim Majority Country Practices*. New York: Springer.

Hasan, Z. (2014). *Islamic Banking and Finance: An Integrative Approach*. Oxford: Oxford University Press.

Hassan, A. and Mollah, S. (2018). *Islamic Finance: Ethical Underpinnings, Products, and Institutions*. London: Palgrave Macmillan.

Hassan, M. and Lewis, M., eds., (2014). *Handbook on Islam and Economic Life* Cheltenham: Edward Elgar Publishing.

Housby, E. (2011). *Islamic Financial Services in the United Kingdom*. Edinburgh Guides to Islamic Finance Series. Edinburgh: Edinburgh University Press.

Ibn Ashur, M. (2006). *Ibn Ashur: Treatise on Maqasid Al-Shariah*. London: International Institute of Islamic Thought.

International Islamic Financial Market (2018). IIFM Annual Sukuk Report, 7th edition available at www.iifm.net/system/files/private/en/IIFM%20Sukuk%20Report%20%287th%20Edition%29_0.pdf accessed August 24, 2018.

International Islamic Financial Market (2017). IIFM Annual Sukuk Report, 6th edition available at www.iifm.net/system/files/private/en/IIFM%20Sukuk%20Report%20%286th%20Edition%29_2.pdf accessed August 24, 2018.

Iqbal, K. (2009). *The Right to Development in International Law: The Case of Pakistan*. Routledge Research in Human Rights Law. New York: Routledge.

Islamic Corporation for the Development and Thomson Reuters (2016). 'ICD-Thomson Reuters Islamic finance development report 2016' available at www.salaamgateway.com /en/story/report_icdthomson_reuters_islamic_finance_development_report_2016-salaamo6122016021157/ accessed August 18, 2018.

Islamic Development Bank (2016). Lives and Livelihoods Fund available at www.isdb.org /partnership/lives-and-livelihoods-fund accessed August 18, 2018.

Islamic Development Bank (2018). 'The Islamic Development Bank Launches New Innovation Hub and Accelerator Fund to Fuel Economic Growth in The Developing World' available at www.isdb.org/announcement/press-releases/the-islamic-development-bank-launches-new-innovation-hub-and-accelerator-fund-to-fuel-economic-growth-in-the-developing-world accessed August 18, 2018.

Islamic Development Bank About IsDB available at www.isdb.org/who-we-are/about accessed August 18, 2018.

Islamic Development Bank (2014). Annual Report 1435H available at https://thatswhy.isdb.org /irj/go/km/docs/documents/IDBDevelopments/Internet/English/IDB/CM/Publications/ Annual_Reports/40th/IDB_Annual_Report_1435H_English.pdf accessed September 18, 2018.

Islamic Development Bank (2017). 'Towards 2030: Exploring the Alignment of the Islamic Development Bank Group's 10-Year Strategy and the Sustainable Development Goals' available at www.unosd.org/content/documents/3439IDBG%20and%20SDGs%20(Ahmad %20and%20Khotamov%20Session%204).pdf accessed October 30, 2018.

Kahf, M. (2010). *Islamic Finance Contracts*. Dubai: Al Manhal.

Karim, S. *The Islamic Moral Economy: A Study of Islamic Money and Financial Instruments*. Florida: Universal-Publishers.

Kettell, B. (2011). *Case Studies in Islamic Banking and Finance*, 550 vols. Chichester: John Wiley & Sons.

Khan, M. and Porzio, M., eds., (2010). *Islamic Banking and Finance in the European Union: A Challenge, Studies in Islamic Finance, Accounting and Governance*. Cheltenham: Edward Elgar Publishing.

Khan, N. and Jareen, S. (2015). The Waqf and Human Security in Muslim Majority Countries: Traditions, Modern Practices, and Challenges. In S. Hasan, ed., *Human*

Security and Philanthropy: Islamic Perspectives and Muslim Majority Country Practices. New York: Springer.

Khazanah Nasional Berhad (2017). 'Khazanah to Issue Second Tranche of Sustainable and Responsible Investment (Sri) Sukuk' Press Release available at www.khazanah.com.my/Media-Downloads/News-Press-Releases/2017/Khazanah-to-issue-second-tranche-of-Sustainable-an accessed August 24, 2018.

Leeuwen, R. (1999). *Waqfs and Urban Structures: The Case of Ottoman Damascus,* Volume 11 of Studies in Islamic Law and Society. Leiden: Brill.

Mohieldin, M., Iqbal, Z. Rostom, A. and Fu, X. (2012) The Role of Islamic Finance in Enhancing Financial Inclusion in Organization of Islamic Cooperation Countries. *Islamic Economic Studies* 20, 55–120.

Malaysia World's Islamic Finance Marketplace (MIFC) (2017). 'Sukuk Going Green: Malaysia Continues to Drive Innovation' available at www.mifc.com/index.php?ch=28&pg=72&ac=187&bb=uploadpdf accessed August 24, 2018.

McChesney, R. (2014). *Waqf in Central Asia: Four Hundred Years in the History of a Muslim Shrine, 1480–1889.* New Jersey: Princeton University Press.

Miura, T. (2015). *Dynamism in the Urban Society of Damascus: The Ṣāliḥiyya Quarter from the Twelfth to the Twentieth Centuries.* Leiden: Brill.

Moffat, G., Bean, G. and Dewar, J. (2005). *Trusts Law: Text and Materials Law in Context.* 4th ed. Cambridge: Cambridge University Press.

Mugasha, A. (2007). *The Law of Multi-bank Financing: Syndicated Loans and the Secondary Loan Market.* 2nd ed. Oxford: Oxford University Press.

Noor, Z. and Pickup, F. (2017). 'The Role of Zakat in Supporting the Sustainable Development Goals' available at www.id.undp.org/content/indonesia/en/home/library/sustainable-development-goals/the-role-of-zakat-in-supporting-the-sustainable-development-goal.html accessed August 31, 2018.

The Qur'an.

Rahman, I. and Sulfia, D. (2015). *Islamic Banking and Finance.* Hamburg: Anchor Academic Publishing.

Ruttan, V. (2003). *Social Science Knowledge and Economic Development: An Institutional Design Perspective.* Michigan: University of Michigan Press.

Sadiq, R. and Mushtaq, A. (2015). The Role of Islamic Finance in Sustainable Development. *Journal of Islamic Thought and Civilization,* 5, 46–65.

Safari, M., Ariff, M. and Mohamad, S. (2014). *Sukuk Securities: New Ways of Debt Contracting.* The Wiley Finance Series. Singapore: John Wiley & Son.

Seear, M. and Ezezika, O. (2017). *An Introduction to Global Health.* Toronto: Canadian Scholars' Press.

Tag El-Din, S. (2013). *Maqasid Foundations of Market Economics,* Edinburgh Guides to Islamic Finance. Edinburgh: Edinburgh University Press.

The Economist Intelligence Unit (2015). 'Mapping Africa's Islamic Economy' available at www.eiuperspectives.economist.com/sites/default/files/MappingAfricasIslamicEconomy.pdf accessed August 4, 2018.

The Standing Committee for Economic and Commercial Cooperation of the Organization of the Islamic Cooperation (COMCEC) (2017). Report on the Special Program for the Development of Africa (SPDA) available at www.comcec.org/en/wp-content/uploads/2017/04/33-FC-IDB-SPDA.pdf accessed August 18, 2018.

Ullah, K. and Al-Karaghouli, W. (2017). *Understanding Islamic Financial Services: Theory and Practice.* London: Kogan Page Publishers.

United Nations (2014a). 'Report of the Intergovernmental Committee of Experts on Sustainable Development Financing' available at www.un.org/esa/ffd/wp-content /uploads/2014/10/ICESDF.pdf accessed October 30, 2018.

United Nations (1987). 'Report of the World Commission on Environment and Development: Our Common Future' available at www.un-documents.net/our-common-future.pdf accessed August 4, 2018.

United Nations (2015). 'Transforming Our World: the 2030 Agenda for Sustainable Development' available at www.un.org/ga/search/view_doc.asp?symbol=A/RES/70/1&Lang=E accessed October 30, 2018.

United Nations (2014b). 'World Investment Report 2014: Investing in the SDGs: An Action Plan' available at http://unctad.org/en/PublicationsLibrary/wir2014_en.pdf accessed August 4, 2018.

Visser, H. (2009) *Islamic Finance: Principles and Practice*. Cheltenham: Edward Elgar Publishing.

Visser, H. (2013). *Islamic Finance: Principles and Practice*. 2nd ed. Cheltenham: Edward Elgar Publishing.

Weber, B, Alfen, H. and Staub-Bisang, M. (2016). *Infrastructure as an Asset Class: Investment Strategy, Sustainability, Project Finance and PPP*, The Wiley Finance Series. 2nd ed. Chichester: John Wiley & Sons.

World Bank and Securities Commission Malaysia (2017). 'Report on Islamic Finance and Public-Private Partnership for Infrastructure Development' available at http://documents .worldbank.org/curated/en/792701518619005045/pdf/123425-WP-P157703-PUBLIC.pdf accessed August 24, 2018.

World Bank Group: Ahmed, H., Mohieldin, M., Verbeek, J., and Aboulmagd, F. (2015). 'On the Sustainable Development Goals and the Role of Islamic Finance Policy Research Working Paper 7266' available at http://documents.worldbank.org/curated/en/442091467999969424/ On-the-sustainable-development-goals-and-the-role-of-Islamic-finance accessed August 24, 2018.

World Bank (2014). 'Global Financial Development Report 2014: Financial Inclusion' available at http://siteresources.worldbank.org/EXTGLOBALFINREPORT/Resources/ 8816096–1361888425203/9062080–1364927957721/GFDR_2014_Concept_Note_Final.pdf accessed August 5, 2018.

World Bank (2008). 'MIGA and Islamic Finance: Doraleh Container Terminal Project, Djibouti (English)' available at http://documents.worldbank.org/curated/en/869821468026341157/MIGA-and-Islamic-finance-Doraleh-Container-Terminal-Project-Djibouti accessed August 18, 2018.

World Bank (2017). 'Mobilizing Islamic Finance for Infrastructure Public-Private Partnerships' available at http://documents.worldbank.org/curated/en/898871513144724493/Mobilizing-Islamic-finance-for-infrastructure-public-private-partnerships accessed August 18, 2018.

15

Developing Countries' Business Schools and Socially Conscious Business Leaders

Nubi Achebo

15.1 INTRODUCTION

It is very difficult to separate ethics, corporate social responsibility (CSR) and sustainability because all the three concepts are intricately linked today. Over the decades there has been a convergence of ethics, CSR and sustainability in business and business school curricula. The terms are also interchangeably used in the literature. Due to pressure from society and accrediting bodies, business schools are gradually moving toward integrating all three areas in their curricula to address challenges in the business environment. Business schools are teaching how managers should be adept at handling the moral responsibility of businesses to society through organisational policies and actions while at the same time paying attention to the economic, social and environmental impact of their actions on society. The 2013 Association to Advance Collegiate Schools of Business (AACSB) standard states that "a school must demonstrate a commitment to address, engage, and respond to current and emerging social responsibilities issues ... through its policies, procedures, curricula, research and/or outreach activities" (2013).

Business leaders are pivotal in engineering the successful adoption and implementation of CSR or sustainability in organisations. Despite the negative activities of some rogue business leaders in the past few decades, business managers still have the responsibility for managing organisational strategy and ensuring profitability. This implies that good or bad, the steering of businesses enterprises will always be handled by business leaders. For this reason, it is imperative to be concerned about how business schools develop ethically responsible business leaders who would take the triple bottom line (considerations of people, planet and profit in strategic organisational decisionmaking) seriously in organisational decisionmaking. While this is not addressed in the literature, business schools effectively creating programs for producing responsible business managers and minimize financial crises, reputational damage or irreparable damage to the environment, is intrinsically linked with how well they handle the issue of proper development for business leaders.

CSR is a concept that has gained currency worldwide (Baumgartner, 2014) and even in emerging markets over the past decades because of its utility as a tool to address organisational challenges and afford organisations the opportunity to be good corporate citizens. This paper looks at ethics, corporate social responsibility and sustainability education as concepts on a continuum that is constantly evolving. Business schools are becoming cognizant of the role in business, the need to act responsibly in the management of the business, and also growing and fostering sustainable businesses in making a shift toward the integration of these concepts in the curricula. Tied to all these is the role of the business leader as a catalyst for ensuring that sustainability happens based on the acquisition of knowledge, skills and attitudes for navigating the terrain of adopting and sustaining such organisational innovation.

Companies have taken to the concept either because of regulatory dictates, expediency, or genuine concerns about the operational environment and a need to justify their legitimacy to operate. Companies are now also held accountable for the impacts of their operations and actions as it affects their sphere of influence (Rasche and Escudero, 2010).

Despite external pressures, the adoption and success of CSR/sustainability initiatives are sometimes hinged on the receptive leadership of organisations. CSR decisions are made by leaders who act on behalf of corporate entities. When CSR/sustainability decisions go wrong, the corporation is liable for the actions of their business leaders. This could have financial and reputational damage implications for the organisations. It is imperative then for business leaders to have the sensitivities and be well versed in dealing with stakeholders on CSR issues. Management education programs are not adequately preparing managers to assume decisionmaking roles when it comes to CSR issues, especially in emerging market countries, and this is a huge risk for organisations as the concept gains wide acceptance.

15.2 BACKGROUND

Nigeria, an emerging market economy, is the largest and most populous nation in Africa. It currently has close to 198 million people as a projected number from the last credible census figures (Nigerian Population Commission, 2018). There are some characteristics associated with emerging market economies: low incomes, rapid growth, high volatility, weak capital markets and higher return on investments (Mwenda, 2000). The same characteristics that make emerging markets attractive for investments are the same factors that seem to hamper their path toward imbibing CSR and sustainability principles. While we are familiar with the global financial and economic scandals, the levels of decay in the developing economies of the world are enormous and a hindrance toward sustainability.

There have been several egregious scandals around the world in the past decades and the culprits are usually MBA graduates from business schools around the world

(Dickson et al., 2013). This has led to a series of questions about the ethical background and preparation of professionals in business schools. Are business schools dropping the ball in preparing MBA students for challenges on the job, especially in relation to issues such as social responsibility, human rights, equity and fairness to all stakeholders? Why do scandals persist despite the efforts being made? For emerging market economies, the question is even more pertinent. As business schools address social responsibility issues beyond teaching profitability for businesses. What can business schools in emerging market economies do differently to address the economic, social and environmental issues around them?

CSR and sustainability are complex concepts and an attempt to incorporate them into organisational strategies increases the complexity (Aguinis and Glavas, 2012). There have been debates in roundtable discussions about the role of business schools in preparing professionals for the job market. There is no doubt that business schools are central to the development of business leaders and as such should be in the forefront of ensuring that their graduates are ready to deal with the complexity inherent in the world today. Institutions have reacted in different ways. While some introduced ethics and CSR into existing curricula, others have created new courses that would address the ethical challenges posed in the emergent business world. Some institutions have also taken the bold step of creating master's and MBA programs devoted solely to churning out sustainability management business leaders.

15.3 DEFINITION AND IMPORTANCE OF CSR AND SUSTAINABILITY EDUCATION

CSR or sustainability education is defined as a set of instruction and exposure to a knowledge base to foster the articulation of appropriate and ethical positions in order to implement socially conscious initiatives, while taking into consideration financial, social and environmental issues. This type of education is designed for individuals who are being prepared as middle-level business leaders and leaders already in a responsible position who are able to affect decisionmaking in an organisation.

Starkey and Welford (2001) indicated that business schools are lagging behind the industry on CSR and sustainability issues. But it appears that things are beginning to change gradually since that publication of that research study even though Lozano et al. (2015) opined that business schools are still lagging behind industries in integrating sustainability into their programs despite the strides made already. Demand for business managers who are adept in managing CSR and sustainability is beginning to increase (Haanaes et al., 2012) thus putting pressure on business schools to up the ante in reviewing curricula and introducing courses and program components to produce qualified candidates. New programs have also emerged devoted solely to producing sustainability managers as opposed to having a few electives in the MBA curricula. Neam and Neal (2010) indicate that in spite of the high interest in CSR and sustainability in business schools, most programs are still focused on teaching ethics rather than integrating sustainability into MBA courses. According to Nicholls et al. (2013), very few institutions have integrated ethics, CSR and sustainability into their programs. This is a gap that requires immediate remedy as we move toward a sustainable society.

Economies worldwide face economic, social and environmental challenges but emerging market economies face very unique challenges as articulated by the United Nations Sustainable Development Goals (SDGs): poverty, hunger eradication, strengthening institutions, responsible consumption, quality education and good health, clean water, decent work, industry innovation, gender equality; among other SDG Goals. Even though the SDGs are targeted at governments of the world, the United Nations also calls on businesses to get involved in the actualization of these Goals adopted in 2016, especially by identifying opportunities and preparing the organisation to capitalize on such opportunities, aligning organisational strategies to stakeholder needs, while stabilizing societies and markets.

15.4 CSR/SUSTAINABILITY CHALLENGES IN THE NIGERIAN BUSINESS ENVIRONMENT

The Nigerian business environment is very tough on entrepreneurs and established businesses. While there are multinational companies operating in Nigeria, it is the small or medium enterprises (SMEs) that really are the bulwark of the economy (Fox, 2004). When CSR/sustainability is well established in most multinational companies operating locally, SMEs are still struggling with the acceptance and adoption of sustainability. According to Crane et al. (2013) CSR activities are more "nuanced" in some emerging economies that previously reported.

15.4.1 CSR Education in Lagos Business School

Lagos Business School (LBS) is the foremost business school in sub-Saharan Africa. The institution was established as a Center for Professional Communications to fill the void in management education some decades ago through the offering of business management courses. It has since blossomed into a full-fledged degree-awarding institution in 1992. The institution offers MBA degree and executive programs to the business community. Even though some question the place of ethics (Swanson and Frederick, 2005) in business education, LBS has seen ethics as central to the development of socially responsible business leaders. The goal has always been to be an oasis of sanity in Nigeria through propagating strong ethical values that will transform business leaders to act responsibly in business management.

Although there is no formalized and institutional program for ensuring that sustainability and/or CSR principles are part of the program offerings of Lagos Business School, the leadership of the institution is quite conscious of the need to instill these principles. So what has emerged over the years is an uncoordinated yet cohesive structure embedded in courses and programs to ensure that business leaders passing through the institution imbibe these principles. These programs are delivered through the academic units as well as through the First Bank Sustainability Center.

Lagos Business School identifies strongly as a sustainable campus because it clearly understands CSR initiatives. In all operational activities, the institution is conscious of its sustainable development goals – recycling, switching off power when office or classrooms are not in use, use of energy saving bulbs, solar energy for lighting in the library and outdoors, use of gas in its kitchen among other initiatives. The university is also a signatory to the United Nations-sponsored Principle of Responsible Management Education (PRME) initiative.

The First Bank Sustainability Center was established to empower individuals and organisations to take up the responsibility of promoting sustainable development and growth. The Center offers programs to organisations and also provides consulting for organisations that are on the sustainability path. The Center has organised workshops anchored in Nigeria and in partnership with foreign institutions, with a view to providing not just local perspectives but internal exposure to sustainability issues. Promoting dialogue on sustainable business strategies is also a key function of the Center.

To develop responsible and effective business leaders, it is imperative to have a strong theoretical and practical background in ethical issues. It is in recognition of this imperative that all degree and open enrolment courses in the institution have ethical considerations built in to address the myriad of ethics, CSR and sustainability issues. These courses undergo the usual rationalization process through the curriculum review process and Senate approval. Their courses are carefully designed to address specific issues based on the type of program being offered to participants. Ethics across the curriculum is the approach adopted by the institution because it is rationalized that business leaders encounter ethical issues not just in the financial sector but in all functional areas of business. Faculty members are mandated to explore the ethical issues in the topical content of the courses being offered.

The leadership of Lagos Business School has also created a program to inculcate the spirit of giving back and also showing concern for the community where they operate through a Personal Social Responsibility program. MBA candidates are exposed to the principles of CSR, ethical responsibility and sustainability during a brush-up session design to bring candidates up to speed to be in a position to succeed in the program. MBA candidates are required to select a CSR/sustainability project in groups of five to seven during the brush-up period and the implementation of the project will be for the 18-month duration of the program. Each group is supervised by a faculty member depending on the topical area selected by the group. A quarterly report is expected from each group to ensure that students are on track with their respective project activities. They are also required to submit a final report before graduation.

The feedback from the Personal Social Responsibility program over the years has been very positive. Students saw the project as an opportunity to interface with the community – understanding the social and economic issues confronting each target population and designing solutions using the knowledge garnered from the academic program.

15.5 FUTURE DIRECTIONS FOR CSR EDUCATION IN EMERGING MARKETS

Ethics is currently a basic requirement for all Association to Advance Collegiate Schools of Business International (AACSB)-accredited business schools. Since this is an accreditation sought after by top business schools around the world, schools pay attention to signals from the accreditation body. The Association has already signaled that corporate social responsibility and sustainability are two areas that are being looked at as requirements from AACSB-accredited institutions (AACSB International, 2013).

The principles of curriculum development emphasize the need to articulate a goal for any curriculum. The ultimate goal for the curricula would be to produce change agents with competencies that would enable them to serve as sustainability managers, decisionmakers, educators, influencers who are capable of moving organisations through the arduous task of transitioning to sustainable organisations. Judging from the different focus and level of CSR and integration of sustainability education worldwide, it would be very presumptuous to prescribe a specific path for business schools. As is the case for a sustainability concept that is highly contextual (Matten and Moon, 2008), business schools will have to determine how best to tailor the integration to achieve best results.

Hesselbarth and Schaltegger (2014) identified the following competency areas as critical for developing sustainability managers: making the sustainability business case, preferring sustainable solutions, integration of sustainability into strategy, conducting sustainability audits, measuring sustainability outcomes, providing support to advance sustainability initiatives, creating a network for partnerships and communicating with credibility. The first point for any institution seeking change would be that of addressing the issue of what should be the focus of CSR/sustainability education based on the realities of the context.

As a starting point for any institution, there needs to be an articulation of the goal of CSR/sustainability education. There has to be some clarity about where the institution is headed with its plan. Some institutions have gone as far as embedding this in their strategic pillars and vision statement as a way of demonstrating the seriousness of their resolve. Institutions will be at different points when they set out for this journey, which should be seen as a point in a continuum. Having a structure to manage sustainability initiatives is very critical. The role of a CSR/Sustainability Officer should reside at a higher level depending on the structure of the institution. In situations where business schools are tied to the university system, this position should report to the Vice Chancellor/President while in autonomous business school structures, the Dean. This kind of strategic placement provides the necessary authority required to initiate, implement and drive sustainability initiatives.

It is imperative that the plans be worked into the strategic plan of the institution if the meaningful outcome is to be expected. Embedding the plans of the institution into strategic goals signals the seriousness and commitment to ensure that results are delivered. Institutional strategic plans outline how stated goals are going to be achieved and what activities need to be instituted to make this happen. The document is usually dynamic in the sense that it is periodically reviewed for progress made and areas of challenges in implementation. Some institutions have gone a step further by revising their vision statement to reflect a new direction toward the path of achieving sustainability.

While some institutions have adopted a course level approach, others have created standalone degree-awarding CSR/sustainability programs. Unfortunately, the critical mass is not there in emerging markets for the development of full-fledged sustainability programs since organisations are just beginning to adopt sustainability. The consideration should be on how courses can be created and embedded in existing or new courses. Sometimes it is not enough to focus on the use of courses to inculcate strong identification with sustainability principles. There should also be a focus on extracurricular activities designed to expose students to situations that will enhance and reinforce classroom instruction.

Faculty buy-in is a critical success factor, especially in situations where CSR/sustainability is embedded into existing courses. The implication is that the faculty, in most cases, will be tasked with revising the course to accommodate the added

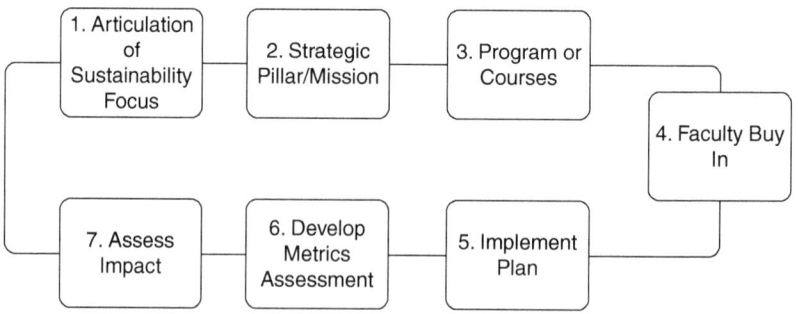

FIGURE 15.1 Embedding CSR/sustainability process
Source: Author

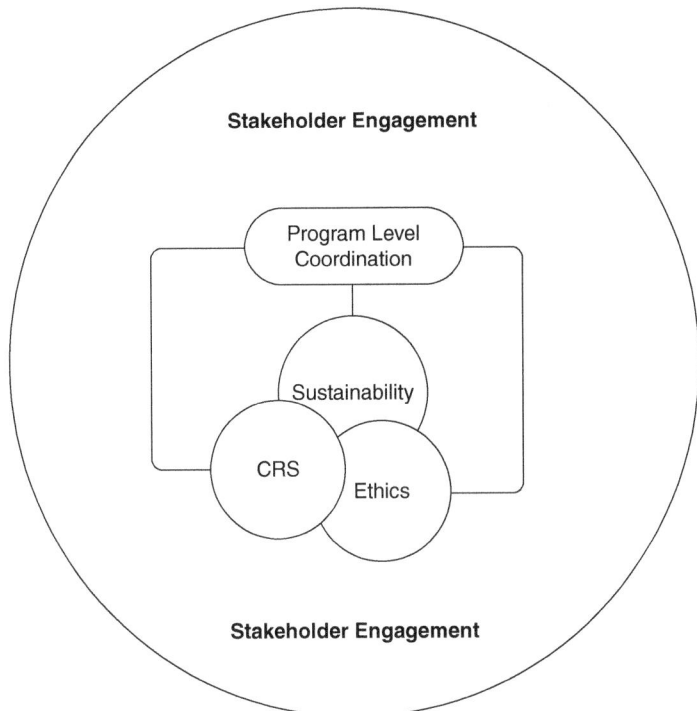

FIGURE 15.2 CSR/sustainability integration model
Source: Author

focus of the courses. Faculty will also have to teach and assess the courses. Faculty members are usually resistant to change in the way they teach so how this is introduced is critical. When new policies are part of the mission and strategic plan, it is much easier to sell to faculty. Schools should also not underestimate the innovative faculty who are pushing the envelope in ensuring the success of such initiatives. There has to be some incentive and encouragement to foster wider acceptance and development of such innovation.

The only way for business schools to ensure a move toward incorporating sustainability into the curricula is to start from a curriculum review or change perspective. A curriculum review through the Curriculum Committee will help the institution identify gaps that need to be plugged. The review process should look at students, faculty and stakeholders within and outside. The immediate business community is a good resource for teasing out ethics, CSR and sustainability challenges. Accreditation bodies are beginning to demand changes so institutions should look beyond the current guidelines to determine what should be included in the curriculum. Having an overall program coordination unit is strategic because this unit will be in a position to direct all activities and monitor implementation timeliness and success.

Developing metrics for assessing the program is important. The assessment tool should be based on the stated institutional goals. The outcome of the assessment will inform the institution whether that are succeeding or failing. Data gathered from the assessment process can be invaluable for fine tuning or making changes in order to achieve good results.

The success of any institutional program can be determined by how graduates will fare in the business world. It is important to conduct a program impact assessment at periodic intervals after graduation.

REFERENCES

Amaeshi, K., Adegbite, E., Ogbechie, C., Idemudia, U., Seny-Kan, K. A., Issa, M. and Anakwue, O. I. J. (2016). Corporate social responsibility in SMEs: a shift from philanthropy to institutional works? *Journal of business ethics*, 138(2), 385–400.

Aguinis H. and Glavas A. (2012). What we know and don't know about corporate social responsibility: a review and research agenda. *Journal of Management* 38(4), 932–968.

Baumgartner, R. J. (2014). Managing corporate sustainability and CSR: a conceptual framework combining values, strategies and instruments contributing to sustainable development. *Corporate Social Responsibility Environmental Management*, 21(5), 258–271. http://dx.doi.org/10.1002/csr.1336

Benn, S. and Dunphy, D. (2009). Action research as an approach to integrating sustainability into MBA programs: an exploratory study. *Journal of Management Education*, 33(3), 276–295.

Dickson, M.A., Eckman, M., Loker, S. and Jirousek, C. (2013). A model for sustainability education in support of the PRME. *Journal of Management Development*, 32 (3), 309–318.

Fox, T. (2004). Corporate Social Responsibility and Development: In quest of an Agenda. *Development*, 44(3), 29–36.

Haanaes, K., Reeves, M., Strengvelken, I., Audretsch, M., Kiron, D. and Kruschwitz, N. (2012). "Sustainability Nears a Tipping Point", MIT Sloan Management Review Research Report. North Hollywood. Winter 2012.

Hesselbarth, C. and Schaltegger, S. (2014). Educating change agents for sustainability – learnings from the first sustainability management Master of Business Administration, *Journal of Cleaner Production*, 62, 24–36. https://doi.org/10.1016/j.jclepro.2013.03.042.

Matten, D. and Moon, J. (2008). "Implicit" and "explicit" CSR: A conceptual framework for a comparative understanding of corporate social responsibility. *Academy of Management Review*, 33(2), 404–424.

Mwenda K. (2000). Securities Regulation and Emerging Markets: Legal and Institutional Issues for Southern and Eastern Africa. Available at http://classic.austlii.edu.au/au/journals/MurUEJL/2000/13.html accessed August 15, 2018.

Nigerian Population Commission (2018). Nigeria's current estimated population. http://population.gov.ng/accessed August 21, 2018.

Rasche, A. and Escudero, M. (2010). Leading change – the role of the principles of responsible management education, *Journal of Business and Economic Ethics*, 10(2), 244–50.

Starkey R., and Welford, R. (2001). Conclusion. Win–win revisited: A Buddhist perspective. In R. Starkey and R. Welford, eds., *Business and sustainable development*, London: Earthscan, pp. 353–357.

16

Corporate Participation in Climate Change Mitigation in Developing Countries: 'Green Capitalism' as a Tool for Sustainable Development

Kikelomo Kila

16.1 INTRODUCTION

Climate change is arguably one of the biggest environmental challenges of the modern era and its far-reaching global consequences on food and energy security, environmental sanctity and displacement of people has become a recurring theme of global concern (UNEP, 2014). Developing countries are particularly vulnerable to climate change shocks owing to their poorly developed infrastructural capacity to cope with the deleterious effects of climate change such as food shortages, displacement of populations and other environmental impacts (Ravindranath and Sathaye, 2002). Therefore, notwithstanding the relatively lower contributions of developing countries to carbon emissions globally,[1] they have a larger stake in devising ways to mitigate and adapt to climate change, as they are most vulnerable to its adverse impacts and they bear a disproportionate burden of climate change shocks.[2] Pursuing climate change mitigation policies will not only help to ensure a cleaner environment in developing countries, but also ensure the actualisation of the Sustainable Development Goals (SDGs) 2015 with particular focus on Goal 13 (climate action) and its linkage with some of the key areas of concern for developing countries encapsulated in Goals 1 – 7 of the SDGs 2015.[3]

The ever-expanding discussion on global climate change mitigation has extended beyond governments and international environmental institutions to the corporate sector. The Governor of the Bank of England, Mark Carney, in a speech to insurers and capital investment firms highlighted the growing threat of climate change to businesses and corporate organisations, especially insurance firms covering

---

[1] The top three greenhouse gas emitters – China, the European Union and the United States – contribute more than half of total global emissions, while the bottom 100 countries only account for 3.5 per cent. See World Resources Institute Carbon Emissions Map 2017, www.wri.org/blog/2017/04/interactive-chart-explains-worlds-top-10-emitters-and-how-theyve-changed accessed 9 December 2017.

[2] See the 2016 Environmental Performance Index (EPI), produced by the Yale Centre for Environmental Law & Policy, http://epi.yale.edu/ accessed 8 December 2017.

[3] Goals 1–7 cover no poverty, zero hunger, good health and well-being, quality education, gender equality, clean water and sanitation and affordable and clean energy respectively. See UN SDGs 2015 www.undp.org/content/undp/en/home/sustainable-development-goals.html accessed 9 October 2018.

properties and other utilities with the potential to be affected by natural disasters linked to climate change shocks (Clark, 2015). Carney's speech indicates the growing concerns amongst the business and finance sectors about the broader effects of climate change such as displacement of people and attendant humanitarian crisis, impacts on businesses and other commercial ventures and stoking environmental conflicts across the globe. As a result, climate change is no longer being viewed as a sole concern for governments and policymakers, but its broader effects have led to calls by major business leaders for the involvement of the business and finance sectors in climate change mitigation efforts (UNEP, 2014).

Beyond the increasing recognition of the impact of climate change on corporations' business objectives, involvement in climate change mitigation is increasingly recognised as part of the CSR of corporations (Idemudia, 2011) and the inclusion of environmental goals in the CSR agenda of corporations has become an integral way of making a contribution to improving the governance, social, ethical, labour and environmental conditions of the developing countries in which they operate, while remaining sensitive to prevailing religious, historical and cultural contexts (Visser et al., 2007).

In an ideal situation, therefore, corporations, as important stakeholders in climate change and SDG goals, will be active contributors to climate change mitigation efforts, through financial investments, without the need for any form of legal compulsion or prescriptive regulatory requirements. However, there is a general apathy among corporations towards investing in climate change mitigation projects, particularly in developing countries, as they tend to focus on profit and economic motives at the expense of climate change goals (Rowlands, 2000). For instance, for several decades after the elevation of climate change concerns into the international limelight in the 1980s, the major multinational oil corporations, led by Exxon Mobil, denounced any move towards instituting stricter regulations of carbon emissions, worried about its impacts on the costs of production and profits (Ans Kolka and David Levy, 2001). This focus on capitalist objectives to the detriment of environmental sanctity underlies the response of corporations to climate change concerns for the past decades.

For developing countries, the challenge of minimising corporate capitalist pursuits at environmental expenses is even tougher owing to the lack of strong regulatory frameworks and lack of political will to effectively control the excesses of these corporations (Eaton, 2011). Not only are the developing countries unable to regulate such huge and powerful organisations, but they are often obliged to lower existing regulatory standards, a race to the bottom destined to boosting domestic competitiveness for foreign investments (Rwabizambuga, 2007). In recent times, however, there is an increasing amount of literature espousing the concept of green capitalism which focuses on the possibility of restructuring capitalism to incorporate environmental criteria (Pulver, 2007) and ensuring profitable corporate action on climate change (Foster and York, 2004; Mol and Buttel, 2002). While wary of the potential 'greenwashing'[4] of corporate investments to appear environmentally compliant, the shift towards incorporating environmental objectives in capitalist pursuits can steer corporations in the direction of environmental sustainability and the achievement of the SDGs in developing countries.

This chapter analyses the role of corporations in the achievement of the SDGs in developing countries through investments in climate change mitigation. It discusses the contributions corporations make to the growing climate change concern globally and why developing countries often bear the brunt of corporate apathy to environmental concerns. It examines the concept of green capitalism and how it can become a veritable tool for corporations to improve their green credentials and commitment to CSR in developing countries and in doing so assist developing countries to achieve the SDGs. The chapter argues that while the weak regulatory frameworks in developing countries encourages corporations to adopt capitalist pursuits at the expense of environmental objectives, green capitalism allows corporations to merge capitalist pursuits with environmental objectives in a manner that enables these corporations to be more environmentally friendly without minimising their profits. However, to prevent the potential for 'greenwashing', developing countries should adopt more cooperative climate policies and less adversarial climate policies. While the former involves corporations in the climate policy framework as integral stakeholders, the latter seeks to use strict regulatory measures to compel corporations to invest in climate change mitigation and raises the potential for the corporations to adopt environmental rhetoric in cosmetic compliance with the regulatory measures without any real 'real change' in firm operations or real time benefits to achievement of the SDGs.

The chapter is divided into three sections. The first section sets the scene by examining the definition of developing countries within the context of the discussions in this chapter relying on the criteria set out by the International Monetary Fund (IMF), the United Nations Development Programme (UNDP) and the World Bank. The second section builds on the first by examining the role of corporations in the global climate change debate and the extent of corporate involvement in climate change issues in developing countries. The third section analyses the green capitalism concept and its impact on the pursuit of SDG goals in developing countries.

16.2 DEFINING DEVELOPING COUNTRIES WITHIN THE SDGS FRAMEWORK

While 'developing countries' is often used as a convenient label for countries with poor socioeconomic and infrastructural conditions, it is not a definitive description of the actual level of development of countries referenced. As the United Nations

---

[4] 'Greenwashing' refers to the tendency of corporations to adopt an environmental rhetoric to cover up ongoing environmentally destructive practices.

states, 'the designations "developed" and "developing" are intended for statistical convenience and do not necessarily express a judgement about the stage reached by a particular country or area in the development process' (UN, 2011).

As a descriptive label, 'developing countries' is also not a term uniformly employed by key international institutions like the IMF, UNDP and World Bank, as different terms are employed by these bodies to reference countries within certain brackets of socioeconomic and infrastructural development (Nielsen, 2011). While the IMF uses the term 'emerging and developing countries', UNDP uses 'developing countries' and the World Bank uses 'low-income and low-middle-income countries' (IMF, 2018; UNDP, 2018; World Bank, 2018).

In determining the criteria for classifying countries within these brackets, the UNDP relies on the Human Development Index (HDI) – countries below 75 per cent in the HDI distribution are regarded as developing countries (UNDP, 2018); the World Bank relies on Gross National Income (GNI) per capita – countries with less than US \$6,000 GNI per capita are regarded as low-income and middle-income countries (World Bank, 2018). IMF does not rely on any explicit criteria but uses relative, flexible criteria in determining 'emerging and developing countries' which rely on the annual economic and infrastructural performance of a country within specified periods (IMPF, 2018).

As a result of the different criteria used by these organisations, the countries classified as 'developing countries' (or similar nomenclature) are not the same and a number of countries that are excluded from this classification by one organisation are included in the classification by the other. While 149 countries are classified as 'developing countries' by the UNDP, only 85 countries fall under the 'low and middle income' classification by the World Bank. The IMF, on the other hand, lists 155 countries under its 'developing countries' classification, including 70 countries that do not fall within the World Bank classification and 6 countries that do not fall under the UNDP classification. The biggest area of variance in the classification is in Europe where the different standards lead to different results regarding the classification of countries like Bulgaria, Hungary, Poland and Romania, for instance, that are excluded from the 'developing countries' classification by the World Bank and UNDP but included by the IMF. In addition, 10 European countries included in this classification by the UNDP are excluded from the category by the World Bank.[5]

The reason for this disparity can be attributed to the nature of the classification standard employed. Generally, developing countries have four key challenges in common – high levels of poverty (low income); human resources weakness, economic instability and infrastructural underdevelopment (UN, 2018; Fialho and Van Bergeijk, 2017). By restricting its classification to GNI per capita, the World Bank's classification criteria focus on only one of the general features of developing

---

[5]   Albania, Azerbaija, Belarus, Bosnia, Georgia, Kazakhstan, Montenegro, Serbia, Macedonia and Turkey.

countries – low income levels – and is, therefore, the most restrictive, resulting in having the fewest numbers of countries within the classification. The IMF, on the other hand, has the broadest criteria encompassing a wider range of common challenges facing developing countries and its classification is, therefore, more reflective of the grouping of countries within the 'developing countries' category.

This lack of uniform standards for referencing developing countries undermines effective international development study as appropriate classification serves an analytic and operational purpose. Analytically, classification helps to understand and disentangle problems in an increasingly complex and heterogeneous world: how and why do countries differ in their developmental achievements and pro- cesses? Operationally, classifications are important for evidence based differential treatment of groups of countries: which kind of country gets what conditions and what resources? (Fialho and Van Bergeijk, 2017). For instance, the implementation of the common but differentiated responsibilities in respect of climate change obligations under international instruments like the Kyoto Protocol, 1992 is broadly based on the bifurcation of developed and developing countries in the global arena. As a result, the 39 countries listed in Annex B of the Kyoto Protocol commitments to limit or reduce quantified carbon emissions are all 'developed countries or upper and middle-income countries' within the World Bank and UNDP classifications. The few amongst them that fall within the IMF 'developing countries' classification – e.g. Romania, Poland, Hungary and Bulgaria – are all indicated in Annex B as countries 'that are undergoing the process of transition to a market economy'.

The United Nations Framework Convention on Climate Change (UNFCCC) also emphasises the differentiated nature of obligations on developing countries by making voluntary some of the commitments to climate change mitigation, financing and projects in relation to the global carbon emission reduction projects (see Article 12(4) for instance). This approach was also adopted in the Paris Climate Change Agreement 2015 which, in its preamble, acknowledged the unique importance of accommodating the 'specific needs and special circumstances of developing country parties'. Article 9 of the Paris Agreement encapsulates this approach by providing for 'developed country parties shall provide financial resources to assist developing country parties with respect to both mitigation and adaptation in continuation of their existing obligations under the Convention'. The classification of a country within the 'developing country' bracket is, therefore, an important step in the analysis of its obligations in relation to sustainability and other environmental concerns under the international legal regime (Sarvajayakesavalu, 2015).

Within the SDG framework, a significant number of the SDGs address the core challenges facing developing countries, particularly Goals 1–10 covering the most pressing challenges of hunger, health, inequality, income and infrastructures (UN, 2015). Developing countries are, therefore, central to the SDGs framework and addressing these goals in developing countries is vital to the achievement of the SDGs as developing countries is 'the battleground where the Sustainable

Development Goals will be won or lost' (UNCTAD, 2018). In its 2015 Stakeholders Forum on the SDGs, the UN acknowledged that 'some of the individual goals and targets have been particularly shaped and calibrated to express the needs and aspirations of developing countries; and others express the responsibilities of the developed world to assist the development process in the developing world' (UN, 2015).

To appropriately encapsulate the 'developing countries' category, it is necessary to adopt the IMF classification for its broad and flexible criteria encompassing the various indices underlying the 'developing countries' classification including the economic, human, environmental and infrastructural factors. Thus, the 155 countries within the IMF categorisation are adopted as representing the developing countries category within the context of this chapter. Because this classification includes all countries within several continents, it is easier to identify the category by the continents rather than listing the individual countries. In this context, 'developing countries' refer to all of – Africa; Asia excluding Japan, Singapore and South Korea; Central America and the Caribbean's; Oceania excluding Australia and New Zealand and parts of Europe.

This categorisation makes it easier to understand the scope of the discussions in relation to corporate involvement in achievement of the SDGs within developing countries, as the attitude of corporations to the SDGs and other sustainability issues within these countries is influenced by the common challenges facing these countries such as low income, weak regulatory and institutional capacities and particularly economic vulnerability and human resources weaknesses.

16.3 CORPORATIONS AND THE SUSTAINABILITY CHALLENGE IN DEVELOPING COUNTRIES

In developing countries, issues with corporate participation in environmental sustainability stem from two major problems – general corporate apathy to climate change matters, and a glaring lack of legal regulations of corporate activities with respect to sustainability. Corporate apathy to sustainability efforts is a more significant problem in developing countries because weak legal and regulatory systems ensure that these corporations are likely to go unaccountable. Moreover, there is a glaring disparity in transnational treatment of sustainability objectives by corporations in developed and developing countries (Ong, 2015). While corporations in developed countries are subjected to stricter regulatory standards, which are regularly enforced, developing countries usually lack the means to strictly enforce regulatory standards on corporations, particularly the large multinational corporations with huge financial budgets operating in areas vital to the economic survival of these countries (Ong, 2015). The Volkswagen scandal, for instance, which sent ripples across the corporate sector in the USA, Europe and other Western countries and resulted in severe repercussions for the culprit, is a common occurrence in developing countries with no outrage or repercussions for the culprits (Bill & Melinda Gates Foundation, 2016).

In developing countries, these corporate obstructionist activities are compounded by regulatory weaknesses as revealed in different factual situations. For instance, the Koko Toxic Waste Dump in Nigeria in 1988 which resulted in the mass dumping of toxic waste imported from Europe in a small village in the Niger Delta region of Nigeria was the result of regulatory inaction by the environmental agency in Nigeria which failed to prevent the multinational company responsible from carrying out such dumping (Amao, 2011). Also, Nigerian regulatory authorities declined to act despite evidence that the local franchisee of the global multinational, Coca Cola, was selling beverages containing very high levels of benzoic acid preservative within Nigeria (Giuliani and Macchi, 2014). Also, in Cote D'Ivoire, the dumping of harmful waste by a multinational company (Trafigura) which caused personal injuries and environmental damage was facilitated by the country's inefficient regulatory institutions and occurred after several other countries refused to permit Trafigura to offload the toxic waste (Amnesty International, 2006). In Turkey, Akyildiz (2006) examined the Eurogold/Normandy Mining Company's activities in the country and how its disregard for regulatory controls negatively impacts the country's carbon emissions strategies for curbing climate change impacts.

Even where legal regulations are in place to impose standards on corporations in respect of their contributions to sustainability, there is a general proclivity of corporations to undercut such legal regulations and adopt obstructionist positions within national and international legal regimes. Recent incidents such as the Volkswagen Emissions Scandal in 2015, the Exxon Mobil climate change suppression scandal in the United States and the wanton flaring of gas by the multinational oil corporations in Nigeria are pointers to the obstructionist role of corporations in climate change mitigation efforts. The Volkswagen Emission scandal broke in 2015 revealing the deliberate development and installation of a software by Volkswagen car manufacturer in their cars to understate the actual level of carbon emissions made by their cars and thus mislead the environmental regulators in the USA and European Union and enable the company's cars to emit much more carbon into the atmosphere than reported in their official disclosures (Hotten, 2017). This action undermined legal efforts to cut down on carbon emissions by cars and was done to maximise profits by the company at the expense of climate change mitigation efforts.

The availability of fiscal mechanisms such as climate bonds, which combine economic benefits for corporations with climate change mitigation should be an avenue for corporations to wholeheartedly invest in climate change mitigation. The Climate Bonds Initiative estimates that more than US$100 billion can be raised from climate bonds annually, which can be invested in climate change mitigation projects around the globe to shore up the shortfalls in financial contributions from states (Climate Bonds Initiative, 2014). Voluntary and self-regulatory guidelines can be instituted by corporations to harmonise such investments in climate change without any need for legal intervention by the state and its regulatory apparatus.

Some of the broader effects of climate change which specifically affect corporations include the rising costs of production and insurance of assets owing to threats to properties by climate change-induced natural disasters, increased governmental regulation and restrictions based on climate change mitigation efforts, and costs of adapting to environmentally friendly activities such as fuel-switching to cleaner energy sources (UN, 2015). Mark Carney's speech, therefore, also serves to awaken the consciousness of business leaders towards the contemporary realities of the link between climate change and the business/financial sector and the need for proactive involvement of the corporate sector in global efforts towards tackling the climate change problem.

To buttress this point, the CEO of Unilever, one of the world's largest multinational corporations involved in a variety of consumer goods, confirmed in an interview in 2014 that natural disasters linked to climate change cost his company about US$330 million a year (Catanoso, 2014). Consequently, corporations, as an integral part of the private sector stakeholder forum, have an important role to play in tackling the climate change concern, particularly through investments in cleaner energy sources and other climate change mitigation projects such as renewable energy projects and carbon capture and storage projects. Therefore, while government and policymakers around the globe grapple with the legal and policy responses to the climate change problem, as epitomised by the Paris Change Climate Agreement of 2015, corporations contribute to climate change mitigation efforts through financial investments in mitigation projects and other financial mechanisms that help to achieve a transition to a low-carbon, greener society (UNFCCC-COP 21, 2015). In this vein, the United Nations Environmental Programme (UNEP) instituted programmes seeking partnership with corporations in designing financial systems that will enable effective contribution of the corporate sector to climate change mitigation, through innovative fiscal mechanisms like climate bonds (UNEP, 2015). Climate bonds, also known as green bonds, are bonds issued by financial institutions which are exclusively ringfenced for investing in climate change and other environmental projects. Their attractiveness to corporations is the opportunity they present to reap economic rewards from the bonds while contributing to climate change and environmental protection projects (Reichelt and Davies, 2015).

The non-committal attitude of corporations to climate change in developing countries is further accentuated by the disproportionate impacts of climate change in developing countries. The World Bank states that the poorest people in developing countries are the worst affected by climate change shocks even though these developing countries contribute the least to climate change causes (World Bank, 2014).[6] As a result, developing countries have even more reasons to impose stricter

---

[6]   Historically, developed countries contributed 79 per cent of the carbon emissions from 1850 to 2011.

standards on corporations with regard to their activities and investments in climate change.

Notwithstanding this corporate attitude, corporations control substantial technological, financial and organisational resources which, if applied appropriately, could play a major role in contributing to sustainability through climate change mitigation and carbon emissions projects (Rugman and Verbeke, 2000). Importantly, seeing the focus on capitalist pursuits that exists within corporations, business opportunities exist for them to seize possible economic opportunities arising from the climate issue by reducing risks and costs, anticipating regulation, developing green capabilities through new products or markets and strategic behaviour vis-à-vis competitors (Kolka and Levy, 2001). In essence, corporations can demonstrate a business case for sustainable development by ensuring the 'convergence between commercial interest and environmental imperative' (Anderson and Leal, 1991) in a form of green capitalism or what Prudham (2009) refers to as 'a mash-up of environmentalism with capitalism'.

16.4 GREEN CAPITALISM AND CORPORATE INVOLVEMENT IN SUSTAINABILITY

Capitalism is the bedrock of the free market enterprise in the modern world and has profit-maximisation as its iron-clad objective (Smith, 2015). As global market enterprise grows and expands, corporations increasingly seek out new avenues for investments and instruments that guarantee the best profit returns and fewer risks (Watts, 2002). In the aftermath of the global financial crisis of 2008, corporations began looking for means to diversify their investment portfolios from volatile stocks but still guarantee profit returns. This period coincided with the increasing awareness of the financial imperatives for achieving global sustainability through investment in climate change mitigation and other environmental sustainability projects (Tienhaara, 2013).

The growing climate change concern at the international level created a form of 'ecological crisis' which corporations capitalised upon to commodify environmental and other ecological resources into investment portfolios with profit-making targets. Sullivan (2015) argues that capitalism thrives on crisis and the ecological crisis arising from these climate change mitigation pressures is itself generating crisis in the global economy; and that this ecological crisis itself has become a major new frontier of value creation and capitalist accumulation. Criticising corporate incursion into ecological services, Sullivan argues that 'economic exploitation and the profit motive, in driving production and transformed consumption of "natural resources", is causing and contributing to ecological crisis'. He cited the Climate Exchanges in London and Chicago as examples of the rush by corporations to commodify and trade in ecological goods. He based his opposition to green capitalism on the grounds that payments for the environmental services produced by nature's labour do not go to the environment itself, but to whoever is able to capture this newly priced value. This argument forms the platform upon which the major objections to green capitalism are based (Schnaiberg, Pellow and Weinberg, 2002; Klein, 2008).

The involvement of corporations in ecological services and commodification of sustainability goods is generally referred to as green capitalism, which is an introduction of capitalist structures, objectives and frameworks into the pursuit of environmental sustainability through the provision of capital investments in sustainability projects. The major objective originally focused on the profit returns, but over time, corporations began incorporating such ventures within their CSR portfolios as part of their contributions to environmental sustainability within their areas of operations, particularly relating to their contributions to climate change mitigation (Bulkeley and Newell, 2015).

Green capitalism can be described as 'nominally free markets and market-based instruments, enclosures of various kinds, and capital investment and entrepreneurial innovation, all aimed at redressing environmental problems (however defined and measured)' (Prudham, 2009). Also referred to as 'market environmentalism', it encapsulates the wide range of modern financial and investment tools that corporations utilise in channelling financial investments into sustainability projects including environmental projects (broadly defined) and climate change mitigation projects (Friedmann, 2005). Foster and York (2004) consider it the modern dominant corporate way of linking environmental health with economic development, while it is also considered a way of ensuring profitable corporate action in the face of climate change (Pulver, 2007).

Green capitalism ensures that capital flows from corporate vaults are available to finance the wide range of sustainability projects that societies and governments consider essential to meeting the various sustainability objectives (Mol and Buttel, 2002). However, the aim of this capital flow into sustainability projects is often to provide profit returns to the corporate investors and not necessarily out of altruistic social goals by the corporations. This profit-making goal has caused green capitalism to be viewed as the commodification of environmental goods and a modern form of converting the environment into a capitalist tool. Smith (2015) considers green capitalism an oxymoron, arguing that

> the project of sustainable capitalism was misconceived and doomed from the start because maximizing profit and saving the planet are inherently in conflict and cannot be systematically aligned even if, here and there, they might coincide for a moment. That's because under capitalism, CEOs and corporate boards are not responsible to society, they're responsible to private shareholders. CEOs can embrace environmentalism so long as this increases profits. But saving the world requires that the pursuit of profits be systematically subordinated to ecological concerns: For example, the science says that to save the humans, we have to drastically cut fossil fuel consumption, even close down industries like coal. But

no corporate board can sacrifice earnings to save the humans because to do so would be to risk shareholder flight or worse. I claim that profit-maximization is an iron rule of capitalism, a rule that trumps all else, and this sets the limits to ecological reform – and not the other way around as green capitalism theorists supposed.

In a way, green capitalism appears to bring together two antagonistic notions; while environmental sustainability prioritises the health of the ecosphere, and focuses on curbing greenhouse gases and preserving biodiversity; capitalism, on the other hand, focuses on production and accumulation of goods and services for economic ends, treating the environmental goods and the natural environment as mere inputs to economic goals. Nevertheless, Smith (2015)'s analysis of the unsavoury role of capitalism in 'saving the planet' overlooks the critical process of ecological systems that capitalism impacts and the ever-evolving manner in which environmental goods and processes have come to rely on financial investments from the private sector to thrive in the absence of available public resources. Also, Smith's argument overlooks the increasing pressure on businesses to serve social and environmental goals through CSR activities in order to maintain their brand and appeal to an increasingly environmentally conscious society (Ramesh et al., 2018).

This socio-environmental pressure means that, contrary to Smith's analysis, corporations often have to pursue environmental sustainability goals even where it affects their profit bottom line in the short term. This 'contested dynamics of the economy-environment interface' was referred to as an 'environment contestation approach' by Pulver (2009). Pulver argues that the 'environment contestation approach' explains the move by corporations to differentiate their business from their competitors by incorporating contemporary social and environmental concerns into their business objectives. He argued that this explained the move by British Petroleum (BP) and Royal Dutch Shell to break away from the consensus of international oil corporations towards fossil fuel dependence when, in 1996, both oil giants announced their support for increased regulatory steps to cut down fossil fuel dependence, which was detrimental to the business of the oil companies (Pulver, 2009: p. 45).

In recent times, this environment contestation approach has proven a reliable explanation for the behaviour of corporations towards environmental and sustainability objectives. Corporations currently strive to outdo their competitors by imbibing environmental goals as a way of improving their brand name by improving its green credentials (Ramesh et al., 2018). For instance, Greenpeace has listed a number of vehicle manufacturers that have pledged to phase out fossil-fuel reliant cars in favour of 100 per cent electric cars by a specified timeline (Thaysen, 2018). Also, a number of corporations including Starbucks, American Airlines etc. have committed to ditching plastic straws in view of their deleterious impacts on marine biology and conservationists' efforts to clean up the oceans.[7] Admittedly, these actions by the corporations may not significantly impact on their financial bottom line – as the alternatives they are switching to will not likely be more expensive – but it is a pointer towards the effectiveness of the environment contestation approach on influencing corporate decisions in favour of environmental sustainability and not mere profitability.

Smith (2015)'s claim that 'no corporate board can sacrifice earnings to save the humans because to do so would be to risk shareholder flight or worse' is largely correct, as corporations will not sacrifice their economic bottom line for environmental sustainability. But Smith's assumption that corporate investment in sustainability always comes down to these mutually exclusive goals is faulty. Firstly, corporate profitability and environmental sustainability are not always mutually exclusive goals. In fact, the very essence of green capitalism is to create various frameworks where these two goals can mutually co-exist and be accommodated under one platform (York, Rosa and Dietz, 2003). This is often created within frameworks that commodify environmental objectives – sustainability goals such as climate change mitigation projects, investments in cleaner energy etc. – and convert them into tradable units whereby trading in these commodities results in increased investments in the environmental objectives, which in turn results in actualisation of these objectives. An illustration of how such schemes work can be seen in the EU Emission Trading Scheme which commodifies carbon emissions and converts them into trading units amongst carbon-emitting corporations within specific industries.[8] The aim is the reduction in carbon emissions which advances the climate change mitigation goal of capping carbon emissions at specified limits.

The corporate participants in these schemes derive financial benefits from the scheme because of the manner in which the frameworks are set up with capitalist structures. The objection to the profiting of corporations from the commodification of environmental objectives is purely idealistic and based on moral foundations, not on any practical impacts this has on the fulfilment of the environmental goals. While it is understandable to frown upon corporate profiteering from environmental objectives, where there is tangible evidence that this structure helps in the achievement of the environmental and sustainability objectives, then such idealistic objections become impractical and naïve. This leads directly to the second flaw in Smith (2015)'s argument – overlooking the relevance of green capitalism in achieving sustainability goals. Achieving sustainability objectives requires adequate funding and the lack of available financing for sustainability projects is one of the major hindrances to achieving these objectives. The UN estimates that in order to achieve Goal 13 of the SDGs, for instance, there is the need to 'jointly mobilise over

---

[7] 'These 8 Companies Are Ditching Plastic Straws. Here's How They Are Replacing Them' http://fortune.com/2018/07/11/ditching-plastic-straws-replacements/ accessed 26 October 2018.

[8] For details of how the EU Emission Trading Scheme works, see 'EU Emissions Trading System (EU ETS)' https://ec.europa.eu/clima/policies/ets_en accessed 2 November 2018.

$100 billion annually by 2020 from all sources to address the needs of developing countries in the context of meaningful mitigation actions and transparency on implementation and fully operationalize the Green Climate Fund through its capitalization as soon as possible' (UN SDGs, 2015).

As can be seen here, developing countries are the focus of most funding requirements geared towards achieving the SDGs because of the common challenge these countries face from high poverty, low income, economic vulnerability and infrastructural underdevelopment. While developed countries are expected to contribute significant part of this fund, there is a realisation that achieving this target is not feasible without the involvement of the public sector. Many developed countries pledge huge sums to fighting climate change and other environmental concerns but the release of such funds is usually caught up in bureaucratic red tape or lack of political will of the pledging government (Ong, 2015). Also, international politics and geopolitical considerations often affect the release of such funds to tackle climate change issues, for instance, the pulling out of the USA from the Paris Climate Change Agreement has significantly affected its pledged contribution to global climate change mitigation.

As noted by the head of the UN's Green Climate Fund in September 2015, the USA and other countries have failed to pay up their US$5.8 billion worth of outstanding pledges towards climate change mitigation.[9] Even other corporate pledges by leading personalities around the world are not guaranteed to be redeemed and cannot therefore form the basis of any sustainable long-term climate change mitigation planning. For instance, a US$3 billion pledge by Richard Branson of Virgin Group of companies in 2006 has yet to be redeemed, almost eight years after the pledge.[10]

Consequently, private sector involvement in environmental sustainability is indispensable for the actualisation of these objectives. Article 6(8) of the Paris Climate Change Agreement 2015 also recognises the importance of enhancing private sector involvement in funding of climate change objectives. Because corporations are private entities, with their main obligation being towards profit returns to their shareholders, they cannot be expected to contribute to environmental sustainability in any long-term, sustainable way without economic returns to the corporations. On the other hand, their obligation to the society means they cannot exploit the environment for their economic benefits without commensurate benefits to environmental sustainability. In this regard, green capitalism integrates the goals of

---

[9] 'Climate change: western states fail to fulfil pledges to developing countries', *The Guardian*, 4 September 2015 www.theguardian.com/global-development-professionals-network/2015/sep/04/climate-change-western-states-fail-to-fulfil-pledges-to-developing-countries accessed 10 March 2016.

[10] 'Richard Branson failed to deliver on $3bn climate change pledge', *The Guardian*, 13 September 2014 www.theguardian.com/environment/2014/sep/13/richard-branson-failed-climate-change-pledge accessed 15 March 2016.

environmental sustainability and economic benefits in one framework, leading to
the actualisation of both objectives (Wallis, 2009).

In developing countries, green capitalism is of great importance in achieving
sustainability as it provides the vital capital flows which these countries require to
invest in sustainability projects, rather than rely on financial handouts from developed countries with the attached conditions, real or perceived (Niyonkuru, 2016 and
Apodaca, 2017). The manner in which the green capitalist tools are structured
ensures that they are insulated from the political control of the developing countries,
are available for long-term strategic investments in sustainability projects and guard
against misappropriation of the investments for other non-sustainability projects by
developing countries eager to address other areas of developmental concerns.

To buttress this point, it is necessary to briefly examine a major green capitalism
tool for sustainable projects in developing countries – green bonds.

16.5 GREEN BONDS AND SUSTAINABLE CORPORATE INVESTMENTS

Green bonds are theme bonds[11] with environmental goals as the specific theme of
such bonds. The concept of 'green bonds' arose from the increased recognition of
the need to protect the environment and mitigate climate change impact on humans
and the society by financing specific projects targeted at achieving environmental
objectives. They are also known as climate bonds[12] or green infrastructure bonds in
that they are targeted at climate change mitigation projects or environmentally
friendly infrastructural projects and proceeds of the bond are 'ringfenced' for financing climate change or renewable energy and other environmental projects. The
main objective of green bonds is achieving a triple bottom line of economic,
environmental and societal benefits in that the bonds satisfy the needs of issuers,
bondholders and the environment (Climate Bonds Initiative, 2015).

Green bonds are an increasingly attractive mechanism for both private and public
sector organisations to raise capital for projects, assets or other activities that benefit
the economy, environment and society. The global green bond market is growing
rapidly. Before 2007, green bonds did not exist, but fast forward to 2014 and the value
of green bonds stood at over US$37 billion dollars, a figure which tripled by 2015
with total green bonds issued standing at US$100 billion dollars (Climate Bonds
Initiative, 2015). Thus, from a modest US$0.81 billion dollars' worth of green bonds
issued in 2007 when the European Investment Bank (EIB) first issued its Climate
Awareness Bond (the first publicly issued green bonds) to a record US$100 billion
dollars' worth of green bonds issued in 2015, the green bonds market has grown
prodigiously within the space of eight years and has become one of the leading

[11]   Theme bonds are bonds issued for investments in marked-out areas seen as important to the issuer and
      that have the same credit risk and returns profile as standards bonds.
[12]   Although a slight distinction exists between green bonds and climate bonds – climate bonds are
      a subset of green bonds, while green bonds encompass all environmentally friendly bonds.

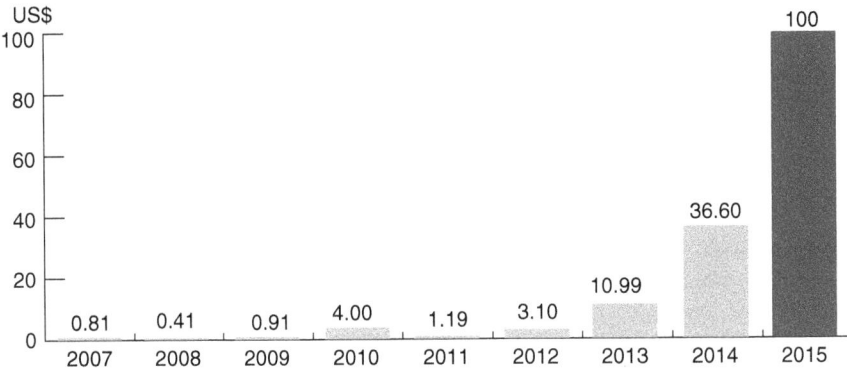

FIGURE 16.1 Green bonds market growth 2007–15
Source: KPMG 2015

sources of funding for environmental projects and particularly climate change projects.

As shown in Figure 16.1, although the green bonds market witnessed inconsistency and fluctuations between 2007 and 2012 owing to uncertainty by financial institutions over its effectiveness and financial returns, from 2012 onwards, it has experienced a consistent and astronomical rise in its value and this reflects the confidence of major financial institutions in its economic and environmental effectiveness, leading to a significant rise in the number of financial institutions partaking in the initiative and a consequent rise in the total value of green bonds issued annually. From 2012 onwards, the total worth of green bonds issued has tripled annually – from US$3.10 billion in 2012 to US$10.99 billion in 2013; from US$10.99 billion in 2013 to US$36.60 billion in 2014; and from US$36.60 billion in 2014 to over US$100 billion in 2015 (Environmental Finance, 2015) and this trend is projected to be maintained over the coming decade as more financial institutions and government bodies join the growing community of green bonds issuers (KPMG, 2015).

Financing climate change mitigation through the green bonds initiative has the benefit of ensuring sustainability of funds for the longer term. Most green bonds are issued for lengthy terms ranging between 30 to 100 years and this ensures that funds are available for long-term climate change mitigation planning. The invested funds are immediately available for application of the proceeds to planned projects and in light of the popularity of green bonds and the eagerness of investors to subscribe to them, issuers of green bonds can embark on long-term projects which can significantly impact on the environment and reduce carbon emissions (for climate bonds).

In addition, green bonds are well structured in corporate finance ways and are therefore non-government reliant with the attendant bureaucracies involved in release of funds by governments. Also, utilising green bonds to tackle climate change enhances an issuer's and investor's reputation as a stakeholder in the financing of climate change mitigation. Issuing and subscribing to green bonds is an effective way for organisations to demonstrate their green credentials by showing commitment to the environment and improving their environmental performance.

16.6 LIMITATIONS ON GREEN CORPORATE INVESTMENTS IN SUSTAINABILITY

While corporate involvement in sustainability projects in developing countries is desirable for actualisation of the SDGs, there are two areas of caution necessary for managing the capitalist tendencies of corporations in sustainability issues – the tendency for so-called greenwashing and the over-reliance on market forces for sustainability growth within developing countries.

Greenwashing is a real issue in the involvement of corporations in sustainability issues. Greenwashing is the process of presenting a project as 'green' to attract funding or commendation, whereas the project actually has very minimal environmental sustainability benefits (Grene, 2015). In a short form, it's a form of green window dressing and the green outlook portrayed in respect of the project represents nothing more than mere symbolic gestures. While 'greenwashers' can refer to companies that adopt an environmental rhetoric to cover up ongoing environmentally destructive practices (Pulver, 2009) or companies that surface paint projects with a green outlook when in real fact no real green benefits accrue from such project; it also includes situations where corporations appear to change their attitude towards sustainability in their business dealings, but no real strategic changes are made in their procedures, products and services.

For instance, subsequent to Shell's 1996 break away from the oil companies' consensus opposing regulatory reduction in fossil fuel usages, Greenpeace's investigation accused the company of changing 'its attitude' but not the company's 'business trajectory'. 'Shell's renewable energy investments are miniscule compared to its fossil fuel expenditure' (Greenpeace, 1998: p. 2). Greenpeace's investigations revealed that 'Shell's new renewable investment of $500 million over five years is only 0.4% of its total annual business turnover of US$123.8 billion' and that 'for every $1 Shell plans to spend on renewables, it currently spends $77 per year on oil and gas'. Similarly, BP that professed its commitment to green investments alongside Shell, spent more than 50 times its US $20 million renewable energy investment on capital expenditures and acquisitions related to oil and gas exploration (BP, 1998). In these instances, the investment in sustainability by these corporations is far outweighed by their investments in environmentally injurious projects, thus cancelling out the benefits from their sustainability investments.

Greenwashing is a challenge for corporations because of the strong capitalist leanings of corporations, which sees them prioritise projects with better profit returns to the company even while striving to be environmentally compliant by investing in sustainable projects. This limits the extent that corporations can invest their capital in sustainable projects, especially since these sustainable projects, e.g. renewable energy projects, are not likely to have the same economic returns as the conflicting fossil fuel project, for instance.

The solution to the potential for greenwashing is tighter regulation of corporate involvement in sustainability through a mix of prescriptive and other fiscal measures that sets the benchmark for corporate investments in environmentally beneficial projects while incentivising such investments by making them more financially attractive to the corporations, e.g. through tax breaks for investments in specific sectors (Bulkeley and Newell, 2015). Such cooperative regulatory policies are essential in developing countries owing to the lack of strong regulatory enforcement mechanisms, especially against the powerful multinational corporations. Ensuring the cooperative participation of the corporations in regulating their involvement in sustainability investment is likely to be more productive than an adversarial regulatory approach which will either be difficult for these developing countries to enforce – thereby rendering it ineffective – or, where stringently pursued, could potentially drive away the corporations from investing in these jurisdictions, an outcome the developing countries seek to avoid (Sarvajayakesavalu, 2015).

Another limitation on green capitalism is the need to prevent an over-reliance of developing countries on market-forces or market-based approaches to achieving sustainability. There is a tendency for developing countries to become 'regulatory states' by their increased reliance on markets and private providers (corporations) to deliver traditional government services, and the accompanying increase in the use by the state of regulatory techniques to control and influence that service delivery (Windholz, 2018).

To discourage what Levi-Faur (2012) termed 'regulatory capitalism' – the takeover of regulatory functions by capitalist institutions – focus should always be on public sector investments in sustainability policies and projects with corporate involvement merely serving a complementary role in achieving the sustainability objectives. This approach is endorsed in the Paris Climate Change Agreement, 2015 which acknowledges the importance of integrated, holistic and balanced non-market approaches to implementing sustainable development projects and policies and encourages developing countries to develop frameworks for non-market approaches to sustainable development.[13]

By doing so, developing countries can ensure they keep control of their public services institutions in relation to sustainability projects and ensure adequate regulation of corporations' involvement in sustainable development projects.

16.7 CONCLUSION

Corporations are capitalist institutions that thrive on wealth creation and maximisation of profits for their owners and shareholders. Often, this profit-making goal

---

[13] Arts. 6(8) and (9).

conflicts with other moral objectives including the preservation of the environment and advancement of sustainable development goals. Developing countries are particularly vulnerable to the relentless capitalist structures of corporations owing to their weak regulatory and enforcement frameworks for controlling the manner of corporate involvement in environmental projects.

However, with the increasing availability of green capitalist tools such as green bonds, the economic interests of corporations can be integrated with the sustainable development goals in developing countries in a symbiotic mutually beneficial manner, ensuring the availability of much-needed capital investment from corporations to fill the loophole in public funding while creating another avenue for corporations to expand their wealth creation and accumulation tools. While this can be viewed as a commodification of ecological goods for capitalist objectives, its practical relevance in advancing the sustainable development objectives oversha-dow its seeming moral repugnance.

While the focus in this chapter has been on environmental sustainability and climate change mitigation projects, the analysis has wider implications for the other SDGs, particularly in core areas where developing countries share common chal-lenges – hunger, health, low income, inequality, labour, clean water and sustainable cities and communities. Corporations can commodify various aspects of these SDGs and introduce investment tools that will see to the provision of these services in developing countries by the corporations in a manner that reaps financial rewards for the corporations. For instance, Goal 7 (affordable and clean energy) and Goal 9 (industry, innovation and infrastructure) of the SDGs can be turned into investment tools in partnership with the public authorities in a public private partnership (PPP) model whereby corporations invest in building necessary infrastructures/clean energy facilities, manage them for a certain number of years and reap the profits before handing them over to the public authorities.

In the end, green capitalism, where adequately managed and regulated, can be a veritable model for the actualisation of the SDGs in developing countries while allowing public funds to be focused on other areas of pressing developmental needs and creating a viable business platform for corporations.

REFERENCES

Akyildiz, F. (2006). The Failure of Multinational Companies in Developing Countries in Sharing Environmental Responsibilities: The Case of Turkey. *Social Responsibility Journal* 2(2), 12.
Amao, O. (2011). *Corporate Social Responsibility, Human Rights and the Law: Multinational Corporations in Developing Countries*, London and New York: Routledge.
Anderson, T. L. and Leal, D. R. (1991). *Free Market Environmentalism*, New York: Palgrave Macmillan.
Apodaca, C. 'Foreign Aid as Foreign Policy Tool' (2017). *Oxford Research Encyclopedia of Foreign Policy Analysis*. http://doi: 10.1093/acrefore/9780190228637.013.332.

Bill & Melinda Gates Foundation (2011). Ethics left behind as drug trials soar in developing countries, *The Guardian* (London, 4 July) www.theguardian.com/global-development /2011/jul/04/ethics-left-behing-drug-trials-developing accessed 6 April 2016.

Barrett, P. (2016). Can ExxonMobil Be Found Liable for Misleading the Public on Climate Change? *Bloomberg* (New York, 7 September) www.bloomberg.com/news/articles/ 2016–09-07/will-exxonmobil-have-to-pay-for-misleading-the-public-on-climate-change accessed 12 May 2017.

Bulkeley, H. and Newell, P. (2015). *Governing Climate Change* 2nd ed. Routledge.

Catanoso, J. (2014) UNILEVER CEO: We need to do more to fight climate change, *Business Insider* (New York, 8 December) http://uk.businessinsider.com/unilever-ceo-speaks-on-climate-change-2014–12?r=us&ir=t accessed 28 January 2017.

Clark, P. (2015) Mark Carney warns investors face 'huge' climate change losses, *Financial Times* (London, 29 September), www.ft.com/content/622de3da-66e6-11e5-97d0-1456a776a4f5 accessed 15 October 2016.

Climate Bonds Initiative, 'Year 2014 Green Bonds Final Report' (Washington, 2015) www .climatebonds.net/year-2014-green-bonds-final-report-0 accessed 15 March 2016.

Dimitris Tsitsiragos (2016). 'Climate Change is a threat- and an opportunity- for the private sector' (World Bank, 13 January) www.worldbank.org/en/news/opinion/2016/01/13/climate-change-is-a-threat-and-an-opportunity–for-the-private-sector accessed 20 May 2016.

Eaton, J. (1997). The Nigerian Tragedy, Environmental Regulation of Transnational Corporations, and the Human Right to a Healthy Environment. *Boston University International Law Journal* 15, 261.

Environmental Finance (2015). 'Green bond market to grow by $100bn this year', www .environmental-finance.com/content/news/green-bond-market-expected-to-grow-by -$100bn-this-year-after-smashing-records-in-2014.html accessed 15 October 2015.

Fialho, D. and Van Bergeijk, Peter A. G. (2017). The Proliferation of Developing Country Classifications. *Journal of Development Studies* 53(1).

Foster, J. B. and York, R. (2004). Political Economy and Environmental Crisis. *Organization & Environment*, 17(3), 293–5.

Friedmann H. (2005). From Colonialism to Green Capitalism: Social Movements and Emergence of Food Regimes. *Research in Rural Sociology and Development* 11, 227–64.

Giuliani, E. and Macchi, C. (2014). Multinational Corporations' economic and Human Rights Impacts on Developing Countries: A Review and Research Agenda. *Cambridge Journal of Economics* 38(2), 479–517.

Grene, S. 'The Dark Side of Green Bonds', www.ft.com/cms/s/0/16bd9a48-0f76-11e5-b968 -0014fcabdco.html#axzz42b8cbfzw accessed 13 March 2015.

Hall, S. (2015). Exxon Knew about Climate Change almost 40 years ago, *Scientific American* (Washington, 26 October) www.scientificamerican.com/article/exxon-knew-about-climate -change-almost-40-years-ago/ accessed 12 May 2017.

Hotten, R. (2015). Volkswagen: The scandal explained, *BBC* (London, 10 December), www .bbc.co.uk/news/business-34324772 accessed 20 March 2017.

Idemudia, U. 'Corporate social responsibility and developing countries moving the critical CSR research agenda in Africa forward' (2011) Progress in Development Studies.

Klein, N. (2008). *The Shock Doctrine: The Rise of Disaster Capitalism*, London: Penguin.

Kolk, A. and Levy, D. L. (2001).Winds of Change: Corporate Strategy, Climate change and Oil Multinationals. *European Management Journal* 19(5), 501–9.

KPMG 'International 2015 Report'.

Levi-Faur, D. (2012). From 'Big Government' to 'Big Governance' in D. Levi-Faur ed., *The Oxford Handbook of Governance*, Oxford: Oxford University Press,pp. 3, 5.

Mol, A. and Buttel, F., eds., (2002). *The Environmental State under Pressure*, Amsterdam: Elsevier Science.

Mol, A. and Spaargaren, G. (2000). Ecological modernization theory in debate: A review. *Environmental Politics*, 9(1), 17–49.

Nielsen, L. Classifications of Countries Based on Their Level of Development: How It Is Done and How It Could Be Done, IMF Working Paper Strategy, Policy, and Review Department WP/11/31 February 2011.

Niyonkuru, F. (2016). Failure of Foreign Aid in Developing Countries: A Quest for Alternatives. *Business and Economics Journal*, 7, 231.

Ong, D. (2015). Regulating Environmental Responsibility for the Multinational Oil Industry: Continuing Challenges for International Law. *International Journal of Law in Context*, 11(2), 153–73.

Prudham, S. (2009). Pimping Climate Change: Richard Branson, Global Warming, and the Performance of Green Capitalism. *Environment and Planning*, 41, 1594–613.

Pulver, S. (2007). Making Sense of Corporate Environmentalism: An Environmental Contestation Approach to Analyzing the Causes and Consequences of the Climate Change Policy Split in the Oil Industry. *Organization & Environment*, 20(1), 44–83.

Ravindranath N. H. and Sathaye J. A. (2002). Climate Change and Developing Countries. In *Climate Change and Developing Countries. Advances in Global Change Research*, Dordecht: Kluwer Academic Publishers.

Reichelt, H. and Davies, C. (2015) 'Getting to Know the Green Bond Market', World Bank Treasury Department Publication, available at http://treasury.worldbank.org/cmd/pdf/get tingtoknowthegreenbondmarket_pensionfundservice.pdf accessed 23 March 2015.

Rowlands I. H. (2000). Beauty and the Beast? BP's and Exxon's Positions on Global Climate Change. *Environment and Planning*, 18, 339–54.

Rwabizambuga, A. (2007). Negotiating Corporate Social Responsibility Policies and Practices in Developing Countries: An Examination of the Experiences from the Nigerian Oil Sector. *Business and Society Review*, 112(3), 407–30.

Sarvajayakesavalu, S. (2015). Addressing Challenges of Developing Countries in Implementing Five Priorities for Sustainable Development Goals. *Ecosystem Health and Sustainability* 1(7), 1–4.

Schnaiberg, A., Pellow, D. N. and Weinberg, A. (2002). The Treadmill of Production and the Environmental State. In A. Mol and F. Buttel, eds., *The environmental state under pressure* Oxford: Elsevier Science.

Smith, R. (2015). *Green Capitalism: The God that Failed*, British Columbia, Canada: World Economics Association Book Series.

Sullivan, S. 'Green capitalism, and the cultural poverty of constructing nature as service provider' http://eprints.bbk.ac.uk/6016/1/Sullivan,_radical_anthropology_2009.pdf, accessed 21 July 2019.

Thaysen, M. (2018). 'A handy list of car companies that are ditching diesel', Greenpeace, 5 October, available at www.greenpeace.org.uk/handy-list-car-companies-ditching-diesel/ accessed 25 October 2018.

Tienhaara, K. (2013). Varieties of Green Capitalism: Economy and Environment in the Wake of the Global Financial Crisis. *Environmental Politics*, 23(2), 187–204.

UNEP (2015). 'Inquiry into the Design of a Sustainable Financial System; Policy Innovations for a Green Economy'.

UNEP (2014). 'Financial Institutions Taking Action on Climate Change' (Inquiry into the Design of a Sustainable Financial System).

United Nations Framework Convention on Climate Change (UNFCCC) (2015). Conference of the Parties, Twenty-first session, Paris, 30 November to 11 December 2015: Draft decision

-/CP.21 FCCC/CP/2015/L.9/Rev.1 https://unfccc.int/resource/docs/2015/cop21/eng/l09r01 .pdf accessed 15 January 2017.

Valdmanis R. and Smith, G. (2016). 'Several companies that claim to support climate-change initiatives are actually funding climate sceptics', Business Insider (*Reuters*, 6 September) available at http://uk.businessinsider.com/r-us-companies-tout-climate-policies-fund-climate-skeptics-2016-9 accessed 1 June 2017.

Visser, W. (2008). Corporate Social Responsibility in Developing Countries. *The Oxford Handbook of Corporate Social Responsibility*.

Wallis, V. (2009). Beyond 'Green Capitalism'. *Monthly Review*, 61(9), 32–48.

Watts M. (2002).Green Capitalism, Green Governmentality. *American Behavioral Scientist*, 45, 1313–17.

Windholz, E. (2018). *Governing through Regulation: Public Policy, Regulation and the Law*, New York, London: Routledge.

World Bank (2014). 'Climate Change affects the poorest in developing countries' (Washington, 3 March). www.worldbank.org/en/news/feature/2014/03/03/climate-change-affects-poorest-developing-countries accessed 23 May 2016.

World Economic Outlook (2018). *World Economic Outlook October* (2018). Challenges to Steady Growth, October, pp. 134–5.

World Energy Council (2016). 'Defining Measures to Accelerate the Energy Transition' (World Energy Trilemma 2016, March). www.worldenergy.org/wp-content/uploads/2016/ 05/World-Energy-Trilemma_full-report_2016_web.pdf accessed 20 October 2017.

York, R., Rosa, E. and Dietz, T. (2003). Footprints on the Earth: The Environmental Consequences of Modernity. *American Sociological Review*, 279–300.

17

Ethics Issues in Outsourcing to Emerging Markets: Theoretical Perspectives and Practices

Rose Hiquet and Won-Yong Oh

17.1 INTRODUCTION

Offshoring (i.e. international outsourcing), which refers to the practice of multi-national corporations (MNCs) from developed countries migrating business processes overseas to reduce costs without sacrificing product and service quality (Venkatraman, 2004), has become increasingly popular. Emerging markets, such as countries in Asia, Africa and Latin America, have been regarded as attractive locations for offshoring (Javalgi et al., 2009). Driven by the pressures to reduce operating costs and the challenges of competition, MNCs across the globe have continued to outsource their value chain activities such as manufacturing, business processing and customer services. In spite of the economic benefits of offshoring, scholars have pointed out various ethical issues related to international outsourcing (e.g. Feng et al., 2017), such as poor working conditions, child labour and environmental pollution.

As shown in the case of Foxconn's employee suicide scandals (Xu and Li, 2013), MNCs should be cautious when choosing outsourcing location in countries where the regulations regarding the rights of workers and the protection of the natural environment are different from those in their home countries. Furthermore, MNCs should be aware that offshoring productions in developing economies are also involved with offshoring pollution (i.e. the transfer of toxic emission from the domestic plants to plants abroad) (Li and Zhou, 2017).

These ethical issues are especially concerning, given that MNCs' outsourcing locations are usually in emerging countries where institutional environments are generally weak (Adobor, 2012). However, due to increasing institutional and social pressures stemming from various stakeholders (Waddock et al., 2002), MNCs have begun to integrate the concept of corporate social responsibility (CSR) into their offshoring activities (e.g. Oh et al., 2015). As a result, MNCs began to make changes to be more responsible: setting up ethical initiatives for MNCs such as the Ethical Trading Initiative (ETI), implementing a code of conduct for the suppliers and collaborating with NGOs. Even though such initiatives have contributed to establishing more responsible business practices, they also have invited criticism because those initiatives have limitations in resolving ethical concerns completely (Lund-Thomsen and Lindgreen, 2014). As a result, 'local stakeholders seem to increasingly perceive MNCs as a source of social and environmental problems' (Zhao et al., 2014: p. 655).

Therefore, in this chapter, we first review the theoretical perspectives relevant to ethical issues of offshore outsourcing to analyse MNCs' motivations for being socially and environmentally responsible. Then, based on these various theoretical views, we propose a number of guidelines for sustainable offshoring practices for MNCs. By doing so, we hope that this chapter will help to address the issue of how to establish ethical practices in MNCs' offshoring operations.

17.2 THEORETICAL BACKGROUND

Prior literatures have suggested a number of theoretical perspectives for analyzing MNCs' motivations for being socially and environmentally responsible: (1) institutional, (2) instrumental and (3) normative. The institutional perspective argues that firms act responsibly in order to enhance and maintain their legitimacy. The instrumental perspective suggests that firms try to gain financial benefits (e.g. increasing revenue or profits) from socially responsible actions. The normative perspective argues that firms engage in responsible decisionmaking mostly based on ethical considerations and moral principles.

17.2.1 *Institutional Perspective*

One of the main tenets of institutional theory is that organisations try to maintain and increase their legitimacy vis-à-vis their environment (DiMaggio and Powell, 1983). Thus, when MNCs lower their production costs by outsourcing overseas, they need to do so in a legitimate way. Otherwise, MNCs run the risks of damaging their legitimacy in a way that will be detrimental to their organisational image and reputation (Kostova and Zaheer, 1999). In a related vein, institutional theory focuses on the concept of isomorphism (e.g. Oh and Barker, 2018), which refers to the mechanism by which organisations become similar by imitating each other.

Organisations are exposed to isomorphic pressures, and such pressures drive organisations to be similar (e.g. industry norms) in order to gain legitimacy (e.g. Ji and Oh, 2014). The prior literature (e.g. Scott 1995) has identified three distinct sources of institutional pressure: (1) coercive, (2) isomorphic and (3) normative. Coercive pressure corresponds to the various legal and regulatory requirements that demand compliance with an ethical standard. The coercive pressure is thus enforced by local and international laws and regulations in offshoring operations. Isomorphism is the mimetic pressure that is largely imposed by peer groups, such as competitors. In particular, the mimetic pressure is more prevalent in environments that are characterized by a high level of uncertainty. For instance, if MNCs conduct offshoring activities in an area where the institutional environment is not well-defined (e.g. there is a lack of clarity regarding regulation and ethical standards), they may follow the norms that are defined and adhered to by other MNCs in that geographic area. The last type of isomorphic pressure is the normative pressure, which refers to the similar approaches taken, and attitudes held by professional groups, associations and accreditations. In the offshoring context, membership of the Ethical Trading Initiative and the Fairtrade Certification Mark licensed by Fairtrade organisations are examples of this normative pressure.

Organisations *strategically* respond to these various types of institutional pressures, thus leading to different organisational behaviours (Oliver, 1991). For example, some organisations proactively conform to the institutional pressures, while others resist them. In this sense, the institutional perspective allows for the identification of which pressures drive MNCs to behave ethically and how MNCs respond differently to such pressures (Carrigan et al., 2017; Pedersen and Gwozdz, 2014). For instance, some MNCs in the clothing industry can conform and thus comply with ethical standards by signing up for the ETI Base Code, an internationally recognized set of labour standards. On the contrary, other MNCs can resist such pressure by not signing up for the ETI Base Code. Some firms deliberately mislead stakeholders by engaging in 'greenwashing' (Testa et al., 2018), that is, they adopt responsible practices only at the surface level, while disguising their real level of commitment to ethical standards.

Most of the studies of offshoring that draw on the institutional perspective have highlighted that MNCs are subjected to both global and local pressures, thereby inducing complex responses in their activities (Jamali and Neville, 2011; Marano and Kostova 2016; Yang and Rivers, 2009). Therefore, it is important for government, policymakers, NGOs and industry associations to create institutional pressures for more responsible practices in MNCs' offshoring operations.

17.2.2 *Instrumental Perspective*

The premise of the instrumental view is that socially and environmentally responsible actions are economic value-creating levers (Chang et al., 2013; Scherer and Palazzo, 2011). Even though there is no clear consensus on whether ethical decisionmaking in foreign markets is truly beneficial to MNCs, previous studies (e.g. Oh et al., 2015) have focused on how to maximize the economic benefits from being a responsible corporate citizen. For MNCs, this view assumes that firms should align their social initiatives with their global strategy in order to create economic value and strengthen their competitive advantage. Therefore, the CSR practices of MNCs and their ability to maximize the economic benefits of CSR are likely to vary depending on the strategic orientations they pursue (e.g. cost leadership) and their market position in their host countries (Husted and Allen, 2006; Park et al., 2015; Rathert, 2016; Young and Thyil, 2014).

Prior studies have described how firms utilize their corporate citizenship as an instrumental vehicle. Socially and environmentally responsible actions may aim at transforming the value chain activities (Park et al., 2015) to improve operational efficiency. Also, firms use corporate philanthropy strategically (e.g. MNCs donate to local charities or NGOs to increase brand awareness) to enhance their competitive position (Porter and Kramer, 2002). As such, according to the instrumental perspective, 'strategic CSR' takes the form of various activities, but the ultimate objectives remain the same: using social and environmental initiatives as a vehicle for increasing wealth creation and developing a competitive advantage over time.

17.2.3 *Normative Perspective*

The normative perspective stipulates that MNCs act responsibly because of intrinsic ethical and moral motives, namely, that MNC are socially responsible because it is the right thing to do. This view is grounded in ethical theories (Gonzalez-Perez, 2013) and its advocates have attempted to justify it through arguments based on various theories, such as Libertarian theories, with their concepts of freedom, rights and consent (Freeman and Philips, 2002), Kantian capitalism (Bowie, 1991) and theories of property and distributive justice (Donaldson and Preston, 1995).

Other scholars (e.g. Sheehy, 2015), while acknowledging the value of the normative perspective, have criticized it for lacking a clear and solid theoretical framework, arguing that consequently, the concept is ill defined and difficult to apply in business contexts. Likewise, other studies (e.g. Bondy et al., 2012; Yin and Jamali, 2016) have expressed concern that this perspective is limited in its ability to explain why and how MNCs act responsibly. In most cases, MNCs do not act responsibly solely based on a normative foundation (e.g. ethical values and moral standards).

17.2.4 *Implications*

These theoretical views suggest different implications for developing guidelines for sustainable offshoring. Institutional theory focuses on institutional pressures to describe why MNCs may establish ethical operations in offshoring (Scott, 1995). Thus, it is important to create institutional mechanisms to encourage MNCs to maintain ethical standards in their offshoring operations. For example, setting environmental, health and safety laws and regulations (i.e. coercive pressure); creating ethical practices as an industry standard (i.e. mimetic pressure); and encouraging an accreditation process for professional groups and associations (i.e. normative pressure) can improve the ethical concerns about offshoring.

The instrumental perspective suggests that MNCs will act responsibly if such engagement leads to improved financial outcomes. Thus, according to this view, it is important to create incentive mechanisms that lead to economic benefits. For example, customer boycott movements contributed to changes in consumers' perceptions of the fast fashion industry (e.g. H&M, Zara and Uniqlo), where a business model relies heavily on offshoring production in emerging economies (Hiquet et al., 2018). As a result, a few companies in the fast fashion industry began to take steps to establish ethical practices in their foreign operations and did so because the ethical production of clothes was seen as necessary to generate sales.

The normative view suggests that MNCs will act responsibly because it is the ethically and morally correct thing to do. While the key objective of offshoring is to reduce operating costs, MNCs should realize that offshoring is also a matter of human rights. For example, in 2013, the collapse of the Rana Plaza building in Bangladesh (Neate, 2014) was an example that received global attention on unsafe and unhealthy working environments in the supply-chain activities of MNCs. In this tragic accident, 1,138 garment workers lost their lives and more than 2,000 were injured. The building, largely used to manufacture fashion products, was constructed with materials of sub-standard quality and extra floors were added without proper permits. Even though there was evidence that the building was unsafe, employees were still forced to work there. This example shows that MNCs, as corporate citizens of society, should recognize their fundamental responsibility to meet ethical standards in their offshoring practices.

17.3 GUIDELINES FOR SUSTAINABLE PRACTICE

Based on the review of these theoretical perspectives, we provide practical guidelines for both MNCs and policymakers. These guidelines include (1) re-designing governance, (2) establishing industry-level actions and (3) developing institutional capacity.

17.3.1 Re-designing Governance

Previous studies on the relationship between MNCs and their suppliers (e.g. Chang et al., 2017; Gimenez and Sierra, 2013; O'Rourke, 2014; Paulraj et al., 2017; Vurro et al., 2009) suggest that designing appropriate governance structures, both public and private, is important to ensure sustainability. Public (i.e. governmental) forms of economic governance have been criticized because regulatory and legal standards at the international level are generally weak, and enforcing them has been challenging (Mayer and Gereffi, 2010), especially in emerging economies where most offshoring activities are conducted.

As such, it is necessary to strengthen private governance such as company codes of conduct, process standards, product certifications and other voluntary, nongovernmental forms of regulation (Mayer and Gereffi, 2010). Such types of private governance have proliferated as a response to social pressures driven by globalization and a perceived inadequacy of governmental involvement in emerging economies.

However, a number of scholars (e.g. Bartley, 2007; Locke et al., 2009; Vogel, 2007) have argued that there are some limitations to the ability of private governance to make a social and environmental impact. In the context of offshoring, these weaknesses mainly stem from the limited incentives to enforce and adopt private governance mechanisms in its value chain activities (e.g. Oh et al., 2018).

Thus, it is necessary to improve some forms of public governance globally; at the same time, private governance should be linked to broad multi-stakeholder institutions in order to increase its impact. From the MNCs' perspective, it is necessary to be proactive in setting up and participating in various forms of public and private governance mechanisms. Developing a form of governance that ensures sustainability implies not only considering the direct relationship between MNCs and their suppliers (i.e. vertical governance) but also taking into account relationships within the industrial cluster (i.e. horizontal governance) (Gereffi and Lee, 2016). Thus, it is critical for MNCs to play a more active role in raising the ethical standards within the outsourcing networks through both their relationships with suppliers and their relationships with other organisations operating in the same industrial cluster. For instance, Microsoft (1) ensures that its suppliers embrace high ethical standards through their supplier code of conduct (Microsoft, 2016) and (2) acts within its industrial cluster through its membership in the Global Network Initiative (GNI).

17.3.2 *Establishing Industry-Level Action*

In emerging economies, MNCs face major business challenges due to a lack of state regulation (Braithwaite and Drahos, 2000). In such cases, industry-level initiatives complement weak governance, thus filling the so-called 'governance gaps'. As such, industry-level action may be a form of private governance, as we discussed in the previous section. Industry-level action can play an important role in ensuring responsibility in offshoring activities. Establishing industry-level action is particularly important because each MNC has different stakeholders with different perspectives on offshoring.

Firm-level action is beneficial, but it creates heterogeneity among suppliers (e.g. offshoring companies) because suppliers act in accordance with the policies of each individual firm. In contrast, industry-level action contributes to the development of common ethical standards across the entire industry, resulting in clear guidelines and standards for offshoring companies. The idea of collaborative action at the industry level is effective as it addresses what public governance cannot solve with formal laws and regulations. Specifically, it has been argued that 'most of the issues we face today are neither owned nor solved by individual stakeholders anymore. With growing interdependence comes a growing need to search for collaborative approaches' (Van Huijstee, 2012: p. 8).

For example, Baumann-Pauly and colleagues (2017) investigated how multi-stakeholder initiatives (MSI) can actually lead to the setting up and maintaining of common ethical standards across an industry. Their analysis relied on the case illustrations of the Fair Labour Association (FLA) and the Global Network Initiative (GNI), both MSIs that focus on human rights. As such, these initiatives fill governance gaps between corporate practices and human rights. Therefore, MNCs should engage in a cooperative approach at the industry level by including all relevant stakeholders in the cooperative paradigm (Lund-Thomsen and Lindgreen, 2014).

17.3.3 *Developing Institutional Capacity*

MNCs from developed countries should provide resources and capacity to local communities to support efforts to lessen ethical violations in emerging markets. For example, MNCs can provide financial assistance, physical resources and education to outsourcing companies and their communities. Ultimately, this support will enhance the outsourcing company's capabilities. In the long run, this may also benefit MNCs by improving the productivity, satisfaction and sustainability of the outsourcing company. In order to support institutional capacity, MNCs should shift their paradigm from one of *compliance* to one of *cooperation*. This paradigm shift would mean that MNCs not only ask their suppliers to improve the working conditions of their employees and environmental standards (i.e. compliance), but also that they would proactively provide resources and support to their suppliers to make those improvements (i.e. cooperation).

Furthermore, institutional capacity can take different forms, such as financial resources, employee training and management support (Lund-Thomsen and Lindgreen, 2014). Some support is tangible (e.g. physical and financial assets), often labelled *hard capabilities*. However, scholars (e.g. Langaas et al., 2007) have highlighted the equal importance of intangible support for institutional capacity building. The intangible support consists of social skills, tacit knowledge and other forms of non-physical assets such as norms, values and culture. These are also called *soft capabilities*. For example, LG Electronics provides CSR risk management training to the suppliers that have been identified through their CSR risk assessment (LG Electronics, 2016).

In particular, a number of studies related to offshoring (e.g. Ding et al., 2018; de Vargas Mores et al., 2018) have emphasized the importance of 'collaboration capacity'. Collaboration capacity is defined as 'understanding each other, exchanging information, drawing and sharing group values, solving problems, and new reasoning' while working together (van Hoof and Thiell, 2014: p. 239). For example, offshoring manufacturers can implement pollution reduction more efficiently if MNCs with a high level of collaboration capacity provide the necessary technical support. As such, MNCs should change their paradigm from one based on individual effort to one based on joint actions to achieve common objectives that have a positive social and environmental impact.

17.4 DISCUSSION

Emerging economies have continued to be an attractive destination for MNCs' offshore outsourcing (Urry, 2014). The symbiosis between MNCs from developed countries and outsourcing contractors in emerging economies should be sustained without neglecting the ethical and moral concerns, which are increasing regarding the social and environmental conditions in which products are manufactured and the services that are offered. With workers in emerging economies being forced to work under highly exploitative and unsafe conditions (e.g. the massive collapse of Bangladesh's Rana Plaza factory in 2013), there have been an increasing number of voices arguing that MNCs should strive to establish ethical standards in their offshoring practices. As a result, MNCs have begun to realize the social and environmental challenges they face, as mimetic, coercive and normative pressures increase. Also, stakeholders reward companies that respond to such pressures proactively, and punish those that fail to achieve legitimacy and act irresponsibly (Ogunfowora et al., 2018). As such, MNCs should realize that economic motivations (i.e. cost-saving efforts) and ethical motivations are not substitutes; rather, they can complement each other.

In order to alleviate ethical concerns, we provide different sets of practices: re-designing governance, establishing industry-level action and developing institutional capacity. These practices are commonly based on the 'cooperative paradigm' (Lund-Thomsen and Lindgreen, 2014), which emphasizes closer cooperation and frequent interaction between the MNCs and outsourcing parties. Specifically, the re-design of governance implies not only the combination of vertical governance (i.e. governance of the relationships between MNCs and their suppliers) and horizontal governance (i.e. governance of the relationships within the industrial cluster), but also a joint form of governance between private and public. The establishment of industry-level action involves the participation of all the relevant stakeholders in the industries in which MNCs operate. The development of institutional capacity presumes that MNCs are developmentally inclined in that they are willing to improve their ethical standards by providing support for outsourcing companies and local communities, instead of expecting outsourcing companies to shoulder the costs.

17.5 LIMITATIONS AND FUTURE RESEARCH

This chapter provides practical guidelines to improve ethical issues in emerging economies. However, it also has some limitations. First, there are positive impacts of offshoring in terms of corporate ethics. Venkatraman (2004, pp. 14–15) noted that offshoring is 'the creative and careful leveraging of new and available pools of skilled labour and exploiting the power of communication technologies to create new sources of competitive advantage'. For example, the economic benefits of offshoring may increase the availability of financial resources for subsequent organisational activities (e.g. investment in environmental protection).

Second, this chapter focused on the ethical issues in international markets, mostly emerging economies. However, offshoring also leads to ethical issues in the domestic markets where the MNCs' headquarters are located (i.e. mostly in developed countries). For example, the availability of comparable workforces elsewhere at a lower cost leads to the shifting of jobs from domestic markets to markets abroad. As such, offshoring has put downward pressure on job availability and workers' compensation in the home countries. The result is the creation of the ethical problem of unemployment, low wages and a failure to stimulate economic growth in the home (or domestic) economy. Future studies may benefit from exploring the ethical issues in 'domestic' markets, instead of foreign markets.

17.6 CONCLUSION

In a globalizing-localizing world, ethical principles apply not only to developed countries, but equally to host countries in emerging economies where offshoring is conducted. As such, MNCs have a social and environmental responsibility to customers, suppliers, governments and the public in both the home and host countries. As a response, numerous approaches to establishing ethical operations in offshoring have been discussed in academic writing, but in practice, have not been implemented appropriately. To overcome this problem, in this chapter, we have proposed a set of guidelines for both MNCs and policymakers. These guidelines consist of three types of measures: (1) re-designing governance, (2) establishing industry-level actions and (3) developing institutional capacity. MNCs need to create more responsible relationships with their outsourcing companies. In order to do so, it is important to develop both public (government) and private governance mechanisms such as a corporate code of conduct and product certification (i.e. re-designing governance). Also, MNCs should engage in collective action at the industry level to address ethical issues, rather than at the level of the individual firm (i.e. establishing industry-level action). Lastly, MNCs should provide resources and capacity to outsourcing companies and local communities that may contribute to alleviating ethical concerns in emerging markets (i.e. developing institutional capacity). We hope these practical guidelines can provide some insights that will help contribute to changes in the practices of MNCs' offshoring in emerging economies.

REFERENCES

Adobor, H. (2012). Ethical issues in outsourcing: The case of contract medical research and the global pharmaceutical industry. *Journal of Business Ethics*, 105(2), 239–55.
Bartley, T. (2007). Institutional emergence in an era of globalization: The rise of transnational private regulation of labour and environmental conditions. *American Journal of Sociology*, 113(2), 297–351.

Baumann-Pauly, D. Nolan, J. van Heerden, A. and Samway, M. (2017). Industry-specific multi-stakeholder initiatives that govern corporate human rights standards: Legitimacy assessments of the Fair Labor Association and the Global Network Initiative. *Journal of Business Ethics*, 143(4), 771–87.

Bondy, K. Moon, J. and Matten, D. (2012). An institution of corporate social responsibility (CSR) in multi-national corporations (MNCs): Form and implications. *Journal of Business Ethics*, 111(2), 281–99.

Bowie, N. (1991). New directions in corporate social responsibility. *Business Horizons*, 34(4), 56–65.

Braithwaite, J. and Drahos, P. (2000). *Global business regulation*. Cambridge: Cambridge University Press.

Carrigan, M. McEachern, M. Moraes, C. and Bosangit, C. (2017). The fine jewellery industry: Corporate responsibility challenges and institutional forces facing SMEs. *Journal of Business Ethics*, 143(4), 681–99.

Chang, Y. K. Oh, W. Y. and Messersmith, J. G. (2013). Translating corporate social performance into financial performance: Exploring the moderating role of high-performance work practices. *The International Journal of Human Resource Management*, 24(19), 3738–56.

Chang, Y. K. Oh, W. Y. Park, J. H. and Jang, M. G. (2017). Exploring the relationship between board characteristics and CSR: Empirical evidence from Korea. *Journal of Business Ethics*, 140(2), 225–42.

de Vargas Mores, G. Finocchio, C. P. S. Barichello, R. and Pedrozo, E. A. (2018). Sustainability and innovation in the Brazilian supply chain of green plastic. *Journal of Cleaner Production*, 177, 12–18.

DiMaggio P. J. and Powell, W. W. (1983). The iron cage revisited: Institutional isomorphism and collective rationality in organizational fields. *American Sociological Review*, 48, 147–60.

Ding, H. Huang, H. and Tang, O. (2018). Sustainable supply chain collaboration with outsourcing pollutant-reduction service in power industry. *Journal of Cleaner Production*, 186, 215–28.

Donaldson, T. and Preston, L. E. (1995). The stakeholder theory of the corporation: Concepts, evidence, and implications. *Academy of Management Review*, 20(1), 65–91.

Feng, Y. Zhu, Q. and Lai, K. H. (2017). Corporate social responsibility for supply chain management: A literature review and bibliometric analysis. *Journal of Cleaner Production*, 158, 296–307.

Freeman, R. E. and Phillips, R. A. (2002). Stakeholder theory: A libertarian defense. *Business Ethics Quarterly*, 12(3), 331–49.

Gimenez, C. and Sierra, V. (2013). Sustainable supply chains: Governance mechanisms to greening suppliers. *Journal of Business Ethics*, 116(1), 189–203.

Gereffi, G. and Lee, J. (2016). Economic and social upgrading in global value chains and industrial clusters: Why governance matters. *Journal of Business Ethics*, 133(1), 25–38.

Gonzalez-Perez, M. A. (2013). Corporate social responsibility and international business: A conceptual overview. *Advances in Sustainability and Environment*, 11, 1–35.

Hiquet, R. Brunneder, J. and Oh, W. Y. (2018). Consumer acceptance of, and resistance to, fast fashion. In M. Heuer and C. Becker-Leifhold, eds., *Eco-friendly and fair: Fast fashion and consumer behaviour*. New York: Routledge.

Husted, B. W. and Allen, D. B. (2006). Corporate social responsibility in the multinational enterprise: Strategic and institutional approaches. *Journal of International Business Studies*, 37(6), 838–49.

Jamali, D. and Neville, B. (2011). Convergence versus divergence of CSR in developing countries: An embedded multi-layered institutional lens. *Journal of Business Ethics*, 102 (4), 599–621.

Javalgi, R. R. G. Dixit, A. and Scherer, R. F. (2009). Outsourcing to emerging markets: Theoretical perspectives and policy implications. *Journal of International Management*, 15(2), 156–68.

Ji, Y. Y. and Oh, W. Y. (2014). An integrative model of diffusion and adaptation of executive pay dispersion. *Journal of Managerial Issues*, 26(1), 70–85.

Kostova, T. and Zaheer, S. (1999). Organizational legitimacy under conditions of complexity: The case of the multinational enterprise. *Academy of Management Review*, 24(1), 64–81.

Langaas, M. D., Odeck, J. and Bjorvig, K. (2007). 'The concept of institutional capacity building and review of road sector projects', Paper presented to the 23rd PIARC World Road Congress, Paris, 17–21 September.

Li, X. and Zhou, Y. M. (2017). Offshoring pollution while offshoring production? *Strategic Management Journal*, 38(11), 2310–29.

Locke, R. Amengual, M. and Mangla, A. (2009). Virtue out of necessity? Compliance, commitment, and the improvement of labor conditions in global supply chains. *Politics & Society*, 37(3), 319–51.

Lund-Thomsen, P. and Lindgreen, A. (2014). Corporate social responsibility in global value chains: Where are we now and where are we going? *Journal of Business Ethics*, 123(1), 11–22.

Marano, V. and Kostova, T. (2016). Unpacking the institutional complexity in adoption of CSR practices in multinational enterprises. *Journal of Management Studies*, 53(1), 28–54.

Mayer, F. and Gereffi, G. (2010). Regulation and economic globalization: Prospects and limits of private governance. *Business and Politics*, 12(3), 1–25.

Neate, R. (2014). Bangladesh factory collapse: Big brands urged to pay into help fund. *The Guardian* (24 February) available atwww.theguardian.com accessed 26 June 2018.

Ogunfowora, B. Stackhouse, M. and Oh, W. Y. (2018). Media depictions of CEO ethics and stakeholder support of CSR initiatives: The mediating roles of CSR motive attributions and cynicism. *Journal of Business Ethics*, 150(2), 1–16.

Oh, W. Y. and Barker III, V. L. (2018). Not all ties are equal: CEO outside directorships and strategic imitation in R&D investment. *Journal of Management*, 44(4), 1312–37.

Oh, W. Y., Chang, Y. K. and Kim, T. Y. (2018). Complementary or substitutive effects? Corporate governance mechanisms and corporate social responsibility. *Journal of Management*, 44(7), 2716–39.

Oh, W. Y., Choi, K. J. and Chang, Y. K. (2015). A new perspective on Corporate Social Responsibility for MNEs: Real options theory. In A. Camillo, ed., *Global enterprise management: New perspectives on challenges and future developments*. New York: Palgrave Macmillan, pp. 107–20.

Oliver, C. (1991). Strategic responses to institutional processes. *Academy of Management Review*, 16(1), 145–79.

O'Rourke, D. (2014). The science of sustainable supply chains. *Science*, 344(6188), 1124–27.

Park, Y. R. Song, S. Choe, S. and Baik, Y. (2015). Corporate social responsibility in international business: Illustrations from Korean and Japanese electronics MNEs in Indonesia. *Journal of Business Ethics*, 129(3), 747–61.

Paulraj, A. Chen, I. J. and Blome, C. (2017). Motives and performance outcomes of sustainable supply chain management practices: A multi-theoretical perspective. *Journal of Business Ethics*, 145(2), 239–58.

Pedersen, E. R. G. and Gwozdz, W. (2014). From resistance to opportunity-seeking: Strategic responses to institutional pressures for corporate social responsibility in the Nordic fashion industry. *Journal of Business Ethics*, 119(2), 245–64.

Porter, M. E. and Kramer, M. R. (2002). The competitive advantage of corporate philanthropy. *Harvard Business Review*, 80(12), 56–68.

Rathert, N. (2016). Strategies of legitimation: MNEs and the adoption of CSR in response to host-country institutions. *Journal of International Business Studies*, 47(7), 858–79.

Scherer, A. G. and Palazzo, G. (2011). The new political role of business in a globalized world: A review of a new perspective on CSR and its implications for the firm, governance, and democracy. *Journal of Management Studies*, 48(4), 899–931.

Scott, W. R. (1995). Introduction: Institutional theory and organizations. In W. R. Scott and S. Christensen, eds., *The institutional construction of organizations*. Thousand Oaks: Sage, pp. 11–23.

Sheehy, B. (2015). Defining CSR: Problems and solutions. *Journal of Business Ethics*, 131(3), 625–48.

Testa, F. Boiral, O. and Iraldo, F. (2018). Internalization of environmental practices and institutional complexity: Can stakeholders pressures encourage greenwashing? *Journal of Business Ethics*, 147(2), 287–307.

Urry, J. (2014). *Offshoring*. Cambridge: John Wiley & Sons.

van Hoof, B. and Thiell, M. (2014). Collaboration capacity for sustainable supply chain management: Small and medium-sized enterprises in Mexico. *Journal of Cleaner Production*, 67, 239–48.

Van Huijstee, M. (2012). Multi-stakeholder initiatives: A strategic guide for civil society organizations. Centre for Research on Multinational Organisations, Amsterdam, www.somo.nl/wp-content/uploads/2012/03/Multi-stakeholder-initiatives.pdf accessed 21 July 2019.

Venkatraman, N. V. (2004). Offshoring without guilt. *MIT Sloan Management Review*, 45(3), 14–16.

Vogel, D. (2007). *The market for virtue: The potential and limits of corporate social responsibility*, 2nd ed. Washington: Brookings Institution Press.

Vurro, C. Russo, A. and Perrini, F. (2009). Shaping sustainable value chains: Network determinants of supply chain governance models. *Journal of Business Ethics*, 90(4), 607–21.

Waddock, S. A. Bodwell, C. and Graves, S. B. (2002). Responsibility: The new business imperative. *The Academy of Management Executive*, 16(2), 132–48.

Xu, K. and Li, W. (2013). An ethical stakeholder approach to crisis communication: A case study of Foxconn's 2010 employee suicide crisis. *Journal of Business Ethics*, 117(2), 371–86.

Yang, X. and Rivers, C. (2009). Antecedents of CSR practices in MNCs' subsidiaries: A stakeholder and institutional perspective. *Journal of Business Ethics*, 86(2), 155–69.

Yin, J. and Jamali, D. (2016). Strategic corporate social responsibility of multinational companies subsidiaries in emerging markets: Evidence from China. *Long Range Planning*, 49(5), 541–58.

Young, S. and Thyil, V. (2014). Corporate social responsibility and corporate governance: Role of context in international settings. *Journal of Business Ethics*, 122(1), 1–24.

Zhao, M. Tan, J. and Park, S. H. (2014). From voids to sophistication: Institutional environment and MNC CSR crisis in emerging markets. *Journal of Business Ethics*, 122(4), 655–74.

18

Promoting Sustainability in Business and Management Education

Ijeoma Nwagwu, Chris Ogbechie and Franklin N. Ngwu

18.1 INTRODUCTION

Following the 2008 financial crisis and subsequent recession, there is a broad consensus that unethical practices contributed to the crisis and still feature in the world of today's businesses. It is clear in many cases that business leaders and entrepreneurs fail to understand their fiduciary responsibilities to care for the ecosystem on which lives and businesses depend. Not only do they enjoy the benefits of the free market, they also seem to take advantage of weak governance and institutional settings especially in developing and emerging economies (DEEs). Consequently, developing and emerging economies, in addition to the problem of unethical corporate practices, are also constrained by the challenges of nurturing the leadership necessary for sustainable and inclusive human development (Goldsmith, 2001; Hope Sr. and Chikulo, 2000; Rotberg, 2004). Unethical practices and poor leadership have contributed to large scale economic crises and unsustainable resource depletion resulting in poverty, hunger, inequality and environmental degradation in many countries.

With such increasing negative outcomes and efforts to curtail the impacts, sustainability is gradually being reckoned as a very important agenda in the corporate world and business schools. Sustainability emphasizes the purpose of business as economic advancement but with concerns for socio-environmental well-being and offers some direction towards filling the ethical gap in management education and corporate praxis. For instance, as the World Business Council for Sustainable Development (WBCSD) identifies within its Vision 2050 the desire that some 9 billion people will be able to live well and "within the limits of the planet" (Muff, 2013: p. 488; WBCSD, 2010), the efforts of the business and management education institutions in achieving such a goal need to accelerate along those lines.

Given the central role of education in advancing the sustainability agenda, there is therefore the need to properly examine how sustainability agenda and education can be embedded and promoted more deliberately in business and management education institutions in DEEs. In line with institutional theory, there is a need to understand and enhance the processes through which business and management education can be used as a vehicle to drive and instil both the awareness and practice of the sustainability agenda in DEEs. Moreover, as the educational institutions are located in DEEs, the issues, challenges, priorities and opportunities of sustainability in DEEs will be better examined and understood to enhance the required buy-in, sense of responsibility, ownership and consensus to achieve a more sustainable and inclusive economies.

The aim of this chapter therefore is to examine and further understand through the lens of institutional theory, the ways in which business schools in DEEs can be better positioned and organised to serve as the fulcrum for the lasting awareness and practice of sustainability agenda across DEEs. With a retrospective inclination, the chapter will examine the ways and strategies through which the educational institutions in DEEs have helped and can better develop, shape and monitor the views and behaviors of present and future corporate managers and entrepreneurs, to enable them to be ethical and responsible towards the society, economy and environment. It will explore possibilities for giving sustainability, responsibility and ethics more prominent role in business and management education; recognizing the context of sustainable development challenges and institutional voids in DEEs.

The remaining sections of the chapter will proceed as follows: in line with the pivotal role of educational institutions in the sustainability agenda, Section 2 will provide a brief review of the role of business and management education and then the concept of sustainability and sustainability education. Building on the sustainability education, the third section will examine the institutional theory as a framework for understanding sustainability education and how business schools can be used to further define the institutional issues. While Section 4 reexamines the roles of educational institutions in the sustainability agenda of DEEs and the pedagogical strategies that can be used in sustainability education. Section 5 provides the conclusion.

18.2 THE ROLE OF BUSINESS AND MANAGEMENT EDUCATION IN THE SUSTAINABILITY AGENDA

With the revelation that the causes of the 2008 financial crisis can be attributed among other factors to unethical practices of businesses, there is a question as to what extent are business and management education institutions effectively performing their tasks. Of particular concern is the commitment and capability of these institutions in developing and producing responsible, sustainable and ethical business managers that understand their responsibility in creating shared value for the firms and society. While business and management education institutions seem to appreciate the need to think beyond preparing leaders and managers just for business profitability and reconsider their role in enhancing the well-being of the society, it is not altogether very clear how it should be done. Besides being institutions where competencies and skills needed for effective management are delivered, business schools could play a role in aligning business with societal interests.

There is a need for a deeper appreciation and understanding that the sustainable growth of most successful economies to a large extent depends on the tripod framework and relationship of the government, the academia and the private sector. The middle position of the academia (institutions) is not accidental! It is strategic and normally protected and supported meticulously. Reason being that academia performs a kind of fiduciary duty to society. Through robust conceptual, theoretical and empirical research, academia generates the ideas and policies used by both the government and the private sector. The academic institutions and individuals are a kind of powerhouse of ideas and innovation: a guardian, protector and trustee for a better society. As they are called the citadel of learning, they are a place where all kinds of skills and human capital are trained and developed. An environment where effective and visionary leaders are identified, properly trained, molded and announced to wider society for effective utilization to achieve the common good of the society.

As the institutions have an extensive reach and profound impact on the financial and commercial domains (Weybrecht, 2015), and their students are seen as future initiators of sustainable value for business and society influencing the organisations and teams they work with (Pradini, Vervoort and Barthelmess, 2012), therefore, business and management education institutions should create learning environments to foster responsible management knowledge, skills and attitudes. Beyond training business and management students, the institutions can afford, through their faculty and diverse student groups, an environment to create much-needed knowledge, craft and test inventive ideas and solutions and present a space to have conversations about company-tailored and global challenges (Weybrecht, 2015).

The onus lies on the business and management education institutions to prepare future business leaders and equip them with skills required to drive ethical business, inclusive and sustainable development. There is a need for these institutions to contribute in rebuilding the global economy with new practices such as moving from economic growth that rests on resource consumption and biodiversity degradation to markets based on long-term value creation and the ability of business to make sustainability an easier choice for consumers and partner companies (Muff, 2013: p. 488). Arguably while performing such salvific tasks, academic institutions can be priceless resources for organisations of all sizes in their sustainable development journeys, and a proper understanding of the concept of sustainability and sustainability education are pertinent.

18.3 SUSTAINABILITY AND SUSTAINABILITY EDUCATION

Sustainability emerged as a component of corporate ethics in response to perceived public discontent over the long-term damage caused by the impact of organisational pursuits for profit maximization at the cost of workers, host community and the environment. The term sustainability is broadly defined as meeting the needs of the present generation without compromising the ability of future generations to meet their own needs (Brundtland Commission, 1987). It involves "finding a balance between economic prosperity, environmental quality, and – the element which business has tended to overlook – social justice, which moves organisations into an absolute state of sustainability" (Elkington, 1999).[1]

Sustainability is often used to describe how organisations display a sense of responsibility in managing their financial, social and environmental impacts and obligations. In this sense, it reminds businesses of their fundamental responsibilities in promoting human rights, fair labour practices, decent jobs, environment conservation, anti-corruption and more. The concept of sustainability has evolved and expanded over the years (Soderstom and Weber, 2011). As a result, sustainability is split into domains (e.g. climate change, water quality, human population growth and social inequality) and theoretical approaches (Bansal, 2005).

Of the different approaches to sustainability, a very prominent one is CSR which Sattiraju (2016) posits as a powerful tool for advancing sustainable development. Corporate social responsibility has had a long history as business ethics, but in the 1990s moved more directly into the core operations of the business, rather than looking as secondary effects of business outcomes.

Sustainability Education: Sustainability has made inroads into education broadly under terms such as Sustainability Education (SE), Education for Sustainability (EfS) and Education for Sustainable Development (ESD), being interchangeable terms describing the practice of teaching sustainability. ESD is the term most used internationally and by the United Nations. Sustainability Education is often referred to as Education for Sustainable Development (ESD). According to UNESCO (2014), "Education for Sustainable Development allows every human being to acquire the knowledge, skills, attitudes and values necessary to shape a sustainable future."

The Cloud Institute for Sustainability Education *defined* Sustainability Education as a transformative learning process that equips students, teachers and school systems with the new knowledge and ways of thinking needed to achieve economic prosperity and responsible citizenship while restoring the health of the living systems upon which our lives depend. Sustainability education utilizes applied learning models that connect real-world circumstances with the broader human concerns of environmental, economic and social systems (GEF Institute, 2018). ESD has both methodological and indeed pedagogical implications. As such, it is described as teaching, training and learning methods that enlighten, encourage and empower learners to shift their perspectives and patterns and become proactive for sustainable development. To achieve this, ESD is theorized as implying changes

---

[1] Elkington (1999): triple P (planet, people, profit).

in the way education is practiced today, and promotes competencies like critical thinking, imagining future scenarios and making decisions in a collaborative way. Arguably, there are both instrumental and intrinsic elements of ESD. It is instrumental in the sense that it is an approach through which sustainability issues are developed and communicated or taught. But it does not stop in learning or teaching ESD. There is something deeper suggesting that it is beyond just learning about sustainability. It appeals to our conscience somehow signifying or emphasizing that it is the appropriate way or approach to use in our business and individual pursuits. There is an implicit demand for ESD to be seen and appreciated from an intrinsic disposition due to its universal benefits. For ESD to be effective, it means that both the instrumental and intrinsic objectives must be robustly achieved. As educational institutions are the key platforms through which ESD is communicated, taught and instiled, it is important that all the relevant issues or factors that might enhance or constrain such institutions from achieving the expected sustainability task are properly understood and captured.

18.4 INSTITUTIONAL THEORY AS A FRAMEWORK FOR UNDERSTANDING SUSTAINABILITY EDUCATION

Institutional theory has been used extensively in several studies, showing remarkable versatility from its roots in sociology. The theory has been embraced for the platform it provides scholars to explain the influences underlying practices in organisations including influences such as culture, social environment, regulation and history, while also giving attention to resources (Baumol et al., 2009; Brunton et al., 2010). The strength of the theory is that it explains why some practices are established in an organisation without a necessary link to economic return (Glover et al., 2014; Hoffman and Jennings, 2015). Institutional theory also examines organisational forms and explains why there are homogenous features/characteristics in organisations that are within the same "organisational field." According to DiMaggio and Powell (1983), an organisational field consists of those organisations that together make up a recognized area of institutional life.

Applied to business and management education, the organisational field of business schools include students, student bodies, faculty and staff, accreditation bodies, industry (employers of labour and/or subject/contributors of knowledge), international organisations government and other regulators. This is in line with UN Principles of Responsible Management Education (PRME). Institutional theory considers organisations such as business schools as operating within a social framework of values, norms and assumptions about what makes up acceptable behavior (Carpenter and Feroz, 2001). It explains that institutional pressures create and drive isomorphism in organisations' strategies, structures and processes. By definition, "isomorphism is a constraining process that forces one unit in a population to resemble other units that face the same set of environmental conditions" (DiMaggio and Powell, 1991: p. 66).

According to Hanson (2001), organisations become more alike when they conform to institutional pressures because institutional practices are diffused throughout space and time. Hanson (2001) further stated that when the pressures become greater, there is less degree for change. As such, the factors or pressures surrounding a business school as an organisation, with all its ties that bind, is dynamic and capable of changing expectations around the observance or neglect of sustainability education.

Institutional pressures which drive isomorphism have been categorized into three: namely mimetic, coercive, normative and pressures (DiMaggio and Powell, 1983).

Mimetic Pressure: Business schools face mimetic pressure around responsible management education. What this means is that business schools tend to model their commitment on what other schools have done in this area. Mimetic isomorphism occurs when one educational organisation follows the path of another that it believes to be more successful in the eye of the public. According to Hanson (2001), the intention to mimic can be constantly encouraged and reinforced by (a) educational consultants who vigorously propagate innovation and changes across institutions, (b) academic conferences that function as marketplaces for innovations and (c) the movement by administrators between schools near and far.

A good example of the effect of mimetic pressures in the field of business and management education is when prestigious schools like the London Business School became a signatory of PRME. It legitimized the underlying agenda of the PRME movement and made it desirable, and also attractive to new adopters. Rasche and Gilbert (2015) also stated that media coverage of curriculum updates can motivate other schools to follow suit because they will come to believe that doing nothing to change may cause them to lose not only their recognition but their patronage and relevance. In July of 2007, a new framework for responsible management education was established, when traditional business school education (Rasche and Escudero, 2009) was partly blamed for the economic crisis that began in that year (because many of the people who contributed to the crisis had been educated in one way or the other by business schools). This spelt the first organised relationship between the United Nations and management education institutions (Kell and Haertle, 2011; Perry and Win, 2013; Waddock et al., 2011). These beliefs are collectively known as Principles for Responsible Management Education (PRME) (Kell and Haertle, 2011; Perry and Win, 2013; Waddock et al., 2011). The initiative had grown to more than 650 leading academic institutions from over 85 countries across the globe (UNPRME, 2017). "The level of support obtained has been judged a remarkable achievement given the speed with which institutions have been recruited and the worldwide interest in the initiative" (Perry and Win, 2013: p. 51).

PRME embodies a set of **voluntary ideals** which management institutions and programs agree to abide by in the interest of nurturing future leaders with the needed awareness, skills and proficiencies to deal with matters that business and other organisations are facing (Rasche and Escudero, 2009; Waddock et al., 2011). The mimetic actions undertaken by schools under the influence of international organisations such as PRME, CEEMAN, ABIS, AshokaU etc. demonstrate structuration, or connectedness, around a stable set of governance procedures, information sharing, interactions, contractual relationships etc. The PRME is an initiative that intends to motivate and support responsible management education through "research, engagement, and thought leadership" (Haski-Leventhal, 2014: p. 29). Further, the PRME are intended to help instruct future managers and leaders who can quite clearly link social and environmental concerns directly to business issues to nurture a more cohesive and inclusive global economy (Waddock et al., 2011). That is, it aims to develop future managers and leaders who can combine profitability with sustainability, ethics and social responsibility (Alcaraz and Thiruvattal, 2010; Kell and Haertle, 2011; Perry and Win, 2013).

Coercive Pressure: This includes formal and informal pressures towards compliance. According to Hanson (2001) the pressures exerted can be explicit, visible, formal and forceful rules that schools are required to develop or comply with or the pressures can be relatively invisible and informal but no less powerful. Government and other organisations, e.g. the accreditation bodies, can constitute a source of coercive pressure on business and management schools to adopt principles and practices that would promote responsible management education. These pressures can be implied in diverse ways, for example, by implying that neglecting relevant practices would result in some form of sanction.

According to Caravella (2011), accreditation agencies can be considered as one important source of coercive pressure in the context of higher education. There are three main business school accreditation organisations: the Association of Advanced Collegiate Schools of Business (AACSB International), the European Foundation for Management Development (EFMD) and the Association of MBAs (AMBA) – all three of which are members of the PRME Steering Committee. Business schools around the world put significant resources into accrediting their programs using one or several of these organisations, and therefore put an emphasis on embedding the standards across their schools. In recent years, all three have begun to incorporate sustainability language and/or related standards into their accreditation criteria. This has had a strong impact on encouraging schools to examine these topics. However, the standards need to be clarified, further expanded and contextualized. Robust accreditation standards that put sustainability front and center could have a significant impact on schools moving forward. Six business schools on the African continent are AACSB-accredited and thereby forced to self-audit on CSR and sustainability strategy and activities. These leading schools include Lagos Business

School (Nigeria), Gordon Institute of Business Science (GIBS, South Africa), University of Cape Town (South Africa), University of Stellenbosch (South Africa), ESCA Ecole de Management (Morocco) and the American University of Cairo.

It is important that accreditation bodies and other regulators of business schools institute and enforce rules and standards that would promote the adoption of responsible management education by schools and which would discredit schools not conforming to such standards. It is also necessary that these rules and standards are continually updated to meet up with emerging global changes and differences in local context.

Normative Pressure: Another source of institutional pressure is normative, that is, responsible management education is considered to reflect a proper course of action. The organisational environment of business schools has signaled in a variety of ways that integrating sustainability into curricula is the right thing to do. Normative drivers therefore exert influence because of a social obligation to comply, rooted in social necessity or what an organisation or individual should be doing (March and Olsen, 1989). First, professional networks such as the NBS (Network of Business Sustainability), GRLI (Global Responsible Leadership Initiative) and PRME develop norms that define what counts as desirable behavior (GRLI, 2014). Faculty leaders from different schools when organised in such networks would propagate these values and norms in their organisations. Also, in line with the statement of Rasche and Gilbert (2015), student organisations can play the role of public advocates, advocating that schools become fully committed to imbibe sustainability into their curriculum and operations. Judgments about the appropriateness of reforms are framed as being aligned with the value system of the majority of students (Net Impact and The Aspen Institute, 2011). In addition to this, publications in trusted media outlets can be used to call on schools to change their educational frameworks.

With the identified institutional pressures, institutions can define what is appropriate or legitimate, and thus render other actions inappropriate and unacceptable (Zucker, 1987). This will then affect how decisions are made. Institutional theory therefore helps provide insight into the role of several actors in the imbibing of sustainability as a core part of the knowledge being disseminated in business and management institutions and their institutional tasks in achieving conformity among business schools in different regions across the globe. The institutional perspective helps to understand the role of conformity, regulatory and social pressures in driving organisational actions (Glover et al., 2014; Westphal et al., 1997).

18.5 RETHINKING THE ROLE OF SCHOOLS IN THE SUSTAINABILITY AGENDA OF DEES

Sustainability education or Responsible Management Education (RME) can be thought of as being part of the larger organisational field of management education

(Hoffman, 1999). This field is made up of a community of organisations, which, even though they may have different purposes, interact around a common theme. Relevant actors in this field include business schools, governmental regulators, accreditation agencies, providers of rankings (for instance, *The Financial Times*), employers of labour, student organisations and professional networks (the GRLI).

Fulfilling the task of developing future business leaders requires business schools to engage with learners around educational content such as theories, ideas, business cases as well as simulations. It also requires a combination of different teaching mechanisms ranging from lectures, case discussions, experiential tours, team projects and report writing (Vance, 1993). Business schools are also required to find out an optimal combination of the different teaching styles (Boisot and Fiol, 1987): such as conceptual versus practical, individual versus collective, and under instruction versus via self-study. As an institutional field, business schools where RME is utilized can through structuration born of institutional pressures resemble one another and share similar program offerings (e.g. MBA programs, EMBA level, other executive programs such as advanced management programs), research structures (contributing to common international journals, developing industry research), teaching methods (case studies, online courses, competitions, simulations etc.).

RME as an emerging institutional context consisting of various institutionalized practices (e.g. curriculum change and new pedagogies). These practices define what is commonly considered to reflect appropriate behavior. Schools cannot simply ignore the emergence of such demands, particularly if they want to be seen as legitimate actors. As earlier explained, the adoption of RME can be through mimetic, coercive or normative pressures (Rasche and Gilbert, 2015).

In line with the above, business schools in DEEs can through RME play a critical role in advancing sustainability such as the UN Sustainable Development Goals (SDGs). For instance, business schools can contribute to poverty reduction by educating business managers and executives on the implementation of inclusive or social business models, which provide opportunities for the well-being of the poor and environmental sustainability while offering commercial benefits to business (Rigoglioso, 2012). The potential for management schools to play a role in driving the emergence of responsible business (business that serves and empowers the poor) is pertinent in DEEs particularly in Africa where the bulk of the population falls within the demographic described as "Bottom of the Pyramid" (BoP) (Prahalad, 2012; Nwagwu and Ogbechie, 2017). Rigoglioso (2012) posits that research and teaching methods provide the foundation tools for alleviating poverty within the BoP populations. That is, while researchers examine ideas and results for tackling extreme poverty, faculty members and students can pursue answers to crucial questions that are essential to understanding poverty reduction and economic growth within the BoP market (Rigoglioso, 2012; Stanford Report, 2014).

The particular role business schools can play within their organisational fields in DEEs must necessarily grapple with context. According to Amaeshi et. al (2016), DEEs are characterized by weakness in institutional arrangements that protects the bonds of accountability between robust government, markets and civil society. In more developed economies, it is assumed that CSR, sustainability and indeed management education occur within an enabling institutional environment for synergized relationship and benefits. On the contrary, in DEEs where such institutional safety nets are not guaranteed, the work of business schools is to adapt CSR curriculum to orient leaders and managers to lay the institutional foundations for development action through the markets, nurturing collaborative relationships with government and civil society. Key levers, such as private morality, were identified as drivers of CSR in developing countries, enabling companies to emerge as sustainability champions despite institutional voids (Amaeshi et al., 2016). Business and management education need to understand and strengthen these opportunities in the institutional fields. Notably, local accreditation agencies need to evolve a regulatory approach and vocabulary to promote CSR and sustainability. Business schools, based on their interactions with international accreditation agencies as well as other international organisations, can share such frameworks to suit the local environments and educate the business community about key sustainable development goals and the role of business in advancing them.

While the need for business schools in DEEs to be champions of RME is not in doubt, it is important also to appreciate some inherent challenges. It is recognized that there is a growing strain between business schools' open pledge to sustainability, ethical or responsible management education and the complexities around its implementation (Rasche and Gilbert, 2015). That is, it is easy to define the principles of responsible management education on an abstract level, however, there is much work to do for these principles to be broken down into concrete instruction and learning scenarios (Pradini, Vervoort and Barthelmess, 2012; Weybrecht, 2015). In their study, Rasche and Gilbert (2015) reveal that while several deans and faculty of business schools believe that relevant discussions on sustainability education have been fully integrated into their organisations, about 75 percent of these courses remain electives detached from business school courses. Further, while existing research has boosted knowledge about changes in educational methods, course content and curriculum design to reflect sustainability management education, little is known about whether management schools' commitment to sustainability management education affects business schools' core organisational practices (Rasche and Gilbert, 2015). However, amidst the known, emerging and unknown challenges that business schools in DEEs might face in pursuit of the sustainability agenda, what is crucial is their commitment and determination to the agenda. With such commitment and determination, innovative strategies will emerge to address the challenges given the compelling belief in the mission and vision of sustainability. Moreover, across educational institutions, there are identifiable and possible strategies that can be adopted and adapted by business schools in DEEs to advance sustainability education and agenda.

18.6 PEDAGOGICAL STRATEGIES FOR ADOPTING SUSTAINABILITY EDUCATION

Just as academic institutions differ to a large extent among themselves, the extent to which they incorporate RME into their activities also varies greatly. According to Weybrecht (2015), some institutions have put in place new courses and electives, established student clubs and organised a series of events and conferences around RME. Others are establishing research centers that focus on ethics, responsible leadership and sustainability; and their individual faculties publish papers with some reference to RME. "More engaged" schools are developing a growing elective and core course collection on RME in their curricula. Audits and surveys are conducted to determine where their institutions stand. Encouragingly also, a number of business schools are making changes to their mission statements and core values to reflect the importance of training students in the area of RME. Sustainability-focused degrees, certificate and specialization programs, a rebranding of business degrees to be "sustainable" are ways other business schools are engaging in RME (Weybrecht, 2015).

As business schools provide society with two unique sets of outputs – their graduates and the research they produce, it is important that they continuously explore a wide range of innovative methodologies, both inside and outside the classroom, to develop and instil the competencies needed by their students and business leaders. Business and management education institutions should not look for a checklist when it comes to embedding sustainability but should value flexibility in implementation in order to develop programs based on their strengths and interests. This is because, despite their similarities in approach and structure, every school has different drivers and pressures, different cultures and different people. Given these vast differences, no single model to implementing sustainability in management education can be argued as the best or more desirable.[2] There are however some systematic approaches or strategies that can help in the effective integration of sustainability education that business and management institutions can possibly learn from:

i **Single Core Course or Module**: Although students are increasingly being exposed to sustainability through a broad range of activities throughout their degree programs, the most valuable of these is what is taught in the classroom. Students today have a better understanding of sustainability compared to their predecessors, and are most likely introduced to sustainability or ethics through

---

[2] "State of Sustainability in Management Education", prepared by Giselle Weybrecht, Special Adviser to the PRME Secretariat.

a single core course or module, often towards the beginning of a program. Sustainability tools (knowledge, skills, mindset) need to be comprehensively introduced in one or several dedicated core courses and then reinforced across the curriculum. In this way, the connections between different disciplines and the importance of sustainability can be made and specific sustainability issues can be explored in more detail within the relevant business context.

ii **Multidisciplinary Programs or Course Integration:** This method involves merging of business or management courses with CSR/sustainability-related courses. This method has been effective in sustaining several courses that have nearly lost popularity in the education system. For instance, several institutions have regained the interest of their students to study history by merging the course with political science or public administration. In the same manner, CSR/sustainability-related courses can be merged with other courses.

iii **Technocrats Inclusion or Guest Speakers:** Sustainability subjects are new in academia, thus, students' interest in these subjects hugely depends on the expertise of those that teach the subjects. This implies that business and management education institutions may engage the services of technically skilled CSR/sustainability practitioners to teach the students from the position of strength and help them to shape their career path towards CSR/sustainability.

iv **Excursion/Site or Company Visits:** Experiential learning technique is one of the teaching tools that has the ability to embed sustainability education in students' training. This can be achieved through immersion courses that require student teams to visit some sustainability-driven businesses or sites to engage in hands-on consulting projects that focus on sustainability issues; that is engaging students in real life projects and sharing experiences relating to successes, failures, needs or limitations with the students.

v **Elective Courses:** This approach requires the introduction of sustainability as an elective course in different disciplines. It can also take another dimension, with sustainability being integrated across required courses to show students how they can apply sustainability values in their core disciplines.

vi **Sustainability Research and Thought-Leadership Centers:** Another approach to make sustainability an integral part of business and management education is the creation of special centers or institutes in different academic institutions. These centers signify a level of investment in the topic beyond that implied by curriculum content requirements and go beyond academics and students to the generation of knowledge that society needs and that can help business leaders implement sustainability. They not only educate business leaders and managers but serve as a platform for businesses to engage with others on key principles of sustainability. This requires organising sustainability business forum, workshops, conferences, roundtables and events that bring together students, the academic and business communities to mainstream discussions and thought leadership on sustainable business, poverty, unemployment and related topics. Such forums are a viable platform to disseminate research findings, collaborate with business in consulting projects and can help to build avenues for dialogue between businesses and business schools. A growing number of business schools have put in place research centers focused on ethics or sustainability, which explore these topics in more depth and regularly engage with a range of stakeholders. An example of these special centers is the Lagos Business School Sustainability Centre; one of the flagships of Lagos Business School that runs a research project supported by the Bill & Melinda Gates Foundation titled *"Sustainable Business Models for Delivering Digital Financial Services to Lower Income Unbanked Citizens of Nigeria."* The project seeks to understand better the delivery and access constraints the poor face in relation to the financial system and explore appropriate Digital Financial Service (DFS) business models to enhance access and financial inclusion. The project features numerous stakeholder forums bringing together industry practitioners, policymakers, academia, FinTech companies, as well as financial sector experts to discuss opportunities and challenges in digital financial services for reaching the un-banked and under-banked.

vii **Research Centers:** A growing number of schools are focusing on entrepreneurship and social entrepreneurship, providing students (and alumni) with the opportunity to create and test business ideas around social and environmental challenges and provide a range of resources, such as venture labs, access to investors, office space and advisory support. For instance, the Oikos-PRME Research Hub is designed to support this dynamic by providing a platform to share finalized or ongoing research on sustainability in economics, finance and management and explore what others are doing in the field. This will enhance information sharing, participation and impactful outcomes.

viii **Sustainability School/Student Clubs:** This involves organising students clubs with focus in sustainability-related topics. For instance, Students in Free Enterprise (SIFE) and Net Impact are international non-profit organisations that work with university students who want to change their communities positively and learn practical knowledge to become socially responsible business leaders. The students form teams in their campuses and use business model to make better the quality of life and standard of living for people in need.

ix **Certificate Programs:** Business and management education institutions can promote sustainability education by offering certificate and specialization programs, as well as minors and majors focused on sustainability. Some institutions have adopted this by rebranding their business degrees to be "sustainable."

18.7 CONCLUSION

With the revelation that unethical practices contributed to the 2008 financial crisis, there is an implicit guilt and attendant challenge on educational institutions, especially business schools, to rethink their role and expected contributions to society. As their contribution to the 2008 financial crisis is related to their role as developers and shapers of ideas and business leaders, they have a fiduciary responsibility to guide, shape and develop society in such a way that the unethical factors with wide negative socioeconomic conse-quences such as the 2008 financial crisis are not repeated. Addressing such unethical factors demands a higher understanding, commitment, advocacy and contribution in the awareness and practice of sustainability. Given that they are citadels of learning, business and management institutions are centrally posi-tioned to enhance sustainability awareness and practice, not only in their management strategies or behaviors, but also in their research, teaching and engagement with the business community and wider society. Referred to as sustainability education, educational institutions – especially business schools in DEEs – can advance sustainability through effective and robust application of sustainability in all that they do. Interestingly, through a combination of or mono-mimetic, coercive and normative institutional pressures, wide and far-reaching involvement of many business schools can be achieved to build the required consensus and impact. As sustainability and coordination challenges can be argued to be presently more prevalent in DEEs, strategies or approaches that are said to have proven reasonably effective in developed economies can be adopted and, if necessary, reviewed to better suit the institutional peculiarities of DEEs. Such strategies include creation of local rating agencies, collaboration and membership of established sustainability forums and networks in addition to the adoption or creation of other pedagogical methods to advance the teaching and practice of sustainability. These include single sustainability core course, multidisciplinary programs or course integration with substantial sustainability input, involvement and use of technocrats as guest speakers in teaching sustainability. Other strategies include establishment of sustainability research centers, creation of sustainability student clubs and certificate pro-grams. Arguably, with the involvement of majority of business schools in DEEs within the sustainability agenda, the practice of sustainability is expected to improve and global sustainability targets such as the UN Sustainable Development Goals (UN SDG) better achieved.

REFERENCES

Alcaraz, J. M. and Thiruvattal, E. (2010). An Interview with Manuel Escudero the United Nations' Principles for Responsible Management Education: A Global Call for Sustainability. *Academy of Management Learning and Education*, 9(3), 542–550. http://doi: 10.5465/AMLE.2010.53791834.

Alon, I. and Mcintyre, J. R. (2005). *Business and management education in China: Transition, pedagogy and training*. New Jersey: World Scientific.

Amaeshi, K., Adegbite, E. and Rajwani, T. (2016). Corporate social responsibility in challenging and non-enabling. Institutional contexts: do institutional voids matter? *Journal of Business Ethics*, 134(1), 135–53. http://doi: 10.1007/s10551-014-2420-4.

Bansal, P. (2005). Evolving sustainably: A longitudinal study of corporate sustainable development. *Strategic Management Journal* 26(3), 197–218.

Baumol, W. J., Litan, R. E. and Schramm, C. J. (2009). *Good capitalism, bad capitalism, and the economics of growth and prosperity.* New Haven: Yale University Press.

Boisot, M. and Fiol, M. (1987). Chinese boxes and learning cubes: Action learning in a cross-cultural context. *Journal of Management Development*, 6(2), 8–18.

Brunton, G. D., Ahlstrom, D. and Li, H. L. (2010). Institutional theory and entrepreneurship: where are we now and where do we need to move in the future? *Entrepreneurship Theory & Practice*, 34(3), 421–440.

Caravella, D. K. (2011). "Mimetic, Coercive and Normative Influences in Institutionalisation of organisational Practises: The Case of Distance Learning in Higher Education". Dissertation submitted to the Faculty of The College for Design and Social Enquiry, Florida Atlantic University, 2011.

Carpenter, V. L. and Feroz, E. H. (2001). Institutional theory and accounting rule choice: An analysis of four US state governments' decisions to adopt generally accepted accounting principles. *Accounting, Organizations and Society*, 26(7), 565–596.

DiMaggio, P. J. and Powell, W. W. (1991). Introduction. In W. W. Powell and P. J. DiMaggio, eds., *The New Institutionalism in Organizational Analysis.* Chicago: University of Chicago Press, pp. 1–38.

DiMaggio, P. J. and Powell, W. W. (1983). The iron cage revisited: Institutional isomorphism and collective rationality in organizational fields. *American Sociological Review*, 48(2), 147–160.

Elkington, J. (1999). *Cannibals with forks: The triple bottom line of 21st century business.* Gabriola Island: New Society Publishers.

Glover, J. L., Champion, D., Daniels, K. J. and Dainty, A. J. D. (2014). An institutional theory perspective on sustainable practices across the dairy supply chain. *International Journal of Production Economics*, 15(2), 102–111.

Goldsmith, A. A. (2001). *Risk, Rule and Reason: Leadership in Africa.* New Jersey: John Wiley & Sons, Ltd.

Green Education Foundation Institute (2018). What is Sustainability Education? Available at www.gefinstitute.org/what-is-sustainability-education.html accessed July 1, 2018.

Hanson, M. (2001). Institutional theory and educational change. *Educational Administration Quarterly*, 37(5), 637–661.

Haski-Leventhal, D. (2014). MBA student values, attitudes and behaviors: a cross-cultural comparison of PRME signatory schools. *SAM Advanced Management Journal*, Autumn, 29–41.

Hoffman A. J. (1999). Institutional evolution and change environmentalism and the US chemical industry. *Academy of Management Journal*, 42(4), 351–371.

Hoffman, A. J. and Jennings, P. D. (2015). Institutional theory and the natural environment: Research in (and on) the Anthropocene. *Organization & Environment*, 28(1), 8–31. https://doi.org/10.1177/1086026615575331.

Hope, K. and Chikulo,B. (2000). *Corruption and development in Africa: Lessons from country case studies.* London: Palgrave Macmillan.

Kell, G. and Haertle, J. (2011). UN global compact and principles for responsible management education: The next decades. *Global Focus: The EFMD Business Magazine*, 5(2), 14–16.

March, J. G. and Olsen, J. P. (1989). *Rediscovering institutions: The organizational basis of politics*. New York: The Free Press.

Muff, K. (2013). Developing globally responsible leaders in business schools. *Journal of Management Development*, 32(5), 487–507. http://dx.doi.org/10.1108/02621711311328273

Net Impact & The Aspen Institute (2011). Business Skills for a Changing World: An Assessment of What Global Companies Need from Business Schools. Available at https://netimpact.org/sites/default/files/documents/business-skills-changing-world-2011.pdf accessed February 10, 2019.

Nwagwu, I. and Ogbechie, C. (2017). The role of management education in Africa's emerging economies: Reaching the bottom billion through inclusive business models, In M. Gudic, T. K. Tan & P. M. Flynn, eds., *Beyond the bottom line: Integrating the UN global compact into management education*. Saltaire: Greenleaf Publishing.

Perry, M. and Win, S. (2013). An evaluation of PRME's contribution to responsibility in higher education. *Journal of Corporate Citizenship*, (49), 48–70.

Prahalad, C. K. (2012). Bottom of the pyramid as a source of breakthrough innovations. *Product management & management association*, 29(1), 6–12.

Prandini, M., Vervoort I. P. and Barthelmess, P. (2012). Responsible Management Education for 21st Century Leadership. *Central European Business Review*, 1(2), 16–22.

Rasche, A. and Escudero, M. (2009). Leading change: The role of the principles for responsible management education. *Zeitschrift für Wirtschafts- und Unternehmensethik*, 10(2), 244–50.

Rasche, A. and Gilbert, D. U. (2015). Decoupling responsible management education – Why business schools may not walk their talk. *Journal of Management Inquiry*, 24(3), 239–252. http://doi: 10.1177/1056492614567315.

Rigoglioso, M. (2012). End of the American dream? Income disparities are widening the achievement gap. *Stanford Educator*, Summer, 4–5.

Rotberg, R. I. (2004). *When states fail: Causes and consequences*. Princeton: Princeton University Press.

Sarkis, J., Zhu, Q. and Lai, K. H. (2011). An organizational theoretic review of green supply chain management literature. *International Journal of Production Economics*, 130, 1–15.

Sattiraju, N. (2016). "CSR: an underrated approach to sustainable progress". Available at https://yourstory.com/2016/09/csr-sustainability accessed July 20, 2019.

Soderstrom, S. and Weber, K. (2011). Corporate sustainability agendas from the bottom up. *European Business Review*, 6–9.

Stanford Report (2014). "The Poverty and Inequality Report 2014". Available at https://web.stanford.edu/group/scspi/sotu/SOTU_2014_CPI.pdf accessed July 20, 2019.

United Nations Educational, Scientific and Cultural Organization [UNESCO] (2014). *UNESCO Roadmap for Implementing the Global Action Programme on Education for Sustainable Development*, UNESCO, Paris.

Vance, R. E., Cooper, B. S. and Hite, S. J. (1999). Understanding the politics of research in education. *Educational Policy*, 13(1), 7–22. https://doi.org/10.1177/0895904899131002.

Waddock, S., Rasche, A., Werhane, P. and Unruh, G. (2011). The principles for responsible management education: Implications for implementation and assessment. In D. L. Swanson and D. G. Fisher, eds., *Ethics in practice: Toward assessing business ethics education*, pp. 13–28. Charlotte: Information Age Pub.

Westphal, J. D., Gulati, R. and Shortell, S. M. (1997). Customization or Conformity? An institutional and network perspective on the content and consequences of TQM adoption. *Administrative Science Quarterly*, 42(2), 366–394.

Weybrecht, G. (2015). *The sustainable MBA: A business guide to sustainability, Second Edition*. New Jersey: John Wiley & Sons, Ltd.

World Business Council for Sustainable Development (2010). *Vision 2050: The new agenda for business*. Conches-Geneva. Switzerland: WBCSD.

World Commission on Environment and Development (1987). *Our common future*. Oxford: Oxford University Press.

Zucker, L. (1987). Institutional theories of organizations. *Annual Review of Sociology*, 13(1), 443–464.

19

Sustainable Finance, the Law and Stakeholders: Towards Responsible Social Movements

Radek Stech[1]

19.1 INTRODUCTION

The long-standing thinking is that enriching business practices with CSR will result in a more sustainable world. Recently, the focus has gradually turned to a wider spectrum of 'organisations', including not-for-profit, away from large multinational enterprises and a narrow business (ISO, 2017; Golubovic, 2018). However, whilst social movements played an important role in forging this thinking and operationalising it into policies, very little has been said and proposed about the social movements' responsibility for its actions (Carroll and Shabana, 2010). This chapter will provide an original and innovative insight into sustainable finance by analysing social movements' interaction with complex finance dynamics (CFDs) through elements of trustworthiness. In doing so, the chapter will draw on data from an empirical qualitative study that traced the involvement of social movements in shaping three major legal CFDs, namely project finance, bond finance and pension finance on the sustainable finance market between 2015 and 2018. It will argue that social movements, who are, by tradition, in conflict with dominant paradigms, pose a perceptible competitive challenge to major stakeholders who shape the finance dynamics. Whilst the utilisation of the trustworthiness analytical framework proves useful in uncovering the conflict, it serves the main purpose of demonstrating the analytic competition between social movements and the major stakeholders. I argue that social movements should take a more responsible stance towards sustainable

[1] Founder of Sustainable Finance, the Law and Stakeholders (SFLS) Network, Senior Lecturer in Law, Exeter Law School. The initial research findings were presented at the Law and Society Association's Annual Meeting (law and theory panel) in New Orleans, USA in June 2016 and the Law and Society Association's Annual Meeting (banking and finance law panel) in Mexico City in June 2017. I held several conversations aimed at testing the findings with NGOs, private and public organisations and investors between 2016 and 2018. Thanks are due to the Economic and Social Research Council for funding (grant ES/R004293/1) that enabled the completion of this research in 2018. I wish to thank all research participants and the practitioner reviewers for their insightful comments. I am also grateful to M. Nicolas J. Firzli, Dr James Griffin, Professor Bob Lee, Professor Andrea Lista, Dr Onyeka Osuji and Mr Darryl Wilkins for their comments on the earlier drafts of this chapter and to Ms Elzbieta Slota NRPSI, for her assistance. The usual caveat applies.

finance and, logically, adopt a form of responsible principles that will govern their relationship with the major stakeholders shaping the CFDs. Further, I draft principles in this chapter and argue that, if adopted by social movements, these will improve their competitive advantage on the fast-paced sustainable finance market.

The originality and innovation of this chapter stems from the fact that no other scholar has conducted a similar research through the lenses of the social movements' interaction with three major CFDs in the context of sustainable finance. The research to date has focused on the interaction between social movements and particular stakeholders such as the multilateral finance institutions (Dawson and Bhatt 2001; Clark, Fox and Treakle, 2003; O'Brien et al., 2009), or corporations in the context of shareholder activism (King and Soule, 2007). There is also ample research on the interaction between NGOs and finance institutions (Fox and Brown, 1998), and banks (Lawrence, 2008). This research usually positions social movements (or NGOs) as a weaker player vis-à-vis organisations such as the World Bank or large investment banks. However, I have taken a completely different approach to this study by focusing my attention on the interaction between the social movements and the three CFDs to facilitate the development of the main argument. These dynamics are complex arrangements that cover the operation of the large cross-section of the financial systems, as opposed to focusing on the role of individual organisations herein. Conceptually, I introduce the notion of complex finance dynamics and the global sustainable finance market (GSFM). The former conveys the dynamic nature of these finance structures that are based on a series of legal deals shaped by several stakeholders; whereas the GSFM reflects an evolving nature of the sustainable finance market that, at these early stages, must remain aligned with the global agendas, co-created by several stakeholders and adaptable to specialised contexts. This conceptualisation serves a purpose of positioning social movements as competitive rather than weak players on the GSFM. Moreover, the novelty of this research lies in employing the elements of trustworthiness as an analytical framework to analyse the rich qualitative data collected through participant observation and interviews between 2015 and 2018. This enabled me to move beyond identifying conflict between social movements and major stakeholders towards uncovering analytic competition. Given these findings, I argue that social movements must become more responsible to take the full competitive advantage of the CFDs. This responsibility (alongside the proposed draft principles for social movements) is not going to deprive the social movements of their raison d'être; rather, it will empower them so that they can take the advantage of CFDs for sustainable finance and contribute to advancing the GSFM.

This research which is presented in this chapter has already made tangible impact and will be relevant to several high-profile stakeholders in the emerging markets. On an operational level, the launch of this research coincided with establishing the Sustainable Finance, the Law and Stakeholders (SFLS) Network at the University of Exeter under my leadership. I am currently focusing my impact on a rapidly growing sector of a global financial industry. My research and ongoing engagement with key industry players (responsible for trillions of dollars of assets) led to the formation of a high-level expert group. This group is currently working on deepening and further integrating environmental, social and governance matters into the investment practices. The group is also developing robust sectoral standards that will be available publicly in due course. I am the overall coordinator of the group and co-head of the 'Finance Systems and Regulation' portfolio/theme.[2] The sustainable finance agenda is still novel, as the UN completed its first investigation in 2015, when this research commenced (McDaniels et al., 2016). Recent years have seen an introduction of novel and dedicated market sources of finance for sustainable development such as green/climate/social/ sustainability bonds. This has coincided with the introduction of government tax credits and incentives to stimulate investment in sustainable and environmentally friendly projects (UK Government, 2016, McDaniels et al., 2016). There is a clear demand created by the multilateral financial organisations, central banks and governments for new data relating to the operation of sustainable finance markets and 'intellectual leadership' (Bank of England, 2018: p. 5).[3] This research is doing exactly this in relation to the important theme of social movements' engagement and participation. On a more practical level, sustainable finance agenda is driven by the Sustainable Development Goals (2015) which aim at eradicating poverty, hunger and increasing growth. Hence, this research is directly relevant to the emerging markets and, more specifically, such institutions that put stakeholder engagement at the top of their agenda as the World Bank, the African Development Bank and the Asian Development Bank. The nature of CFDs is such that this research will be relevant to several private and public stakeholders engaged in shaping project finance, bond finance and pension finance. Naturally, this chapter will be useful to social movements and NGOs that constantly seek ideas as to how to improve their engagement strategies.

My overall argument is that social movements, whilst projecting their conflict with the dominant players, play a competitive role on the GSFM, and, to improve their competitiveness, they need to adopt responsibility principles. The first section of the chapter will conceptualise the role of social movements on the GSFM. I will position social movements as heterogenous and evolving entities that can play a tangible role, which does not necessarily have to include conflict, on the GSFM. I will propose an original notion of the GSFM which should be governed by the following principles: alignment, co-creation and adaptability. Section 2 will provide an overview of the project by firstly explaining the innovative and rigorous research design that involved data collection from places where three distinct CFDs were shaped over a three-year period of time. Section 3 will offer an analysis through the trustworthiness analytical framework that will prove useful in uncovering the conflict. However, it will serve the

---

[2] Due to confidentiality restrictions, which will be lifted in Winter 2019, I am unable to provide more details.

[3] See for example the Bank of England's willingness to be a leader in the field reflected in its commitment to form a Climate Financial Risk Forum (actually established in March 2019).

main purpose of demonstrating the analytic competition between social movements and the major stakeholders. In Section 4, I argue for and propose principles of responsible social movements and draft the key elements they could contain.

19.2 CONCEPTUALISING THE ROLE OF SOCIAL MOVEMENTS ON THE GLOBAL SUSTAINABLE FINANCE MARKET

The sustainable finance agenda is shaped by several dominant actors,[4] such as international organisations (UN), sovereign states (e.g. through the G20), multilateral finance organisations (the World Bank), national central banks and large investment banks, alongside niche players such as values-based banks.[5] The purpose of this section is to argue that social movements can play a tangible role (beyond conflict) in shaping this agenda before turning to discussing the empirical findings through which that role will be developed and explained to a greater detail (Sections 2–4). I need to make this argument because I reject such an understanding of social movements that often reduces them to NGOs or equates them with the general public. Rather, I turn to the origins of this concept and take a broader approach, recognising that they are heterogenous entities constantly evolving with time – conglobates that bring together various groupings, organisations or individuals that are connected by a shared agenda. To further advance my argument, I offer an explanation of sustainable finance; however instead of taking a descriptive approach that summarises countless definitions,[6] I will explain the sustainable finance agenda through an original notion of the GSFM and its governing principles. The GSFM is a meeting place for diverse actors that must remain aligned with the sustainable development agenda; co-created; and adaptable to different contexts. Such a market should provide a fertile environment for social movements to shape the sustainable finance agenda.

19.2.1 *Social Movements as Heterogeneous and Evolving Entities*

The concept of social movements is elusive and used interchangeably with the narrower terms 'social movement organisations', non-governmental organisations (NGOs), non-profit organisations (NPOs); or extremely broad concepts which align

---

4   Dominant in a sense of overall influence and resourcefulness combined with their interest in shaping sustainable finance mechanisms such as the World Bank's Environmental and Social Framework (2017) and the International Finance Corporation's (IFC) Performance Standards (2012); or the Equator Principles, the International Capital Market Association's (ICMA) Green/Social/Sustainability Bond Principles (2018).
5   See for example the GABV Principles of Values Based Banking (2011).
6   My approach not to explain sustainable finance through the descriptive approach, which would require a presentation of several existing definitions, is also informed by the empirical findings. In the course of the research, I observed several high-profile discussions, which ended prematurely because the discussants were unable to proceed further due to the disagreements over the definitions. Not only is my approach to explaining sustainable finance through his original notion of the sustainable finance market more analytical, but it also serves as a basis for productive and actionable debates.

with the general public such as 'civil society' (McCarthy and Zald, 1977; Hilson, 2002, O'Brien, Goetz and Scholte, 2009) and by the participants in this study.[7] On the one hand, those labels constitute useful scholarly analytical lenses that permit a focused investigation of social movements. On the other, such categorisations could be no more than an 'epistemological mistake', whereby investigators seek 'unitary empirical objects' (Melucci, 1996: p. 5) to prove their originality when conducting research.

I reject those narrow and broad definitions of social movements and turn to the origin of the meaning to emphasise they are heterogenous and evolving in time. Thus, one important characteristic of social movements is that, rather than being static, they are constantly evolving, and, through this transition:

> acquire[s] organisation and form, a body of customs and traditions, established leadership, an enduring division of labour, social rules and social values – in short, a culture, a social organisation, and a new scheme of life (Blumer 1951: p. 168)

Social movements often move through a 'sequence' from initial forms of unrest, through collective action, some form of organisation and finally leading to 'institutionalisation' (Smelser, 1962: 18). It is therefore inappropriate to associate social movements with the wider public as it usually does not have an organisational structure.[8] It is even more difficult to associate social movements with NGOs (or even social movement organisations[9]), as such movements do not have to necessarily move towards acquiring an organisational structure.[10] Such a narrow understanding of social movements would also render this chapter counterproductive as there is already an ongoing discussion over the responsibility of NGOs and non-for-profits. Since the NGOs usually rely on charitable status, there are existing channels to improve their responsibility through state policies and regulations or even through the international initiatives.[11] However, as we will see in Section 4, these developments shed light on developing principles for responsible social movements on the global sustainable finance market.

Next, there are numerous labels that one could attach to social movements – radical, reformative, violent, progressive, global, European, local, religious to name a few. Social movements can be given birth to today (Crossley, 2003; Fominaya and Cox, 2013) and move from 'old' to 'new' – the former works around loosely defined economic struggles (e.g. a labour movement), whereas the latter represents the post-materialistic and post–World War II interests of, for instance, gays and lesbians, women, the

---

[7] Such as 'ordinary citizens', 'savers', 'the people'. Reports from the participant observations and the interviews conducted as part of the research.
[8] Unless, of course, we consider 'state' as the 'organisation' which goes beyond the scope of this research project (see for example Art. 1 of the Montevideo Convention).
[9] Which come next if the social movement decides to establish them (Edwards and McCarthy, 2004)
[10] Such movements may remain loose for a considerable period of time without acquiring organisational structures such as online communities (see for example Rheingold (2001), Kraut (2016)).
[11] See for example the current debates in the Council of Europe (2018).

environment or animals. This means that social movements are also diverse in terms of their focus, which might sometimes be conflicting.

Diani, following an extensive review, offered the following four elements that, in his view, explain the social movement dynamics: a) 'the presence of informal interactions involving individuals, groups and organisations'; b) 'shared beliefs and solidarity'; c) 'collective action on conflictual issues' emphasising that 'the notion of conflict is understood in very different ways by different scholars' and may relate to 'negotiable issues'; and d) 'action which displays largely outside the institutional sphere and the routine procedures of social life' and may include protest and organisations which are 'loosely structured' (Diani, 1992).Hence we turn to another significant characteristic of social movements, that is conflict.[12] Such movements have often been described as *anti-something or pro-something*, for example anti-capitalist or pro-global justice (Kitschelt, 1986; Klein, 2002; Crossley, 2002; Crossley, 2003; Porta, 2007) which denotes the inherently embedded contention and the need to change the state of current affairs acting as the raison d'être of social movements (see also WBG, 2017). However, grievances could be generated by the available financial resources, where supporting organisations might not be concerned with the conflict at all, thus putting into question the honesty of some of the contention (McCarthy and Zald, 1977). Thus, one can argue that the importance of funding[13] which is so critical for social movements reveals that the conflicts reside on the surface of some of the social movements' rationale for action. The empirical part of this chapter will prove that, within the contours of my research, it is analytic competition which dwells beneath the apparent conflict, at least in this context. Logically, we need to turn to the research contours that will be defined through the notion of the global sustainable finance market.

19.2.2 *Towards Aligned, Co-created and Adaptable Global Sustainable Finance Market (GSFM)*

It would be counterproductive to conceptualise sustainable finance through the review of existing definitions, because, at least at this stage, we would arrive at a list of sometimes vague or conflicting concepts. Such haste risks multiplying these definitions and spawning endless debates, similar to those centred on the nomenclature for sustainable development.[14] To move on, it is enough to note that, broadly, sustainable finance was defined through the integration of social, environmental

---

[12] For the purpose of this research, conflict should be understood in its ordinary meaning as indicated by the Cambridge Dictionary: 'an active disagreement between people with opposing opinions or principles', https://dictionary.cambridge.org/dictionary/english/conflict.

[13] Resources include financial resources but also moral, infrastructure, social networks, labour and cultural resources, see Edwards and McCarthy (2004).

[14] Broadly speaking, sustainable development (SD) thinking emerged from the attention to the harmful environmental and social impacts associated with traditional development and ways of producing growth and wealth (Ross, 2009). There is no single definition of sustainable development and the

and governance matters (European Commission, 2018), green finance (Böhnke at al., 2015) social finance (Kaeufer, 2010, Weber and values-based banking GABV, 2011), values-based intermediation (Bank Negara Malaysia, 2018), impact investment (Mudaliar et al., 2017). These definitions are sometimes vague as they embrace concepts (such as environment or human rights), which are themselves not settled, and their meaning fluctuates depending on the context.[15] Rather, it will be more productive to agree on a set of principles that define and promote the tenets of sustainable finance through the GSFM. The meaningful and effective allocation of finance on the GSFM is fundamental and this means that sustainable finance must be aligned with the overarching global agendas; co-created and adaptable.

First, through alignment with global agendas such as the SDGs and the climate change objectives, sustainable finance naturally embeds substantive elements such as better governance, transparency and disclosure, stakeholder involvement (including the interest of future generations) and integration of the three SD pillars. By doing so, it implements the thinking and practices of corporate or organisational social responsibility and the environmental and human rights laws and policies that have been taken up by global multilateral institutions. The alignment of sustainable finance with the UN's agenda is, for example, clearly visible in the recently adopted UN Principles for Responsible Banking and the first principle, entitled 'Alignment':

> We will align our business strategy to be consistent with and contribute to individuals' needs and society's goals, as expressed in the Sustainable Development Goals (SDGs), the Paris Climate Agreement and relevant national and regional frameworks. We will focus our efforts where we have the most significant impact. (UN, 2018)

However, alignment moves beyond substantive themes towards collaborative approaches evident through the seventeenth SDG Goal, emphasising:

> Urgent action is needed to mobilize, redirect and unlock the transformative power of trillions of dollars of private resources to deliver on sustainable development objectives. (UN, 2015)

Logically, the GSFM must be co-created by several players. Aligned with this urgency, many international initiatives emphasised the importance of effective finance for sustainable development from various sources at international, regional

concept has been highly confusing for policymakers during the attempts to frame its various interpretations into legislation (Stech, 2013). There are two main, and not mutually exclusive, approaches to SD: one which focuses on the inter-generational and intra-generational equity (Brundtland at al., 1987), and the other which highlights the importance of integrating the three pillars of development, i.e. social, economic and environmental coupled with a long-term thinking (UN World Summit on Sustainable Development). Following earlier international developments, such as the UN Millennium Development Goals and the UN Agenda 21, the UN adopted 17 Sustainable Development Goals in 2015 relating to, inter alia, poverty, food security and inequality.

[15] For example, our understanding of the environment and environmental justice was framed over decades, see Taylor (2000).

and local level. In July 2015, the World Bank, other multilateral banks and the IMF committed to moving from 'billions to trillions' in financing development and emphasised an increasing role of private sector and investors in achieving this goal (World Bank Group and other multilateral development banks, 2015), including the world's wealthiest billionaires (Jopson, 2015) and NGOs (FAO, 2015). However, this co-creation moves beyond mere invitations to unlock more money to include initiatives that shape complex finance dynamics. CFDs are finance structures that are based on a series of legal deals shaped by several stakeholders and include project finance, bond finance and equity finance.[16] The structure of project finance, which is non-recourse or limited recourse 'allocates risks associated with a project and defines the claims on rewards' (World Bank, 1994: p. 98). It hinges upon contractual legal relationships between the project sponsor, lenders and the project company and is surrounded by, and dependant upon, many more actors such as governments, government agencies, commercial operators (insurance companies, banks, credit rating agencies), quasi-commercial or quasi-governmental agencies (e.g. credit export agencies or sovereign investment funds), the public (e.g. as the recipient of energy outputs) and NGOs. All of these actors bring something unique to the structure, be it equality or loans, technical expertise, political support or guarantees (Dugue, 2000). Bond finance is a form of lending albeit its structure is different to lending by banks in project finance as lenders (investors) are spread across capital markets rather than confined to banks. The clear advantage of using bonds to support large projects lies in the possibility of sourcing finance from a large pool of investors who can be located anywhere on the globe.[17] The principal structure relies upon a legal relationship between the issuer of a bond, an underwriter of the bond (an investment bank) and both institutional and (rarer) retail investors (Hudson, 2013). Pension finance hinges upon a legal relationship between the beneficiaries (or savers), the pension fund and the companies in which the fund trustees invest to maximise returns for the savers. The legal relationship is under-pinned by the fiduciary duty which governs what pension funds' trustees can and cannot do with the beneficiaries' money and the relationship between the invest-ment advisers and their clients. The pension finance structure, often called an investment chain, has undergone intermediation following the development of electronic trading and the demise of individual shareholding,[18] which led to the erosion of trust and confidence (Kay, 2015; O'Malley, 2015; Sullivan et al., 2017). Pension money is ultimately invested into various asset classes and the complex

[16]   These will be discussed more in detail in Sections 3–4 of this chapter.
[17]   Though it can be qualified at certain period of times depending on the regulation, see Chris O'Malley, 2015.
[18]   This was eloquently captured by Kay: 'The decline in the role of the individual shareholder has been paralleled by an explosion of intermediation. Between the company and the saver are now interposed registrars, nominees, custodians, asset managers, managers who allocate funds to specialist asset managers, trustees, investment consultants, agents who "wrap" products, retail platforms, distributors and independent financial advisers. Each of these agents must employ its own compliance staff to

fiduciary relationship governs the direction of the money, which can also include large infrastructure projects. Here, the striking feature is that the pool of pension holders includes ordinary people on whose behalf institutional investors (pension funds) invest the money in capital markets.

These CFDs are currently underpinned with several co-created sustainable finance schemes including binding and soft-law standards initiated by the international organisations (e.g. UNEP Finance Initiative and UN Principles for Responsible Banking), multilateral banks (e.g. the World Bank Environmental and Social Framework and the International Finance Corporation's Performance Standards), private financial organisations/associations (such as the Equator Principles, the International Capital Market Association's Green Bond Principles and the Social Bonds Principles and Global Alliance for Banking on Values' (GABV) Principles of Values-based Banking) and not-for-profits (e.g. the Climate Bonds Initiative's Climate Bonds Standard and the Principles for Responsible Investment (PRI)). These standards, co-created by several players, integrate a wide array of sustainability factors into financial structures, including the CFDs, with various degrees of focus and enforcement.

Finally, the GSFM must be adaptable to specialised contexts which include the CFDs, jurisdictions and industries. The mere fact of multiple standards in place rather than a 'one-size-fits-all' reflects the complexity of finance dynamics and the multiplicity of interests involved. Hence, currently, there is no wide appetite for merging these mechanisms into one widely accepted scheme despite instances of collaboration[19] and voices for consolidation (G20 Insights, World Bank and UNEP, 2017, WWF, 2016). Rather each mechanism takes its own pathway through updates and newer versions[20] suggesting that there is a market for these mechanisms and the initiators are in competition with one another.[21] These mechanisms uncover existing complexities which are inherently embedded within the finance systems, complex finance dynamics, and the existing environmental, social and governance rules. Adaptability creates more choice for sustainable finance players best explained by the developments on the bond market. Hence, whereas Green Bond Principles (GBP) were launched in 2014, International Capital Market Association has recently introduced the Social Bond Principles (SBP) and the Sustainability Bond Guidelines (SBG). Hence, green bonds support investments into environmentally

monitor consistency with regulation, must use the services of its own auditors and lawyers and earn sufficient to remunerate the employees and reward its own investors', Kay Review, p. 4.

[19] For example, the Equator Principles use certain definitions set out by the IFC (Equator Principles, n. 106, p. 15).

[20] Some of these updates are reflected in new published versions (e.g. Equator Principles, third version, Green Bonds Principles, 2017 edition) whereas others are updated on a regular basis (e.g. GABV 'Principles of Sustainable Finance' were recently renamed to 'Principles of Values-based Banking').

[21] For example, Climate Bonds Initiative highlighted on its website that '[t]he 2016 update of the Green Bond Principles have been fully integrated' suggesting it has a cutting edge through its certification programme. www.climatebonds.net/standards/about accessed 1 September 2017.

sound projects, social bonds focus on social projects whereas sustainability instruments combine both environmental and social benefits. These were introduced to meet investor demand but may lead to 'bond cannibalisation' (Ridley and Barnshaw, 2019) when issuers limit the availability of, for example, green bonds in favour of social bonds. Whereas cannibalisation sounds threatening to the market, it only reflects different appetites that investors have in relation to sustainable finance hence 'bond adaptability' is a better term that may explain these developments. Similarly, GSFM must be adaptable to different jurisdictions such as Islamic finance banking that, unlike conventional banking, prohibits investments in alcohol (Bank Negara Malaysia, 2018) and economic sectors such as forestry (FAO, 2015). Further, the specialised contexts include some values-based banks that favour approaches which elevate the positive impact of banks (with associated exclusion of certain investments) and certain large investment banks that prefer to focus on reducing negative impacts and a gradual shift towards carbon neutral investments. The line between these approaches is not easy to draw (neither conceptually nor practically) because of the lack of uniform measures and globally agreed understanding of impact. Nevertheless, the adaptability permits a co-existence of the GABV Principles of Values-based Banking (2011) that focus on the positive impact in the first instance and the UN Principles for Responsible Banking (2018) that favour a gradual shift.

19.2.3 *Role of Social Movements on the GSFM*

I need to conclude this part with an optimistic view that heterogeneous and evolving social movements can play a tangible role that does not have to necessarily be based on conflict on the GSFM. The GSFM is still in the early stages of development that cannot be defined by a single nomenclature; requires involvement from several players and must remain adaptable to different contexts. The global sustainability and climate change agenda is very close to the social movement's central thinking relating to broad justice; however, the shift towards that agenda cannot occur instantaneously. Social movements are conglomerates of various organisations, groups and communities and, as they evolve over time, we cannot predict their future forms on the evolving GSFM. In this sense, social movements should move forward on the growing wave of sustainable finance rather than try to cut through this wave or even flatten it.

However, the GSFM embeds several complex finance dynamics such as project finance, bond finance and pension finance that have been underpinned with sustainable finance initiatives. These dynamics cannot be dominated by one player, let alone governed by social movements, which, because of their nature, may evolve into something else in the future. Let us now turn to the part of the chapter which is based on a three-year empirical project which traced the involvement of social movements into shaping the CFDs.

19.2.4 *Innovative SFLS Project*

19.2.4.1 Project Overview and Methods

The objective of the study was to trace the involvement of social movements into shaping the CPDs in the context of sustainable finance and develop a new concept of an investment opportunity framework.[22] The starting point for this project was to choose the complex investment dynamics and gain access to contexts in which social movements could interact with those dynamics. Project finance, bond finance and pension finance are ideal in my view because they relate to distinct segments of the financial markets and thus offer enough diversity in terms of the social movements' involvement. These CFDs have been underpinned with the sustainable finance standards,[23] which integrate sustainable finance elements into these structures with various degrees of focus and enforcement. Hence, for example, the Equator Principles touch upon all ESG elements but are entirely voluntary[24] whereas WB's ESF covers all these matters in a much more comprehensive manner and is binding on the borrowers. Both Green Bond Principles and Climate Bonds Initiative (CBI) are environmentally oriented but the former is voluntary whereas the latter includes a certification process that adds a layer of legal enforceability and the potential for dispute resolution.[25] I have therefore carefully chosen an appropriate research field which creates opportunities for rigorous, original, innovative and significant empirical study.

I conducted inductive preliminary research between April 2015 and September 2016, and subsequently engaged in the main empirical data collection between October 2015 and December 2016 and between September 2018 and

---

[22] I intended to analyse the data through theories of opportunity structures which I am currently completing. My original idea was to develop a new Investment Opportunity Framework (IOF) for social movements. However, my views on social movements changed following the writing stage for this chapter and I intend to frame the IOF as a notion that will sit in the context of sustainable finance rather than in the field of social movements studies.

[23] For example, the Equator Principles www.equator-principles.com/index.php/ep3 accessed 1 April 2015, (p. 3) apply to project finance but also to corporate loans relating to projects and bridge loans whereas the World Bank's Environmental and Social Framework (ESF) applies to 'investment project financing'. For further explanations, see Operational Manual, https://policies.worldbank.org /sites/ppf3/PPFDocuments/090224b0823064b7.pdf, at 1. ESF Standard 9 applies also to 'project finance, corporate finance, medium and small enterprise finance, micro-finance, housing finance, leasing, and trade finance' (p. 91).

[24] This is further supported by the following statement: 'In a situation where there would be a clear conflict between applicable laws and regulations and requirements set out in the Equator Principles, the local laws and regulations prevail' (Equator Principles, above (n. 23), p. 11).

[25] The certification process is based on a legal agreement between the bond issuer and the Climate Bonds Initiative (see, for example, clause 16 'The Applicant agrees that if the Bonds become non-conformant with the Climate Bond Standard, then the Applicant must promptly (within one month of the becoming aware of the non-conformance) provide written notice to CBI of the fact of non-conformance.' www.climatebonds.net/files/files/Certification%20Agreement%20-%20May2016.doc accessed 1 September 2017.

December 2018. The second, shorter, empirical stage included a few interviews following the testing stage which included participation in the events (without formal data gathering) and informal conversations with the key participants and academics. I needed to include the second empirical stage in 2018 because of internal changes at the University of Exeter Law School[26] and a need to further test the findings. I managed to establish a relationship with the World Bank Group and the International Monetary Fund civil society teams and attend formal meetings between these organisations. Such meetings are held biannually in April and October and I included three such meetings (between October 2015 and October 2016) and one Annual Meeting in 2018 into this research. Some of the individual sessions were formal and official (organised by the WBG/IMF) whereas other sessions were organised (or co-organised) by social movements and other partners. In practice, my project design yielded results as it was relatively easy to identify social movements as heterogeneous and evolving entities engaging with the institutional investors, multilateral banks and other institutions at the WBG-IMF meetings through the project finance dynamic. There were several large, medium and small NGOs attending these events alongside individuals, academics and think-tanks that joined them. The social movements' involvement was further reinforced by the occurrence of protests and manifestations outside the formal and informal negotiations taking place inside the building. It was clearly noticeable that the observed social movements resemble the social movement dynamics as noted by Diani (1992).

In May 2015, I became an observer of Green Bond Principles and this status offered me an opportunity to attend several events relating to bond finance, bringing together the key stakeholders including social movements. However, the character-istics of social movements engaging in bond finance were least aligned with the description provided by Diani (1992) and thus least heterogeneous. I noticed only a handful of NGOs attending rather than a substantial social movement. I also attended relevant events which included discussions on green bonds organised by one environmental consultancy firm and by the UN at the UN Climate Change Conference in Paris (COP21) in Paris and COP24 in Katowice.

I attended several events around pension finance, one organised by the Principles of Responsible Investment (PRI) and another by a small UK NGO. Social move-ments were also prominent in relation to pension finance. However, whereas Principles for Responsible Investment (PRI) offered an access route to the pension finance dynamic, the social movement seems not to rely on it directly and were keen to self-organise and engage with investors directly. One explanation of such an approach is that the PRI is arranged by a non-profit organisation (albeit supported

---

[26]   I was seconded to do intensive teaching away from my main department at the beginning of the main empirical global stage, which caused significant delays further down the line for this research. This meant that the grant from ESRC that commenced in September 2018 enabled me to complete this research.

by the UN) and there might be a degree of competition between various organisations.

Overall, most events were broken into one to two-hour sessions and I managed to take notes from 58 such sessions with the majority held by the WBG/IMF (38). It is not possible to provide exact numbers of events linked to a single complex finance dynamic as many meetings related to more than one and I did not intend to conduct a quantitative study. Moreover, I conducted 36 usable interviews with senior/executive members of social movements (15), institutional and individual investors (12) and public bodies such as multilateral finance institutions, municipalities and governments (9) between October 2015 and December 2016 lasting between 30 minutes and one and a half hours and many more, off-the record,[27] informal conversations. I also conducted a further five interviews with institutional and individual investors and three with multilateral finance institutions between September 2018 and December 2018 specifically for this project.[28] I paid particular attention to anonymising the data, given the sensitivity of the project, in line with the appropriate ethical guidance and approvals at the University of Exeter.[29] Even though many events were held during WBG/IMF meetings, the participants' observations and/or interviews must not be assumed to represent the views of the WBG because of the focus on the CFDs.

19.2.4.2 Data Analysis

It became clear through initial observation that the interactions between social movements and dominant players shaping the CFDs were manifested by conflict (Diani, 1992) and I sought a framework which would help me in continuing the data collection and analysis. I investigated the notion of trust since conflict implies the lack of it and trust is 'the expectation that arises within a community of regular, honest, and cooperative behavior, based on commonly shared norms, on the part of other members of that community' (Fukuyama, 1995: p. 26). I consciously rejected using a legal concept of trust and confidence, which would be dependent on a particular jurisdiction and this research was not intended to focus on a legal regime, as it would in fact be impossible. I decided to use 'conceptions of trustworthiness' (Hardin, 2006: p. 16) that can further be broken down into the constitutive elements that facilitate the data analysis, namely: reliance, risk, expectations and confidence, knowledge ability, honesty and reliability, and transparency (Fukuyama, 1995; Irwin, 1995; The BSE Inquiry 2000; Hardin, 2006; Meijboom, Visak and Brom, 2006).[30]

---

[27] I did not record the informal conversations and did not take them into account during the data analysis. These off-the record conversations reflect the fact that I established deep and trustworthy relationships with many participants.

[28] The final interviews intended primarily at validating the my concept of the Investment Opportunity Framework (IOF) which will be published elsewhere.

[29] Ethics certificates were obtained in 2015 and 2018.

[30] Reliance because if one trusts another person it means that one can rely on that person; risk as one tends to trust another person if there is no risk of suffering a loss; expectations and confidence as one

19.3 SOCIAL MOVEMENTS AND CFDS: FROM CONFLICT TO ANALYTIC COMPETITION

This empirical part is a result of a rigorous analysis of the rich data through the above elements of trust rather than presentation of a general research report. I start with the data analysis through *reliance* to prove that social movements chose to rely on dominant players to a great extent with their little exploration of opportunities embedded in the CFDs. Those positive instances of utilising CFDs are found in relation to pension/bond finance. Often high and unclear demands that social movements attached to reliance shift their relationship with the dominant players towards one manifested by conflict. These relationships are further complicated by the inherent conflicts within the social movements' community. Thereafter, I turn to analysing the data through *knowledge ability, risk, honesty, expectations* and *transparency* elements of trust to identify observable conflict between social movements and dominant players. I argue that that conflict dwells on the surface of these interactions, whereas competition resides beneath that visible layer of struggle, which I subsequently frame as analytic competition. I will then make a logical progression to Section 3 where I argue that social movements should be more responsible on the GSFM.

19.3.1 *Reliance on Dominant Players*

The analysis of the research findings suggests that social movements (especially those focused on project finance) aspire to rely on the World Bank Group institutions that clearly manifested at meetings relating to various aspects of project finance. However, social movements attach high and often unclear demands to this aspirational reliance that cannot be fully met by the WBG, which, in turn, leads to conflict. Let us look at a few examples to prove this argument. First, social movements expressed their wish that the World Bank, and other multilateral financial institutions, would 'do something', 'take further action' and 'be more decisive'.[31] They demanded more robust grievance mechanisms at the country project level[32] and WBG level[33] to improve the viability of the projects but, most importantly, often requested projects to be stopped. Secondly, social movements

---

tends to trust another person if the latter can fulfill the former's expectation that may turn into confidence; and knowledge ability as one tends to trust more in another person if that person is knowledgeable, especially in relation to their profession. Further elements of trustworthiness such as honesty and reliability and transparency were also used in data analysis but to a lesser extent.

[31] Reports from the Participant Observations, WBG-IMF Annual/Spring Meetings.

[32] See for example The Grievance Redress Service website available at http://projects-beta.worldbank.org/en/projects-operations/products-and-services/grievance-redress-service accessed on 1 September 2018; and the role of the Compliance Advisor Ombudsman at the website available at www.cao-ombudsman.org/.

[33] See for example the role of the Independent Evaluation Group at the website available at http://ieg .worldbankgroup.org/.

petitioned actively the WBG to 'do something'[34] over various laws and policies in developing countries including human rights laws, environmental laws, informational laws and even NGO laws.[35] Thirdly, social movements required the WBG to 'do something' to influence the conduct of financial intermediaries that receive funding from the WBG with a view to channelling that funding to development projects. Such requests, coined as a 'bottom-up approach'[36] were primarily focused on improving the projects because such financing can indeed pose problems with tracing spending and allocating the accountability in case of environmental or human rights violations. These demands included requests to stop financing these projects as soon as possible. This clear aspirational reliance was somewhat reduced by political protests and manifestations outside the WBG premises during the meetings. It certainly exacerbated tensions between social movements and the dominant players (mainly WBG) and introduced a possibility of further protests should the demands were not met.

Reliance was much more subtle with regard to pension finance and bond finance with clearer instances of social movements forging alliances with key investors and institutions ('key partners') to improve their campaigns during the dedicated bond and pension finance meetings. There was evidence of aspirational reliance where social movements expressed their willingness to collaborate subject to investors meeting certain demands relating to the definition of green bonds or disinvestment practices. Principles for Responsible Investment (PRI) has been marketed as a non-profit movement relying on the support and participation of high-profile stakeholders such as the UN. For bond finance, established NGOs and think-tanks relied mostly on their networks.[37] However, during interview, smaller NGOs and organisations expressed problems with relying on well-established NGOs (both project finance and equity finance).

19.3.2 Missing the Core of CFDs

It is clear that social movements targeted the top and dominant finance players (especially with regard to project finance) and, in my view, such social movements should show more appreciation of the complex finance dynamics. Logically, social movements cannot easily alter the project finance structure by issuing demands to

---

[34] Social movements frequently said 'you [multilateral financial institutions] have to do something over [human rights laws, gay rights etc.]'. Reports from the Participant Observations, WBG-IMF Annual/Spring Meetings, explanations added by the author.

[35] The last point related to, for example, the 2009 Ethiopian Proclamation to Provide for the Registration and Regulation of Charities and Societies which restricts rights of NGOs in the country and the issue over the NGOs and the Financial Action Task Force (FATF). See also, Chapter 3 of the report by the Secretary General of the Council of Europe (2017).

[36] Reports from the Participant Observations, WBG-IMF Annual/Spring Meetings. The 'bottom-up approach' includes reliance on the existing ESG standards to strengthen the projects.

[37] Reports from the Participant Observations, Green Bonds/Pension Finance.

the dominant players. These demands often requested the WBG to stop a given project, as if these projects were simple limited companies that can be put under administration. Rather, social movements should be engaging these dominant players (alongside other key stakeholders) into the complexity of the dynamic at various stages of its existence, from initial scoping stage through to operation and maintenance. This should be done by channelling the discussion on the content of memoranda of understanding, contracts and guarantees, the role of syndication and intermediation and the relevant legal opportunities and limitations. Social movement demands could be framed as vague, which naturally led WBG officials to clarify several times that the WBG was not a 'political institution'[38] and often invoked Article IV, section 10 of the Articles of Agreement:

> The Bank and its officers shall not interfere in the political affairs of any member; nor shall they be influenced in their decisions by the political character of the member or members concerned. Only economic considerations shall be relevant to their decisions, and these considerations shall be weighed impartially in order to achieve the purposes stated in Article I.[39]

Social movements (attending the WBG-IMF meetings) had little appreciation of bond finance at some discussions that explored the connections between bonds and project finance. Social movements (both at WBG meetings and bond meetings) targeted large investment banks for their alleged inaction in developing the green bond market, whereas, the latter expressed a need for restraint and incremental advancement of the market. The preference for the gradual developments can be explained by the huge risks that investment banks assume legally when entering into a subscription agreement with the issuer of the bond. Such agreements usually compel the investment banks to 'acquire any securities which are left unpurchased means they are putting their own money on the line when they advise the issuer' (Hudson, 2013: p. 916). Any negative information about the bond issuance, irrespective of the potential success of the financed project, may be hugely detrimental to investment banks and the whole I-owe-you (IOU) structure. The dominant players on the bond market appreciated this complex finance dynamic and leveraged the relationship with other dominant market players (i.e. large issuers, states, investment banks, institutional investors and multilateral financial institutions). Whereas this research did not trace the development of the ICMA Social Bonds (2017), one senior respondent emphasised in 2016 that the trigger for their development came from 'Nordic pension funds and not from NGOs'.[40]

---

[38] Reports from the Participant Observations, WBG-IMF Annual/Spring Meetings.
[39] IBRD Articles of Agreement http://siteresources.worldbank.org/EXTABOUTUS/Resources/ibrd-articlesofagreement.pdf accessed 15 October 2017. Art. 1 of the Articles of Agreement refers to the overall economic goals of the World Bank to facilitate the development through broad categories of investment tools such as loans, guarantees or providing leverage to attract private investment.
[40] Interview with Respondent 29.

I observed instances of social movements moving closer to the core of the pension finance dynamic. I also observed social movements issuing demands towards asset large institutions such as pension funds, sovereign funds and asset managers along-side some appreciation of the role of pensioners themselves. As one respondent highlighted:

> we engage with institutional investors and policy-makers [. . .] but, we also talk to savers, they should know where their money is being invested, it is an issue of transparency; [. . .] but they [*the savers*] should also be able to influence the direction of their money, there is so much they could do if they knew . . . and we try to help them.[41]

Some of the key initiatives which underpin the complex finance dynamics are driven by not-for-profit organisations that employ some business-like professional mechanisms to drive the ESG agenda (e.g. Climate Bonds Initiative or the UN-supported Principles of Responsible Investment). Such organisations are targeting the 'core' of the CFDs which differs from the instances to influence the dominant players, who are constrained by the structures of these dynamics as to what they can do. Social movements must comprehend the core of the CFDs, that is the consti-tuent series of deals which in turn, should trigger a measured response leading to the incremental developments.

19.3.3 Observable Conflicts

Undoubtedly, I uncovered the participant observation that social movements were conflicted, with the dominant stakeholders shaping project finance, bond finance and pension finance. This conflict, understood as 'an active disagreement between people with opposing opinions or principles',[42] was especially marked during the WBG/IMF meetings that were characterised by tense emotional debates. Usually, social movements and NGOs would portray themselves as the representatives of the vulnerable with clear demands towards the institution to 'do something'. This conflict was less pronounced, yet still visible, at meetings relating to bond finance and pensions finance during which the social movements stressed the need to move urgently away from the financial bottom line and towards social and environmental aspects of sustainable finance. The social movements favoured disinvestment approaches, i.e. the shift towards the processes that exclude certain asset classes from sustainable finance.

The conflict is especially visible through the *risk* element of trustworthiness at the WBG-IMF and bond meetings. Social movements often emphasised the social and environmental risks resulting from the current 'mainstream' agenda. They typically called for greater articulation of social and environmental matters by the dominant

---

[41] Interview with Respondent 21.
[42] https://dictionary.cambridge.org/dictionary/english/conflict.

players, including stronger enforcement. The sustainable finance agenda was said to be threatened by the alleged inadequate integration of environmental, social and governance matters into the project finance and bond finance. Public institutions and institutional investors seemed to be aware of these risks, yet they would usually try to emphasise and explain the role of the existing mechanisms governing these matters (e.g. environmental permits, margin of appreciation embedded in human rights laws, environmental risk assessments). Clearly, these dominant players showed appreciation of the proposed principles governing the GSFM. Interviews with social movements' representatives and public institutions confirmed findings from the participant observation. However, interviews with investors showed another side of the coin – some investors perceived social movements as a risk to pursuing the current green agenda. Some respondents described NGOs as 'cynical' organisations that 'destroy the market',[43] as 'unhelpful'[44] and 'obstructive'.[45] One senior respondent who initiated the green bonds developments was adamant about the NGOs' initial contributions: 'They [NGOs] wanted to kill the market! Just when we started it!'[46] Conflict was also visible through the *expectation and confidence* elements of trustworthiness. The movements and NGOs urged much more decisive and quicker actions including litigation, greater accountability and clearer definitions (e.g. what 'green' means under green bonds). The expectations relate mostly to the urgency of actions ('we need to act now' that has been uttered by many participants including some non-profits driving the bond market and the PRI). Such expectations received largely reserved feedback from the institutions and investors who emphasised the complexity of finance, the policymaking and the market-forming mechanisms.[47] Interviews confirmed findings from the participant observation. Similarly to the above, some institutional investors emphasised that the social movements' expectations exceeded the current possibilities. One interviewee representing a large management consultancy firm (thus advising and working on a variety of project finance matters) emphasised that for social movements 'nothing is perfect' and that they tend to 'still criticize' after certain concessions are made.[48]

The analysis of the *knowledge-ability* element of trustworthiness uncovers further active disagreements. Several events during the WBG-IMF meetings included presentations of research findings by social movements and public institutions. Most of the presentations were criticised (by social movements or institutions) based on flawed methodologies, flawed sampling or even inadequate personnel conducting the research. Such criticism led to cutting the substantive discussions prematurely. Further, social movements complained that they were not understood

43 Interview with Respondent 31.
44 Interview with Respondent 7.
45 Interview with Respondent 9.
46 Interview with Respondent 31.
47 Reports from the Participant Observations, WBG-IMF Annual/Spring Meetings, Pension/Equity finance, Green Bonds.
48 Interview with Respondent 17.

due to some multilateral banks employing highly specialised economists struggling to engage with civil society. There were a few occasions during which the officials referred to the progress made to expand on social and environmental agendas within the multilateral financial institutions, hence, confirming the social movements' anxieties.[49] However, several meetings between the social movements and the officials revealed that some of the latter struggle themselves to engage with senior colleagues. This created a platform for mutual understanding between the social movements and the dominant players that also opened the door for some collaboration:

> X [*name removed*] himself met with the wall in Y [*name of the organisation removed*] ... you know ... he wanted to help us; he pushed for the environment, but they moved him around so we could not ask him again ... however, he was very keen to meet with us and talk to us.[50]

However, I also observed instances of collaboration in relation to *knowledge-ability*. The second day of the small UK NGO's event included a workshop during which social movements could share their experience and expertise on finance dynamics and how to effectively campaign. Emphasis was made on the need to 'use the language of finance'[51] when engaging with the pension funds or asset managers. There was a positive culture of learning from each other that appreciated that complexity – the more experienced NGOs would train the less experienced groups how to engage with active and passive asset managers; the difference between banking and equity and pension finance; how to gain the media's attention, to name a few. Further, the social movements were very keen to draw the expertise from the former finance experts who worked for large institutional investors; the interviews confirmed that some of the social movements' representatives 'opted out' from corporate finance to join the social movements.[52]

Turning to *honesty*, there were a few instances where institutions or investors were very honest in relation to their past actions (e.g. relating to finance through inter-mediaries): 'we know we made mistakes in the past' and 'we are going to make mistakes in the future'.[53] The institutions and investors seemed honest in relation to social movements' frequent calls to exclude investments into certain companies (e.g. through 'negative screening') with a transition slowly towards green finance: 'we don't want to exclude those who struggle initially'.[54] Social movements were also adamant about the need to define clearly what 'green' means under 'green bonds' to which the dominant stakeholders would respond: 'there are different shades of green'.[55] Social

49 Reports from the Participant Observations, WBG-IMF Annual/Spring Meetings.
50 Interview with Respondent 5.
51 Reports from the Participant Observations, Pension/Equity finance.
52 Ibid.
53 Reports from the Participant Observations, WBG-IMF Annual/Spring Meetings.
54 Reports from the Participant Observations, Pension/Equity finance.
55 Reports from the Participant Observations, Green Bonds.

movements were often honest about their feelings of anger, disappointment and sadness when presenting serious cases of human rights violations or environmental campaigners facing death or rape threats.

The interview data provided further insights into honesty. Social movements often described investors and institutions as those who struggle with being honest and forging and maintaining hidden agendas. One respondent referred to high 'compensation [remuneration] schemes'[56] as a real driver of the current sustainable finance agenda as opposed to the honest environmental and social stewardship.

These relationships are further complicated by the internal conflicts within the social movements' community. There was some emphasis on the need to firstly forge adequate alliances among the social movements in the first instance and reliance on the WBG civil society teams to help in organising such alliances. In addition, the participant observation notes prove that the alliances were challenging due to the inadequate coordination and ill-representation of smaller movements, groups and individuals especially from the developing countries. The lack of adequate internal representation manifested itself at each WBG/IMF meeting with instances of respondents from developing countries challenging the well-established larger NGOs for hijacking the communication with the dominant players for their own benefit (e.g. by arranging one-to-one meetings with the multilateral finance organisations or institutional investors).[57]

19.3.4 *Competition Beneath the Conflict*

Yet, my argument is that this apparent conflict was only dwelling on the surface of these interactions – a finding arising mainly from the limitations of participant observation. There is a much more subtle competitive interaction between the social movements and the dominant players shaping the CFDs that I uncovered mainly through interviews, testing the findings and my own reflection. Competition does emphasise a rivalry between the parties with the potential for collaboration[58] that raises questions over the equivalency and complementarity of actions. Starting with honesty, some institutional investors uncovered NGOs' alleged hidden competitive agendas as a key driver of their high expectations. One senior institutional investor noted:

> [T]hey are doing this for money . . . they need to apply for funding . . . I know that as they told me![59]

The competition is clearly visible by analysing the *knowledge-ability* and *responsibility* elements of trustworthiness through the interviews from respondents shaping

---

[56] Interview with Respondent 2.
[57] Ibid.
[58] As noticed above, there were instances of collaboration.
[59] Interview with Respondent 31.

the project finance. The analysis suggests that the gaps in knowledge-ability are inevitable given the complex finance dynamics and the background of the stakeholders. The social movements were said to include very specialised NGOs and even described as ' . . . very unsophisticated'[60] with emphasis on the critical role of funding. Following on from this trail, one investor responded to the question whether they would sponsor some of the social movements' activities in the following manner:

> Yes, but they would need to have a proper plan . . . you know . . . a business plan; what will be done and when . . . otherwise our funding could kill them! They wouldn't know what to do with such money![61]

One institutional investor was very keen on collaborating with social movements as long as they 'bring something that we haven't thought through, yet'[62] and another respondent emphasised his trust in 'the market forces'[63] to find solutions to the sustainable finance dilemmas. The confidence in the market forces opens the opportunity for social movements if they can prove their competitive advantage. Further, I interviewed two mathematicians[64] (one involved in project finance, another in pension finance during the global financial crisis) who both noted the knowledge gaps between the social movements and investors/institutions and the apparent knowledge gaps within the specialised institutions during the financial crisis. Finally, it is worth noting that one respondent (met at the WBG meetings) made a conscious shift from being a member of 'civil society' to actively pursuing 'business opportunities' by engaging with the multilateral financial institutions and investors.[65]

Competition intensified when I looked at the data through the *transparency and traceability* elements of trustworthiness. Social movements demanded more transparency by frequently complaining that multilateral financial institutions, institutional investors and other institutions often invoked confidentiality to hide their practices. However, one respondent representing a large NGO claimed full confidentiality that prevented them sharing certain information during an interview with myself. Further, one respondent who has recently moved from the civil society to becoming an entrepreneur saw advantages in getting a competitive edge through withholding information. A closer analysis of the interview transcripts suggests that social movements do not petition for absolute transparency and recognise the need to balance the interests of the investors/institutions with the public interest. Interviews with multilateral financial institutions, investors and other institutions show that confidentiality is a necessary element embedded in complex finance

---

[60] Interview with Respondent 11.
[61] Interview with Respondent 6.
[62] Interview with Respondent 30.
[63] Interview with Respondent 31.
[64] Interviews with Respondent 15 (now a small-scale investor).
[65] Interview with Respondent 9.

dynamics. Further, coming back to reliance, there was one request that focused on a need to 'do something' through covenants and made by larger and more sophisticated NGOs.[66] The analysis of the interview scripts suggests that such requests were present on the agenda of these experienced NGOs and frequently expressed directly during the one-to-one meetings, unofficial or specifically arranged meetings outside the WBG-IMF Annual/Spring meetings. However, the same large NGOs attended the WBG-IMF meetings and, for unexplained reasons, did not share their expertise with smaller organisations. In my view, this can only be explained by the existence of competition between organisations forming the social movements that I observed during various meetings.

Conflict dwells on the surface of interactions between social movements and dominant players and within the social movement communities. However, competition resides beneath that visible layer of conflict and I will now frame this competition as analytic competition.

19.3.5 Analytic Competition: from a Cog to a Sustainable Finance Citizen

So far, the term 'analytic competition' has been used in the company context to denote a largely quantitative advantage (Davenport and Harris, 2007), with very limited application to the interaction between NGOs and WTO and the NGOs involvement in the investment treaty arbitration processes (Esty, 1998; Ishikawa, 2010). It needs to be taken to the next level to fit the requirements of the GMSF, which is a meeting place for various stakeholders who shape, inter alia, the CFDs and the innovative underpinning mechanisms that unlock and advance finance for sustainable development. Analytic competition serves as a source of competitive advantage for social movements on the sustainable finance market.

I propose that the aligned, co-created and adaptable GSFM requires two critical analytic ingredients from the players: unique explicit and tacit sustainable finance knowledge and the holistic predisposition to navigate effectively through this market. Knowledge includes understanding of finance, CFDs, environmental and social issues alongside methodological approaches inclusive of quantitative and qualitative approaches. It will be a challenge for a single dominant player (say a single multilateral finance institution or a single state) to acquire this vast knowledge base and the very nature of CFDs in the sustainable finance context necessitates the collaborative approaches. Clearly, as captured by this research, social movements possessed distinct knowledge on environmental and social issues and some were willing to acquire finance knowledge. Similarly, the dominant players, with access to finance and legal knowledge, were inclined to engage with social movements on social and environmental matters. This knowledge includes tacit knowledge which embraces expertise and skills that cannot be easily formulated (Polanyi, 1969), but also confidential

---

[66] Reports from the Participant Observations, WBG-IMF Annual/Spring Meetings.

information and 'tricks of trade' (Collins, 2001: p. 72). Obviously, tacit knowledge can be acquired by groups through experience (Baumard, 1999 and has been acknowledged as one of the key social movements' resources (Edwards and McCarthy, 2004). My research proves that all players on the GSFM possess some confidential information that they may not want to express publicly. Yet, whilst this is understandable, social movements need to acknowledge they also possess such confidential information or tricks of the trade that they cannot share without appropriate transfer agreements. My research also proves that social movements find it difficult to express their tacit knowledge by issuing high and unclear demands that I discussed at the beginning of this section (*reliance*).

However, unique sustainability explicit and tacit knowledge is not enough to gain the competitive advantage on the GSFM. Knowing *your stuff* and *how to do your stuff* may actually lead to isolation on the market or even self-inflicted exclusion from it. Obviously, the exclusion from the GSFM does not mean that the player is doomed or in a somewhat disadvantaged position. My argument is that those relying solely on explicit and tacit knowledge may not be able to fully participate on the aligned, co-created and adaptable GSFM, yet, they can provide services for the components of that market; remain an important a cog in a sustainable finance machine. I argue that true participation is a form of sustainable finance citizenry that requires the holistic predisposition to navigate effectively through this market. It is a willingness to move from the comfort of one's knowledge base onto a territory of another CFDs, unique jurisdiction (such as Islamic finance) or industry (from conventional banking to values-based banking). This predisposition is not another form of tacit knowledge. Rather, it is a form of consciousness and virtue which serves as a lubricant that helps navigating through this vast sustainable finance knowledge base and the GSFM. It is a form of tolerance on the individual level – even if one disagrees with the opposing industry, one recognises that that industry is moving towards sustainable finance (through alignment and co-creation). In this area, however, the dominant players are still way ahead of the social movements, with some exceptions among individual highly specialised NGOs (e.g. Climate Bonds Initiative). The dominant players co-created the standards and initiatives that provide pathways for other players to contribute to shaping the CFDs. Hence, social movements could attend the WBG/IMF Spring meeting or join, as observers, the Green Bond Principles. This explains why the dominant players interviewed by me were willing to engage with social movements provided that the latter were not obstructive and had something concrete to bring to the table. It also justifies their apprehension about involving the social movements in shaping the CFDs given some perceptions, as noted above, that social movements may 'kill the market'.[67] This understanding of analytic competition leads to the final point that social movements must become more responsible in their engagement with CFDs.

[67] Interview with Respondent 31 (see p. 382).

19.4 TOWARDS RESPONSIBLE SOCIAL MOVEMENTS

19.4.1 *Responsible Social Movements for Sustainable Finance*

The dominant players that shape the CFDs have created pathways for the social movements' engagement with the CFDs that have also enabled me to conduct the research. These players are clearly driving the sustainable market by involving other stakeholders that can enhance the debate. They are not without fault, which they admitted ('we made mistakes'[68]) and they also face their own analytic competition distinct challenges (e.g. inadequate internal processes; excessive macro-economic language). Yet, the social movements were much less inclined to such self-reflective admissions, often creating noise aimed at evoking emotional reactions. On the surface, they portrayed themselves as a beacon of justice and fairness in conflict with the dominant players whilst, behind the scenes, they struggled to obtain funding to continue their actions or express their demands in a professional manner.

Hence, social movements must become more responsible to improve their analytic competition for the benefit of the GSFM. This means they need to continue working on improve their knowledge base; yet, most importantly acquire the holistic predisposition to navigate effectively through this market. By doing so, the social movements will not lose their principal driving force (or soul) because, by their very nature, social movements tend to move from loose groupings towards obtaining an organisational structure (Blumer, 1951). Through this they align with the evolving GSFM as pointed out in the conclusion of Section 2 of this Chapter and become the citizens of sustainable finance.

19.4.2 *Principles for Responsible Social Movements*

As I argued in Part 2, social movements are conglomerates of various organisations, groups and communities, and do not possess an organisational structure early in their development. The current attempts at the international level to develop stronger accountability mechanisms for NGOs (Golubovic, 2018) are therefore insufficient. There is a need for an initiative that broadly aligns with the notion of descriptive or stakeholder accountability (Kovach, Neligan and Burall, 2003; Dekker, 2011).

My argument is that social movements should be more explicit about their responsibility by adopting collective responsibility principles and codes of conduct at the early stages of their engagement on the GSFM. These principles should be place-based, that is, closely tied to specific places where the engagement is going to take place such as the WBG/IMF meetings, the Climate Change conferences or meetings with investors. They could also be revised and accepted during subsequent meetings because, as we said, social movements are heterogeneous and evolving in

---

[68] See n. 52 above.

time, same for the GSFM. Such an approach will serve as a self-reflective exercise for various groupings, organisations and individuals and as a possibility for them to learn more about the evolving GSFM. The principles could include the following elements:

Under alignment with sustainable finance: the reason for forming the movement, the strategic objectives of the movement, and a statement on their alignment with global sustainability and climate agendas could be agreed upon and announced/ published at the sustainable finance agenda.

Under co-management: identification of the CFDs that they primarily want to engage with, and through this, the stakeholder analysis of the key dominant (and lesser) stakeholders shaping these dynamics; the knowledge base needed to make an effective engagement and the principles governing this engagement (e.g. effective inclusion of smaller groups; communication channels with dominant players).

Under adaptability: a form of an impact assessment; relevance of their actions for other CFDs (e.g. interactions between pension finance and project finance; influence on other distinct markets such as in the developing countries or Islamic finance countries; corporations making the transition to sustainable finance and smaller investors intending to scale up their actions for SD; or, self-reflection on social movement becoming a social enterprise or a business).

19.5 CONCLUSION

This chapter offered an original and innovative insight into sustainable finance by analysing social movements' interaction with complex finance dynamics (CFDs) through elements of trustworthiness. My overall argument is that social movements, whilst projecting their conflict with the dominant players, play a competitive role on the global sustainable finance market (GSFM), and, to improve their competitiveness, they need to adopt responsibility principles.

To develop this argument, I positioned social movements as heterogeneous and evolving entities that can play a tangible role on the GSFM which does not necessarily have to include conflict. We are still at the early stages of sustainable finance and I resisted a temptation to define the market through a summary of several vague and (sometimes) conflicting definitions. Instead, I proposed an original notion of the GSFM which should be governed by the following principles: alignment, co-creation and adaptability. Hence, the market remains aligned with the global sustainability agenda; co-created by various parties that shape, inter alia, the CFDs; and adaptable to different contexts such as Islamic banking or specialised contexts such as niche values-based banking or forestry. I then moved to the empirical part of the chapter by firstly explaining the innovative and rigorous project design that involved data collection from three distinct CFDs over a three-year period of time. My analysis used a trustworthiness analytical framework that proved useful in uncovering the conflict. However, it served the main purpose of demonstrating the analytic competition between social movements and the major stakeholders. I offered original conceptualisation of the analytic competition to include explicit and tacit unique sustainable knowledge and the holistic predisposition to navigate effectively through this market. I explained this holistic predisposition as a form of consciousness and virtue which serves as a lubricant that helps players to navigate through this vast sustainable finance knowledge base and the GSFM. My argument is that those relying solely on explicit and tacit knowledge may not be able to fully participate on the aligned, co-created and adaptable GSFM, yet, they can provide services for the components of that market; remain an important a cog in a sustainable finance machine. I argue that the true participation is a form of sustainable finance citizenry that require the holistic predisposition to navigate effectively through this market. I argued that social movements struggle with this virtue and, to acquire or improve it, they need to become more responsible about their actions. This led to me proposing principles of responsible social movements and drafting the key elements of such a code through the lenses of the GSFM. To close the loop, I think that the adoption of such principles would be a form of an exchange on the GSFM where, in response to large industry commitments, social movements commit to acting sustainably vis-à-vis the CFDs. This exchange should lead to increasing trust between social movements and the dominant players in the long term.

REFERENCES

Asian Infrastructure Investment Bank (2016). Environmental and Social Framework, available at www.aiib.org/en/policies-strategies/framework-agreements/environmental-social-framework.html accessed 1 April 2016.
Bank Negara Malaysia (2018). Value-Based Intermediation. Financing and Investment Impact Assessment Framework, available at: www.bnm.gov.my/index.php?ch=57&pg=137&ac=734&bb=file accessed 1 November 2018.
Bank of England (2018). Transition in thinking: The impact of climate change on the UK banking sector, available at www.bankofengland.co.uk/-/media/boe/files/prudential-regulation/report/transition-in-thinking-the-impact-of-climate-change-on-the-uk-banking-sector.pdf accessed 18 March 2019.
Baumard, P. (1999). *Tacit Knowledge in Organisations*. London: Sage Publications.
Blumer, H. (1951). Collective Behavior. In A. M. Lee, ed., *New Outline of the Principles of Sociology*. New York: Barnes & Noble, pp. 167–222.
Brundtland, G. H., Khalid, M. and Agnelli, S. (1987). *Our Common Future: Brundtland Report*. Oxford: Oxford University Press.
Carroll, A. B. and Shabana K. M. (2010). The Business Case for Corporate Social Responsibility: A Review of Concepts, Research and Practice. *International Journal of Management Reviews*, 12(1), 85–105.
Clark, D., Fox, J. and Treakle, K. (2003). *Demanding Accountability. Civil Society Claims and the World Bank Inspection Panel*. London: Rowman & Littlefield Publishers.
Collins, H. M. (2001). Tacit Knowledge, Trust and the Q of Sapphire. *Social Studies of Science*, 31(1), 71–85.
Crossley, N. (2003). Even Newer Social Movements? Anti-Corporate Protests, Capitalist Crises and the Remoralization of Society. *Organization*, 10(2), 28788.

Crossley, N. (2002). Global Anti-Corporate Struggle: A Preliminary Analysis. *British Journal of Sociology*, 53(4), 667.

Davenport, T. H. and Harris, J. G. (2007). *The New Science of Winning*. Boston: Harvard Business School Press.

Dawson, C. T. and Bhatt, G. D. (2001). *The IMF and Civil Society Organisations: Striking a Balance*. Washington, DC: International Monetary Fund.

Dekker (2011). Socially Responsible NGOs? A European Perspective. In Y. Li, ed., *NGOs in China and Europe: Comparisons and Contrast*, 1st ed. London: Routledge.

Della Porta, D. (2007). *The Global Justice Movement: Cross-National and Transnational Perceives*. London: Paradigm Publishers.

Denzin, N. K. and Lincoln, Y. S. (2005). *Sage Handbook on Qualitative Research*. London: Sage, p. 22.

Diani, M. (1992). The Concept of Social Movement. *The Sociological Review*, 40(1), 1.

Dugue, C. (2000). Dispute Resolution in International Project Finance. *Transactions. Fordham International Law Journal*, 24, 1064.

Edwards, B. and McCarthy, D. J. (2004). Resources and Social Movement Mobilisation. In A. D. Snow, A. S. Soule, H. Kriesi, eds., *The Blackwell Companion to Social Movements*. Oxford: Blackwell Publishing.

Equator Principles (2013). *The Equator Principles*, available at https://equator-principles .com./wp-content/uploads/2017/03/equator_principles_III.pdf, accessed 17 August 2017.

Esty, D. C. (1998). Non-Governmental Organizations at the World Trade Organization: Cooperation, Competition, or Exclusion. *Journal of International Economic Law*, 1, 123.

Flesher Fominaya, C. and Cox L., eds. (2013). *Understanding European Movements: New Social Movements, Global Justice Struggles, Anti-Austerity Protest*. Abingdon: Routledge.

Food and Agriculture Organisation of the United Nations [FAO] (2015). *Sustainable Financing for Forest and Landscape Restoration. Opportunities, Challenges and the Way Forward*. Rome: FAO.

Fox, A. J. and Brown, D. L., eds., (1998). *The Struggle for Accountability. The World Bank, NGOs and Grassroots Movements*. Massachusetts: The MIT Press.

Fukuyama, F. (1995). *Trust. The Social Virtues and the Creation of Prosperity*. London: Penguin Books.

G20 Insights (2017). Fostering Sustainable Global Growth through Green Finance – What Role for the G20? available at www.g20-insights.org/wp-content/uploads/2017/04/ Climate_Green-Finance_V2.pdf accessed 1 September 2018.

GABV Principles of Values Based Banking (2011). Available at: www.gabv.org/about-us/our-principles accessed 1 September 2018.

Goldsmith, H. (2015). Actors and Innovations in the Evolution of Infrastructure Services. In A. Picot et. al., eds., *The Economics of Infrastructure Provisioning: The Changing Role of the State*. Massachusetts: MIT Press.

Golubovic, D. (2018). International Standards Relating to Reporting and Disclosure Requirements for Non-Governmental Organizations. Council of Europe, available at https://rm.coe.int/expert-council-conf-exp-2018–3-review-ngo-reporting-requirements /16808f2237.

Haberman, S. and Sibbett, T. A. (1995). *History of Actuarial Science*. Vol. 1. London: William Pickering.

Hannigan, J. A. (1995). *Environmental Sociology: A Social Constructionist Perspective*. London: Routledge.

Hardin, R. (2006). *Trust*. Cambridge: Polity Press.

Hilson, C. (2002). New Social Movements: The Role of Legal Opportunity. *Journal of European Public Policy*. 9(2), 238.

Hudson, A. (2013). *The Law of Finance*. London: Sweet & Maxwell.

ICMA (2018). Green, Social and Sustainability Bond Principles, available at: www.icmagroup.org/green-social-and-sustainability-bonds/ accessed 1 September 2018.

ICMA (2019). 'Membership' available at www.icmagroup.org/green-social-and-sustainability-bonds/membership/.

IFC (2012). Performance Standards, available at: www.ifc.org/wps/wcm/connect/topics_ext_content/ifc_external_corporate_site/sustainability-at-ifc/policies-standards/performance-standards/performance-standards accessed 17 August 2017.

Irwin, A. (1995). *Citizen Science: A Study of People, Expertise and Sustainable Development*. London: Routledge.

Ishikawa, T. (2010). Third Party Participation in Investment Treaty Arbitration. *International and Comparative Law Quarterly*. 59(2), 373–412.

ISO 26000 and OECD Guidelines (2019). Available at: www.iso.org/files/live/sites/isoorg/files/store/en/PUB100418.pdf accessed 1 March 2019.

Jopson, B. (2015). COP21 Paris Climate Talks: Billionaires Join Forces in Energy Push. *The Financial Times*, available at: www.ft.com/content/1fcae3aa-96f5-11e5-9228-87e603d47bdc accessed 30 November 2015.

Kaeufer, K. (2010). *Banking as a Vehicle for Socio-economic Development and Change: Case Studies of Socially Responsible and Green Banks*. Cambridge: Presenting Institute.

Kay, J. (2012). The Kay Review of UK Equity Markets and Long-Term Decision Making, p. 9, available at www.gov.uk/government/consultations/the-kay-review-of-uk-equity-markets-and-long-term-decision-making accessed 1 April 2015.

King, G. B. and Soule, A. S. (2007). Social Movements as Extra-Institutional Entrepreneurs: The Effect of Protests on Stock Price Returns, *Administrative Science Quarterly*, 52(3).

Kitschelt, H. (1986). Political Opportunity Structures and Political Protest: Antinuclear Movements in Four Democracies. *British Journal of Political Science*. 16, 57.

Klein, N. (2002). Farewell to 'The End of History': Organization and Vision in Anti-Corporate Movements. *Socialist Register*. 1–13.

Kovach, H., Neligan, C. and Burall, S. (2003). *Power without Accountability? The Global Accountability Report 1*, London: One World Trust.

Kraut, R. (2016). *Building Successful Online Communities: Evidence-Based Social Design*. Massachusetts: MIT Press.

Lawrence, R. (2008). NGO Campaigns and Banks: Constituting Risk and Uncertainty. In G. De Neve, P. Luetchford, J. Pratt, and D. C. Wood, eds., *Hidden Hands in the Market: Ethnographies of Fair Trade, Ethical Consumption, and Corporate Social Responsibility*. Vol. 28 of *Research in Economic Anthropology*. Emerald Group Publishing Limited, pp. 241–69.

McCarthy, J. D. and Zald, M. N. (1977). Resource Mobilization and Social Movements: A Partial Theory. *American Journal of Sociology*. 82(6), 1212.

McDaniels, J., Robins, N., Strauss, D., Thoma, J. and Dupre, S. (2015). Building a Sustainable Financial System in the European Union. UNEP Inquiry and 2° Investing Initiative, available at http://unepinquiry.org/wp-content/uploads/2016/04/Building_a_Sustainable_Financial_System_in_the_European_Union.pdf accessed 1 January 2017.

Melucci, A. (1996) *Challenging Codes: Collective Action in the Information Age*. Cambridge: Cambridge University Press, p. 5.

Meijboom, F. L. B., Visak, T. and Brom, F. (2006). From Trust to Trustworthiness: Why Information Is not Enough in the Food Sector. *Journal of Agricultural and Environmental Ethics*, 19(5), 427–42. http://doi 10.1007/s10806-006-9000-2.

Mudaliar, A., Schiff, H., Bass, R. and Dithrich, H. (2017). 2017 Annual Impact Investor Survey: The Global Impact Investing Network available at https://web.archive.org/web/20170708185027/https://thegiin.org/assets/GIIN_AnnualImpactInvestorSurvey_2017_Web_Final.pdf Archived from the original (PDF) on 2 June 2016, accessed 14 March 2017.

O'Brien, R., Goetz, A. M. and Scholte, J. A. (2009). *Contesting Global Governance. Multilateral Economic Institutions and Global Social Movements.* Cambridge: Cambridge University Press.

O'Malley, C. (2015). *Bonds without Borders. A History of the Eurobond Market.* Chichester: John Wiley & Sons.

Polanyi, M. (1969). Tacit Knowing: Its Bearing on Some Problems of Philosophy. In M. Grene, ed., *Knowing and being. Essays.* London: Routledge and Kegan Paul, Chapter 11, pp. 159–80. Originally published in *Reviews of Modern Physics* (1962) 34, 601–61.

Rheingold, H. (2001). *The virtual community: Homesteading on the electronic frontier.* New York: Harper Perennial.

Ridley, M. and Barnshaw, P. (2019). Green Bond Insights. 2019 Market Outlook: Rise of the ESG Investor. HSBC Global Research available at www.research.hsbc.com/C/1/1/254/wGBzQcL accessed 21 July 2019.

Ross, A. (2010). Modern Interpretations of Sustainable Development. *Journal of Law and Society.* 36(1), 32.

Secretary General of the Council of Europe (2017). Report on the State of Democracy, Human Rights and the Rule of Law, available at www.theioi.org/ioi-news/current-news/council-of-europe-2018-report-on-the-state-of-democracy-human-rights-and-the-rule-of-law accessed 1 July 2019.

Smelser, N. J. (1962). *Theory of Collective Behaviour.* New York: Free Press, p. 18.

Stech, R. (2013). Think before you Act: Sustainable Development Bill in Wales. *Journal of Environmental Law.* 25(1), 137–44.

Sullivan, R., Martindale, W., Feller, E. and Bordon, A. (2015). Fiduciary Duty in the 21st Century. PRI, UNEP FI, UNEP Inquiry, UN Global Compact, 11. Available at: www.fiduciaryduty21.org/about.html accessed 1 August 2017.

Taylor, D. (2000). The Rise of the Environmental Justice Paradigm. Injustice Framing and the Social Construction of Environmental Discourses. *The American Behavioral Scientist*, 43(4), 508.

UK Government Guidance (2016). Social Investment Tax Relief. Updated 23 November 2016. Cabinet Office, HM Revenue and Customs, HM Treasury. Available at: www.gov.uk/government/publications/social-investment-tax-relief-factsheet/social-investment-tax-relief accessed 1 December 2016.

UNEP Finance Initiative (2017). Regional Roundtables on Sustainable Finance. Available at www.unepfi.org/events/regions-events/regional-roundtable/regional-roundtables-2017/ accessed 17 August 2017.

UNEP Finance Initiative Banking (2017). Available at www.unepfi.org/banking/banking accessed 17 August 2017.

United Nations (1992). Agenda 21. United Nations Conference on Environment & Development Rio de Janerio, Brazil. Available at https://sustainabledevelopment.un.org/content/documents/Agenda21.pdf accessed 1 July 2015.

United Nations (2002). *Johannesburg Declaration on Sustainable Development. World Summit on Sustainable Development*, available at www.un-documents.net/jburgdec.htm accessed 12 April 2016.

United Nations Environment Programme (2016). Available at http://web.unep.org/north america/news/2016/g20-financial-leaders-commit-exploring-green-finance-options accessed 17 August 2017.

United Nations (2012). The Future We Want. Resolution adopted by the General Assembly on 27 July 2012. Available at www.un.org/ga/search/view_doc.asp?symbol=A/RES/66/288&Lang=E accessed 1 July 2015.

United Nations Global Compact (2017). Available at www.unglobalcompact.org/ accessed 17 August 2017.

United Nations (2015). Millennium Development Goals. Available at www.un.org/millennium goals/ accessed 1 July 2015.

United Nations (2016). Goal 17: Revitalize the Global Partnership for Sustainable Development. Sustainable Development Goals. Available at: www.un.org/sustainabledeve lopment/globalpartnerships/ accessed 1 July 2016.

Volz, U., Böhnke, J., Knierim, L., Richert, K., Röber, G.-M. and Eidt, V. (2015). *Financing the Green Transformation: How to Make Green Finance Work in Indonesia*. Basingstoke: Palgrave Macmillan.

Weber, O. (2014). Social Banking: Concept, Definitions and Practice. *Global Social Policy*, 14 (2), 265.

World Bank (1994). *World Development Report 1994: Infrastructure for Development*. New York: Oxford University Press.

World Bank (2017). *World Development Report*. Governance and the Law. Available at: https://openknowledge.worldbank.org/bitstream/handle/10986/25880/210950ov.pdf accessed 3 April 2017.

World Bank and UNEP (2017). *Roadmap for a Sustainable Financial System*, available at http://documents.worldbank.org/curated/en/903601510548466486/pdf/121283–12-11–2017-15–33-33-RoadmapforaSustainableFinancialSystem.pdf accessed 1 September 2018).

WWF (2016). Green Bonds Must Keep the Green Promise. A Call for Collective Action toward Effective and Credible Standards for the Green Bond Market, available at http://d2ouvy59p0dg6k.cloudfront.net/downloads/20160609_green_bonds_hd_report.pdf accessed 13 June 2016.

World Bank (2017). *Environmental and Social Framework*, available at http://documents .worldbank.org/curated/en/383011492423734099/pdf/114278-WP-REVISED-PUBLIC-Environmental-and-Social-Framework.pdf accessed 17 August 2017.

Zimmermann, R. (1996). Non-Recourse – The Most Condemnable of Loan Transactions. *Project Finance International*, 100, 62–3.

20

Sustainable Consumption, Consumer Protection and Sustainable Development: Unbundling Institutional Septet for Developing Economies

Onyeka K. Osuji and Ugochi C. Amajuoyi[1]

20.1 INTRODUCTION

This chapter investigates the role of consumption in sustainable development and, drawing on the institutional and stakeholder theoretic models, examines its institutional implications for developing economies. Against the backdrop of concerns about consumerism and responsible business practices, the chapter seeks to identify consumer protection measures that can facilitate a symbiotic relationship between consumption and sustainable development within the framework of the Sustainable Development Goals (SDGs) (United Nations, 2015). These consumer protection measures can assist in protecting 'present' (proximate) consumers and 'future' generations in line with the definition of sustainable development as providing for 'the needs of the present without compromising the ability of future generations to meet their own needs' (United Nations, 1987). The measures can be employed in providing a balance between economic development, social development and environmental protection as the pillars of sustainable development emphasised by the Johannesburg World Summit on Sustainable Development (United Nations, 2002).

Although the linkage between consumption and sustainable development seems widely acknowledged, there has been limited attention on deploying consumer protection rules to advance sustainable development. This chapter therefore provides an original contribution to the debate on sustainable consumption and production in three main ways. Firstly, it studies sustainable consumption through a new theoretical lens which combines the legal institutional and stakeholder perspectives. Thus far these theoretical models have only been considered separately and in addition, they have not been considered in combination to analyse the developing country context. Secondly, the chapter draws on the SDGs to recommend a septet of foundational components of sustainable consumption and development within the context of developing countries. Thirdly, it is argued that a more interventionist consumer protection approach involving a mix of recognition of

[1] We thank Professor Chris Willett for commenting on earlier drafts of this chapter.

consumer vulnerabilities, consumer private law rights, stakeholder rights and responsibilities and administrative enforcement powers can be utilised to align consumption with sustainable development in developing countries.

Before expanding on these arguments, it is useful to underline the contemporary significance of sustainable consumption and production, especially ongoing legitimate concerns over its role and operationalisation in sustainable development in local and global contexts. Originally, the concept of sustainable development was narrowly focused and primarily conservation-driven. This is exemplified by the International Union for Conservation of Nature and Natural Resources (IUCN), which helped to bring the concept to global consciousness. IUCN formulated the World Conservation Strategy with 'the overall aim of achieving sustainable development through conservation of living resources' (IUCN, 1980). The SDGs, however, underline a shift to a more expansive conception of sustainable development that encompasses a range of other matters including poverty reduction, health and well-being, sustainable consumption and production, labour standards, gender equality, anti-corruption and international cooperation. Prior to the SDGs, the United Nations Conference on Environment and Development 1992 highlighted some linkages between consumption and environmental protection. The Johannesburg World Summit on Sustainable Development 2002 had sustainable consumption and production as one of the main goals for sustainable development. The 2012 United Nations Conference on Sustainable Development (Rio+20) adopted a ten-year framework of programmes on sustainable consumption and production (UN, 2012) that projected the broader notion of sustainable development. In addition to other references (e.g. Articles 5(i), 6 and 7), Part H (Articles 49–60) of the UN Guidelines for Consumer Protection (United Nations, 2016) focuses on sustainable consumption.

Consumption arguably plays a dual role in sustainable development. While in the negative sense, consumption can create demands for, and use of, unsustainable products and production methods, it can also limit and re-align demands and usages to positively contribute to sustainable development. The SDGs highlight this two-fold importance of efficient consumption to sustainable development by including the Goal 12 broad statement of ensuring 'sustainable consumption and production patterns'. Implicit in the statement is, on the one hand, the acknowledgement of consumers as a significant constituency for sustainable development. For example, by encouraging the efficient use of energy resources and reducing wasteful food consumption within households, largely by placing limits on consumption, the SDGs recognise the key role of consumers in procuring the achievement of sustainable development. On the other hand, Goal 12 confirms a growing recognition that businesses can play vital roles in addressing social issues globally, especially in the developing markets. The willingness and participation of corporations in norm-setting for environmental protection (Falkner, 2003: p. 30) and other areas of sustainable development is crucial for investigating, detecting and communicating evidence and adopting appropriate solutions. The SDGs share this aspiration with other international initiatives such as the UN Global Compact 2000, UN Guiding Principles on Business and Human Rights and OECD Guidelines for Multinational Enterprises 2011. Moreover, the exponential growth of corporate and independent reporting initiatives such as the Global Reporting Initiative's G4 Sustainability Reporting Guidelines and certification programmes such as SA8000 is an indication of the heightened interest of corporate constituencies like investors and consumers in sustainable development and other social matters endorsed within the umbrella of CSR.

In addition to the anthropogenic approach of Goal 12, the SDGs also affirm the role of institutions in developing countries. For example, Target 16a of Goal 16 stresses the need to 'strengthen relevant national institutions . . . for building capacity at all levels, in particular in developing countries'. Although a global concern, sustainable development may have developing economy-specific strands. A recent report of Christian Aid (2018: p. 4), while noting the contemporary effects of climate change, observed that '[i]n many developing countries the human cost of climate change to vulnerable communities is much higher than the financial cost'. Nonetheless, despite the gravity of threats from unsustainable practices, the relatively inadequate responsiveness in some developing countries sharply contrasts with the more advanced countries.

We have therefore adopted an improved approach by drawing on the SDGs to make an original proposition about the existence of inceptive components of sustainable consumption and production: (a) sustainable consumption by proximate consumers for future generations; (b) sustainable production for future generations; (c) sustainable consumption by/for proximate consumers; (d) sustainable production for proximate consumers; (e) participation by proximate consumers; and (f) corporate social responsibility. These six elements may present distinctive contextual challenges, hence recognising this developing country context makes for seven key elements in total and completes what we can call the septet of implications for sustainable consumption. This septet framework provides clarity to the concept of sustainable consumption and production by identifying, segregating and linking its constituents. It provides fresh insights in the bourgeoning area of sustainable development, especially in the developing country context where attention has mainly concentrated on poverty reduction. The septet approach is unlike existing studies (e.g. Shove, 2004; Bray and Johns, 2011; Antonetti and Maklan, 2014; Newholm et al., 2015; Carrington et al., 2016) which have largely focused on behavioural analyses of consumer behaviour and lifestyle changes. Similarly, 'circular economy' studies emphasise the involvement of corporations/producers and consumers in recycling processes (Winans et al., 2017; Korhonen et al., 2018). The plastic industry is a prominent example of the circular economy campaigns (see European Commission, 2015, 2018). Here, however, the septet framework will be applicable to both factors: consumer/producer behaviours and industry practices.

The septet approach has facilitated the other two original contributions. It prompts us to ask how consumer law rules should be designed in order to deliver on the key elements of the septet approach to sustainable development. In doing so it is original first in adopting a mixed methodology for understanding the links between consumer law rules and sustainable development; and second, based on these links, in making the argument for a more interventionist consumer protection model to achieve sustainable consumption. Let us now elaborate on this a little. While sustainable consumption can be studied from a range of theoretical lenses, this chapter provides novel solutions to the sustainable development agenda by combining the legal, institutional and stakeholder perspectives. Proceeding on the basis that economic actors such as corporations can be 'distantiated' from responsibility by lack of proximity to stakeholders and regulations (Herlin and Solitander, 2017: p. 10), we argue that delivering on the septet criteria for sustainable development requires a more interventionist consumer protection paradigm in contrast to the current less interventionist and less protective consumer law approach undertaken, for example, by UK and other jurisdictions. However, the current consumer law approach does not achieve this. Rather it involves a less interventionist and less protectionist approach, and crucially, one that does not do enough to promote the key septet criteria for sustainable development. It is important to develop and deepen private participation and enforcement to complement public enforcement within the legal framework for sustainable consumption and production. Drawing on the institutional and stakeholder theoretic models, we demonstrate that consumption is an institution and consumers and corporations are groups of institutional actors for sustainable development. We propose a context-specific interventionist approach to provide a framework for aligning consumer protection to sustainable development in the developing markets. The chapter in particular advances knowledge by integrating regulatory debates and applying them to advocate a 'consumer protection' model that reframes consumer vulnerability, disclosure regulation, contract law, consumer responsibilisation, stakeholder roles, corporate governance, institutional voids and international cooperation for sustainable consumption in developing countries.

The rest of the chapter is organised as follows. First, we examine the meaning of institutions and show that legal rules and frameworks can be categorised as 'institutions' as defined by the institutional theoretic model. This is followed by an outline of the meaning of sustainable consumption which shows that within the institutional theoretic model, sustainable consumption can be classified as an institution and, therefore consumers and corporations are economic and social institutional actors within this theoretical model. The chapter then examines the role of consumption in promoting sustainable development by identifying six foundational components of sustainable consumption and production before considering the developing country context to complete the septet. It then discusses consumer protection, regulatory and stakeholder measures that can positively enhance the role of consumption in promoting sustainable development to show that a symbiotic relationship between consumption and sustainable development is possible within the framework of the SDGs. The final section deals with the key argument as to the importance of strong consumer protection in order to deliver on the septet criteria for sustainable development. So, it shows that for a consumer protection model to be effective within developing countries where regulatory and enforcement mechanisms may be weak or non-existent, it is imperative that it is designed in a way that aligns sustainable consumption and production to sustainable development through the recognition of corporations as social and institutional actors. It highlights that the original septet framework proffered in this chapter enables this by facilitating the idea of private enforcement of international best standards and a strong consumer protection regime.

20.2 INSTITUTIONS AND CONSUMPTION

We will now look at the institutional theoretic model to show that it can be deployed in explaining the role of sustainable consumption and production in sustainable development. This is because the institutional theory attempts to explain the driving factors for the behaviour and interaction of social actors. Within the institutional theoretic model in the institutional economics movement is the implicit rejection of the neoclassical theory that gives little or no attention to the role of institutions in the market process and outcomes (Rutherford, 2001: p. 187). Accordingly, North (1990: p. 3) defined institutions as 'the rules of the game in a society or, more formally, are the humanly devised constraints that shape human interaction'. Hodgson (2006: p. 2) similarly defined institutions as 'systems of established and prevalent social rules that structure social interactions'.

Law is therefore a class of institution within the institutional theoretic model (Modigliani and Perotti, 1997; Beck and Levine, 2005; Hodgson, 2006). However, there are two divergent views on the role of legal institutions in national economic growth. On the one hand, it is argued that legal institutions create enabling environments by providing for and enforcing, among others, property and investor rights. This links economic growth to the nature of legal rules and the quality of their enforcement (La Porta et al., 1997, 1998, 2000, 2008). Another viewpoint, however, suggests that market-led developments can precede and inspire legal rules in countries like the UK and USA (Black, 2001; Cheffins, 2001: pp. 483–4; Coffee, 2001: pp. 65–6; Dam, 2006: pp. 188–9). Nonetheless, it is clear from these two schools that legal institutions can play a critical role in shaping and enforcing rules for the market notwithstanding the initial source of the rules. After all, institutions of different categories provide incentives for the economic behaviour of social actors (Acemoglu et al., 2002; Chang, 2011).

Although these institutional studies focused on economic growth, the lessons can be extrapolated to sustainable development, particularly as its definition (United

Nations, 1987, 2002) suggests balancing present economic development and ethical considerations for present and future generations. It is notable, firstly, that the concept of institutions encompasses both public and private entities. For example, according to North (1990: p. 3) institutions can be 'political, social, or economic' while the categorisation of institutions by Acemoglu et al. (2002) is based on the respective influence of economic incentives, geography and culture on behaviour. Implicit in these is the notion of the capability of private individuals and organisations to shape behaviour in society outside the formal political and legal framework. Another inference is that, despite their coercive powers, state agents do not have an exclusive influence on social behaviour and regulatory outcomes. Thirdly, culture is an essential determinant of individual and organisational behaviour. As Hofsted (1994: p. 116) stated, the behaviour of individuals is influenced by 'a structure in their organisations, institutions, and relationships which makes events clearly interpretable and predictable'. This is a reference to culture which Aghion and Howitt (2009: p. 421) defined as 'individual and collective beliefs, social norms, and various attributes of individuals' preferences that are somehow influenced by their environment, but typically slow moving'. The fourth point is that rules and standards of behaviour can originate from formal and informal non-state agents like individuals, groups and communities who share certain beliefs and values. Sometimes, formal laws and regulations simply manifest pre-existing informal rules, customs and attitudes of private persons in society (Easterly, 2008).

This conceptualisation of institutions suggests that, while consumer protection rules are institutions, consumption can be an institution and consumers institutional actors in the social, economic, cultural senses by influencing or incentivising the economic and other behaviours of businesses and social actors. This can be inferred from Acemoglu's (2009: p. 120) description of economic institutions as comprising 'such things as the structure of property rights, the presence of markets, and the contractual opportunities available to individuals and companies'. Similarly, Hodgson (2006: p. 2) identified 'language, money, law, systems of weights and measures, table manners, and firms (and other organisations)' within the categorisation of economic institutions.

Consumption ultimately drives production and innovation. As Mansvelt (2005: p. 1) observed, '[t]he increased visibility of sites of consumption and the proliferation of consumer goods and images have led social commentators to suggest consumption rather than production is now the driving force in contemporary society'. Consumer tastes and purchasing behaviour influence the emergence, survival and profitability of products and services and the investments needed for their research, formulation and existence. Even in the case of 'new' products and services, their appearance is often linked to expectations of future positive and profitable custom by producers and investors. This also applies to marketing and advertising aimed at influencing consumption which succeeds when consumers are, in fact, attracted to products and services and propel their production patterns. Similarly, when the state encourages or discourages production and consumption along certain lines, the success of the policy depends on the extent of consumption. The long-term prospects of governmental incentives for production is limited if consumption moves in a parallel direction. The institutional approach similarly recognises that economic behaviour is a product of the institutional social actors and their beliefs and values which in turn influence their actions (Greif, 2006).

The institutional approach therefore underscores the role of law and other institutions in promoting desired behaviours and discouraging undesirable ones. It is useful to identify the relevant activity and institutions that can help to influence behaviours towards the achievement of the goal. This section has shown that, while law is one of the institutions that influence consumption and production, private actors like consumers are also institutional actors in that regard. The next part of this chapter examines consumption as an institutional factor for sustainable development.

20.3 SUSTAINABLE CONSUMPTION AND PRODUCTION

To consume would ordinarily refer to purchasing and using products and services. The decision to purchase or use may depend on several factors, including physiological and psychological needs, interests, personal preferences, tastes and beliefs that differ from person to person. These factors can also be influenced by changing sociological circumstances, including law, culture and other institutions. Consequently, it is arguable that 'all human societies have been involved in consumption but the connections between what people do and a sense of them being "consumers" are only found in specific analytic contexts' (Evans et al., 2017: p. 5). Strictly speaking, it may be possible to distinguish between sustainable consumption ('consuming less') and ethical consumption ('consuming differently') (Evans et al., 2017: p. 2) with the former's objective of reduced resource use in production and consumption (Evans, 2011, 2018). Nonetheless, we use sustainable consumption and ethical consumption interchangeably in this chapter since purchasing, using or consuming differently can be influenced by ethical values derived from individual and society orientations.

The notion of sustainable consumption exists within the individualised and sociological context that 'criss-crosses and works through a multitude of consumption-related behaviours and scales' (Hinton and Goodman, 2010: p. 246). Sustainable consumption can be identified from the essentialist, existentialist, performative and descriptive approaches to collective responsibilisation for promoting individual and collective interests in sustainable development. An essentialist approach that highlights certain basic characteristics is Article 49 of the UN Guidelines for Consumer Protection which states that sustainable consumption 'includes meeting the needs of present and future generations for goods and services in ways that are economically, socially and environmentally sustainable'. In the performative and descriptive senses, sustainable development can be part of consumers' 'expressed preferences as "ethical" subjects to other actors involved in making markets including state agents, corporations and regulatory agencies' (Barnett et al., 2011: p. 85). Kysar (2005: p. 641) similarly argued that consumers increasingly purchase 'not only products, but also shares of responsibility in the moral and ecological economy that produces them'.

Nonetheless, the existentialist approach to sustainable consumption seems to dominate scholarly and policy suggestions. The existentialist approach conveys the idea of individual consumption preferences and decisions coupled with individualised responsibility for promoting sustainable development. Evans et al. (2017: p. 3) noted that 'sustainable consumption is commonly thought to be premised on appeals to the responsibilities of consuming subjects'. This is succinctly illustrated by Shove's (2010: p. 1274) ABC framework of 'attitude, behaviour and choice' which she observed 'is an indication of the extent to which responsibility for responding to climate change is thought to lie with individuals whose behavioural choices will make the difference'. While some share Shove's criticism of individualised responsibilisation (see Strengers and Maller, 2015), others have stressed the need to avoid moving 'too far in the other direction' (Whitmarsh et al., 2010: p. 259) of exclusion of individual responsibility for sustainable responsibility.

The middle ground of shared responsibility between the sociological and the individualised approaches to sustainable development avoids governmental abdication of responsibilities for consumers while acknowledging that individual consumption and production patterns can make a meaningful impact. It incorporates the essentialist, existentialist and performative approaches to sustainable consumption and is reflective of the collective approach required for sustainable development. The reality is that sustainable consumption involves how 'one set of collective actors (campaigns, NGOs, charities) engage with other collective actors (retailers, suppliers, corporations) through the real and discursive figure of "the ethical consumer"' (Clarke et al., 2007: p. 238). There is also the private interest dimension suggesting the need to protect consumers' physical and mental well-being in utilising products and services as well as their personal interest in advancing sustainable development even when they may not be directly affected in the short or longer term. The dual protective dimensions are exemplified by Article 18 of the World Health Organisation's Framework Convention on Tobacco Control (WHO FCTC) which reiterates the need for protecting 'the environment and the health of persons in relation to the environment in respect of tobacco cultivation and manufacture'.

Based on the shared responsibility approach to sustainable consumption, we draw on the SDGs to make the original argument that sustainable consumption and production is a multi-constituent concept that needs to be developed further and unbundled for greater clarity and effectiveness. We will therefore now proceed to demonstrate that the foundational elements of 'sustainable consumption and production' consist of: (a) sustainable consumption by proximate consumers for future generations; (b) sustainable production for future generations; (c) sustainable consumption by/for proximate consumers; (d) sustainable production for proximate consumers; (e) participation by proximate consumers; and (f) corporate social responsibility. The application of these underpinning elements in the developing country context completes an institutional septet for sustainable consumption and production as partly mapped out by the SDGs. The remaining part of this section explains these core elements in further detail.

20.3.1 *Sustainable Consumption by Proximate Consumers for Future Generations*

This conveys the orthodox notion of sustainable consumption as requiring 'sustainable lifestyles' (Targets 4.7 and 12.8 of the SDGs). In several respects, the success of the sustainable development agenda can depend on the behaviour and lifestyle choices of individuals and groups (Shove, 2004), hence the recognition of the role of ethical consumption (Bray and Johns, 2011; Newholm et al., 2015). Some consumers favour 'green consumption' and refrain from purchasing products of unsustainable practices (Black, 2010). These 'ethical consumers' may be willing to pay higher prices. Consumers have, for instance, been known for paying more for 'fair trade' products even when cheaper alternatives are available (Castaldo et al., 2009; Andorfer and Liebe, 2015; Campbell et al., 2015). Although there are some doubts on whether purchasing decisions are always aligned with consumers' ethical orientations rather than price and other economic factors (Carrington et al., 2016), consumers are more likely to undertake ethical consumption when they feel that they can make a difference (Antonetti and Maklan, 2014).

Unilever (2017) recently reported that about 33 per cent of consumers prefer to purchase 'sustainable brands' based on their 'environmental and social impact'. The report estimated the global 'opportunity' value of 'sustainability credentials' to be €966 billion. Based on a five-country study, the report significantly noted that a greater proportion of consumers in the emerging economies of India (88 per cent), Brazil and Turkey (both 85 per cent) were influenced by sustainable production than consumers in the more developed markets of the UK (53 per cent) and USA (78 per cent). The attitudinal difference was attributed mainly to the direct impact of unsustainable practices on consumers and residents of the emerging economies and the greater power of social norms that included sustainability scrutiny of purchasing decisions by family and friends of consumers in those countries.

20.3.2 *Sustainable Production for Future Generations*

The critical role of production patterns is highlighted by various provisions of the SDGs (e.g. Targets 2.4, 12.2–12.6, 15.2). Regulations, fiscal incentives and other institutional factors can determine production patterns. For example, the Environmental Audit Committee of the UK Parliament is investigating the environmental and social impact of the fashion industry (House of Commons, 2018). Specifically, the Committee is looking into the 'carbon, resource use and water footprint of clothing throughout its lifecycle' and the recycling of clothes and reduction of waste and pollution.

Nonetheless, consumption can potentially influence the cessation of unsustainable business practices and encourage innovation and adoption of more sustainable products and production methods. In 2003, an Indian non-governmental organisation, the Centre of Science and Environment, reported that the pesticide content in samples of Coca-Cola products being sold in the country far exceeded those allowed in European countries (Bantekas, 2004; Hills and Welford, 2005; Burnett and Welford, 2007); Cedillo Torres et al., 2012). It also reported that Coca-Cola was extracting a large quantity of underground water and was polluting water bodies in its production processes. In the immediate aftermath, the report led to significant reduction in consumer purchase of Coca-Cola products in India and even the suspension of the products by some American universities. While it later denied the allegations in the report in its 2006 Corporate Responsibility Review, Coca-Cola sought to demonstrate changes to its production methods (Altschuller et al., 2010).

While the Volkswagen emissions scandal could be examined by references to breaches of US legislation, the penalties imposed and the sustainable development implications of vehicle emissions for the future generations, there is the additional element of the interest of consumers in promoting sustainable production for the future generations. One of the triggers for the scandal was the apparent corporate mission to influence at all costs, including by false information, the sustainable development – conscious consumers who would be willing to pay a premium for sustainable products and services. These consumers would actively refrain from purchasing 'unsustainable' products especially when alternatives were available. Consumers are being encouraged by several institutional agents to tackle greenhouse gas emissions through reduced and alternative consumption (Cherrier et al., 2012).

20.3.3 *Sustainable Consumption by/for Proximate Consumers*

It is sometimes in the consumer's own interest to engage in sustainable consumption. The interest can be material such as in saving money and resources through 'efficiency in consumption' (Target 8.4 SDGs) or refraining from 'wasteful consumption' (Target 12c SDGs). Consumers can promote their physical and mental well-being by avoiding products such as tobacco. On this note, the SDGs' Target 3A requires the implementation of the WHO FCTC within the Goal 3 promise to 'ensure healthy lives and promote well-being for all at all ages'.

Consumers may also be affected even when there are impacts on the environment or the future generations. In *Guerra v. Italy*,[2] the European Court of Human Rights

---

[2] *Guerra v. Italy* (1998) 26 EHRR 357, [1998] ECHR 7 at [60].

(ECHR) held that 'severe environmental pollution may affect individuals' well-being and prevent them from enjoying their homes in such a way as to affect their private and family life adversely'.

Consumers require information capable of influencing their beliefs, intentions and attitudes (Longo et al., 2019) towards sustainable development and enabling them to make appropriate consumption and lifestyle choices. For example, in holding that a government failed in its duty of informing local populations of environmental pollution risks, the ECHR noted that 'the applicants waited, right up until the production of fertilisers ceased in 1994, for essential information that would have enabled them to assess the risks they and their families might run if they continued to live at ... a town particularly exposed to danger in the event of an accident at the factory'.[3]

20.3.4 Sustainable Production for Proximate Consumers

While consumers can directly benefit from improvements in product quality and innovations that improve quality of life, some products can be harmful to their well-being. There are references in the SDGs (e.g. Targets 2.4, 3.5, 3.9, 3a) to confirm that products and production patterns should consider the well-being of proximate consumers. Tobacco is one example, prompting the EU Tobacco Products Directive 2014 and Directive 2001/37/EC which provide maximum tar, nicotine and carbon monoxide content of cigarettes for export. The content and quality of some products can make them potentially harmful to consumers. For instance, in *Fijabi* v. *Nigeria Bottling Company Plc*,[4] a franchisee of Coca-Cola in Nigeria sold beverages containing benzoic acid preservative at levels the UK and other European countries declared unsafe for consumption. Sustainable development in this type of case requires changes to production processes.

The references to access and affordability in the SDGs (e.g. Targets 7.1, 11.2) show the need to protect proximate consumers' material interest. Inefficient products such as high-fuel consumption vehicles and production and methods can raise costs for proximate consumers. The introduction of carbon emissions vehicle taxes in the UK (HM Revenue and Customs, 2018) is an indication of direct consumer interest in sustainable development in that context. Consumers also are financially affected when products are marketed in such ways to encourage inefficient use and waste. This is the backdrop to the WHO International Code of Marketing of Breastmilk Substitutes. Similarly, regulators like the UK Advertising Standards Authority have been acting against advertisements considered as socially irresponsible for encouraging, or appearing to promote, unsustainable and unhealthy consumer practices.

---

3 *Guerra* v Italy (1998) 26 EHRR 357, [1998] ECHR 7 at [60].
4 *Fijabi* v. *Nigeria Bottling Company Plc* Suit No. LD/13/2008 of 15 February 2017.

Consumers may be directly affected if laws of some jurisdictions prohibit certain products or impose extra financial burdens on consumers for using them. *Bramhill* v. *Edwards*,[5] where a motorhome failed the UK size requirements after complying with the US rules, suggest this possibility in cases of conflicts of sustainable development laws.

20.3.5 *Participation by Proximate Consumers*

The sustainable development agenda requires the inclusion and participation of key stakeholders like consumers. Inclusivity is one of the goals of sustainable development as evidenced by Targets 1.4, 10.2 and 10.3 of the SDGs. While Target 4.7 highlights the imperativeness of appropriate knowledge and skills for inclusivity, Targets 6b, 17.16 and 17.17 provide a linkage to stakeholder participation. The importance of stakeholder participation in environmental policy is highlighted by principle 23 of the World Charter for Nature 1982.[6] A safe environment is linked to the 'rights' to health and participation in environmental decisions (Francioni, 1991: p. 293). Similarly, some government agencies and international organisations have been promoting community participation in public health programmes. Falletti and Cunial's (2018) comparative study of Western Europe and Latin America identified monitoring and policymaking as the two forms of programmatic participation for the community stakeholder groups that could explain the two regions' relatively advanced social welfare systems.

Engagement in sustainable consumption is dependent on consumers' knowledge in addition to their willingness to participate. Although consumers' purchasing decisions are often driven by their 'consumption knowledge' derived from experiences of product use (Clarkson et al., 2013), institutional agents can be influential in shaping new knowledge. In *Guerra* v. *Italy*,[7] the ECHR held that a government's failure to inform the host community of a 'high-risk' chemical factory and the details of the environmental pollution risks, constituted a breach of the residents' right to private and family lives. In other words, the government has a positive duty to identify, collect and disseminate information on relevant corporate activities.

20.3.6 *Corporate Social Responsibility*

While it is increasingly clear that a growing number of consumers have become sustainable development champions through their product purchasing decisions, consumption patterns and lifestyle choices, consumers are in a relatively weak position compared to corporations. In addition to determining production methods

---

5 *Bramhill* v. *Edwards* [2004] EWCA Civ 403.
6 World Charter for Nature adopted in General Assembly Resolution No. 37/7 of 28 October 1982.
7 *Guerra* v. *Italy* (1998) 26 EHRR 357, [1998] ECHR 7.

and processes, corporations enjoy knowledge advantage over consumers. Corporations have better access to scientific knowledge, technology and resources that can identify, track, monitor, evaluate and resolve sustainable development issues. If, according to Blake (1999: p. 271), 'the "public" is best defined in terms of alienation from dominant political or knowledge regimes in a particular context' then consumers are more likely than corporations to be regarded as such. Matters such as 'technical assistance . . ., know-how . . ., product development . . ., and health and safety issues'[8] require 'superior knowledge'. This is applicable to proximate consumers and future generations who are potential victims of harmful unsustainable activities.

The reality is also that corporations are not 'passive and powerless' (Anabtawi and Stout, 2008: p. 1275) in their relationship with state agents. There are several dimensions to corporate power. First, political institutions may be unwilling or unable to impose strong national standards or to demand the observance of international best practices from powerful private actors such as corporations. Secondly, corporations can interfere with formal regulatory processes and engage in 'regulatory capture' that results in weakened substantive rule and enforcement. The ability of tobacco companies to engage in 'dissuasive efforts' and political lobbying against effective regulations of the industry is noticeable even in a country like Switzerland (Maurisse, 2019). This, perhaps, explains why Article 5.3 of the WHO FCTC demands the protection of public health policies from 'commercial and other vested interests of the tobacco industry'. Thirdly, economic actors such as multinational corporations are sometimes not incentivised, including by public and private sanctions, to adopt more sustainable practices even when they are aware of, and may in fact adhere to, such practices in the more advanced countries. This is also applicable to international law (de Jonge, 2011; Omoteso and Yusuf, 2017). Despite the reality that 'companies today operate across the globe through a complex web of subsidiaries and affiliate concerns' (Deva, 2012: p. 4), international law seems to play a 'modest role in holding corporations to account' (van Dam, 2011: p. 225). Soft-law initiatives such as the UN Global Compact and OECD Guidelines for Multinational Enterprises (OECD, 2011) attempt to fill the gaps in international law with limited success.

The emergence of the notion of CSR can be traced to these factors. CSR demonstrates that corporate obligations are not restricted to explicit legal provisions. CSR dictates that corporations should not abuse their knowledge and political power. Corporations are expected to apply their power and influence to address social issues and even undertake some traditional governmental functions (Osuji, 2015; Osuji and Obibuaku, 2016). Scherer and Palazo (2011) argued that corporations are political actors that are recognised as such by non-governmental organisations

---

[8]   *Chandler* v. *Cape Plc* [2012] EWCA Civ 52 [13–16] (Lady Justice Arden relied on these factors to impose a duty of care on a parent company over its subsidiary's employees).

who demand CSR, public governance roles and stakeholder engagement from them.

There exists an emergent evidence of consumers who are motivated by moral considerations (Andorfer and Liebe, 2013; Johnstone and Tan, 2015; Shaw et al., 2016; Perera et al., 2018) and are attracted by positive CSR credentials of a business or a product. Sustainable development is one of those considerations, hence its advertisement as part of CSR can be a significant factor for consumer selection of products and services (Green and Peloza, 2014). Corporations are therefore increasingly expected by consumers and other stakeholders to engage in self-regulation of their operations, supply and purchasing chains while addressing sustainable development and other social issues. For example, Greenpeace's 'Slaughtering the Amazon' campaign compelled Nike and Adidas to stop their operations and supply chains from using leather sourced from the Amazon (Bernd et al., 2016). The 'dirty fuel' movement challenged the 'fiction of clean hands' previously adopted by the European corporate and political institutions (Yoboué and Kaufman, 2018: p. 291). The CSR scheme, therefore, presumes that corporations will refrain from exploiting 'institutional voids' (Karam and Jamali, 2013: Doh et al., 2015; Husted, 2015) triggered by public governance failures, especially in developing countries.

20.3.7 *Sustainable Consumption and Consumer Protection*

This section has shown that, while corporations can promote sustainable development through CSR, consumers can play an institutional role in nudging corporations to adopt appropriate CSR. Consumers need to be aware of this responsibility, and there must be a suitable consumer protection approach for sustainable development to be advanced through CSR, especially in the developing country context which this chapter examines next.

20.4 SUSTAINABLE CONSUMPTION IN THE INSTITUTIONAL CONTEXT OF DEVELOPING COUNTRIES

As noted above, developing countries can present challenges to adapting consumption for sustainable development due to possibilities of institutional voids. This section will show that institutional voids arise from the incapacity of formal institutions that lead to weak substantive standards; and from inadequate enforcement of consumer protection rules which in turn adversely affect the potential role of consumption in promoting sustainable development.

The institutional approach accentuates the role of geography and culture in the identification of institutional needs and structures, because it highlights how these factors can vary the success of sustainable development from country to country. Acemoglu et al. (2005: pp. 399–402), for example, attributed geographical differences as one of the factors for the economic performance of countries. They give the examples of the impact of climate and the disease burden faced by a country, which can impact the productivity, behaviours and incentives of different actors within it. Under the factor of 'culture' and based on a field of anthropological research, they noted that some societies may become 'dysfunctional' because they have adopted a belief system or system of operating which does not promote the success or prosperity of the society. For example, the mentality in one country that public office is an opportunity to amass private wealth rather than correct societal ills is a factor that might influence the actions available to various institutional actors, such as consumers, in a way that differs from the more developed countries.

Despite its global appeal, sustainable development, as underlined by the SDGs (e.g. Targets 3b-3d, 6a, 9.5, 9a, 11c and 12a), presents context-specific issues for developing countries. Some challenges confront consumption and its role in sustainable development in developing countries. While issues such as poverty, diseases and environmental factors may require geography-specific solutions, the formal institutions may be incapable and even prone to exploitation by private and informal institutional actors like corporations. One is political and regulatory incapacity of political institutions as demonstrated by *Fijabi* v. *Nigeria Bottling Company Plc*,[9] where Nigerian regulators declined to even require warning labels for the benefit of consumers.

Similarly, Public Eye reported that Swiss companies sold extremely high sulphur content fuels to consumers in African countries (Guéniat et al., 2016). These high sulphur content fuels are toxic to human health and cause respiratory diseases and deaths, pollute the environment and even impede economic development (WHO, 2006; World Bank, 2013). The companies profited from 'regulatory arbitrage' between the typically restrictive regulations of Europe and lax standards of African countries (UNEP, 2016). In response, the Centre for International Environmental Law (CIEL, 2017) argued that Belgium and the Netherlands were in breach of their international law obligations in allowing dirty fuel exports to African countries.

Another area of inconsistency of standards is tobacco. On the one hand, smoking has fallen by 38 per cent in European countries mainly due to preventative public health campaigns, usage policies and taxation-induced price increases (Maurisse, 2019). On the other hand, the number of smokers in African countries is steeply increasing and predicted to constitute about 40 per cent of the continent's population by 2025 from the current levels of 6.5 per cent. Tobacco-associated deaths will double by 2030. Eighty per cent of smokers now reside in low-income and middle-income countries. Public Eye reported the 'double standards' of Swiss tobacco companies in selling to African markets cigarettes that are more toxic than those sold and smoked in European countries (Maurisse, 2019). These companies were exploiting the fact that Switzerland, not being an EU member state, is not subject to tobacco product rules under Directive 2001/37/EC and allows cigarette content to be

---

[9] *Fijabi* v. *Nigeria Bottling Company Plc* Suit No. LD/13/2008 of 15 February 2017.

determined by the law of the importing country even when the law is weak or promotes unsustainable practices. In countries like Morocco, local authorities had no procedures and measures for investigating and monitoring the ingredients and toxicity of cigarettes.

The Volkswagen emissions scandal also epitomises the developed–developing countries divide. While the scandal has generated a furore among regulators and consumers in the advanced jurisdictions (Crête, 2016), the reaction in developing countries has been muted at best. This leads one to wonder whether Volkswagen vehicles were not sold in developing countries. In some developed jurisdictions, Volkswagen was penalised by regulators and compelled to recall millions of its vehicles for refitting and to compensate consumers. Consumers brought civil proceedings, including class actions in countries like the USA.[10] The EU initiated the Real Driving Emissions test to improve the reliability of emissions testing. The European Commission (2017) has been tightening regulations around the level and testing of vehicle emissions having acknowledged the impact on the environment and people's health and well-being, including linkages between pollutants and premature deaths and respiratory diseases.

The Volkswagen scandal highlights the sharp differences between developing and developed jurisdictions with regard to the consumer protection responsiveness of formal and informal institutions. While Article 2(2) of the United Nations General Assembly Declaration on the Right to Development (1986) 'imposes' responsibility on all, including consumers and other individuals, the reality is that the awareness of this responsibility and the ability to take steps to enforce it differs between jurisdictions. The institutional theoretic model can attribute the jurisdictional differences to the capability of formal institutions such as consumer law, environmental law, legal system and administrative agencies and private institutional actors like consumers.

This is evident in other areas of business activity that potentially affect sustainable development and consumers such as gas flaring in Nigeria's Niger Delta which emits harmful gases linked to the global climate change. The US Environmental Protection Agency's greenhouse gas calculator equated the emissions to driving 3.5 million passenger vehicles and annual operations of four coal-based power plants (Myles et al., 2018). The direct human impact includes lack of conversion for electricity especially in a country where power supply is scarce and erratic, heat and noise pollution, depleted wildlife scared by drastic changes to the environment, reduced farm yield, destruction of farmlands and deprivation of means of livelihood, deprivation of sleep due to perpetual bright light and hot environment, and contaminated water, reduced air quality, non-communicable diseases such as cancer and respiratory infections (Myles et al., 2018).

---

[10] See *People of the State of California v. Volkswagen*, 16-cv-03620 (2016); *In re: Volkswagen 'Clean Diesel'* MDL 15-MD-2672-CRB (JSC).

Although it was officially prohibited in 1984 by the Associated Gas Reinjection Act, gas flaring has persisted in Nigeria. A gradual reduction in the practice would be normally expected over time like in other gas flaring nations, but a recent investigation reported the reverse despite the government's cessation deadline (Myles et al., 2018). The World Bank's Global Gas Flaring Reduction Partnership (2018) ranked it sixth globally from the seventh position in 2017 and second in Africa in terms of gas flaring levels. Multinational oil companies often claim that they could not adopt more sustainable alternatives but curiously ceased gas flaring in the more advanced countries where they also operate. Stakeholders insist that Nigeria's latest 2020 deadline for ending gas flaring is unrealistic due to the government's lack of 'the willpower and sincerity to force the oil companies to use modern equipment' (Myles et al., 2018). Even the uncollected fines from the oil companies between April 2008 and October 2016 are estimated at US$14.298 billion (Myles et al., 2018).

The discussions in this section highlight the need to avoid reliance on formal (public) institutions in developing countries if the sustainable development agenda can be promoted through sustainable consumption and production. Furthermore, private institutional actors can facilitate sustainable consumption and production through the identification and enforcement of appropriate standards. These actors can play a more effective role when they are recognised by legal institutions as being vital for sustainable development.

20.5 SEPTET FRAMEWORK AND CONSUMER PROTECTION FOR SUSTAINABLE DEVELOPMENT

The septet framework developed (above) here has clarified the interconnectedness of sustainable consumption and production to the needs of present and future generations in the overall sustainable development agenda. While the institutional theory acknowledges the potential role of public and private institutions in promoting sustainable development, it is necessary to protect consumers' heterogenous needs and interests in view of the essential elements of sustainable consumption identified above. Although developing countries like Nigeria (Monye, 2018) tend to adopt models from developed jurisdictions due to shared colonial history, a context-specific approach to institutions is imperative as equally demonstrated by Target 16a of the SDGs. The task of this part is therefore to suggest an appropriate consumer protection model for sustainable consumption, especially in the developing country context. We outline below our original arguments for a more interventionist approach that can support the septet approach to using sustainable consumption to promote sustainable development.

20.5.1 *Consumer Protection Law*

While the six foundational elements of the septet framework show that sustainable consumption and production may be pursued for consumers' interest and for the common good, including future generations, the law as an institution has a vital role to play in protecting consumers' role in the consumption chain. Two approaches to protecting consumers through the law can be identified: consumer law and consumer protection law. A key difference between the consumer protection law and consumer law approaches is the latter's individualistic emphasis on consumers' ability to make, and enforce their, free, rational choice (Huffman, 2010: p. 11). In other words, consumer law focuses on information provision at the pre-contractual stage of transactions. The assumption is that consumers need information about different choices (Akinbami, 2011: p. 135) and, if this is available, consumers will make the right or 'rational' choice that promotes market efficiency (Spindler, 2011: p. 317). Consequently, it is more information focused and less interventionist than a consumer protection law approach.

Having shown the relative vulnerability of consumers with respect to the cardinal components of sustainable consumption, we propose a 'consumer protection' approach. The consumer protection approach regards consumers as weaker parties and addresses market failures that impede consumers' ability to maximise their welfare (Huffman, 2010). It uses regulations to protect their interests at the transactional level in a three-fold manner. First, consumers may be protected against businesses to prevent the latter's unscrupulous or exploitative activities (Inderst, 2009). Secondly, the consumer protection approach can apply a degree of paternalism to protect consumers from self-harm. An example is when consumers are protected against taking excessive credit and financial risks (Bar-Gill and Warren, 2008; Gerding, 2009). Thirdly, unlike competition law and other areas of law which rely on administrative enforcement to protect consumers at the macro level, consumer protection provides consumers with private law rights (Huffman, 2010).

Consumer vulnerability therefore seems essential to the consumer protection law approach. The concept of 'vulnerable consumers' is well-known in EU instruments which protect individuals on the basis of age, mental or physical infirmity or credulity.[11] This is, however, criticised for linking the concept to the notion of 'average consumer' and using individual consumer characteristics in the determination of business liability (Incardona and Poncibo, 2007). In contrast, the situational approach to consumer vulnerability canvassed in this chapter reflects consumers' limited knowledge and powers even if a consumer strongly desires to advance sustainable protection. The situational approach is supported by *Buet* which suggested vulnerability as a question of circumstances. The ECJ stated that, being that they are more likely to be behind on their education and wish to catch up and enhance their job prospects, customers of door-to-door educational enrolment

---

[11] Council Directive 2005/29/EC of 11 May 2005 concerning unfair business-to-consumer commercial practices in the internal market and amending Council Directive 84/450/EEC, Directives 97/7/EC, 98/27/EC and 2002/65/EC of the European Parliament and of the Council and Regulation (EC) No. 2006/2004 of the European Parliament and of the Council ('Unfair Commercial Practices Directive') OJ 2005 No. L149/27, Art 5(3).

salespersons may be more vulnerable and open to sales tactics than consumers in most canvassing situations.[12] The court also stated that, because the provision of education is not a consumer service/product to be used daily, a poorly considered purchase could cause the buyer more long-lasting harm than mere financial losses, including low quality or unsuitable training that could harm job and training prospects.[13]

20.5.2 *Interventionist Consumer Protection*

While the consumer protection law approach is a spectrum of interventionism, here, as noted in the introduction, it is argued that a more interventionist consumer protection law approach of a mix of recognition of consumer vulnerabilities, consumer private law rights, and stakeholder rights and responsibilities to complement administrative enforcement is useful for sustainable consumption. According to Llewelyn (1999), 'the concept of "protecting the consumer" is largely protection against the costs of externalities and other market imperfections and failures'. Similarly, a non-interventionist approach to consumer protection will not advance sustainable development which often reflects ethical and selfless goals sometimes for the common good of society and often for protecting future generations. This is evident from the common pool resources studies (Gabaldon and Gröschl, 2015) which reference moral justifications for sustainable development obligations of members of society that may be irrelevant factors for non-interventionism. Non-interventionist approaches are favoured by economists (La Porta et al., 1999) and reflect capitalist orientations (see Baldwin et al., 2012). While it gives self-interest a pre-eminent position and allows little room for morality in the market; pure capitalism can clash with ethical ideals when economic and social actors are confronted by certain matters of society. This was illustrated by the cases of irresponsible lending where the pursuit of profit and personal rewards drove lenders to ignore affordability, consumer needs and other matters that would protect consumers and financial stability (Osuji, 2017).

Norbert Reich (1992) identified 'pre-interventionist', 'interventionist' and 'post-interventionist' philosophies as the broad approaches to consumer protection. Pre-interventionist approaches developed from commercial and competition law and incorporate basic assumptions of civil law like caveat emptor and freedom of contract and provides limited solutions by refraining from imposing specific standards on contractual relations. Regarding information as a key component of consumer autonomy, it promotes improved consumer autonomy through self-help information systems and government-monitored information systems like labelling. The interventionist or regulatory approach reflects a more active role for the state in

---

[12] Case 382/87 R *Buet and Educational Business Services (EBS)* v. *Ministère Public* [1989] ECR 1235, para 13.

[13] Ibid., para 14.

social relations encapsulated in the notion of the 'welfare state'. Under the approach, the welfare state can control and modify traditional principles of freedom of contract, caveat emptor, competition and fault liability that might be unfavourable to consumers. This is complemented by welfare economic theories dealing with the power aspects of market transactions and re-establishment of bargaining power through tools like warranties and restricting exemption clauses.

The post-interventionist approach is a middle ground between interventionism and pre-interventionism. It promotes 'mixed rationality' (Reich, 1992: p. 267) using tools such as product liability for businesses in addition to labelling, instructions and warnings requirements in favour of consumers. Advocate-General Geelhoed implicitly referenced the post-interventionist approach by stating that

> before acquiring a given product (for the first time), a consumer will always take note of the information on the label and that he is also able to assess the value of that information. [A] consumer is sufficiently protected if he is safeguarded from misleading information on products and that he does not need to be shielded from information whose usefulness with regard to the acquisition and use of a product he can himself appraise.[14]

The post-interventionist approach explains the gradual shift in EU consumer policy from consumer protection to consumer law. The focus shifted from protecting the weak consumer to the 'average consumer' (Micklitz, 2012, 2013) except in certain cases of situational vulnerability such as door-to-door selling. Micklitz (2013) criticised the average consumer approach and highlighted four classes of consumer: informed consumers; responsible consumers that can make use of information provided to exercise their rights; circumspect consumers that benefit from market-rectifying mechanisms that grant minimum levels of fairness through mandatory rules; and vulnerable consumers that require the protection of the legal system and can be afforded status-based anti-discrimination and social justice rules. Micklitz (2013) therefore proposed a 'mobile system of rules' and 'conceptual descriptions' that assigns rights and obligations to different classes of consumer.

The differentiated consumer class and remedies approach highlights the fact that consumers are not homogenous and can include vulnerability-based differentiation. Consumer vulnerability is relative to other market participants (Cartwright, 2011). Consumers may be vulnerable in comparison to other market players like traders or in comparison to other consumer groups. Consumers may have the capacity to look after their own interests but still be relatively vulnerable or disadvantaged (Cartwright, 2011). Sustainable consumption can be contextualised in this relative vulnerability or disadvantage by providing a less information-focused approach to empowering the consumer institution in relation to the varied vulnerabilities of consumers and their institutional environment.

---

[14] Case C-239/02 *Douwe Egberts NV v. Westrom Pharma NV and Christophe Souranis*, Opinion of Advocate General Geelhoed of 11December 2003, [54].

20.5.3 *Beyond Disclosure*

While *participation by proximate consumers* and other foundational elements of the septet framework suggest the importance of information availability to consumers, we are demonstrating that the more interventionist consumer protection law approach required for sustainable consumption and production shows that disclosure should not be the focus of regulatory interventions in aid of sustainable development. The role of disclosure regulation in consumer protection is debated (see Howells, 2005; Ben-Shahar, 2009; Nield, 2010; Domurath, 2013; Fejos, 2015; Gardner, 2017; Overton and Fox, 2018; Willett, 2018) within the broader debate on regulatory approaches. Regarding securities regulation, for example, some economists have identified possible alternative regulatory approaches by government through the 'three broad hypotheses' of the 'alternative theories of optimal legal arrangements' (La Porta et al., 2006: p. 1). First, the 'null hypothesis' (Coase, 1960, 1975; Stigler, 1964) is against governmental regulation of any form. The argument is rather in favour of market regulation by private market participants such as investors and stock exchanges who can require and rely on quality disclosure. The market participants can enforce rules and standards through reputation incentives and private legal proceedings based on contract law and tort law. Secondly, economists like Easterbrook and Fischel (1984), having noted the expensive and unpredictable nature of private litigation promoted by the null hypothesis, support government's role in providing standard (model) contracts for market participants which can reduce the costs of private contracting and enforcement and promote certainty of rights and obligations. This school supports governmental disclosure regulation that specifies what to disclose and liability for non-disclosure or defective disclosure. In contrast to the liberal framework of the other two, the third approach supports regulation by state agents and perceives private market regulation as relatively weak (Landis, 1938; Polinsky and Shavell, 2000; Glaeser and Shleifer, 2003). Public regulators such as the US Securities and Exchange Commission are favoured over private regulation due to their relative independence; detachment from political interference; and the ability to provide binding regulations, seek and obtain information and impose sanctions on market participants.

The 'rational choice theory' of consumers in the information paradigm, for example, informed Articles 3, 4, 5 and 6 of the Distance Marketing Directive 2002 of the European Commission. As Howells (2005) however detailed, the information paradigm has several weaknesses. These include the assumption of clarity of information to, and its understanding by, consumers and consumers' tendency to ignore information provided. In addition, disclosure regulation can ignore the imbalance in the business-consumer relationship, including the fact that businesses can limit the effectiveness of information through marketing activities that exploit consumer information weaknesses. Akinbami (2011: p. 135) similarly noted that businesses can 'exploit an unfair advantage they have over their consumers in terms of superior information and expertise'. Businesses can apply 'heuristics' that 'results in cognitive weaknesses in individuals' decision-making, leading them to make inferior decisions with regard to their welfare' (Akinbami, 2011: p. 144). Consequently, the European Union appeared to have been adopting a more interventionist approach rather than exclusive reliance on disclosure regulation in financial consumer law, for example (Cherednychenko, 2010).

One of the consequences of the 2008 financial crisis is a growing realisation of the limited impact of disclosure as an exclusive regulatory method to support business-to -consumer contracting (see Nield, 2010; Osuji, 2017; Aldohni, 2017). As Akinbami (2011: p. 136) observed, the financial crisis demonstrated that the information paradigm of the non-interventionist approach has 'little correspondence with the real world'. The financial crisis, which was partly triggered by consumer over-indebtedness, also created unprecedented levels of consumer debt in several jurisdictions. The OECD (2009) in a Draft Recommendation observed that '[o]ne of the features of the financial crisis is the emergence of inadequately regulated alternatives to traditional credit products, which have exposed vulnerable consumers to unsuitable offers, unfair sales practices, and the purchase of credit products that were clearly inappropriate for them'. One of the fallouts of the crisis was the acknowledgment by the then UK Financial Services Authority (FSA, 2009: para. 6.12) of the need for the law to 'protect consumers from themselves' while the Treasury department stressed that 'every effort must be made to help consumers get the products that are right for their needs and circumstances' (HM Treasury, 2009: para. 8.51).

Consequently, the UK appears to have adopted a more interventionist approach to regulating responsible consumer lending. In this regard, the Treasury Department (HM Treasury, 2011: para. 4.17) explained that regulatory approach 'reflects the fact that different consumers require different degrees of protection, depending on their capability and personal circumstances, the product they are buying, and the channel through which they are buying it' (see also HM Treasury, 2012: paras. 4.11–4.12 for similar comments). This is a form of paternalism which recognises that 'consumers can, and do make inferior decisions with regards to their welfare decisions' (Akinbami, 2011: p. 136) and proceeds by 'using regulatory power over consumers for their own good' (Fairweather et al., 2017: p. 3). In addition to the Unfair Commercial Practices Directive 2005,[15] recital 3 of the Mortgage Credit Directive 2014 and recitals 3, 4, 5 and 6 of the Payment Systems Directive 2015 show the European Commission has similarly adopted a pro-interventionist approach to financial consumer regulation following the 2008 financial crisis.

---

[15]   Directive 2005/29/EC of the European Parliament and of the Council of 11 May 2005 concerning unfair business-to-consumer commercial practices in the internal market and amending Council Directive 84/450/EEC, Directives 97/7/EC, 98/27/EC and 2002/65/EC of the European Parliament and of the Council and Regulation (EC) No. 2006/2004 of the European Parliament and of the Council, OJ 2005 L149/22–39.

These examples show that the rational choice theory basis of information regulation 'will not work for all markets and all consumers all of the time or in all situations' (Akinbami, 2011: p. 136). Libertarianism favours disclosure as a regulatory tool to make consumers to make informed choices. It proceeds on the basis that consumers as 'rational economic creatures' can 'maximise their own self-interests' having 'had complete information, unlimited cognitive abilities and unlimited self-control' to make decisions (Akinbami, 2011: pp. 135, 136). In sustainable consumption, however, consumers may not be able to protect themselves from self-harm and external harm as demonstrated above. Consumers may also have collective interest and even altruistic goals for future generations to consider as institutional agents. This weakens the private contract and private interest basis of the rational choice theory and requires disclosure to be complemented by other regulatory tools.

20.5.4 *Beyond Private Contract Law*

The libertarian school frowns at state intervention with 'limited, if any, regulation or other government intervention' (Akinbami, 2011: p. 136). It supports private contract law as the basis for determining the parties' rights and obligations in business-to-consumer cases. The private contract approach of resolution of rights and obligations is highlighted by the statement of the Privy Council in *MacLeod* v. *MacLeod*,[16] albeit in relation to spousal agreements and financial consequences of divorce, that '[w]e must assume that each party to a properly negotiated agreement is a grown up and able to look after him- or herself.' Notwithstanding Kronman's (1980: p. 473) contention that 'contractual regulation as a method of redistribution', the doctrines of privity of contract and consent (Hevia, 2013) and its 'unreflective understanding of the moral and political significance of contract' (Lucy, 1989: p. 132) demonstrates traditional contract law's private transactional nature. It is founded 'upon a platform of neutrality with respect to distributive outcomes' (Collins, 1992: p. 49). Damages award is normally based on inter-party considerations and not with reference to outcomes on society.[17]

Nonetheless, a corollary to the interventionist approach to sustainable consumption is the recognition of distributive justice as a contract law goal. This requires a shift from the common law's traditional emphasis on corrective justice between contractual parties.[18] A distributive justice reframed contract law can consider different segments of society in its outcomes rather than focusing exclusively on contractual parties (Collins, 1992). This enables a regulated contract law to be used to undertake institutional and public governance functions by imposing predetermined distributive justice goals and outcomes on privately arranged contracts.

---

[16] *MacLeod* v. *MacLeod* [2008] UKPC 64, [2010] 1 AC 298, [42] (Baroness Hale) (noted by Miles, 2009).
[17] See *Golden Strait Corp* v. *Nippon Yusen Kubishika Kaisha, the Golden Victory* [2007] UKHL 12.
[18] For discussions of the corrective and distributive goals of contract law, see Kronman, 1980; Colins, 1992, 2004; Miller, 2013; Fejos, 2018; Hardy et al., 2018.

For example, a duty of care can also be imposed in certain circumstances to promote sustainable consumption. If a duty of care is imposed, it may be possible to impose responsibility for, and provide accountability towards, primary (proximate consumers) and secondary (future generations) victims of unsustainable practices. For example, in *Rabone* v. *Pennine Care NHS Trust*, a patient who was discharged by the defendant hospital as in-patient committed suicide shortly afterwards. The UK Supreme court held that the hospital was in breach of its primary duty of care to the deceased as well as its secondary duty of care to the deceased's parents, noting that '[t]he agony may be made worse by knowing that the loss both could and should have been prevented'.[19]

20.5.5 *Resolving Information Asymmetry*

Although disclosure-focused regulation may be inadequate for sustainable consumption and production, this does not mean that that disclosure has no role in the septet framework. An interventionist approach in the septet framework requires improvements to consumer access to information even within a contractual framework. This requires that disclosure should be regarded as one of the ingredients of substantive regulation and not the exclusive regulatory tool. Better and effective information is also important in that it must be useful for consumers in their diverse role in promoting sustainable consumption. Consumers are unlikely to have access to superior information in contrast to businesses. The Volkswagen emissions scandal highlighted the information asymmetry between businesses (as manufacturers, distributors, retailers or service providers) and consumers in relation to sustainable development when proximate consumers or future generations are potentially victims of unsustainable practices. Consumers generally must rely on the information provided by businesses in making purchasing decisions and are often not able to verify such information in advance and post-purchase. As Lord Wright observed in a different context 'the reliance will be in general inferred from the fact that a buyer goes to the shop in confidence that the trades man has selected his stock with skill and judgement'.[20]

The sustainable development agenda can be promoted when counterparties to consumers are required to disclose certain information related to production, marketing and distribution and business relationships involved in those processes. It may help if the disclosure duty is coupled with consequences for non-disclosure. For example, in *Plevin* v. *Paragon*,[21] the UK Supreme Court held that consumers were entitled to recover compensation from banks that failed to disclose commissions in payment protection insurance contracts they persuaded consumers to take up. A legal duty of

---

[19]   *Rabone* v *Pennine Care NHS Trust* [2012] UKSC 2 (SC) para. 92 (Baroness Hale).
[20]   *Grant* v *Australian Knitting Mills Ltd* [1936] AC 85.
[21]   *Plevin* v *Paragon Personal Finance Ltd* [2014] UKSC 61.

this kind can facilitate the disclosure of information consumers may need to be effective institutional champions for sustainable development.

Timely availability of information to consumers is necessary since the courts may not award remedies if 'undue delay' or 'prejudice to third parties and good administration'[22] occurs even when there are valid grounds for making challenges. For example, while consumers can theoretically promote sustainable development through appropriate positive and negative covenants, they need to be aware of the covenant's prospective and retrospective implications. Generally, contractual parties' ability to police covenants through mandatory and prohibitory injunctions depends on their awareness of the factual and legal circumstances. In *Tabcorp Holdings* v. *Bowen Investments*, for instance, a tenant 'in contumelious disregard of the landlord's rights'[23] secretly replaced an existing structure on the leased commercial premises. This was in breach of the leasehold negative covenant prohibiting alterations to the premises without the landlord's consent. Due to lack of knowledge, the landlord could not seek and obtain a prohibitory injunction against the tenant and was restricted to an award of damages. Contract law can therefore be reshaped to impose disclosure obligations and expand the range of remedies that can prevent surreptitious breach of sustainable development covenants and allow parties to insist on steps to redress unsustainable practices.

20.5.6 Improving Corporate Social Reporting for Sustainable Consumption-Promoting CSR

As discussed in relation to the sixth foundational element of the septet framework, CSR can be linked to sustainable consumption and production. The role of consumers and other stakeholders in using CSR to advance sustainable development is often tied to the quality of CSR reporting, which can be voluntary and mandatory. Reporting of corporate social activities is growing due to the popularity of CSR and the need to promote positive reputation that reflects the expectations of stakeholders like consumers (Osuji, 2012; Osuji and Obibuaku, 2016). As the UK Department for Business, Innovation and Skills noted, this type of reporting can promote transparency and corporate accountability (DBIS, 2010). Nonetheless, being that consumers increasingly rely on corporate social disclosures, which include information on sustainable development policies and practices, to make purchasing decisions, it is problematic when such disclosures lack credibility or are misleading. For example, the Deepwater oil spillage showed that BP's previous positive reputation for environmental protection and CSR generally was unearned (Balmer et al., 2011). When there is a 'dichotomy' (Osuji, 2011) between corporate disclosures and performance, consumers will be unable to play an institutional regulatory role for the promotion of

---

[22] *Whitstable Society* v. *Canterbury City Council* [2017] EWHC 254 [76] (Admin) [129] (Dove J).
[23] *Tabcorp Holdings Ltd* v. *Bowen Investments Pty Ltd* (2009) 83 ALJR 390, para. 4.

sustainable development. To fill this gap, it may be useful to explicitly provide for private law rights for individual consumers and stakeholder organisations to challenge false or misleading reports. A consumer relied on such statutory provisions in a Californian statute in *Kasky* v. *Nike*[24] case but that right was removed in an amendment to the law.

Another source of influence on the purchasing decisions of socially conscious consumers is certification or ecolabelling. Certification can be provided by individual corporations, business associations or by third parties such as government agencies and independent non-governmental organisations. Research suggests that consumers are more inclined to trust third party certification schemes (Darnall et al., 2018). Therefore, it is helpful for the sustainable development agenda to promote credible independent third-party certification schemes.

Sustainable consumption can play a more effective role when corporate social reporting and certification are linked to corporate performance. Improved credibility of sustainable development-related reporting can compel businesses, especially the consumer-facing ones, to promote it throughout their operations, supply and purchasing chains. This relates back to the concept of CSR, the practice of which suggests that it is possible for a business to exercise some due diligence responsibility over legally separate entities and business partners. For example, Nike and Levi-Strauss were compelled by consumer and stakeholder pressure to monitor the labour standards of their supply chains and to voluntarily disclose their suppliers' factories to independent organisations to undertake verifications (Doorey, 2011). This trend is somewhat reflected in the emergent disclosure obligations of anti-modern slavery legislations of the UK, Australia and California, USA.

20.5.7 *Consumer Responsibilisation*

We have already shown that the sixth essential component of sustainable consumption in the septet framework is participation by proximate consumers. Although this involves the recognition of consumers as institutional agents for sustainable development, it is important to demonstrate the level of consumer engagement and participation for the interventionist approach required in the septet framework.

There are two models of engaging the public in public interest matters like sustainable development. These are the rationalist or information deficit and the deliberative or civic models which respectively appeal to passive and active participation (Owens, 2000). As discussed above, the rationalist approach is unsuitable for sustainable consumption due to the combined elements of self-interest, collective interest and altruism. The deliberative model can assist consumers in their interaction with other private and public institutional actors. For example, the UK courts

---

[24] *Kasky* v. *Nike* 27 Cal. 4th 939, 946, 45 P.3d 243, 247, 119 Cal. Rptr.2d 296 (Cal. 2002), 123 S. Ct. 2554 (2003).

have stressed the need for 'a conscious deliberative process'[25] in land use and development cases which requires local councils to comply with formal statutory mechanisms and consider expert and stakeholder evidence before reaching decisions.[26]

Nonetheless, there should be mechanisms for raising consumer awareness of relevant issues and rationalisations for participation and prevent reticence to sustainable consumption. Eckhardt et al. (2010) highlighted three rationalisations for consumer resistance to ethical consumption. The economical rationalisation is when price and other economic factors trump consumers' ethical orientations while institutional dependency is consumers' belief that ethical product regulation is the government's sole responsibility. Development realism is the belief that unethical and unsustainable product development is a necessary component of national or macro-economic development.

Consumers' participation therefore requires their 'responsibilisation' for sustainable development. To responsibilise consumers is to enhance their awareness of their own responsibility for the nature and consequences of their decisions and their role in resolving problems (Shamir, 2008). When couched in the economic sense of 'empowerment' responsibilisation reduces barriers to consumers' market participation and access to key information (Williams, 2007). Responsibilisation can be undertaken through consumer education and helps to improve consumer decision-making skills and ability to benefit from disclosure and other remedies. Nonetheless, when responsibilisation is designed to empower consumers to seek private means of protecting their interests, it can encourage individualism and erode solidarity in social policy (Williams, 2007). It may not address public and collective goods issues and the need for collective information and action (Kidd Jr and Daughtrey Jr, 2000: p. 224).

The rationalist responsibilisation model of individual empowerment is therefore inappropriate for sustainable development. As discussed, sustainable consumption, from the consumer perspective, is not only about protecting the individual proximate consumer's interest and may seek to protect future generations. Furthermore, the rationalist model does not allow institutional and stakeholder perspectives which are necessary for promoting sustainable development. The 'emergent sense of distributed responsibility' (Evans et al., 2017: pp. 9–10) therefore offers a better alternative and follows the shared responsibility approach highlighted by Article 50 of the UN Guidelines for Consumer Protection. Distributed responsibility also suggests the need for the participation of all segments of society and prevents key

---

[25] *R (on the application of Goodman) v. Secretary of State for Local Government & Rural Affairs* [2015] EWHC 2576 (Admin) [29] (Dove J).

[26] See *R (Midlands Co-operative Society Ltd) v. Birmingham City Council* [2012] LGR 393 [122–123]; *Western Power Distribution Investments Limited v. Cardiff City Council* [2013] EWHC 1407 (Burton J); *R (on the application of Goodman) v. Secretary of State for Local Government & Rural Affairs* [2015] EWHC 2576 (Admin) (Dove J); *Faraday Development Limited v. West Berkshire* [2016] EWHC 2166 (Holgate J); *Whitstable Society v. Canterbury City Council* [2017] EWHC 254 [76] (Admin) (Dove J).

actors like governments from abdicating their own responsibility for consumers. Similarly, the OECD's Draft Recommendation on Consumer Credit (OECD, 2009) 'calls for a balanced policy focus on financial education and consumer protection, and reinforces the importance of financial literacy as a necessary complement to (rather than a substitute for) a sound framework for financial market regulation and prudential supervision'. The principles the Draft Recommendation encapsulates are applicable to other areas where it is desired that consumers should have an active role in addressing issues they raise.

20.5.8 Stakeholder Rights and Obligations

Two strands of the more interventionist consumer protection we have argued here are the need for consumer private law rights and the need for recognising other stakeholder rights and responsibilities. The concept of sustainable consumption as unpacked by the septet demonstrates that consumers are a stakeholder group for sustainable development in line with Freeman's (1984: p. 46) popular definition of 'stakeholder' as 'any group or individual who can affect or is affected by the achievement of the organisation's objectives'. The definition further suggests that consumers are not only a stakeholder group for sustainable development and the discussions so far implicitly show that governments and corporations are equally stakeholders among others. While the dynamic nature of the concept of stakeholder (Miles, 2017) makes it adaptable to different contexts, what it means for sustainable development needs to be unpacked. The first issue is the identity of relevant stakeholders. Fassin's (2009) analysis of the stakeholder model is helpful here. Fassin identified three classes of stakeholders: (real) stakeholders like consumers that are directly affected by corporate actions; stakewatchers like pressure groups and non-governmental organisations; and stakekeepers who are regulators that enforce formal rules. These classes of stakeholder can play different roles in promoting sustainable consumption and production within the septet framework.

Following the identification and classification of stakeholders, the next issue is therefore whether they have or can have legal rights or obligations within the septet framework. In this regard, public interest organisations and other independent stakeholder groups play a multi-faceted role in promoting the public interest as shown, for example, by the *Kasky* case. Following its 1990s sweatshop scandal, Nike agreed to independent verifications of its suppliers' factories to ensure compliance with international best practices (Osuji, 2012). In the aftermath of its 2003 Indian scandal, Coca-Cola engaged local and international non-governmental organisations in addressing the water usage issues and to restore consumer and public trust (Altschuller et al., 2010). Nike and Coca-Cola experiences are instructive although the involvement of independent organisations was not backed by law. The legitimacy of these stakewatchers to act as claimants and interveners in public interest cases on behalf of consumers can be recognised by the law and public authorities.

Independent organisations can promote legal accountability by representing and demanding protecting of the rights of stakeholders who may not have appropriate knowledge and resources.

Generally, enforcement of rules and standards can be carried out by public agencies or by private market participants if legally permitted to so do (Coffee, 2007; Jackson and Roe, 2009). Nonetheless, the relative competence of public authorities in developed jurisdictions like UK and EU suggest their reliance on administrative procedures. Experiences from consumer law and other fields of public interest also suggest the need to avoid relying exclusively on public enforcement. For example, having argued that the anti-corruption efforts of public agencies achieved modest success at best, Heilbrunn (2004: p. 3) asserted the need to 'forge broad coalitions that can endure efforts of an organised opposition if they hope to succeed in the fight against corruption'. Similarly, the need for 'partnerships' of stakeholders cutting across individual firms, industries and sectors of society is increasingly being recognised in environmental protection policy and scholarship (Stadler and Lin, 2019).

The stakeholder enforcement approach can apply to corporations as well. If corporations are legally recognised as direct or indirect stakewatchers, a business may be required to ensure that its supply and purchasing chains reflect the best consumer protection practices, including in the provision of sustainable development-related information. For example, in *Argos* v. *Leather Trade House Ltd*,[27] the English High Court held that a furniture supplier must reimburse two retailers for millions of pounds in compensation they paid to consumers. While the supplier had assured the retailers that an anti-mould chemical in its products had no adverse effect on human health, consumers complained of skin irritation and respiratory problems. In *Webster* v. *Liddington*,[28] the defendant doctors' brochure contained drug information supplied by its manufacturers. The doctors were held to have committed misrepresentation when it was found that the information excluded the side effects.

Corporate insiders, like employees, can act as sustainable development stakewatchers but they may be open to reprisals when they report wrongdoings. Whistleblowing protection is therefore necessary to encourage corporate insiders to disclose wrongdoings, unethical policies and practices to appropriate persons within and outside the organisation. A recent example of whistleblowing as a regulatory tool is the CRR Firms: Whistleblowing Amendment Instrument 2018 of the UK Prudential Financial Authority. A whistleblowing policy can make use of appropriate financial incentives to incentivise stakewatchers in making disclosures. The use of financial incentives to encourage whistleblowing is gaining traction although some jurisdictions like the UK are reluctant to adopt the approach. In

---

[27] *Argos Ltd & Others* v. *Leather Trade House Ltd (formerly BLC Leather Technology Centre Ltd)* [2012] EWHC 1348 (QB).
[28] *Webster and others* v. *Liddington and others* [2014] EWCA Civ 560.

contrast, in the USA the Dodd-Frank Wall Street Reform and Consumer Protection Act 2010 permits the transfer of a percentage of financial penalties paid by wrong-doers to whistleblowers who facilitated the investigation and detection of misconduct (Laming, 2017).

20.5.9 *Independent Determination of Standards*

A particular example of the recognition of stakeholder rights and responsibilities in the more interventionist consumer protection approach of the septet framework is the legal provision for an independent stakeholder determination of sustainable development standards. In contrast, the courts composed of mainly legally qualified judges may not be able to determine, in an effective way, some technical issues surrounding sustainable development, especially as it applies to sustainable consumption and sustainable production. There may not be courts with specific jurisdiction for sustainable development and, even when there are consumer courts, the judges may not be specially trained in the diverse and often complex issues.

The expert stakeholder determination of appropriate standards is similar to some commercial dispute resolution practices that provide for third party experts to make binding decisions for parties. Expert determination has been applied in historical and contemporary commercial dispute resolution regarding issues such as product quality and product price.[29] Traditionally, contract law permits parties to provide for third party determination of contractual terms despite the fundamental rule that contractual terms need to be clear and certain to be enforceable.[30] Nonetheless, unlike commercial dispute resolution where expert determination of technical and factual issues is usually based on the parties' prior agreement that defines the issues to be addressed,[31] the stakeholder determination in consumer protection can be imposed by law.

20.5.10 *Recognising 'Agency Problem' in Sustainable Consumption*

As discussed, one of the central features of the more interventionist approach in the septet framework is the recognition of stakeholder rights and responsibilities. We argue here that this requires the acknowledgement of the agency problem as a result of conflicts of interests in the consumption chain and its resolution through the application of the stakeholder model. Furthermore, corporate governance needs to be aligned with the stakeholder model in order to advance sustainable development through sustainable consumption and production.

---

[29] Nigel Blackaby et al., *Redfern and Hunter on International Arbitration* 6th ed. (Oxford University Press, 2015) 4.

[30] See *Foley v. Classique Coaches* [1934] 2 KB 1; *Sudbrook Trading Estate Ltd v. Eggleton* [1983] 1 AC 444, [1982] 3 WLR 315; *Jacobs UK Ltd v. Skidmore Owings & Merrill LLP* [2012] EWHC 3293 (TCC).

[31] *Portland General Electrical Co. v. U.S. Bank Trust National Association*, 218 F.3d 1085, 1090 (9th Circuit 2000).

The sustainable consumption chain includes manufacturers and their operations, supply and purchasing chains, distributors, retailers and consumers. Consumers can be differentiated from the others in the motivation, power and control of product and service quality. Unlike consumers that may be driven by personal needs and tastes, businesses on the sustainable consumption chain are usually profit-motivated and able to prospectively bargain on, and determine, the production processes and outcomes. Therefore, a conflict of interest potentially exists between consumers and businesses on the sustainable consumption chain.

The need for the resolution of conflicts of interests is implicit in Adam Smith's statement in *Wealth of Nations* (1776: para. V.1.107) that company directors 'being the managers rather of other people's money than of their own, it cannot be well expected that they should watch over it with the same anxious vigilance'. This statement is often referenced in corporate governance discourse, specifically the separation of ownership and control of companies (Berle and Means, 1991), to illustrate the 'agency problem'. The agency theory has emerged to propose measures for reducing opportunities for conflicts of interests and to align the interests of 'agents' (often corporate directors and managers) as closely as possible to those of the principals (usually identified by economists as the shareholders). According to the agency theory there are three levels of conflict of interest in a business context (Jensen and Meckling, 1976; Armour et al., 2017). First, the classic case highlighted by Adam Smith is the conflict of interests between corporate directors and managers on the one hand and shareholders on the other hand (Enriques et al., 2017a). Secondly, it has been recognised that a conflict of interests exists between majority shareholders and minority shareholders (Enriques et al., 2017b) and, if unchecked, majority shareholders can promote their own self-interest to the detriment of minority shareholders. The third example of agency problem is divergence of interests between corporate 'insiders' such as managers, directors and shareholders and others regarded as corporate 'outsiders' (Roe, 2000; Enriques et al., 2017b). Being the ones in control of the corporation, corporate insiders can ignore the interests, and even act to the detriment, of the outsiders.

The Anglo-American corporate governance model (Keay, 2010) traditionally regards non-shareholder groups like employees, creditors and consumers as outsiders who have no participation and representation rights. This 'shareholder primacy' model exclusively recognises the shareholder class in corporate governance and prioritises shareholders' interests over and above the interests of other corporate constituencies. The model also equates shareholders' interest with profit-making and, as a result, directs corporate managers and directors to pursue profit maximisation. Accordingly, Milton Friedman (1970) argued that 'there is one and only one social responsibility of business – to use its resources and engage in activities designed to increase its profits so long as it stays within the rules of the game, which is to say, engages in open and free competition without deception or fraud.' Similarly, in *Dodge* v. *Ford Motor Co*, the court stated that 'a business corporation is organised and carried on primarily for the profit of the shareholders ... and the powers of the directors are to be employed for that end'.³²

Clearly, the shareholder primacy model has little room for representing the interests of non-shareholders like proximate consumers and future generations in corporate governance. The alternative stakeholder model offers protection of sustainable development in corporate governance. This is highlighted, for example, in *Lyonnais Bank* v. *Pathe Communications*³³ where the court upheld a corporate 'obligation to the community of interests that sustained the corporation, to exercise judgment in an informed, good faith effort to maximize the corporation's long-term wealth creating capacity'. The stakeholder corporate governance model can provide opportunities for representing the interests of proximate consumers, future generations and stakewatcher groups in various ways, including voting and veto rights, membership of, and nomination to, the board of directors, incorporation of interests in directors' duties, accountability of directors, consultation rights and disclosure requirements.

20.5.11 International Cooperation

As discussed above, the septet framework is completed by the consideration of the developing country context, including possible existence of institutional voids. We draw on the SDGs and the UN Guidelines for Consumer Protection to argue that international cooperation is necessary for implementing appropriate standards for sustainable consumption and production, especially when developing countries are involved. While Targets 6a and 16a of the SDGs and Part VI (Articles 79–94) of the UN Guidelines for Consumer Protection stress the need for 'international cooperation' especially in the developing country context, lack of coordination between different national political institutions, especially those sharing geographical and socio-cultural affinities is problematic. The presumption against extraterritoriality of regulation and enforcement³⁴ has aggravated the existence of institutional voids in some developing countries. The dirty fuel and toxic tobacco cases and their Africa-specific products highlight international or regional coordination as one of the obstacles to sustainable consumption in developing countries. This creates regulatory arbitrage that some businesses can exploit to provide harmful products or use unsustainable production systems. International cooperation can facilitate improved regulatory standards which, for example, resulted from the dirty fuel campaign (Yoboué and Kaufman, 2018).

International cooperation can help to improve the effectiveness of enforcement of standards. This is one of the justifications of the EU Consumer Protection

---

³²   *Dodge* v *Ford Motor Co.* [1919] 170 NW 668, 684.
³³   *Lyonnais Bank Nederland, N.V* v. *Pathe Communications Corp* Civ A. No. 12150, 1991 WL 277613 (Del. Ch. Dec. 30, 1991).
³⁴   *Kiobel* v. *Royal Dutch Petroleum Co.*, 133 S Ct 1659 (2913) 1669.

Cooperation Regulation 2006/2004.[35] It may therefore be helpful for groups of developing countries to enter into agreements covering matters like administrative and technical cooperation, information sharing, formulation and application of rules and standards and the enforcement of decisions.

20.6 CONCLUSION

The septet framework developed in this chapter provides the basis for fresh insights that challenge conventional approaches in consumer protection, contract law and regulatory standards and enforcement. It is argued that the concepts of consumer vulnerability, disclosure regulation, contract law, consumer responsibilisation, stakeholder, corporate governance, institutional voids and international cooperation can be reframed to advance the six essential dimensions of sustainable consumption in developing countries. The septet framework promotes shared responsibility for sustainable consumption and production between consumers and other institutional actors like governments, corporations and public interest organisations.

The notion of sustainable consumption and production, which has become increasingly popular as demonstrated by the SDGs and the UN Guidelines for Consumer Protection, shows that consumers can make a real difference to the sustainable development agenda as institutional champions. Consumption can encourage sustainable individual behaviour and business practices and protect the interests of future generations. Sustainable production is indeed one of the pro-social activities expected of businesses by stakeholders like consumers, including within the umbrella of CSR. In turn, the pursuit of sustainable development can make a significant difference for consumers, especially in developing countries. Proximate consumers and future generations are potential victims of unsustainable business practices. This is particularly the case in some developing countries which, due to institutional voids, provide inadequate substantive consumer protection standards and enforcement.

Unlike existing studies that focus mainly on consumer behaviour and lifestyle choices, this chapter draws on the legal, institutional and stakeholder perspectives to uniquely unbundle the concept of sustainable consumption and apply it to the developing country context. The chapter shows that the concept of sustainable consumption and production has six foundational components: (a) sustainable consumption by proximate consumers for future generations; (b) sustainable production for future generations; (c) sustainable consumption by/for proximate consumers; (d) sustainable production for proximate consumers; (e) participation by proximate consumers; and (f) corporate social responsibility. The developing country dimension caps the novel septet approach adopted by the chapter which stresses the need to fill

---

[35] Regulation (EC) No 2006/2004 of the European Parliament and of the Council of 27 October 2004 on cooperation between national authorities responsible for the enforcement of consumer protection laws (the Regulation on consumer protection cooperation) OJ 2004 L364/1–11.

institutional voids that can impede sustainable development. To illustrate the practical relevance of the septet framework, the chapter maps it out with the SDGs' provisions on sustainable consumption and production.

The chapter provides original proposals for an interventionist consumer protection model for sustainable consumption that includes public interest-oriented disclosure regulation, distributive justice-oriented contract law, resolution of business-to-consumer information asymmetry, credible corporate social reporting and certification standards, distributed/shared consumer responsibilisation model, stakeholder enforcement rights, obligations and protection, independent stakeholder determination of standards, resolution of related agency problem through a stakeholder approach to corporate governance and international cooperation in regulatory standards and enforcement. A consumer protection approach to sustainable development can promote stakeholder engagement and meaningful CSR by corporations.

The chapter therefore demonstrates the roles of consumers as institutional actors and consumption as an institution within the institutional theoretic model are context-specific. It is important to consider the institutional environment, especially where consumers are disadvantaged due to the legal and political institutions and the stronger position of economic institutions like corporations. Consequently, there is a need to align sustainable consumption and production to sustainable development in developing countries by designing and implementing an effective consumer protection model that may depart from the typical approaches of the more developed countries. The septet framework for sustainable consumption and production can facilitate private enforcement of international best standards and a consumer protection regime with horizontal impact, even when vertical regulation and enforcement is weak.

REFERENCES

Acemoglu, D. (2009). *Introduction to modern economic growth*. Princeton: Princeton University Press.

Acemoglu, D., Johnson, S. and Robinson, J. (2005). Institutions as a fundamental cause of long-run growth. In P. Aghion and S. Durlauf, eds., *Handbook of Economic Growth* Volume 1A, Amsterdam: Elsevier, pp. 386–472.

Acemoglu, D., Johnson, S. and Robinson, J. A. (2002), Reversal of fortune: Geography and institutions in the making of the modern world income distribution. *Quarterly Journal of Economics*, 107(4),1231–94.

Aghion, P. and Howitt, P. (2009). *The economics of growth*. Cambridge: MIT Press.

Akinbami, F. (2011). Financial services and consumer protection after the crisis. *International Journal of Bank Marketing*, 29(2),134–47.

Aldohni, A. (2017). The UK new regulatory framework of High-Cost Short-Term Credit: Is there a shift towards a more 'Law and Society' based approach? *Journal of Consumer Policy*, 40(3),321–45.

Altschuller, S. A., Lehr, A. and Orsmond, A. J. (2010). Corporate social responsibility. *The International Lawyer*, 45(1),179–89.

Anabtawi, I. and Stout, L. (2008). Fiduciary duties for activist shareholders. *Stanford Law Review*, 60(5),1255–308.

Andorfer, V. and Liebe, U. (2013). Consumer behavior in moral markets. On the relevance of identity, justice beliefs, social norms, status, and trust in ethical consumption. *European Sociological Review*, 29(6),1251–65.

Andorfer, V. and Liebe, U. (2015). Do information, price, or morals influence ethical consumption? A natural field experiment and customer survey on the purchase of fair trade coffee. *Social Science Research*, 52,330–50.

Antonetti, P. and Maklan, S. (2014). Feelings that make a difference: How guilt and pride convince consumers of the effectiveness of sustainable consumption choices. *Journal of Business Ethics*, 124(1),117–34.

Armour, J., Hansmann, H. and Kraakman, R. (2017). Agency Problems and Legal Strategies. In R. Kraakman, J. Armour, P. Davies, L. Enriques, H. Hasnmann, G. Hertig, K. Hopt, H. Kanda, M. Pargendler, W. Ringe and E. Rock, eds., *The anatomy of corporate law: A comparative and functional approach*. Oxford: Oxford University Press, pp. 29–48.

Baldwin, R., Cave, M. and Lodge, M. (2012). *Understanding regulation: Theory, strategy, and practice* 2nd ed. New York: Oxford University Press.

Balmer, J., Powell, S. and Greyser, S. (2011). Explicating ethical corporate marketing. Insights from the BP deepwater horizon catastrophe: The ethical brand that exploded and then imploded. *Journal of Business Ethics*, 102,1–14.

Bantekas, I. (2004). Corporate social responsibility in international law. *Boston University International Law Journal*, 22,309–47.

Bar-Gill, O. and Warren, E. (2008). Making credit safer. *University of Pennsylvania Law Review*, 157(1),1–101.

Barnett, C., Cloke, P., Clarke, N. and Malpass, A. (2011). *Globalizing responsibilities: The political rationalities of ethical consumption*. Oxford: Wiley-Blackwell.

Beck, T. and Levine, R. (2005). Legal institutions and financial development. In C. Menard and M. Shirley, eds., *Handbook of new institutional economics*, Dordrecht: Springer.

Ben-Shahar, O. (2009). The myth of the 'Opportunity to Read' in contract law. *European Review of Contract Law*, 5(1),1–28.

Berle, A. and Means, G. (1991). *The modern corporation and private property*. London: Transaction Publishers.

Bernd, H., Spraul, K. and Ingenhoff, D. (2016). Under positive pressure: How stakeholder pressure affects corporate social responsibility implementation. *Business & Society*, 55 (2),151–87.

Black, B. (2001). The legal and institutional preconditions for strong securities markets. *UCLA Law Review*, 48(4), 781–856.

Black, I. (2010). Sustainability through anti-consumption. *Journal of Consumer Behaviour*, 9 (6),403–11.

Blake, J. (1999). Overcoming the 'value – action gap' in environmental policy: Tensions between national policy and local experience. *Local Environment*, 4,257–78.

Bray, J. and Johns, N. (2011). An exploratory study into the factors impeding ethical consumption. *Journal of Business Ethics*, 98(4),597–608.

Burnett, M. and Welford, R. (2007). Case study: Coca-Cola and water in India: Episode 2. *Corporate Social Responsibility and Environment Management*, 14(5),298–304.

Campbell, C. L., Heinrich, D. and Schoenmüller, V. (2015). Consumers' reaction to fair trade motivated price increases. *Journal of Retailing and Consumer Services*, 24,79–84.

Carrington, M. J., Zwick, D. and Neville, B. (2016). The ideology of the ethical consumption gap. *Marketing Theory*, 16(1),21–38.

Cartwright, P. (2011). The vulnerable consumer of financial services: Law, policy and regulation. Available at www.nottingham.ac.uk/business/businesscentres/gcbfi/documents/resear chreports/paper78.pdf. accessed 10 December 2018.

Castaldo, S., Perrini, F., Misani, N. and Tencati, A. (2009). The missing link between corporate social responsibility and consumer trust: The case of fair trade products. *Journal of Business Ethics*, 84,1–15.

Cedillo Torres, C. A., Garcia-French, M., Hordijk, R., Nguyen, K. and Olup, L. (2012). Four case studies on corporate social responsibility: Do conflicts affect a company's corporate social responsibility policy? *Utrecht Law Review*, 8(3),51–73.

Centre for International Environmental Law [CIEL] (2017). Are Belgium and the Netherlands in breach of their international obligations under the Basel Convention and customary international law due to their export of high sulfur fuels to certain developing countries in Africa that are Parties of the Bamako Convention? Available at www.ciel.org /wp-content/uploads/2017/02/High-sulfur-fuels_CIEL-legal-opinion-23_01_2017-.pdf. accessed 10 December 2018.

Chang, H. A. J. (2011). Institutions and economic development: Theory, policy and history, *Journal of Institutional Economics*, 7(4),473–98.

Cheffins, B. (2001). Does law matter? The separation of ownership and control in the United Kingdom. *Journal of Legal Studies*, 30(2),459–84.

Cherednychenko, O. (2010). Conceptualizing unconscionability in the context of risky financial transactions: How do converge public and private law approaches? In M. Kenny, J. Devenney and L. Fox O'Mahony, eds., *Unconscionability in European Private Financial Transactions*. Cambridge: Cambridge University Press, pp. 246–74.

Cherrier, H., Szuba, M. and Özçağlar-Toulouse, N. (2012). Barriers to downward carbon emission: Exploring sustainable consumption in the face of the glass floor. *Journal of Marketing Management*, 28(3/4),397–419.

Christian Aid (2018). *Counting the cost: A year of climate breakdown.* 27 December 2018. London: Christian Aid.

Clarke, N., Barnett, C., Cloke, P. and Malpass, A. (2007). Globalising the consumer: Doing politics in an ethical register. *Political Geography*, 26(3),231–49.

Clarkson, J. J., Janiszewski, C. and Cinelli, M. D. (2013). The desire for consumption knowledge. *Journal of Consumer Research*, 39(6),1313–29.

Coase, R. (1960). The problem of social cost, *Journal of Law and Economics*, 3,1–44.

Coase, R. (1975). Economists and public policy. In J. F Weston, ed., *Large corporations in a changing society*, New York: New York University Press.

Coffee, J. C. (2001). The Rise of Dispersed Ownership: The Roles of Law and the State in the Separation of Ownership and Control. *Yale Law Journal*, 111,1–82.

Coffee, J. C. (2007). Law and the Market: The Impact of Enforcement. *University of Pennsylvania Law Review*, 156(2),229–312.

Collins, H. (1992). Distributive justice through contracts. *Current Legal Problems*, 45(2),49–67.

Collins, H. (2004). Regulating contract law. In C. Parker, C. Scott, N. Lacey and J. Braithwaite, eds., *Regulating law*. Oxford: Oxford University Press, pp. 13–32.

Crête, R. (2016). The Volkswagen scandal from the viewpoint of corporate governance. *European Journal of Risk Regulation*, 7(1),25–31.

Dam, K. (2006), *The law-growth nexus*. Washington DC: Brookings Institution.

Darnall, N., Ji, H. and Vázquez-Brust, D. A. (2018). Third-party certification, sponsorship, and consumers' ecolabel use. *Journal of Business Ethics*, 150(4),153–69.

de Jonge, A. (2011). Transnational corporations and international law: bringing TNCs out of the accountability vacuum. *Critical Perspectives on International Business*, 7(1),66–89.

Department for Business, Innovation and Skills [DBIS] (2010). *Corporate law and governance. The future of narrative reporting: a consultation*. Available at www.gov.uk/government/consultations/the-future-of-narrative-reporting-a-consultation accessed 10 December 2018.

Deva, S. (2012). *Regulating corporate human rights violations*, London: Routledge.

Doh, J. P., Littell, B. and Quigley, N. R. (2015). CSR and sustainability in emerging markets: Societal, institutional, and organizational influences. *Organizational Dynamics*, 44 (2),112–20.

Domurath, I. (2013). The case for vulnerability as the normative standard in European consumer credit and mortgage law – An inquiry into the paradigms of consumer law. *Journal of European Consumer and Market Law*, 2(3),124–37.

Doorey, D. (2011). The transparent supply chain: From resistance to implementation at Nike and Levi-Strauss. *Journal of Business Ethics*, 103,587–603.

Easterbrook, F. and Fischel, D. (1984). Mandatory disclosure and the protection of investors, *Virginia Law Review* 70,669–715.

Easterly, W. (2008). Institutions: Top Down or Bottom Up? *American Economic Review: Papers and Proceedings*, 98(2),95–9.

Eckhardt, G. M., Belk, R. and Devinney, T. M. (2010). Why don't consumers consume ethically? *Journal of Consumer Behaviour*, 9(6),426–36.

Enriques, L., Hansmann, H. and Kraakman, R. (2017a). The interests of shareholders as a class. In R. Kraakman, J. Armour, P. Davies, L. Enriques, H. Hasnmann, G. Hertig, K. Hopt, H. Kanda, M. Pargendler, W. Ringe and E. Rock, eds., *The anatomy of corporate law: A comparative and functional approach*, 3rd ed. Oxford: Oxford University Press, pp. 55–88.

Enriques, L., Hansmann, H. and Kraakman, R. (2017b). The basic governance structure: Minority shareholders and non-shareholder constituencies. In R. Kraakman, J. Armour, P. Davies, L. Enriques, H. Hasnmann, G. Hertig, K. Hopt, H. Kanda, M. Pargendler, W. Ringe and E. Rock eds., *The anatomy of corporate law: A comparative and functional approach*, 3rd ed. Oxford: Oxford University Press, pp. 89–114.

European Commission (2015). *Closing the loop – An EU action plan for the Circular Economy*. COM(2015) 614 final. Available at https://eur-lex.europa.eu/resource.html?uri=cellar:8a8ef5e8-99a0-11e5-b3b7-01aa75ed71a1.0012.02/DOC_2&format=PDF accessed 10 December 2018.

European Commission (2017). *EU action to curb air pollution by cars: Questions and answers*. http://europa.eu/rapid/press-release_MEMO-17-2821_en.htm accessed 10 December 2018.

European Commission (2018). *A European strategy for plastics in a circular economy*. COM (2018) 28 final. Available at https://eur-lex.europa.eu/resource.html?uri=cellar:2df5d1d2-fac7-11e7-b8f5-01aa75ed71a1.0001.02/DOC_1&format=PDF accessed 10 December 2018.

Evans, D. (2011). Thrifty, green or frugal: Reflections on sustainable consumption in a changing economic climate. *Geoforum*, 42(5),550–7.

Evans, D. (2018). What is consumption, where has it been going, and does it still matter? *The Sociological Review*. Available at https://doi.org/10.1177/0038026118764028 accessed 10 December 2018.

Evans, D., Welch, D. and Sawffield, J. (2017). Constructing and mobilizing 'the consumer': Responsibility, consumption and the politics of sustainability. *Environment and Planning*, 49(6), 1396–1412,1–17.

Fairweather, K., Grantham, R. and O'Shea, P. (2017). *Credit, consumers and the law: After the global storm*. Abingdon: Routledge.

Falkner, R. (2008). *Business power and conflict in international environmental politics.* Palgrave Macmillan: Basingstoke.

Falletti, T. G. and Cunial, S. L. (2018). *Participation in social policy: Public health in comparative perspective.* New York: Cambridge University Press.

Fassin, Y. (2009). The stakeholder model refined. *Journal of Business Ethics*, 84(1),113–35.

Fejos, A. (2015). Achieving safety and affordability in the UK payday loans market. *Journal of Consumer Policy*, 38(2),181–202.

Fejos, A. (2018). Social justice in EU financial consumer law. *Tilburg Law Review*, 24 (1),68–88.

Financial Services Authority [FSA] (2009). Mortgage market review. Available at www .fsa.gov.uk/pubs/discussion/dp09_03.pdf accessed 15 August 2018.

Francioni, F. (1991). Exporting environmental hazard through multinational enterprises: Can the state of origin be held responsible? In F. Francioni and T. Scovazzi, eds., *International responsibility for environmental harm.* London: Graham & Trotman, pp. 275–98.

Freeman, R. E. (1984). *Strategic management: A stakeholder approach*, 1st ed. Boston: Pitman Publishing.

Friedman, M. (1970). The social responsibility of business is to increase its profits. *New York Times* (13 September).

Gabaldon, P. and Gröschl, S. (2015). A few good companies: Rethinking firms' responsibilities toward common pool resources. *Journal of Business Ethics*, 132,579–88.

Gardner, J. (2017). High-Cost credit in the UK: A philosophical justification for government intervention. In K. Fairweather, R. Grantham and P. O'Shea, eds., *Credit, Consumers and the Law: After the Global Storm*, Abingdon: Routledge, pp. 132–52.

Gerding, E. F. (2009). The subprime crisis and the link between consumer financial protection and systemic risk. *FIU Law Review*, 5,93–122.

Glaeser, E. and Shleifer, A. (2003). The rise of the regulatory state. *Journal of Economic Literature*, 41,401–25.

Gray, R., Owen, D. and Adams, C. (1996). *Accounting & accountability: Changes and challenges in corporate social and environmental reporting.* London: Prentice Hall.

Green, T. and Peloza, J. (2014). Finding the right shade of green: The effect of advertising appeal type on environmentally friendly consumption. *Journal of Advertising*, 43(2),128–141.

Greif, A. (2006). *Institutions and the path to the modern economy: Lessons from medieval trade.* Cambridge: Cambridge University Press.

Guéniat, M., Harjono, M., Missbach, A. and Viredaz, G. (2016). *Dirty diesel. How Swiss traders flood Africa with toxic fuels.* A Public Eye Investigation, Lausanne: Public Eye.

Hardy, G., O'Malley, K. and Brindle, B. (2018). *The domino effect: Exposing the knock-on effects of consumer problems.* Citizens Advice.

Heilbrunn, J. (2004). Anti-corruption Commissions: Panacea or Real Medicine to Fight Corruption? World Bank Institute Working Paper Series 37234. available at http://sitere sources.worldbank.org/WBI/Resources/wbi37234Heilbrunn.pdf. accessed 15 August 2018.

Herlin, H. and Solitander, N. (2017). Corporate social responsibility as relief from responsibility: NPO legitimizations for corporate partnerships in contested terrains. *Critical Perspectives on International Business*, 13(1),2–22.

Hevia, M. (2013). The distributive understanding of contract law: Kronman on contract law and distributive justice. In *Reasonableness and responsibility: A theory of contract law.* Law and Philosophy Library, 101. Dordrecht: Springer Netherlands, pp. 19–32.

Hills, J. and Welford, R. (2005). Case study: Coca-Cola and water in India. *Corporate Social Responsibility and Environmental Management*, 12(3),168–77.

Hinton, E and Goodman, M. (2010). Sustainable consumption: Developments, considerations and new directions. In M. Redclift and G. Woodgate, eds., *International handbook of environmental sociology* 2nd ed. Cheltenham: Edward Elgar. pp. 245–61.

HM Revenue and Customs (2018). Carbon emissions tax. Available at: www.gov.uk/govern ment/publications/carbon-emmisions-tax/carbon-emmisions-tax accessed 10 December 2018.

HM Treasury (2009). Reforming financial markets, Cm 7667.

HM Treasury (2011). A new approach to financial regulation: building a stronger system, Cm 8012.

HM Treasury (2012). A new approach to financial regulation: securing stability, protecting consumers, Cm 8268.

Hodgson, G. (2006). What are institutions? *Journal of Economic Issues*, 40,1–25.

Hofsted, G. (1994). *Cultures and organizations*. London: HarperCollins.

House of Commons Environmental Audit Committee. Sustainability of the fashion industry inquiry. Available at: www.parliament.uk/business/committees/committees-a-z/commons-select/environmental-audit-committee/inquiries/parliament-192017/sustainability-of-the-fashion-industry-17-19/ accessed 26 November 2018.

Howells, G. (2005). The potential and limits of consumer empowerment by information. *Journal of Law and Society* 32(3),349–70.

Huffman, M. (2010). Bridging the divide? Theories for integrating competition law and consumer protection. *European Competition Journal*, 6(1),7–45.

Husted, B. (2015). Corporate social responsibility practice from 1800–1914: Past initiatives and current debates. *Business Ethics Quarterly*, 25(1),125–41.

Incardona, R. and Poncibò, C. (2007). The average consumer, the unfair commercial practices directive, and the cognitive revolution. *Journal of Consumer Policy*, 30,21–38.

Inderst, R. (2009). Retail finance: Thoughts on reshaping regulation and consumer protection after the financial crisis. *European Business Organization Law Review*, 10(3),455–64.

International Union for Conservation of Nature and Natural Resources [ICUN] (1980). *World conservation strategy: Living resource conservation for sustainable development*. Gland, Switzerland: International Union for Conservation of Nature and Natural Resources. United Nations Environmental Programme and World Wildlife Fund.

Jackson, H. and Roe, M. (2009). Public and private enforcement of securities laws: Resource-based evidence. *Journal of Financial Economics*, 93(2),207–38.

Jensen, M. C. and Meckling, W. H. (1976). Theory of the firm: Managerial behaviour, agency costs and ownership structure. *Journal of Financial Economics*, 3(4),305–60.

Johnstone, M.-L. and Tan, L. P. (2015). Exploring the gap between consumers' green rhetoric and purchasing behaviour. *Journal of Business Ethics*, 132,311–28.

Karam, C. M. and Jamali, D. (2013). Gendering CSR in the Arab Middle East: An institutional perspective. *Business Ethics Quarterly*, 23(1),31–68.

Keay, A. (2010). Stakeholder theory in corporate law: Has it got what it takes. *Richmond Journal of Global Law and Business*, 9(3),249–300.

Kidd Jr, D. L. and Daughtrey Jr,W. H. (2000). Adapting contract law to accommodate electronic contracts: Overview and suggestions. *Rutgers Computer and Technology Law Journal*, 26,215–80.

Korhonen, J., Honkasalo, A. and Seppälä, J. (2018). Circular economy: The concept and its limitations. *Ecological Economics*, 143,37–46.

Kronman, A. T. (1980). Contract law and distributive justice. *Yale Law Journal*, 89, 472–511.

Kysar, D. A. (2005). Preferences for processes: Process/product distinction and the regulation of consumer choice. *Harvard Law Review*, 118,525–641.

La Porta, R., Lopez-de-Silanes, F. and Schleifer, A. (2006). What works in securities laws? *Journal of Finance*, 61(1),1–32.

La Porta, R., Lopez-de-Silanes, F. and Schleifer, A. (2008). The economic consequences of legal origins. *Journal of Economic Literature*, 46(2),285–332.

La Porta, R., Lopez-de-Silanes, F., Schleifer, A. and Vishny, R. W. (1997). Legal determinants of external finance. *Journal of Finance*, 52(3),1131–50.

La Porta, R., Lopez-de-Silanes, F., Schleifer, A. and Vishny, R. W. (1998). Law and finance. *Journal of Political Economy*, 106(6),1113–55.

La Porta, R., Lopez-de-Silanes, F., Schleifer, A. and Vishny, R. W. (2000). Investor protection and corporate *governance*. *Journal of Financial Economics*, 58(1–2),3–27.

La Porta, R., Lopez-de-Silanes, F., Schleifer, A. and Vishny, R. W. (1999). The quality of government. *Journal of Law, Economics and Organisation*, 15(1), 222–79.

Laming, H. (2017). Should the UK pay financial rewards to whistleblowers? *Banker*, 167 (1096),12–12.

Landis, J. (1938). *The administrative process*. New Haven: Yale University Press.

Llewelyn D., (1999). The Economic Rationale for Financial Regulation. Financial Services Authority FSA Occasional Papers on Financial Regulation. Available at www.fsa.gov.uk /pubs/occpapers/op01.pdf accessed 15 August 2018.

Longo, C., Shankar, A. and Nuttall, P. (2019). 'It's not easy living a sustainable lifestyle': How greater knowledge leads to dilemmas, tensions and paralysis. *Journal of Business Ethics*, 154 (3),759–79.

Lucy, W. N. R. (1989). Contract as a mechanism of distributive justice. *Oxford Journal of Legal Studies*, 9(1),132–47.

Mansvelt, J. (2005). *Geographies of consumption*. London: Sage.

Maurisse, M. (2019). The blazing success of Swiss cigarettes in Africa: An investigation by Marie Maurisse, winner of Public Eye's investigation award. Available at: http://stories .publiceye.ch/tobacco/ accessed 18 February 2019.

Micklitz, H. (2012). The expulsion of the concept of protection from the consumer law and the return of social elements in the civil law: A bittersweet polemic. *Journal of Consumer Policy*, 35,283–96.

Micklitz, H. (2013). Do consumers and businesses need a new architecture of consumer law? A thought-provoking impulse. *Yearbook of European Law*, 32(1),266–367.

Miles, J. (2009). Agreements for grown-ups. *Cambridge Law Journal*, 68(2),285–8.

Miles, S. (2017). Stakeholder theory classification: a theoretical and empirical evaluation of definitions. *Journal of Business Ethics*, 142(3),437–59.

Miller, D. (2013). *Justice for earthlings*. Cambridge: Cambridge University Press.

Modigliani, F. and Perotti, E. (1997). Protection of minority interest and the development of security markets. *Managerial and Decision Economics*, 18(7),519–28.

Monye, F. (2017). An overview of consumer law in Nigeria and relationship with laws of other countries and organisations. *Journal of Consumer Policy*, 41(4),373–93.

Myles, P., Schick, L. and Okonta, O. (2018). Special report: Nigeria's gas flare increase ahead 2020 deadline. *Premium Times*, Nigeria 25 November. Available at www.premiumtimesng.com /news/headlines/297472-special-report-nigerias-gas-flares-increase-ahead-2020-deadline.html accessed 25 November 2018.

Newholm, T., Newholm, S. and Shaw, D. (2015). A history for consumption ethics. *Business History*, 57(2),290–310.

Nield, S. (2010). Responsible lending and borrowing: Whereto low-cost home ownership? *Legal Studies*, 30(4),610–32.

North, D. (1990). *Institutions, institutional change and economic performance.* Cambridge: Cambridge University Press.

OECD (2009). *Draft recommendation of the council on good practices on financial education and awareness relating to credit.* Available at https://one.oecd.org/document/C(2009)62/en/pdf accessed 15 August 2018.

OECD (2011). *OECD guidelines for multinational enterprises 2011 edition.* Available at www.oecd.org/corporate/mne/oecdguidelinesformultinationalenterprises.htm accessed 15 August 2018.

Omoteso, K. and Yusuf, H. (2017). Accountability of transnational corporations in the developing world: The case for an enforceable international mechanism. *Critical Perspectives on International Business,* 13(1),54–71.

Osuji, O. (2011). Transnational corporations and the protection of human rights: Non-financial reporting as an option. In D. Nault and S. L. England, ed., *Globalization and human rights in the developing world.* New York: Palgrave Macmillan, pp. 83–117.

Osuji, O. (2012). Corporate social responsibility: Fairness and promise as the fundaments for juridification of social disclosures. *Contemporary Issues in Law,* 12(1),46–76.

Osuji, O. (2015). Corporate social responsibility, juridification and globalization: 'Inventive interventionism' for a 'paradox'. *International Journal of Law in Context,* 11(3), 1–34.

Osuji, O. (2017). Responsible lending: Consumer protection and prudential regulation perspectives. In K. Fairweather, P. O'Shea and R. Grantham, eds., *Credit, consumers and the law: After the global storm.* Abingdon: Routledge, pp. 62–85.

Osuji, O. and Obibuaku, U. (2016). Rights and corporate social responsibility: Competing or complementary approaches to poverty reduction and socioeconomic rights? *Journal of Business Ethics,* 136(2), 329–47.

Overton L. and Fox, L. (2018). Stakeholder conceptions of later-life consumer vulnerability in the financial services industry: Beyond financial capability? *Journal of Consumer Policy,* 41 (3), 273–95.

Owens, S. (2000). Engaging the public: Information and deliberation in environmental policy. *Environment and Planning,* A32(7),1141–8.

Perera, C., Auger, P. and Klein, J. (2018). Green consumption practices among young environmentalists: A practice theory perspective. *Journal of Business Ethics,* 152, 843–64.

Polinsky, M. and Shavell, S. (2000). The economic theory of public enforcement of law. *Journal of Economic Literature,* 38,45–76.

Reich, N. (1992). Diverse approaches to consumer protection philosophy. *Journal of Consumer Policy,* 14(3), 257–92.

Roe, M. J. (2000). Political conditions to separating ownership from control. *Stanford Law Review* 53(3), 539–606.

Rowan, S. (2009). Protecting contractual expectations: An Australian perspective. 68(2) *Cambridge Law Journal,* 68(2),276–78.

Rutherford, M. (2001). Institutional economics: Then and now. *Journal of Economic Perspectives,* 15(3),173–94.

Scherer, A. and Palazzo, G. (2011). The new political role of business in a globalized world: a review of a new perspective on CSR and its implications for the firm, governance, and democracy. *Journal of Management Studies,* 48(4),899–931.

Shamir, R. (2008). The Age of responsibilization: On market-embedded morality. *Economy and Society,* 37,1–19.

Shaw, D., McMaster, R. and Newholm, T. (2016). Care and commitment in ethical consumption: An exploration of the 'attitude-behaviour gap'. *Journal of Business Ethics,* 136, 251–65.

Shove, E. (2004). *Changing human behaviour and lifestyle: A challenge for sustainable consumption?* London: Elgar Publishing.

Shove, E. (2010). Beyond the ABC: Climate change policy and theories of social change. *Environment and Planning*, A 42(6),1273–85.

Smith, A. (1776). *An inquiry into the nature and causes of the wealth of nations.* London: W. Strahan and T. Cadell.

Spindler, G. (2011). Behavioural finance and investor protection regulations. *Journal of Consumer Policy*, 34,315–36.

Stadler, L. and Lin, H. (2019). Leveraging partnerships for environmental change: The interplay between the partnership mechanism and the targeted stakeholder group. *Journal of Business Ethics*, 154(3),869–91.

Strengers, Y. and Maller, C., eds., (2015). *Social practices, intervention and sustainability: Beyond behaviour change.* London: Routledge.

Thøgersen, J., de Barcellos, M. D., Perin, M. G. and Zhou, Y. (2015). Consumer buying motives and attitudes towards organic food in two emerging markets: China and Brazil. *International Marketing Review*, 32(3/4),389–413.

Unilever (2017). Report shows a third of consumers prefer sustainable brands. 5 January 2017. Available at www.unilever.com/news/press-releases/2017/report-shows-a-third-of-consumers-prefer-sustainable-brands.html accessed 15 August 2018.

United Nations (2002). 'Report of the world summit on sustainable development'. Johannesburg, South Africa, 26 August-4 September 2002. A/CONF.199/20. Available at www.un-documents.net/aconf199-20.pdf accessed 15 August 2018.

United Nations (2012). A 10-year framework of programmes on sustainable consumption and production patterns. A/CONF.216/5. Available at www.un.org/ga/search/view_doc.asp?symbol=A/CONF.216/5&Lang=E. accessed 15 August 2018.

United Nations (2016). United Nations guidelines for consumer protection. New York: United Nations.

United Nations Environment Programme (UNEP). (2016). *Diesel fuel sulphur levels: Global status June 2016.* Available atwww.unep.org/Transport/New/PCFV/pdf/Maps_Matrices/world/sulphur/MapWorldSulphur_June2016.pdf accessed 30 December 2016.

United Nations. (1987). 'Report of world commission on environment and development: Our common future' (Brundtland Report). Available at www.un-documents.net/our-common-future.pdf accessed 1 December 2018.

United Nations. (2015). Transforming our world: The 2030 agenda for sustainable development. Available at: www.un.org/ga/search/view_doc.asp?symbol=A/RES/70/1&Lang= accessed 15 August 2018.

Van Dam, C. (2011). Tort law and human rights: brothers in arms. *Journal of European Tort Law*, 2(3), 221–54.

Vogel, D. (2005). *Social Responsibility.* Washington, DC: Brookings Institution Press.

Whitmarsh, L., O'Neill, S. and Lorenzoni, I. (2010). Climate change or social change? Debate within, amongst, and beyond disciplines. *Environment and Planning*, A43,258–61.

Willett, C. (2018). Re-theorising consumer law. *Cambridge Law Journal*, 77(1),179–210.

Williams T. (2007). Empowerment of whom and for what? Financial literacy education and the new regulation of consumer financial services. *Law & Policy*, 29(2),226–56.

Winans, K., Kendall, A. and Deng, H. (2017). The history and current applications of the circular economy concept. *Renewable and Sustainable Energy Reviews*, 68(1), pp.825–833.

World Bank/Institute for Health Metrics and Evaluation University of Washington, Seattle (2013). *The Cost of air pollution strengthening the economic case for action.* Washington DC: World Bank.

World Health Organization [WHO] (2006). WHO Air quality guidelines for particulate matter, ozone, nitrogen dioxide and sulfur dioxide Global update 2005. Summary of risk assessment. Geneva: WHO Press. Available at http://apps.who.int/iris/bitstream/10665/69477/1/WHO_SDE_PHE_OEH_06.02_eng.pdf accessed 30 November 2018.

Yoboué, M. and Kaufman, J. (2018). Inside the dirty fuels campaign: Lessons for business and human rights. *Business and Human Rights Journal*, 3(2),291–7.

Corporate Social Responsibility and Sustainable Development in Developing and Emerging Markets: Looking Forward

Franklin N. Ngwu, Onyeka K. Osuji and Dima Jamali

21.1 INTRODUCTION

The contributions to this work reveal two major issues; one is clear while the other seems unclear. On the one hand, what is clear and unquestionable is that the field of Corporate Social Responsibility (CSR) is rapidly changing and its relevance in day-to-day activities and interdisciplinary discourse is undeniable. On the other hand, what remains uncertain, but intriguing, is the extent to which the influence of CSR can go and has gone. If this is the case, it means that even the existing meanings, understandings and applications of CSR are arguably tentative. It will be recalled that this book sets out to examine four main questions:

(1) What are the linkages between CSR and sustainable development?
(2) What does or can CSR mean for developing or emerging economies and in what ways does this deviate from orthodoxies and universalist approaches?
(3) What institutional factors and actors influence or can influence the effectiveness of CSR in developing and emerging economies?
(4) How can developing and emerging economies promote a flexible, diverse and reconstructed CSR that promotes inclusive and sustainable development?

The 20 chapter contributions not only significantly addressed the questions, they enriched our understanding of CSR issues and its wide and increasing importance and interconnectedness. However, the deep examination of the issues exposed further questions not caused by the contributors but perhaps prompted by the emerging and absorbing intricacies of CSR, especially as it applies to the developing and emerging markets (DEMs). As will be further demonstrated, the better understanding of CSR and the further questions that emerge can be attributed mainly to a desire for higher CSR and sustainable development among DEMs that are characterized by intriguing complexity and heterogeneity. This relates to the differences in the contextual and institutional peculiarities of DEMs. In comparison to developed societies where contexts, while important, might not significantly change the strategies and outcomes, the case of DEMs is insightfully very different. Due to the contextual and institutional peculiarities, no two developing or emerging markets seem to be similar and as they vary so will macro, meso and micro CSR and sustainable development issues differ especially as they apply to the key questions of this book. These issues will be more apparent as we examine the findings and implications emanating from the three sections and contributions.

21.2 PART I: INSTITUTIONS, CSR CONCEPTUALIZATIONS AND SUSTAINABLE DEVELOPMENT

With six chapters focusing on the meanings, theorizations and scope of CSR and implications for DEMs, Pilato in Chapter 2 leads with an investigation of the institutional theory and CSR. While affirming that the meaning, understanding and practice of CSR in DEMs are moderated by their respective institutional and contextual peculiarities, she uses a review of the institutional theory to propose a new theoretical approach for CSR in DEMs. As existing comparative institutional models such as Varieties of Capitalism (VOC) or National Business Systems (NBS) have been used mainly for developed markets, she maintains that a combination of Varieties of Institutional Systems (VIS) and the heterogeneous expressions of CSR in developing and emerging markets provides a better model for the understanding and practice of CSR in DEMs. The interesting aspect of this proposition is that it allows firms to choose specific expressions of CSR based on their assessment of DEMs' VIS compositions. While there is no doubt regarding the opportunities for a better CSR understanding and practice through the VIS model, there are also challenges. A key one is that the institutional make-up of every DEM is dynamic and even heterogeneous within specific DEMs, especially the plural ones such as Nigeria. The question therefore is in the selection of the institutional factors that will consist the institutional basket of a DEM and the inherent varieties even within particular DEMs.

In addressing the above challenge, useful assistance comes from Chapter 3 through Okoye's focus on how CSR can be used as an allocative device to enhance the sustainable development of DEMs. Relying on the effectiveness of CSR laws and regulations, she alludes to the possibility of allocating some societal development challenges to business. As CSR is more of relationship between business and society, the link can be enhanced through legal support of the two ways through which firms practise their CSR. These include firms' actions to ameliorate their impacts on society and their other contributions to societal well-being. In line with Sen's Development as Freedom, which focuses on how sustainable development can be enhanced through the creation of an environment that supports the achievement of the identified capability needs, CSR contribution of firms can be better pursued through legal support and a focus on the capability needs of society. In identifying common development challenges of DEMs such as optimal health, education and unemployment which are in line with capability demands and needs of majority of the populace in DEMs, the challenge of VIS as highlighted in Chapter 1 can be better managed. But as this depends on the support, robustness and effectiveness of the legal system, there is a further challenge given the duality and sometimes plurality of legal systems in DEMs. As a consequence of colonization, most DEMs transplanted and adopted the legal systems of their former colonizers in addition to their respective informal and normative legal systems. Expectedly, this leads to a legal system challenge requiring possible harmonization of the legal systems to enhance their effectiveness (See Menski, 2006). In supporting CSR practice with legal systems, the challenge and question is which should the legal system use, given the formality of the adopted ones and the higher acceptance, internalization and compliance of the normative and informal ones (see Cooter, 2002; Menski, 2006).

Possibly appreciating the legal system challenge, Osuji and Abba in Chapter 4 'Domestic Adjudicative Institutions, Developing Countries and Sustainable Development: Linkages and Limitations' emphasize the importance of adjudicative institutions in promoting CSR and sustainable development. Without allocating superiority to any of the three key institutional frameworks – regulatory, normative and cognitive/cultural, they underline their importance and influence in sustainable development through their knowledge and communicative attributes. They maintain that the adjudicative institutions perform different functions. These include the constitutionalization of sustainable development through the adjudicative institutions' regulatory role, internalization and transmission of sustainable development values via their normative roles and refining local practices through alignment with global expectations and corporate governance based on their cognitive tasks. With suggestions on how the challenges to effective use of adjudicative institutions in sustainable development can be better managed, they identify and appreciate some inherent challenges such as lack of explicit provisions, narrow focus on compensatory remedies, locus standi, *forum non conveniens* and choice of law. To better understand how these challenges play out especially in DEMs, Chapter 5 by Adeola, Eigbe and Muritala is helpful. With a focus on SMEs, which dominate the economies of most DEMs, they further affirm that the peculiarities of DEMs such as the lack or low formalization, weak accounting and governance procedures and other attributes of SMEs in DEMs affect their understanding, approach and practice of CSR. As CSR is presently more in the formalized segment of economies, promoting CSR in DEMs dominated by informal economic activities of SMEs will require interventions to enhance social capital (trust, reputation and legitimacy), culture and combine with proper legislation to achieve a better CSR outcome especially through SMEs. The interesting contribution of this chapter is its revelation of the dominance of DEMs by SMEs in the informal economic sub-sector and their inherent peculiarities which influence their engagement and practice of CSR.

To further elucidate the relevance of contextual and institutional peculiarities, the examination of 'Human Resource Management and Political CSR in Global

Supply Chains: Causes and Consequences of host Communities' Enduring Struggles in Chapter 6 by Knoll and Ahen is revealing. Focusing on one of the world's largest multinational palm oil producers, they found out, contrary to existing views and literature, that while CSR is more of a firm's contribution or response to their impacts, the socioeconomic demands from low income developing countries can be linked or understood as the communities' response to the shocks from the disruptive activities of multinational corporations (MNCs). Captured as '5Ds', they include dispossession of land; displacement of people; destruction of the environment; desperation and de-democratization through disenfranchisement. Torn between restitution demands of the host communities and profit pursuits of the MNCs, HR managers mutate into reconciliation agents but with a bias in favour of MNCs. Given the wide negative impacts of MNCs on the life of the host communities which sometimes might be unavoidable and which the MNCs and other firms might not be able to respond to comprehensively, the task then is how to identify the best strategy or sector that can be focused on to achieve the maximum positive impact.

This is the focus of Chapter 7 by Motilewa, Ebes and Ngwu. While appreciating that firms can respond to CSR demands in varied ways, they maintain that with the increasing relevance of social issues on CSR discourse and required actions, it is important for firms to identify intervention strategies with the most pervasive positive impact on all the key stakeholders. Considering that the two most important stakeholders in the CSR discourse are arguably the host communities and the firms, they maintain that interventions in the human capital development of the society seem to be most convincing and impactful. Affirming this suggestion are the outcomes from the interventions of General Electric (GE) and Private Sector Health Alliance of Nigeria (PHN) in Africa's human capital development chal-lenges. While the GE intervention focused on science, technology, engineering and mathematics (STEM) subjects of South Africa, Mozambique and Nigeria, PHN has contributed to the improvement of Nigeria's health sector through interventions for enhancing the skills of health workers. While their view that human capital chal-lenge is common in all DEMs and their findings that interventions such as that of GE and PHN benefit both the firms and society are convincing, there are questions that demand attention. First is whether such interventions can be replicated across all DEMs? Second is can all firms execute such interventions and third is whether human capital development is the priority of every society. The issues will require deeper investigation of societal CSR demands and firms' activities in DEMs as pursued in the second part of the book.

21.3 PART II: CSR AND SUSTAINABLE DEVELOPMENT: CROSS-COUNTRY STUDIES

From the first seven chapters, it is apparent that CSR issues are wide and varied especially in DEMs due to differences in contextual and institutional peculiarities.

As understanding these differences will help in identifying both common and unique strategies that can be applied across, or in, particular DEMs, the following deeper cross-country examinations are pertinent. Starting the investigation are Ren, Feng, Xiao, Hongyan and Liu, who used a multiple stakeholder perspective to examine firm ownership and CSR in China. Utilizing data from publicly listed firms from 2011 to 2016 and appreciating that resources are often limited, they examined how firms attend to the five key stakeholders' interests. Their findings are interesting, suggesting that the area of CSR focus can be deduced from ownership types. While privately owned firms might likely focus more on social orientation issues, foreign-owned firms arguably will prioritize issues relating to investor, consumer and environmental orientations. The deduction that can be made from their findings is that the type of ownership has a central influence on the selection of, trade-off between and decisions relating to the stakeholders' interests that firms make. As this is the case in China, the challenge is whether the same can be said of other DEMs. Moreover, as ownership is significantly influenced by the legal system and the laws of society, a further question is whether the CSR activities, priorities and performance of firms are largely influenced by the prevalent legal system of the society in question.

Focusing on India, Tamvada in Chapter 9 maintains that culture, values, religion, traditions and the role of Dharma are important factors influencing CSR in India. Tracing the evolution of CSR from Gandhian orientation, the chapter shows that CSR in India has transformed into a more strategic inclination particularly due to FDI and MNCs' entry and growth in India. To manage such competing and transforming challenges and their impacts on firms, India had to legislate CSR. However, as the legislation applies only in India and with the absence of a global code on CSR, India further intervened to ensure that CSR activities of firms address local needs. While the interventions of India in CSR legislation and focus on local needs are commendable and offer other DEMs insights on how CSR activities can be managed, the Indian challenge especially in dealing with global CSR issues especially as it pertains to MNCs seems similar for many DEMs. This however depends on the nature of the economy and the extent of influence of MNCs in the economy. Expectedly, the influence of MNCs will be more in emerging economies with higher FDI and MNCs than in developing economies with limited FDI and MNCs. Even in developing economies, the Indian challenge especially in dealing with MNCs might not be a priority if the economy is mainly informal and dominated by SMEs. This seems to be the case in Nigeria as demonstrated by Uzo and Shittu in Chapter 10. They emphasize that as the economy is largely informal, the focus should be on improving the CSR practices of the informal actors especially the SMEs. Identifying inherent CSR practices such as apprenticeship and credit sales, they maintain that these CSR practices are part of the day-to-day activities of the informal economy and, as the economy is dominated by SMEs, improvements in their CSR understanding and practices should resultantly lead to higher sustainable development of the country.

With a slightly different inclination, Cupido in Chapter 11 through the examination of salvage contracts demonstrates that the inclusion and observance of environmental issues in the shipping sector of South Africa is of a secondary concern as compared to the commercial interests of the contracting parties. Identifying three interrelated pillars of sustainable development as economic development, social development and environmental protection, the chapter, while highlighting that salvage operations should involve at least two of these identified pillars, further affirms that sustainable decisions are made based on the competing interests of stakeholders. Focusing on three key stakeholders – salvors, property owners and the state – Cupido interestingly shows that the position of salvors is most challenging given their expectation to consider and balance both environmental and commercial interests. As the contracts are weak in protecting the environmental interests of third parties, the chapter maintains that a better outcome where the conflicting interests of all stakeholders can be better managed can be achieved through proper legislation especially through the use of *stipulatio alteri*. While this suggestion on how to address the institutional void is encouraging, the challenge is how to ensure that all parties or key stakeholders are inclined to sustainable development consideration in their negotiations. A related challenge be on who will lead the negotiation, integration and provision of the required institutional gap.

The insights from Chapter 12 by Wesley, Dau and Moore on how MNCs can help in filling institutional voids in DEMs can be helpful. Through a deep historical analysis of institutional challenges in Thailand especially issues of slavery and child labour, Chapter 12 illustrates that even with failures in international and domestic policy efforts, a multinational firm, Nestlé, has positively addressed some of the institutional voids through their operations and activities, such as Seafood Task Force, that tackle human right abuses at the source. The chapter shows truly that where there is a will, there is a way. Recalling that Thailand is a country with all the negative attributes of a developing country such as corruption and abuse of power, the success of Nestlé shows that addressing institutional voids or sustainable challenges can be achieved once a critical stakeholder is involved and committed to a goal. Relatedly, as firms' decisions are considered and approved by boards and senior management of firms, it is helpful to understand if the composition of board/senior management of firms contributes to their involvement in addressing institutional voids or sustainability performance of the firms. This challenge was undertaken in Chapter 13 by Acar and Gozum focusing on gender composition of top firms listed in the Istanbul Stock Exchange. Their findings show that firm sustainability performance is influenced by the board composition with a positive improvement recorded when three or more women are included on the boards or senior management of firms. As the study focused on the top 100 firms, the findings, if applicable in other DEMs, provide an encouraging strategy that can be used in improving the sustainability performance of firms.

Going through these preceding chapters reveals interesting facts. First is that the variation in the CSR needs and challenges of DEMs is unquestionable. Second is that a key and common challenge across most DEMs is the presence of institutional voids manifesting in different forms and segments of society. Third is that addressing the institutional voids can be started not only by the government but also by any of the critical stakeholders. Fourth is that formal legislation while important in regulating CSR might not be very effective due to duality or plurality of legal systems that affects the understanding, acceptance, internalization and compliance with the laws and legislation. Based on contextual and institutional peculiarities, a better outcome can be achieved through the combination of formal legislation with informal laws or even only with informal laws (culture, norms and values) given their higher understanding, acceptance, internalization and compliance than the formal laws and legislation, especially in DEMs with economies that are largely informal. Fifth is that CSR and sustainability decisions are largely affected by the interests of the stakeholders in terms of their costs and benefits. These issues are further examined in Part III.

21.4 PART III: NORMATIVE AND UTILITY PERSPECTIVES

Properly started by Alshaleel in Chapter 14 with a convincing explanation of the similarities between the goals and attributes of Islamic finance and Sustainable Development Goals (SDGs) and as such how the latter can be financed by the former. As SDGs require substantial financing especially in the DEMs, Alshaleel argues that the ideology, attributes, principles and products of Islamic finance such as asset-backed finance and prohibition of interest are in line with the social and ethical orientation of SDGs. While the findings of the chapter are appealing and can be helpful in addressing the development challenges of DEMs, there are impediments. For instance, how to ensure the effective utilization of the funds especially in DEMs with weak institutions resulting in pervasive institutional voids is one obstacle. In the absence of an effective institutional framework, the reverse might be the case, with Islamic finance contribution becoming unsustainable. Another challenge will be how to achieve good understanding of CSR and sustainable concerns among the critical stakeholders in DEMs. To address some of the identified difficulties, Achebo in Chapter 15 argues that business schools in DEMs have a role to play. Drawing from theories of CSR and CSR education, the chapter critically shows how CSR issues and education are acquired and the ways through which business schools are performing their task of developing CSR leaders and what can be done to enhance CSR education.

Advocating for higher knowledge and understanding of the attributes and benefits of green capitalism, Kila in Chapter 16 maintains that it offers a fascinating option for effective integration of both sustainable interest of society and the economic/profit interests of firms, especially in issues of climate change mitigation. Noting the avoidance of environmental sustainability by firms in the DEMs, the chapter suggests that its effective inclusion and integration in the business decisions of firms can be achieved by making investment in environmental sustainability economically attractive to firms, so that they can directly or indirectly contribute to sustainable development goals of DEMs. The chapter maintains that with the success so far achieved in the issuance and usage of green bonds for environmental projects, a green capitalist approach is indeed a good partner in the pursuit of the SDGs in the DEMs. It also suggests some regulatory steps that can be used to remedy or prevent abuse of the opportunities and benefits. Related but focusing on ethical issues in outsourcing is Hiquet and Oh's contribution in Chapter 17. They maintain that while outsourcing has economic benefits to the outsourcing firms, there are ethical issues such as poor working conditions, child labour and environmental pollution that should not be ignored. To address these ethical issues, some institutional reforms are suggested and include re-designing governance, establishing industry-level action and developing institutional capacity. And these reforms should be done in both public and private sectors. While the public sector reform will focus on regulation, the private sector one should be on corporate governance and how to achieve better outcomes. MNCs are encouraged to collaborate and take industry level action and provide support to both outsourcing companies and local communities so that they can help in addressing ethical challenges.

While the suggestions of Chapters 16 and 17 can be helpful to other DEMs, the reliance on legislation and regulation brings back the memories of the 2008 financial crisis and the need to rethink deeply all the causes of ethical problems and to go beyond laws and regulation in finding solutions. As the financial sector is perceived as a properly regulated sector, the disturbing ongoing question is how such a crisis and consequent recession happened even with volumes of laws and regulation. Concerned about such outcomes, Nwagwu, Ogbechie and Ngwu in Chapter 18 lay the blame not only on financial institutions but also educational institutions that teach and develop business leaders, again returning to business schools as done in Chapter 15. To prevent a recurrence of the 2008 crisis, they suggest that it is pertinent for educational institutions, especially business schools, to rethink their role and responsibility as citadels of learning for the good of society. This will require a rethink not only in their curriculum but also in their mission, vision, activities and engagement with the wider society and stakeholders. Focusing on business schools in DEMs, they maintain that through mimetic, coercive and normative pressures either solely or combinatorically, a better orientation and practice of sustainability and sustainability education can be achieved.

Possibly expanding the idea that stakeholders that can effectively influence and enhance sustainable development, Stech in Chapter 19 calls for more involvement of social movements especially in promoting sustainable finance. Focusing on social movements' interaction and involvement in three complex finance dynamics – project finance, bond finance and pension finance for sustainable finance, he maintains that social movements can act as an effective competitive challenge to major stakeholders that determine finance trajectories. Expectedly through the competition and conflict that will arise, even the major finance stakeholders will adjust their strategies and be better inclined towards ethical concerns and sustainable development. Envisaging challenges in his appeal for more social movements' involvement in finance issues, he provides insightful guidelines that can be used to enhance the competitive advantage of social movements.

Expanding the options for a better CSR and sustainable development, Osuji and Amajuoyi in Chapter 20, the penultimate chapter, approaches the discussion from a slightly wider theoretical but interesting approach with a focus on sustainable consumption, consumer protection and sustainable development. Gaining from sustainable development goals, legal, institutional and stakeholder perspectives, they developed a septet framework to enhance our circumstantial examination and understanding of issues in sustainable consumption and production. Disaggregating sustainable consumption and production into six primary elements, the existing understanding of issues in consumer vulnerability, disclosure regulation, contract law, consumer responsibilization, stakeholder, corporate governance, institutional voids and international cooperation is expanded and questioned. This is due to a better exposition of the six primary elements that include (i) sustainable consumption by proximate (existing) consumers for future generations; (ii) sustainable production for future generations; (iii) sustainable consumption by/for proximate consumers (iv) sustainable production for proximate consumers; (v) participation by proximate consumers; and (vi) corporate social responsibility. Suggesting the need for an interventionist 'consumer protection model', they argue that better sustainable development and CSR can be achieved through a more involving stakeholder engagement that might emerge. With the broader theoretical inclinations, the findings and suggestions, the chapter is indeed a penultimate chapter. It intuitively expands the discussion incorporating the earlier approach of the previous chapters, which focus mainly on the firms, with new discussions on how consumer behaviour can contribute to better CSR and sustainable development. With the inclusion of consumers as a critical stakeholder, it means that consumers or other stakeholders outside the firms can indeed act as lead agents in the pursuit of CSR and sustainable development.

21.5 CONCLUSION

While there is no doubt that our exposition and understanding of issues in CSR and sustainable development in DEMs have been enriched with the contributions to this book, there is however a doubt which is to be expected. Should the contributions have stopped at the penultimate chapter by Osuji and Amajuoyi in Chapter 20? This is due to the issues raised, the findings that emerged and the suggestions proffered. The consolation though is that the issues, findings and suggestions might not have come to the fore without this book and the four questions that it has focused on. Another key benefit of the book is that it has set the stage for the issues raised to be further examined, especially given the increasing relevance and awareness of CSR and sustainable development in the DEMs.

With the awareness and practice of CSR so far achieved in DEMs, the positive linkage between CSR and sustainable development is well established and accepted across DEMs. However, given the wide differences in contextual and institutional peculiarities of DEMs, pursuing CSR and sustainable development from one-size-fits-all might be inappropriate. A further investigation of the possibility of arriving at some general principles and guidelines which can moderate CSR practices across DEMs might be helpful. With such macro guidelines, the understanding, involvement and practice of CSR may improve due to the better alignment of CSR and sustainable development with the contextual and institutional peculiarities of DEMs. It will engender the required flexibility that will accommodate even the internal pluralities within specific DEMs. As institutional make-up and development are critical for effective CSR practices, a further investigation will be required to properly understand the kind of critical institutions and stakeholders most relevant to and required by DEMs. For instance, as both formal and informal laws (values, norms, culture) are important institutional factors for CSR and sustainable development, further research on the kind of combination between formal and informal institutions might be necessary to enhance CSR and sustainable development in the DEMs. This is also the case with the kind of CSR that might be applicable to both formal and informal sub-economies of DEMs. Recalling that CSR is dynamic and relatively emerging in DEMs, the need for further research on some of the issues, findings and suggestions provided in this book cannot be overemphasized.

REFERENCES

Cooter, R. D. (2002). *The strategic constitution*. Princeton: Princeton University Press.
Menski, W. F. (2006). *Comparative law in a global context: The legal systems of Asia and Africa* 2nd ed. Cambridge: Cambridge University Press.

For EU product safety concerns, contact us at Calle de José Abascal, 56–1°, 28003 Madrid, Spain or eugpsr@cambridge.org.

www.ingramcontent.com/pod-product-compliance
Ingram Content Group UK Ltd.
Pitfield, Milton Keynes, MK11 3LW, UK
UKHW020434240426
470322UK00017B/502